PREACHING THE LECTIONARY
A Workbook for Year B

Also by Perry H. Biddle, Jr.

**Preaching the Lectionary
A Workbook for Year A**

PREACHING THE LECTIONARY

A Workbook for Year B

PERRY H. BIDDLE, Jr.

Westminster/John Knox Press
Louisville, Kentucky

Scripture quotations from the Revised Standard Version of the Bible are copyrighted 1946, 1952, © 1971, 1973 by the Division of Christian Education of the National Council of the Churches of Christ in the U.S.A. and are used by permission.

Material on pages 15–17 is reprinted in altered form from "Preparing to Preach," in *Hallelujah!* No. 6, a publication of the Section on Worship of the General Board of Discipleship of The United Methodist Church, by permission of the General Board of Discipleship of The United Methodist Church.

Book design by Gene Harris

First edition

Published by Westminster/John Knox Press
Louisville, Kentucky

PRINTED IN THE UNITED STATES OF AMERICA

9 8 7 6 5 4 3 2 1

Library of Congress Cataloging-in-Publication Data

Biddle, Perry H., 1932–
 Preaching the lectionary : a workbook for Year B / Perry H. Biddle. — 1st ed.
      p.   cm.
  ISBN 0-664-25104-8

   1. Bible—Homiletical use.   2. Common lectionary.   3. Preaching.
I. Title.
BS534.5.B544   1990
264′.34—dc20   89-49191

DEDICATED TO

ROBERT H. CRUMBY

MY BROTHER IN CHRIST

FRIEND AND ENCOURAGER

Contents

Preface

I offer this preaching workbook to you the working pastor for use in Year B of the Common Lectionary. As I look back on the beginning of my pastoral ministry thirty-one years ago, I recall how difficult it seemed to select a passage of scripture for each Sunday's sermon. The Common Lectionary now provides a more balanced guide for preaching many of the major passages of the Bible. I have used and researched the biblical texts in my preparation of this manuscript. I have also used most of these materials in preparation for preaching each week to the congregation of the First Presbyterian Church, Old Hickory, Tennessee. Therefore this workbook is the result of the weekly task of sermon preparation.

In August 1989, before completing the manuscript, I was critically injured in an auto accident in Louisville, Kentucky. I am especially grateful to Harold Twiss for assuming more than the usual duties of an editor in bringing this manuscript to completion. I am also appreciative of the patience and support of the editorial board of Westminster/John Knox Press. I want to thank those who have used my previous workbooks and have made useful comments. David Buttrick continues to provide help and encouragement. And thanks to Sue for our shared life.

October 10, 1989   P. H. B., Jr.
Baptist Hospital Rehab Center
Louisville, Kentucky

Introduction

This workbook is designed by a working pastor for use by working pastors in preparing to preach one or more times each week. While many of us hesitate to write in our books, this one invites you to write in its margins and underline passages as you use it week by week. Take a few minutes to become familiar with its design and intended purpose. Too often we attempt futilely to use a new gadget and *then* turn to the instructions to find out why it doesn't work! By purchasing this book you have made a commitment to improve your preaching skills. Find out what it has to offer before digging in to develop a sermon for a particular Sunday.

Weekly Materials

Step 1. The scripture for each Sunday is listed at the beginning of the material for each week, including one or more psalms appropriate for singing or reading or for use as a responsive reading. (No commentary is offered on the psalms, however.) Many readings are prescribed by the Consultation on Common Texts, an ecumenical body. When there are no variations from this reading, no symbol is placed after it. However, when there are variations,

(C) indicates the Common Lectionary reading,
(L) indicates the Lutheran reading,
(RC) indicates the Roman Catholic reading, and
(E) indicates the Episcopal reading.

Often the only difference is the length of the reading or the omission of verses. The commentary always deals with the longer passage; you, as the preacher, have the option of selecting the shorter pericope if this is preferable. Be sure to read the passages preceding and following the pericope in order to see it in its context. There may be times when you will want to read in the service *more* than the lectionary calls for, in order to give the full sense of a passage. You should be aggressive in asking why the shapers of the lectionary omitted certain verses, particularly those dealing with judgment and eternal punishment. By doing this, you will help preserve the meaning of the passage as we have received it.

Step 2. The **Meditation on the Texts** is designed to help you "pray through the scriptures" in preparation for reading the commentary. Listen for God's word as you meditate on the scripture. In addition to reading the meditation, it is helpful to read the lectionary selections and pray for God's wisdom and guidance in handling the texts and preparing to preach.

Step 3. Now make a copy of the **Preparing to Preach Worksheet** found at the end of this section and fill it out, following the suggestions that immediately precede it. This should be done *before* going to commentaries, because the commentaries may answer questions you have not asked or may blur your vision of a question that should be asked. By first working through the worksheet you will gain critically important insights into what to look for in your commentary work and related study. This exercise will help you examine three vital aspects of the preaching task: (1) the world of the living word; (2) the world of you, the preacher, and (3) the world of the community.

Step 4. Next, turn to the **Commentary on the Texts** in the workbook and, after reading it over, consult two or more commentaries; several are suggested under Preaching Resources for Year B. While studying other commentaries, you may want to make notes in the margins of this workbook. Among other tools, you will need Bible wordbooks, a Bible dictionary, a concordance, the original Hebrew or Greek texts if you are able to work in them, and an atlas of the Bible lands. Write notes gleaned from this study in your workbook or on a separate pad as your sermon preparation moves forward. Doing this study early in the week—Monday or Tuesday—will give you adequate time to reflect on the texts during the week and to let your subconscious mind ruminate on the meaning of the passage and its application for the congregation. Artists are very much aware of the need for time in which to let the creative process take place before painting a scene, composing a poem, or writing a chapter of a novel. Preachers, who rely on the guidance of the Holy Spirit in sermon preparation, should also allow time for the Spirit to work in the creative process.

Read the commentary for all the texts for a particular Sunday even though you select only one for the basis of the sermon. Note the word study and theme of the sermon in the section **Recommended work.** Also read the paragraph entitled **Theological Reflection,** which gives a brief summary of each passage and seeks to relate common themes.

Step 5. The **Children's Message** is usually based on one of the passages from the lectionary. You will need to flesh out the suggestions for the talk. They are not object lessons, nor do they seek to draw a moral from the text. Rather, the message seeks to enable the children to think with the preacher about some aspect of church life or life in general in the light of scripture teaching. The relationship developed between preacher and children is a very important aspect of the message.

Step 6. The hymns listed for each Sunday are related to one or more of the lectionary texts. Read or sing them as another way of reflecting on the themes of the lectionary pericopes. One or more of the hymns may be selected for use in worship, to be used before or after the sermon. Many hymnals have a listing of hymns according to the scripture passages on which they are based. This is an additional resource for shaping the worship in following the theme of the sermon. The *Handbook of the Christian Year,* edited by Hoyt L. Hickman and others, is useful in planning worship throughout the Christian year.

Other Materials

In addition to the materials for each week, this workbook includes an **Overview of the Gospel of Mark.** After read-

ing this section, you will benefit from reading one or more similar introductions to Mark in order to get a better grasp of this Gospel's structure and themes and the audience for whom it was written. We need to remember that the Gospels were written to be *heard;* someone would read them aloud in a worship service or group study of scripture because few people could read and write.

A bibliographic listing of additional commentaries and other resources appears in the section titled **Preaching Resources for Year B.**

Celebrating the Christian Year introduces the two centers of the Christian year: Advent/Christmas/Epiphany and Lent/Easter/Pentecost. These two centers developed independently in the history of the church in different times and places. A valuable tool to use in preparation for following the lectionary is the *Handbook for the Common Lectionary,* edited by Peter C. Bower. It describes the two basic patterns for text selection for lectionaries, explains the advantages and disadvantages of using a lectionary, gives brief summaries of the texts for each Sunday, and suggests hymns, anthems, and musical settings for the psalms.

Shaping a More Creative Message

One church that used a computer for designing each Sunday's worship bulletin habitually put instructions for worshipers down the left-hand side, indicating when to "stand," "sit," or "kneel." One day an unauthorized person got into the computer memory and put an additional cue to the congregation just to the left of the sermon: "Sleep!"

One of the chief criticisms from sermon listeners is that sermons are boring, more likely to induce sleep than to make one sit up and take notice. One reason for this is that sermons are often predictable. The sermon with three points and a poem (which was a standard homiletical product in the past) usually engaged the congregation in a rational argument. The scripture text was reduced to a proposition, which was developed into a neat three-point message, each point leading logically to the next. The sermon ended with a conclusion and often a poem or a hymn stanza on the theme.

This stock homiletic developed during the eighteenth and nineteenth centuries at the same time that the scientific method was further developed, and it is no accident that a rationalistic, objective approach to preaching resulted. A topic was isolated for study, all too often on Saturday night. A general deduction followed by a descriptive statement and some illustrations was shaped into a sermon. One professor I had in seminary confessed that when he was preaching during the 1920s he would have given $5 on many a Saturday night for a good illustration. The preacher might also exercise some sanctified imagination in altering the rational points of the sermon. Thus a romantic notion of inspiration was wedded to a rational methodology, the homiletic still found in most books on preaching.

However, a fresh new approach has appeared in the homiletical world in recent years. David Buttrick has stated the case for this new approach better than anyone else in *Homiletic*. This book on how language forms in human consciousness, and what this has to say about the way in which sermons are shaped, is extremely valuable.

Buttrick asks four things of the scripture passage. What is its form? What is the plot, structure, or shape of the passage? What is the field of concern? What is its logic of movement? The passage is viewed as a moving picture rather than a proposition containing religious truth according to the rationalistic approach. The preacher asks: What is the world this scripture addresses and what is the passage trying to do?

This dynamic approach to scripture and preaching sees sermons as plotted sequences of language units. However, the "movements" of the sermon need not follow the sequence of moves found in a biblical passage. Nor is the sermon bound by the biblical form. Buttrick says the preacher should be a combination of poet, exegete, and theologian.

Images are critical in this method of preaching, images that not only form in the consciousness but motivate the hearer to do something. The human psyche is ever in flux, made up of a movement of images of many kinds, both visual and nonvisual. Our goals as persons come out of this flow of moving imagery. We cannot underestimate the power of images in shaping our values, hopes, and future. The prophets describe the new age which God is bringing about. God is a God of the future who is drawing us forward through images of the new Eden when the kingdom is consummated.

People enjoy hearing and telling stories because of the power the stories have to form memorable images. The point of view of the sermon, as in fiction, is very important. For this reason you should be cautious about using the pronoun "I" in the sermon, since this causes a shift in the point of view from third person to first.

At the end of each commentary on a lectionary passage there are a few sentences suggesting possible moves the sermon may take that are influenced by the scripture. Only the preacher who knows the congregation, the scripture passage, and himself or herself can properly develop a sermon for a congregation. However, the suggested moves may serve as a foil, against which you will react as you wrestle with the text, or as a catalyst to help bring a sermon into being. This paragraph at the end might be compared to a jump start for a car. It is intended to get you going so you can develop the sermon on your own.

One of the many advantages of following the lectionary in preaching is that it enables you to plan ahead. Many preachers find that keeping a file for each Sunday with text and theme for six weeks in advance allows them to collect images, illustrations, and ideas for the sermon. This also allows for advance planning with the church musician(s) and the worship committee. This file would include illustrations the minister has gathered from conversations and observation of life. Other illustrations may be gathered from reading novels and short stories, attending plays, and watching movies and selected television programs that give insights into the contemporary mind and values. You may want to make up illustrations as Jesus made up parables, indicating in some way to the congregation that these are not factual stories. Keeping a notebook for each year with observations, stories, and images can be a valuable resource for more creative preaching. You may use only 40 percent of the material, but what is used will be fresher and more interesting than canned illustrations from sermon illustration books.

A sense of humor is important in creative preaching. The most effective humor often comes spontaneously from a playful mindset. Playing around in the mind with an idea or image can enable you to come up with a fresh view of a problem or issue or of the way the Gospel speaks to you. This playfulness should also be combined with the focus of one's thinking, relating images and illustrations to a particular theme or thrust of the sermon. Sermons must be dynamic and moving if they are to move the hearers. Humor can crack a door in a closed mind and enable a fresh point of view to enter. Humor, of course, should be used sparingly and for a purpose; it should not simply be humor for humor's sake. That preacher demeans the pulpit who tries to compete with stand-up comedians or late-night television show hosts in making people laugh. Jokes don't work in sermons, because jokes are not open-ended, to hook on to what follows, but are a closed system with a beginning, a middle, and an end.

Creative preaching depends ultimately upon our listening to God speaking in and through scripture to us as preachers who interpret the message for our hearers. This calls for an openness to God in prayer, meditation on scripture, and seeing where and how God is working in human events today as well as in past history. Preachers would do well to look for places where God is working and call God's people to join in working for justice, peace, and love. In an interview with Bishop Desmond Tutu in South Africa a few years ago we prayed for "the hot spots of the world." We should pray for these hot spots. Creative preaching calls for helping people to see the world through the eyes of faith and become engaged in the work of the kingdom here and now.

The lectionary should be used as a tool for preaching rather than as a legalistic system to which the preacher must adhere. For example, during the nonfestival season, from Pentecost to the end of the church year, the preacher may choose to develop a series of sermons on the Lord's Prayer, on the Apostles' Creed, on the Ten Commandments, or on a book or section of the Bible. This is another way of becoming more creative in preaching. A series should run from two to seven sermons. Or after preaching through the Gospel lessons one year during the nonfestival season, the preacher may preach next on the epistle lessons and on the third cycle of Year B preach from the Old Testament lessons. The lectionary was created by a particular group of Christians, and thus it reflects their own view of scripture and Christian thought. The preacher should be aware of this limitation and seek to supplement the lectionary by preaching on the minor

prophets, Esther, and other passages that the lectionary passes over or treats only briefly. The lament and complaint psalms should also be included.

The greatest challenge for the preacher is to do justice to the biblical material in applying it to current concerns of the congregation. Only you, the preacher in your particular congregation, know the *Sitz im Leben,* the place in life, and can shape the sermon so that it is a faithful proclamation of God's word to your hearers. The workbook's philosophy of seeing the scriptures and sermon as dynamic, moving process rather than as static, propositional truth can enable you to keep the sermon crackling with excitement from beginning to end.

Seek to engage your hearers in asking, What is the message of this scripture for our lives as a congregation and for my life in particular? This is the thrust of the parables Jesus told. The listener was caught up in a simple story that had a hook and offered a challenge to make a decision for or against the kingdom of God. The parable of the waiting father (prodigal son) is a prime example of what faithful preaching should do. The parable concludes without telling us whether or not the elder brother repented and went in to the feast that had been prepared for the prodigal son. Each hearer must respond to the challenge: Will I repent and enter God's kingdom and fellowship with brothers and sisters at God's banquet of love? Another aspect of being creative in preaching is responding to events in the congregation, the community, and the world through an "occasional sermon." This may call for breaking with the lectionary for one or more Sundays. However, if the sermon is based on a Gospel text, you might continue the regular lectionary readings for the epistle and the Old Testament, explaining what is being done. This might be the case on a special Sunday like Mother's Day or in response to a community crisis or other event. While the lectionary is a very helpful guide for preaching through the scriptures, it should not become an obstacle to following the leading of the Holy Spirit in preaching for special occasions.

While some people seem to be inspired most by deadlines and by the necessity of producing a sermon, a piece of art, or a novel, many people find this kind of pressure counterproductive. They become too anxious and cannot do their best. Starting early in the week to study for the sermon, and allowing the sermon idea to roll around in the mind while they attend to other pastoral work, frees them to be their most creative. Each preacher must work out her or his own system for sermon preparation. But whatever the process, it should enable you to find satisfaction, a sense of affirmation in obeying God's call to preach, and even occasional joy in the task! We do best those things which we like to do and which reinforce us in what we are doing. The preacher who dreads the task of preaching after doing it for a few years should probably consider another expression of ministry. Few preachers earn much money, but they have the privilege, as one professor of preaching put it, of "rolling in the scriptures" each week, a privilege allowed few other Christians by time or energy.

Moving from Text to Sermon

The following suggestions for shaping the sermon in the light of the world of scripture, the world of the preacher, and the world of the community are adapted from *Hallelujah!* No. 6 (1988), in an article by Rev. Michael Williams and Rev. Andy Langford of the Section on Worship of the General Board of Discipleship of the United Methodist Church. Use the worksheet at the end of this introduction to answer these questions. (Permission is granted to copy this material, in whole or in part, from *Hallelujah!*)

The World of the Living Word (Scripture)

After you select the text for the sermon, read it aloud with passion, as if reading to the congregation who will hear it later. Then answer the following questions on a copy of the form that follows this section.

1. Where is the event taking place and what is the setting in which the scripture arose?
2. When did the scripture occur, the time and occasion?
3. Who are the characters in the text? What people (and other parts of creation) are present, both seen and unseen?
4. What objects are present? Examine the narrative and list both seen and unseen things found in it.

5. What is the sequence of scenes or themes? In what order do the events or ideas occur?
6. What strikes you as strange or unexpected in the passage?
7. What words appear to be most important? Are any unusual verbs, nouns, or catch phrases used?
8. Why was this passage written? What caused the writing, and why did the community of faith preserve it?
9. Do you find an invitation in the scripture? Is it explicit or implicit to the audience?

The World of the Preacher

Again, read the scripture aloud using the voices of the different characters in the text. Ask yourself the following questions and note them on the form that follows.

1. With which characters do I identify most closely? With which am I most comfortable? With which am I most uncomfortable?
2. When have I experienced this scripture, if ever? Do I have life experiences that parallel this text?
3. What is my reaction to the text? What feelings and thoughts are produced by the situation related in the text?
4. What is God inviting me to be or to do through this text? How do I hear God's call to me through it?

The World of the Community

Listen to the scripture as a member of your congregation would and then answer the following questions, seeking to relate your community to the scripture. Try to include the whole of the church universal in your community.

1. When have individuals in my community experienced an event similar to this text? Are there persons in my community who have lived or now live this story?
2. When does or did my community as a corporate body experience a similar event?
3. When does or did my community experience this scripture through its shared oral tradition? In my community are there stories that are parallel to this text?
4. When does or did my community ex-

perience this event through its culture? Are there media (books, TV, movies) that are familiar to my community which parallel this scripture?

5. What is or was my community's reaction to this event and how do or did people respond?

6. How does God invite my community through this text, and what grace does God offer my community through it?

Review the answers you gave to the foregoing questions. Then ask yourself: What more do I need to know about the scriptures? What perceptions do I need to evaluate? What more do I need to know about myself and what perceptions do I need to evaluate? What more do I need to know about my community and what perceptions of it do I need to evaluate? Seek answers and write them on your worksheet.

Having followed this process, next select the sermon focus. It may be the basic image, thrust, theme, statement, or impact that guides the sermon and will direct the service. State this focus in a short declarative sentence. If you do this several weeks in advance you will then be able to collect ideas and illustrations for the sermon and place them in a folder. (A period of eight weeks in advance is advocated by Williams and Langford.) Then select other aspects of the worship and persons to participate in it. Select visuals.

Additional guidance for preaching may be found in *Preaching Pilgrims,* by Michael E. Williams. This is a self-study book for preachers using a variety of approaches to preaching.

The preacher following the lectionary might use the foregoing process and share insights with a lectionary preaching group that meets weekly to share insights and illustrations on the text. For guidance in working in a lectionary preaching group, see *Preaching Peers,* by Michael E. Williams. Many ecumenical lectionary preaching groups of two to seven preachers are finding this a stimulating method of sermon preparation.

Preparing to Preach Worksheet

It is suggested that you make several copies of this form at one time, using one for each sermon.

Date: _____ Day of the Christian Year: _____

Scripture: _____

World of the Living Word

Where:

When:

Characters:

Objects:

Sequence:

The Unexpected:

Words:

Why:

Invitation:

World of the Preacher

Characters:

Experiences:

Reactions:

Invitation:

World of the Community

Personal Experiences:

Community Experiences:

Oral Traditions:

Culture:

Reactions:

Invitation:

Sermon Focus

Overview of the Gospel of Mark

This overview can only be a brief look at the Gospel of Mark as a whole and the context in which it was written. For a more detailed discussion of the questions of authorship and date, its relation to the other Gospels, and its outline, you will want to turn to commentaries such as *Saint Mark,* by D. E. Nineham (Westminster Pelican Commentaries) and *The Gospel According to St. Mark,* by C. E. B. Cranfield (Cambridge Greek Testament Commentary). (These and other resources are listed in Preaching Resources for Year B.)

Author and Place of Writing

Scholars are not fully agreed on the identity of the author of Mark. But several, including Cranfield, agree with the ancient tradition that the author is the Mark who was the associate of Peter and also the Mark of the Pauline epistles. They say that this Mark was a Gentile who had become a strongly committed Christian. Although he had a strong intellectual ability, he did not have the formal education that would have enabled him to express himself in sophisticated Greek. Other scholars, such as Werner Kelber, say that Mark was written by an anonymous Jewish-Christian author. Tradition has it that Rome was the place where Mark was written, but the arguments for this are not conclusive. Others claim that Antioch was the place of writing. More recently, a scholarly focus on the internal logic of the Gospel rather than external evidence points to Galilee or southern Syria as a likely place for the writing of Mark.

Date

Many scholars agree that Mark seems to be the first Gospel to have been written. Some recent studies, however, have questioned this assertion, claiming that Mark is derived from Matthew and Luke. In support of the traditional assumption of the priority of Mark, over 90 percent of Mark's verses are found in Matthew and over 50 percent in Luke. In those cases where the text of either Matthew or Luke differs from Mark, the other Synoptic Gospel usually agrees with Mark. Also, the date of the writing of the Gospel seems to have been sometime in the latter part of A.D. 65–70, earlier than the usual dates given for the writing of Matthew or Luke. One factor in support of this view is that Mark does not seem to reflect in any way the fall of Jerusalem to the Romans, which occurred in A.D. 70.

Purpose of the Author

The author of Mark has not attempted to describe the whole of the life of Jesus, as if it all had been recorded with an audio or video recorder as it happened. Rather, he has put together a series of essentially independent stories that had been preserved and to some extent modified through their use in the church's life and worship. Because the Gospel of Mark consists of these stories which were in use by the church, it gives us a picture of the beliefs and understandings about the ministry of Jesus prevalent in the church at the time of the writing of the Gospel.

Mark, like the other Gospels, is intended to convey a religious message and to demand a religious decision. If one reads Mark straight through, as the preacher is urged to do before beginning a study of individual sections, one is impressed with how Jesus is presented as the mysterious Son of God. Jesus is shown as one who works to bring home to his contemporaries the conviction that the End time was near. Jesus sought to hasten the coming of the kingdom of God by his ministry and death.

The Gospel of Mark was written for Greek-speaking people living in various parts of the Mediterranean world. Therefore the author explains Aramaic terms and does not dwell on Jewish customs. These people were already Christians, and the Gospel was written to give them a brief account of the facts about Jesus of Nazareth and to encourage them to remain faithful in the face of persecution. Because Mark was written for this audience, the understanding of Jesus and his work of salvation presented by Mark is closely related to that in the letters of Paul addressed to the same audience. Therefore the letters of Paul help us to understand the religious message of Mark. Insofar as Mark was written for this Gentile audience, and probably before the other Gospels, we must refrain from reading Matthean or Lukan or Fourth Gospel elements into our interpretation of Mark's Gospel.

Structure

An overview of the outline of Mark makes plain that the primary emphasis in Mark is on the passion of Jesus, with the second part of the Gospel devoted almost wholly to that.

A. Ministry in Galilee (1:1–8:26)
   1. Baptism of Jesus
   2. Beginning of Jesus' ministry in Galilee
   3. Developing opposition
   4. Parables of Jesus
   5. Sending out of the Twelve
   6. Jesus' visit to Tyre and Sidon

B. Ministry in Judea (8:27–13:37)
   1. Announcement of Jesus' approaching death
   2. Journey from Galilee to Judea
   3. Palm Sunday and the cleansing of the temple
   4. Other teaching in Judea

C. The last week; death and resurrection (chs. 14–16)

Mark falls into two rather sharply divided parts, each of which contains its own characteristics. In the first part (1:1–8:26), the emphasis falls more on the miraculous deeds of Jesus than on his teaching. Whatever teaching is described was directed to the crowd, not to the disciples. This teaching is concerned with the coming of God's kingdom and often is couched in parables. Jesus seeks to prevent the recognition of his Messiahship (the messianic secret), and there is almost no teaching about it.

The story of the Great Confession is the pivotal point. It comes when Jesus and the Twelve are alone near Caesarea Philippi (8:27–30). Peter speaks for all the disciples to say that Jesus is the Messiah (8:29). His assertion is recognized as the first affirmation of Jesus' Messiahship by human beings. Although Jesus continued to hide his Messiahship from outsiders who might misunderstand it, he changed his tactics after being recognized for what he was by the disciples.

After 8:31 this change is reflected in the Gospel. Accounts of miraculous healings are very rare, and the emphasis is now on Jesus' teaching, directed for the most part to the disciples. He tried to lead them to an understanding that the Messiah was also the suffering Son of man. Jesus explains how the Messiah's work will involve grievous suffering both for the Messiah himself and for his followers. But the final outcome of this suffering will be the glorious triumph of God's cause which the Messiah was expected to bring.

The conclusion of the Gospel (16:9–20) as it appears in most versions of the Bible is generally considered to be a later addition to the Gospel by the early church.

Preaching Themes and Emphases

Some of the themes and emphases have already been noted, but specific themes will be highlighted here.

Jesus as both human and divine. This affirmation is part of the Nicene Creed and has been supported by the church through the ages. Mark begins his Gospel with "The beginning of the gospel of Jesus Christ, the Son of God." He portrays Jesus as both human and divine. He describes Jesus as feeling anger, pity, sorrow, and so forth. Jesus was tempted. He prayed like any human being and experienced despair on the cross. But he was also the Son of God who forgave sin, cast out demons, calmed storms, healed the sick, and raised the dead.

Action thrust of Jesus' ministry. Mark shows us Jesus as always on the move. "Immediately" ("straightway" in the King James Version) is a common word in Mark. Jesus tried to do as much as possible in the little time left before the End. Mark portrays him as teaching not only by words but by his life and works. Jesus is often addressed as "Teacher" in Mark, and he taught not only in parables but by his miracles and life itself. Jesus had divine power to do wonderful things for people. Mark gives more place to miracles than any other Gospel does. Miracles express Jesus' authority and power. But his greatest power was revealed in his death for the sins of the world.

The centrality of the cross. As early as the account of the arrest of John the Baptizer (1:14), we can see a foreshadowing of the arrest of Jesus, since John was his forerunner. The increasing opposition to Jesus, as indicated in 2:1–3:36, culminates in a plot to put him to death. His rejection by his hometown (6:1–6a) foreshadows his rejection by the people in general. The story of the passion and resurrection forms the climax of Mark, dominating the latter portion of the Gospel (8:27–16:8). From the time of Peter's confession, the references to Jesus' approaching passion and resurrection become more and more plain. Jesus came to suffer and die for human beings so that they might be reconciled to God and so that the kingdom of God might come. The conflict between Jesus' opponents and Jesus reaches a peak on Good Friday at the cross.

The great emphasis that Mark put on the cross and the resurrection is revealed by the amount of space and material devoted to this theme. As the preacher works through the Gospel of Mark, he or she should take into account this focus on the cross and the resurrection. This is the heart of the Gospel and should be proclaimed in some form *every preaching occasion*.

Preaching Resources for Year B

(* = highly recommended)

Commentaries on the Gospel of Mark

Achtemeier, Paul J. *Mark.* Proclamation Commentaries. 2d ed., rev. and enl. Philadelphia: Fortress Press, 1986.

Cranfield, C. E. B. *The Gospel According to St. Mark.* Cambridge Greek Testament Commentary. Cambridge: Cambridge University Press, 1959.

Grant, Frederick C. "Introduction" and "Exegesis" on Mark. In *The Interpreter's Bible,* Vol. 7.

*Hamilton, Neill Q. *Recovery of the Protestant Adventure.* New York: Seabury Press, 1981. (While not a commentary in the usual sense, this book is an excellent resource for preaching from Mark.)

Kee, Howard Clark, and others. *The Gospels. Interpreter's Concise Commentary.* Vol. 6. Nashville: Abingdon Press, 1983.

*Kelber, Werner H. *Mark's Story of Jesus.* Philadelphia: Fortress Press, 1979. (Excellent brief introduction to Mark's Gospel.)

Mann, C. S. *Mark.* Anchor Bible. Garden City, N.Y.: Doubleday & Co., 1986.

Martin, Ralph P. *Mark.* Knox Preaching Guides. Atlanta: John Knox Press, 1982.

Moule, Charles F. *The Gospel According to Mark.* Cambridge New English Bible. Cambridge: Cambridge University Press, 1965.

*Nineham, D. E. *Saint Mark.* Westminster Pelican Commentaries. Philadelphia: Westminster Press, 1978.

Schweizer, Eduard. *The Good News According to Mark.* Atlanta: John Knox Press, 1974.

*Williamson, Lamar, Jr. *Mark.* Interpretation: A Bible Commentary for Teaching and Preaching. Atlanta: John Knox Press, 1983.

Additional Commentaries and Resources

Achtemeier, Elizabeth. *Preaching from the Old Testament.* Louisville: Westminster/John Knox Press, 1989.

Achtemeier, Elizabeth, ed. *Proclamation 3,* Series B. Philadelphia: Fortress Press, 1984.

Barrett, Charles V. *The First Epistle to the Corinthians.* Harper New Testament Commentary. San Francisco: Harper & Row, 1968.

———. *The Second Epistle to the Corinthians.* Harper New Testament Commentary. San Francisco: Harper & Row, 1974.

Barth, Marcus. *Ephesians.* Anchor Bible. Garden City, N.Y.: Doubleday & Co., 1966, 1970.

*Brown, Raymond E. *Epistles of John.* Anchor Bible. Garden City, N.Y.: Doubleday & Co., 1966, 1970.

———. *The Gospel According to John.* Anchor Bible. 2 vols. Garden City, N.Y.: Doubleday & Co., 1966, 1970.

Cox, James W., ed. *Biblical Preaching: An Expositor's Treasury.* Philadelphia: Westminster Press, 1983.

Craddock, Fred B., and others. *Preaching the New Common Lectionary,* Year B. 3 vols. Nashville: Abingdon Press, 1984, 1987, 1988.

*Crenshaw, James L. *Story and Faith: A Guide to the Old Testament.* New York: Macmillan Co., 1986.

Fuller, Reginald H. *Preaching the Lectionary: The Word of God for the Church Today.* Rev. ed. Includes cycles A, B, C. Collegeville, Minn.: Liturgical Press, 1984.

The Interpreter's Bible: The Holy Scriptures in the King James and Revised Standard

Versions. George A. Buttrick, commentary editor, and others. 12 vols. Nashville: Abingdon Press, 1951–1957. Pertinent volumes.

*Jeremias, Joachim. *New Testament Theology.* New York: Charles Scribner's Sons, 1971.

C. Leslie Milton. *Ephesians.* New Century Bible Commentary. Wm. B. Eerdmans, 1981.

Laymon, Charles M., ed. *Interpreter's Concise Commentary.* 8 vols. Nashville: Abingdon Press, 1971–. Pertinent volumes.

McCurley, Foster R. *Proclaiming the Promise.* Philadelphia: Fortress Press, 1974.

*Old Testament Library. Philadelphia: Westminster Press, 1961–. Pertinent volumes.

Plaut, W. G. *The Torah: A Modern Commentary.* New York: Union of American Hebrew Congregations, 1981.

Sloyan, Gerard S. *A Commentary on the New Lectionary,* A, B, C. Paramus, N.J.: Paulist Press, 1975.

Westcott, B. F., ed. *The Epistles of John.* Marcham Manor, 1966.

One-Volume Commentaries

*Black, Matthew, and H. H. Rowley, eds. *Peake's Commentary on the Bible.* Nashville: Thomas Nelson & Sons, 1962.

*Brown, Raymond E., and others, ed. *The Jerome Biblical Commentary.* Englewood Cliffs, N.J.: Prentice-Hall, 1968.

The Church Year

Allen, Horace T., Jr. *A Handbook for the Lectionary.* Philadelphia: Geneva Press, 1980.

*Bower, Peter C. *Handbook for the Common Lectionary.* Philadelphia: Geneva Press, 1987.

Common Lectionary: The Lectionary proposed by the Consultation on Common Texts. New York: Church Hymnal Corp., 1983.

*Hickman, Hoyt L., and others, eds. *Handbook of the Christian Year.* Nashville: Abingdon Press, 1986.

An Inclusive-Language Lectionary: Readings for Year B. Rev. ed. Atlanta: John Knox Press; New York: Pilgrim Press; and Philadelphia: Westminster Press, 1987.

Old, Hughes Oliphant. *Guides to the Reformed Tradition: Worship.* Atlanta: John Knox Press, 1985.

Recommended Translation

The New Oxford Annotated Bible with the Apocrypha, Expanded Edition, Revised Standard Version. Edited by Herbert G. May and Bruce M. Metzger. New York: Oxford University Press, 1977.

Other Resources

Burghardt, Walter J. *Preaching: The Art and the Craft.* New York: Paulist Press, 1987.

*Buttrick, David G. *Homiletic.* Philadelphia: Fortress Press, 1987.

Craddock, Fred B. *As One Without Authority.* 3d ed. Nashville: Abingdon Press, 1979.

*———. *Preaching.* Nashville: Abingdon Press, 1985.

Davis, Henry Grady. *Design for Preaching.* Philadelphia: Muhlenberg Press, 1958.

Efird, James M. *How to Interpret the Bible.* Atlanta: John Knox Press, 1984.

Fant, Clyde. *Preaching for Today.* San Francisco: Harper & Row, 1977.

Hallelujah! No. 6. Nashville: General Board of Discipleship, United Methodist Church, 1988.

Keck, Leander E. *The Bible in the Pulpit: The Renewal of Biblical Preaching.* Nashville: Abingdon Press, 1978.

McKim, Donald K., ed. *A Guide to Contemporary Hermeneutics: Major Trends in Biblical Interpretation.* Grand Rapids: Wm. B. Eerdmans Publishing Co., 1986.

Smith, D. Moody. *Interpreting the Gospels for Preaching.* Philadelphia.: Fortress Press, 1980.

*Williams, Michael E. *Preaching Peers.* Nashville: Discipleship Resources, 1987.

*———. *Preaching Pilgrims.* Nashville: Discipleship Resources, 1988.

Celebrating the Christian Year

Almost all Christians follow the Christian year to some extent. Some observe only Christmas and Easter; others follow the church calendar from the first Sunday of Advent all the way through the year to Christ the King Sunday. The growing use of the Christian year in planning worship and preaching is a result of the modern liturgical movement, which continues to influence both Protestant and Roman Catholic worship.

The lectionaries used in this workbook are based on the Christian calendar, which begins with the first Sunday of Advent, the Sunday nearest to November 30. We may divide the Christian year into two roughly equal parts: the special seasons that celebrate events in sacred history, and what is called ordinary time, the "Sundays of the year." The special or festal seasons begin with the first Sunday of Advent and continue through the feast of Epiphany, they pick up again with Ash Wednesday and go through the Day of Pentecost. The Sundays after Epiphany and after Pentecost are called ordinary time, with the following exceptions. The Sunday after Epiphany is known as the Baptism of Our Lord, and in some churches the last Sunday of that season is known as the Transfiguration of Our Lord, the first Sunday after Pentecost is called Trinity Sunday, and the final Sunday of the church year is called Christ the King.

During much of ordinary time we find readings of scripture in sequence. In Year B, parts of Mark and Ephesians are used in this way. Note that the Gospel of John and other books of the New and Old Testaments are read where they seem most appropriate, and the psalms generally are harmonized with the lessons. However, the Common Lectionary follows a course reading during ordinary time in the Old Testament lessons and so does not usually have a common theme with the Gospel, while the Lutheran readings in the Old Testament are chosen for their relevance to the Gospel reading. The preacher should be aware of the differences in the lectionaries and not try to force the readings for a particular Sunday to harmonize when they do not do so.

The origin of the lectionary seems to go back to a time in Judaism after Jesus' ministry when there were two readings for each Sabbath, one from Torah (the Pentateuch) and one from the Prophets. Some Jewish scholars think this practice existed as early as Jesus' ministry, and Luke may have assumed that Jesus was reading a proscribed reading at Nazareth as recorded in Luke 4:18–19. History does not tell us exactly how or when lectionaries came into use in the Christian church, but some scholars think that Mark, Matthew, and John were shaped on the plan of the Jewish liturgical year and were intended to be read in sequence. The earliest lectionaries in the Western Church date from the fifth century as certain books of the Bible came to be associated with specific seasons of the year. There were gradual changes during the Middle Ages, and various lectionaries emerged, but all of these were similar to one another and were based on a one-year cycle. This eliminated many passages from being read. John Calvin advocated reading a single passage in each service, a custom many Reformed churches follow, while the more radical Protestant churches rejected lectionaries entirely. But following Vatican II and the modern liturgical renewal, many ministers and churches are adopting the practice of following the lectionary for some if not all of the Christian year. The major reason for doing this is to enable the congregation to hear many parts of the Bible read in public in a systematic fashion over the three-year cycle of Years A, B, and C. A church may begin following the lectionary at any time and need not wait until Year A or even until Advent 1 to do so. However, the congregation should be prepared for the use of the lectionary, and appropriate explanations should be given.

The Common Lectionary, noted as (C) in this workbook, was prepared by the North American Committee on Calendar and Lectionary. The Consultation on Common Texts, an association of representatives of most of the major denominations of the United States and Canada, has commended the present Common Lectionary for use until 1992. Some adjustments may be made in readings after that time. Where there are longer and shorter readings in this workbook, the longer one is used, leaving you, the preacher, the option of selecting the reading of your denomination, which may be shorter.

Both the Jewish and Christian lectionaries reveal a tendency common to many religions to have a cycle of annual festivals and fasts. In primitive religions there were myths about the eternal return of the seasons, and one goal of religion was to ensure that this cycle was observed properly. Following the cycle of the Christian year is helpful both psychologically and educationally for preacher and people. But rather then seeing the cycle as a mere repetition of the same texts and celebrations, we should view the cycle each year as a kind of *spiral* moving toward Christ, fostering growth and greater faithfulness in the Christian life. The cycle of the Christian year reminds us that there is an aspect of the Christian faith that stays the same, while the structure of worship and sermon and the church's life is apt to change over the years. One purpose of the lectionary is to help Christians see by faith that in scripture we have one continuous story of God's dealing with the human race which reveals God's nature and purpose. The ultimate purpose of all preaching and worship, of course, is to unite us more fully to God through Christ.

Color alone can often be the most effective symbol for use in the worship setting. We should understand that such visual symbols are more than mere decorations. They serve as visual proclamations of the gospel. The meaning of the colors of the year should be given the worshipers in either written or spoken form. Often a visual image will remain in the worshiper's mind long after spoken words are forgotten. Visual aspects of worship should be chosen with care; they can be an integral part of the service and not just decoration.

While the colors used on specific days and seasons were first formally set forth in 1570 in the reformed missal under Pius V, a few changes have been made in recent times. The colors of the Christian year are as follows (see J. G. Davies, ed., *The Westminster Dictionary of Worship* [Philadelphia: Westminster Press, 1972], p. 140):

Advent to Christmas Eve	Violet/Blue/Black
Christmas to Epiphany	White/Gold
Sundays after Epiphany	Green
Septuagesima to Ash Wednesday	Violet/Blue/Black
Throughout Lent	Veiling of colors
Passion Sunday to Easter Eve	Red/Rose
Easter	White/Gold
Pentecost	Red
Trinity	White/Gold
Sundays after Trinity	Green
Ordinary weekdays	Green
Blessed Virgin Mary	White/Red
Apostles, evangelists, martyrs	Red
Saints (except martyrs)	White/Yellow
Baptisms/confirmation	White/Red
Ordination/marriage	White
Funeral	Violet/Blue/Black
Dedication of a church	White

In the Roman Catholic Church the post-Vatican II *Ordo Missae* (1969) in general reaffirmed the current practice:

White for Easter, Christmas, feasts of Christ (other than the Passion), All Saints, feast of Mary, and so forth.
Red for Passion/Palm Sunday, Good Friday, Pentecost, feasts of the Passion of Christ and of martyrs.
Violet for Advent and Lent and possibly for funeral masses in place of black.
Rose for Gaudet Sunday and Laetare Sunday.
Green for other times.

For additional suggestions for use of liturgical colors and visual effects in the Christian year, see Hoyt Hickman and others, *Handbook of the Christian Year,* p. 36. It notes that purples, grays, and blues may be used for seasons of a preparatory and pentitential character, while white and gold are used for celebrating joyous seasons and events that have a special christological emphasis.

The Seasons of Advent and Christmas/Epiphany

There is a powerful thrust in the theology of the seasons of Advent and Christmas/Epiphany, which are viewed here as a unity. The underlying theology unites the celebration of the expectation and birth of Jesus, and the waiting for his return, with his life, suffering, death, and resurrection. The incarnation and the atonement cannot be separated; they are both aspects of God's saving action in Christ Jesus. The purpose of Jesus' birth was to make God known to all humanity through Jesus' life, death and resurrection.

The central message of this season is expressed in the words of John's Gospel: "The Word became flesh and dwelt among us" (John 1:14). We learn from church history that the original special day of this season was not Christmas but Epiphany. This was the day for celebrating the manifestation (epiphany) of God's light and power in Christ. Along with Easter and Pentecost, it was the third great celebration of the Christian calendar for the church, beginning around the fifth century. The focus in the earliest lectionaries and sermons for Epiphany was placed on John 1:1–2:11. Among the themes associated with Epiphany were light, Jesus' advent (coming) into the world, his baptism, and the miracle of changing water into wine at Cana. The one theme running like a red thread through all these events was the affirmation that God was in Christ manifesting God to human beings to the ends of the world.

Advent

Color: Purple.

The season of Advent begins with the fourth Sunday before Christmas, which is the Sunday nearest November 30, and continues to Christmas Eve. The season combines themes of both threat and promise. Its primary concern is eschatology, or the events of the End, including Christ's return in glory, the last judgment, and the consummation of the kingdom.

Advent looks both backward to Jesus' first coming at Bethlehem and forward to his coming again at the End. Thus we begin the Christian year by reflecting on the End of history. Consider the message of the many Advent hymns that have a note of threat and promise in contrast to Christmas carols. This emphasis points up the thrust of the readings and sermons of Advent, which deals not so much with preparation for Christmas as with the *expectation* of Christ's return in glory to rule, judge, and save. The prayer of this season is expressed in the phrases of the Lord's Prayer: "Thy kingdom come, thy will be done, on earth." There is a strong prophetic note in this season announcing judgment upon evil, combined with an emphasis on hope and the expectation of Christ's coming reign in glory.

Some leaders of denominational worship programs suggest that Advent hymns may be sung *before* Advent begins, that is, on the Sundays of November when sermons deal with the End time and the coming rule of Christ as King. Then, during the Advent season proper, appropriate Christmas hymns and carols may be interspersed with Advent hymns. Not to sing Christmas hymns during Advent, as liturgical purists insist, is to confine the singing of Christmas carols and hymns to Christmas Eve and Christmas Day only. A compromise might be to sing only Advent hymns on the first Sunday of Advent and then intersperse Christmas hymns with Advent hymns on the other three Sundays.

Christmas

Color: White, yellow, and gold, and combinations of these.

The color of white signifies joy and is used for Christmas Eve and Christmas Day. The Christmas celebration begins on Christmas Eve (which is counted as an integral part of the following day, as Jews do with the Jewish Sabbath). Many congregations celebrate on Christmas Eve with a candlelight Communion service and again with worship and Communion on Christmas Day. Christmas should focus on the incarnation and its meaning. The celebration should not become a sentimental service of child worship but should connect the incarnation with the atonement. The Christ who was born was born to die as our redeemer. Preaching during this season should lift up the joy that Christ brings into our lives by forgiving our sins and giving us eternal life. This joy, a gift of the Holy Spirit, is independent of outward circumstances and passes all understanding. The fulfillment of Old Testament prophecies of Messiah in the birth of Jesus highlights God's continuing plan of salvation.

In the hymn "O Little Town of Bethlehem" the words "Cast out our sin, and enter in, be born in us today" are the prayer of Christmas. The goal of preaching in this season is to enable people to so hear the gracious word of God that they may invite the living Christ to be born anew in their lives.

In the time between Christmas and Epiphany some early churches celebrated the Sacrament of Baptism, with an emphasis second only to that of the Easter Vigil and the Great Fifty Days. In the Roman Catholic tradition, the feasts of martyrs and saints are observed during this time, which reminds us of the connection between Christmas/Epiphany and our dying to sin and being raised to new life in Christ.

Epiphany

Color: White, gold, and yellow for Epiphany Day, the Baptism of Our Lord, and the Transfiguration of Our Lord.
Green is used on other Sundays of Epiphany.

The word "epiphany" comes from a Greek word meaning "manifestation." The thrust of this day and season is the revelation of God in Jesus Christ, the Light of the World. White, which is used during this season, symbolizes joy and celebration. Green, which is also used, symbolizes growth in our knowledge and love of God in Christ. Epiphany Day itself is a celebration of the act of Jesus manifesting God to the world. The Wise Men, who represent the whole human race, come bearing precious gifts, and Jesus manifests God to them. It is a day of splendor and light. Two events also associated with Epiphany are Jesus' baptism and the wedding at Cana.

January 6 was chosen as Epiphany Day because it was the winter solstice in the East and it was on this day that the birth of the sun-god was celebrated. Later, Christians substituted Epiphany for the solstice, and Jesus is sometimes referred to as the Sun of Righteousness, carrying out this symbol of light and the return of more sunlight. No wonder light and its rebirth are ancient themes of Epiphany.

One way to celebrate this season of more light is through a renewed emphasis on evangelism. Christ, the Sun of Righteousness, shines in the darkness of this world's evil to cast it out. Notice that the thrust of Transfiguration is on worship as the disciples experienced worship on that occasion.

Two symbols that may be used effectively are the Epiphany star and candle. The star represents the star that guided the Wise Men to the stable and that can guide us to the Christ-child. The candle sends forth light into a world of darkness and gives its light by burning itself up. Thus we find in the burning candle a symbol of Christ himself who "burned himself out" on the cross as the Light of the World.

Notice that the number of weeks in Epiphany depends upon the date of Easter. Thus the length of the season may vary. It may consist of six to nine Sundays, since the former pre-Lenten season of three Sundays was incorporated into Epiphany in the new lectionary.

Psalm 80:1–7 (C)
Psalm 80 or 80:1–7 (E)

1 Corinthians 1:3–9

Isaiah 63:16–64:8 (C)
Isaiah 63:16b–17; 64:1–8 (L)
Isaiah 63:16–17, 19; 64:2–7 (RC)
Isaiah 64:1–9a (E)

Mark 13:32–37 (C)
Mark 13:33–37 (L) (RC)
Mark 13:(24–32) 33–37 (E)

Meditation on the Texts

We give thanks to you, O God, always for the grace you have given us in Christ Jesus, a grace that has enriched us in him with all speech and knowledge so that we are not lacking in any spiritual gift. We wait expectantly for the revealing of our Lord Jesus Christ who will sustain us to the end, guiltless in the day of our Lord Jesus Christ. We thank you for your faithfulness and for calling us into the fellowship of your Son, Jesus Christ our Lord. As we wait for the return of Christ at the End we pray that we may always be watching like a doorkeeper watching for the return of the master. May we be faithful in our daily tasks, waiting for Christ's return at any moment, though we do not know the day or the hour. We remember the words of the prophet Isaiah, "Thou, O LORD, art our Father, our Redeemer from of old." We urgently pray that you will come down, O God, and make your name known to your adversaries, that the nations might tremble at your presence! We have sinned and become like one who is unclean, and all our righteous deeds are like a polluted garment. Yet you are our Father and we are the clay and you the potter. Be not exceedingly angry, O Lord, and do not remember our iniquity forever. We thank you for the assurance that in Christ our sins are forgiven and we are made a new creation. Amen.

Commentary on the Texts

Mark 13:32–37 (C)

Mark 13:33–37 (L) (RC)

Mark 13:(24–32) 33–37 (E)

Our readings are part of vs. 3–37, a section that deals with the End of the age.

There is a parallel to v. 32 in Acts 1:7: "He said to them, 'It is not for you to know times or seasons which the Father has fixed by his own authority.' " Some scholars have questioned whether v. 32 is an authentic saying of Jesus and have claimed that it is a Jewish saying to which a redactor has added "nor the Son, but only the Father." It is very unlikely, however, that the early church would have created this assertion about Jesus' ignorance regarding the time of the End of the age. The saying was an offense to the church early on, as indicated by the fact that Luke omits it entirely and many ancient authorities in the Matthew parallel omit "nor the Son." When the Arian controversy was going on, this saying about Jesus' ignorance of the timing of the End was an embarrassment for the orthodox. This verse has been a topic of a great deal of discussion from early times. The meaning here is that although the Parousia (the coming of Christ) is imminent, its precise date is not known. The fact that Jesus did *not* know the day or the hour of the End of the age is a mark of Jesus' true humanity and thus an aspect of the glory of the incarnation.

The term "that day" appears to have been a Christian technical term for the day of judgment. This may originally have been an independent saying about the day of judgment.

Verse 32 is a final warning against sign-watching and time-charting. Because only God knows the day or the hour of the End, all people should be alert and cautious.

This passage seeks to guard against two dangerous extremes: misguided enthusiasm on the one hand and careless indifference on the other. The point made here is that the test of a disciple's faithfulness is not the accuracy of the disciple in the prediction of the End time but rather the disciple's patience and endurance in watching.

Notice the repetition of the command to "watch" in vs. 33, 35, and 37. Earlier, Jesus had been teaching the four disciples, but now his teaching is to all the disciples, which means the whole church. The disciples are to watch as Jesus watched in Gethsemane. Here in the command "Watch" is Jesus' final command to all disciples *in every century*.

Reflect on how v. 37 sums up vs. 33–36 and also sums up the whole discourse from v. 5 on. The meaning of this watching for the returning Lord might be said to sum up the whole duty of Christians. The meaning of watching is drawn out by the three parables found in Matthew 25:

1. To watch for Christ's return is to make sure that our faith is not a counterfeit one that will vanish at the last crisis. To watch is to have true faith which will enable us to take our place beside Christ, the "bridegroom" who comes at an hour one does not expect.

2. To watch is to use the time before Christ returns in the work of winning others for Christ.

3. To watch is to see Christ in the intermediate comings in the persons of the least of Jesus' brothers and sisters.

Thus, to watch is not to have anxiety over heavenly cataclysms but to be obedient to the Christ who has assigned the task to watch.

This exhortation to watchfulness is reinforced by a parable that in vs. 35–36 shades off into direct advice to the disciples and to everyone. Scholars generally agree that the parable has been put together from parable material in other sources, with one being basic, namely, Luke 12:35–48. The master who had gone to a wedding might come home at any hour late at night, but no oriental traveler would return from a trip at night, as our parable says he would. The assigning of work to various servants reminds us of the parable of the talents but seems irrelevant to the point of this parable. The central thrust is the command to the porter to "watch." The figures in the parable are only thinly veiled representations of the persons for whom the teaching is intended. Consider how the distinction between parable and direct teaching has almost disappeared in this parable. The hours are those used by the Romans in dividing the night into four parts: evening, midnight, cockcrow, and morning.

The things that seem implausible may be explained if we realize that the parable pictures a situation somewhat like that of 2 Thessalonians. The early Christians were conscious that Christ was still away, perhaps for a longer time than they had expected. But they are warned to be constantly on the alert for his return, not in an excited or impatient way, but by devoting themselves to faithful service which has been assigned to each of them. We see this spelled out in 2 Thessalonians 3:6–13, which urges Christians, "Brethren, do not be weary in well-doing." Also see Ephesians 4:11ff. for another admonition to use gifts and to grow to maturity in Christ.

The first hearers of Mark's Gospel may have been in a state of excited expectation caused by and culminating in the fall of Jerusalem in A.D. 70. But these events had not brought the Second Coming, and while the people should not abandon their expectation of Christ's return, their expectations needed to be calmed and moralized.

The one theme that unifies the whole chapter is the command to be on the alert. However, the kind of alertness and the things causing the alertness vary from section to section of the chapter.

This passage speaks to Advent hopes, saying to those who are excited by calculations that the day has been determined that only God knows the time. It speaks of Advent hope to those who have a jaded skepticism and see no intervention of God taking place in the future. So this Advent message speaks both to the blandness of contemporary religious life and particularly to the apathy with which so many people face the future. Here is the good news that God will intervene in the future when the One we experience primarily as absent will come with great power and glory. Therefore we are to *watch!*

Recommended work: Study the parable in vs. 34–37 and related parables. Do a word study of watch.

The thrust of the sermon should be that although the time of Christ's return is unknown to all except God, our hope should nevertheless be alert and cautious. The audience today may be compared to that of Mark's writing, people who are bereft of their Master, who are in charge of their lives now, and who must give a full account of their stewardship when he returns. All disciples then and now are charged by Christ to "Watch!" The sermon should mention that the first observance of Advent was focused on the Second Coming, not on Christmas or Christ's birth. This is an opportunity to reshape the understanding of many people regarding Advent and the movement of history toward Christ's return in power and glory.

Isaiah 63:16–64:8 (C)

Isaiah 63:16b–17; 64:1–8 (L)

Isaiah 63:16–17, 19; 64:2–7 (RC)

Isaiah 64:1–9a (E)

We will deal with the inclusive passage of Isaiah 63:16–64:9a. This is part of a psalm of intercession that runs from 63:7 to 64:12. The preacher will need to read the entire psalm to grasp the background for our pericope. It begins with a historical prologue in 63:7–14 recalling Israel's deliverance from bondage in Egypt. God calls Israel, protects, exalts, delivers, and safely leads Israel through Sinai into Canaan. But the Israelites rebelled, causing God to oppose them. Then in 63:15–16 the psalmist prays to God to look down from heaven and see and have compassion.

This psalm is one of lament. It is a lament and prayer of the whole community which the prophet offers to God. Such laments were usually spoken by a religious leader on behalf of the people to God. Compare the motifs here to those in Psalm 74.

A prayer for pity begins with 63:15 and continues through 64:5b. In it the people in disaster turn to ask God to look in compassion on them. They pray to God to show strength and jealousy for the people. The thrust of 63:16 is that God alone, who is Father to the people, is their guardian, not Abraham and Israel their ancestors.

The message of 63:17 is that the present distress of the people is judgment in which it seems that God has entirely rejected the people who belong to God. Note that 63:18 calls the period of Solomon's temple of some 375 years "a little while." Some scholars suggest that this phrase should be amended to read that "the adversaries of Israel only a little while ago dispossessed Israel." This would point to the recent disaster of 586 B.C.

Then in 64:1–5b there is a prayer that God would reveal Godself in power as in days of old. Humans cannot approach God, but God comes to humans. In this appeal the prophet recalls the ancient manifestations of God's power—earthquakes and other terrible things that were evoked by the divine presence.

As in Second Isaiah, the appeal here is to God who is the only one who will act "for those who wait for him" (64:4). The prophet prays that God may meet those among his people who work righteousness and remember his ways.

The prophet in behalf of his people confesses their sin and hopelessness in 64:5c–7. This sin had already been suggested in the charge brought against God in 63:17. In the psalms of lamentation we see a progression from the exile onward in the way the charge brought against God falls more and more into the background, until finally it disappears from the prayer. The result is that greater importance is given to the confession of sin.

In 64:8–12, which goes farther than our pericope, the prophet makes his final petition and pleads that the Lord put away anger and have compassion on desolate Jerusalem and the destroyed temple. Whereas in 63:16 the stress was on God being a Father, here in 64:7–8 the stress is on the fact that the speakers are children. They have the status of creature, and this means belonging, trusting, and taking refuge.

The point of 64:9 is that the praying ones ask, not that God simply cancel their sin which has aroused God's anger, but that in spite of it it should be possible for them to go on living. Some scholars suggest that 63:17b, which is not in context where it is, should be placed after 64:9.

Recommended work: Do a word study of lament. Read a brief history of this period in Israel's life, around 530 to 510 B.C. Compare God's concern for the exiles in Isaiah 40–55 with a parallel comforting assurance to Zion in Isaiah 56–66. Note the sobering realities in the restored community and the emphasis on cultic matters as the Servant motif disappears.

The sermon might compare Israel's sin at that time to the sin of contemporary culture, then draw upon the images of the text of potter and clay, Redeemer and Father, and the uniqueness of God to express God's mercy to repentant sinners. The prayer for the Lord not to remember iniquity was fulfilled in Christ's death on the cross to redeem us from bondage to sin.

1 Corinthians 1:3–9

In v. 3 we have a part of the salutation in which Paul uses "grace," a Greek term, and "peace," a Hebrew term, in praying God's blessings on the Corinthians. These two terms sum up the whole of Paul's theological outlook. All of God's saving activity toward humans is contained in the word "grace," meaning unmerited love. As believers experience God's grace they find "peace," which means well-being, wholeness, and welfare. Note how peace flows out of grace and both come from God and are made effective in human history by our Lord Jesus Christ.

With v. 4 the thanksgiving begins, and it ends with v. 9. Note the themes that Paul develops further in the letter as he deals with them in a critical way: the Corinthians' knowledge of the gospel, their speech or eloquence, and the variety of their spiritual gifts.

Paul says the readers are not lacking in any spiritual gift as they wait for the revealing of our Lord Jesus Christ who will sustain them to the end. They will not only be sustained but declared guiltless in the day of our Lord. Here are two references to Christ's second coming: the end and the day of our Lord, the central theme of Advent which relates to our Markan pericope.

Recommended work: Do a study of grace, peace, day of the Lord, speech, knowledge, and spiritual gift.

The sermon should be one of thanksgiving for the hearers and confidence that God will sustain them to the end, guiltless in the day of our Lord. It might develop the meaning of grace and peace as hearers experience these gifts.

Theological Reflection

There is a theme of expectancy in all three pericopes. The Isaiah passage looks forward to the time when God will return to God's servants and meet those who joyfully work righteousness. The theme of Mark's reading is "Watch!" and in 1 Corinthians, Paul gives an assurance of God's sustaining believers until the End, making them guiltless in the day of our Lord Jesus Christ.

Children's Message

The talk with the children might be about the meaning of Advent and the Advent wreath and its candles. A child might be asked to light the first Advent candle.

Hymns for Advent I

Watchman, Tell Us of the Night; O Come, O Come, Emmanuel; O God of Every Nation.

Advent 2

Psalm 85:8–13 (C)
Psalm 85 (L)
Psalm 85:9–14 (RC)
Psalm 85 or 87:7–13 (E)

Isaiah 40:1–11 (C)
Isaiah 40:1–5, 9–11 (RC)

2 Peter 3:8–15a (C)
2 Peter 3:8–14 (L) (RC)
2 Peter 3:8–15a, 18 (E)

Mark 1:1–8

Meditation on the Texts

We thank you for sending your Son, Jesus Christ, to deliver us from our sins, O God. As we wait with eager expectation for his return at the End of the age we repent of our sins, trusting in Christ's death for forgiveness. We thank you for John the Baptizer who prepared the way for Christ by preaching a baptism for the forgiveness of sins and by baptizing in the Jordan. We know that one day is as a thousand years and a thousand years as one day in your sight. We thank you for being forbearing in bringing the day of the Lord so that all should reach repentance. May we be found living lives of holiness and godliness, waiting for and hastening the coming of the day of the Lord. May we be zealous to be found by him without spot or blemish and at peace. We have heard your gracious words of "Comfort, comfort my people" and the good news that our time of service in bondage has ended. Although human life is fragile and passes away, we rejoice that your word will stand forever. We have experienced in Christ your very presence as the Good Shepherd who feeds and cares for us his flock, gently leading us in his paths. Amen.

Commentary on the Texts

Mark 1:1–8

Our pericope describes the activity of John the Baptizer who prepared the way for Jesus. John's ministry of preparation is one of the traditional themes of Advent. John called people to repent and turn to God in the light of the coming One who will baptize with the Holy Spirit. John's message applies to hearers in our time who are preparing for Christ's second coming which may occur at any moment and who are preparing to celebrate his birth and first coming in Bethlehem. This celebration is not a memorial to someone now dead but is a celebration of the presence of the living Christ who meets us in the preaching of the word and in the Sacraments.

Note that v. 1 is in the title of the Gospel and that Mark is the only Gospel writer to entitle his book "the good news." When Paul uses the Greek word for "good news" it means either the act of proclaiming the good news or the content of the good news, namely, salvation in Christ. See how Mark, like Paul, identifies the good news with Christ. In calling his book "the gospel, or good news," Mark means that it is a proclamation of the risen Christ in which Christ is *again made present* rather than being primarily an account *about* Christ. This is a crucial point for both preacher and hearers of the gospel. The living Christ comes to those who are waiting and expectant. Advent introduces the whole Christian year and is a training in how to live expectantly throughout the whole year, actively waiting for Christ's second coming and open to his presence in the here and now.

Note that the Gospel begins with John's call to repentance. Repentance is not only a turning from sin but a turning to God. The action that takes place is this: John preaches, the hearers repent of their sin, and God forgives. The Greek word for "repent" means "to change one's mind." The Hebrew verb that lies behind it means "to turn around," carrying the thrust of "to change one's heart, will, and way of living." Notice that in v. 5 we learn that John's audience respond by confessing their sins. The translation in Today's English Version stresses the practical, behavioral element of repentance and words it "Turn away from your sins." In a sermon on this text, the preacher needs to show its central thrust, nuances, and the way it relates to the problem of guilt. Repentance is not just being sorry for getting caught in some wrongdoing. Repentance is, like the heavenly kingdom, *the gift of God.* So much preaching is bad news in that it calls on hearers to do something about getting out of bondage to sin rather than announcing the good news that God has already done the crucial thing to free us. The preaching of John and Jesus calls hearers to repent so that they may receive the reconciliation which is offered to them.

William J. Bouwsma, a contemporary historian, has this insight into the issue as expressed by John Calvin:

> But anxiety had also a part to play, for Calvin, in the spiritual life. It is the means by which the law prepares for the gospel: by threatening punishment the law stimulates an anxiety that inhibits sin and promotes repentance, "All who have at any time groped about in ignorance of God," Calvin wrote, "will admit that the bridle of the law restrained them in some fear and reverence toward God until, regenerated by the Spirit, they began wholeheartedly to love him" (*Institutes of the Christian Religion* by John Calvin, Westminster Press, II, vii, 11). . . . He [Calvin] was approaching, though he avoided the term, the Scholastic doctrine of attrition, according to which a crude fear of punishment is the first step toward reconciliation with God. But he also had something more subtle in mind; the conception suggested a way of reclaiming for Christianity what the Stoics considered the two great obstacles to human happiness: fear and hope. . . . Hope, one of the theological virtues, thus depends on anxiety. The insight anticipated the modern insight that anxiety is evidence of the life of the spirit. (William J. Bouwsma, *John Calvin, A Sixteenth-Century Portrait* [New York: Oxford University Press, 1988], p. 44)

Mark's Gospel follows the pattern of the preaching of the apostles (Acts 1:22; 10:37) in introducing the gospel proclamation with John's ministry in the wilderness. John's ministry is a prelude to God's saving act in Jesus who came as the Messiah. John points to a mightier one who is yet to come, and his preaching is a fulfillment of Old Testament prophecy, says Mark.

Note that v. 2 refers to "as it is written in Isaiah," but some manuscripts read "in the prophets" and thus avoid the problem that the quotation is an adapted form of Malachi 3:1 plus the quotation from Isaiah 40:3 beginning with Mark 1:3. The quotation from Isaiah (see the Isaiah pericope for today) in the original version has the voice cry, "In the wilderness," but Mark changes this to read "the voice of one crying in the wilderness" which makes the prophecy fit John more closely. In the Hebrew Scriptures it was God for whom the forerunner was to prepare, but changes have been made to make the quotations refer to Christ. This is not dishonesty, since Jews and Christians did not approach the Hebrew Scriptures as modern critical scholars do. Both saw such passages as referring to God's breaking into human history. Christians saw this event in the person of God's Messiah, Jesus. Today we would use an exegetical note rather than changing the text to indicate the same thing.

The messenger (v. 2) is identified as Elijah in Malachi 4:5, the one who is to come to purify Israel before the day of the Lord. We can apply this text to John only when we affirm that Jesus is now the Lord. Thus John is the forerunner. But in John 1:21, John disclaims that he is the forerunner. And in Matthew 11:14, Jesus declares that John the Baptist is Elijah! (For a solution to this, see *The Jerome Biblical Commentary,* p. 24.)

Mark has "the voice of one crying" refer to John, believing that Jesus is the Lord whose way is being prepared, thus giving a Christian interpretation to the Hebrew Scriptures.

John was certainly a historical figure who was famous for his powerful moral teaching; his ministry is noted by Josephus the Jewish historian. John expected the imminent coming of the kingdom of God, as indicated in Matthew 3:2, where John declares, "Repent, for the kingdom of heaven is at hand.'' What John promised was that if people repented of their sins, then John's baptism in water might be an effective sign of the cleansing of their souls from guilt and thus they would become members of the New Israel, ready for God's judgment. John may have confronted people with the choice: either my water baptism now for forgiveness or quite soon the Messiah's fire baptism, which means condemning judgment.

Some think that John's baptism was one in which individuals immersed themselves in the Jordan while John witnessed it. If huge crowds went out to be baptized, as Mark indicates, then this form of baptism was very likely the one used, since individual baptisms by John would have been almost impossible for all the people of the country of Judea and Jerusalem. (See Joachim Jeremias, *New Testament Theology,* p. 51.)

The Isaiah 40 text should be studied as background for this pericope, and the image of preparing the highway for the king or god is an image to use in preaching on the Markan text. John dresses as a prophet in clothes of camel's hair and wears a leather girdle. He prepares the way for Jesus the king, even as servants prepared Babylonian highways for the king or god. John's preparation does not involve grading roads and leveling hills and filling in valleys but rather confession of sins and repentance. This means turning from sin and turning to God. So John prepares the way of the Lord and affirms two things about him. He, John, is unworthy even to remove Jesus' sandals, which was slave work. This may allude to the crowds who took off their sandals to wade into the Jordan for baptism by John. By putting Jesus in a higher position than his own, John suggests but does not actually define who Jesus is. A second thing John says is that the coming One, Jesus, will baptize them with the Holy Spirit. Recall the role of the Holy Spirit in Jesus' life of descending upon him at baptism (vs. 9–11), driving him into the wilderness, where he is tempted by Satan (vs. 12–13), and promising the Holy Spirit to the disciples when they are brought to trial (13:11). This promise of the Spirit stands unfulfilled in Mark, waiting for fulfillment at Pentecost, as Luke indicates, or in John's report of the risen Christ breathing the Holy Spirit upon his disciples.

Recommended work: Study Isaiah 40:1–11 as background. Study John the Baptizer in a Bible dictionary, and do a word study of Holy Spirit.

The sermon should focus on the role of John the Baptizer (the title ''Baptizer'' indicates his function and is currently being used more than ''Baptist''). John's role is the traditional theme for the second Sunday of Advent as he prepares the way of the Lord by preaching repentance for the forgiveness of sins. The preacher may want to draw on the Luke 3:1–20 text for some of the message of John's call to repentance which may be interpreted for today's audience: a call to repent of specific sins. The sermon should prepare hearers for Christ's second coming at any moment (see the 2 Peter text) as well as for celebrating the birth of Jesus and celebrating his presence in the here and now in the preaching of the word and in the Sacraments.

Isaiah 40:1–11 (C)

Isaiah 40:1–5, 9–11 (RC)

This text is background for the Markan pericope for today, which may be mentioned when preaching on the Isaiah passage. Our pericope is the prologue to the major work of Second Isaiah found in 40:1–44:13. In addition to the prologue, we find hymns to the Lord's Redeemer (40:12–48:22) and hymns to the New Jerusalem (chs. 49–55). The setting of our pericope is a solemn convocation of the heavenly council in which God commissions the prophet. Compare this to Isaiah 6 and the call of First Isaiah. God speaks to a gathering of angels and commands them to ''comfort, give comfort'' to Jerusalem, announcing that the exile is nearly over. The double imperative of ''comfort, comfort'' is the first of many others (51:9, 17; 52:1; 57:14).

The prophet announces God's coming and the good news that the exiles' time of service in exile is nearly over. To ''speak tenderly'' literally means to ''speak to the heart,'' indicating that the words are deeply felt and earnestly spoken, much as a lover would speak to the beloved. Remember that at this time Jerusalem is in shambles. So God is speaking to an ideal Jerusalem, an ideal kingdom bound to God personally. Note that "my people" and "your God" are covenant words and the thrust in this is to remind the people of God's covenant promises. Instead of "warfare" in v. 2, a preferred translation is "time of service" (RSV footnote). The mention of "double for all her sins" may refer to the law in Exodus 22:7–8 requiring double restitution, or it may suggest that God has already punished Israel more for its sins than was to be expected.

Then in vs. 3–5 we have the image of preparing a highway in the desert for God's coming, an image reflecting Babylonian practice of building highways for the processionals of gods or the king (see *The Jerome Biblical Commentary,* p. 368). Their "glory" was revealed much as a president or ruler today reveals herself or himself in an open car in a parade. For Isaiah, the voice cries, "In the wilderness prepare," but in Mark 1:3 the author has changed this for his purposes to read "The voice of one crying in the wilderness: Prepare the way of the Lord" and has John speaking this in the wilderness.

"The glory of the LORD shall be revealed" is the good news as God acts to deliver the people from bondage in exile and returns them, much as in the first exodus to the promised land. The "voice" contrasts the immutability of God's word with the temporal nature of all living things such as grass, flowers, and all flesh. Note that for the first, and perhaps only, time the prophet speaks in the first person. A mood of despondency comes through in this strophe (vs. 6–8). Contrast this with the preceding verses on the divine glory.

Jerusalem is called to speak as a herald of good tidings to the cities of Judah, calling them to "Behold your God!" (v. 9). This God comes in heavenly grandeur and yet is a compassionate God. Note in vs. 9–10 the mounting crescendo. Now Jerusalem is hailed as the home of God on earth and the center of world redemption.

Then in v. 11 there is an easy transition from "king" to "shepherd," which in scripture can be synonymous (see Jer. 3:15). The king governed people as a shepherd governed sheep. The prophet describes God as a shepherd/king who not only attracts his people but carries them as a shepherd carries lambs.

Recommended work: Do a word study of shepherd and king. Review this period of Israel's history for the setting of our passage. Study comments by Claus Westermann in his commentary *Isaiah 40–66,* Old Testament Library (Philadelphia: Westminster Press, 1969).

The sermon may follow the moves and the images of the passage as they reveal God's coming, a theme of our Advent lessons. The sermon should show how this was fulfilled in Jesus' coming and will be completed in his coming in power and glory at the End time. The images of king/shepherd fulfilled in Jesus the Good Shepherd and "King of kings" should also be included. The sermon should be one of hope and confidence in God in spite of the outward circumstances of death and destruction in the world, for God is coming in power and glory.

2 Peter 3:8–15a (C)

2 Peter 3:8–14 (L) (RC)

2 Peter 3:8–15a, 18 (E)

Our pericope is part of a chapter whose theme is the day of the Lord. While scoffers ridicule the Christian hope of Christ's return, the delay in the Second Coming is not sufficient proof that Christ will not return, since God measures time differently from humans. Note that in v. 8 the author addresses the readers directly, as "beloved," which indicates that believers had a problem with the delay of the End also. The very fact of the delay points to God's patience and God's desire that all have time to repent and turn to God their maker and redeemer. The time of Christ's coming will be unexpected, like a thief in the night. Therefore Christians should wait in holiness and godliness. God's forbearance is a characteristic attributed to God in Exodus 34:6 and onward in Hebrew Scriptures and given more prominence in the New Testament. This undergirds the concern here about the delay, saying that it is due to the universal salvific will of God.

Note that v. 10 is the only passage in scripture pointing to a final fire which will destroy all things, an idea that was widespread at the time, and that had originated in Persia. Scripture draws on a wide variety of images, but the acceptance in faith of the truth revealed in such images does not require acceptance of the worldview from which they are drawn.

Recommended work: Do a word study of day of the Lord, holiness and godliness, and zealous.

The sermon may follow the movements of the text, focusing on the certainty of the day of the Lord, although delayed until now, and the need to live lives of holiness and godliness, without spot or blemish, and at peace.

Theological Reflection

The Markan text focuses on John's role in preparing the way of the Lord by preaching a baptism of repentance for the forgiveness of sins and pointing to Jesus who will baptize with the Holy Spirit. The 2 Peter text calls hearers to renewed expectation of the day of the Lord and godly living until that time. The Isaiah passage stresses God's coming to return the exiles and to reveal God as a shepherd/king who deals compassionately.

Children's Message

The talk might be about John the Baptizer preparing people for Jesus by calling them to repent and turn to God. Describe repentance as not only being sorry for doing wrong but turning from it to God and God's love for us in spite of our doing wrong. Repentance is more than being sorry for getting caught in not doing what we should or in doing something we shouldn't. It includes turning to God to follow the way of love.

Hymns for Advent 2

Heralds of Christ; Comfort, Comfort You My People; Come, Thou Long-expected Jesus.

Advent 3

Luke 1:46b–55 (C)
Luke 1:46–54 (RC)
Psalm 126 or Canticle 3 or 15 (E)

Isaiah 61:1–4, 8–11 (C)
Isaiah 61:1–3, 10–11 (L)
Isaiah 61:1–2, 10–11 (RC)
Isaiah 65:17–25 (E)

1 Thessalonians 5:16–24 (C)
1 Thessalonians 5:(12–15) 16–28 (E)

John 1:6–8, 19–28 (C)
John 1:6–8, 19–28 or John 3:23–30 (E)

Meditation on the Texts

We thank you, O God, for sending John to bear witness to the light so that all might believe through him. We pray that we may follow his example of being witness to Jesus the Light of the World so that others might believe in Christ. May we always remember that we are servants of Christ whose sandals we are not worthy to untie. May we be faithful in calling people to repent and turn to you, O God, thus making straight the way of the Lord. As we await Christ's return at the End we rejoice always, pray constantly, and give thanks in all circumstances. Help us to abstain from every form of evil. Keep us blameless until the coming of our Lord Jesus Christ. We remember the mission of your Servant described by Isaiah which Jesus fulfilled by bringing good tidings to the afflicted, freeing the prisoners, and proclaiming the year of the Lord's favor. We look forward to the new heavens and a new earth you have promised. We pray for the time when peace will reign and there will be no weeping or cry of distress. Amen.

Commentary on the Texts

John 1:6–8, 19–28 (C)

John 1:6–8, 19–28 or John 3:23–30 (E)

Our pericope overlaps two sections: the Prologue (vs. 1–18) and the testimony of John (vs. 19–34). It is part of the first half of the Gospel of John, which may be called the Book of Signs, and corresponds to the Synoptic narrative of Jesus' public ministry.

Note that the Fourth Gospel stresses John's role as a witness more than his ministry as a baptizer. Some scholars think that vs. 6–7 were the original opening of the Fourth Gospel and that they were displaced when the Prologue was added. Consider that the words "There was a man sent from God" would be the normal beginning of a historical narrative (see Judg. 13:2; 19:1; and 1 Sam. 1:1). Also, if the core message of vs. 6–7 came just before 1:19, there would have been a good sequence of thought: v. 7 says John was a witness to the light and vs. 19ff. are an account of his testimony to Jesus, the Light. While light can ordinarily be plainly seen and needs no testimony, in our pericope John testifies before those who are hostile and have not yet seen Jesus.

Verses 6–9 appear to have been sandwiched in between the second strophe, which deals with the creation by the Word and the gift of life and light and the attempt by the darkness to overcome the light, and the third strophe, which deals with the Word's coming into the world to defeat the darkness. John the Baptist has a role of preparing people for the coming of the Word and the light.

John was sent from God as were the prophets of old and Jesus himself, and it is this divine sending that gives relevance to John here. John's testimony is the final prophetic voice to announce the appearance of the Word among human beings. While v. 7 says that John came as a witness to testify, vs. 19ff. give an account of his testimony and the conditions under which it is given.

Verse 8 has a motif all its own: the refutation of the exaggerated claims by the followers of John the Baptist. Apparently they formed a sect that may have thought of John as the light. Some scholars think that Luke 1:68–79 was originally a hymn to John, later adapted to Christian use. While v. 9 is not a part of our pericope, it is a transition used by the editor to adapt vs. 6–8 to their present place in the Gospel.

The testimony of John is found in vs. 19–34. Verses 19–28 form the first section of this testimony concerning the coming One. In vs. 19–23 we have the first questioning of John the Baptist by priests and Levites, and John disclaims traditional roles. Then in vs. 24–28 we have the second questioning of John and his description of his own baptism as preliminary, and he exalts the One to come.

In the RSV, v. 19 begins with "And this is . . . ," but it might be translated "Now this is . . . ," and this may have opened the Gospel, or vs. 6–8 may have immediately preceded it. John came to testify to the light, vs. 6–7 tell us, and now we have his testimony. While we expect John to testify to Jesus, this will come on the following day (vs. 29–34). We can probably account for this by the work of an editor or editors. John first clarifies who he is himself to the Jews who sent priests and Levites from Jerusalem to question him. John's testimony is so important for the Fourth Gospel partly because of the necessity of clarifying his relation to Christ in his own words for some of his followers who continued a movement independent of Christianity (Acts 19:1–7).

The Jews sent priests and Levites to ask John about his baptizing, since they were specialists in ritual purification. John uses the term "Jews" as a reference to the religious authorities hostile to Jesus, especially the leaders in Jerusalem (see Raymond E. Brown, *The Gospel According to John I–XII,* pp. lxx–lxxiii). The Synoptics, however, do not mention any such embassy to John, but Mark 1:5 and Matthew 3:7 do bring out the opposition between John the Baptist and the Jewish leaders.

The priests and the Levites ask John, "Who are you?" (v. 19), which is also the question asked of Jesus in 8:25 and 21:12. Recall that in John's Gospel, Jesus says "I am" a number of times and now the Baptist says twice "I am not." The most significant aspect of this negative confession is in v. 20 when the Baptist says he is not the Christ (Messiah). John "confessed," a word usually reserved for confessing faith in Christ.

Two additional roles are proposed for John, but he denies both: Elijah and the prophet. While Jesus says that John fulfilled the mission of Elijah (Matt. 11:14), John was not literally Elijah come back to life; thus his reply here is correct. John was not fully aware of Jesus' messianic character and therefore he was less able than Jesus to evaluate his own relationship to Christ. The Jews of that time believed that the prophet Elijah would return to earth to take part in establishing God's kingdom (Mal. 4:5) or that a prophet like Moses would appear and play an important role in establishing the kingdom that the Messiah would inaugurate.

John the Baptist declares that he was simply the "voice of one crying in the wilderness, 'Make straight the way of the Lord.' " Thus he refuses to relate himself to any person but is merely the voice heralding the good news which comes in Jesus' life, death, and resurrection (see Matt. 3:3). John was in a desert region when he raised his voice; therefore the New Testament writers found the Greek version of Isaiah more suitable for their purposes, since it put the voice crying in the wilderness, while the Hebrew text reads, "A voice crying out, 'Prepare the road of the Lord in the desert.' " John sees his role as similar to that of road builders of ancient Babylon of Isaiah's day who prepared royal highways for processions of the king or statues of the gods. John prepares the way for Jesus by calling the people to repent and turn to God and baptizing them in preparation for God's kingdom breaking into human history.

Now more emissaries, this time from the Pharisees, question John. Since priests and Levites ordinarily were not Pharisees, this raises problems, but the solution seems to be that the editor of the Gospel has combined in this section more than one interrogation of John. Thus the questioners of vs. 24ff. are not the same as those of vs. 19ff.

Various kinds of baptismal rites were in use then, such as proselyte baptism and the

Essene baptism of initiates. John justifies his baptism as a preparation for Messiah who is already in their midst but they do not know him. John declares that he is not worthy to do a slave's task of unfastening the sandal straps of Messiah. There was a rabbinic saying that a disciple might do any task for his teacher that a slave was required to do for his master *except* this lowly task of unfastening his sandals. Thus John puts himself in the lowest of relationships to Messiah.

There is a problem about the location of Bethany. It is not the one near Jerusalem, and some manuscripts indicate that the place is Bethabara.

Recommended work: Do a word study of testimony, witness, and baptism. Review Isaiah 40:1–11 from last week's pericope.

The sermon might be on John the Baptist's role as witness to Jesus the Messiah. Grünewald, in one of his altarpieces of the crucifixion, takes poetic license in placing John the Baptist at the foot of the cross pointing to Jesus with a crooked finger of his right hand while holding the Hebrew Scriptures in his left. At his feet stands a lamb with a cross by its head. The artist shows us John as the one bearing witness to Jesus as the lamb of God who takes away the sin of the world (1:29). John is a model for the Christian preacher in pointing to Christ while humbling himself. The sermon might deal with the questions that people had about who John was and his mission to prepare the way of the Lord by calling people to repent and turn to God.

Isaiah 61:1–4, 8–11 (C)

Isaiah 61:1–3, 10–11 (L)

Isaiah 61:1–2, 10–11 (RC)

Our pericope is part of the section of vs. 1–11 that describes the mission to Zion. It reminds us of the Servant Songs of Isaiah 42–53, particularly 50:4–11. The mission of the prophet of God is to bring encouragement to the exiled and oppressed, whom he will strengthen to become like mighty oaks. We should compare this passage to Luke 4:16–20 and Matthew 11:5 and Luke 7:22. The Luke 4:16–20 pericope describes Jesus' sermon in Nazareth at the synagogue and has been called the "Christian Manifesto." In preaching our pericope for today, the preacher should show how it was fulfilled in Christ upon whom the Spirit of the Lord came and who brought good tidings to the afflicted (the poor).

This poem may have been the inaugural calling of one of the leaders of the early postexilic members of the school of Isaiah. Notice how rich each phrase is in biblical tradition. The word "Spirit" always points to a mighty work of God. Prophets of this period ordinarily avoided the term as they stressed the interior rather than the exterior wonders of God's work. Recall that the Spirit had been promised to the messianic king in Isaiah 11:1–2. Recall that in Genesis 1:2 the spirit creates God's new paradise.

The Lord anointed the prophet. The Word is linked to the preaching and hearing of the word of faith which enlightens hearers to know God's word and to follow the Word. "Anoint" is used here in a nonliteral sense. It means "to give full authorization." The anointing and the endowment of the spirit occur together in other passages where the reference is almost always to kings who are designated God's "anointed." The anointing of priests came later. This is the prophet's commissioning.

The prophet's task is to speak, and in and through this speaking he is to effect a change on those to whom he is sent. For the Hebrew way of thinking, to proclaim salvation is almost as much as to summon it into existence or to bring it about as to talk about it. Fresh prophecy made a beginning in the work of Third Isaiah (chs. 56–66), as he takes up the task of Second Isaiah. He brings good tidings to the poor (see 40:9 and 52:7). In these other two passages from Second Isaiah the proclamation is of an event that has already come about. The people who bring such good tidings are *not* the prophet but the watchers! Some think that Third Isaiah mistakes the bringers of good tidings for the prophet.

The message of the prophet is destined to heal wounds and bring liberty to captives and to bind up the broken-hearted. Prisoners are led out of dark dungeons to full daylight. The abundance of metaphors here serves the basic idea of the total salvation of God's people both bodily and spiritually, individually and corporately (see Matt. 11:4–6).

The year of the Lord's favor means that the messianic jubilee has arrived (see 49:8).

The liberation of captives refers to people in prison for debts and other offenses, not to the exiles. With the dawning of the time of jubilee and its salvation there will be a change for the better in the personal suffering of the great number of people suffering at that time. So the prophet compares his proclamation to that of a herald announcing release to those in slavery because of debts.

No specific event is mentioned. But God's favor is God's turning in grace, which will happen at some indeterminate but near point in time. "Vengeance" (v. 2) might better be translated "rescue," since God will rescue those who are oppressed and in prison. The final task of the prophet is to comfort all who mourn, a phrase found a number of times in Third Isaiah.

This comforting will take place as God gives a garland instead of ashes and the oil of gladness instead of mourning and the mantle of praise instead of a faint spirit (v. 3). The outcome of this is that the oppressed will be called "oaks of righteousness" by which God is glorified. The prophet is convinced he has been sent by God with a message to his nation of such conviction and freedom.

Verses 4–11 describe the seed that God blesses, and they connect directly with the messenger's proclamation in 61:1ff. In v. 4, which should be joined with vs. 7–11 because they deal with the same theme, there is a change in Judah's fortunes: what was destroyed is raised up, and ruined cities are repaired.

Then in vs. 8–11 we are told that all nations will see God's covenant faithfulness and blessing, and the prophet in vs. 10–11 identifies himself with Zion, rejoicing in Zion's salvation. God is a God of justice who hates wrongdoing and will judge offenders. As surely as the earth produces vegetation, so will God's righteousness and praise spring forth before all the nations (v. 11).

Recommended work: Do a word study of Spirit, vengeance, justice, and righteousness.

The sermon may draw upon the rich images and metaphors of the text as it follows the movements of the passage. The preacher will want to link it with Luke 4:16–20 and Jesus' fulfillment of the role of the Servant described here. Through Jesus' death and resurrection he has set free those who were bound in sin and has brought to all who mourn comfort through the hope of the resurrection. God continues to act in history to work for justice and righteousness, and this may be related to Jesus as Lord of history who is working still. This text might be the first choice for a sermon this Sunday, since the text from John continues the theme of John the Baptist and centers more on his identity than on Christ.

Isaiah 65:17–25 (E)

The thrust of this passage is that heaven and earth will be transformed by God, and God will rejoice with Jerusalem now that Jerusalem's former troubles are forgotten. The pericope should include v. 16b, which begins the thought continued in v. 17. The new creation is a miraculous one, and the world is designated by "heavens and . . . earth." Note that v. 17b repeats the thought of 16b that former troubles are to be forgotten. This idea of a fresh creation is a bit odd here, since it is a basic idea in later apocalyptic writing. It may be intended in a figurative sense here.

In vs. 19b–24 we are told specifics about this fresh creation in which there will be no more weeping, and no premature deaths, because of the blessing of God, a connection between God and humans that never breaks.

In this new creation even animals are to live at peace with one another (v. 25). Artists have painted this scene of the "Peaceable Kingdom," and the preacher may want to refer to this image which artists have sought to capture.

In contrast to ordinary life, the fresh creation will be one in which life is lived to the end by everyone. Everyone will have long life in the new era of salvation (v. 20). The person who does not reach one hundred years will be the exception! And in vs. 21–22 we learn that there will be no more work that is done in vain. Salvation will occur in space and time, according to this prophet's message. Human beings are blessed by God and their lives are like a tree (v. 22). When humans call on God, they will be given an answer; thus there will be free access to the spring of life, the Creator God. In fact, God will anticipate the call of people and answer *before* they call! Such is the gracious providence of Israel's God. The Lord will protect this new creation, and nothing shall hurt or destroy in God's holy mountain.

Recommended work: Compare our text with Isaiah 11:6–9 and the image of the fresh creation. Compare it with the Genesis image of the first creation before the Fall.

The sermon might follow the images and the movement of the text itself, holding up the picture of the fresh creation with its peaceable kingdom. The emphasis that God, not humans, will create it and protect those who live in it should be a thrust of the message. God in Christ began this new age within the boundaries of present history and we have this hope which leads us forward into the future. The sermon should be one of strong hope in God for God's creation.

1 Thessalonians 5:16–24 (C)

1 Thessalonians 5:(12–15) 16–28 (E)

This pericope is part of the conclusion of the letter in which Paul exhorts the Thessalonians to rejoice, pray, and give thanks. He tells them in v. 19 not to quench the Spirit, and in v. 20 he tells them much the same thing in saying they should not despise prophesying, which probably meant speaking the word of God in a coherent way. He wrote the Corinthians (1 Cor. 14:37–40) to channel the Spirit without despising the ecstatic ways in which it is expressed.

Note that v. 23b picks up the theme of Christ's coming again, a major thrust of Advent which, like a theme in music, appears again and again. God's faithfulness is affirmed.

In vs. 26–28, Paul gives his farewell. We know little about the holy kiss, but it seems to have been a customary part of early Christian worship. It is generally interpreted today to mean a gesture of peace such as a handclasp or an embrace and not exclusively a kiss as such. Paul emphasizes that the letter is to be read to "all the brethren," which may indicate that some factions had developed.

Recommended work: Compare this benediction with others of scripture. Do a study of Spirit in Paul's other letters.

The sermon might take one verse and develop it, or it might deal with the entire passage as an exhortation to hearers today. The mention of the Second Coming should be included as a theme of Advent.

Theological Reflection

There is a theme of expectation of God's breaking into human history to bring about a new creation. Both of the Isaiah passages point to such an age. John the Baptist points to Jesus as Messiah, disclaiming that he himself is Messiah, and the 1 Thessalonians passage refers to the coming of our Lord Jesus Christ, a major theme of Advent.

Children's Message

The third candle may be lighted by one of the children, with conversation about Advent as a time of expectation and preparation for celebrating Jesus' birth and his coming again in glory.

Hymns for Advent 3

Let All Mortal Flesh Keep Silence; Joyful, Joyful, We Adore Thee; Rejoice, Rejoice, Believers.

Advent 4

Psalm 89:1–4, 19–24 (C)   **Romans 16:25–27**
Psalm 89:1–4, 14–18 (L)
Psalm 89:2–5, 27, 29 (RC)   **Luke 1:26–38**
Psalm 132 or 132:8–15 (E)

2 Samuel 7:8–16 (C)
2 Samuel 7:(1–7), 8–11, 16 (L)
2 Samuel 7:1–5, 8–11, 16 (RC)
2 Samuel 7:4, 8–16 (E)

Meditation on the Texts

O God, as we recall your establishing an everlasting "house" and kingdom for David, we remember the fulfillment of this promise in the birth of Jesus. We thank you for the mystery of salvation disclosed through the prophetic writings and now made known to all nations, the mystery made public through Jesus Christ to bring about the obedience of faith. As we prepare to celebrate the miracle of Jesus' birth we remember the example of Mary his mother who said to the angel, "Let it be to me according to your word." During this holiday season and in the days and years ahead may we become more obedient to your word, following the One whose name was called Jesus. We rejoice that he was given the throne of his father David and of his kingdom there will be no end. Amen.

Commentary on the Texts

Luke 1:26–38

The annunciation is the theme of our pericope, a theme often depicted in religious art. The foretelling of the birth of Jesus in vs. 26–38 is the second half of the section of vs. 5–38 which tell of the births of both John the Baptist and Jesus. Examine how closely the two halves correspond to each other, since the core of each is a divine birth announcement resembling descriptions of divine revelations in the Hebrew Scriptures. For an outline of such a revelation of a coming birth, see Charles H. Talbert, *Reading Luke* (New York: Crossroad, 1982), p. 18. In all such forms the emphasis is always on the child as the fulfillment of divine promise, *not* on the parent(s). Thus, in our reading, the stress is not on Mary but on Jesus who is to be born to her.

There are two points of emphasis here. One is on the relationship of Jesus to John the Baptist, his relative (traditionally thought to be a cousin). This implies continuity between the ministry of John and that of Jesus in salvation history. Recall that a major thrust of Luke/Acts is establishing a continuity between Jesus and the church on the one hand and Israel on the other. It is foreshadowed here in the annunciations of the births of John and Jesus. Note the superiority of Jesus over John, which is another theme of Luke's Gospel.

A second point of emphasis is on the unusual nature of Jesus' conception. Here is one point on which Roman Catholics and Protestants, conservatives and more liberal Christians differ. While Luke does *not* address the issues that arose later in church history, such as the miraculous birth of the child (meaning giving birth while Mary's physical organs remained intact, and also the perpetual virginity of Mary), Luke does speak of Mary's virginity before giving birth: she conceives Jesus without benefit of husband Joseph (vs. 34–35).

Verses 32–33 declare that Jesus will be the Davidic Messiah, who was expected to save Israel from its enemies. Hence, v. 31 says his name shall be called "Jesus" (meaning "Yahweh saves"). Then in v. 35 we learn how this will come about. Jesus will be conceived by the Holy Spirit. Some paintings of the annunciation show the Holy Spirit speaking into Mary's ear with a kind of cartoon "balloon." This seeks to indicate that Jesus was conceived by the word of God, not by a human father. The point that Luke is making here is that Jesus entered the status of divine Sonship by a new creative act of the same Holy Spirit which in the Genesis creation story brooded over the waters of chaos. Now a new creation takes place, which is the real miracle of Jesus' birth and the theme of the angel's annunciation and Mary's awe. And the miraculous character of this event is not affected by the question of whether Jesus had one human parent or two.

The miraculous conception of Jesus, or virgin birth as it is called, has functioned in a variety of ways in the theology of the church through the ages. It has been used to confront those who claimed that Jesus only seemed to be human (Docetists). Jesus' birth was a sign of his true humanity. Early writers after Matthew and Luke appeal to the birth of Jesus by the Virgin Mary as proof of his real humanity (not divinity, as is commonly claimed). Augustine and others claimed that since all human beings are infected by original sin, Jesus, in order to be Savior from sin, must be sinless and to do this he must *not* inherit Adam's sin. Thus the Holy Spirit conceives Jesus as the means by which Jesus avoids original sin and is the sinless Savior. Some Protestant orthodox scholars put the proof of the truth of Christianity in the miracles of Jesus and in the fulfillment of biblical prophecy in Jesus' life and mission. They see the virgin birth as a biological miracle that fulfills Isaiah 7:14 and so claim this as the ultimate proof for Jesus' divinity and thus the truth of Christianity. For them, to deny the virgin birth as a biological miracle is to deny Christianity itself.

In Luke's thought the miraculous conception of Jesus functions to explain Jesus' later life, as such miraculous births in Greek and Roman biographies did. According to this view, Jesus was what he was, divine and human, because he was divinely begotten. Note also the Christology of Luke, who uses an "exaltation Christology." In our text we are told that Jesus is the descendant of David and thus is heir to the promises of the Hebrew Scriptures. By his resurrection Jesus was raised to the exalted status of God's Son and given divine power. This exaltation theology of the church served to present Jesus as the present Lord who rules from heaven and as the historical figure whose story we have in the Gospels. Accordingly, the risen Christ reigns from heaven because of his resurrection from the dead, and his unique earthly life may be explained by his miraculous birth. The greatness of Jesus' life was not a human achievement but was the result of God's intervention by the Holy Spirit. Thus Jesus was God's act, an act of God's grace which excludes all human merit.

We should note that the Latin Vulgate translation of the Greek text has contributed to the veneration paid to Mary. The angel's greeting to her is translated into English as "Hail, Mary, full of grace," while the RSV puts it, "Hail, O favored one." The idea expressed by the Vulgate (the Roman Catholic translation of the Greek into Latin) is that Mary is full of grace and so is able to dispense from the fullness of this grace to others the grace they ask for. But the Greek does not allow any such interpretation, for it has Mary addressed simply as the favored one who is the beneficiary of God's sovereign choice.

If we are to believe that the virgin birth was simple history, then we must affirm that the story ultimately came from Mary herself. Mary's response to the announcement that she would bear a son is the only response anyone can properly make to the free and gracious gift of God's favor: the response of humble obedience which acts in faith. In understanding this account, we must remember that Luke is not revealing a diary as if he had come into possession of a young Jewish girl's diary but rather is offering a gospel of salvation.

Mary thus stands as a model for Christians through the ages when confronted by God's favor and call to obedience. In this scientific age we too often ask with Mary, though, "How shall this be . . . ?" and thus seek a rational explanation of what is promised. She sees no possibility for a child, since she has no husband. But with God all things are possible, and the angel Gabriel announces that God will act to make it possible.

with each other and with those of the Hebrew Scriptures. Compare Mary's response to the annunciation to that of other biblical characters who obeyed or disobeyed God's call, such as Isaiah, Jeremiah, David, the rich young ruler, and Zacchaeus.

The sermon might focus either on who Jesus is as revealed in the annunciation story or on Mary as the model of obedience to God's call. The sermon might seek to lead hearers to open their hearts to Christ to be born anew within them this Christmas season, obeying God's leading as Mary did. Or the sermon might focus on Jesus as the Davidic Messiah whose identity was fully revealed by his death and resurrection and exaltation to the right hand of God. As exalted Lord he intercedes for us and is Lord of our lives and of history, and the sermon might relate him as such to hearers.

2 Samuel 7:8–16 (C)

2 Samuel 7:(1–7), 8–11, 16 (L)

2 Samuel 7:1–5, 8–11, 16 (RC)

2 Samuel 7:4, 8–16 (E)

The key to understanding our pericope, and in fact the whole of chapter 7, is the play on the various meanings of "house." Note that in vs. 1–2 it means "palace"; in vs. 5–7, 13 it means "temple"; in vs. 11, 16, 19, 25–27, 29 it means "dynasty"; and finally in v. 18 it means "family status."

This oracle of Nathan is the basis of royal messianism in the Hebrew Scriptures. Notice that Nathan reverses his first word that the king should build a temple and says later that instead of David building a house (read temple) for the Lord, the Lord will build a house (read everlasting dynasty) for him!

In reading this passage, we may pick up a somewhat hostile attitude, or at least an apathy, toward the temple and a preference for the "old-time religion" of the desert. But in v. 13, which may be a later addition, there is a favorable attitude toward the temple.

This chapter's purpose is to explain why David was not chosen to build the temple, and it seems to be based somewhat on Psalm 89. Although the historical Nathan does not appear in the Early Source material until 12:1, we have Nathan the prophet used as a mouthpiece of the author in our pericope. Note that in v. 6 the author ignores the temple at Shiloh.

God makes a personal promise to David to continue his line forever, thus making his dynasty an everlasting one, assuring Israel that it will enjoy peace and security (vs. 10–11). In v. 13 we have a reference to Solomon's act of building the temple and God's promise to establish David's dynasty forever.

The Lord will make this permanent house of David, and the verses up to v. 16 seem to be a commentary on a previous textual passage. God promises personal protection of the eternal dynasty of David, and the sins of the future king not only will be taken seriously but will be punished accordingly. But it will be a relationship like a father who chastises a son, not a relationship to destroy the sinner.

According to the author of 1 Chronicles 22:7–10 it is not David the man of many wars who is to build the temple with hands stained with the blood of his enemies but another, whose name is Solomon (note hint of the word *shālōm,* meaning "peace"). There will be not only a temple house but a definite succession of men to bear David's authority. The fulfillment of this promise comes when the Word of the Son of David, Jesus Christ, who is the Son of God, makes his dwelling with us (John 1:14). He tabernacles with human beings. Compare this to our Lukan passage for today of the annunciation.

Recommended work: Review the life and lineage of David in a Bible dictionary. Do a word study of "house," which is the key word of the passage. Read the prayer of David in vs. 18–29 which he offers in response to God's promise of a "house."

The sermon might develop the theme of David's house being a dynasty, not a temple, which is fulfilled in Jesus, the Davidic Messiah. This passage should be related to our

Lukan reading for today and show how Jesus fulfilled the role of kingly messiah, not as an earthly king but as a messiah/king who rules from the cross by the power of love. The sermon should stress the presence of the living Christ here and now who rules our hearts by love, not by force.

Romans 16:25–27

This is the finest of Paul's doxologies. Paul ascribes glory to God who has given to human beings the gospel of Christ and sustains the constancy of deeds in the Christian way of life. Note that the term "preaching" is another word for "gospel." Paul's gospel is the good news that he has made known in preaching Jesus Christ. He says that the prophetic writings, the Hebrew Scriptures, held a secret (v. 25) which became known only when Christ appeared. This text is illustrated by the 2 Samuel and Lukan readings for today. The prophecy of the everlasting dynasty of David was fulfilled in Christ, the Davidic Messiah who reigns forever.

Paul prays to God "who is able to strengthen you." The word for "able" in the Greek is from the same root word from which we get the word "dynamite." God is more than able to strengthen us. God strengthens us by the preaching of Jesus Christ. The gospel of Christ sets us free from bondage to sin and death and gives us power for daily living in obedience to God's leading.

The manifestation of the divine plan (v. 26) is the plan of salvation which includes all humans, Jew and Greek alike. Paul is anxious to link the revelation of this mystery plan with the Hebrew Scriptures. In v. 26 the Greek word for "manifested" is a first aorist passive participle and has the thrust of to make plain as a completed action.

Paul's statement that this manifestation was according to the command of the eternal God indicates that he affirms that God is in charge of the redemptive work and gives orders to carry it out. The same word "eternal" used here of God is used of eternal life and eternal punishment in Matthew 25:46. In this verse Paul may be alluding to his call as an apostle of the Gentiles so that he could make the mystery, hidden until that time, known to all the nations (see 1 Tim. 1:1; Titus 1:3).

Then Paul praises the "only wise God," which is the high point of the doxology. Note that praise is offered to God *through* his Son Jesus Christ. A better translation is "to God alone wise."

Recommended work: Do a word study of mystery, revelation, and obedience.

The sermon might follow the text and its moves, leading up to the climax at the end "to God alone who is wise," which is the high point of the pericope. The sermon may be one of encouragement for those who are despairing and weak. It might also relate the other two texts for today, showing how the prophetic writings such as 2 Samuel 7 were fulfilled in Christ as described in the Lukan text. The purpose of this revelation is to bring about the obedience of faith which is the heart of the Christian faith. The sermon might emphasize this.

Theological Reflection

The 2 Samuel passage foretells the Davidic dynasty which shall be unending, and we see this fulfilled in Christ who is described by Luke as the Davidic Messiah. Thus the two passages link with each other nicely. The Romans passage speaks of the mystery kept secret for long ages but now disclosed through the prophetic writings and made known to all nations, namely, the plan of salvation in Jesus Christ. The goal of the plan is to bring about the obedience of faith.

Children's Message

The conversation with the children, who are becoming very excited about the nearness of Christmas on this last Sunday in Advent, might be about the annunciation and Mary's response. The meaning of Jesus' name, "God saves," and how he fulfilled this by his death and resurrection might be discussed. And Mary's humble obedience in faith should be held up as the model for all of us to follow. She heard God's word and obeyed.

Hymns for Advent 4

Come, Thou Long-expected Jesus; Lo, How a Rose E'er Blooming; O How Shall We Receive You.

Christmas 1

Psalm 111 (C)
Psalm 128:1–5 (RC)
Psalm 147 or 147:13–21 (E)

Isaiah 61:10–62:3 (C)
Isaiah 45:22–25 (L)
Sirach 3:2–6, 12–14 (RC)

Galatians 4:4–7 (C)
Galatians 3:23–25; 4:4–7 (E)
Colossians 3:12–17 (L)
Colossians 3:12–21 (RC)

Luke 2:22–40 (C)
Luke 2:25–40 (L)
John 1:1–18 (E)

Meditation on the Texts

We rejoice in you, O God, for you have clothed us in the garments of salvation and covered us with the robe of righteousness through Jesus Christ. We thank you that in Jesus Christ you have caused righteousness and praise to spring forth before all the nations. We know that only in you, O Lord, are righteousness and strength. Your word has gone forth in righteousness in Jesus Christ, a word that shall not return. We thank you that when the time had fully come you sent forth your Son, Jesus, born of a woman and born under the law, to redeem those who were under the law. We rejoice that we have received adoption as children by faith in Christ and so are no longer slaves but children and heirs of yours. We thank you for the Spirit of Christ in our hearts crying, "Abba! Father." We pray that whatever we do in word or deed we may do in the name of the Lord Jesus, giving thanks to you, our God, through him. May we put on love which binds everything together in perfect harmony. We remember the obedience of Mary and Joseph who took Jesus to the temple and offered sacrifice and the recognition of the child Jesus by Simeon and Anna. And we recall with thanksgiving that Jesus as a child grew and became strong, filled with wisdom, and that your favor was upon him, O God. Amen.

Commentary on the Texts

Luke 2:22–40 (C)

Luke 2:25–40 (L)

Our pericope is part of vs. 21–52, a section whose common theme is obedience to the Jewish law and some pious customs of the Jews. It is also part of the larger portion of 1:57–2:52, whose theme is Jesus' birth and early life. In v. 21 Jesus' circumcision on the eighth day as obedience to Jewish law is described.

In the reading of vs. 22–40 we have two traditional Jewish practices that Jewish law required: vs. 22–24 describe the purification of a mother after childbirth following the instructions of Leviticus 12:6, 8. Luke tells us that the family offered birds, not a lamb, for her purification, which indicates that she was poor. Jesus was from a poor family, and throughout his life he was an advocate for the poor and oppressed.

Note that vs. 22b–23 refer to presenting Jesus, the firstborn son, to the Lord. In Exodus 13:2, 12, 13, and 15 we learn that the firstborn belongs to God and must be redeemed; thus Mary and Joseph are acting according to the law.

The law of Moses provided for three rituals after the birth of a male child (Leviticus 12; Ex. 13:12; Num. 18:16): (1) Circumcision was required on the eighth day from birth, usually the occasion for naming the child, as in Jesus' case ("Jesus" is Greek for the

Hebrew word meaning "Yahweh is salvation"). (2) In the case of a firstborn, Jewish law required that he be redeemed by the payment of a five-shekel offering, anytime after the first month. (3) The purification of the mother after forty days which involved the sacrifice of a lamb and a turtledove or a young pigeon, but in the case of the poor a second dove or pigeon could be sacrificed in the place of the lamb. It appears that Luke has confused the second and third ceremonies. This is not surprising, since Luke did not have a deep personal interest in the details of Jewish ceremonial law. However, he mentions five times in our pericope that the purification was carried out in accordance with Jewish law.

The implication of this account is that Jesus was brought up according to the strictest tradition of Jewish piety. Then Luke introduces two other persons, Simeon and Anna, who have similar loyalty to the law and piety. Their devotion to the law had made them eager for God's coming intervention. Simeon was "righteous and devout, looking for the consolation of Israel, and the Holy Spirit was upon him" (v. 25). Anna "did not depart from the temple, worshiping with fasting and prayer night and day" (v. 37). When people properly understood the piety of the Hebrew Scriptures they became eager for the coming of the Gospel in Jesus the Messiah.

There was an old Jewish custom in which parents brought their child to the temple for an aged rabbi to bless and pray for the child. This may be the reason that Simeon took Jesus up in his arms and blessed God and spoke what is now called the Nunc Dimittis. Simeon, like a slave addressing his king, asks for dismissal from duty. He was looking for "the consolation of Israel," which was a standard rabbinic description of the messianic age. In the opening words of Isaiah 40–55 we find the basis for this prophecy. Much of Simeon's song is drawn from these prophecies. The "consolation of Israel" has now become visible in this child of a peasant maid. Until this moment Simeon may have thought of the future glory of Israel as liberation from its enemies and the restoring of the kingdom of David. But now with the Messiah in his arms, Simeon paints a darker picture, one reflecting the Isaiah prophecies. The kingdom of this Messiah will not come about in an easy or superficial triumph, but he will bring it about through suffering. His mother's heart will be pierced. He will be the center of controversy. The reference to the fall and the rising of many in Israel has been interpreted in various ways, but perhaps the best interpretation is that the Messiah must walk with Israel the pathway of suffering on the way to glory. Even Jesus' best friends, the chosen Twelve, had to be humbled by failure. But because Jesus had chosen to share their humiliation, they were able to rise with him after his resurrection.

In vs. 32ff. we learn that Mary and Joseph do not understand the true meaning of their son's destiny as Messiah. Luke describes their response as one of marveling at what was said about him. Compare this with vs. 48–50, where we see that the reaction of Jesus' parents was one of joy and anticipation mixed with perplexity and amazement.

In v. 33 "his father" is replaced in some manuscripts by "Joseph," probably to uphold the virgin conception. But we should remember that Matthew and Luke recognized Joseph's fatherhood both legally and realistically as they followed Semitic thought patterns. Jesus' Messiahship rests firmly on his Davidic heritage, while no meaning is drawn from Mary's possible descent from the tribe of Levi. But for Luke and Matthew, this was not inconsistent with the fact that Joseph was not Jesus' natural father. We have in Levirate marriage (Luke 20:28) a partial parallel in which the son by the wife of a deceased brother is nevertheless viewed as *the brother's son!*

In vs. 36ff. we are told of Anna, a prophetess who was very old. The text does not make it clear whether she was eighty-four years old or had been a widow for eighty-four years. She may have belonged to an order of widows with specific religious duties in the temple. The fact that she has been a widow for a long time was a mark of honor. She was a prophetess, one who spoke for God and was given a recognition rare in Jewish history. In Hebrew Scriptures only seven prophetesses prophesied to Israel: Sarah, Miriam, Deborah, Hannah, Abigail, Huldah, and Esther. Anna gave thanks to God and then spoke of Jesus to all who were looking for the redemption of Jerusalem, meaning the coming of Messiah. She, like Simeon, recognized the infant Jesus to be the longed-for Messiah to redeem Israel.

Recommended work: Study in a Bible dictionary the three Jewish customs related in vs. 22–40. Do a study of consolation of Israel, redemption of Jerusalem, and Messiah.

The sermon might follow the images and the moves of the text, pointing to the devotion of Jesus' parents in following Jewish law and to Simeon and Anna who were eagerly awaiting the Messiah and who recognized in the infant Jesus the fulfillment of their dreams. The sermon might relate our dreams for peace, for freedom from oppressive forces, and for the new era of God's rule to the longing of Simeon and Anna and other devout Jews, showing how Jesus' death and resurrection have begun this new era.

John 1:1–18 (E)

See Christmas 2, (C).

Isaiah 61:10–62:3 (C)

In Isaiah 61:10–11 the prophet identifies with Zion. He rejoices in Zion's salvation which is as sure as the vegetation growing up in a garden when it is sown with seeds. Compare this passage with 51:1–3. The prophet acknowledges God's salvation and recognizes that what is to happen in the future with Israel is the work of the Lord who will cause righteousness and praise to spring forth.

Then 62:1–3 is the beginning of a new section, vs. 1–12, describing the New Jerusalem, and it repeats themes common to chapters 40–55 and 60–61. Zion, which stands for Jerusalem founded on Mt. Zion, is the object of God's prophecy. Note that God speaks in the first person here. The prophet continues to declare Zion's approaching vindication in vs. 1–3. The "new name" of v. 2 denotes a new status. The name meant the nature or character of a person or a nation. (Recall Abram's name change to Abraham: Abram=exalted father; Abraham=father of a multitude, Gen. 17:5.)

The thrust of this chapter is encouragement, and the image in v. 3 of Zion becoming a crown of beauty in the hand of the Lord and a royal diadem gives the people of Israel a vision of hope. It tells of the New Jerusalem which is to be the religious capital of the world. No longer will Jerusalem be called Forsaken but rather Married and My delight is in her (v. 4).

Recommended work: Read the background of Israel in the period of Third Isaiah and compare chapter 61 with the Servant Songs of Isaiah 42–53, especially chapter 50.

The sermon may relate this hope for God's approaching vindication of Jerusalem to the hope of Simeon and Anna of our Lukan text, a hope realized in the birth of Jesus the Messiah. The Lord God in Jesus Christ caused righteousness and praise to spring forth before all the nations. And Israel will be called by a new name: the church, the New Israel.

Isaiah 45:22–25 (L)

The thrust of this passage is the call to let all nations bow before God and sing God's praises. There is only one requirement for salvation, which is to turn to God in humble devotion and trust in God alone. God asserts that there is no other God.

God speaks to Israel in exile in a foreign country as a righteous and helping God. God's action in history continues as though Israel had never met with disaster. The nations who had conquered Israel have fallen to the same fate of defeat and exile. But instead of jubilation on the victor's part over the defeated gods, those among the nations who survived are invited to participate in God's salvation. God intervened by means of Cyrus, which involved a radical change in God's way of operating in history. Since God is the creator of the whole world, God's purpose is not the destruction of the nations. Rather, God's victory involves something entirely new, namely, the convincing of the nations that God, indeed, is the only God.

In vs. 23–25 the goal is set forth of God's dealings with all humanity: free confession and trust which springs from conviction on the part of those who realize that Israel's God is the only true God: "To me every knee shall bow, every tongue shall swear." Here "every" means every individual. Those who once were God's enemies and fought against God now participate with Israel in God's salvation. To bow the knee to God and confess

God to be the one true God demands a free decision on the part of the individual who confesses his or her faith.

Recall that this text is taken up in the New Testament in Romans 14:11 and Philippians 2:10–11. Both citations maintain the original thrust of the passage. The author of the Isaiah passage believes that all human beings are invited to partake in the divine salvation. Membership in the people of God is now based on the free confession of those who have discovered that the God of Israel alone is God. These two very important factors, which we see are already present in Second Isaiah, became significant for the Christian understanding of the church.

Recommended work: Compare this passage with the Romans and Philippians passages noted above which cite it. Reflect on how this passage's prophecy is fulfilled in the church.

The sermon might describe the setting of the prophecy and how this was good news not only to Israel but to all human beings. The preacher might relate this to the New Testament citations and to the church. The sermon should call the hearers to see God's invitation as one to all people to partake of God's salvation, conditioned on the free confession of those who trust in Israel's God now revealed in Jesus Christ.

Sirach 3:2–6, 12–14 (RC)

The theme of this passage is the duty of children to parents and its reward. Jewish doctrine said that the observance of the Mosaic law was meritorious. Note that Sirach says that honoring one's parents, the fifth commandment, "atones for sins" (v. 3). This belief was supplanted by Jesus' teaching that "when you have done all that is commanded you, say, 'We are unworthy servants; we have only done what was our duty'" (Luke 17:10). The New Testament clearly rejects the notion of earning God's favor by good deeds and declares that salvation is by faith alone (Gal. 2:16).

The meaning of "will refresh" (v. 6) is "will grant rest from anxieties."

Adult children are commanded to help their parents in their old age and not to grieve them, even if their minds fail them (v. 12). The declaration that kindness to a father will be credited against one's sins continues the thought of v. 3 but is not a New Testament teaching, as we just noted. Salvation is by grace alone, and we cannot earn it or lay up credits upon which to draw against sins. But the notion of credit is found also in 35:1: "He who keeps the law makes many offerings; he who heeds the commandments sacrifices a peace offering."

Recommended work: Compare and contrast the notion of merit for obeying the fifth commandment with the teaching of Paul in Galatians and Romans which emphasizes justification by grace alone, not by works of the law.

The sermon should stress the importance of honoring and caring for the physical and spiritual needs of one's parents but not to lay up merit or to atone for one's sins, since Christ died once for all for our sins. The sermon might deal with the needs of the elderly and how individuals and society are seeking to meet their needs and develop a more caring community. The need for patience and kindness should be stressed. These virtues are the fruit of a life transformed by Christ's death and resurrection.

Galatians 4:4–7 (C)

Galatians 3:23–25; 4:4–7 (E)

In Galatians 3:23–25 we have a contrast between the law which acted as a custodian and salvation by faith which came with Christ and frees us from being under the custodian, the law. The key word here is "custodian." A custodian was a household assistant, often a slave, who supervised the life of a minor child. Paul compares the law to such a custodian and makes two points: (1) The law's function is to impede sin, as indicated in Romans 7:7–25; and (2) its tenure was limited until Christ came and faith was revealed.

The thought of 3:23–25 continues in 4:4–7 which contrasts freedom in Christ with bondage under the law. Christ came at the right time, a time determined by God in order to ransom those under the law. There is a parallel to "when the time had fully come" (4:4) in "the date set by the father" (4:2). Both terms express the purposefulness of God in sending the Son in fulfillment of the promises made to Abraham (see 4:4).

In 4:4–7 we have the strongest declaration of the incarnation in all of Paul's letters. He stresses that Jesus was "born of woman, born under the law" to make the incarnation even more real, showing Jesus as part of all humanity. But the major emphasis in these verses is on the purpose of Christ's coming: (1) to redeem those under the law and (2) to make possible their adoption as children of God. This passage is a good corrective to the notion of merit in the Sirach reading for today, for it points out that Christ redeemed those born under the law.

God has acted in Christ to redeem and set free those born under the law. They are freed from the self-defeating struggle to earn God's favor and from a self-centered anxiety about being worthy of salvation. God gives freedom to live, not under a custodian, but in freedom as mature sons and daughters and heirs of God's promises. The mention of adoption includes the bestowing of the full rights as heirs and complete access to God.

Recommended work: Do a word study of faith, law, custodian, redeem, and adoption.

The sermon might contrast life under the custodian (the law) with life lived in freedom as children of God by faith in Christ and heirs of God. This text is especially timely as we reflect on Christ's birth which came at the time set by God, reflecting God's divine purpose in salvation. The sermon might describe the futility of trying to earn God's favor by obeying laws and customs in contrast to the gift of salvation by Christ's death and resurrection which results in freedom and joy and peace.

Colossians 3:12–17 (L)

Colossians 3:12–21 (RC)

The passage of vs. 12–27 spans two sections: 3:1–17, which deals with the true Christian life, and 3:18–4:6, which deals with the duties of a Christian.

In v. 10 Paul has spoken of the new nature of the Christian which is being renewed. Now in vs. 12–13 he describes the qualities of this new nature. He moves from the indicative, where he indicates there is a new nature, to the imperative: "Put on then . . . " (v. 12). Consider the contrast between the five characteristics of this new nature with the two fivefold lists of vices already presented (vs. 5, 8). These virtues belong to the new nature, and the Christian should strive to practice them. Non-Christian writers often listed all but one of these virtues as qualities to strive for. But "meekness" or lowlines when used by non-Jewish and non-Christian writers was always called a vice, not a virtue! Christ by his example of lowliness revealed the true meaning of this virtue.

The significant thing about the list of virtues is not its content but the context in which they are presented: they describe the life of one who is raised with Christ and who is being renewed. The Colossians are "God's chosen ones, holy and beloved" (v. 12); in the Hebrew Scriptures these terms are applied to Israel, but Paul uses them in his letters. They refer to the call of God which set God's people apart for service and obedience to God and to God's worship.

In v. 13 the author appeals to the readers' experience of the forgiving love of God which was made real in their baptism. Note that in v. 12 all the qualities have a bearing on human relationships. Now in v. 13 this is continued with a stress on forgiveness even as the Lord has forgiven.

Then in vs. 14–15a love is held up as the supreme quality. (Compare with 1 Corinthians 13.) Love binds life together, giving it meaning, vitality, and integrity. The Greek word translated "perfect harmony" connotes wholeness and completeness. Thus love creates wholeness not only within the Christian community but within the lives of Christians and within the whole of the cosmos.

"Put on love" (v. 14) means surrender one's self to the rule of Christ. The peace of v. 15 is far more than inner psychic tranquillity. It reaches cosmic dimensions and is God's gift to the whole community of believers. A Christian is called into the community of believers. Thus "in your hearts" points to the depth and sincerity of commitment to Christ's rule which marks one's new life. It is not the place where Christ rules, for that is the community of faith.

Then in vs. 15b–17 thankfulness is urged. The Christian life is not one of drudgery or joyless burden bearing. Rather, thankfulness is at the heart of the Christian life, thankfulness to God which is expressed in joy and a continuing attitude of gratefulness. Such thankfulness is closely related to faith, for both indicate dependence upon God and trust for the future. Thankfulness is expressed in public worship and in daily living.

The "word of Christ" (v. 16) has been variously interpreted to mean Christ's own preaching, the gospel about Christ, and Christ himself. The difference in meaning is slight, and the point is that where the church is, there God is working for the mutual growth of all believers.

The early church had a rich hymnody of psalms, hymns, and spiritual songs. It is not clear whether or not these were distinct types of music. Much of the church's music was influenced by the Hebrew Scriptures and their psalms, but some was taken over from secular sources or newly composed. (See 1:15–20, which may have been based on an early Christian hymn.)

Then in v. 17 there is an admonition to give thanks in all of one's life. The process of giving thanks to God is the only proper way to live out one's response to God for God's magnificent gift in Christ Jesus.

In vs. 18–21 Paul gives instructions about the Christian household which continue on to 4:1. This may be the earliest example of what has been called a "table of household duties." For other examples, see Ephesians 5:21–6:9; 1 Peter 2:13–3:12; and Titus 2:1–10. They may be drawn from the general ethical teaching of that time and only slightly made over in a Christian mold. But they do emphasize the need for mutual respect and consideration within a household: husbands and wives, parents and children, slaves and masters.

The key word in all of these instructions is "Lord," which is repeated seven times in eight verses (vs. 17–24). As one obeys the Lord, putting on love in all relationships, one will carry out one's duties in the household properly. Notice that the emphasis is on carrying out duties, not on asserting one's rights in the household.

Recommended work: Compare the list of household duties (vs. 18–21) with others. Do a word study of love, peace, and thankfulness.

The sermon may apply the qualities of the new nature to life today, following the movements of the text, climaxed with v. 17 and thanksgiving to God.

Theological Reflection

The Isaiah 61:10–62:3 passage conveys Jerusalem's expectation of God's coming vindication. The Isaiah 45:22–25 reading calls all the nations to bow before God and sing praises to God. There is a promise that God's word shall not return but shall be effective for righteousness and strength. The message of the Sirach reading is a call to obedience to the fifth commandment to honor one's parents, with the promise of God's favor for doing so. The reading from Luke describes the fulfillment of the promise of Messiah in Jesus, which was recognized by two devout Jews, Simeon and Anna, and the obedience of Mary and Joseph to Jewish law and customs. In the Galatians passage Paul contrasts life under the law with life in Christ, saying that God sent the Son at the right time to redeem those who were under the law. The law served a purpose until Christ's coming, but now believers are justified by faith, not by works, and are made adopted children of God and heirs of God. The Colossians reading describes the true Christian life, after one has put on the new nature. It is a life in which both individuals and the community are bound together by love. The passage describes how the new life is to be lived in the household between various persons, with love as the guiding principle.

Some of the passages point forward to God's promised new era of righteousness, the Lukan reading describes God's act in Jesus inaugurating this new era, and the Colossians and Galatians readings show how this new era of God's rule is to be lived in daily life. The Sirach passage commands kindness and patience, honor and love for one's parents.

Children's Message

The conversation with the children might be about Simeon and Anna who recognized that the child Jesus was the Messiah, the fulfillment of their dreams for Israel. Simeon felt that his life was complete when he took the child Jesus in his arms, and he asked the Lord to let him depart in peace (die), since he had seen God's salvation. Anna, a devout widow who spent her life in the temple worshiping, with fasting and praying gave thanks when she saw the child Jesus. She saw in him the redemption of Jerusalem. We have just celebrated the birthday of Jesus. We see Jesus as our Savior and Lord who saves us from our sins and guides our lives.

Hymns for Christmas 1

Lord, Dismiss Us with Your Blessing; Now Thank We All Our God; Let All Mortal Flesh Keep Silence.

Psalm 147:12–20 (C)
Psalm 147:12–15, 19–20 (RC)
Psalm 84 or 84:1–8 (E)

Jeremiah 31:7–14 (C)
Isaiah 61:10–62:3 (L)
Sirach 1:3–6, 15–18 (RC)

Ephesians 1:3–6, 15–18 (C)
Ephesians 1:3–6, 15–19a (E)

John 1:1–18 (C)
Matthew 2:13–15, 19–23 or Luke 2:41–52 or
Matthew 2:1–12 (E)

Meditation on the Texts

We praise you, O God, for sending forth your Son, Jesus Christ, the Word who became flesh and dwelt among us, full of grace and truth. From fullness have we all received grace upon grace. We thank you that in him was life and the life was the light of all humanity, and that although the light shines in the darkness, the darkness has not overcome it. We thank you, O God, for blessing us with every spiritual blessing in Christ, choosing us in him before the foundation of the world. You destined us in love to be your sons and daughters through Jesus Christ according to the purpose of your will. Grant us a spirit of wisdom and of revelation in the knowledge of our Lord Jesus Christ, and may we know the hope to which he has called us. We thank you for the promise to Isaiah that your people shall be satisfied with your goodness, and in Christ we have found our soul's satisfaction. Amen.

Commentary on the Texts

John 1:1–18 (C)

Our pericope is the Prologue or overture to the Fourth Gospel. It introduces the major themes of John's writings. A key word in this passage is "word" (*logos* in Greek). This word has origins in Jewish tradition. However, John must have been aware of the relevance of this word to Hellenistic thought. In Hellenistic (Greek) thought the word meant divine speech, emanation, and mediation, while in the Hebrew Scriptures it has the meaning of the revelation of God. This could be revelation in creation, acts of power and grace, or in prophecy. It means more than speech, however. It is God in action creating, revealing, and redeeming. John draws together these meanings and shows that Christ, the incarnate Word, is the complete revelation of God. Recall the personification of the wisdom of God (see our Sirach reading for today) in the late Hebrew Scriptures. A second strand of background of "word" is the glorification of the law in rabbinical Judaism. But Christ is the true word of God who exists from all eternity. It is through Christ, not the law, that grace and truth come (v. 17).

The Prologue is in the form of a hymn which celebrates God's revelation of the divine nature to the world. Some scholars think this hymn existed independently before John placed it at the beginning of his Gospel. He has added several prose comments that we would put in as footnotes. They anticipate the witness to God's Word which will unfold in the chapters that follow. In vs. 6–8 we have the testimony of John the Baptist as the final prophetic voice to announce the coming of the Word. Then in vs. 12–13 John inserts the belief of the new people of God who are God's children, not by reason of natural birth or race, but by their faith in God's Word. A third insertion is v. 17 in which John declares that, in Jesus the Word, God surpassed even the glory of grace and truth which was revealed earlier to Moses when God gave the law at Mt. Sinai.

There has been much discussion of the source of this prologue hymn, and it is undoubtedly related to Genesis 1, the creation song, and possibly to Mark 1:1, which speaks of the beginning of the gospel. There is an imitation of this in 1 John 1:1–4. Recall that in Genesis, God "said" and it was done. God spoke and it was done in creation, in the giving of the law, and in the message of the prophets. God spoke and created the world, giving it life for fellowship with God and light for knowledge of God. However, these gifts of life and light have been resisted or even ignored by God's creation, and sometimes they have even been rejected by God's chosen people. But the Word revealed God's glory in a supreme way by becoming a man of flesh like other human beings. God revealed in the person of Jesus Christ the character of the eternal God in all the fullness of God's love and truth.

Darkness (v. 5) is total evil which is in conflict with God but cannot overcome God. Darkness is the antithesis of light and represents a world bound over to sin (see 3:19). Humans are in darkness but are not darkness itself. God's light has been present down through history to enlighten human beings, although they invariably succumbed to the darkness.

John the Baptist is a witness to the light but is not the light. Some had misunderstood John's role. He was the forerunner of God's kingdom, not its inaugurator.

Jesus, the Word, came as the true light. In Hebrew thought, "true" characterizes the divine order.

In v. 10 "the world" refers to the world of human beings and their affairs, a world subject to sin and darkness. The world knew not the Word. John uses "know" in the full Semitic sense of *personal involvement,* not merely perceiving or being aware of someone or something.

The climax of the hymn comes in v. 14, where John states the ultimate purpose of the manifestation of God's Word: "The Word became flesh and dwelt among us." Notice the paradox in this climax. There is a newness in this revelation which can be best appreciated by comparing it with Isaiah 40:6–8 and similar passages in which the Word of God is contrasted with flesh, namely, all that is transitory, mortal, and imperfect and that seems incompatible with God. There is tremendous mystery in the incarnation: the eternal Word took on our exact human nature and identified completely with us except for sin. Note that John chose the word "flesh" deliberately; it connotes humans in their fallen, concrete state. So the Word became human flesh in the fullest possible sense, and this is the very essence of the incarnation. Redemption is the result of this. John says the Word not only became flesh but "dwelt among us" (literally, "pitched his tent among us"). Glory is a term from the Hebrew Scriptures for the presence of God visibly manifested, especially in relationship to the Tent of Meeting and the Tabernacle.

God was an invisible God and could not be seen by human beings (v. 18). But in the incarnate Word, God has been revealed completely (Col. 1:15). Because only the Son sees God, it is through the Son that we too see God with the eyes of faith.

Recommended work: Do a word study of Word, glory, flesh, life, and light. Compare this new creation with Genesis 1:1ff.

The sermon might focus on the mystery of the incarnation, developing v. 14 in particular. The sermon might show how John is describing the new creation which began in Jesus, the Word become flesh, in contrast to the first creation. It might develop the images of light, flesh, life, and darkness to show how Jesus has made God known in personal experience, not just in perception of the word "God."

Matthew 2:13–15, 19–23 or Luke 2:41–52 or

Matthew 2:1–12 (E)

We will deal only with Matthew 2:13–15, 19–23, which is part of the account of the slaughter of the innocents and tells of the flight into Egypt and the return.

Note that the dream plays a role both in departing for Egypt and in returning. The story of the flight into Egypt serves the purpose of Matthew by indicating that the Hebrew Scriptures were fulfilled both by the sojourn in Egypt and by the return to Nazareth. The author of Matthew practiced a greater freedom in interpreting scripture than we do, as is evident in the comments on both events. The reference to "out of Egypt" (v. 15) is a quotation from Hosea 11:1. While the original refers to the call of the exodus, Jesus is portrayed here as the new Israel who reenacts the life of the first Israel, including the call out of slavery in Egypt.

The Sinai Peninsula was a part of Egypt then, so its nearest part was not far from Bethlehem. By the second century A.D. there was a Jewish story that Jesus learned magic in Egypt. Christians in the early centuries often thought of the exodus as a type of Christian redemption, and the rabbis thought it foreshadowed the messianic age, when all of its miracles would be reenacted.

The shapers of the lectionary omit the verses that tell of the slaughter of the children (vs. 16–18), although v. 13 indicates that Herod is about to search for the infant Jesus to destroy him. Herod murdered many people, including his own son and other relatives. So the slaughter of the innocents was not out of character for him. There are similar stories of the infancy of Heracles, Sargon I, Cyrus, Romulus and Remus, and Cypselus. The fact that the male children two years and younger were to be killed indicates that the astrologers first saw the star two years before that time.

The slaughter of the innocents foreshadows the death of Jesus, the innocent one, for the sins of the world. In the escape to Egypt, Jesus' life is spared and the infants die "in his place," since Herod is seeking his life. But on the cross Jesus does not escape, and the innocent one dies for the guilty to destroy the power of evil which leads tyrants of every age to slaughter children and adults alike.

We cannot be certain of the scripture referred to in v. 23, but it may be an allusion to Isaiah 11:1, where the Messiah is described as a *netzer,* a Hebrew word meaning sprout or shoot. This implies that although the dynasty of David has been cut down, it will grow up once more like a shoot or branch of a felled tree and David's kingdom will be reestablished. Since only consonants were used in Hebrew, Matthew was able to take the consonants of *netzer* and interpret them as a prophecy referring to Nazareth. Although this method of interpreting scripture may seem fanciful and farfetched to us today, it was a common method among the rabbis of Matthew's time.

Recommended work: Reflect on the place and meaning of the slaughter of the innocents in the Gospel. Compare Jesus' coming out of Egypt to Israel's coming out.

The sermon might follow the movement of the text, showing the obedience of Joseph and Mary to God speaking to them through dreams. It might include the tragedy of the slaughter of the innocents which foreshadows Jesus' death when he does not escape from his destiny on the cross.

Jeremiah 31:7–14 (C)

Our pericope describes the homecoming when God will gather all the dispersed in their homeland (see Isa. 35:5–10 and Ps. 23:2–3). This will be the new exodus. As the exiles march through the desert, there is reason for great joy for both those coming home and the foreign nations. They come home from the north country, Assyria, where they have been kept captive. These people are the remnant, the small number who escaped the calamity of 721 B.C. and who have been purified through experiences of the exile and now make up the New Israel which is faithful to God.

Notice that the caravan is composed of those who are weak—namely, the blind, the lame, woman with child and woman in travail—together with a great company. This indicates the miraculous nature of the new exodus, for they could not return on their own power. There is a mixture of joy and tears (vs. 7 and 9), which reminds us of Psalm 126, which also deals with the return from exile.

The reference to the brooks of water is an echo of the rock from which Israel drank on the first exodus (Ex. 17:1–7), but now it is a stream of water and not an occasional spring which supplies water. The march is on straight and level road, in contrast to the first exodus.

Then in v. 9 God declares, "I am a father to Israel, and Ephraim is my first-born," an idea first used to stress the covenant that God made with Israel. Hosea (11:1) used fatherly love as a symbol of God's love for Israel during the exodus.

Distant people are invited to witness this return of God's people. Notice especially the symbolism of the shepherd and his flock (v. 10), a theme symbolizing God's saving action which Jeremiah uses.

All shall join in praising God for delivering Israel (v. 12). The bountiful produce of the land will characterize this new age, and the priests as well as the people will share in the prosperity. God will turn their mourning into joy and comfort them.

Recommended work: Compare this exodus with the first exodus.

The sermon might relate this announcement of the new exodus of the remnant from Assyria back to Zion to the deliverance that Jesus made possible by his death and resurrection. Both reflect the first exodus from Israel's bondage in Egypt. All three deliverances are the work of God in redeeming God's people.

Isaiah 61:10–62:3 (L)

See last Sunday's material.

Sirach 1:3–6, 15–18 (RC)

Background for this reading is v. 1, which declares that all wisdom comes from the Lord. The reference to the height of heaven (v. 3) draws on the cosmogony of Genesis (see Ps. 103:11). The author of Sirach personifies wisdom (v. 6). Wisdom is described as an intermediate creature between God and the rest of creation (see Prov. 8:22–31). While wisdom has her origin in God, she is not identical with God.

Then in vs. 15–18 the store of treasures of those who fear God are described. The fear of the Lord is the crown of wisdom, making peace and perfect health to flourish. "Peace" translates a Hebrew word meaning general well-being and prosperity, not mere absence of conflict. Such wisdom is based on the proper relationship with God which will bring a long and full life.

Recommended work: Do a word study of wisdom, peace, and health.

The sermon might deal with the relationship between the fear of the Lord which gives wisdom and a healthy, full, peaceful life. Medical studies show a correlation between living in right relations with others and good health. The sermon might point out that wisdom is more than mere knowledge. It concludes an awe of and relationship with God which is the source of wisdom.

Ephesians 1:3–6, 15–18 (C)

Ephesians 1:3–6, 15–19a (E)

Our pericope overlaps two sections: 1:3–14, in the form of an introductory hymn, deals with the mystery hidden from eternity, and 1:15–2:22 deals with the mystery revealed to the church. In 1:15–23 there is a prayer for understanding the mystery. The mystery is God's plan to make Christ the head of a new community of humankind, including both Jew and Gentile.

Many contemporary scholars reject the Pauline authorship of the Letter to the Ephesians because of differences in language and style, and doctrinal emphasis and content, from the letters accepted as genuinely from Paul. There is also a question about the relationship of this letter to the Letter to the Colossians and other Pauline letters. For convenience' sake, we will call the author "Paul," although the author may have been a disciple of Paul's.

Ephesians does not begin with the usual Pauline "thanksgiving" related to the church to which the letter is directed. Instead, it begins at once with the praise of God for revealing God's plan of salvation. The hymn begins with v. 3 and a traditional Hebrew form of thanksgiving to God, namely, that of pronouncing a blessing and following it with a list of God's mighty deeds and favors. This is not a blessing from God to humans but an act of praise expressed by humans before God for some action on God's part which has already been performed or is now desired. This kind of prayer was used by devout Jews on occasions such as a meal, when it was recited over bread. Recall that Solomon's long prayer at the temple in Jerusalem (1 Kings 8:15, 56) opens and closes with a ''blessing'' prayer formula. Here the word ''blessed'' is in the aorist which denotes a single action in the past. It may refer in this verse either to the saving action of Christ or to baptism in which this saving action is appropriated by a believer. Since there are numerous other references to baptism in this letter, some scholars think the reference here is to baptism.

Note that the initiative is taken by the God and Father of our Lord Jesus Christ to inaugurate the mystery. The term ''in the heavenly places'' (v. 3) is an expression found only in Ephesians and refers to the unseen spiritual world behind and above the material universe. A place is mentioned because the Hebrew mind thought of God as acting out of one of the spheres of the universe. The thrust of this verse is that God's ordered plan of salvation is now brought into human activity.

The term ''in Christ'' (v. 3), in various forms such as ''in him,'' is repeated some thirty times in Ephesians. This term emphasizes the unity that Christians have in Christ through their incorporation into a visible community, the church, under Christ's leadership. When a student asked the late Karl Barth whether there was an authentic Christian mysticism, he replied that there is, but only in the sense of Paul's use of a person being ''in Christ'' and so united to God in this vital relationship. As used in Ephesians, the term lacks the more profound sense that Paul often gives it in which it expresses a Christian's identification with Christ and with one another. Here the meaning seems to be more instrumental, meaning ''through or by means of Christ.''

''He chose us'' (v. 4) indicates the contents of the blessing which motivates the praise offered to God. Note that this is the first verb in the indicative mood in the passage. The object of the choice is ''us,'' namely, the church made up of both Gentiles and Jews united in Christ. But the choice was made before the foundation of the world (v. 4). The reference to the choice existing from all eternity is a typical Hebrew thought form to emphasize the importance of the choice. This formula was also used of the law, the name of Messiah, and so forth. The really significant thing here is that the identity of the members of the church is declared to be preexistent from all eternity. They are one with Christ and equally part of God's eternal purpose for the world.

The words ''holy'' and ''blameless'' are almost synonymous and create the image of sacrificial victims.

Then v. 5 virtually repeats v. 4 but describes the life lived as a result of being chosen by God in terms of sonship rather than blamelessness. In both, the stress is on status conferred rather than on moral goodness. In this verse, ''purpose,'' as in the RSV, is better than ''favor'' or ''good pleasure'' which might be used.

The predestination described is not an individual one but refers to those chosen to be saved in and through a community in Christ, but this does not rule out individual salvation in some other way.

''The praise of his glorious grace'' introduces a theme that recurs in the letter, that humans who understand God's plan should praise God and give thanks. In the Hebrew Scriptures, Israel seeks to live for God's praise. This praise is a strong indication that we are dealing with material designed for use in worship, based on liturgical models. The form is Jewish. Note that the word ''Beloved'' has a strong baptismal reference (see Mark 1:11).

Then in vs. 15–19a we have a thanksgiving that is typical of a letter of Paul's. The point of this passage is to pray that the blessings referred to in the blessing may be fully accepted by Gentile Christians who are addressed. Thus it points back to the blessing mentioned in v. 3 and following. The passage does not make any totally new points. This seems to be a liturgical piece also. The verses express with majestic language the Lordship of Christ over all and especially over the church.

The word ''called'' (v. 18) is a common and important term used by Paul to indicate a deliberate choice by God which brings both individuals and the church into relationship with him. God will fulfill this inheritance which is heaven, among the believers (saints) at the Last Day.

Recommended work: Do a word study of blessed, praise, and love.

The sermon might develop the images of the text, relating them to the congregation's own life, images of being chosen by God for salvation, being made holy and blameless before God, giving us grace in the Beloved. The sermon should include both praise and thanksgiving for God's gracious saving acts in Christ.

Theological Reflection

The passage from John describes the new creation in which the Word became flesh in Jesus Christ. The Ephesians passage praises God for choosing us in Christ for salvation. Matthew tells of the escape of Jesus and his parents to Egypt and their return. Isaiah points to God's saving action in a new exodus.

Children's Message

The talk with the children might be about the fact that no one has ever seen God but that Jesus has made God known to us as a God of love.

Hymns for Christmas 2

Joy to the World; O Word of God Incarnate; The Lord's My Shepherd.

Baptism of Our Lord

(Epiphany 1)

Psalm 29 (C)	**Acts 19:1–7 (C)**
Psalm 45:7–9 (L)	**Acts 10:34–38 (L) (RC) (E)**
Psalm 29:1–4 (RC)	
Psalm 89:1–29 or 89:20–29 (E)	**Mark 1:4–11 (C)**
	Mark 1:7–11 (RC) (E)
Genesis 1:1–5 (C)	
Isaiah 42:1–7 (L)	
Isaiah 42:1–4, 6–7 (RC)	
Isaiah 42:1–9 (E)	

Meditation on the Texts

O God who created the heavens and the earth and whose Spirit was moving over the face of the waters, we praise you for the revelation of yourself to us in Jesus Christ. Thank you for putting your Spirit upon Jesus at his baptism and equipping him for his mission as the suffering servant. You gave him as a covenant to the people and a light to the nations to heal and release those who are oppressed. We thank you that Jesus was baptized by John in the Jordan for our sins and that he submitted to the baptism of death on the cross for our forgiveness. Even as you gave the Holy Spirit to come upon the disciples in Ephesus, so may your Spirit so fill us with wisdom, truth, and power that we may faithful speak forth your word in our time. We remember that you show no partiality but that everyone who fears you and does what is right is acceptable to you through Christ. We rejoice in the good news that Jesus, when anointed with the Spirit at his baptism, went about doing good and healing all that were oppressed by the devil. May the living Christ make us whole and release us from the power of Satan. Amen.

Commentary on the Texts

Mark 1:4–11 (C)

Mark 1:7–11 (RC) (E)

Jesus' baptism is the last of the pericopes in the birth narrative cycle of the liturgical year. The early church, like the church today, had difficulty with the notion of Jesus, the sinless One, undergoing baptism for the forgiveness of sins. This issue should be dealt with in the sermon on Jesus' baptism, since it continues to raise difficulties for believers.

It might even be the "hook" to get the hearer's attention, leading into the meaning of Jesus' baptism for us today.

Although vs. 1–11 may seem to focus on John the Baptist, they have much to say about the credentials of Jesus, pointing as they do to John as the forerunner of the Messiah. The message of vs. 2–3 is essential for understanding the passage, although these verses are omitted from our pericope, for they show that the Messiah would be preceded by a forerunner, according to the prophecy of the Hebrew Scriptures. Note that v. 4 should be taken closely with vs. 2–3, using a dash, as the RSV does, or a comma at the end of v. 3 rather than a period.

The point of mentioning that John lived and worked in the wilderness is to show that he fulfilled the prophecy. The wilderness was associated with the messianic End time. It was believed that the Messiah would appear in the wilderness; thus, revolutionary messianic groups were attracted to the wilderness (recall the Qumran sectarians). There was a debate about whether Messiah would appear in the wilderness of Judea or the wilderness of Sihon and Og to the east of the Jordan River. (For more background on this pericope, see C. E. B. Cranfield, *The Gospel According to St. Mark,* pp. 40f.)

The implication of John's baptism which was derived from proselyte baptism was that Jews did *not* have a right to membership in the people of God simply because they were Jews, since by their sins they had become as Gentiles. They needed to repent as the Gentiles did in order to have any part in God's salvation. Thus John was trying to shake his fellow Jews out of their false sense of security, calling them to turn from their sins and turn to God. Although proselyte baptism was primarily a means of ritual cleansing, it seemed to have some ethical meaning also. John's baptism had a very clear ethical meaning. John preached a baptism of repentance for the forgiveness of sins. The Greek word for "repentance" used here translates a word in the Hebrew Scriptures that means to turn back or to return. It involves a new attitude toward everything. There are two movements in repentance: turning from sin and turning back to God. The prophets called the people to return to God with their whole being and to trust God, not pagan gods or foreign alliances. Repentance is something that in the final analysis comes from God, not from human beings.

The goal of baptism of repentance was the forgiveness of sins and salvation in the coming judgment of God. So there was an element of gospel in John's message. In their basic thrust John's message and Jesus' message were not as different as some claim. Both proclaimed God's breaking into human history to judge and to forgive the repentant. John may have thought of his baptism for forgiveness as having some real effectiveness toward forgiveness. At least, it was a pledge of forgiveness. "The forgiveness of sins" is a main theme throughout Mark's Gospel.

In his preaching, John pointed forward to the One who is mightier than he who will baptize with the Holy Spirit. Thus John confesses the vast superiority of the coming One over himself. John administers the End time sacrament of baptism. But Messiah will actually give the End time gift of the Spirit. The early church closely associated the gift of the Spirit with baptism. Note carefully that the contrast is between the persons of John and Jesus, not between John's baptism and Christian baptism. It is not that John baptized with water and the Christian baptizes with water and the Spirit. All the Christian minister does is baptize with water, since it is God in Christ, not the celebrant, who bestows the Spirit. There is a real continuity between John's baptism and Christian baptism.

The baptism of Jesus by John is viewed by most scholars as historical, although Jesus' submission to a baptism of repentance embarrassed the early church. It is unlikely that the church would have invented Jesus' baptism, since it created a problem in interpreting it. The sequel of the heavens opening, the Spirit descending, and the voice from heaven may be interpreted as a visionary experience, however. The account we have of it appears to have come from Jesus himself, and it appears to be based on primitive tradition.

A clue to understanding why Jesus submitted to a baptism of repentance is found in v. 11. Its quotation from Isaiah 42:1 (a reading for today) speaks of the Servant of the Lord, whose mission is also described in Isaiah 52:13–53:12. The significance of the baptism of Jesus is that his submission was part of his mature self-dedication to his mission of self-identification with sinners, which ultimately would involve his "baptism" on the cross. In his baptism, Jesus took the place of human beings and "repents" for them. It is likely that Jesus was already aware at the baptism in the Jordan that this foreshadowed another, more bitter, baptism. Jesus consecrated baptism in his own body so that we might share it with him.

Proselyte baptism seems to have been self-administered before witnesses. Some scholars think that John's baptism followed this procedure, while others think John actually administered baptism.

The imagery of the vision goes back to the Hebrew Scriptures and Judaism. The comparison of the Spirit to a dove seems to go back to Genesis 1:2, where the Hebrew word used for "moving over" suggests the brooding of a bird. The Holy Spirit was sometimes compared to a dove. In the Judaism of that time the giving of the Spirit almost always meant prophetic inspiration. A person is grasped by God, and God authorizes the person to be God's messenger and preacher. Thus when the Spirit descends upon Jesus, the meaning is that Jesus is called by God to speak for God.

Joachim Jeremias argues the possibility that the voice at the baptism is not a composite quote of Psalm 2:7 and Isaiah 42:1, as some scholars have claimed, but is limited to Isaiah 42:1 (Joachim Jeremias, *New Testament Theology,* pp. 54–56). In the Judaism of that time it was a regular practice to quote only the beginning of a passage, with the continuation of it kept in mind. The really decisive clause from Isaiah 42:1: "I have put my Spirit upon him," does *not* appear in the Mark 1:11 quotation. The meaning seems to be that what Isaiah 42:1 has promised has now just been fulfilled. The implication of the message of the voice from heaven being only from Isaiah 42:1 is twofold, according to Jeremias: (1) All the emphasis is on the event of the communication of the Spirit. (2) The proclamation originally had nothing to do with the enthronement of the king or adoption rites, as a Psalm 2:7 quotation would indicate. The emphasis of the message therefore is not upon the Messiah as king but on the scriptural statements about the Servant of the Lord.

To sum up: At his baptism Jesus experienced his call. From that time forward he knew that he was grasped by God's Spirit and that God was taking him into God's service. God was equipping him and authorizing him to be God's messenger. And God was setting him apart as the inaugurator of the time of salvation.

Recommended work: Do a word study of repentance, baptism, and beloved Son. Reflect on the Isaiah 42:1 passage and Jesus' life and ministry.

The sermon might relate the meaning of Jesus' own baptism to the baptism and lives of the hearers, showing how he was baptized for us, the sinless for sinners. It should also relate his "baptism" on the cross to forgiveness and the sacrament of baptism. The sermon might give some background of the meaning of John the Baptist's baptism and relationship to Christian baptism.

Genesis 1:1–5 (C)

This reading relates to the Markan account of Jesus' baptism in which Jesus saw the Spirit descending on him like a dove. Rabbis interpreted the Spirit of God "moving over the face of the waters" as being like a bird brooding on its nest. Notice that vs. 1 and 2:4a form an *inclusio:* "In the beginning God created" and "when they were created." The whole cosmos came into being because of the sovereign divine activity. God's personal will is expressed in God's word: "And God said . . . ." This ties in with Jesus, the Word, through whom all things were made (John 1:3). Some scholars see in these verses the three persons of the Trinity: God who creates by speaking the Word (Jesus Christ) and the Spirit moving over the face of the waters. God bridges the chasm between God and formlessness, first producing light, the most sublime of all the elements. Note that light is created *before* the sun, implying that light is independent of the sun and therefore the sun is not to be worshiped, as some pagan religions do. Rather, God, who created light, is the object of true worship. Light stands in sharp contrast to the dark chaos, which humans have always feared. Light symbolizes the good, wisdom, and God's presence. God saw how good creation was. God names the light "Day" and the darkness "Night," which can be done only by one who has control over them, according to the Semitic mind. The evening is followed by morning to form one day, again following the Hebrew concept of a day beginning at sundown and ending at sundown.

Recommended work: Do a word study of Spirit, create, and light and darkness.

The sermon might follow the movement of the passage, but drawing on John 1:1ff. to point out the role of Jesus the Word through whom all things were created by God. All was created good in God's sight. The sermon might relate the goodness of original creation to the destruction and misuse of creation caused by human sin expressed in greed, war and preparation for war, and the poisoning of our environment. Jesus' death to redeem all creation should be related to the present condition of the spaceship earth, indicating ways Christians can work with God to renew creation.

Isaiah 42:1–7 (L)

Isaiah 42:1–4, 6–7 (RC)

Isaiah 42:1–9 (E)

In vs. 1–4 we have the first song of the Suffering Servant. The verses are in the style of other Servant Songs that are quiet, terse, and concentrated. There is even a melancholy note to them, in contrast to other hymns which are usually lyrical, exultant, and expansive. Note that vs. 5–7 combine both styles; some scholars question whether these verses belong to the first song. (Other songs are found in 49:1–6; 50:4–11; and 52:13–53:12.) Biblical scholars hold a variety of opinions about the identity of the Servant, some claiming the reference to be to an individual, others claiming it refers to Israel as a corporate body, and still others asserting that the Servant incorporates both individual and corporate identities. The Servant does represent the finest qualities of Israel and its leaders. The Servant, as the chosen one of God, fulfills the role of Davidic king, messianic king, and prophet. The role of the Servant, Israel, is to bring about God's teaching and restore justice to the nations. This he will do with all patience. His role is set in contrast to that of the military tactics of Cyrus.

God speaks to the heavenly court, and God's words go out to include foreign nations as well, including all the distant isles. The Servant accomplishes his role modestly and quietly, not by human force but by transforming them within. Note that the meaning of "wait" in v. 4 is "strive for." It is an energetic striving for life, not a passive waiting.

The thrust of vs. 5–9 is the victory of justice. The author insists on the power of God's Word in re-creating the universe (compare this to our Genesis pericope). What God did at the beginning continues now.

In v. 7 God commissions the Servant to bring light to those in darkness and freedom to prisoners. Humans must first recognize their blindness and imprisonment *before* they can be healed and freed.

It is difficult to explain the "former things" of v. 9, but they may be the exodus events. The "new things" may point to the messianic glory surrounding the victorious march of Cyrus and his edict of freedom granted to the Jews. The author of Second Isaiah did not distinguish a time lag between the return from exile and the final day of salvation. While God reveals the future, God does not do it in a mathematical way. Fulfillment will come suddenly, springing forth (v. 9) and taking people by surprise.

Recommended work: Do a word study of Suffering Servant of the Lord, covenant, and justice.

The sermon might focus on the identity and mission of the Servant and show how Jesus fulfilled this role as God's messenger. The sermon might relate this passage to the Markan account of Jesus' baptism when Jesus is called by God to begin his ministry. The preacher may want to relate this role of Israel to that of the church as the New Israel, empowered by God for mission in the world.

Acts 19:1–7 (C)

This is part of the account of Paul's long ministry in Ephesus contained in vs. 1–40, covering more than two years. The disciples mentioned here belonged to John the Baptist, while the disciples elsewhere in Acts refer to Christians. This pericope ties in with the Markan text in which the baptism of John is contrasted with Christian baptism, including the gift of the Holy Spirit. These disciples at Ephesus had *not* received the Holy Spirit, which in his preaching John promised the coming One would give. The upper country refers to inner Asia.

Paul's ministry in Ephesus begins with these twelve isolated and immature Christians, who, like Apollos (18:24f.), knew only the baptism of John. Some scholars say these twelve were disciples of John who later became Christian. The point seems to be that they were Christians but were immature in their understanding of Christian baptism and its implications.

Among Christians a new outpouring of the Spirit was understood as an essential of the Christian experience, incorporating human beings into the church. All who read the Hebrew Scriptures would know of a Holy Spirit. So it may be that the reference here is to their lack of awareness of the outward sign of the Spirit's presence, as evident at Pentecost.

In the reference to John's baptism of repentance there is an echo of Acts 13:24–25. Recall that the reference to "the one who was to come after him" points to Mark 1:7 of our Markan pericope.

They were baptized "in the name of the Lord Jesus" (v. 5). The new baptism is superior to John's baptism not only because of the gift of the Holy Spirit but also because of the saving name which can now be pronounced. For Luke, Christian baptism and the Spirit are inseparable. However, the distinction between the reception of baptism and the reception of the Spirit has always been a problem.

Paul laid hands on the Twelve and the Holy Spirit came upon them. This may imply that the imposition of hands meant they were given a charismatic office to be exercised in the church. They spoke with tongues and uttered prophecies.

Recommended work: Do a word study of Holy Spirit and baptism.

The sermon might focus on the meaning of baptism and the gift of the Holy Spirit in the church today. The preacher may want to refer to John the Baptist's baptism in our Markan reading and to the difference and similarities between John's baptism and Christian baptism. The message should stress baptism as a sign and seal of initiation into the Christian community and the gift of the Spirit as God's empowering of believers for service.

Acts 10:34–38 (L) (RC) (E)

Our pericope is part of the section of vs. 1–48, which deals with the conversion of Cornelius. The whole section should be studied in order to interpret the pericope.

In vs. 34–43 we find the last great discourse of Peter in Acts, the classic message of the gospel to the Gentiles. This particular discourse, however, has nothing to do with the topic of the episode as such. It follows a pattern of other sermons of Peter in Acts. Some scholars think the "sermon" was composed by Luke in order to fulfill a literary and theological task rather than to give a historical account of Peter's message. Luke wants to show what Christian preaching is and ought to be. We can discern three parts of the whole speech: (1) the introduction, vs. 34–35, (2) the kerygma or message, vs. 36–41, and (3) the conclusion and appeal to the Hebrew Scriptures, vs. 42–43.

In vs. 34–35, which serve as an introduction, Luke seeks to relate the discourse to the situation in which Peter finds himself. The literal meaning of the Greek translated "God shows no partiality" is "God accepts no one's face," meaning God is not one showing favors (see Deut. 10:17).

In v. 35 Peter seems to imply that a person could fear God and do what is right and thus be acceptable to God even if that person were not a Jew. The meaning of "the word" in v. 36 is the proclamation that was first made to the children of Israel but will eventually be made to the Gentiles. The reference to peace in v. 36 alludes to Isaiah 52:7. Then in vs. 37–39 Peter gives a résumé of Jesus' ministry, a résumé paralleling to some extent the Synoptic Gospels.

In vs. 36 and 37 the reference to "you know the word" is directed to the reader of Acts, not to Cornelius, since he is a Gentile and is not likely to know the essence of the Christian message now being described to him.

The reference to Jesus' baptism by John and the anointing of Jesus ties in with our Markan reading for today. Jesus' baptism is seen as an "anointing" with the Holy Spirit. But for Luke this does not mean that Jesus becomes the Messiah at his baptism. Then in v. 38 Peter outlines the mighty works that Jesus did because God was with him.

Recommended work: Do a word study of anointed, peace, and baptism.

The sermon might follow the movements of the passage, building up to the description of Jesus' mighty works after his baptism and anointing by the Spirit. The sermon might describe in more detail some of Jesus' healings and "doing good" and casting out demons, and then point to the church's mission today to carry forth this ministry, empowered by the same Holy Spirit.

Theological Reflection

It is not surprising that on this day, which celebrates the baptism of our Lord the passages relate to that event. The Genesis passage mentions the Spirit moving (brooding) over the waters, and in the Markan reading the Spirit comes like a dove upon Jesus. The voice heard from heaven speaks a verse from Isaiah 42:1 about the empowering of the Servant for mission. Acts 19 deals with the baptism of early disciples, and Acts 10 is an account of Peter's sermon, with a reference to Jesus' baptism, receiving the Spirit, and mission.

Children's Message

This would be a splendid occasion to talk with the children about the meaning and the process of baptism as all are gathered around the baptismal font or pool. Stress that Jesus, though sinless, was baptized for us and that by his baptism we are cleansed of our sin.

Hymns for Epiphany I

Morning Has Broken; Hail to the Lord's Anointed; Descend, O Spirit, Purging Flame.

Ordinary Time 2

Psalm 63:1–8 (C)   **1 Corinthians 6:12–20 (C)**
Psalm 67 (L)   **1 Corinthians 6:13–15, 17–20 (RC)**
Psalm 40:2, 4, 7–10 (RC)   **1 Corinthians 6:11b–20 (E)**

1 Samuel 3:1–10 (11–20) (C)   **John 1:35–42 (C)**
1 Samuel 3:1–10 (L)   **John 1:43–51 (L) (E)**
1 Samuel 3:3–10, 19 (RC)

Meditation on the Texts

O God who called prophets and apostles of old, we pray that we may hear your call to us in our time to be your obedient messengers. May we not only hear but obey your call to faithful services in the kingdom, as the boy Samuel obeyed. May we not be like the sons of Eli whose iniquities were great. May our eyes and ears be open to behold Christ, the Lamb of God who takes away the sin of the world. And when Christ calls us to "come and see," may we follow him in grateful obedience. We pray that we, like Andrew, may lead others to Christ and thus find salvation. We know that our body is the temple of your Holy Spirit. We are not our own but have been bought with the price of Jesus' death on the cross. May we never confuse Christian freedom with licentiousness but rather shun immorality. We pray that we may always glorify you in our bodies. Amen.

Commentary on the Texts

John 1:35–42 (C)

John 1:43–51 (L) (E)

Our longer pericope, vs. 35–51, is the testimony of Jesus' first disciples. It follows an event the previous day when John the Baptist declared to his disciples when he saw Jesus, "Behold, the Lamb of God, who takes away the sin of the world!" Note that our pericope is linked with the events of that day by the words that John repeated, "Behold, the Lamb of God!" On the first occasion John had indicated more of the meaning of the title "Lamb of God." John the Baptist saw Jesus as the sacrificial One whose death will take away the sin of the world. The artist Grünewald in his Isenheim altarpiece has taken poetic license to place John the Baptist at the foot of the cross, although John was beheaded at the beginning of Jesus' ministry. John stands there dressed in camel's hair, with a leather girdle about his waist, pointing with a bony finger toward Jesus on the cross. Under his left arm he holds a book, the Hebrew Scriptures. At his feet stands a lamb, and there is a small cross by the shoulder of the lamb. Thus the artist portrays what John the Baptist has said to his disciples: "Behold, the Lamb of God, who takes away the sin of the world!"

The events of our pericope occur on the "third day" of the new creation which the Fourth Gospel describes, paralleling in some ways the first creation of Genesis. Two of John's disciples turn from following John to follow Jesus after John repeats the words, "Behold, the Lamb of God" which he used to describe Jesus the day before. These two eventually accept that Jesus is the Lamb of God, the Messiah (Christ in Greek). Before coming to know him as Messiah, they followed Jesus as disciples following a teacher. One of the disciples was Andrew, but the other is not named. There is some basis for identifying him as John, the beloved disciple, as tradition has done. All the Gospels indicate that John the Baptist had disciples, a group set apart by his baptism with their own prayer and rules for fasting. While some left John to follow Jesus, apparently others continued to follow John even after his death (Acts 19:3).

The word for "looked at" in v. 36 means gazed at with penetration and insight. It is also used in v. 42.

Jesus' question to the new followers, "What do you seek?" (v. 38) is a question Jesus puts to everyone who would follow him. It has greater meaning than simply why they are walking after Jesus. The question goes to the basic need of human beings that causes them to turn to God. The answer of the disciples also has a deeper meaning than merely asking about his address when they ask, "Where are you staying?" Human beings wish to stay, abide, dwell with God. There is within the depths of the human soul a drive to escape this world of change, death, and time and to find the One who is lasting. Studies of world cultures and religions indicate this drive.

Jesus' answer to their question of where he was staying is a challenge to faith: "Come and see." Throughout John's Gospel the theme of "coming" to Jesus is used to describe faith in Jesus, and "seeing" is another way John describes faith. Thus those who come to Jesus, see Jesus, and believe in Jesus are engaging in the same faith activity. Here in this calling of the disciples their training begins as they go to Jesus and see where he is staying and believe in him. This training for discipleship is completed when they see his glory and believe in him (2:11). It points forward to Jesus' words in 12:26: "If any one serves me, he must follow me; and where I am, there shall my servant be also; if any one serves me, the Father will honor him." There are motifs here from the Wisdom of Solomon regarding the way one finds Wisdom (see Wisd. 6:12, 13, 16). Also note in Proverbs 1:20–28 that Wisdom cries aloud in the street. Some find her. Some do not. John tells us that the disciples who found Jesus go out at once to announce to others what they have found (1:41, 45). This section is a gold mine for preaching to the continuing human search for God and God's revelation in Jesus, the Lamb of God.

The tenth hour (v. 39) was four o'clock in the afternoon. Some scholars think that it was Friday, just before Sabbath began and the disciples would not be able to travel any distance until Sabbath was over at sunset on Saturday.

We are not told when Andrew found his brother, Simon, to bring him to Jesus. It may have been the same day, or a day later, but John sets it on the same day to keep the connection with the "Lamb of God" identification by John. The point describing Andrew's bringing Simon to Jesus (vs. 40–42) is that this is the model for what all disciples must do: bring others to Jesus. This is an excellent text for a sermon on the way in which most people are brought into church membership: by family member or friend inviting them. When Andrew finds Simon, Andrew refers to Jesus as the Messiah, a title some scholars related to "Lamb of God." However, note that Andrew and the other disciple call Jesus Rabbi or teacher before their stay with Jesus and then they call him Messiah. In this Gospel, Andrew first confesses Jesus as Messiah, but in the Synoptics it is Simon Peter who does this. Also, in this Gospel the change of names from Simon to Peter takes place at the beginning of Jesus' ministry, while in Matthew it takes place over halfway through it.

Remember that in the Hebrew Scriptures the giving of a new name to a person indicated the role the person would play in salvation history (Abraham, Isaac, etc.). John stresses that Jesus gave Simon the new name because of his insight into Simon as he "looked at him." The names Cephas and Peter are both nicknames and not normal proper names. Calling Simon by Peter is in effect like calling him "Rocky." This use of the name would have to be explained by what Jesus saw in his character or envisioned for his career.

Then in vs. 43–51 we have an account of Philip and Nathanael coming to follow Jesus. Note that Jesus called Philip to follow him (v. 43). Philip is the third disciple to be named in John's Gospel and is from the same town as Andrew and Peter, Bethsaida. Nathanael asked, "Can anything good come out of Nazareth?" This may have been a local proverb and a putdown of the village, since Nathanael was from Cana a town nearby Nazareth. Nathanael is named only in John, and his name means "God has given." The early church fathers suggest that he was *not* one of the Twelve, however. Some scholars think he is the same person as the Bartholomew mentioned in Matthew 10:3; Mark 3:18; and Luke 6:14. John seems to use Nathanael as a symbol of Israel coming to God, but he is more than a symbolic figure here.

We cannot be sure what caused Jesus to say there was no guile in Nathanael. Some suggest that it means that Nathanael was one who was worthy of the name of Israel. Jesus may have been saying that Nathanael had none of the qualities of Jacob before he became Israel. What Jacob had only seen in a vision (Gen. 28:12) has now become a reality in Jesus.

Nathanael addressed Jesus, "Rabbi, you are the Son of God! You are the King of Israel!" (v. 49). The disciples called Jesus Son of God after the resurrection. Jesus then refers to himself as Son of man (v. 51). Son of man as a title is rooted in Ezekiel and Daniel. All the Gospels agree that Jesus used this title to designate himself. In fact, it seems to have been used more often by Jesus of himself than any other title. The Son of man was a messenger from heaven to make God known on earth and to be the final judge. Most of the passages that use Son of man in John are concerned with his future glory. The final judgment is mentioned in one of them. The reference to seeing the heaven opened reminds us of the descent of the Spirit at Jesus' baptism.

Recommended work: Do a word study of Lamb of God, Messiah, God of God, Son of man, and Andrew. Compare this account of calling the disciples with those in the other Gospels.

The sermon might focus on Jesus' calling the disciples and their testimony to Jesus as the Messiah. It might refer to God's call to Samuel as another example of one who hears and obeys. Following Jesus means abiding and staying with him all through life. To come to Jesus and see Jesus is to believe in him. The sermon might point to evangelism as a sharing of the good news of Jesus as Andrew, the soul winner, brought his brother Simon to Jesus. He also brought the Greeks to him and the lad with loaves and fish. The sermon might cite evidence that the great majority of people who join a church have been brought there by a friend or a relative, thus continuing the pattern of Andrew bringing Simon to Jesus. The sermon could challenge the hearers to become more conscious of their opportunities to tell others about Jesus and to invite them to know him as Lord and Savior. What greater gift can one give another?

1 Samuel 3:1–10 (11–20) (C)

1 Samuel 3:1–10 (L)

1 Samuel 3:3–10, 19 (RC)

The call of Samuel continues through v. 18, followed by vs. 19–21 describing Samuel as a prophet. This call of Samuel to be a prophet is combined with a denunciation of the house of Eli which has blasphemed against God and committed gross iniquities.

The setting is the sanctuary at Shiloh, where earlier Samuel's mother had prayed for a son (ch. 1). Tradition says that Samuel was twelve years old when he was called, the same age as Jesus when he discoursed with the scholars of the law at the temple in Jerusalem. Samuel is sleeping near the Ark when he hears his name called, and he naturally thinks that Eli his master is calling him. But on the third call, Eli realizes that it is God who is calling and instructs Samuel to reply the next time with, "Speak, Lord, for thy servant hears."

It may be that Samuel slept in the temple so that he could tend the lamp that burned there or to serve as a watchman. The text mentions that the "lamp of God" had not gone out, implying that it was not yet morning, when the oil would have burned out. A lamp was to burn in the sanctuary throughout the night (Ex. 27:20–21; Lev. 24:3). The Hebrew word for "hears" has the meaning of "is ready to hear." Remember that in Hebrew thought to hear includes also obeying.

The call of Samuel should be understood against the background of the sins of the house of Eli which apparently was the reason the word of the Lord was rare in those days and there was no frequent vision (v. 1). The sins of the clergy are ever with us and block the hearing of God's word they are to transmit to the people. This pericope is another instance in which the lectionary reading fails to deal with the negative side of the story being told and so the preacher should include it by dealing with the alternate vs. 11–20 of the (C) reading. Verse 19 indicates that Samuel grew and the Lord blessed him. The story of the birth and childhood of Samuel must have been in the thoughts of Luke as he wrote the story of Jesus' birth and childhood.

Recommended work: Do a word study of vision, word, and hear. Compare this call to the calls of persons before him, such as Moses, Gideon, and Samson.

The sermon might follow the movement of the text itself as it builds to the climax in v. 10, where Samuel asks God to speak, for he is ready to hear. The sermon may deal with how we hear God's word for our lives and respond to it in faithful obedience. It might deal with the consequences of failing to hear as Eli's house failed and contemporary religious shysters fail to hear and obey God's word.

1 Corinthians 6:12–20 (C)

1 Corinthians 6:13–15, 17–20 (RC)

1 Corinthians 6:11b–20 (E)

The theme of vs. 12–20 is the evil of sexual sins. In an age that has confused freedom with license, this is a very relevant text. Corinth was a city notorious for its sexual license. There was a saying that one must have a lot of money to visit Corinth because of the excesses there.

The libertines then, like those today, saw sex as a drive like hunger. Satisfying the sexual desire was like eating food to relieve hunger. It was a natural desire to be satisfied. But Paul rejects this argument, declaring that immorality involves the whole body of a person in a way quite different from eating food. It involved the whole personal life of the one engaging in sexual activity. Sexual intercourse means becoming one flesh with the partner in sex: "Therefore a man leaves his father and his mother and cleaves to his wife, and they become one flesh" (Gen. 2:24). Jesus declared, "And the two shall become one flesh" (Matt. 19:5b).

Those who were claiming their rights in Christian liberty to justify their immorality were probably converts from paganism. Apparently they had taken over Paul's aphorism that "All things are lawful for me" and made it into a principle of libertinism which says anything goes. "Doing your own thing" regardless of principles or other persons is the contemporary way of putting it. Paul had applied the aphorism to Jewish dietary laws, asserting that Christians were no longer bound by them.

The main point of Paul's argument is that a Christian has been united to Christ and thus his or her body is a member of Christ. The sin of fornication lies in uniting the members of Christ in an intimate relationship with a prostitute. In having sexual relations with a harlot, the Christian enters into a "one flesh" relationship with her and thus disowns membership in the body of Christ. The risen Christ is the model and principle of the glorious relationship destiny of the Christian's body.

In addition, the fornicator sins against the body (v. 18). The Christian's body is a temple of God's Spirit and therefore belongs to God. Because the Christian is bought from slavery to sin by the death of Christ, the Christian belongs to God, not to self. Therefore the Christian should glorify God in his or her body by refraining from sexual immorality.

Recommended work: Do a word study of body, immorality, and glorify.

The sermon might follow the movements of the passage, climaxing with "You were bought with a price" (v. 20), pointing out that a Christian belongs to God, not to self. The sermon should contrast the difference between what is called the "new morality" of anything goes with biblical principles of sexual morality. The Christian has died to sin and been raised in Christ and united to Christ's body and thus is under the command of Christ, not of self.

Theological Reflection

The 1 Samuel passage and the John passage deal with calls and responses. Samuel hears God in the night and responds in obedience. Jesus calls disciples and they follow.

These are examples of the biblical theology of God's calling people to obedience and their response of acceptance or rejection of that call. The 1 Corinthians reading is a call to sexual morality because one has been called by Christ and incorporated into Christ's body and no longer belongs to self but to God in Christ.

Children's Message

The talk with the children might be about names and nicknames and their meaning: "Speedy," a nickname for a fast runner; "Shorty," for someone small. A girl might be named "Grace" or "Precious" because of her parents' special feeling about her. Jesus gave Simon a new name, Peter, meaning "Rocky." Other new names for biblical characters might be mentioned, such as Abraham and Isaac, and their meaning.

Hymns for Epiphany 2

Jesus Calls Us; We Are One in the Spirit; God Himself Is with Us.

Epiphany 3

Ordinary Time 3

Psalm 62:5–12 (C)   **1 Corinthians 7:29–31 (32–35) (C)**
Psalm 62:6–14 (L)   **1 Corinthians 7:29–31 (L) (RC)**
Psalm 25:4–9 (RC)   **1 Corinthians 7:17–23 (E)**
Psalm 130 (E)

Mark 1:14–20

Jonah 3:1–5, 10 (C)
Jeremiah 3:21–4:2 (E)

Meditation on the Texts

We thank you, O God, for sending your Son Jesus Christ into the world, preaching the gospel and saying, "The time is fulfilled, and the kingdom of God is at hand; repent, and believe in the gospel." We remember Jesus' call to the disciples to follow him and the promise to make fishers of human beings. May we not only hear his call to follow but obey his command to bring others to the living Christ. May we not be like Jonah who, when he first heard your call to go to Nineveh, fled in the opposite direction. And when we obey and preach repentance, may we rejoice when sinners repent, turn to you, and are saved from judgment. We remember that you promised Israel that if the people returned to you, the nations would bless themselves in Israel and glory in Israel. May we of the church, the New Israel, trust your promises, repent, and turn to you in faithful obedience. We know the time has grown very short and the form of this world is passing away. We have been bought with a price, Christ's death on the cross. May we lead the life you have assigned us and to which we have been called by your Spirit. Amen.

Commentary on the Texts

Mark 1:14–20

All of Mark's Gospel is an expansion of vs. 14–15 which summarize Jesus' message. Note the events up to this point: John the Baptist, the messianic herald, has appeared, and Jesus the Messiah himself has been designated and he has secretly entered on the first stage of what will be his final battle with the forces of evil (vs. 12–13). Now the stage is set for Jesus to declare himself publicly and to call men and women to share in the kingdom and in the remaining stages of the battle with evil. The note that "after John was arrested" (v. 14) indicates that John's work is completed, and now Jesus' work is to begin. The forerunner's work of preparing the way of the Lord is finished. Now the time has come for Jesus, the Messiah, to begin his work.

Our pericope is composed of two sections: vs. 14–15, which deal with the theme of the gospel of God, and vs. 16–20, which tell of the call of the first disciples. The first section (vs. 14–15) serves as a transition from the prologue in the wilderness (vs. 1–13) to Jesus' public ministry which begins in Galilee and is described in 1:16–8:21. These two verses resemble a pronouncement story as well as serving as a summary of Jesus' characteristic activity.

The first half of Jesus' ministry is in Galilee, and v. 14 indicates that Jesus "came into Galilee." In addition, vs. 14–15 give the themes of fulfillment and kingdom which are especially prominent in the passion narrative. There is also the call to repent and believe, themes that underlie the ongoing communication between the reader and the text throughout Mark's Gospel.

Mark says Jesus came preaching, which indicates Jesus' role as herald of the kingdom of God. Both preaching and teaching are basic activities of Jesus in Mark's Gospel, and no clear distinction is drawn between them in this Gospel. Recall that Jesus' authoritative deeds were other ways of proclaiming the arrival of God's kingdom. The content of Jesus' preaching is ''the gospel of God.'' Contrast this with ''the gospel of Jesus Christ'' in the title of the Gospel (v. 1). ''Gospel'' in Mark means the good news *about* Jesus Christ. But in v. 14 ''gospel'' refers to what Jesus preached about the kingdom of God.

There is a symmetrical structure to the content of Jesus' preaching in vs. 14–15:

1. Announcement
   a. ''The time is fulfilled''
   b. ''The kingdom of God is at hand''
2. The earnest plea
   a. Repent
   b. Believe in the gospel

The coming of Jesus fulfilled God's plan for history. A different era began with Jesus' preaching following John's work as prophet preparing the way. Mark also ties the turning point in time to the preaching of Jesus: this is decision time, to be for or against God's rule.

The kingdom is both present and yet in the future. Those who are confronted by the power of God in Jesus' words and works experience God's kingdom as present but still hidden, since its full manifestation lies in a future that has now drawn near. Jesus calls hearers to repent and believe the gospel. To repent is to turn from sin and to turn to God and a new life. This turning to God is the primary meaning of repent in this verse. Note carefully that the climax of this unit is ''believe the gospel.'' Where Jesus is, there is the rule, power, and kingdom of God actively at work. While Jesus was active in the flesh then, he is present and active in the word of proclamation now. The preacher today continues to call people to repent and believe the good news of Jesus Christ.

We find in vs. 16–20 the group that will be the second major concern of the entire Gospel story, the disciples. As soon as Jesus announces the kingdom of God, he calls people to enter it, to follow him, and in turn to invite others to enter by becoming ''fishers of men.'' The kingdom is corporate in Mark as it is in Matthew's thought. There is no individualist approach to the rule of God as if the kingdom was only a ''Jesus in my hand'' kind of religion.

Notice the five personal names, the mention of the Sea of Galilee, nets, boats, hired servants, the activity of casting, mending, and following—all very sharp details about this episode. According to Mark, this is the *first* encounter of Jesus and his disciples. Notice that the only words spoken are those of Jesus calling the disciples and charging them to become ''fishers of men.''

Mark does not describe the day or the countryside but focuses rather on the primary interest of the Gospel, namely, Jesus' authority and the response of the disciples. This action of Jesus' calling and the disciples' response reflects the two focal points of the entire Gospel: Jesus' presence and words, and the response to Jesus' call to discipleship. Jesus is king, and where he is, there is the kingdom of God. Jesus' call to these four disciples not only prepares for the further preaching of the kingdom of God but also *exemplifies* the kingdom in human experience.

The literal meaning of the Greek words translated ''Follow me'' is ''Come [plural] after me.'' Contrast this with Jesus' command to Peter in Mark 8:33: ''Get behind me, Satan! For you are not on the side of God, but of men.''

Jesus not only calls the disciples but gives a promise that defines the content of the call: ''and I will make you fishers of men.'' See how Jesus uses figurative language which is appropriate to these fishermen. The purpose of God's gospel is to lead the hearers/readers to become faithful disciples of Jesus Christ. Faithful discipleship is summed up in following Jesus. Jesus' call to follow him confronts each person who hears it with a decision regarding life's ultimate loyalty: to Jesus or to material possessions, other people, or centers of loyalty. Notice that the four fishermen model response to Jesus' call by immediately leaving their nets and following Jesus. They turn their backs on this past in order to move out into a new future with Jesus.

Recommended work: Compare the call of the disciples here with that in the other Gospels, especially in John 1:35–51 of last Sunday's Gospel. Do a word study of kingdom, repent, and believe.

The sermon might follow the movement of the text, drawing on images in the text. The goal of the sermon might be to lead hearers to repent and believe in the gospel and to follow Jesus in faithful discipleship. A note of urgency should be included, since the "time is fulfilled" and God's kingdom is at hand for us today.

Jonah 3:1–5, 10 (C)

Our pericope is part of the second mission of Jonah in chapters 3–4. Recall that Jonah had been rescued by the merciful Lord when he tried to evade his call to go to Nineveh to preach repentance. There is no mention by the Lord of Jonah's resistance to the first call, and there has been no change of heart on Jonah's part. He merely complies with the Lord's call because he has found escape impossible. He goes reluctantly and grudgingly to Nineveh.

The Lord's message is found in vs. 1–2. Consider how vs. 1–3 are modeled on 1:1–3. We are told that Nineveh was three days' journey in breadth, which may not be too great an exaggeration, since the city could embrace the so-called Assyrian triangle of Khorsabad in the north to Nimrud in the south, a distance of some twenty miles. One of the mounds marking the site of ancient Nineveh is called Nebi Yunus, meaning "the prophet Jonah."

Jonah's brief message is unlike that of other prophetic books which are full of judgment speeches and actions, plus oracles of admonition and doom. Jonah merely cries, "Yet forty days, and Nineveh shall be overthrown!" (v. 4) and this message is delivered in the Lord's name, as v. 2 says. The forty days remind us of the forty days of the flood and of the exodus.

Take note of the amazing reaction of the Ninevites, who immediately repent, believe God, and proclaim a fast from the greatest to the least. Even the king and the beasts respond (vs. 6, 7). The king even asks, "Who knows, God may yet repent and turn from his fierce anger, so that we perish not?" (v. 9).

The repentance and conversion of the people from sin moves God to repent of the evil intended for Nineveh (v. 10). The Lord's oracles of doom are conditional. Jeremiah taught a similar understanding of God's judgment and repentance as the people repented (Jer. 18:7–8; 26:3). Some scholars think that the issue of whether divine oracles will be fulfilled is the fundamental teaching of this book. But the thrust of the whole Jonah story is not whether Jonah's threat of destruction is fulfilled but whether the Lord's mercy extends even to Nineveh. It does, which is a theme of Epiphany with its emphasis on God's revelation to the nations.

Recommended work: Read the Book of Jonah in its entirety. Consider treating the story as a parable.

The sermon may follow the movement of the text. It should be prefaced with what has taken place earlier in Jonah, since some hearers may not be familiar with this book, although they may know the name Jonah. The emphasis of the sermon may be on God's mercy which extends to all nations today as it did to the wicked city of Nineveh. There should be a call to repentance and turning to God in obedient faith.

Jeremiah 3:21–4:2 (E)

Notice Jeremiah's twofold mission: (1) to root up and to tear down and (2) to build and to plant. Earlier, in 2:2–37, Jeremiah carried out the first part. Now he deals with the second, that of building up and planting. The thrust of this whole section is the working out of conditions that are necessary for bringing about reconciliation between Israel and the Lord God.

"On the bare heights" was the site of pagan idolatry, from which come cries of profound repentance and determination to return to God. Genuine repentance will be expressed in the removal of pagan shrines, recognition of God's exclusive claim by swearing in God's name only, and the cleansing of their hearts.

The nations who see the sight of the glory given by God to Israel will desire to serve God also: ''Nations shall bless themselves in him.'' Here is a theme of Epiphany: the revelation of God to the nations. As Israel is true to its faith, it will bring forth the promises made to the patriarchs (Gen. 12:3; etc.).

Recommended work: Read 2:2–37 and compare it with our pericope. Compare God's repenting here with that in the Book of Jonah.

The sermon might apply the call to repentance to hearers today with the promise that God will forgive and restore. The sermon might follow the action in the text, with the climax being God's enabling the nations to bless themselves through God's forgiveness of God's people. The purpose is that the nations might glory in God, a theme of Epiphany.

1 Corinthians 7:29–31 (32–35) (C)

1 Corinthians 7:29–31 (L) (RC)

Paul expresses in these verses his conviction that the last period of salvation history was running its course. Christ might return at any moment. For this reason the Christian must live as the Lord has admonished, in prayer and watchfulness (Matt. 24:43–44). Paul repeats what he has said earlier about marriage. He justifies his caution with a reference to the shortness of the time which makes it desirable for Christians not to be involved in the distracting obligations of marriage and family. The Christian must keep detached from the form of this world which is passing away. Even the married should live with detachment. They can fulfill the duties of marriage without attaching their hearts to this world which is passing away.

Recall that the author of 1 John 2:18 cautions that this is ''the last hour.'' With the Lord's resurrection and the gift of the Spirit at Pentecost the last days of salvation history have begun. Time is rapidly pressing on to the consummation of redemption.

Note the strong eschatological perspective of this passage as it focuses on the future End time which is breaking into the present. Those who clearly see the future of God's salvation will live now in the present by radically altered values as to what counts and what does not.

Recommended work: Do a word study of ''form.'' See a detailed exegesis of this passage in Gordon D. Fee, *The First Epistle to the Corinthians* (Grand Rapids: Wm. B. Eerdmans Publishing Co., 1987).

The sermon might focus on ''hanging loose'' to this world in the light of the coming salvation of God which is breaking in from the future. The sermon could raise consciousness regarding the passing of this world and the permanence of God's kingdom which is breaking in. It should challenge hearers to reorder their priorities and daily living in the light of God's promise of Christ's return at the End.

1 Corinthians 7:17–23 (E)

The thrust of this passage is similar to 1 Corinthians 7:29–31 with its stress on the imminent return of Christ and Paul's advice to remain in one's present condition rather than try to change it. Paul was dominated by the conviction that the form of this present world is passing away and the time has grown very short. Therefore Christians should concentrate on the Lord's affairs, since their lasting well-being with God depends on it, rather than focusing on the relations of this world. Paul reminds them they were ''bought with a price,'' namely, Christ's death. Those who are slaves are free in Christ. Those who are free are nevertheless slaves of Christ.

Recommended work: Compare this passage with others in the New Testament that advise Christians regarding marriage and family life.

The sermon should put this passage in the context of the expectation of the imminent return of Christ of the early Christians. The sermon might focus on freedom in Christ and slavery to Christ as it applies to Christian living today.

Theological Reflection

The theme of call and response is found in the passages from Mark and Jonah. The theme of repentance on God's part as people repent of sin is also found in the Jonah and Jeremiah passages. The two 1 Corinthian passages focus on the radically different lifestyle of Christians in the light of the shortness of time before Christ's return. In the passage from Mark, Jesus announces that the rule of God is at hand, calling people to repent and believe in the gospel.

Children's Message

The talk might be about Jesus' disciples who were fishermen but who left their old way of living and working in order to follow Jesus. You might describe some people who have left comfortable lives in order to obey God's call to service in another part of the world. The congregation's missionary partners or other Christians and their work might be described.

Hymns for Epiphany 3

They Cast Their Nets in Galilee; The Light of God Is Falling; Take Thou Our Minds, Dear Lord.

Ordinary Time 4

Psalm 111 (C)   **1 Corinthians 8:1–13 (C)**
Psalm 1 (L)   **1 Corinthians 8:1b–13 (E)**
Psalm 95:1–2, 6–9 (RC)   **1 Corinthians 7:32–35 (RC)**

Deuteronomy 18:15–20   **Mark 1:21–28**

Meditation on the Texts

We thank you, holy God, for raising up a prophet like Moses who was more than a prophet, for he is our Savior and Lord. You put your words in his mouth and he spoke all that you commanded him. We acknowledge that there are many gods and idols but there is only one God from whom are all things and for whom we exist and one Lord, Jesus Christ, through whom are all things and in whom we exist. Whether single or married, we pray that we may be free from anxieties as we put our trust in you our God. We pray that we may give our undivided devotion to you, O Lord, for we know that the form of this world is passing away and the appointed time has grown very short. We recall that Jesus cast the unclean spirit out of the man at Capernaum who recognized Jesus as the Holy One of God. We pray that we may be cleansed of all our sins by the power of Christ's Spirit and so enabled to bear a bold witness to Christ's power over evil. Amen.

Commentary on the Texts

Mark 1:21–28

It is significant that Jesus' first miracle was an exorcism, which demonstrated his power over evil. Earlier, Jesus had announced that "the kingdom of God is at hand" (v. 15), and in this miracle Jesus shows that God's rule is at work. The major thrust of this pericope is Jesus' authority in word and deed. The question of the people after the healing goes right to the heart of our passage: "What is this? A new teaching! With authority he commands even the unclean spirits, and they obey him" (v. 27). The focus on Jesus' teaching and authority is expressed by the structure of the text itself.

The general setting is Capernaum, on the northwest shore of the Sea of Galilee, which Jesus apparently chose as the headquarters of his mission. All four Gospels testify to Jesus' loyalty to the synagogue of his time. Jesus worked to purify the old order of worship, not to establish a new type. The synagogue has been compared to an English parish church in that every village or town of any size had one. Sacrificial rituals were done in the temple in Jerusalem. Christian worship was strongly influenced by the synagogue service. It consisted of various praises, blessings, prayers, and readings from the Hebrew Scriptures which were often expounded by a preacher. But there was no ordained ministry in our sense of the term. There were elders who were responsible for the synagogue, and one or more rulers among them who arranged for and might lead worship. There was also a paid official who might teach and fulfill a number of other duties. But any male Israelite who was qualified was allowed to deliver the sermon. It seems Jesus was often invited to do this by synagogue rulers. Later his disciples did the same, which gave them one of their best opportunities for spreading the gospel.

Mark gives us the precise setting of Jesus' teaching: on the Sabbath in the synagogue of Capernaum. When Jesus taught, the response was astonishment and recognition of his authority in teaching. This is followed by the exorcism. Note that Mark uses one of his favorite words, "immediately," to introduce the teaching and the healing events. This gives the text and actions a note of urgency and movement. The exorcism takes place in the synagogue, and the problem is an unclean spirit. The spirit, or demon, was called unclean because the effect of the condition was to separate the person from the worship of God. But the word translated "unclean" sometimes means "vicious," and so Mark may be describing an evil spirit. Mark uses "unclean spirit," "evil spirit," and "demon" synonymously. While they have the same denotation, they have different connotations. Unclean or evil spirit indicates ritual impurity. A demon indicates satanic power. All of these terms denote an invisible being that is alienated from and hostile to God.

The solution to the problem of the unclean spirit was Jesus' healing word: Be silent and come out of him! The evidence of the cure was the man's convulsion and his shouting with a loud voice. The response was amazement and the recognition of Jesus' authority. Mark gives a general conclusion to both the teaching and the healing: Jesus' fame spread everywhere throughout Galilee.

Consider that Mark uses the words "teaching" and "authority" in both v. 22 and v. 27 to tie together these two events of teaching and healing to form a single passage. While an exorcism is not a new teaching, Mark links Jesus' power in both word and deed to show Jesus' amazing authority.

In the ancient world, sickness was ascribed to evil spirits. Many of Jesus' miracles are described in terms of exorcisms. It was commonly thought that a person was at the mercy of the demons unless under the protection of some stronger spiritual power. We do not know whether or not Jesus believed in demon possession, but in order to heal persons who did believe, he would have needed to seem to believe in it, whether he actually did or not. A common feature of miracle stories was the description of the gravity of the sufferer's affliction. This is indicated here by the man's cries and the details of the cure (v. 26).

A distinctive feature of Mark is that the demons recognize Jesus as Holy One of God, or the Messiah, while the people around Jesus do not. But the reader of the Gospel is given a clue to Jesus' identity by the demons. The possessed man cried out, "Have you come to destroy us?" and Mark's clear answer is yes he has. Some scholars think this verse should be read not as a question but as an exclamatory declaration. The demons knew who Jesus was (v. 24). To know the name of one's adversary was to gain magical power over the adversary. Note that the demons name Jesus twice: Jesus of Nazareth, and the Holy One of God, meaning a charismatic prophet like Elijah. But Jesus' real identity is kept secret from the crowds (the so-called messianic secret of Mark's Gospel). Mark wants to reveal gradually to the reader what the crowds did not know. All through this Gospel *only* the demons recognize Jesus for who he really is. Mark uses this technique of dialogue with the demons to keep the reader fully informed.

Jesus' rebuke is not a denial of the title given him by the demons in the man; rather, it is a suppression of it. Jesus constantly says to demons who recognize him, "Be silent." This is Mark's way of dealing with the question asked in his time of why Jesus wasn't recognized as the Son of God during Jesus' earthly ministry. Only the demons recognized him, says Mark, and he silenced them. One goal of Mark's Gospel is to allow us today to participate with the first disciples in gradually coming to recognize who Jesus is until we reach the conclusion to which the demoniac already points.

Hearers of this story today are invited to ask the same question as the onlookers in the synagogue: "What is this?" although we know the answer to what happened in the healing. Mark continually confronts us with the basic questions and then leads us to fresh perceptions. The challenge of the preacher is to help the hearer recognize that Jesus of Nazareth was indeed who the demoniac said he was, "the Holy One of God." Thus Mark confronts each hearer with the decision of faith.

Recommended work: Do a word study of unclean spirit, demon, evil spirit, and Holy One of God. Compare this healing with other exorcisms in Mark and note their differences and similarities.

The sermon might follow the movements of the text leading up to the question of "What is this?" thus confronting the hearers with a faith decision. The sermon should focus on Jesus' authority over evil revealed in this healing and the recognition of his authority in his teaching. The good news of Jesus' power to heal broken and bound lives today should be stressed. In the light of recent reports of medical science of the relationship of mind and body in healing, this miracle takes on greater meaning. Studies show that one personality type is more likely to have cancer, another is more likely to have a heart attack, and the destructive force of the emotions in resentment is well known. Jesus can and does heal personalities and thus heal physical diseases as well as mental illnesses.

Deuteronomy 18:15–20

Our pericope is part of the longer passage of vs. 9–20 dealing with the role of the prophet. The issue being dealt with is the vital link between God and people. While nature religions sought to control and influence the god of nature, the Hebrew sought to live by obedience to God's saving word. In the preceding vs. 9–14 the Israelites are warned not to resort to pagan divination. Two sorts of abominable pagan practices were condemned here: burning son or daughter as an offering, and various forms of communication with the occult, such as divination of the future, fixing of curses or spells, and communication with the dead.

Then in our pericope the role of the true prophet stands in sharp contrast to these pagan practices. (The new interest in the occult in recent years could be noted in the sermon.) The pericope begins with Moses announcing that God will raise up a prophet for the people. The context implies that this is not just one prophet but the prophetic office, which will be filled by a succession of prophets. More than one prophet will have to establish credentials as a true prophet in the eyes of the people.

Prophecy for Israel is the great means of mediation between God and Israel in contrast to pagan religions. The author of this passage thinks of the prophetic office as being founded at Horeb (Mt. Sinai) and its being an office like that filled by Moses himself. Deuteronomy outlines the function of this prophet to be the mouth of God for Israel. We should not think here of the pattern of the great prophets like Isaiah, Jeremiah, Amos, and others but of the way in which Moses carried out his duties according to Deuteronomy's understanding of the role. This involves interceding, suffering as a representative, and actually dying. Thus this description of a prophet is in harmony with that of the Suffering Servant of God described in Second Isaiah.

At Mt. Sinai, Israel had begged to be spared the experience of hearing God's voice directly. So Moses listened to God and then gave Israel an account of what he heard. Thus the prophetic office of mediator came into being in the role of Moses.

Verse 18 was interpreted in later Judaism as applying to a figure coming at the End of the age. The Christian church saw it fulfilled in Christ.

The penalty for a prophet speaking in the name of other gods or speaking a false word from Israel's God is death. The final test of whether or not a prophet spoke in God's name was a simple one but sometimes required a long period of time: whether or not the prophecy came true. If a serious matter came up, how could the question of the authority of the prophet be left in suspense until the test of time proved it to be true? Jeremiah based his claim upon the tradition of prophets before him (Jer. 28:8–9).

Recommended work: Do a word study of prophet and Moses. Reflect on ways in which people today can determine true and false prophets among television evangelists, preachers, and others who claim to speak for God.

The sermon might focus on the issue of how we can know God's will for our lives and for the nation. It could outline the problem that Israel faced and the solution in v. 22, but pointing out our need for other criteria to judge prophets immediately as to the truth or falsity of their message. The sermon could raise the consciousness of people, pointing to Jesus as the true prophet who was "the Word made flesh" and who gave his life in carrying out this mission for God. The role of scripture, one's willingness to suffer for one's message, prayer, and the role of councils of the church in hearing and interpreting God's will for people today, might be presented. The sermon should be concrete and specific and relevant for the hearer's daily living.

1 Corinthians 8:1b–13 (E)

The thrust of this passage is whether or not a Christian may eat food consecrated to a pagan god. Much of the meat sold in the marketplace at that time had come from animals sacrificed in pagan temples. The Christian might be invited to a social gathering at a pagan temple or to a home in which meat offered to idols was served. As a result, there were problems for a convert to Christianity. So Paul deals with knowledge and love as they relate to this problem.

Some Corinthians said it did not matter if one ate meat offered to idols, and Paul seems to be agreeing with them when he quotes their sayings in v. 1a and v. 4. But he knows that this argument is being used by Gnostics, who are libertines, to justify their actions. Paul recognizes two kinds of wisdom: the kind some Corinthians think they possess fully and the true knowledge which a Christian does not possess now but which will be given by God eventually as a result of being known by God.

Paul has two principles governing his solution to the problem of eating meat offered to idols: a Christian is free from slavery to the law, the world, and Satan; and love is the controlling power in Christian morality. Paul points out that in eating meat offered to idols some converts from paganism will be led to relapse into paganism. To eat this meat may be a morally indifferent act for some, but for others the circumstances make the act a sin against a weaker Christian. Paul is ready to follow the principle of love in the matter and to abstain from meat forever in order to avoid scandalizing a brother or a sister in the faith.

1 Corinthians 7:32–35 (RC)

This passage should be read in the light of vs. 25–34 and in the context of the whole New Testament teaching on marriage and family life. Our pericope repeats Paul's earlier counsel about marriage in the light of the shortness of the time before Christ's return. In view of the imminent return of Christ, Paul counsels people not to get involved in the distracting obligations of family life. Paul seems to be idealizing the effectiveness of a celibate Christian's witness. We should keep in mind Paul's basic affirmation stated earlier: "But each has his own special gift from God" (v. 7). While most Christians do not have the gift of celibacy, some do. Those who marry may find that the witness of a Christian marriage and family to the world outweighs the divided interests that marriage demands. There is a challenge to grow in Christian love which marriage creates even as one struggles with demands upon time of both the family and the affairs of the Lord.

Recommended work: Read other New Testament teachings regarding celibacy and family life.

The sermon should deal with this text in the light of the biblical teaching that God created humans as male and female and ordained marriage and in the light of the expectation of the imminent return of Christ as the End of the age. The sermon might deal with the conflicting demands that both celibates and persons who have chosen to marry have on their time and energies. Both married and unmarried persons can glorify God and be obedient to Christ in their particular status.

Theological Reflection

The theme of the passage from Mark is Jesus' authority and power over the forces of evil. The passage from Deuteronomy focuses on the prophetic office as a means of knowing God's will. In the 1 Corinthians 8 passage Paul deals with knowledge and love and the responsibility that stronger Christians have for weaker ones. The 1 Corinthians 7 passage deals with Paul's counsel not to marry in the light of the imminent return of Christ so that the Christian may devote his or her undivided attention to the affairs of the Lord.

Children's Message

The conversation with the children might be about Jesus' custom of worshiping and teaching in the synagogue and his desire that people have good health. Jesus is recognized as having a special relationship with God which gives him authority and healing power. Jesus heals boys and girls today through the loving care of doctors and nurses. The words "holy," "health," and "whole" are closely related. Jesus wants us to be holy and whole.

Hymns for Epiphany 4

Rejoice, the Lord Is King; The Light of God Is Falling; Songs of Thankfulness and Praise.

Epiphany 5
Ordinary Time 5

Psalm 147:1–11 (C)
Psalm 147:1–13 (L)
Psalm 147:1–6 (RC)
Psalm 142 (E)

1 Corinthians 9:16–23 (C)
1 Corinthians 9:16–19, 22–23 (RC)

Mark 1:29–39

Job 7:1–7 (C)
Job 7:1–4, 6–7 (RC)
2 Kings 4:(8–17) 18–21 (22–31), 32–37 (E)

Meditation on the Texts

We thank you, gracious God, for Jesus Christ who preached, taught, and healed many who were sick with various diseases and who cast out demons. We recall that he withdrew to a lonely place to pray. May we never become so busy doing religious chores that we neglect communing with you through prayer. Although we preach the gospel, this gives us no ground for boasting. We have heard and responded to your call to preach. Help us to adapt ourselves to all kinds of people in order to preach the gospel to them and thus share its blessings. Sometimes we have become so burned out in ministry that we have felt like Job of old who had months of emptiness and nights of misery. We too have had long nights of tossing until the dawn. We thank you that when Christ descended into hell he experienced all the despair and separation from you that one can experience and that he was raised from the dead victorious. As we recall the kindness of the Shunem woman and her husband to Elisha, we pause to give thanks for the gracious hospitality that people have shown us. We pray that we may never be ungrateful for even the least act of kindness shown to us, nor forget to show kindness to others. Amen.

Commentary on the Texts

Mark 1:29–39

Our pericope is the conclusion of vs. 14–39 describing the beginnings of Jesus' activity in Galilee. Our pericope consists of three major incidents: the healing of Simon's mother-in-law (vs. 29–31), the healing of the sick at evening time (vs. 32–34), and Jesus' extension of his ministry to other places (vs. 35–39).

The healing of Simon's mother-in-law is the very first *physical healing* in Mark as distinct from the earlier exorcism. This involved a woman with a fever. Her faith is not mentioned, and the only detail about her is that after she was healed, "she served them." This story is alien to the understanding of women's place in home and society in the perspective of women's liberation. But we must read it in the context of the culture of Jesus' day. Note carefully, however, that Mark makes women the model of discipleship here and elsewhere. This woman responds to being healed by serving. She represents the right response to Jesus, in contrast to the male disciples who are increasingly insensitive and misunderstand Jesus and his mission.

In the preceding incident we saw that Jesus healed a man with an unclean spirit. Now we see Jesus dealing with other forms of sickness. In Jewish thought there was a tendency to think of all illness as due to personal forces. That explains why so many of the healing stories in the Gospels seem like accounts of exorcism. These demons were hostile to God; therefore the establishment of God's kingdom involved their overthrow by

Messiah. In the last incident, Jesus healed through a word, but here it is through an action: he took her by the hand and lifted her up. No word is reported.

Jesus' actions in healing Simon's mother-in-law were similar to those used by rabbis, according to records of the Talmud. In fact, the phrase "lift up" was the usual term for cure or heal in this literature. The comment that "the fever left her" was also found in contemporary accounts of healings. Mark uses a Greek verb for "lifted her up" that was used often of Jesus' resurrection (cf. Mark 14:28). The early church may have thought of this miracle as a foreshadowing of the coming resurrection of Jesus and the coming general resurrection at the End of time.

Mark says that after being healed she served them, which indicates the completeness of her cure and the service expected of those who have been healed of sin and saved by Christ.

Compare this healing with our pericope in Job 7, where Job complains of hard labor and sleepless nights, disease, and the shortness of this hopeless life. For Job, all of life was a fever.

Then in vs. 32–34 Jesus heals the sick at evening time, when the Sabbath was over at sundown. The notation of time stresses that Jesus did not exercise his power until the Sabbath was over and it was again lawful to carry the sufferers through the streets. They brought the sick and those possessed with demons. Jesus would not permit the demons to speak because they knew him. Thus Jesus deliberately makes it more difficult for people to figure out his identity from his works. But the reader or hearer of the story is given another clue to Jesus' identity, confirmed by the supernatural insight of the demons (v. 24). According to Jesus, miracles are the activity of God and are the manifestation of God's kingdom, inspired by God's Spirit. They are evidence that Satan has been bound and that Jesus is the promised coming One. But they are not compelling proofs, since some of the cities in which Jesus worked miracles did not repent and the disciples often misunderstood him.

There may have been a period of activity between the events described in vs. 21–34 and v. 35. Verse 39 seems to be a summary of the section of vs. 21–34. Jesus went out to a lonely place a great while before day. The early morning was a favorite time for prayer among pious Jews. In Mark's Gospel, Jesus' praying is mentioned here at the beginning of his ministry, again in the middle of it (6:46), and at the end in Gethsemane. Each time he prays in the dead of night. Luke mentions Jesus praying more often but omits this reference. Each time he prays it is a time of stress connected with the true nature of his role as Messiah.

It appears that Jesus went out to pray because of the false messianic hopes that his miracles had created. Reflect on the rhythm of work, rest, and prayer in the life of Jesus. Jesus, in Mark's Gospel, often prays alone, which reveals not only his Jewish piety but his humanity as he turns to God in times of stress, temptation, and decision. (Read Heb. 4:14–5:10 and note 5:7 especially as it sheds light on the role of prayer in Jesus' life.)

Simon and those with him (here they are not called disciples) tell Jesus that the crowd is searching for him. It may be that Mark avoids the title "disciple" here because they are not acting like disciples but are in opposition to Jesus. The word for "searching" is used in nine other places in Mark and always in a derogatory sense. When this word is used, it points either to finding Jesus in order to persecute him or to seek him in a way both wrong and unacceptable. Simon implies that Jesus should stay longer in Capernaum and capitalize on the popularity his miracles have stirred up. But Jesus refuses either to stay in one place or to encourage a false understanding of Messiah.

Jesus tells Simon and the others that he wants to go to the next towns in order to preach there also, for that is his mission. The word for "towns" means small towns, the small market towns in the neighborhood. Note the emphasis on preaching as the divine commission given to Jesus. Compare this with Paul's sense of commission in our 1 Corinthians 9 text for today. Jesus said he came out to preach, which may refer to his having left Capernaum (v. 35), but more likely means he came from heaven to earth to preach.

Recommended work: Do a word study of demons, prayer in Jesus' life, and Messiah. The sermon might take one of these three major incidents and develop it. Or the preacher might deal with the pericope as a whole, focusing on Jesus as the proclaimer of the kingdom of God. The sermon might show Jesus as both proclaiming and embodying the kingdom. Note the prayer of Jesus, the faith of Jesus, and his steadfast obedience to God's commission. These are qualities the sermon might encourage hearers to emulate in their own lives. The demons we encounter in our daily lives might be mentioned and the good news that Jesus can cast them out!

Job 7:1–7 (C)

Job 7:1–4, 6–7 (RC)

Our pericope is part of the section of chapters 6–7, which contains Job's reply to the first discourse of Eliphaz. In our passage Job says that the life of a human being is in general comparable to that of a slave who longs for the shadow (death). Such a life is transitory, which is an additional source of anguish (v. 6). Job compares human life to that of forced military service, to the work of a day laborer, and to that of a slave. These were three wretched states of life in that period. This is Job's reply to Eliphaz' easy optimism in 5:17, where he says, "Behold, happy is the man whom God reproves; therefore despise not the chastening of the Almighty." Job brings out the abrasiveness inherent in biblical faith, over against the romantic view of life set forth by Eliphaz which is still prevalent today. "Inspirational books," Hollywood movies, and television commercials paint a picture of life always turning out all right. But Job protests that this just isn't so.

Job's suffering moves him to explore the universal human condition and to describe it as one of misery (v. 3b). His friend Eliphaz had attributed human trouble to human sinfulness (5:6–7), but Job here attributes it to other causes. So in vs. 1–6 Job outlines the miserable slave conditions of human life. No wonder so many people have appreciated the Book of Job through the ages, for Job "tells it like it is" and deals in the realities of human oppression and distress. Then in vs. 7–21 Job accuses God of the rough treatment that humans receive. This hints that in 3:17–19 the terms "wicked," "taskmaster," and "master" all refer to God!

Note that the word for "hard service" in v. 1, which is so translated about 480 times in the Bible, refers to military service. Only in Job and in Isaiah 40:2 and Daniel 10:1 does the word refer to slave service. Since both Job and Second Isaiah use this word in this rare fashion, we can relate the plight of Job to that of Israel in exile. This suggests that we might explore Job in the light of Second Isaiah and vice versa.

Verse 7 begins a prayer that continues through v. 21. In v. 7 Job prays to God to remember that his life is a breath. In 4:7 Eliphaz used "remember" in speaking to Job. Now Job uses it in addressing God. The tone of this first address to God is *not* the penitential plea that Eliphaz had recommended in 5:8. Job was accustomed to an untroubled relationship with God. Now he appeals implicitly to the love that God has for him. While his friends have failed him, Job looks to God his divine friend, but he is afraid it is too late: "My eye will never again see good." There is a note of mockery in Job's prayer, for it implies that God will act when it will be too late. Job had heard of people who had descended into the underworld, where they were denied any return to this world.

Recommended work: Read a summary of the Book of Job in a Bible dictionary. Compare this speech to Eliphaz' discourse in chapters 4–5 to which Job is replying here.

The sermon should speak to the disillusioned people of today who find life empty. T. S. Eliot's "hollow men" of *The Wasteland* reflect the same idea. The sermon should seek to identify with the sense of emptiness that many people have today and the anguish of many who spend sleepless nights in hopelessness. The preacher should bring the gospel to bear on this sense of emptiness by showing how Jesus came that we might have life and have it abundantly. The sermon should point to the hope we have through Jesus' death and resurrection which has enabled us to overcome the last enemy, death.

2 Kings 4:(8–17) 18–21 (22–31), 32–37 (E)

Our pericope contains two incidents in the account of Elisha and the Shunem woman's son who was restored to life (vs. 8–37). We have in vs. 8–17 a favorite theme of the birth of a child late in life to a woman who has been barren to this point. Such a birth was considered a special favor from God. The unusual birth was thought to symbolize the importance of the person later in life. The second part of this story (vs. 18–37) is a parallel to the account of Elijah's resuscitation of a child (1 Kings 17:17–24).

Elisha is shown kindness by the Shunem woman and her husband who build a permanent roof chamber for him and equip it so he can stay there on his visits. This "prophet's chamber" not only ensured Elisha's privacy but completely safeguarded the family below from the consequences of contact with the "holy" man of God. When the Shunem couple's child was grown, he became ill in the field and was brought home, where he died on his mother's lap. She took him up to the prophet's chamber and laid him on Elisha's bed, shut the door and went out.

When Elisha came to the house he saw the child lying dead on his bed. His parents had not called Elisha earlier, because it was neither new moon nor Sabbath (v. 23), more propitious times to visit holy men to ask for help. The magic means of restoring the child used by Gehazi, Elisha's servant, did not work (v. 31). By contrast, Elisha crouches over the young man and his contact with hands, mouth, and eyes suggests a rite of contactual magic by which the life-giving powers of one person were transferred to another (a kind of human "jump start," as one might connect car batteries). Some scholars think that popular tradition might have exaggerated in describing the unconsciousness of the boy as actual death.

After Elisha restored him to life, the boy sneezed seven times, a token of life (literally, "breath") in the boy. Recall that breath in the nostrils of Adam gave him life (Gen. 2:7). The sneezing seven times indicates a possible popular elaboration.

After the miracle, Elisha walked once to and fro in the house, probably a means of relaxing after the intense physical and spiritual concentration which had exhausted him.

Recommended work: Compare this to 1 Kings 17:17–24. Do a word study of Elisha's life.

The sermon should sketch the whole story in order to make sense of the two passages. The sermon should point to God as the creator of life who can restore life. The preacher will want to relate Jesus' death and resurrection, which restores our lives from the "death" of bondage to sin to new life in him. God's Spirit raises to life those who are dead in bondage to substance abuse, to spiritual pride, and to apathy.

1 Corinthians 9:16–23 (C)

1 Corinthians 9:16–19, 22–23 (RC)

Our readings are part of a larger section, vs. 15–27, in which Paul waives his apostolic rights. Paul says he deserves no credit for preaching the gospel, since he is divinely commissioned to do so. But he does take pride in preaching without compensation, not making full use of his right in the gospel (v. 18). He is confident that he will have a special recompense from the Lord for renouncing pay for preaching. The "woe" he would experience if he did not preach is not some kind of inner distress; rather, he would stand under divine judgment if he failed to fulfill his commission from God. He cannot boast in the task of preaching the good news to the Gentiles, because that is precisely what God has commissioned him to do.

Then in vs. 19–23 Paul returns to the topic of chapter 8, namely, Christian freedom in everything except the obligation to love. We must take this passage in this context. It expresses Paul's consideration and tact, not cowardice and compromise. For an excellent treatment of this whole pericope, see Gordon D. Fee, *The First Epistle to the Corinthians* (Grand Rapids: Wm. B. Eerdmans Publishing Co., 1987), pp. 418–433.

Recommended work: Compare Paul's ministry as a "slave" to that of Jesus (Phil. 2:5–8; Gal. 4:4–5).

The sermon might follow Paul's discussion, pointing to the example of Christ as "servant" or slave as the expression of the believer's relationship to others. The sermon's goal should be to "save some" by hearing and responding to the gospel.

Theological Reflection

The Job reading expresses Job's sense of emptiness and despair over life which is so brief. It points up the need of the gospel and the hope of eternal life in Christ. The 2 Kings reading is an account of a miracle of God through Elisha by which a young man is restored to life. Mark tells of Jesus' healings and exorcisms and his preaching in Galilee, pointing to his authority and the breaking in of the kingdom of God. Paul waives his apostolic rights in the 1 Corinthians reading, declaring his need to preach the gospel because of his divine commission.

Children's Message

The children's message might focus on Jesus' need to pray and our need to pray also. Jesus prayed especially in times of temptation and stress as our passage from Mark indicates. The children should be encouraged to ask God's help when tempted in order to do the kind and loving thing and reject the mean and destructive.

Hymns for Epiphany 5

At Even, When the Sun Was Set; We Would See Jesus; I Look to Thee in Every Need.

Epiphany 6

Ordinary Time 6

Proper 1

Psalm 32 (C)	1 Corinthians 9:24–27 (C)
Psalm 32:1–2, 5, 11 (RC)	1 Corinthians 10:31–11:1 (RC)
Psalm 42 or 42:1–7 (E)	
	Mark 1:40–45
2 Kings 5:1–14 (C)	
2 Kings 5:1–15ab (E)	
Leviticus 13:1–2, 44–46 (RC)	

Meditation on the Texts

Merciful God, who sent your Son Jesus into the world with authority over demons and illness, we thank you for his healing power. While we were yet sinners he died for us, the ungodly, that through faith in him we might have life and have it abundantly. We thank you for Jesus' pity which moved him to heal the leper and made him clean. We recall Elisha's healing of Naaman the leper of Syria. Although he doubted at first, he obeyed the prophet's commands and was restored to health. Forgive us when we have doubted your word and in our pride have tried to heal ourselves. As we compete in the race of life we pray that we may so run that we may obtain the prize. May we discipline ourselves, that we may not be disqualified after preaching the gospel but may receive the imperishable prize of eternal life. Amen.

Commentary on the Texts

Mark 1:40–45

This account of the healing of the leper seems to be composed of two earlier accounts that were joined together. One account depicted Jesus' pity, the other his anger. The miracle serves to illustrate Jesus' power to save even a person excluded from the people of God by the Mosaic law. Leprosy not only was a loathsome disease that disfigured a person but also involved ritual uncleanness and complete segregation of the leper from the community and religious life. Persons suffering from AIDS today may identify with the treatment of lepers. Note that the law could do nothing for the leper; it could only protect the rest of the community.

There are a number of problems in the text, some of which are concealed in the English translation. Instead of reading ''moved with pity,'' it seems we should read ''moved with anger'' or ''indignation,'' as many manuscripts do. Many recent commentaries think the more difficult reading of anger is correct and it fits well with the harshness of v. 43, where the literal Greek could be translated ''He snorted at him and cast him out.'' The other Gospel writers found anger in the text and omitted any reference to Jesus' motivation. However, both pity and anger have good manuscript support and witness to a truth about Jesus. He was angry toward sickness, sin, and alienation. He was irritated in being interrupted. But Jesus also had both human and divine compassion toward suffering human beings.

The Greek translated ''sternly charged'' implies indignant displeasure. The word translated ''sent away'' has the thrust of ''drive out'' and is often used in connection with demons. In v. 45 the RSV assumes that the first half of the verse refers to the leper who was healed, but the Greek could just as well be translated, ''And he [Jesus] went out and preached [the gospel]." This would in some aspects be the more natural interpretation of the original Greek.

This miracle story is a prime example of miracle stories which follow a certain pattern: (1) a problem (v. 40), (2) a solution (vs. 40b–42), (3) evidence of the cure (vs. 43–44), and (4) public acclaim over the miracle (v. 45). Although the healing is reported in a very concise manner, the comments that follow are expanded and call attention to it.

This healing miracle witnesses to the Lordship of Jesus and also draws attention to the role of faith in healing, two themes common in Mark. While faith is not explicitly mentioned in our pericope, the leper's words, "If you will, you can make me clean," affirm his confidence and trust which is genuine faith. He trusts Jesus and knows that Jesus can heal if he will.

Jesus stretched out his hand and touched the leper, an unthinkable action at the time. It brought ceremonial defilement. But we are given a new insight into Jesus' ministry by this action of touching, namely, his deep compassion for the outcast who found himself rejected and despised by other human beings and believed himself to be despised and rejected by God also. Jesus' touch was a new and exquisite expression of the pity and love which the prophets had demanded.

Jesus dismissed the demon that caused the leprosy (v. 43). Jesus told the man to say nothing about the healing, which is in accord with the messianic secret. The remainder of v. 44 is in accord with Leviticus 13 and 14 (see the Leviticus pericope for today). Mark shows Jesus' regard for the law and thereby sets the stage for the controversies of 2:1–3:6. Although Jesus will later break certain Jewish laws, here he shows that he respects his Jewishness and does not flout Mosaic law. The real issue here, as in the verses that follow, is Jesus' implied claim to divine authority.

Then Jesus commanded the man to offer sacrifice which would allow him to reenter society. Note that the word "clean" appears four times in this passage. The first three instances refer to the healing of the disease, while the fourth indicates ceremonial purification. The thrust of this whole passage is that Jesus was concerned to restore the man physically, spiritually, and socially. The command to offer sacrifice indicates again Jesus' compassion for the man.

Recommended work: Do a word study of leprosy in a Bible dictionary. Read Leviticus 13 and 14. Compare this healing with that of Naaman the leper.

The sermon might develop moves that reveal the moves of the text, from problem to healing to evidence of cure to public acclaim. One application of the text would be to faith healing today and the excesses of some television evangelists and faith healers. Christians today must be cautious not to use faith healing to win converts, gather crowds, raise money, or boost personalities. The church has a continuing ministry of healing in the name of Jesus, inviting all to come to Jesus as the leper did and say, "If you will, you can make me clean." Jesus' death and resurrection cleanse us of our brokenness and restore us to right relationship with God and others. This is the greatest healing miracle of all!

2 Kings 5:1–14 (C)

2 Kings 5:1–15ab (E)

In reading this passage, we should recognize the humor which the Hebrew storyteller must have enjoyed. Naaman the commander of a foreign army, a mighty man of valor, is struck by one of the most dreaded diseases, leprosy, and the weakest member of society, a little Hebrew slave girl of his wife, provides the clue to his healing. Here is power contrasted with powerlessness. But the little maid is proud of Elisha the prophet of her land and promises he could cure Naaman. The great Syrian commander of the army serves the king, while the little maid serves his wife. Both are servants, but one is powerful, the other is weak. Then what glee the storyteller would have in relating the conflict between the king of Israel and the king of Syria. The king of Israel, probably Jehoram, thinks the plea for a cure is a trick to create a quarrel with him. He rent his clothes and asked, "Am I God, to kill and to make alive?" (5:7). The greatest humor is found when Naaman comes to Elisha's house and Elisha refuses to come out and do some dramatic act to cure him. Rather, he sends a messenger with a simple prescription. Naaman turned away in a rage and was about to return home without a cure. But his servants (powerless people) persuade him to obey the directive. When he did, he was made clean and his flesh became like that of a little child (a powerful man of war is given the flesh of a powerless child!). The preacher may find other bits of irony and sources of humor. These should not be lost in preparing the sermon.

Leprosy is a term that covered a variety of scabious diseases, some curable and others not. It seems Naaman could remain in society because his leprosy had not advanced to the point of his being quarantined. Or it may have been one of the more minor types of skin diseases which did not create a barrier to social interaction.

See how the huge gift that Naaman gathers to take with him gets our attention and develops anticipation. Giving gifts to prophets was the usual custom. Notice that the king of Syria fails to mention the prophet in Samaria, and this comic complication gives the reader a good laugh at the bureaucratic fumbling. The king of Israel makes an important confession, that he is not God, but defines God as one who kills and makes alive.

When Naaman arrives at Elisha's house, Elisha takes matters into his own hand and breaks through the government mixup. In vs. 8–10 the action is back on track moving toward Naaman's cure. But in spite of all of Naaman's horses and chariots and huge gift, Elisha is unimpressed and does not come out to work a dramatic and miraculous cure. Elisha puts Naaman in his place by refusing to come out to see him and sends a messenger instead. Later, in v. 15, they will meet face-to-face.

Naaman is given a classic test in such stories: go do something that seems silly. Naaman's anger in vs. 11–12 almost defeats his mission. It seems he will fail the test. Note the egocentric objection in v. 11. In the Hebrew the pronoun is emphasized. Naaman expected some magical hocus-pocus to be performed. He also downgrades the little Jordan River, which was so much less than the rivers of Syria. The Jordan was a joke even then because of its size and pollution. Naaman still does not realize that there is a prophet in Israel whose power lies in God, not in the prophet's magic. But his prophets get him back on track (v. 13). He is healed, which is the climax of the initial problem. The story continues with Naaman's conversion in vs. 15–19, which perhaps should be mentioned in the sermon, although it is beyond the bounds of our pericope.

Recommended work: Compare this healing with that in our Markan reading for today. Both are the result of God's power working through God's messenger. Naaman is skeptical, while the leper in Mark expresses faith in Jesus. Do a word study of leprosy.

The sermon should capture the humor of this delightful story while at the same time showing the outcome of the healing, found in v. 15, namely, Naaman's conversion. The sermon should contrast the powerful people (Naaman and the two kings) with the powerless (the slave girl and the servants). There is a not too subtle ridicule of military might, trust in riches, the omnipresent provincialism and egotism in the story. This is a sermon to provoke some laughter while sinking home the message that God heals even lepers outside the people of God who are desperate for help. And this one is even converted!

Leviticus 13:1–2, 44–46 (RC)

The thrust of this whole chapter is the diagnosis of leprosy. The next chapter deals with the cleansing of it. This was not the leprosy we know now. Leprosy was a generic term that included various skin diseases as well as blemishes affecting garments and buildings. We cannot determine the exact nature of the illness described in our pericope. The role of the priest was not that of a physician, since no treatment was prescribed. He was the judge and interpreter of the law. His favorable decision was required before purification rites permitting reentry into the community could be begun. If there was a doubtful case, then the person was quarantined, sometimes for a week, or at most two weeks. During this time the diseased person had to remain outside the city, give notice of his or her disease by customary signs such as torn garments, long, flowing hair, covered head, and the cry of "Unclean!"

Recommended work: Read an article on leprosy in a Bible dictionary.

The sermon should relate this passage to that of 2 Kings and the Markan passage rather than seek to develop a message from the text alone. The healing power of Jesus Christ through his death and resurrection which restores the broken person to wholeness should be stressed.

1 Corinthians 9:24–27 (C)

The thrust of this passage is that Christian zeal and prudence call for sacrifice and self-renunciation. Corinth was the site of the famous Isthmian games held there every two years. From these sporting contests Paul draws the images of this passage. Paul's use of sporting images suggests to the preacher the value of drawing images from contemporary sports in building the sermon. One well-known preacher always included at least one illustration from golf.

The perishable crown of v. 25 refers to the laurel wreath given the victors in the Olympic Games at Athens and the Pythian Games at Delphi. At Corinth a wreath of pine branches was given. Paul says he does not run aimlessly, but keeps his eye on the goal which is salvation, an imperishable gift of God.

He pommels his body (v. 27). The Greek verb here means "I strike under the eye" or, in modern slang, "I uppercut." In Greek boxing, the blow under the eye was considered the knockout blow. Paul applies this to himself in a figurative sense. Paul says he subdues his body lest after preaching he should be disqualified. This may be an allusion to the custom of humiliating the vanquished boxer. The winning boxer would throw a rope around the defeated opponent and drag him about the arena to the jeers of the crowd. Paul does not tell us how he got mastery over his body, but in 2 Corinthians 6:4–10 he tells of fasts and vigils in addition to the persecutions, hardships, and sufferings that he endured in the line of duty as an apostle of Jesus Christ.

Recommended work: Read a brief article on the Greek games of Paul's era. Read other passages that relate how Paul disciplined himself.

The sermon might appeal especially to young people and sports-minded hearers with images from contemporary athletes. The sermon might compare the Christian way of living to a race in the Olympics which demands self-discipline, keeping one's eye on the goal and exercising self-control. While salvation is a gift from God, appropriating it calls for response on the part of the Christian in living a life of obedience to God. The sermon should avoid works righteousness, while stressing the need for self-discipline in living the Christian life.

1 Corinthians 10:31–11:1 (RC)

Our pericope is part of the larger section of 10:23–11:1 which returns to the topic of chapter 8, the question of whether or not a Christian may eat food consecrated to a pagan god. In 10:31–33 Paul concludes with an exhortation to live so as to give glory to God in all that one does and being careful not to give offense. Giving offense means placing an obstacle in the way of the conversion of Jew and Greek (Gentile) and in the way of the growth of the church. The church of God is thought by some to refer to the universal community of believers.

As the believers imitate Paul they will be imitating Christ, who is the perfect example of renunciation for the salvation of human beings. Note that Paul says he tries to "please all men in everything I do" which in other passages is anathema to Paul (1 Thess. 2:4; Gal. 1:10). Here Paul is not concerned to please people, as charlatans do, but to make his conduct such that he will not stand in the way of others being saved.

Recommended work: Compare Paul's "pleasing" statement here to his other statements about pleasing people.

The sermon might follow the movement of the text, climaxing with "being imitators of me, as I am of Christ." Christ is our example, but we need human models to help us imitate Christ.

Theological Reflection

Continuing the Epiphany theme, the Markan, 1 Corinthians 10:31–11:1, and 2 Kings texts have a theme of revealing God to others. Mark shows how Jesus' healing of the leper spread the news and people came to him. The 1 Corinthians 9 text is concerned with self-discipline for more effective living and preaching the gospel. Leviticus gives laws regarding leprosy.

Children's Message

The talk with the children might be about getting in shape for sports, developing Paul's message in 1 Corinthians 9:24–27. Local sports stars might be mentioned and their constant training to stay in shape for winning. The Christian faith calls for discipline of study in church school, worship, prayer, and loving others.

Hymns for Epiphany 6

Amazing Grace; Love Divine, All Loves Excelling; Lord Jesus, Think on Me.

Epiphany 7

Ordinary Time 7

Proper 2

Psalm 41 (C)
Psalm 41:2–5, 13–14 (RC)
Psalm 32 or 32:1–8 (E)

Isaiah 43:18–25 (C)
Isaiah 43:18–19, 21–22, 24–25 (RC)

2 Corinthians 1:18–22

Mark 2:1–12

Meditation on the Texts

Gracious God, we thank you that you have done a new thing in sending Jesus Christ to die for our sins. We confess that we have burdened you with our sins and wearied you with our iniquities. We failed to call upon you and we have been weary of you, O God. We thank you for the promise of water in the wilderness and rivers in the desert, that we may drink and declare your praise. We recall that as you are faithful to us your word has not been a Yes and No but always a Yes! You have established us in Christ and commissioned us. You have put your seal upon us and given us Christ's Spirit in our hearts as a guarantee. We recall Jesus' healing of the paralytic who was let down through the roof to be healed. We thank you for the faith of his friends and the faith of our friends. We are grateful for the forgiveness of our sins through Christ's death and resurrection. May we rise up and glorify you, O God, in our daily lives. Amen.

Commentary on the Texts

Mark 2:1–12

This account of the healing of a paralytic is part of the section of 1:40–9:50 dealing with Jesus' ministry and the controversy that resulted, mainly in Galilee. Parallels to this account are found in Matthew 9:1–8 and Luke 5:17–26. The setting is a house in Capernaum to which Jesus had returned. So many people had gathered inside and around the door of the house to hear Jesus that no more people could get in or even stand around the door! Jesus was preaching the word to them. The "word" included everything Jesus had to say to human beings about God's purposes.

This healing miracle shows the growing opposition to Jesus, leading up to the Pharisees' plot in 3:6. It is a part of 2:1–3:5, a unit revealing the controversy with the Pharisees. There is a question about the composition of this account. It may have been a single event. Or the passage may be composed from a miracle story in vs. 3–5, 11–12, and a pronouncement story in vs. 6–10 which associated forgiveness of sins with faith. The chief difficulty in the text is in v. 10 which involves a shift in the persons addressed and thus breaks the unity of the passage. It is out of character for Jesus to disclose himself so early in his ministry as the Son of man with authority to forgive sins, especially since this revelation is made to hostile scribes. But v. 10 may not be a genuine saying of the earthly Jesus but a parenthetical comment placed here by the Christian church, inspired by the risen Christ, and addressed to the Christian reader to explain the significance of the healing. If this is the case, then the passage does form a perfect literary unit. Its purpose is to establish Jesus' effectiveness in forgiving sins not by a verbal claim but by a miracle whose meaning is revealed only to those who have faith. But notice some other artificial elements. The scribes do not speak their feelings, but Jesus perceived "in his spirit that they thus questioned within themselves" (v. 8). Thus Jesus is portrayed as discerning these feelings by supernatural insight. They are representative Jewish reactions to the Christian claim that sin could be forgiven, and in the name of Jesus. (For more detailed discussion of problems in the passage, see D. E. Nineham, *Saint Mark,* pp. 89–94.)

The essential thing to note in vs. 3–5 is the connection between the faith of the paralytic and his four friends and Jesus' declaration of forgiveness. While Jesus' words in v. 5 may have meant simply, "God has forgiven your sins," we see in vs. 7 and 10 that Jesus' words are reported here in the light of the church's faith in the resurrected Christ who has power to forgive sins personally. Mark was undoubtedly influenced by the fact that he and other Christians of his time experienced forgiveness "through" or "in the name of" Jesus Christ.

We also note that Jesus saw their faith which was necessary for a miracle. But before the resurrection this could not mean faith in Christ as a divine person. The authors of the Gospels who write as Christian believers tend to give "faith" a specifically Christian content, a content to which "faith" was leading during Jesus' earthly ministry. Faith during Jesus' ministry meant an openness to God's healing word proclaimed by Jesus in word and deed, along with a confident self-abandonment to God who was working in and through Jesus.

Note that it is the faith of the friends as well as the paralytic's faith that Jesus takes into account. "My son" is a term of endearment. While it is sometimes thought that the scribes taught that God could not and does not forgive sin from free grace, this is not the case. Nor did they teach that a person could not be forgiven by God until the person had achieved some merit by works of the law. Understand that their opposition to Jesus in this event lies in his claiming for himself what they thought was the sole prerogative of God.

The roof of the house was probably made of wattle and daub, not clay tiles as were used in Rome. Mark literally says "unroofed the roof." There would have been an outside staircase to the roof. Before the rainy season the roof of sticks and packed earth would have been repaired. It is possible that the Greek words translate an Aramaic phrase that literally meant "brought him up to the roof." In this case, the story of making an opening may be an addition inspired by the false translation of the original Aramaic in which the story was first told.

The pallet was the poor man's bed and could be carried fairly easily, which helps explain the comment that he took it up and went out (v. 12).

Jesus asks in v. 9 whether it is easier to say "Your sins are forgiven" or "Rise, take up your pallet and walk." Jesus took sin so seriously that it is somewhat surprising that he would describe forgiving sin as "easier" than healing. Some scholars take Jesus to be assuming that healing is the easier, but this makes it difficult to follow the logic of the passage. The "you" of the verse could not refer to the scribes but is addressed to the Christian readers for whom the miracle is being recounted. This verse seems to be a Christian editorial on the miracle.

Consider the relationship of sin to paralysis, of forgiveness to healing in this miracle, and of faith to both healing and forgiveness. No sin or guilt of the paralytic is mentioned, but Jesus' offer of his word of forgiveness shows that he perceives sin to be the man's real problem. But we cannot deduce from this that all illness is the result of sin, for sin is not mentioned in connection with some dozen other healings and exorcisms in Mark. The connection of sickness and sin is ruled out in John 9:2 and Luke 13:1–5. This event of the forgiveness and healing of the paralytic is one among several examples of the good news that Jesus came to proclaim which readers of Mark are invited to believe. Jesus has the authority both to forgive and to heal, two dimensions of the wholeness which marks the kingdom of God. Remember, however, that a person may be healed and not forgiven, or forgiven and not healed. But here both occur. The major thrust of this passage is the miracle as a witness to God's forgiveness and to Jesus' authority. The preacher should place the emphasis here rather than trying to explain the miracle in terms of psychosomatic medicine and hysterical paralysis which may be relieved by forgiveness. Relate this text to our Isaiah 43:18–25 text for today, which tells of God's gracious forgiveness which is not dependent on the worthiness of God's people.

The scribes charged Jesus with blasphemy, since in Jewish thought only God can forgive. But in Mark's theology Jesus is the incarnation of God's Spirit (1:9–11) and therefore can forgive sins. Jesus, the Son of man, came to judge the world and clearly has authority to forgive sins now. The phrase "Son of man" is a Jewish idiom meaning simply "man." See Psalm 8:4 or Ezekiel 11:2. However, in later Jewish thought "Son of man" came to denote a superhuman being coming out of the clouds to deliver the righteous from their enemies. In Mark's Gospel, Jesus avoids using this term in its technical sense of "messiah" until his recognition by the disciples at Caesarea Philippi (8:27ff.).

Jesus' cure was demonstrated when the man took up his pallet and went out. The cure substantiated the forgiveness of sins and symbolized the spiritual health of the forgiven sinner. The people who saw the cure were amazed and glorified God. But they failed to see the miracle as a sign of Jesus' power to forgive sins, in contrast to v. 9. This is another reason for considering v. 10 to be an addition to the original account and not a saying spoken by Jesus. There are parallels to the cure in accounts of pagan stories of healing at that time.

Recommended work: Do a word study of Son of man, forgiveness of sins, heal, and faith.

The sermon may follow the dynamic movement of the text from illness to cure and from forgiveness of sins to demonstration of the cure and the amazement of the people. The sermon should enable the hearers to get inside the story and become a living word so that they can in their imaginations be let down right into the middle of the crowd surrounding Jesus and be forgiven and healed by him. Voltaire's famous quote, "God will forgive, that's his business" might be used to refute the notion of cheap grace. The sermon should point to the cross and the cost by which we are forgiven by God.

Isaiah 43:18–25 (C)

Isaiah 43:18–19, 21–22, 24–25 (RC)

Our pericope is part of the section of 43:14–44:5 which deals with the redemption and restoration of Israel. The preacher should read the whole section before studying this pericope in depth. In vs. 16–17 there is an allusion to the passing through the sea of the exodus. These verses could be thought of as corresponding to the part of a community lament known as "the review of God's former acts of salvation." The "new thing" (v. 19) is the return of Israel to Palestine. The new and greater exodus is an important theme in Second Isaiah. The way in the wilderness was part of the exodus story. While Second Isaiah was greatly devoted to the redemptive acts of the past, more so perhaps than any other prophet, he warns in v. 18 against so glorying in the past that one does not have time for application to the present. He stresses that what is to be remembered as a continuous redemptive action is the new exodus.

The prophet is saying in effect, "Stop looking back mournfully, looking only to the past. Rather, open your minds to the fact of a new, miraculous act of God which still lies in the future." This new thing that God is about to do is something that Israel had ceased to hope for or believe in. Israel thought that God's saving actions were all in the past.

Note in vs. 19b–20 the correspondence between the new thing that God is about to do and the exodus of old, the new exodus from exile and the exodus from Egypt. Although God will take an entirely new way of doing this new thing, the same God of the exodus will deliver and liberate God's chosen people. This new deliverance will become a reality by means of a new journey through the wilderness during which it will be transformed. God will give water in the wilderness so abundantly that the wild animals there will share in it. God's action of creation and redemption are thus illustrated to be one.

Notice that Second Isaiah takes the deliverance of the exodus and places it in the wider context of God's action in creation. Israel must be shaken out of a complacent faith that had nothing to learn about God's activity and therefore nothing to learn about the future which was breaking in on Israel. This speaks to a faith today that is rote and dogmatic and has ceased to expect anything new from God.

The act of the new exodus is to be praised by those who experience it (v. 21). History moves forward and the new thing will not bring in complete salvation, since praise would have no meaning unless history goes on and there are those who need to hear of God's miraculous works. This praise is the means by which the acts of salvation will be spread.

Verses 22–25 are part of a division of vs. 22–28 dealing with God versus Israel and God's accusation that Israel has burdened God.

All worship consists in something said and something done, but Second Isaiah says that Israel's worship never, in fact, reaches God (v. 22). This verse introduces the disputations that follow on the subject of Israel's worship. The clearest expression of worship was sacrifice. In vs. 23–24a the most important sacrifices are listed, and v. 23b sums up Israel's worship: their offerings were not true service, not genuine worship offered to God.

Instead, as v. 24b points out, Israel gave God toil and trouble with its iniquities and sins. While preexilic prophets protested against particular aspects of corruption or depravity in Israel's worship, Second Isaiah passes a verdict on *all* Israel's preexilic worship. But this verdict is not a condemnation in principle, since some worship had been genuine and effective and was accepted by God. Second Isaiah points out that Israel could not depend upon services of worship as works to please God. As a result of Israel's sin, God has had to let judgment come upon Israel (v. 28).

But at the heart of Second Isaiah's message is forgiveness (v. 25). This message, however, must be heard against the background of vs. 22–28. (Note that vs. 26–28 should be included and are an example of the shapers of the lectionary creating a romantic view of God and the world versus the abrasive reality of divine judgment.)

Recommended work: Read the whole section and the story of the exodus in Exodus 14 and 15. Reflect on the wordplay on the Hebrew verb for "to serve or to work" in vs. 23b and 24b in which God says, "I did not make you serve (work) and you made me serve (work)" (see KJV). If God is made into a servant, then God's divinity is taken away.

The sermon might be given the title "God, Servant or Lord?" It might develop the images of the text of offering worship in an effort to please God but in reality burdening God with sins and iniquities. God's revelation in Jesus Christ in which God takes our burden of sins and frees us should be included.

2 Corinthians 1:18–22

In v. 18 we have an introductory formula for an oath: God is faithful. Paul's critics have accused him of vacillating, speaking yes and no. Paul says he could not vacillate, because Jesus Christ was absolute truth who through his life and work brought to fulfillment God's previous promises (vs. 19, 20). The Hebrew for "yes" is "amen." Paul says the goal of God's revelation is divine glory manifested through God's people. Only by God's grace are we moved to give God glory. God gives help to those who believe. Paul lists three effects of our initiation into the Christian life (vs. 21–22): (1) God has commissioned us, (2) God has put God's seal upon us, and (3) God has given us the Spirit as a guarantee or pledge. The seal was a personal mark put on a piece of property by its owner. A pledge was a down payment ensuring that the rest would be paid later. The pledge here is God's Spirit which points forward to the messianic bounty yet to come (Eph. 1:13–14). God will finish what God has begun. And the Spirit within Paul is a guarantee of his sincerity.

Recommended work: Do a word study of commissioned (anointed), seal, and guarantee (pledge).

The sermon might be given the title "God's Yes!" It might deal with the ways in which we are assured of salvation through baptism, assured that God's final word is a "yes" in Jesus Christ who was baptized for us in the Jordan and on the cross.

Theological Reflection

The Isaiah passage assures us that God is forgiving in spite of our false worship and sins which are a burden for God. The 2 Corinthians passage stresses that Jesus Christ is God's "yes" for us in spite of our sins. The Markan passage describes Jesus' healing and forgiving of the paralytic, thus manifesting his Lordship over sin and illness. Jesus demonstrates God's "yes" for suffering humanity.

Children's Message

The story might be about the man who was paralyzed but whose friends carried him to Jesus. Point out that the faith of the friends as well as the sick man's was involved in his healing. Jesus both forgave him and healed him, and he can do this for us too.

Hymns for Epiphany 7

Where Cross the Crowded Ways of Life; O Where Is He That Trod the Sea?; New Every Morning Is the Love.

Epiphany 8

Ordinary Time 8

Proper 3

Psalm 103:1–13 (C)
Psalm 103:1–4, 8, 10, 12–13 (RC)
Psalm 103 or 103:1–6 (E)

2 Corinthians 3:1–6 (C)
2 Corinthians 3:1b–6 (L)
2 Corinthians 3:(4–11) 17–4:2 (E)

Hosea 2:14–20 (C)
Hosea 2:14–16 (17–18), 19–20 (L)
Hosea 2:16–17, 21–22 (RC)
Hosea 2:14–23 (E)

Mark 2:18–22

Meditation on the Texts

We thank you, O God of the covenant, for the gift of the kingdom which breaks in like new wine and bursts old wineskins of human traditions. We thank you for Christ the bridegroom who brings joy into our lives. We rejoice in his presence by the Spirit, but we long for his coming again at the End of the age. While we await his coming, we fast and pray and work expectantly. We pray that we may be living letters from Christ written not with ink but with the Spirit of the living God on tablets of human hearts. We know that while the written code kills, the Spirit gives life. We thank you that where the Spirit of the Lord is, there is freedom. May we continually be changed into the likeness of Christ, from one degree of glory to another. Since we have this ministry by your mercy, O God, may we not lose heart. May we never practice cunning or tamper with your word. But by the open statement of truth may we commend ourselves to every human being's conscience in your sight, O God. You have loved your people as a merciful husband loves his wife and made a covenant with us. You have promised to betroth your people forever in righteousness, justice, steadfast love, mercy, and faithfulness. And so may we know you, the Lord. Remove the pagan idols from our minds and midst so that we may join together to praise you and say, "Thou art my God." Amen.

Commentary on the Texts

Mark 2:18–22

Our pericope is the second section in the first part of three major parts in the Galilean ministry. This first part extends from the call of the first four disciples in 1:16–20 to 3:6, the plot by the Pharisees and the Herodians to kill Jesus. In this major part there are five controversy stories. In these controversy stories, we have a record of growing hostility to Jesus by the religious leaders. People ask why Jesus and why his disciples behave as they do. The answers are authoritative words of Jesus which apparently were used in the early church as responses to adversaries and as a guide to living in the Christian community.

Our pericope tells of the question put to Jesus about why the disciples of John the Baptist and those of the Pharisees fast but his own disciples do not fast. At the moment when the question was asked, pious Jews were observing a fast. But Jesus' disciples did not join them as was expected of anyone really concerned about the kingdom of God.

As we examine the passage, note that some scholars think that vs. 18–20 and vs. 21–22 were originally independent units that were brought together as the tradition was passed along, and Mark includes them as integral parts of the account here. There are two parables in vs. 21 and 22 whose significance seems broader than the question posed in vs. 18–20. Notice that Mark does not use a link at the beginning of v. 21. This may indicate that he is aware that the parable of cloth and the parable of wine were not in the original historical context. But in commenting on the passage, we will take vs. 18–22 as belonging to a single section of Mark, since he clearly intends this.

Jesus' attitude toward fasting would have been a concern of the early church. It appears that the parables in vs. 21–22 were relevant to the struggle about the relation of the church to Jewish law. But we need not assume that they are a product of the early church, since the tone of them is clearly that of Jesus.

The followers of John fasted because their master had been taken from them and beheaded. But for Jesus' disciples, fasting was not appropriate, since he was still with them. The followers of John may have made up a sect that was in competition with Jesus' followers. John's followers and the Pharisees stand for a kind of rigor in piety which Jesus' disciples did not practice.

To his critics Jesus replies with a cluster of analogies, that of the bridegroom and the wedding guests. See how Jesus answers the question of his critics with another question: "Can the wedding guests fast while the bridegroom is with them?" (v. 19a), which is found in the other two Synoptic Gospels also. But Mark alone has added, "As long as they have the bridegroom with them, they cannot fast" (v. 19b).

Neither in the Hebrew Scriptures nor in Judaism was the bridegroom a figure of the Messiah. But here we have the image of Christ as the bridegroom, which is found in other New Testament passages also (Eph. 5:21–33; Rev. 19:9). The image of Christ as the bridegroom connotes *joy* in the presence of the Lord and the realized presence of the kingdom of God. Notice, next, that in v. 20 there is a second aspect of the bridegroom analogy. It points to a future time when the bridegroom, Christ, will be taken away from them. That will be the appropriate time for the disciples to fast. Fasting indicates sorrow over the absence of the Lord and is quite appropriate for the "between the times" period of the church then and now. There is a definite "not yet" dimension to the kingdom although Jesus inaugurated it in his coming.

The two parables of cloth and wineskins speak of the newness of that which has come into the world in Jesus. They show the incompatibility of new and old. A new piece of unshrunk cloth sewn on an old garment will shrink and tear it when washed. An old hardened wineskin will burst when new wine still fermenting is put into it and expands. Note the additional clause of "new wine is for fresh skins" (v. 22). This is the *main point* of the entire paragraph. The reason Jesus' disciples do not fast is that the message of the kingdom of God is a fresh, new force which calls for appropriate forms or else it will burst the old. The major thrust of the two parables is that the old has passed away in Jesus' coming and the new has arrived. But in one the concern is to save the old garment. In the other, pliable new wineskins are needed to preserve new wine. Consider the paradoxical aspect of these wisdom sayings. One parable may be true in one situation and the other in another, and each expresses a diametrically opposite principle. Sometimes the old must be preserved. But on other occasions the old must be discarded in favor of the new.

We cannot be certain what the exact original interpretations of these parables were, however. Do they mean that God's kingdom cannot be confined within the limits of Judaism? Or do they speak of the need for rebirth? Or of the uselessness of halfway measures, pointing to the folly of trying to mend one's old life with a patch of the new? The preacher may discover other possible original meanings.

Recommended work: Reflect on the exclusivism of Judaism versus the inclusive nature of the kingdom of God. Reflect on the role of joy in the kingdom of God indicated here and in other places by doing a word study of joy.

The sermon might deal with the joy of the kingdom, in the light of Christ's presence by the Spirit, in tension with the need for fasting over Christ's physical absence as we await his return at the End. Or the sermon might deal with the subject of exclusivism in the church community, which may not be religious in nature but be based on ethnic, economic, or social prejudice. The preacher may want to point to the example of Jesus and the disciples who ate with tax collectors and sinners. Jesus heals relationships by eating with alienated people, for he came to call sinners, not the righteous.

Hosea 2:14–20 (C)

Hosea 2:14–16 (17–18), 19–20 (L)

Hosea 2:16–17, 21–22 (RC)

Hosea 2:14–23 (E)

We will deal with vs. 14–23, the thrust of which is the message that the Lord will woo Israel back. God renews the covenant with Israel and betroths her to himself forever.

Verse 14 begins with the third "therefore" used in this chapter. Each "therefore" section is a refraction of Hosea's message of God's love. Each is related to the others by Hosea's knowledge that God will not let this people go. The first, in v. 6, introduces a description of how God will disrupt Israel's pursuit of her lovers. The second "therefore," in v. 9, begins the account of how God will strip Israel of the imagined benefits of her harlotry (her idolatry). Now in the passage beginning with v. 14 we see God's determination to do what is necessary to restore the original relationship. God promises to assume the responsibility for the reconciliation of his faithless wife. The third announcement thus fulfills and completes the other two, bringing to a consummation the pleading with which the sequence opened in v. 2 of the chapter. In this allegory, God is the husband who sets out to woo back the woman he has lost.

The Hebrew word translated "allure" means entice or persuade irresistibly so as to overwhelm the resistance and will of another person. The verb is used of the seduction of a virgin or of the divine constraint that grips and holds Jeremiah the prophet powerless. Even as a lover might plot to take his beloved to a place to be alone with her, so God vows to take the woman (Israel) into the wilderness. Here wilderness is more than a geographical place. It symbolizes the time and situation in which the pristine relationship between God and Israel was untarnished and Israel depended completely on God. It represents the point of a new beginning. And in the wilderness God will make love to Israel, God will speak to her heart! The word for "speak tenderly" (literally, "speak to the heart") is used in Genesis 34:3 and Ruth 2:13. Recall that Hebrew religion was averse to any speaking of God in sexual terms, but here is an exception. Here is a daring portrayal of the passion of God, a passion that condescends and does not hold back in its seeking to woo back the beloved elect.

The Valley of Achor (v. 15) was the place where Israel sinned when entering the promised land. The name meant "valley of trouble." So Hosea makes a wordplay on the name: the valley of trouble is made the door of hope (v. 15). Once again Israel will be a fresh chaste girl with Egypt behind her and the promised land ahead (v. 15). In that day Israel will call the Lord "My husband" and not "My Baal." Baal means lord or master and was the name of the leading Canaanite deity. The word "Baal" comes from a verb meaning to own or to have rights over. In relationship to a wife, it stresses the husband's legal rights as possessor of the woman (Ex. 21:3). But Israel will call God "My husband," showing her change of heart. There is a subtle play on words in the Hebrew of the words for "baal" and "husband," both of which can mean husband. The Hebrew word for "husband" means one who is a partner and counterpart of the woman (Gen. 2:23). By contrast as we have seen, "baal" comes from a verb meaning to possess or to own. So Israel will give herself to God as a woman gives herself to her husband whom she loves and not to one whom she is only bound to by a legal commitment.

God promises to make a covenant on that day which includes all living creatures, and God will bring peace and safety (v. 18).

God will betroth Israel to himself forever (v. 19). Now the metaphorical situation changes and God speaks directly to Israel as the intended bride. The promise includes the three elements of marriage: the finality of the marriage, the bride price, and the fulfillment of the purpose of the marriage. The bride price in marriage customs in Israel was the final step in concluding a marriage and included the payment by the groom of the bride price which binds the arrangement and commits all parties involved. It is a public legal act, and only actual cohabitation remained to seal the marriage relationship.

Notice the five attitudes and actions of God which are the bride price that establishes this marriage of God with Israel: righteousness, justice, devotion, compassion, and faithfulness. However, there is no father to receive the payment. These five attitudes sum up what Israel could look for from its covenant Lord. Although the old covenant is broken and finished, here is the promise of a new and unexpected grace. Now Israel will know God. To know God is inclusive of what God expected of Israel as the covenant people, for it means the whole response of Israel to God's acts and words. See how God through this metaphor of marriage institutes a new covenant with Israel and takes up the responsibility for its integrity and permanence. It points to the new covenant of Jeremiah (Jer. 31:3f.) and to the church as the bride of Christ in the End time (Eph. 5:23–31).

Then in vs. 21–22 there is another image of the time of salvation: the blessings of a fertile land which are a means of knowing God, thus linking this section to v. 20. The prophet announces that an appeal to God has been heard and will be answered. "'In that day'" is an End time formula pointing to God's future action. God will sow Israel into the land as if God was the farmer and Israel the seed, and the harvest will surely be abundant. The children of Hosea named "Not pitied" and "Not my people" (1:8) had symbolized Israel under judgment. Now there is a new covenant and God has pity on "Not pitied" and calls "Not my people" "You are my people" and Israel responds "Thou art my God."

Recommended work: Read chapters 1; 2; and 3. Scan the remainder of Hosea to get an overview of our pericope's setting.

The sermon might develop the images used by Hosea to indicate Israel's alienation from God and God's initiatives in making a new covenant with Israel. The sermon might show how God in Jesus Christ has taken the initiative to restore us through the new covenant in his death and resurrection. Hosea's message of the covenant foreshadows this new one by which we know the Lord.

2 Corinthians 3:(4–11) 17–4:2 (E)

See Transfiguration of Our Lord, (L).

2 Corinthians 3:1–6 (C)

2 Corinthians 3:1b–6 (L)

Our pericope is part of a chapter in which Paul contrasts his ministry with that of Moses, and the new covenant in Christ with the old one made with Israel through Moses. Those disturbing the church had overstressed the role of the Hebrew Scriptures and understressed the kingdom which is new in Christ. Notice that in vs. 1–6 Paul sets forth the basis of his argument by introducing a set of contrasts between the old way with Moses and the new way with Christ. Paul says in vs. 1–6 that life comes from the Spirit. He continues the defense of his ministry.

Paul uses the image of letters which were used then as now when traveling to introduce a person to a mutual friend. Paul tells the Corinthians they are his letter of recommendation written on their hearts to be known and read by all. This letter is written not with ink but with the Spirit of the living God, written not on tablets of stone, as the Ten Commandments of Moses' day were, but on tablets of human hearts (see Jer. 31:33; Ezek. 11:19). The church at Corinth was the work of God, and Paul was only the instrument (v. 5). God has made Paul and his associates competent to be ministers of a new covenant. While the written code kills, the Spirit of God gives life.

Recommended work: Read the whole chapter to see how Paul develops the theme introduced in vs. 1–6. Do a word study of law, Spirit, and ministry.

The sermon might follow the moves of the text, developing the image of Christians as living "letters" from Christ written on tablets of human hearts. The sermon might contrast the ministry of a new covenant in Christ which gives life in the Spirit with the written code of behavior which kills.

Theological Reflection

The old covenant which kills is contrasted with the new covenant which gives life in all three pericopes. It is an appropriate Epiphany theme of manifesting God in Christ to the world by the Spirit which gives life.

Children's Message

You might talk about letters and how we like to receive them from friends and family. God writes his letter on our hearts with the Spirit for all to read. Are we letters of kindness, love, forgiveness, patience, and truth?

Hymn for Epiphany 8

There's a Wideness in God's Mercy; Praise to the Lord, the Almighty; We Are One in the Spirit.

Transfiguration of Our Lord
Last Sunday After Epiphany

Psalm 50:1–6 (C) 2 Corinthians 4:3–6 (C)
Psalm 27 or 27:5–11 (E) 2 Corinthians 3:12–4:2 (L)
  2 Peter 1:16–19 (20–21) (E)

2 Kings 2:1–12a (C)
1 Kings 19:9–18 (E) Mark 9:2–9

Meditation on the Texts

O God who has said, "Let light shine out of darkness," we thank you that you have shone in our hearts to give us the light of the knowledge of the glory of God in the face of Christ. May we always preach Jesus Christ as Lord, with us as your servants for Jesus' sake, and not preach ourselves as the center or content of preaching. We know that where the Spirit of the Lord is there is freedom. We pray that we may be changed into the likeness of the glory of the Lord. May we not lose heart, for we have this ministry by the mercy of God. O God, we ask that we may have a vision of the risen Christ and may listen to him. For Christ is your beloved Son. We recall your servants Elijah and Elisha who by words and actions proclaimed your message. We ask for the gift of your Spirit, that we may fulfill our tasks. May we always be zealous for you, O Lord. Although we may feel that we are alone left as your faithful prophet, we know that you are with us in all the difficulties and challenges of life. And with your Spirit we can face and overcome the abrasive and hostile culture around us as we minister in your name. Amen.

Commentary on the Texts

Mark 9:2–9

The transfiguration began as prayer, as noted by Luke: "And as he was praying, the appearance of his countenance was altered, and his raiment became dazzling white" (Luke 9:29). Matthew describes the transfiguration in terms of a vision: "And as they were coming down the mountain [after the transfiguration], Jesus commanded them, 'Tell no one the vision, until the Son of man is raised from the dead' " (Matt. 17:9). It appears that all three Synoptic accounts mean to describe a vision of Jesus in heavenly glory as the Messiah. This revelation of Jesus to the three disciples which foreshadows his resurrection appearances is a fitting climax to the Epiphany season with its emphasis on making Jesus known to the world. Notice the link with the 1 and 2 Kings passages which describe the ministry of Elijah. The prophet Elijah was expected to appear on earth *before* the Messiah appeared, as noted in Malachi 4:5–6. Elijah represents the prophets. Moses, who also appeared, represented the law and traditionally was thought to be the author of the first five books of the Bible which formed the basic authority of Judaism. More recent scholarship has, of course, rejected the tradition regarding authorship.

While it is impossible to reconstruct the original event of the transfiguration, it is based on experiences that enabled the three disciples to recognize that although Jesus' Messiahship involved suffering and death (8:31), he was surely the Son of man whose full glory would be revealed in the resurrection. Notice that this account uses motifs found in the Sinai revelation of God: the cloud which overshadowed, the mountain, the awesome majesty, Moses' presence, and the tent. It also draws on apocalyptic appearances of the Son of man found in Daniel 7; 8; 9 and in apocryphal books. These appearances involve visions, Elijah's presence, the fear, the command to secrecy, the bright shining clothing, and the conversation.

We should understand that the transfiguration text here and in the other Synoptics is one of the *central* messianic texts. Notice its similarities to the baptism of Jesus passages, namely, the heavenly voice and its message. Compare it with the Gethsemane story: the same three disciples of the inner circle, the mountain (Mount of Olives), the cry "Abba! Father!" which corresponds to the heavenly voice saying "This is my beloved Son." Also note the prominence of Peter and the incomprehension of Peter in both the transfiguration and the Gethsemane texts.

Our pericope begins with a mentioning of "six days" which is very unusual. There is no parallel for such a precise noting of time in Mark's Gospel; thus he must have included it for a specific reason. It appears to bind this event with the preceding episode, and one must be interpreted in the light of the other. There may be a link with the Sinai revelation when the cloud covered the mountain six days and on the seventh God called out to Moses. It may also link up with the traditional length of time of six days required for preparation and self-purification *before* a close approach to God.

We are not told the name of the mountain. Some scholars have thought it was Mt. Tabor, others Mt. Hermon, which is snow-covered at the top and is a "very high mountain." The high mountain is an allusion to Sinai and seeks to show Jesus as the new Moses radiant in God's presence on the new Sinai.

The meaning of "transfigured" (v. 2), is literally to be transformed or to change one's form. The idea here and in v. 3 seems to be that Jesus temporarily exchanged the normal human form he had during his earthly life for the unique glorious form he was believed to possess after he was exalted to heaven as the risen Christ. Believers hoped to be clothed in a similar way after Christ's second coming (Phil. 3:21 and other texts). At that time, "glory" was thought of as an actual shining ethereal substance, the kind of body that belonged to heavenly beings and especially to God. The idea included clothing as well as the body shining with glory (Revelation and Enoch record this). The implication of this is that the disciples were given a glimpse of Jesus in his final state of Lordship and glory to which he would be exalted later. The appearance of Moses and Elijah point in this direction, since it was believed that various characters from the Hebrew Scriptures would appear at the End of the world and play an important part in the events leading up to it. Elijah was the most frequently mentioned of these persons. The appearance of Moses and Elijah symbolizes that for Christians the Law and the Prophets both testify to Christ.

Peter told Jesus, "Master, it is well that we are here," indicating their joy which is explained in the following verses. The "booths" were used in the Feast of Tabernacles, a joyous festival. Peter thinks that the End time has come that was promised in Hosea 12:9: "I will again make you dwell in tents, as in the days of the appointed feast." Peter wants to capture for eternity this End time experience of God's presence. Compare Peter's loss for words here with that in Gethsemane as he contemplates the mystery of Christ. Mark comments on how naïve Peter is in thinking that Jesus needed earthly tents.

There are two possible meanings to Peter's comment "It is well that we are here." One is that they have an opportunity to serve Jesus and the heavenly visitors, but the second and more likely meaning is that it is an experience Peter and the other two would like to prolong. The Greek more probably should be translated, "How good it is to be here!"

Elijah is mentioned first and given special place. He, like Moses, experienced a manifestation of God at Sinai (Horeb). While the language of our pericope is primarily that of a theophany or manifestation of God to humans, the vision of Jesus in glory described is apocalyptic and eschatological in nature, revealing hidden things and End time events.

Be aware of the holy fear the disciples experienced (v. 6). Whether we take this account as a vision, a displaced resurrection appearance (likely), or the collective experience of the early Christian community, the affective power is powerful. Verses 2–8 give an account of an experience of transcendence, while vs. 9–13 (extending our pericope) reflect on its meaning.

The voice from heaven tells the disciples that Jesus is God's beloved Son (Isa. 42:1), reminding us of the words that Jesus heard at his baptism (1:9–11). "Beloved" has a meaning similar to "chosen." The command echoes Deuteronomy 18:15 and suggests that Jesus is the prophet of the End time, like Moses and Elijah.

The disappearance of Moses and Elijah, leaving Jesus, indicates that Jesus replaces them in the new order. Note that in v. 9 we have a clue that this vision (the word that Matthew uses in his parallel account) was not known until *after* the resurrection.

Recommended work: Compare this account with parallels in Matthew and Luke and with baptism accounts. Do a word study of transfigured, Moses, Elijah, and Son of man.

The sermon might approach the transfiguration as a vision that the disciples shared with Jesus on the high mountain in which they saw his glory as the Son of man who also must suffer as Messiah. The sermon might deal with the contemporary sense of the absence or death of God and the longing of the religious mind for a manifestation of God. The three disciples were given a glimpse of what we can know by the Spirit speaking through scripture of God revealed in Christ. The sermon might show Jesus as the fulfillment of the Law and the Prophets of the Hebrew Scriptures who is God's chosen One.

1 Kings 19:9–18 (E)

Both the pericopes from 1 and 2 Kings deal with Elijah, who figures in the Markan account of the transfiguration. Note that 1 Kings 19 deals with Elijah's burnout as a prophet and his being recommissioned. The story is really about Elijah's attempt to relinquish his prophetic office and God's refusal to accept his resignation and insistence that Elijah continue. Carefully note that the focus is on Elijah and his mission, not on the presence or absence of God, as is commonly thought. Compare this to Jeremiah's complaint to God and the responses he received (Jer. 11:18–23).

Richard Nelson has given a fresh insight into this passage. The preacher should study it in detail, pointing out that nothing is said about God's presence being in the enigmatic small voice. "The fact is that while God is associated with the first three events (though not 'in' them), nothing relates the fourth event to God one way or the other" (Richard D. Nelson, *First and Second Kings* [Atlanta: John Knox Press, 1987], p. 124). Nelson stresses that the fireworks of the wind, earthquake, and fire are contrasted with the quiet calm that followed. It is not a contrast between God's presence and absence.

In v. 14 the word translated "jealous" should be translated "zealous," as the Douay version does, which is more in accord with the modern usage of the two words.

Also note that in v. 18 the Hebrew text refers to the future. One translation might be "Yet I shall keep a remnant in Israel." This anticipates the remnant of Isaiah 10:20 and 11:11–16. There will always be a small but loyal nucleus of those who are faithful to God.

The new commissioning of Elijah is found in vs. 15–17 in metaphorical language. Elijah fulfills only one command and does not literally anoint Elisha. The major thrust of this passage is the interplay between human despair and God's call, a message that speaks to us today as it did to the exiles. God can be counted on to provide. The therapy for prophetic burnout included the assignment of new tasks and the promise of a certain future which would transcend the success or failure of the prophet. So God gave Elijah tasks to be done away from the womblike safety of the cave at Horeb. Because of the hope of a new future, life was worth living, and so Elijah journeyed into the wilderness of Damascus.

Recommended work: Study theophany, prophet, and remnant.

The sermon might follow the movement of the text but should avoid the trap of focusing on the still small voice as the source of God's presence. The sermon should deal with our call to faithful service in our vocations and our despair and burnout. The sermon should help listeners hear God's call anew and find a future of hope and new tasks for God.

2 Kings 2:1–12a (C)

Our pericope is part of a chapter whose theme is Elisha's inheriting Elijah's mantle. Elijah is aware that his work is finished and asks Elisha to remain at Gilgal, a town near the

Jordan. Some scholars think the town was not the Gilgal between Jericho and the Jordan but one on the high road from Shechem to Bethel, seven miles north of Bethel.

Elisha asks for a double share of Elijah's spirit (v. 9), the customary share which the firstborn heir received of a father's goods. The prophet's mantle was made of skin and covered with hair. It might be a goat's skin, with the hair side outward. It was the distinctive clothing of a prophet and was the physical means by which Elijah's prophetic powers were transferred to Elisha. While we today might see this as only symbolic of the transfer of prophetic power, the ones telling the story at that time probably accepted the mantle as an object through which or by means of which special power was transferred. Elisha receives the wonder-working power of Elijah through the mantle and parts the waters of Jordan with it (v. 14).

Then in the middle of their conversation the climax of the story suddenly appears like a bolt of lightning. A chariot and horses of fire, suggesting the fire of a manifestation of God, separated Elijah from Elisha. Elijah is caught up in the whirlwind. Note carefully that he was not taken up in a chariot of fire, as the common misunderstanding has it. Elisha cried out to Elijah that he was Israel's sure defense against their better-armed enemies, addressing him as father. The narrative tension of v. 10 is now resolved as Elisha witnesses Elijah's translation and Elijah was seen no more. The focus of the text is as much on Elisha's ability to see and his reaction as it is on the whirlwind and the fire of chariots and horses. Thus the story supports Elisha's claim to succeed to Elijah's office and to complete his incomplete mission (1 Kings 19:15–16, part of our other 1 Kings pericope). Elisha shows the wonderful mantle of Elijah, and he proves himself also to be Israel's chariots and horses (13:14).

Recommended work: Compare this pericope with 1 Kings 19:9–18 above. Read stories of Elijah and Elisha in a Bible dictionary. Reflect on the nature of change in leadership in church and political structures such as moderators and presidents and the fact that God is the author of change.

The sermon might deal with change in the church and society as leadership roles are passed from one person to another. The election and installation of church officers might be a fitting time to preach on this text. The point of the sermon might be that change is both meaningful and bearable because God is the author of change who not only created but is working still. Each generation of the church must discover the continuity of divine purpose and carry on the divine commission.

2 Corinthians 3:12–4:2 (L)

2 Corinthians 4:3–6 (C)

The two pericopes overlap and will be dealt with together. The first is part of 3:4–18, a section that deals with the new covenant. The second reading is part of 4:1–18 whose theme is the apostle's ministry.

In 3:12–18 we have one of the most difficult passages in this letter, caused partly by uncertainties as to its translation. The RSV seems as acceptable as any. The preacher is referred to an academic, critical commentary for details.

Paul is speaking from Exodus 34:29–35 and is concerned with the veil on Moses' face which was always worn except when he was speaking with God in the Tent of Meeting or had come out of it to tell the Israelites what God had said to him. It seems that Moses wore the veil because his face shone with the glory or splendor of God and the Israelites were therefore afraid to come near him. But Paul uses the veil of Moses in a different way, pointing out that Moses wore it to keep the people from seeing the glory gradually fade from his face after he had come from speaking with God. Paul then moves from the veil on the face of Moses to the minds of the Israelites, applying the idea of the veil to the Hebrew Scriptures. The veil on the minds of the Israelites through the years represented their failure to find Christ in the Hebrew Scriptures and the failure of many Jews in Paul's time to accept Christ when he was preached to them. Paul looks forward to the time when the fullness of the Gentiles will come to Christ, and after that the Jews will come also. The veil was removed from Paul's mind by his conversion, but he fears the veil has not been removed from his opponents in Corinth who still keep the law as the center of their teaching.

Paul declares that "the Lord is the Spirit" (3:17), by which he does not simply identify the risen Lord and the Spirit. In other passages Paul speaks of the Lord and the Spirit as separate (13:14). The Lord Christ is too closely identified with the earthly Jesus to permit the full identification of the Lord Christ with the Spirit. The two are so closely associated because the Lord is the risen Jesus who now has a spiritual body and has become a life-giving spirit (1 Cor. 15:44–45). But the two are one in nature and share in the guidance of the church. So Paul neither identifies them nor clearly separates them. By saying that the Lord is the Spirit, Paul means that as the Spirit the Lord can be with his people wherever they are. He gives them freedom.

When Christians see Jesus they are changed (3:18). Christ changes us from one degree of glory to another until we are entirely transformed into his likeness and glory. Recall that this transformation of the Christian is one of Paul's constant themes (Rom. 12:2; 8:29; etc.). The same Greek word is used for "transformed" as for "transfigured" in our Markan text for today.

Then in 4:1–6 Paul deals with the ministry of light against darkness. He says he has his ministry by the mercy of God, and therefore does not lose heart. In this chapter "we" refers mainly to Paul and only secondarily to others. Paul's conversion, call to service, and effective work are not to his personal credit, since all come only by the mercy of God. In his work Paul has made honest and diligent use of his gifts from God and has rejected deception and dishonesty.

But not all who hear Paul believe. Some are perishing, blinded by the god of this world. Paul compares the brilliant light at his conversion with the light that God created at the beginning, light that gives the knowledge of the glory of God in Christ.

Recommended work: Read Exodus 34:29–35.

The sermon might follow the movement and images of the text, leading up to the knowledge of the glory of God in Christ of 4:6. There should be a clear call to decision for faith in Christ and a rejection of the god of this world.

2 Peter 1:16–19 (20–21) (E)

The theme is the factual basis of the apostolic testimony. The facts are those of the transfiguration, our Markan text. Except for the Synoptics, 2 Peter is the only book to use this tradition in this way.

The author asserts that "we," the apostles, did not follow myths. The Gnostics abhorred history and claimed speculation to be the essence of truth. In vs. 17–18 there is a reference to the transfiguration (see the Markan text for today and parallels in Matt. 17:1–8 and Luke 9:28–36). The testimony of the transfiguration confirms the prophecies of the Hebrew Scriptures which must be studied diligently until Christ returns at the End of the age.

"You will do well" (v. 19) means please pay attention. The image of a light shining in a dark place is used of Elijah, of John the Baptist, and of the word of Christ. Here it refers to the message of the apostles who saw the glory before its due time. The day is the coming of the glory of God, when all creation will be transformed.

Recommended work: Compare the transfiguration accounts with our pericope. Read an article on gnosticism in a theological wordbook.

The sermon might contrast the myths of today of the new age religion and other cults with the apostolic witness to Christ. The sermon should enable hearers to make critical judgments about the biblical witness to Christ in contrast to cleverly devised myths.

Theological Reflection

The transfiguration is the theme of Mark and 2 Peter. The 1 and 2 Kings readings deal with Elijah, who represented the prophetic tradition and appeared in the transfiguration. The 2 Corinthians readings focus on the new covenant and the apostle's ministry.

Children's Message

You might tell the story of Elijah from the 1 Kings 19 passage, pointing out that he became greatly discouraged and was ready to quit being a prophet for God. We all get down at times and feel like Elijah. But God did not give up on him, but gave him new work to do and preserved a remnant of Israel who did not worship false gods.

Hymns for Transfiguration

Fairest Lord Jesus; All Hail the Power of Jesus' Name; At the Name of Jesus.

The Seasons of Lent and Easter/Pentecost

The focus of this part of the Christian year is on the heart of the Christian faith: the life, suffering, death, resurrection, and ascension of Jesus and the gift of the Holy Spirit. The Lent and Easter/Pentecost cycle and the previous one of Advent and Christmas/Epiphany, which centered on the incarnation, are the two festival cycles of the Christian church's calendar. The incarnation celebrates the act of God by which "the Word became flesh and dwelt among us" (John 1:14). Now in this season we are reflecting on the meaning of the atonement, the act by which God in Christ made us at one with God by grace through faith. God sent forth the Son in the fullness of time (incarnation) to suffer and die and be raised (atonement) for our salvation. The risen Christ ascended into heaven, from which we expect his return in power and glory, a major theme of the Advent season. Thus we see that the festival season of the church year is especially intertwined with common themes. The gift of the Holy Spirit is the gift of the living Christ, bringing the power of Christ's death and resurrection to human lives.

Since the very beginnings of Christian worship the celebration of Easter has been the highlight of the Christian year. Easter, along with Jesus' passion and death, shaped the life and worship of Christians for each week. The celebration of these saving events of God in Christ shaped the life of community and individuals. We can rightly observe the seasons of Lent, Easter, and Pentecost only as we reflect on their relationship to one another and to the mystery of salvation in Christ. Lent and Easter/Pentecost are formed by the pattern of Jesus' death, resurrection, and the gift of the Spirit which offer eternal life to all who believe.

The Season of Lent

Color: Purple.

The word "lent" is related to the words "long" and "lengthen." It came into use in reference to the lengthening of the hours of sunlight in the springtime. This season has been referred to as "the Easter penitential period" in order to keep the focus on *Easter* rather than on Lent itself. During this season the joyous Gloria and Alleluia are omitted from worship.

Note carefully that the Sundays during the Lenten season are *not* considered an integral part of Lent because Sundays are a celebration of the resurrection. Therefore we speak of Sunday *in* Lent, not *of* Lent. The beginning of Lent is determined by the date of Easter. Lent begins on Ash Wednesday, which comes forty-six days before Easter, and the season itself lasts forty days.

The intention of the season of Lent is to imitate Jesus, who following his baptism, fasted for forty days, but the church also recalls in this fast the forty days Moses fasted on Mt. Sinai (Ex. 34:28), Israel's forty years of wandering in the wilderness, and Elijah's forty days on his journey to Mt. Horeb (Sinai) (1 Kings 19:8). By the second century, Christians were already observing a two-day grief-inspired fast as they prepared for celebrating Easter. The first Ecumenical Council of Nicaea (A.D. 323) refers to a forty-day period of preparation for Easter that was familiar to all churches by that time.

The fast of Lent was first observed by the eating of only a single meal each day, in the evening. Later the fast included abstinence from meat and wine, and then even later dairy products and eggs. The practice continued until the Middle Ages and later. Recall that fasting for medical reasons was not uncommon for the Greeks and the Romans of the ancient world. For Christians of the early church fasting was a source of fervor in prayer. The prayer of a person fasting was compared to the soaring of a young eagle, in sharp contrast to the prayer of one who did not fast.

The central purpose of observing Lent was to *prepare for receiving the Spirit.* The Spirit was a powerful ally in the fight against evil spirits. Fasting was also preparation of candidates for baptism and the Eucharist. Denying oneself food during Lent was a way of freeing up money to give to the poor. But the church was always aware of the danger that fasting could become a mere external formality. It recalled Jesus' warnings in the Sermon on the Mount regarding fasting for fasting's sake and public show of piety.

The Roman Catholic Church's Vatican II Council gave directions for observing Lent which put special emphasis on the recalling of baptism or preparation for it and on penance. The purpose of Lent continues to be the preparation of the faithful for Easter. To do this the Christian is called to repent and turn from sin, with hatred for it because it is an offense against God. The Vatican II statement indicates that penance should be not only internal and individual but also external and social and should be adapted for different regions and individual circumstances.

Ash Wednesday, the beginning of Lent, is so named because on this day penitents put on penitential clothes and had ashes sprinkled on them, both of which were familiar Old Testament practices. In about the twelfth century the rule developed that the ashes used either to sprinkle on the heads of men or to mark a sign of the cross on the foreheads of women should come from the burning of palm branches left from the previous year's Palm Sunday celebration. In many communities of faith Ash Wednesday is still observed as a day of fasting on which ashes are distributed. But Vatican II relaxed some of the strictness of traditional Lenten observances, and now Catholics are allowed to eat meat on Fridays and to eat breakfast before a Communion.

Many congregations observe Lent with special services, such as a noonday luncheon followed by worship once a week. As people better understand the meaning of Lent and its purpose they can find in its discipline a means of self-discipline and self-denial in preparation for celebrating Eastertide and Pentecost. Lent is a period during which many Christians examine their spiritual development and give more time to devotional reading, to service in the programs of the church and community, and to special worship services. Thus it is a time of growth in service both to God and to others.

As pastor and people join in planning and carrying out Lenten programs of worship the time can be one of spiritual journey of the congregation as they engage in "the work of the people," the literal meaning of the word "liturgy."

Holy Week

Holy Week is also called Passion Week to indicate Jesus' suffering and death and is observed in Protestant as well as Roman Catholic churches. Some hold special midday or evening services each day of this week following the themes of Jesus' movement each day. Tradition tells us these are the themes:

Monday	Cleansing of the temple
Tuesday	Jesus' verbal conflict with opponents
Wednesday	Day of silence and retreat to Bethany
Thursday	Jesus' final conversations with the disciples
Friday	The crucifixion
Saturday	Jesus' body in the tomb

Maundy Thursday is so called because the word "maundy" is derived from the new "mandate" or "commandment" Jesus gave the disciples to love one another and his commandment to celebrate the Lord's Supper until he returns. The occasion is usually observed with a candlelight service of worship in which the Lord's Supper is celebrated.

Good Friday is another occasion for special services, often a three-hour service of worship from noon until 3 P.M. The practice began in the Roman Catholic tradition in the seventeenth century and is now often observed in Protestant congregations as a way of remembering Jesus' suffering on the cross during that time. Often congregations in a community join together for a union Good Friday service in which different speakers present brief meditations on Jesus' seven last words from the cross or on another theme. In strict liturgical observance of Good Friday the altar is stripped, candles are left unlit, and the cross is veiled in black to remind all of Jesus' death on this day.

The official end of Lent is at noon on Saturday before Easter. The period from sunset on Maundy Thursday until sunset on Easter Day has come to be known as Triduum, a time in which the early church, following a long rigorous fast, celebrated the saving work of Christ on Easter Eve and on into Easter Day in one unified service.

The themes of exodus, deliverance from death, liberation from slavery—all themes that come to a focus during the passover-Easter period—have special appeal to black congregations. Other ethnic groups have special traditions that enrich not only their worship but the worship of the church worldwide as they are shared.

Easter

Color: White or gold. Gold expresses the prominence of this peak of the Christian year.

The first purpose of Easter preaching is proclamation of the resurrection of Jesus from the dead and its meaning for faith and life. Faith in Jesus' resurrection was universal in the Christian community from the beginning. Through the ages the celebration of Easter in worship has been the high point of the whole Christian year. The church declares in word and sacrament that the Christ who was crucified, dead, and buried has been raised from the dead and exalted to the Godhead. We celebrate the presence of the living Christ in our midst by the power of the Holy Spirit. The first day of the Christian week is the Lord's Day, celebrating Christ's resurrection on the first day of the week. Therefore Easter may be thought of as a "big Sunday" rather than Sunday thought of as a "little Easter."

The dominant mood is joy. Jesus' death and resurrection are the central focus of the Easter celebration.

Notice that although Easter is the *climax* of the church's worship and is concentrated on one day, the celebration of the resurrection continues throughout Eastertide, which continues until Pentecost.

Be aware of the contrast between Lent and Easter/Pentecost. Lent is penitential, with a mood that is sober, reflective, and watchful. Standing in dramatic contrast is Easter/Pentecost, whose mood is exuberant. The joyful mood of this season should be expressed in all aspects of worship, including music, visual images, and the sermon itself.

We should be aware of the tension involved between Christ's death and resurrection and the gift of the Holy Spirit. Easter has been referred to as the "Eighth Day," which ushers in the End time and brings promise of the light of eternal life. The risen Christ is the New Adam whose resurrection is the beginning of the new humanity and new creation. Worship and preaching during this season should keep in focus the tension between the death/resurrection of Jesus and the gift of the Holy Spirit.

Pentecost

Color: Flame red; other bright colors, such as gold.

Pentecost celebrates the outpouring of the Holy Spirit on the day of Pentecost when the church was no longer desolate, since the living Christ had returned by the Spirit to the disciples. Thus Pentecost, in a sense, is a reliving of the meaning of Eastertide, which runs from Easter until Pentecost. One of the major church festivals, Pentecost ranked second only to Easter until greater emphasis was placed on Christmas. Pentecost includes three festivals of the church: Ascension, Pentecost, and Trinity Sunday. It is the great climax of the Easter/Pentecost season. It is particularly fitting to celebrate the Lord's Supper with great joy on this day and to join in special gatherings and a festive common meal. It is also a time for dramatizing the first Pentecost experience by having several people read different texts simultaneously in several languages, and then experience the unity of speech heard in the preaching of the gospel.

Ascension Day comes forty days after Easter and is not completely separate from the celebration of Pentecost. In fact, until the end of the fourth century the ascension of Christ and the descent of the Spirit were celebrated on the *same* Lord's Day. Thus the exaltation of the risen Christ is linked in an integral fashion with his giving of the Holy Spirit. The color for Ascension Day is white.

Trinity Sunday is observed on the Sunday immediately after Pentecost. It celebrates the mystery of the Godhead: Creator, Son, and Holy Spirit, one God in three persons. The color for this Sunday is white. Use of the Nicene Creed is appropriate in worship this Sunday, since it has special emphasis on the nature of Jesus Christ as well as setting forth the Trinity. This can be a challenging day to preach as you seek to declare the scriptural understanding of the Godhead.

Psalm 25:1-10 (C)　　　**1 Peter 3:18-22 (C)**
Psalm 6 (L)　　　　　　**Romans 8:31-39 (L)**
Psalm 25:4-9 (RC)
Psalm 25 or 25:3-9 (E)　**Mark 1:9-15 (C)**
　　　　　　　　　　　　Mark 1:12-15 (L) (RC)
Genesis 9:8-17 (C)　　　**Mark 1:9-13 (E)**
Genesis 22:1-18 (L)
Genesis 9:8-15 (RC)

Meditation on the Texts

Gracious God who made a covenant with Noah and set the rainbow in the cloud as a sign of it, we thank you for keeping covenant with your people through the ages. We thank you that the bow of war now is a sign that your wrath has abated and you have made a gracious covenant with every living creature. As we recall Abraham's obedience and your sparing of Isaac's son from being sacrificed, we thank you for blessing all the nations through Abraham and his descendants. For the revelation of yourself in Jesus Christ, who was baptized in the Jordan for our sins, though sinless himself, we offer praise and thanks to you, O God. We rejoice that Jesus came preaching the gospel and declaring that your kingdom is at hand. May we repent and renew our faith in the gospel. We declare our faith in the assurance that nothing can separate us from your love in Christ Jesus our Lord. We are more than conquerors through Christ who loved us. We thank you that Christ died for sins once for all, the righteous for the unrighteous, that he might bring us to you, O God of our salvation. We recall our baptism which saves us as an appeal to you for a clear conscience through the resurrection of Jesus Christ. He reigns in heaven with you, O God, and we thank you that all angels, authorities, and powers are subject to him. Amen.

Commentary on the Texts

Mark 1:9-15 (C)

Mark 1:12-15 (L) (RC)

Mark 1:9-13 (E)

Since vs. 4-11 were dealt with in the Baptism of Our Lord (Epiphany 1), and vs. 14-20 were dealt with for Epiphany 3, we will comment here only on vs. 12-13, an account of the temptation of Jesus. However, a brief overview of the whole pericope will be given.

The baptism of Jesus (vs. 9-11) was the event in which Jesus was manifested as the "beloved Son" with whom God is well pleased. The heavens opened and the Spirit descended on Jesus, empowering him for his mission as Son of God. Jesus is revealed as the Messiah who will fulfill his role through suffering and humiliation after the pattern of the Servant of the Lord of Second Isaiah. But Jesus was not only given the messianic Spirit. Immediately (a favorite term of Mark's) he was driven into the wilderness to be tested by Satan. There Jesus was victorious, but it was not the final battle with Satan. It would continue in the various activities of Jesus, such as exorcisms and the Gethsemane prayer and in the lives and sufferings of the early Christians as well. After being tested by

Satan and prevailing, Jesus began his ministry, preaching the gospel of God and pro-claiming that the time of God's rule was at hand. Jesus called people to repent and believe in the gospel. Jesus is the messianic herald who in vs. 14–15 sums up the substance and essential meaning of his whole public ministry. For Mark it is a kind of manifesto. In preaching the gospel of God, Jesus is ultimately referring to himself. With this overview, we will now direct our attention to the testing of Jesus in vs. 12–13.

Parallels to the testing of Jesus are found in Matthew 4:1–11 and Luke 4:1–13. It seems, however, that we have two independent accounts, one told by Matthew and Luke and the other by Mark. It is not recorded in John. Matthew and Luke put an emphasis on the moral temptation, but this should not be used as a key to understanding Mark's account. From Mark's account the testing had nothing to do with the inner experience of Jesus. Rather, it points to the belief at that time in Jewish thought that the Messiah was the divine agent for overthrowing Satan and evil powers. This would occur in a great battle or trial of strength between Messiah and Satan in the last days. The Greek word used here for "testing" is more inclusive than our word "tempt" and can include testing or trying. It may include a moral temptation here but only as part of a wider test of strength with Satan. The great End time battle has begun! The details indicate that Jesus was success-ful and his miracles of exorcism and healing which follow reveal his power over demons and evil which causes illness.

Part of the reason for the telling of this story of testing by the early church was to enable readers to see the real nature of Jesus' ministry, which followed, and the life of the ongoing church, which was carrying on and completing this decisive battle with the powers of evil. Notice that the reader is let in on the nature of this battle of Jesus with Satan about which the actors in the Gospel do not yet know the truth.

The wilderness was especially associated with demons. Wild beasts also point to the loneliness and awfulness of the desert. Recall Israel's forty years in the wilderness, Moses' forty days on Sinai, and Elijah's forty-day trip to Horeb (Sinai). The common factor in all of these wilderness experiences was a sense of the absence of God. But God is present there! (Deut. 2:7). Israel tested God in the wilderness (Ex. 17:7), and now Satan tests Jesus in the wilderness.

The Greek word for "testing" can mean enticement to sin or putting to the test. Every other use by Mark of this Greek verb indicates a putting to the test without any reference to temptation to sin. Thus the thrust of the verb here is a test of strength between Jesus and Satan representing the forces of evil. Note that there is no reference in Mark to fasting or hunger. The angels ministered to him, probably supplying Jesus with food as the angels did for Elijah.

Consider the figures in the testing story in addition to Jesus, who is the only human being present: the Spirit, Satan, beasts (who coexisted with Adam and Eve in Eden), and the angels. Divine providence by the Spirit sent Jesus into the wilderness. The Spirit made it clear to Jesus that the acceptance of his Servant role must lead him by way of a testing with Satan. The word for "drove" has a note of compulsion or violence which is usually used of Jesus' expulsion of the demons.

The cosmic struggle which is described is one that is continuous and underlies the whole Gospel of Mark. For the reader who has ears to hear, the victory of Jesus over Satan is clear, although the defeat is yet to take place. It might be compared to D day of World War II which signaled the beginning of the end for the Nazi powers, although many battles remained to be fought before the unconditional surrender of the Nazis to the Allied Forces.

Recommended work: Compare this testing with that of Abraham in Genesis 22:1–18 and with Mark 8:11; 10:2; 12:15; and 14:38. Reflect on the theme of Lent of self-examination and growth in resisting evil. Compare the preparatory nature of Lent of forty days with Jesus' forty days. Reflect on God's parental love and the function of testing and trials in our life.

The sermon might begin with identifying the "civil war" going on in the life of each of us between good and evil. Jesus was tested and was victorious in the wilderness and on the cross; therefore the outcome of the battle within us and in the world has been determined: Jesus is Lord! (the earliest Christian creed). The sermon should deal with testing as a means of growth which we cannot avoid, but God's Spirit is with us in our wilderness and will not allow us to be defeated by evil.

Genesis 9:8–17 (C)

Genesis 9:8–15 (RC)

Recall the promise made to Noah in 6:18. Now God makes a covenant with Noah, the first one that is explicitly described. For the editor of this tradition a covenant marks the end of one world epoch and the beginning of another. Notice that God's covenant with Noah does *not* require anything on his part, and thus is unilateral. It includes all creation, and its sign is a natural thing, a rainbow. For the ancient people, the rainbow was thought of as a divine bow from which arrows of lightning were shot (Ps. 7:12–13; Hab. 3:9–11). It was used by the gods to inflict punishment on humans. The editor has taken this rainbow symbol and used it as a sign of divine appeasement.

Contrast this covenant with that made with Abraham which presupposes his trust in God and includes only his descendants and has circumcision as its sign. The covenant that God made with Israel is restricted to the nation Israel, and its sign is Sabbath observance (Ex. 24:7–8). Notice the progression in covenants from a wide one including all creation to a more intimate one between God and human beings.

The content of the covenant with Noah is the merciful assurance of history's continuation, for there will never again be a flood that ends a world epoch. This new age that opens with Noah includes a renewal of the blessing given at creation (v. 7; cf. 1:28). Now God guarantees that the natural order will be preserved from the waters of chaos. The three sons of Noah are considered the ancestors of all the nations (ch. 10).

Recommended work: Reflect on this covenant with Noah and other covenants in the Bible with a word study of covenant.

The sermon might give an overview of the evil in Noah's time, the building of the ark and the flood, and the landing of the ark. Now our text begins with the assurance that God's wrath has abated, even as the waters were abated, and the rainbow is a sign of this. The sermon should point to the cross which is the supreme sign of God's mercy to all and should call for faith in Christ's death and resurrection as the way of salvation from destruction now and in the future.

Genesis 22:1–18 (L)

This is the account of the testing of Abraham by God. Compare it with our Markan text of Jesus' testing in the wilderness. Here we see a miracle of faith as Abraham shows that he has the faith to surrender his only heir, Isaac, his only means of fulfilling the covenant promise of many descendants. It is a brutal trial of Abraham's faith, and the telling of the story is a literary masterpiece. The story must be read against the background of child sacrifice. The Hebrews knew and practiced human sacrifice, as Deuteronomy 18:9–14 implies.

The story of Ishmael's expulsion prepares the reader for this story, since Ishmael was Abraham's earlier hope of the fulfillment of the promise of many descendants, but he was the son of a slave woman. Notice that Isaac, the reward of faith to both Abraham and Sarah, now becomes the very test of that same faith. Note the paradox here: God demands that Abraham surrender his faith's only basis, since it is now through Isaac that the covenant must be fulfilled (21:12b). God's free choice of Abraham and later Israel and their acceptance of this free choice is at the basis of this poignant and moving story. It is one of the most artistic of all the stories of the patriarchs.

Abraham had cut himself off from his past when he left his homeland. Now he is commanded to give up his entire future! The testing goes to the heart of his life. The reader can endure the horror of the story only because the reader knows that this is a trial, as v. 1 indicates. Abraham's fear of God is shown in his steadfast obedience to God's command, regardless of whether it results in Isaac's death or not. Note that Isaac's deliverance does not invalidate Abraham's act or serve as his reward for risking his future.

Recommended work: Compare this testing of Abraham with God's giving up his Son, Jesus Christ, to die on the cross when there was no ram as a substitute. Compare it to Jesus' testing in the wilderness and during his ministry.

The sermon might focus on testing and its role in our life with God. We are tested, but God does not allow us to be utterly defeated. The sermon might apply the testing of Abraham to our testing in times of crisis, such as illness, business failure, and family crisis. We have the assurance in Christ that we are not alone in the time of testing but that God's Spirit is there to strengthen and guide us to victory.

1 Peter 3:18–22 (C)

The two themes of this passage are the example of Christ and the effect of baptism. Reflect on the reference to Noah's ark (v. 20), which is the Genesis 9 pericope, and the baptism reference which relates to Jesus' baptism for us in the longer Markan reading. The pericope is part of the larger section of 3:13–4:11, which gives instruction on the blessing of uncalled-for persecution. Peter urges the practice of goodness in the face of persecution, remembering that such suffering is really a blessing.

In v. 17, which immediately precedes our pericope, Peter points out that it is better to suffer for doing right, if this is God's will, than for doing wrong. Now in vs. 18–22 Peter gives an exhortation of consolation as a reason for what is recommended in v. 17.

For a detailed treatment of this passage, see Ernest Best, *1 Peter*, New Century Bible Commentary (Grand Rapids: Wm. B. Eerdmans Publishing Co., 1971), pp. 135–150. In v. 18 some translations read "suffered" instead of "died," but the meaning is not changed. Peter says Jesus "was put to death in the flesh," meaning that he really died. He was made alive in the spirit, raised from the dead. Peter proposes Christ's example as a motive for the readers to be patient during their persecution. Peter also stresses the unique nature of Christ's death and its relation of the redemption of human beings.

Note that vs. 19–20 are difficult to understand but may mean that Christ announced his completed work to those who died in the days of Noah and had been very evil.

Then in v. 21 the flood of Noah's day, which destroyed all of life except Noah and his family, is compared to baptism. Whereas water destroyed in the flood, now baptism saves. The right hand of God (v. 22) is the place of honor. A king was said to sit on the right hand of a god, to execute the divine commands. The authorities and powers are angelic beings.

Recommended work: Read the entire section of 3:13–4:11. Compare Jesus' testing and victory over Satan with v. 22, which says Jesus has all powers subject to him.

The sermon might deal either with the example of Christ for those who suffer persecution or with baptism and its effects in the Christian's life.

Romans 8:31–39 (L)

This passage expresses our confidence in God. It is part of the larger section of chapters 5–11 whose theme is the love of God which assures salvation to the justified. Paul has just discussed the various aspects of the new Christian life lived in union with Christ, along with the reasons that give a basis for Christian hope. Now he concludes this section of vs. 1–39 which deals with the Christian life lived in the Spirit and destined for glory. It contains a rhetorical passage and a triumphant hymn to the love of God. Watch for the deep emotion expressed and the rhythm of the phrasing in the passage.

In contrast to life in Western society today with its religious freedom, it was difficult and dangerous to be a Christian in the first century.

Paul begins the passage with the terminology of a lawsuit (v. 31). Compare this to the debates in Job and Zechariah 3. The plan of salvation set forth in scripture makes it very plain that God is for us. Jesus has been called "the man for others." Someone has said that the ultimate question of philosophy is simply, "Is this a friendly universe?" Theology based in scripture replies with an unqualified "Yes." God is for us.

The reference to "who did not spare his own son" may be an allusion to the Genesis 22 account of Abraham taking Isaac his son to offer as a sacrifice. Abraham did not spare even his one and only hope of a future but was willing to offer him up. God did not spare his own Son but gave him up for us all and there was no ram to substitute at the last moment. Since God has pronounced sentence in our favor, we can expect God to "give us all things with him" (Christ).

The punctuation in vs. 33–35 is disputed. Some commentators prefer to take all the sentences as rhetorical questions, while the RSV does not. Each verse may be taken as a question which is answered by an absurdity also placed in the form of a question. The effect is to show that the only ones who have the power to accuse or condemn us are God and God's Son, and these are precisely the ones who protect us!

It may be that the accuser of God's elect is thought to be Satan, as in Job 1:6. Or it may be the law, or possibly the critic in 6:1, 15, and 7:7. As in Jesus' testing by Satan in the wilderness and Jesus' victory, so in the final trial of the Christian the arguments of the defense will far outweigh any offered by the prosecution. There may have been a simple creed in Paul's thought as he wrote v. 34.

Persecution was a real possibility for Christians, as Paul knew firsthand. In v. 36 there is a quote from Psalm 44:22 which is a community lament that bemoans the injustice done to faithful Israel by its enemies. It recalls Israel's fidelity to God and seeks God's aid and deliverance from enemies. Paul quotes this psalm to show that such tribulations are not proof of God's *not* loving the persecuted. Instead, such things are signs of God's love. (See Col. 1:24 and 2 Cor. 11:23–33 for descriptions of Paul's sufferings.) Paul witnessed to his faith in God being for us out of his own sufferings and near-death experiences for the gospel.

Paul says neither human evil nor evil influences can disturb the Christian's salvation, since it is grounded in the love that God has for us. In vs. 38–39 we have perhaps the most compelling statement of the basis of our Christian confidence in all of Paul's writings. Notice the elegance of the New English Bible translation of these verses.

The angels and principalities and powers refer to supernatural powers which were thought to influence human life. The new age religion of contemporary American culture raises some of the same beliefs in supernatural powers. The references to "height" and "depth" are astronomical terms referring to the position of planets in the sky. They may be drawn from ancient astrology, where they would refer to the greatest proximity and remoteness of a star from its zenith, by which the star's influence was determined. The modern resurgence of belief in astrology should be countered by this affirmation of Paul's.

The love of God is the unshakable foundation of the Christian's life and hope. This passage rises to an even higher level of confidence than vs. 28–30. Here the language of love, not election, is used. Love for Paul is the power that causes God to justify sinners. Reflect on its connection with the Spirit of 5:5 and 1 Corinthians 13.

The gnostic religion seems to be reflected in vs. 38–39, which gave initiates the secret of how to escape the perils that the astral powers put in the way of the soul journeying toward God. These powers were called angels, principalities, and powers, and they had to be tricked or mastered in order for the soul to approach God. Paul assures the Romans that nothing can separate them from the love of God in Christ Jesus our Lord, thus refuting the gnostic system.

Recommended work: Do a word study of gnosticism, justifies, and astrology.

The sermon might follow the movement of the text, climaxing in the assurance of v. 39. It might deal with current new age religion and astrology which seek to find salvation and direction for life outside the Christian faith. The sermon might use the rhetorical question style of the text to some extent.

Theological Reflection

The Genesis 9 and 1 Peter texts both deal with Noah and the flood. The 1 Peter text points to baptism which saves as the antitype of the flood which destroyed. The Genesis 22 and Markan readings both deal with testing. Abraham's faith is tested. Jesus is tested by Satan and is victorious. The Romans reading affirms that God in Christ is victorious and nothing can separate us from God's love. God is for us and will give us all things with Christ.

Children's Message

The talk might begin with a question about who has seen a double or triple rainbow and move from there. Then the story of the flood and God's promise never again to destroy creation by a flood might be told. The meaning of the rainbow for the ancients, a bow shooting lightning, and the rainbow as a sign of God's covenant love should be described.

Hymns for Lent 1

A Mighty Fortress Is Our God; Lord, Who Throughout These Forty Days; Lord, from the Depths to You I Cry.

Psalm 105:1–11 (C)
Psalm 115:1, 9–18 (L)
Psalm 116:10, 15–19 (RC)
Psalm 16 or 16:5–11 (E)

Romans 4:16–25 (C)
Romans 5:1–11 (L)
Romans 8:31–34 (RC)
Romans 8:31–39 (E)

Genesis 17:1–10, 15–19 (C)
Genesis 28:10–17 (18–22) (L)
Genesis 22:1–2, 9–13, 15–18 (RC)
Genesis 22:1–14 (E)

Mark 8:31–38 (C)
Mark 9:2–10 (RC)

Meditation on the Texts

We praise you, O God, for the revelation of yourself in Jesus Christ who suffered many things, was rejected and killed, and after three days rose again. We thank you for the gift of life through faith in Christ. We have heard his call to deny self, take up our cross and follow him. We would profit nothing if we gained the whole world and forfeited our life, for there is nothing we would give in exchange for our soul. May we never be ashamed of Christ, so that he may not be ashamed of us when he comes in the glory of you, God his Father, with the holy angels. We thank you for the example of Abraham, who modeled faith for us all in believing against hope. May we, like him, grow strong in our faith as we give you glory. We thank you that our faith is reckoned to us as righteousness, as it was to Abraham. For we believe in you, O God, who raised Jesus from the dead, who was put to death for our trespasses and raised for our justification. We thank you for the everlasting covenant made with Abraham by which he was made the father of a multitude of nations and was blessed with the land of his sojournings. Amen.

Commentary on the Texts

Mark 9:2–10 (RC)

See Transfiguration of Our Lord, (C).

Mark 8:31–39 (C)

Our pericope is one of three passion predictions in the section of 8:31–10:52 whose theme is the way of the Son of man. Our text stands as the theological and geographical fulcrum at the midpoint of Mark's Gospel. At this point the Galilean ministry is essentially completed. From this point on, the action of the Gospel is directed toward Jerusalem. In vs. 27–30 Jesus has asked Peter and the disciples who people are saying he is. Peter's confession that he is the Christ (Messiah) immediately shifts the theological focus to what it means for Jesus to be the Christ (v. 31). And it points to what it means for his followers to be Christians, as defined in v. 34. These themes will be in the forefront in the remainder of the Gospel. Notice also that this is the opening section discussing the meaning of discipleship, a major emphasis in Mark. Mark shows the way of Jesus as the way the disciples are called to follow. Only as we have a correct understanding of Jesus can we have a clear and correct understanding of the meaning of being a disciple. In Mark's Gospel the disciples often stand for the evangelist's church or simply the Christian community, and the Twelve represent church leaders in whatever age. Note the two major foci of Mark's Gospel: Jesus and the disciples. Watch for the repeated misunderstanding of the disciples of who Jesus is. While Peter, for example, calls Jesus the Christ, he rebukes Jesus when Jesus speaks of rejection, suffering, and death. And in 9:34 the disciples discuss who is the greatest in the kingdom of God, again indicating that they have not understood Jesus' teachings about denying self, taking up one's cross, and following Jesus in the way of servant living.

Our pericope should be read and understood in its context. Its immediate context begins with v. 27a and continues through 9:1. The setting is the villages of Caesarea Philippi. Then Peter's confession follows in vs. 27b–30. This background is essential for grasping the meaning of our pericope which follows with the first passion prediction in 8:31–9:1. The prediction itself is in vs. 31–32a, followed by conflict with Peter in vs. 32b–33 and Jesus' instructions on discipleship in 8:34–9:1. *Who Jesus is and what he does* is intimately related to who the disciples are and what is required of disciples.

Our pericope is an example of the omission by the shapers of the lectionary of an integral part of a reading, namely, vs. 27–30. In fact, vs. 27–33 are a unit that gives Peter's profession and Jesus' correction and is the turning point of Mark's Gospel. It climaxes Jesus' revelation of himself and includes the disciples' first recognition of him as Christ (Messiah). More important, it introduces the theme of the suffering Messiah, a theme that is developed in the chapters that follow. In Mark's Gospel, Peter's confession and the first prediction of Jesus' passion form a logical and structural unit in contrast to Matthew 16:17–19 in which the same account is interrupted by the promise to Peter. This section, vs. 27–33, belongs to the preceding passage, since it is the climax of chapters 1–8, but it also is the transition to the next section.

When Jesus said "must" in v. 31 regarding his coming passion and death, he meant this. He used a word that was used in contemporary apocalyptic literature which indicated that certain future events were part of a firmly decreed will of God. Thus for Peter and the disciples to try to tempt Jesus to depart from the will of God, as Satan had done earlier in the wilderness and now Peter will try to do (v. 32), is to pose the basic temptation of Jesus. Both Matthew and Luke describe the temptation of Jesus as basically the same one as set forth here, namely, to try to accomplish the work of Messiah by spectacular means that involve *no suffering*.

At no place in Mark do we find a theory as to why it should be God's will that Messiah and his disciples must suffer. In the End time thought pattern of the early Christians, God's realm in heaven entirely conformed to God's holiness. It stood in sharp contrast over against this age and world ruled by evil values and designs. It was believed that God would judge this world and bring this age to an end, transforming whatever possible to the conditions of his realm. Anyone in God's realm now must expect suffering and misunderstanding from the evil powers and human beings controlled by evil. The true servant of God would not be put off by such suffering but would understand that in some mysterious fashion it was a means by which God's redemptive purpose for this world was being carried out. Isaiah 53, of course, was the classic passage for this idea, but it is not the only one. We must reflect on the disciples' reaction to Jesus' prophecy of rejection and suffering against this background. They had to learn that until the kingdom of God came with power, the law of suffering applied at least as much to the Messiah (Christ) and his followers as it had to earlier representatives of God (see 9:13 and 6:17–29).

"The chief priests and the scribes" was a way of referring to the lay and clerical aristocracy in Jerusalem. Along with the scribes they formed the Sanhedrin. Some think that such a detailed forecast was a "prophecy after the event" which was ascribed to Jesus by the early Christians.

Then in v. 33 Jesus turned and saw his disciples and spoke to Peter a reproof intended for the disciples as well as for Peter. Jesus tells Peter he is on the side of men, not of God. The basic meaning of the word translated "on the side of" is "to be minded," which includes the idea of sharing another's point of view.

Jesus outlines the demands of discipleship in v. 34. He has just told Peter to get behind him. Now he says that to be a disciple means to come after him, to follow him. Recall that Peter rebuked Jesus (v. 32b) and Jesus rebuked Peter (v. 33). Peter has tried to behave like a patron, not a disciple. There is a struggle over control, over who is in charge. Jesus' rebuke of Peter and the disciples reminds them that disciples belong behind him and after him. Disciples are not to guide or possess Jesus in some fashion but are to follow him.

To deny self is not to deny oneself something, as so often the observance of Lent has involved. Rather, it is to deny *self*. This is not asceticism which may focus attention on the self, nor is it self-hatred. It is a denial of the grasping self, in order to liberate the real self.

To take up one's cross refers not to the burdens of life, to the illnesses and misfortunes that befall us, but to the painful, redemptive action that is freely assumed for others in following Christ. The Romans required a condemned criminal to carry part of his own cross to the place of execution, which gives us this metaphor. Jesus' audience would have been familiar with this Roman practice which was normally used only to execute criminals condemned by due process. But it is doubtful that the disciples, before Jesus' own crucifixion, could have caught the allusion here. This points to the possible formulation of this saying by the early church.

To save oneself (v. 35) means to save one's psyche, meaning life or soul or self.

The term "adulterous" is probably a metaphor for idolatrous. Note Isaiah 1:4, 21, Jeremiah 3:3, and Hosea 2:2.

In v. 38 there seems to be a distinction between Jesus and the Son of man, as if there were two separate persons. Jesus is speaking to the crowd (v. 34), and in Mark's view it would have been natural for Jesus to use a form of words that gave no hint of his identity as Son of man. Anyone who is ashamed of the Son of man now will feel the shame of Jesus in the End. Those who wanted to save themselves will stand before the Christ who did not save himself but gave his life for us all.

Recommended work: Compare this passion prediction with others in Mark. Do a word study of passion of Christ, life, and Son of man.

The sermon should begin with v. 27 and continue through 9:1 in order to put our pericope in the proper context. The sermon might focus on the cost of discipleship (v. 34), showing how disciples are to follow the example of Jesus in enduring suffering for the gospel. The sermon might point to Christians who in recent times have lived out this denial of self, taking up their cross and following Jesus. It should call for a commitment of the hearers to do the same.

Genesis 17:1–10, 15–19 (C)

Our pericope is part of the section that describes the covenant of circumcision, Genesis 17. It is another version of the covenant with Abraham, 15:7–21. In reading the passage, notice that the scene is centered entirely on God. Compare the solemnity, ritual concern, style, and vocabulary with that in Genesis 1. This covenant from the Priestly tradition is the third great stage in salvation history, following that of Adam and Noah. See how each introduces a new ritual institution: 2:1–3; 9:4–7. Now circumcision is introduced and a new divine name is revealed (v. 1). For the Priestly tradition, human history is characterized by solemnity and rigidity of liturgical practices.

God reveals Godself in v. 1 as God Almighty, a word that in Hebrew means "God of the mountain" or "God, the One of the Mountains." It was a Mesopotamian name current in the time before Moses. In this covenant, God does not "cut" a covenant but "gives" it.

Abram fell on his face (v. 3). This gesture indicates his acceptance of the covenant that God gives. The content of this unilateral covenant is the promise of a great number of descendants. Note that the change in name indicates the change affected in Abram by the promise. "Abram" means "the father (God) is exalted." This becomes Abraham which is similar to Abram but indicates "father of a multitude." This multitude of nations implies that nations beyond those of Israel alone will be in God's kingdom. Then in v. 7 God extends the covenant to generations yet to come, which is a new item in the covenant. The promise of land (v. 8) is a parallel to that in 15:18. Note well that the covenant with Abraham involves two promises: land and descendants.

Then in vs. 15–19 we learn that Sarai is given a new name, Sarah, meaning princess, and she too will be blessed by God. God will give a son by her and she shall be a mother of many nations, kings, and peoples. No explanation is given of the new name which is the same as the old one in basic meaning. In response to God's promise of a son in their old age Abraham fell on his face and laughed. The laughter motif is connected with Isaac's birth on several occasions as in 18:12–15 and 21:6. There was originally a play on words in that the Hebrew for "Isaac" sounds similar to the word "to laugh." The birth is a necessary part of the divine plan and thus shares in the wonder of the divine intervention.

Abraham asks in vain in vs. 18–19 that the promise be extended to Ishmael, who is already alive, rather than be reserved for a son whose birth is not likely.

Recommended work: Do a word study of circumcision, covenant, Abraham, and Sarah.

The sermon should deal with Abraham and Sarah, who believed against hope, as our Romans 4:18 passage says, and show them as persons who trusted God against all odds. Abraham was justified by his faith, not by works. God gives him the covenant with its promises, an act of sheer grace. God in Christ has given us salvation through the covenant in Christ's death on the cross. We are called to live in covenant obedience in our daily lives.

Genesis 28:10-17 (18-22) (L)

This is the account of Jacob's dream at Bethel, which at that time was unsettled. The ancients believed that oracles could be received by sleeping in a holy place (recall the boy Samuel, 1 Sam. 3:1ff.). Jacob saw in a dream the gate of heaven and received a manifestation of God. Compare this with 35:1–15. Jacob has extraordinary strength which enables him to erect a monolith by himself. He rolled another stone (29:10) from the mouth of a well. Apparently Jacob's strength was legendary. Here he moved a pillar or sacred stone which was often found in sanctuaries. He poured oil on it (v. 18) the next morning, an act that made it holy, set apart for God.

During the dream, God identifies Godself as the God of Jacob's father and grandfather, Isaac and Abraham. God renews the promise. The name, Bethel, house of God, suggests that the ancients believed this was a place where God came down to meet the people.

When Jacob awoke from the dream in which he saw angels ascending and descending he said, "Surely the LORD is in this place; and I did not know it" (v. 16). So he was filled with holy awe and called it the house of God, which is the meaning of the name Bethel.

Recommended work: Compare this event with others in Jacob's life when he met God or had other crisis experiences by reading a brief account of Jacob in a Bible dictionary.

The sermon might follow the movement of the passage, leading up to Jacob's recognition that God was in the place although he did not recognize God at first. The sermon might deal with holy places and times in our lives when God was there but we did not recognize God's presence at that moment but did become aware of God later: critical illness, accidents, marriage, death of a loved one, critical decision in professional or personal life.

Genesis 22:1-2, 9-13, 15-18 (RC)

Genesis 22:1-14 (E)

See Lent 1, (L).

Romans 4:16-25 (C)

This is part of the larger section of vs. 13–25 whose theme is the true descendants of Abraham. They are all those who have faith in Christ, whether Jews or Gentiles, and to them belong the benefits promised to Abraham (Gen. 17:4–6 and 22:17–18 of our pericopes for today). Abraham is declared to be the father of us all in the faith (vs. 16–17).

The promise to Abraham depended on faith, so that it might rest on grace (v. 16), which picks up the thought of v. 13. Since the law and promise cannot coincide, the law must yield to promise. The person who lives by faith lives by grace, and this includes not only the Jew but all who share Abraham's faith as the Hebrew Scriptures teach.

Abraham was the father of many nations (Gen. 17:5 of our pericope for today). The many nations refers to the descendants of Ishmael and of the children born to Keturah according to Genesis, but Paul takes this to mean the Gentiles in general who are children of Abraham by faith. God gives life to the dead and calls into existence "the things that do not exist" (v. 17), referring to the divine power which enabled barren Sarai to conceive Isaac. It points forward to vs. 24–25, describing Jesus' resurrection.

The thrust of vs. 18–25 is that faith is based on the conviction that God is, as vs. 17 and 21 indicate, able to give us a righteousness of faith in the place of our nonexistent righteousness. God is able by God's creative powers to do what seemed impossible, whether bringing Isaac to parents who were near death or raising Christ from the dead (vs. 24, 25).

But Paul does not use the story of the sacrifice of Isaac which would illustrate further Abraham's hope against hope and deep faith. This too revealed his faith that God was "able to do what he had promised" (v. 21).

God creates righteousness where there is the receptiveness of faith, as v. 22 indicates, and the evidence for this is the example of Abraham and the words of promise to him, and the death and resurrection of Jesus. The death and resurrection are two intimately connected phases of one great act of salvation.

Recommended work: Do a word study of righteousness, faith, grace, and hope.

The sermon should draw on the Genesis 17 pericope for today as it points to the example of Abraham's faith. The sermon should point up the sheer absurdity of faith, faith that hopes against hope, rather than describing faith as something we do in a rational manner. God calls faith into existence and thus gives us righteousness through sheer grace. The sermon should raise the consciousness of hearers to the real meaning of faith and lead them to deeper commitment of life to God.

Romans 5:1–11 (L)

Our pericope gives the consequences of justification by faith. They are peace with God (v. 1b), new hope (vs. 2–5), and evidence of God's love (vs. 6–11). Justification calls forth the scene of a law court in which a judge acquits an accused person in view of fresh evidence or a new counsel for the accused. The accused is now freed to resume a new life of freedom. One result is peace with God, not "Let us have peace," as some manuscripts indicate.

The basic human problem is a broken relationship with God, a state of cold war. But God has taken the initiative to make a new relationship of peace or reconciliation possible.

Note carefully that Paul never speaks of God being reconciled to us but always of our being reconciled to God (v. 10). We were enemies toward God, not God toward us. The death of Christ brings about the reconciliation of the enemy, humankind, to God. While in 4:25 justification is ascribed to Christ's death, "raised for our justification," here in v. 10 Paul says we were justified by his death (v. 9). Notice that v. 10 is a repetition of v. 8 but in a more positive way. Reconciliation with God is another way of expressing "peace with God" (v. 1) and justification by God. As Paul uses the term, justification is not so much a judge's acquittal as it is a parent's welcome home to a prodigal son or daughter. There is a reunion with the life of the family. Paul says he rejoices in God. One of the distinctive marks of the Christian life is joy, joy in being reconciled to God and at peace with God.

Recommended work: Do a word study of peace, justification, and reconciliation.

The sermon might develop the images of alienation from God, a state in which we were enemies of God because of sin, and our reconciliation with God which is a gift received through faith in our Lord Jesus Christ. The sermon might use illustrations of family relationships in which the alienated son or daughter returns home and is reconciled to the family and lives in peace.

Romans 8:31–34 (RC) and Romans 8:31–39 (E)

See Lent 1, (L).

Theological Reflection

The theme of justification by faith in God pervades both the Genesis 17 and the Romans 4 and 5 passages. We are put in right relationship with God by a free gift of justification received by faith. The Genesis 28 reading tells of Isaac's vision of the gate of heaven and the renewal of the covenant by God with him and his descendants. The Mark 8 reading defines the meaning of "Christ" and its implications for the Christian life.

Children's Message

The talk might be about our relationship with God being like our relationship in our family. When we disobey family rules and alienate ourselves from our family, we feel angry, lonely, and rejected. But when mother or father hold out their arms in love to receive us back, we are reconciled to our family. This is what God has done in Jesus Christ.

Hymns for Lent 2

When I Survey the Wondrous Cross; My Faith Looks Up to Thee; Jesus, Thou Joy of Loving Hearts.

Lent 3

Psalm 19:7–14 (C)   **1 Corinthians 1:22–25 (C)**
Psalm 19:8–11 (RC)   **Romans 7:13–25 (E)**

Exodus 20:1–17   **John 2:13–22 (C)**
                          John 2:13–25 (RC)

Meditation on the Texts

We thank you, O God, for the gift of Jesus Christ who came to earth, suffered, died, and was raised on the third day. We recall how he purged the temple of those who had made it a house of trade and restored it to be his Father's house, a house of prayer for all nations. While Jews demand signs and Greeks seek wisdom, we thank you for the preaching of Christ crucified, a stumbling block to Jews and folly to Gentiles, but to those who are called, the manifestation of your power and wisdom. For we know that your foolishness is wiser than that of human beings, and your weakness is stronger than we are. All too often we do not understand our own actions. We do not do the thing we want but instead do the very thing we hate. Sin within us moves us to do the evil we do not want. We delight in your law in our inmost self, but we see in our members another law at war with the law of our mind which makes us captives to the law of sin which dwells in our members. Thanks be to you, O God, who through Jesus Christ our Lord have delivered us from this body of death. We recall your mighty act of bringing Israel out of the land of Egypt, out of the house of bondage and giving Israel the Ten Commandments. May we listen for your guiding word in the commandments as we seek to love you with all our heart, mind, and soul, and love our neighbor as ourself. Amen.

Commentary on the Texts

John 2:13–22 (C)

John 2:13–25 (RC)

John places the account of the cleansing of the temple early in Jesus' ministry in contrast to the Synoptics, which put it near the end of his ministry (Matt. 21:12–17; Mark 11:15–19; Luke 19:45–46). Animals were sold in the temple area to be used for sacrifice, and Roman coins were exchanged for Jewish money to pay the temple tax. The Tyrian half-shekel was the only money acceptable in the temple. The meaning of the cleansing of the temple, rather than the date it took place, is the point stressed in both John and the Synoptics.

Our pericope is part of the larger section of 2:12–4:54, which presents the new life in signs, and part of the overall division of 1:19–12:50, which contains the Book of Signs whose theme is faith and unbelief, focusing on Christ the light that shines in the darkness. Our reading is followed by the discourse with Nicodemus on the new birth and baptism in John 3. In our pericope, John presents "The New Temple: The Resurrection Christ." There is an underlying spiritual significance to Jesus' cleansing of the temple which is reproduced from the Synoptic tradition. John takes little note of Jesus' activity in Galilee, and in v. 12 we see that Jesus stayed in Capernaum only a few days before going to Jerusalem for the Passover.

The text refers to "the Passover of the Jews," in contrast to the Christian Passover, known by John and mentioned in 1 Corinthians 5:7. The Jewish Passover was but a type of the Christian one. This is the first of three Passovers mentioned by John (6:4; 11:55). The feasts of the Jewish religion play a major role in the Fourth Gospel, representing as they do the institutions that prefigured Christ.

Jesus "went up" to Jerusalem, the normal term for a journey to Jerusalem, which is situated on a hill. One possible solution to the difference between John's and the Synoptics' dating of this visit to Jerusalem is suggested by Raymond Brown:

> We suggest as a plausible hypothesis that on his first journey to Jerusalem and to the Temple at the beginning of his ministry Jesus uttered a prophetic warning about the destruction of the sanctuary. The Synoptics give evidence that later on this warning was recalled and used against Jesus, although they never tell us at what precise moment the warning had originally been given. On the other hand, it seems likely that Jesus' action of cleansing the temple precincts took place in the last days of his life. (Raymond E. Brown, *The Gospel According to John I–XII,* p. 118)

Several features of the cleansing of the temple are found only in John: the presence of the oxen and sheep, the making of the whip, and the words attributed to Jesus. Some scholars think that the presence of oxen and sheep in the temple precincts is not historical, since no Jewish sources mention such a practice, and the presence of such animals would be extraordinary, since if they got loose, they might get into the sanctuary and violate it. The usual place for animal markets was either in the Kidron Valley or on the slopes of the Mount of Olives. It seems, however, that Caiaphas allowed merchants to set up animal stalls in the temple confines to avenge other merchants who gave hospitality to his enemies. The doves or pigeons were the sacrifices of the poor, which may explain Jesus' milder dealing with the dove sellers.

The Roman coins had to be exchanged, at a small profit for the money changers, for legal Tyrian coinage, the half-shekel, since Roman coins had pagan portraits on them and were not allowed for paying the temple tax. A half-shekel was equal to two denarii, and a denarii was a day's pay for a common laborer. It was equal in value to the drachma.

Since no sticks or weapons were allowed in the temple precincts, the whip made out of cords may have been made from the rushes used for bedding for the animals. The Synoptics do not mention the whip but do say Jesus drove out the sellers of doves. The Synoptics and John seem to draw on a common source which they adopted and expanded for their purposes. It appears that Jesus used the whip on the merchants: "he drove them all" (v. 15). Jesus knocked over their tables. The various Greek manuscripts of John differ slightly on this, but all reflect an attempt by scribes to harmonize with the Synoptics.

But notice how the Jews take Jesus' words, "Destroy this temple," literally, and later at his trial the words were distorted into an imputation of sorcery. Jesus spoke of the temple of his body which refers not only to the resurrection but also to the church, Christ's body (v. 21). The Gospels indicate that the full significance of Jesus' words and deeds was understood only in the light of Jesus' resurrection and the coming of the Holy Spirit. The early church saw Psalm 16:10 as an intimation of the resurrection (see Acts 2:31; 13:35).

Many believed in Jesus' name (v. 23). In Semitic use the "name" was equivalent to the person, so to believe in Jesus' name is to make a commitment to him as a person. There is a mention of signs that Jesus did, and so far John has mentioned only the miracle at Cana. Therefore he must have been referring to the numerous miracles recorded in the Synoptics. Matthew 21:14f. refers to the miracles that had occurred at the time of the cleansing of the temple.

John says that Jesus did not trust himself to the people, since a faith based only on miracles but without a proper recognition of the nature of the person who performed them would reveal itself unstable and inconstant. Note the same idea in 6:2. Jesus has no illusions about the frailty of human nature, for he who is human is endowed with divine wisdom.

Recommended work: Compare this cleansing with that recorded in the Synoptics. Do a word study of sacrificial system, temple, and name.

The sermon might follow the movements of the text, applying the thrust of the text to religious life today. It might point out how religion has been corrupted and made into big business through television evangelism, perverting religion into entertainment in church worship. The sermon might deal with the cross and resurrection as the ultimate sign on which our faith is based, in contrast to miracles which may create a shallow belief. The sermon might contrast the church as either a house of God or a house of commerce, pointing out ways in which religion is misused today.

Exodus 20:1-17

The pericope is the Decalogue, found in two forms, Exodus 20 and Deuteronomy 5:6–21. Attempts have been made to harmonize them. A third form is in Exodus 34:11–26, the so-called Ritual Decalogue.

While there were many law codes before the Decalogue, their basis was casuistic law, meaning "If so and so happens, then the following is the penalty." But the Decalogue is apodictic law: Thou shalt do so and so, or shalt not do so and so, without any kind of introductory conditional element. Some scholars think that the fourth commandment through the tenth represent the original code, with the first three pithy statements supplemented by later traditions. There are slight discrepancies about the way the Decalogue is divided. The chief difference between the Exodus version and that of Deuteronomy is that the latter has a humanitarian motivation added for observing the Sabbath, and there is a reversal of order in Exodus 20:17 and Deuteronomy 5:21. Note in Exodus that "house" is named first and then "wife."

As we examine the Decalogue, we find that the fifth commandment through the tenth contain what are elements of the natural law, commandments found in earlier law codes. But there is a major difference between the Exodus and earlier ones. In the earlier codes, violation against a commandment is a crime against one's fellow, while in the Hebrew Scriptures a violation is a crime against God! Thus, there is an entirely new orientation here.

The reference to "these words" (v. 1) points to the original version in which each commandment was a short utterance, as in vs. 13, 14, and 15. Explanations were later added to those in vs. 4–6 and 8–10. Notice that while Jewish tradition considers v. 2 to be the first commandment, it actually is a preface summarizing the meaning of the exodus. It sets the commandments within the covenant context and God's redemptive action. The Lord is Israel's God who delivered Israel from bondage, and Israel is to be loyal to God alone. God is a jealous God who tolerates no rival, for God is a jealous God (v. 5; 34:14).

One of the things that made Israel's worship unique in the ancient world was its worship *without* images. Other religions personified natural powers. Statues of powers of fertility, nature, and so forth, in animal form were worshiped.

Some interpreters consider vs. 3–6 to be one commandment and then divide v. 17 into two commandments.

The third commandment (v. 7) prohibits misuse of God's name in magic, or false swearing. The ancients believed that one could use a name to exert magical control.

The Sabbath probably existed long before it was expressed in the Decalogue. Keeping it holy means observing it as a day separate from the others, a portion of time that belonged especially to God. Humans are to imitate God whose work ceased on the Sabbath, leaving the Sabbath free from work.

The fifth commandment stresses the obligations that *adult* children have to their aging parents for the care of their physical and emotional needs. Note that this commandment is the first to contain a promise: that your days may be long.

This commandment applies to all children, but it especially applies to the parent's right to care. This emerged out of a variety of different situations and was controlled through several means, such as court, cult, and household. The thrust of this commandment originally was to protect parents from being driven out of the home or abused after they could no longer work (Ex. 21:15; Lev. 20:9). The term "honor" means far more than to obey. It includes the command to prize highly, to show respect, and to care and show affection. It is a term often used to describe a proper response to God and related to worship (Ps. 86:9). This commandment has been thought of as a bridge connecting the obligations to God in the first four commandments with the obligations to human beings in the last six, since the commandment contains a reference to "your God," which is a phrase that occurs only in verses concerning obligations to God.

The sixth commandment raises the difficulty of what is meant by the Hebrew word for "kill." A special kind of killing is intended, and the verb is found only forty-six times in the Hebrew Scriptures, in contrast to other words that mean kill which are found much more frequently. Some have translated this "Thou shalt not murder." The thrust of the word used here is that illegal killing is prohibited, thus protecting the life of the Israelite from illegal, impermissible violence. The word "kill" used here designates those acts of violence against a person which arise from personal feelings of hatred and malice. In its present form the command forbids such an act of violence and rejects any claim of a person to take the law into his or her hands out of a feeling of personal injury. Grounds for opposing capital punishment and killing in war must be found in other places in scripture than here.

The seventh commandment seeks to maintain the sanctity of marriage. The verb used can have either the man or the woman as subject. Private property is safeguarded in the eighth commandment. Some exegetes think this applies primarily to stealing a person and thus seeks to protect an Israelite against being stolen and sold into slavery. It prohibits the enslavement of free Israelites by force either for personal use or for trade.

The ninth commandment is concerned with prohibiting bearing false witness in legal trials. This would take place in the setting of the local legal assembly which met at the gate of a town, a relatively spacious meeting place where all free Israelites belonged. The neighbor refers to the person with whom one lives and comes into contact in the conditions of life.

The final and tenth commandment describes not only the emotion of coveting but also includes the attempt to attach something to oneself illegally. It covers all attempts to gain power over the goods and possessions of a neighbor, whether by theft or various kinds of dishonest dealings. The term "house" can refer in a narrow sense to the house or tent house alone, or it can be used in a wider sense to include everything that is in the house. It begins with wife, who in the Hebrew Scripture law of marriage was the possession of the husband. The commandment ends with the catchall "anything that is your neighbor's."

Recommended work: Read other forms of the Decalogue and compare them. Reflect on how the law that Jesus gave to love God and love neighbor as one's self is spelled out in specific cases in the commandments.

The sermon might deal with the commandments as responses to God's salvation in Jesus Christ which are still binding on every Christian, but not as a means of justifying oneself before God, as some have used them. The preacher might select one commandment to deal with, or treat all ten, showing that they are unique among law codes of human history. Their relevance to contemporary society should be stressed, such as the commandment of adult children to honor and care for the physical needs of their aging parents.

1 Corinthians 1:22–25 (C)

This is part of the larger section of 1:18–2:5, whose theme is that the gospel is not a new philosophy but a message to be accepted and lived out in daily life.

Paul writes that Jews demanded signs, namely, spectacular miracles that showed divine intervention. They looked for a messiah who would inaugurate their nation's rule over the Gentiles by a display of miraculous powers. See Mark 8:11 and its parallels and the Hebrew Scriptures' record of Israel's tempting the Lord, as in Numbers 14:11, 22. This attitude refuses to take God on trust, demanding that God present credentials in the form of visible and identifiable acts. Although this attitude may be expressed in religious forms, it is fundamentally skeptical and essentially egotistical.

Paul says the Greeks demanded wisdom. The wisdom is that of gnosticism, religious thought without the practice of religion, a pretended revelation of God that was actually just human speculation. These Greek philosophies sought to give satisfactory explanations of humans and the cosmos.

Both Jewish and Greek attitudes express those of human beings alienated from God and manifesting their rebellion in self-centered existence.

For the Jews, Christ crucified is a stumbling block, or scandal. The literal meaning is something that trips people up. The cross is a cause of offense and revulsion and an object of vigorous opposition and anger. This is true because in the cross God does precisely the opposite of what Jews expected God to do. Note that Christ crucified refers to the living, risen Christ who was crucified.

The Gentiles find the cross folly because incarnation crystallized in crucifixion means that humans have not speculated their way up to God but rather God has come down to humans where they are.

Christ crucified is the power and wisdom of God in a paradoxical sense. It is God's foolishness, since what God has done in Christ crucified is a direct contradiction of human ideas of wisdom and power. But it achieved precisely what human wisdom and power failed to achieve. It brings the truth about God and humans and delivers humans from their bondage. This power and wisdom comes to those who are called, writes Paul, thus stressing the primacy of God's action in bringing about faith. Humans believe because God calls them.

Recommended work: Do a word study of signs, wisdom, power, and foolishness.

The sermon might contrast human demand for miraculous signs such as those provided by television evangelists and human wisdom expressed in the new age religion and other cults with the power and wisdom of God expressed in Christ crucified and risen from the dead. The sermon should lead hearers to think critically about false religions and come to see that God's "foolishness" is wiser than human wisdom and that God's weakness is stronger than human strength.

Romans 7:13–25 (E)

Our pericope is part of a chapter whose theme is freedom from the law. In our pericope sin is personified as an evil power that enters a human being's life and brings his or her true self into slavery to its rule or law. Paul says that the law is spiritual in nature, meaning that its origin, nature, is holy and divine. Paul Achtemeier in his commentary on Romans (Paul J. Achtemeier, *Romans,* Interpretation series [Atlanta: John Knox Press, 1985], pp. 118f.), says that in this passage what Paul describes is the dilemma of all human beings who seek to follow God's will apart from Christ. While humans know that they ought to do good, they nevertheless stumble under the power of sin into the very evil they seek to avoid. In trying to do the good, they in fact oppose the good until they come to recognize the good in Christ.

Thus the problem the passage discusses is that of those who can do nothing but evil, since the power of sin over them remains unbroken. Christians should reflect on their gratitude to God for delivering them from such enslavement through Christ, God's Son.

While Christians have been set free from bondage to sin, these verses of chapter 7 should serve as a warning of what awaits those who reject that freedom. The Christian is not totally under the dominion of sin as the "I" whom Paul describes here is enslaved but has the chance to follow God's will expressed in Christ. This is the good news we have in Christ, who died to free us from bondage to evil.

Recommended work: Do a word study of law, flesh, and sin.

The sermon might follow the discussion in the text, pointing out that this describes the person who does not know Christ. The sermon should focus on the freedom the Christian has in Christ from the power of sin and the law, in contrast to the old way of life of bondage to the flesh, sold under sin. It should move hearers to be vigilant lest they reject the freedom they have in Christ.

Theological Reflection

The law and its role are themes in the Exodus and Romans readings. The John 2 passage deals with Jesus' cleansing the temple, making it a house of God for worship rather than a house of trade for profit. The 1 Corinthians reading contrasts human wisdom with divine wisdom revealed in Christ, and human power with God's weakness which is stronger than human power.

Children's Message

The talk might be about Jesus' concern for true worship and his action in driving out of the temple those who were making it a house of trade. This might lead to a discussion of what we do in worship, such as pray, which is both speaking to and listening to God, singing praises to God, listening to God's word in scripture and sermon, and giving ourselves and our gifts in the offering and commitment of life in church programs.

Hymns for Lent 3

Be Thou My Vision; God Moves in a Mysterious Way; Judge Eternal, Throned in Splendor.

Lent 4

Psalm 137:1–6 (C)
Psalm 27:1–9 (10–14) (L)
Psalm 137:1–6 (RC)
Psalm 122 (E)

Ephesians 2:4–10

John 3:14–21 (C)
John 6:14–15 (E)

2 Chronicles 36:14–23 (C)
Numbers 21:4–9 (L)
2 Chronicles 36:14–17, 19–23 (RC)

Meditation on the Texts

Gracious God, we thank you that you so loved the world that you gave your only Son that whoever believes in him should not perish but have eternal life. We are grateful that he came into the world, not to condemn the world, but that the world might be saved through him. Even as Moses lifted up the serpent in the wilderness for the healing of the people, we thank you that Jesus was lifted up on the cross that whoever believes in him might have eternal life. Christ, the light of the world, has come into a world of darkness, and people loved darkness rather than light because their deeds were evil. We thank you for calling us to follow Christ by the Spirit who enables us to do what is true and thus come to the light. You are rich in mercy, O God, and loved us while we were yet dead through our trespasses and have made us alive together with Christ. We rejoice that we have been raised up with Christ and made to sit with him in the heavenly places in Christ Jesus. By grace we have been saved through faith, and this not of our own doing. It is a gift from you, O God, not because of works, lest we should boast. We acknowledge that we are your workmanship created in Christ Jesus for good works which you prepared beforehand that we should walk in them. Amen.

Commentary on the Texts

John 3:14–21 (C)

Our reading is part of the section that deals with Jesus and official Judaism (3:1–21). The whole chapter deals with the new birth and baptism, showing how Christ has replaced the institutions of Judaism. This theme was begun in John the Baptist's testimony in 1:26, 33.

The preacher is urged to read the whole chapter, noting that the first twelve verses have Jesus speaking of what should be rather easy to understand, at least by analogies. Then in the verses that follow, Nicodemus disappears from the dialogue and what was a dialogue becomes a monologue. Christ and John, or both, speak in the monologue. (See Bruce Vawter, "The Gospel According to John," in *The Jerome Biblical Commentary* ed. Raymond E. Brown and others, no. 30, p. 419.) Vawter describes how the Johannine dialogues often dissolve into a monologue either of Christ or of the evangelist, as happens here.

The thrust of vs. 13–14 is that Jesus descended from heaven in order to bring eternal life, meaning participation in God's life. He accomplished this by being lifted up on the cross (see the discussion of Num. 21:4–9 in today's comments). Note that v. 13 is integral to our pericope, although omitted from the lectionary reading, since it refers to Jesus, the Son of man, who has both ascended into heaven and descended from heaven. Jesus has just spoken of heavenly things which cannot be grasped by any human being at will. This reminds us of the gnostic mystery religions of that time, which claimed to introduce initiates into a realm of heavenly knowledge. Jesus is the only one who can speak of such heavenly things, because he is the only person who has both come down from heaven, in the incarnation, and ascended into heaven, at his ascension (1:51).

The serpent refers to the incident recorded in Numbers 21:4–9 in which Moses placed the bronze serpent on a standard-bearing pole. Some sources say that he placed the serpent on an elevated place or that he suspended it. The Hebrew word for "standard-bearing pole" is literally the word for "sign." This may be one of the things that influenced John to use the word "sign" for the miracles of Jesus. One of the sources interprets looking on the serpent as meaning turning one's heart toward the presence of God. In Wisdom 16:6–7 the bronze serpent is called the symbol of salvation. In the case of the Israelites and those who looked on Jesus lifted up, salvation came through a "raising up."

Note that the condition of the giving of the Spirit (v. 8) and the introduction of human beings into the heavenly realm is the exaltation of Christ. The raising up has a double significance: his being raised up on the cross, and his glorification in the resurrection and the ascension to God. The Greek word for "raised up" is a key one in John's vocabulary and has a meaning close to that of "be glorified." This seems to be an allusion to the Servant of the Lord, described in Isaiah 52:13. Recall that in Jesus' proclamation of himself there is a unification of the functions of both the Servant and the Son of man.

As a result of the exaltation of Christ, those who believe in him are given healing in him. Compare this with Numbers 21:8 indicating that those who look on the serpent shall live. The Hebrew word for "lifted up," which the Greek word used here translates, has both the meaning of death and glorification, as in Genesis 40:13, 19. The Aramaic word equal to these can mean both to crucify or hang as on a cross, and to raise up. For John, the term "being lifted up" refers to one continuous action of Jesus' return to his Father, an action that begins as Jesus approaches death and continues through his ascension to God in heaven, as in 20:17. We might visualize this as a large *U*, with the left side representing Jesus' incarnation in which the Word became flesh. The right side of the *U* symbolizes Jesus' being lifted up on the cross and continues through his being raised up from death, and is completed when he is lifted up to heaven. Reflect on Jesus' words in 8:28: "So Jesus said, 'When you have lifted up the Son of man, then you will know that I am he.'" Jesus' claim to the name of "I AM" used of God was hardly recognized at the crucifixion but was recognized only *after* the resurrection and ascension. For example, Thomas confessed faith in him as "my God" (20:28). Also, Jesus said in 12:32, "And I, when I am lifted up from the earth, will draw all men to myself." This being "lifted up" included the resurrection as well as being "lifted up" on the cross in death.

When Jesus is so lifted up, then he will give the Spirit which will constitute a flowing source of life for those who believe in him.

John 3:16 marks a subdivision in the second part of the discourse. Now God becomes prominent. However, the theme of Jesus' death, which began in vs. 14–15, continues in v. 16. There is an allusion to the Hebrew Scriptures in which Abraham was commanded to take his "only" son Isaac whom he loved and offer him to the Lord. This may well lie behind the phrase "God so loved the world that he gave his only Son," as many scholars think. The mention of "the world" also fits in with this background, since the purpose of Abraham's sacrifice of Isaac was to bring about a benefit for all the nations of the world. But in contrast to Abraham's sacrifice in which a ram was furnished to take Isaac's place, there was no ram when Jesus was offered up by God on the cross. Abraham's sacrifice is a type that points forward to God's love which offered up Christ.

The love of God for the world is the only explanation we have of the gift of eternal life made possible through Christ's death and resurrection. Compare v. 16 with our Ephesians reading for today. John 3:16 has been called "the gospel in a nutshell" and "the little gospel" and other terms, and many sermons and books have explored the meaning of this infinite love of God in Christ for the world.

The key to receiving eternal life, the life of the age to come, is faith in Christ. The purpose of Christ's coming into the world was not to condemn it, says John, but that the world might be saved through him.

Christ's coming brought the light into the world which is judgment (crisis). Human beings must choose: to believe or not to believe. Willful unbelief results in condemnation. The unbeliever passes judgment on himself or herself. Everyone who does evil hates the light. But the person who *does* what is true comes to the light, says John, that it may be clear that his or her deeds have been wrought in God (v. 21).

Recommended work: Compare the image of the lifting up of the serpent by Moses which brought about healing with the image of Christ being ''lifted up'' on the cross, resurrection, and ascension. Do a word study of eternal life, believe, condemned, judgment, and light.

The sermon might focus on v. 16 alone and develop this familiar verse in its broadest meaning, namely, that God loved the world, not the church alone or Christians alone, but the whole world, and so gave God's Son. The sermon might point to the judgment which Christ's coming brought, to believe or not to believe, and the consequences: eternal life or eternal separation from God. Or the sermon might follow the various images and moves of the passage, contrasting the life which God offers with the darkness, evil, and rejection of the light which leads to death and separation from God. Whatever the tack the sermon takes, it should confront the hearers with the faith decision in a fresh and creative way which motivates them to believe in Christ and do what is true and thus receive eternal life as a gift.

John 6:4–15 (E)

This part is the account of the feeding of the five thousand, the only miracle recorded by all four Gospels. Jesus tested Philip's faith (v. 6), although Jesus knew what he would do. This occurred when the Passover feast was near. This is the second Passover mentioned in John, and John is already thinking of the Eucharist, a theme to be developed.

Barley loaves were the food of the poor. Notice the allusions to Moses in this chapter as Jesus went up on the mountain, as Moses went up Mt. Sinai. Jesus lifted up his eyes. The question of how to feed so many recalls Numbers 11:22, where Moses questions how to feed so great a number of people.

Andrew, who brought the lad to Jesus, also brought his brother Peter to Jesus and later will bring the Greeks to Jesus (12:20). Andrew is an evangelist showing those who hunger for the Bread of Life where to find food. The Gospel authors show us a rare insight into the personality of a disciple in describing Andrew and his actions.

There are allusions to the Eucharist in Jesus taking the loaves, giving thanks, and distributing them, as he also did with the fish. The Synoptics have the disciples rather than Jesus himself distribute the bread. Only John gives the command to gather up the fragments left over. This gathering is a symbol of the gathering of the church. The early church used the same Greek word for gathering the eucharistic bread.

The mention of twelve baskets by John seems to symbolize the presence of the twelve disciples. The people threatened to come and make Jesus a king, a political messiah who would lead them in opposing Rome, but Jesus refuses to accept this (18:36).

The people thus see in this miracle an indication that Jesus is the prophet like Moses who has come to found the New Israel. But the people reach this conclusion purely on the basis of the signs Jesus did rather than on a real depth of perception of who Jesus is. In v. 14 ''signs'' is a preferred translation to ''sign,'' since John is thinking of similar instances in which they were enthused by Jesus' miracles.

Recommended work: Compare this account of the feeding of the multitude with others in the Gospels. Compare them with the Eucharist. Reflect on the thrust of God's gracious feeding of his people so that there is much left over!

The sermon might hold up Jesus' test question to Philip of ''How are we to buy bread . . . ?'' as the question we also ask of how to feed the hungry of the world. But Jesus used what was available, a lad's five barley loaves and two fish and by a miracle fed the multitude. The sermon should relate this to the Eucharist and the heavenly banquet which it foreshadows when God will feed all the people with great abundance.

2 Chronicles 36:14–17, 19–23 (RC)

Our pericope is part of a chapter that describes the last agonies of the doomed nation of Israel. It was apostate, and the goodness of former kings and leaders could not spare Israel from its fate. There is no parallel to v. 14 in 2 Kings, where the blame is laid mainly on the king. Note that the author does not include the Levites and musicians in his condemnation.

In chapter 36 the author sums up the last fifty-eight verses of 2 Kings in just a dozen verses. Then he adds twelve more verses he has composed. The preacher is urged to read the whole chapter and commentaries on it in order better to understand vs. 14–23. Note in vs. 15–16 one of the Chronicler's favorite themes, namely, that of the unheeded prophet: "But they kept mocking the messengers of God, despising his words, and scoffing at his prophets." Then in vs. 17–21 there is a condensation of 2 Kings 25:1–21, with the addition of comments on the establishing of the kingdom of Persia, the prophecies of Jeremiah, and the Sabbaths. In v. 20 the author reflects on the evil of not listening to God's prophets, which culminates in the assertion that the exile would last some seventy years in fulfillment of Jeremiah 25:12.

Finally, in vs. 22–23 the author reproduces the note of hope found in Ezra 1:1–3, where it properly belongs. Remember that the author of 1 and 2 Chronicles describes the downfall of God's people, while Ezra and Nehemiah describe their restoration. In the present arrangement of the Hebrew Scriptures, 2 Chronicles is the *last* book. Therefore an editor appears to have added these verses so that the Hebrew Scriptures would not end on a note of doom but on a note of optimism. This portion of Chronicles was inserted into the canon after Ezra and drew on Ezra.

God uses Cyrus, king of Persia, to enable the temple to be rebuilt at Jerusalem, commanding the exiles to go up to Jerusalem and asking that the Lord God be with them.

Recommended work: Scan the history of Israel leading up to this event in a Bible dictionary or a book on the history of Israel. Compare the destruction of Jerusalem and its temple with the prophecy of and later rebuilding of the temple.

The sermon might follow the moves in the text, showing how God used a pagan ruler, Cyrus, to bring the restoration of the people of God to their land and rebuilding the temple. It might deal with the mystery of God's working in history, often incognito, to bring about God's plan of salvation for the people. The sermon should warn hearers to listen to God's prophets and avoid the punishment that despising God's words brings. The rejection of Jesus and his words is the ultimate example of this, of course. The sermon should call for a decision for Christ, to hear and obey his words as God's prophet and Messiah, and thus be restored to God's house, and avoid destruction.

Numbers 21:4–9 (L)

This text is background for the John 3:14–21 reading for today in that it deals with the serpent scourge and the lifting up of the bronze serpent as a means of healing the people. Note that v. 4 is a brief interruption of the narrative of the journey from Kadesh to Moab.

The serpents were venomous. The attack by the fiery serpents was interpreted as divine judgment upon the people's rebellion. They were called "fiery" because their bite caused inflammation. Archaeology reveals that the cult of the snake was widely practiced in Canaan, most probably in connection with fertility rites. "The bite of a poisonous snake is a frequent symbol for the fear of death or insanity or both" (Joseph L. Henderson and Maud Oakes, *The Wisdom of the Serpent* [New York: Collier Books, 1963], p. 37). A bronze serpent was found in the excavations of Lachish dating from the Late Bronze Age, roughly the age of the exodus. Moses may have learned to make an image of the serpent from his Kenite relatives, whose name means "smith." This incident took place in the area of Punon, one of the major sources of copper in ancient times.

It appears that the cure of the people was a case of sympathetic magic, but the author makes sure the reader understands that it was the work of God. But the bronze serpent never became a permanent part of Israel's worship. In fact, Hezekiah broke it into pieces.

We need to be aware of the two elements in our narrative which stand side by side: one of the bronze serpent said to have been made by Moses to which the Israelites offered sacrifices, as just noted. The other is the idea that the desert is a place of vicious and dangerous serpents and that there was a "fiery serpent" whose name can no longer be explained. It is pictured as a flying serpent, "the viper and the flying serpent" (Isa. 30:6). It is worse than an ordinary serpent.

We see in this passage that the discontentment of the people with the frugal life of the desert wandering leads to punishment of those who have risen against God and Moses. The punishment is by means of the bite of the fiery serpents. The reason for putting an image of the serpent on top of a pole so that everyone could see it was based on the concept that one can annul the power of dangerous creatures by making an image of them and offering some kind of worship to that image (see 1 Sam. 6:4-5). The people looked at the serpent image in order to be released from the fatal consequences of the serpent bites. The representation of the serpent as a god of healing to which one must turn may also play a part.

Recommended work: Read articles on serpents and their symbolism. Compare this text with John 3:14-16 and the symbolism involved in healing.

The sermon should relate this text to the John 3:14-21 text of our Gospel pericope, showing that the lifting up of the serpent image for the healing of the people foreshadows the lifting up of Jesus on the cross, in his resurrection and ascension. The sermon should include the judgment aspect of the text in which God judges the people for their discontent and rebellion against both God and Moses. But God did not utterly reject Israel but provided a means of healing in the bronze serpent. God has provided in Christ the way of healing and salvation.

Ephesians 2:4–10

Our pericope is a section of a chapter whose theme is Christ's benefits for both Gentiles and Jews. The preacher should read the entire chapter in order to see the reading in its context.

The first word of v. 4, "But," is the hinge on which the verses that follow turn, in contrast to the sin of humans described in v. 3. The author contrasts God's initiative in salvation with the evil desires and acts of human beings. Note that the word "rich" is used five times in Ephesians and is characteristic of the author, who places emphasis on the abundance of God's mercy. Grace, of course, is God's unmerited favor shown to human beings in Christ. Compare the good news of this reading with the John 3:14-21 reading.

Then in vs. 5 and 6 three verbs are used: made us alive together with Christ, raised us up with him, and made us sit with him. In the Greek each verb is prefixed by "with," indicating that the Christian's ultimate association is with Christ. Faith is the channel of salvation (v. 8). The author never says "saved because of faith," as if faith were a work we can do. "This" refers to your salvation. Good works are the fruit of salvation, not the means to it. In v. 8 the phrase "by grace you have been saved" points to the future salvation which is now present. The End time events are realized now.

Recommended work: Do a word study of grace, mercy, love, faith, and good works.

The sermon might contrast human sin (v. 3) with God's bold initiative of salvation given in Christ while we were yet sinners. It should stress the superabundance of God's love and relate this to John 3:14-21. It should show that good works are the fruit, not the means, of salvation.

Theological Reflection

It is very appropriate during Lent that the superabundance of God's mercy should be the theme of all our readings for today, since the good news enables the sinner to confess, repent, and turn to God. Christ's coming as the light is judgment in itself.

Those who accept God's love are healed and saved. Those who reject it condemn themselves.

Children's Message

The children might sing "Jesus Loves Me." You might follow this with a talk about God's great love in Jesus for all the world, centering on John 3:16, which should be familiar to the children already. You might lead them in affirming this verse as a simple confession of our faith in God's love.

Hymns for Lent 4

Amazing Grace; Come, Thou Fount of Every Blessing; To God Be the Glory, Great Things He Hath Done.

Psalm 51:10–17 (C)   Hebrews 5:7–10 (C)
Psalm 51:11–16 (L)   Hebrews 5:7–9 (L) (RC)
Psalm 51:3–4, 12–15 (RC)   Hebrews 5:(1–4) 5–10 (E)
Psalm 51 or 51:11–16 (E)

                           John 12:20–33
Jeremiah 31:31–34

Meditation on the Texts

We join with the Greeks who wish to see Jesus. May we through faith have a new vision of the risen and glorified Jesus Christ. And may we, O God, as witnesses to him enable our hearers to see Jesus and thus come to faith. We thank you that Jesus, although he was a Son, learned obedience through what he suffered, and being made perfect he became the source of eternal salvation to all who obey him. For you, O God, designated him a high priest after the order of Melchizedek. We thank you for the promise of a new covenant with the houses of Israel and Judah, a promise we see fulfilled in Christ's death and resurrection. We pray that your law, the law of love, may be written upon our hearts. For you are our God, and we are your people. We look forward in hope to the day when no one needs to be taught the knowledge of you, O God, for all will know you. In Christ you have forgiven our iniquity and you remember our sin no more. We rejoice in the new life you have given us in your kingdom. Amen.

Commentary on the Texts

John 12:20–33 (C)

The whole section of which our pericope is a part continues through v. 36 and has the theme of life in death. Notice that the request of the Greeks (Gentiles) to see Jesus is a fulfillment of the universal triumph of Jesus which was just spoken by the Pharisees: "You see that you can do nothing; look, the world has gone after him" (v. 19). Immediately Greeks, representing "the world," ask to see Jesus! But John does not record that the Greeks actually come into Jesus' presence, which is in keeping with history, since Jesus' earthly ministry was directed exclusively to the Jewish people. But in the discourse that follows, the reader is enabled to "see Jesus," since it pictures him as Savior of the world in the triumph of life over death. Jesus glorifies the Father's name (character) by revealing God to be a God of suffering love, bringing life out of death.

The Greeks who came seeking Jesus were Gentile pilgrims, probably in the group known as God-fearers. They were not Greek-speaking Jews, however, or semiproselytes. Note how their desire to see Jesus puts them in sharp contrast with the Jewish leaders who have just spoken their despair over Jesus' success (v. 19). The fact that the first Gentiles have come to Jesus explains his exclamation that the hour has come (v. 23). The thrust of "to see" here may mean to visit with, to meet, or, as in John's thought, it may well mean "to believe in."

The hour refers to Jesus' self-disclosure which was determined by God. Jesus disclosed himself at the miracle of Cana and at various points during his ministry, but the final manifestation was at the cross (7:30; 8:20; 12:23, 27 [our text]; 13:1; 17:1).

Note that the Greeks' desire to see Jesus was presented to Jesus through Philip and Andrew, the only two of the Twelve who have Greek names. The Jews of Bethsaida were considered Galileans, although it was technically in the territory of Gaulanitis, which adjoined Galilee. Note that Philip and Andrew consult with each other before going to tell Jesus, since there was no precedent for Jesus' dealing with Gentiles.

John says that "Jesus answered them," but this does not require that the Greeks were among those to whom Jesus spoke. He may have spoken to Philip and Andrew and other disciples. The fact that the Greeks are not mentioned again points to their *not* being among those addressed here. Jesus' response is a comment on the whole event rather than a direct answer to either group, Philip and Andrew, or the Greeks. It is not yet time for the Gentile mission (Matt. 10:5–6), although its principle is being revealed at that moment. Remember that John is writing from the standpoint of the early church in which the Gentiles have indeed "seen Jesus" and found salvation through faith in him.

Jesus says the hour has come for the Son of man to be glorified, which is mentioned soon after the acclamation with palms (v. 13) and has a parallel in Luke 19:38, where the multitude shouts "Glory in the highest!" as Jesus enters Jerusalem amid the waving of palm branches. Reflect on the meaning of "glory" as used in scripture in its reference to the aspect of a person or God worthy of praise, honor, or respect. Glory is often represented by brightness or splendor. In John's Gospel, Jesus' glory is preexistent with God and is revealed in Jesus' works as full of grace and truth, which are signs inviting people to believe. But the cross is the culminating sign, the hour of Christ's glorification. And God glorifies Jesus in his resurrection and continues to do so through the work of the Holy Spirit. In the Hebrew Scriptures glory referred to salvation, and in the New Testament glory is revealed in the Messiah's work of deliverance.

Earlier, Jesus stated many times that his hour had not yet come. But now and in the next chapters we are told that Jesus' hour *has come*. While Jesus' life could not be taken away from him involuntarily, now Jesus is ready for the hour of the laying down of his life and the taking of it up again. Note in v. 27 that Jesus resists the temptation to ask God to save him from the hour. Instead, he rejoices at the opportunity for glorifying God which the hour will offer.

Jesus compares his death to the sowing of a grain of wheat, which, unless it falls into the earth and dies, cannot bear fruit. And Jesus warns against loving one's life and by so doing losing it. Instead, a person must hate his or her life in this world in order to keep it for eternal life. To hate one's life is a Semitic usage which likes vivid contrasts in order to express preferences. While the word for "life" here has sometimes been translated "soul," the Jewish thought about human beings did not have a dualism of soul and body. The Greek word used here may mean one's self as it refers to life here. Eternal life is the life which the believer receives from God.

In order to serve Jesus, one must follow him. The principle of sacrifice also holds for anyone who will be a follower of Jesus. Sacrifice explains Jesus' life. God will honor the person who imitates Christ by serving him.

In agony Jesus makes his final decision of obedience unto death in servanthood and sonship (vs. 27–33). This obedience is indeed the glorification of God. God answers in a voice from heaven: "I have glorified it, and I will glorify it again." This is judgment of this world, for Christ's death means the overthrow of Satan.

This passage is the closest Johannine equivalent to the Synoptic narratives of the agony in the Garden (see Mark 14:32–42 and parallels). In the Synoptics, Jesus first asks to be delivered from the necessity of dying but immediately submits his will to the will of his Father. The value of Jesus' sacrifice consists in the *readiness* with which he submitted to it. When Jesus prays that his Father glorify his name, this is Jesus' final answer from his crisis of spirit. Note well that it is a wholehearted acceptance of God's will. And the glorification of the Son is also the glorification of God.

While John does not say that Satan will be destroyed, he does say that Satan will no longer be the ruler of the world, except to the extent that human evil disposition allows it.

Then in v. 32 the paradox is put in a more positive form. Jesus tells the crowd that when he is lifted up from the earth he will draw all to himself. The crowd understands this to refer to his death, and rightly so. But the crowd does not understand that it also refers to his glorification. The death of Christ is part of the glorious realization of God's plan. It is possible that the writer who inserted v. 33 was thinking of crucifixion as not only a lifting up of the body of Jesus on the cross but also as a stretching out of the arms to draw all humans to himself. The death of Christ makes possible the exercise of Jesus' will of universal salvation.

Notice the paradoxes: Jesus' death judges the world, not him; it defeats Satan, not Jesus; and it draws all humans, not repels them, as an ordinary crucifixion would.

Recommended work: Do a word study of glorify. Compare this agony of Jesus over his death with that recorded in the Synoptics. Reflect on the power of the cross in attracting and transforming human lives through the centuries.

The sermon might develop the thrust of v. 32 in which Jesus declares that by his crucifixion he will draw all humanity to himself. It might move from the desire of the Greeks (Gentiles) to see Jesus to show how Jesus' death has drawn people from all parts of the world to see and believe in him. The sermon should lead the hearers to experience God's love in Christ more fully and so be drawn to Christ, to serve and follow him.

Jeremiah 31:31–34

The prophet uses the oldest expression for covenant making, namely, to "cut a covenant." He opposes what had come to be an increasingly limited concept of the Sinai covenant, declaring that God will make a new covenant which will be written on human hearts, in contrast to that written on the stone of the Ten Commandments. This brief oracle might be called Jeremiah's spiritual testament, since his whole message has been condensed into these few words of the new covenant. Note that in v. 31 we have the only instance in which "new covenant" is used in Hebrew Scripture. Only in the New Testament do we see how these words of Jeremiah are to be understood and fulfilled.

Scholars question whether the passage as we now have it is in the precise words that Jeremiah spoke or wrote. It is in the elevated language and style of the prose that is characteristic of much of the editorial and developmental material in this book. Note that the passage represents a concern to express the authoritative word of hope given through Jeremiah concerning the restoration of Israel and that this is set forth in carefully defined theological terms.

There is a question that is not spoken but that nevertheless underlies this section: If the sins of Israel in the past brought such fearful judgment upon the nation so that it came close to being totally annihilated, then what assurance is there that after a future restoration has taken place the same thing will not happen again? The answer is clear and simple: God will by the creative power of divine love write the covenant on the hearts of the people Israel, thus giving an inner power and motivation toward obedience. Although the word "spirit" is not used, it is implied as the motivating force to bring Israel to obedience to God.

Examine the primacy of the interior values such as obedience, love, and knowledge of God set forth in the passage. These make up the condition for a true practice of religion. Like Hosea, Jeremiah thinks of the covenant as basically a reality of love and mercy, symbolized by marriage, which calls for such an interior and sincere relationship.

Israel had broken the old covenant, so that it was no longer in force, as a marriage covenant might be broken (v. 32).

The newness of this covenant is found not in its essentials but in the realm of its realization and its means. The real newness lies in the new means to assure faithfulness to it. It will be thoroughly interiorized as the covenant enters the heart of every member of the community.

No longer will there be a need for teachers, prophets, and priests to teach the knowledge of God, because all will know God in every action and situation. People of all ages will enter this covenant. And God will forgive the people's iniquity and remember their sin no more.

This utopian society that Jeremiah describes does not and cannot exist. He uses motifs and sayings from the past to construct a vision of the future. God will act in the restoring of Israel as a nation to create a kind of society that previous generations failed to achieve, thus giving Israel a hope for an idyll of the future.

140

Recommended work: Do a word study of covenant, and do an overview of Israel's past leading up to this point in its history. Read commentary on this passage in Robert P. Carroll, *Jeremiah, A Commentary,* Old Testament Library (Philadelphia: Westminster Press, 1985).

The sermon might follow the images and the moves of the passage, leading up to the image of the utopian society in which everyone will have a personal knowledge of God and God's forgiveness will be complete. The preacher is cautioned not to read into this text a prediction of the new covenant in Christ's blood but must see it in its context. However, the preacher should interpret this text in the light of the new covenant written on the hearts of humans by the Spirit described in the New Testament. The preacher may want to relate the John and Hebrew texts to this one in the sermon.

Hebrews 5:7–10 (C)

Hebrews 5:7–9 (L) (RC)

Hebrews 5:(1–4) 5–10 (E)

Our pericope is the last part of the section from 4:14 to 5:10 whose theme is Jesus, the compassionate high priest. Note that these verses recall 2:16–3:1 and prepare for the development of Jesus' priesthood in the passages that follow.

Note that v. 5 has a quotation from Psalm 2:7. The "order of Melchizedek" (v. 6) refers to the rank that he held (Ps. 110:4). Melchizedek was a mysterious priest/king who was greater than either Abraham or his descendant, Levi. But his ancestors' birth and death are not recorded in scripture.

In vs. 7–8 we have a description of Jesus' agonizing prayer in Gethsemane (Mark 14:32–42). Compare this with the John reading for today. These verses show us that Jesus is one who can sympathize with sinners because he knew temptation as they do. He shared in our flesh and blood. He knew the trials of human beings, including their fear of death. But after his resurrection, Christ no longer knows weakness. But because he has experienced it, he can sympathize with those who do. The days of his flesh refers to his mortal life on earth.

The author says that Jesus was heard for his "godly fear." The author takes Jesus' deliverance from death as a reference to his resurrection. Recall that Jesus prayed in the Garden of Gethsemane that God might keep him from dying, rather than that he be rescued from death once he had undergone it. Here the author uses "save him from death" in the double sense which is characteristic of John. It is possible that vs. 5–10 were once a hymn to "Jesus the High Priest" which the author used.

In v. 8 we see that the author considers Jesus' Sonship in two ways. He became Son when exalted in the resurrection and ascension. But he was always Son, because he existed with the Father even before being born on earth. The resurrection/exaltation gave Jesus' human nature full participation in his divine nature, according to later theology. The learning through suffering idea is common in Greek literature. Note that here and in Romans 5:19 and Philippians 2:8 are the only New Testament passages where the obedience of Christ in his passion is mentioned explicitly.

Jesus' being perfected means that through obedience he was brought to the full moral perfection of his humanity. Jesus' obedience leads to his priestly consecration. This, in turn, qualifies him to save those who are obedient to him. Jesus brings eternal salvation to his followers because it is based on his eternal priesthood. This salvation is permanent, in contrast to the transitory realities of earth.

Recommended work: Do a word study of high priest, perfect, and obedience.

The sermon might center on Jesus' saving work as high priest and his identification with humans in all their temptations and sufferings. The sermon should point to the cross as the supreme example of Jesus' obedience and suffering by which he became the source of eternal salvation to all who obey him.

God's gracious gift of salvation is a theme common to all three passages. The Jeremiah text points to the new covenant which God will make and put in human hearts. The John passage is a discourse about Jesus' final hour when he will be lifted up on the cross and so will draw all humans to himself. The Hebrews text points to Jesus as the high priest made perfect through suffering who became the source of eternal salvation.

Children's Message

The talk might be based on the Jeremiah passage. You might speak of the different kinds of things we can write on: paper, chalkboard, walls, in the sand, and so forth. But God has promised to write on our hearts the law of love. And in Christ, God has written on our hearts knowledge of God and the law of love.

Hymns for Lent 5

Beneath the Cross of Jesus; Jesus Shall Reign Where'er the Sun; The Head That Once Was Crowned with Thorns.

Lent 6

Palm Sunday/Passion Sunday

Psalm 118:19–29 (C)	Philippians 2:5–11 (C)
Psalm 22:8–9, 17–20, 23–24 (RC)	Philippians 2:6–11 (RC)
Psalm 22:1–21 or 1–11 (E)	
	Mark 11:1–11 (C)
Isaiah 50:4–9a (C)	Mark 11:1–10 (L)
Isaiah 50:4–7 (RC)	Mark 11:1–11a (E)
Isaiah 45:21–25 or 52:13–53:12 (E)	Matthew 26:14–27, 66 (RC)

Meditation on the Texts

We join with those who greeted Jesus as he entered Jerusalem in shouting, "Hosanna! Blessed is he who comes in the name of the Lord!" Save us, O God, from our bondage to self, to pride, greed, and sloth. Set us free to live in joyful obedience to the living Christ. May we do nothing from selfishness or conceit, but in humility count others better than ourselves. Help us to look not only to our own interests but also to the interests of others. Enable us to have the mind of Christ among us. We remember how he did not count equality with you, O God, a thing to be grasped but emptied himself and took the form of a servant, being born in the likeness of human beings. We remember how he humbled himself and became obedient even to death on a cross. But you, O God, have highly exalted him and given him a name which is above every name. We join in confessing that Jesus Christ is Lord, to your glory, O God. We thank you for the Servant who was reviled and persecuted but was not confounded. Rather, he set his face like a flint and trusted in you to vindicate him. For you helped the Servant and you help us. Who will declare us guilty, since Christ died to make us righteous by faith? Amen.

Commentary on the Texts

Mark 11:1–11 (C)

Mark 11:1–10 (L)

Mark 11:1–11a (E)

Our pericope is the account of Palm Sunday and Jesus' entrance into Jerusalem. It is a part of the larger section of chapters 11–15, which is a narrative of the last week of Jesus' earthly life. In reading our pericope, we should first note carefully the expectations of both the Hebrew Scriptures and later Jewish thought which those who first read this account would have had. Second, we should, like those first readers, *not* hold in our mind impressions gained from the accounts of the incident in other Gospels. The account in Mark's Gospel has been leading up to Jesus' arrival at Jerusalem. The first readers or hearers of this Gospel would have looked upon Jerusalem as the holy city of God. And they are bound to have anticipated Jesus' eventual entry into it with some excitement, for they would have recalled that this was the city that slew Jesus. The Mount of Olives was associated with the coming of the Messiah, according to the Jewish historian Josephus. And they would have recalled Zechariah 9:9 and 14:4 as they heard this story. Mark says Jesus sent the disciples to get a colt on which no one has ever sat, corresponding to the Zechariah 9:9 description of the colt which is new, meaning unused.

So in reading this account we must be conscious that Jesus' entry was portrayed in full conformity with the prophecy of Hebrew Scripture and with Jewish expectations. There is a supernatural power and mission suggested here by the miraculous way in which the necessary ass's colt was waiting and Jesus knew where to send the disciples to find it.

The entry into Jerusalem has traditionally been understood as a spectacular festival, with great crowds waving palm branches and shouting "Hosanna!" attracting attention from all Jerusalem. But a rethinking of the text by scholars reveals a different kind of event. While it seems clear that Jesus intended to fulfill the prophecy of Zechariah 9:9, he did it in a way that veiled the assertion of his Messiahship so that it was *not* recognized at the time, although it would be afterward by his disciples. Jesus' riding on the unused colt was a sign of the kind of Messiah he was. The Zechariah passage tells of a king who would speak peace to the nations, not a nationalistic Messiah who would come on a horse as a military leader. Notice that Jesus' royal entry was a piece with the rest of his ministry rather than a sudden break with the messianic hiddenness which characterized Jesus' role to this point. His majesty is hidden under an outward appearance that was far from kingly. Apparently the acclamations and attentions of his followers were so insignificant that the Roman authorities did *not* even notice them. Thus the messianic hiddenness which plays such an important role in Mark's Gospel is maintained. Some commentators say that the demonstration was likely quite small: the Greek word for "many" in v. 8 does not need to imply a very large number. And v. 10, which has a definite messianic flavor, may have been either an expression of the feelings aroused by Psalm 118 and the entry to Jerusalem and the Passover, or it may be a reflection of the later Christian understanding of the entry which Mark has allowed to creep in at this point.

One argument for the entry's being a rather unspectacular event is that the Roman and Jewish authorities did not take any action. The numbers of the followers were small and their words were simply quotations from the current liturgy, and the crowd did not explicitly claim messiahship for Jesus.

According to Mark's account, the entry is closely associated with the Passover, which follows five days later, but this association is based entirely on Mark's artificial chronological scheme. A number of scholars discount the association of the entry with Passover. Rather, they see it as associated with the Feast of Dedication commemorating the redeeming of the temple by Judas Maccabeus in 165 B.C. Now the ceremonies of this feast were modeled on those of the Feast of Tabernacles and so both included the carrying of green branches by the people. The Hallel found in Psalms 113–118 was recited. At various points in the service the branches were waved, and then after the sacrifice there was a procession in which the branches were carried and the "Hosanna" from Psalm 118:25 was intoned. The branches were even called "Hosannas" from the Hebrew word *hoshianna* or *hosanna*, meaning "Save us" or "Save now." Since the branches were difficult to buy in the city, the pilgrims customarily went out into the country to gather them as they drew near to Jerusalem. According to this position, we should assume that as Jesus and his followers approached Jerusalem on their way to the Feast of Dedication the followers responded in an outburst of enthusiasm. The enthusiasm was not over Jesus being the messiah but was expressed in words and actions appropriate to the coming feast! The sight of the city and Jesus' earlier announcements about the nearness of the kingdom would have provoked the enthusiasm Mark records. Thus Jesus' action in riding into Jerusalem was not an obvious and unambiguous assertion of his Messiahship. Neither the crowd nor his disciples were aware of its messianic meaning.

If we take this evidence of more recent scholarship seriously, then we must revise our preaching and celebration of the triumphal entry to conform more realistically to what actually happened rather than reading back into it our faith and enthusiasm in Jesus as the Messiah.

The shout in vs. 9 and 10 of "Hosanna" is from an Aramaic word meaning "Save now." The meaning of "Hosanna in the highest!" is probably "Save now, (O God that dwells) in the highest."

According to Mark, Jesus enters into Jerusalem, goes to the temple and looks things over. But since it is then late in the afternoon he goes back to Bethany with the Twelve for the night. Matthew and Luke do not actually say that the cleansing of the temple took place immediately after Jesus entered Jerusalem, but nothing is mentioned of a night between. Mark's account here is preferred.

Recommended work: Compare the other accounts of the entry into Jerusalem and note similarities and differences. Reflect on the "messianic secret" of Mark and how the entry continues this downplaying of the messianic role.

The sermon might follow the moves of the text, showing Jesus entering Jerusalem as one coming in peace with his Messiahship still hidden. The sermon might point out how we, on this side of the cross, see the entry in a different way than those who spread palm branches and shouted, for we see Jesus as the Messiah, the Prince of Peace, who enters on a colt to inaugurate his kingdom by dying on the cross. This is in contrast to worldly kings who rode horses to establish earthly kingdoms by military might.

Matthew 26:14–27, 66 (RC)

Our pericope overlaps several sections: vs. 14–16 describing Judas' receiving money from the chief priests; vs. 17–19, in which the disciples are sent to prepare the Passover; vs. 20–25, in which Jesus predicts his betrayal by Judas; and vs. 26–29, in which Jesus interprets his death to his disciples.

The value of the thirty pieces of silver is uncertain. Matthew refers to silver shekels. According to one calculation at four denarii to the shekel, the total would amount to 120 denarii, or 120 days' wages for a laborer.

The Last Supper is described in vs. 17–19. Compare this account with that in Mark 14:12–16 and Luke 22:7–13. According to Luke, Jesus directed the disciples to follow a man carrying a water jar and to enter the house he enters. The plans for the Last Supper rest on some prearrangement. Since a man carrying a water jar would be doing woman's work and thus would stand out as unusual, the procedure would be a secret plan to hide the intended place of the meal from Jesus' enemies.

The first day of Unleavened Bread would be the fifteenth of Nisan, the day following Passover. Matthew, however, obviously means the day *before* the Passover. There is some evidence that this could be referred to as the first day of Unleavened Bread. Recall that the Passover could be eaten only in Jerusalem.

At the Passover meal all dipped their hands into a dish. But at other meals they dipped bread into the dish. Although Judas was divinely predestined to betray Jesus (vs. 21ff.), this does not abolish human responsibility. Judas will be judged for what he has done, and his punishment will be so dreadful that it would have been better if he had never existed.

Jesus' actions and words in vs. 26–27 are the normal way of saying grace among the Jews. Jesus blessed God, not the bread. He gave thanks to God.

Jesus then compares the bread which he has broken to his body which will soon be broken when he is put to death. By commanding the disciples to eat the bread (only Matthew includes the actual word "eat") he is offering them a part in the situation which his death will bring about, namely, a place in the kingdom.

Jesus performs the same action with the cup. He commands the disciples to drink it. Notice that Matthew has changed Mark's "and they all drank of it" to a command: "Drink of it, all of you." Matthew interprets the cup as his blood of the covenant (Ex. 24:8; Jer. 31:31; Zech. 9:11). The blood of the covenant here recalls both the covenant that God gave after the exodus from Egypt and the new covenant of the last days which Jeremiah foretold. "Which is poured out" means "about to be poured out," since a prophetic present tense is used. "For many" was a Hebrew way of saying "for everyone." Jesus is dying for the world, so the "many" does not refer to some only but not others.

Recommended work: Compare and contrast this account of the Last Supper with other accounts. Do a word study of Passover and covenant.

The sermon might develop the Last Supper events, focusing on Jesus' giving the bread and the cup, saying "Take, eat; this is my body" and "Drink of it, all of you." This should be related to v. 27, in which Jesus says the cup is the blood of the covenant poured out for many for the forgiveness of sins. Thus the sermon might deal with the meaning of the Last Supper for believers.

Isaiah 50:4–9a (C)

Isaiah 50:4–7 (RC)

Our pericope is part of the third Servant song, which extends from v. 4 to v. 11. While scholars hold differing views about the identity of the Servant here and in the other songs, I take it as referring to the nation, regarded sometimes as an individual and sometimes as a community, and sometimes as both. We do this with Uncle Sam as a symbol of our country. These verses represent the confession of confidence spoken by a mediator of the word. We cannot prove that the Servant is Second Isaiah, but we can see that the prophet regarded the Servant's task, his sufferings, and his relationship to God as those of a prophet.

The Servant is taught by God and conscientiously brings God's comfort to his fellow Israelites (he that is weary). But they treat him despicably, as noted here and in 52:13–53:12. In these verses the prophet may be identifying himself with the Servant.

Note in vs. 7–9 that law court terminology is used as the Servant expresses his confidence that God will vindicate him.

It is the complete acceptance of the blows and shameful treatment which enable the Servant to make his face hard as flint (v. 7).

The question of whether or not there is the slightest possibility of any justification or rehabilitation of the Servant is left open in vs. 4–9. Note that v. 9b expresses the Servant's conviction that his opponents, who can now mock and smite him, will all perish. But this does not answer the question and thus points forward to the final Servant song.

Recommended work: Compare this song with the other Servant songs. Reflect on ways Jesus suffered as did the Servant and was helped and vindicated by God.

The sermon should develop the images and moves of the text and then relate them to Jesus as he spoke for God, suffered courageously, setting his face like a flint, and was vindicated by God by the resurrection. The meaning of this for believers and the church should be spelled out.

Isaiah 45:21–25 or 52:13–53:12 (E)

The Isaiah 45 pericope should begin with v. 20, and the theme of vs. 20–25 is a trial speech in which God confronts the nations or gods of the nations. The nations' gods are powerless. In vs. 20–21a there is a challenge to the nations and their gods to appear in court. Here the people addressed are "the survivors of the nations," and the word "survivor" in Hebrew always presupposes a battle, and a lost battle at that. The prophet is likely thinking of the Babylonians, especially of those who had escaped when the city itself fell. But they stand for the survivors of the nations generally.

Note in v. 22 that the victor does not glory in his triumph. There is no "I told you so" attitude here. Rather, there is an invitation to the survivors to participate in salvation! This invitation is a sign that God's radically new kind of intervention by means of Cyrus brings about a new way of God's working in history. Since God is the creator of the whole world, God cannot have a purpose of destroying the nations. God's victory in the lawsuit against the gods of the nations involves something entirely new. Instead of overthrowing and destroying the enemy, there is now convincing.

God's oath in vs. 23–25 means that the goal to which God's dealings with humanity are directed is free confession which arises from the conviction on the part of those who have come to realize that the only true God is the God of Israel.

Bowing the knee to God and confessing God to be the one God demands the free assent of each individual to God's claims (v. 23). The confession in v. 23b brings the distant and near together. Those who once were God's enemies and fought against God arrive on the scene and along with Israel participate in God's salvation (v. 25).

Notice that this text is taken up in Romans 14:11 and Philippians 2:10–11 (one of our pericopes for today). Second Isaiah believed that in his day a final break had been made between the people of God and any form of an existence as a political entity. Now all human beings are invited to partake in the divine salvation, and membership in the people of God is based on the free confession of those who have come to believe that God alone is God. These two factors which are crucial for the church's understanding of itself are already present in Second Isaiah.

Recommended work: Study the whole section of vs. 14–25 dealing with the conversion of the nations. Compare this to the Romans and Philippians passages listed above.

The sermon might develop the images of God's invitation to all humanity to confess faith and become members of the people of God. This passage should be related to the Christian understanding of confessing faith in God through Christ and becoming a part of the people of God by baptism. God's love invites even God's enemies to salvation.

Philippians 2:5–11 (C)

Philippians 2:6–11 (RC)

The theme of vs. 1–18 is humility and the example of Christ. Note that the ''if'' in v. 1 is rhetorical. There is indeed the encouragement mentioned. Now that the Philippians have Christ's encouragement and they are moved by God's love for them, they are to complete Paul's joy. There is not a sharp break in Paul's thought from the preceding verses. ''So'' of v. 1 looks back to what has been said and builds upon it. Note in 1:27 the mentioning of one spirit and one mind which is now given more increased attention by Paul as he describes a believing community that is in Christ Jesus (2:1–5). Further evidence that vs. 1–11 are continuous with what has gone before is found in the fact that Paul is basing his exhortation here on the two considerations that have dominated this letter thus far: the Christian experiences they all have shared and the relationship of the church to Paul.

In v. 3 there is an indication that Paul fears that the Philippians are somewhat divided by petty jealousies. One is mentioned in 4:2: ''I entreat Euodia and I entreat Syntyche to agree in the Lord.''

With this background to our pericope we can better understand why Paul urges the Philippians to: ''Have this mind among yourselves, which is yours in Christ Jesus'' (v. 5). Having the same mind does not mean agreeing on everything; rather, it means having a common attitude or orientation. Note carefully that the Greek word translated ''mind'' and used twice in v. 2 and once in v. 5 is very important in this letter. It is translated ''feel'' in 1:7, and ''to agree'' in 4:2 (see also 3:15, 19). We don't know what caused the dissension in the church, but it may have been centered in Euodia and Syntyche, or it could have been over Judaizers, or it could have been related to Paul himself.

The thrust of v. 5 is that the Philippian Christians are to act in the light of what and how they think about Christ. Christ is the norm of the mind-set they are to have. This is spelled out in vs. 6–11, which is an early Christian hymn, and which falls into verse patterns. Paul quoted a hymn that is older than the letter.

The first half of the hymn (vs. 6–8) begins with God and descends to the low point of death. Notice that each of the three action verbs focuses on a moment in this downward movement of Christ's obedience. It begins with equality with God, meaning having divine prerogatives, being God's equal. ''Emptied'' (v. 7) is crucial and here means to take the status of a slave. The word should be understood metaphorically. The phrase translated ''being born'' is a free translation of a verb that means ''come to pass'' or ''happen.'' Jesus shared the likeness of humans but did not become just another human being. Jesus, who was equal with God, now became equal with humanity.

He humbled himself (v. 8) and was obedient even unto death on a cross.

The second half (vs. 9–11) begins at the low point of humiliation and then celebrates, in one dramatic act of God, Jesus' exaltation which includes the resurrection and the ascension.

Recommended work: Do a word study of mind, form, likeness, emptied, and exalted. The sermon might follow the downward movement of the text to Christ's death on the cross, and then celebration of his exaltation. The implications of this for Christian living should then be spelled out.

Theological Reflection

Note the themes of obedience to God's will and humility in the Philippians, Mark, and Matthew readings. Isaiah 50:4–9 describe the Servant who brings God's comfort but is treated despicably. Isaiah 45 stresses the uniqueness of Israel's God in contrast to the nations' gods.

Children's Message

The talk with the children might be about Jesus' entry into Jerusalem told from the point of view of a child who was in the crowd and later came to faith in the risen Christ.

Hymns for Lent 6

When I Survey the Wondrous Cross; All Glory, Laud, and Honor; Hosanna, Loud Hosanna.

Easter Day

Psalm 118:14–24 (C)
Psalm 118:1–2, 15–24 (L)
Psalm 118:1–2, 16–17, 22–23 (RC)
Psalm 118:14–29 or 118:14–17, 22–24 (E)

Isaiah 25:6–9 (C)
Acts 10:34–43
or Isaiah 25:6–9 (E)

1 Corinthians 15:1–11 (C)
1 Corinthians 15:19–28 (L)
Colossians 3:1–4 (RC)
Colossians 3:1–4
or Acts 10:34–43 (E)

John 20:1–18
or Mark 16:1–8 (C)
John 20:1–9 (RC)
Mark 16:1–8 (E)

Meditation on the Texts

Gracious God who gave your Son Jesus Christ to die for the sins of the world, we thank you for raising him from the dead. With Mary Magdalene may we witness to the resurrection by word and deed, ''I have seen the Lord!'' When the living Christ calls us by name, may we recognize him and obey his commands. We thank you that you have swallowed up death forever in Christ's death. We look forward to the day when you, O God, will wipe away tears from all faces and take away the reproach of your people from all the earth. Let us be glad and rejoice in your salvation. May we from this time forward seek the things that are above where Christ is, seated at your right hand. For we have died to sin, and our life is hid with Christ, in you, O God. Amen.

Commentary on the Texts

John 20:1–18 or Mark 16:1–8 (C)

John 20:1–9 (RC)

The Markan passage will be dealt with immediately after this commentary. John's account of the empty tomb and the appearance of the risen Christ to the disciples is similar in many ways to the tradition given by Luke, but there are emphases and details that are distinctive to John. For example, while each of the Synoptic Gospels tells of several women coming to the tomb in order to complete the preparation of Jesus' body for burial, here only Mary Magdalene is mentioned. It appears that her reason for visiting the tomb is to express devotion to her buried Lord.

By way of background it should be pointed out that the New Testament reveals that Christian faith in Jesus' victory over death has been expressed in various ways. For example, Hebrews 9 tells how Jesus as a high priest entered the heavenly holy of holies with his own blood offered in sacrifice, which seems to indicate that Jesus progressed from crucifixion to ascension without the resurrection. But resurrection is the usual way in which Jesus' victory over death is expressed. Note carefully that the resurrection is *never pictured* in the New Testament. There are two kinds of material that are most pertinent to the resurrection: (1) the short sayings, often confessional in nature, which arise out of the preaching, teaching, and worship of the early church and (2) the narratives in the Gospels and Acts which tell of the finding of the empty tomb and the appearances of the risen Jesus. Scholars generally agree that the *formulae* provide us with information about the resurrection that is earlier than the narratives. Note that the formulae do not mention the empty tomb and make no attempt to localize the appearances of the risen Christ. This appears only in the narratives, which are later material.

The preacher must also serve as apologist of the resurrection. Our task is exegesis and proclamation of the resurrection, not explanation. Objections to the possibility of resurrection have come from philosophy and science. Their greatest force has been against a crassly *physical* understanding of the resurrection which views it as a *resuscitation.* But they are less convincing in dealing with arguments such as those of Paul, who describes the resurrection body as a radically different kind of body from the physical body but nevertheless a body. As we read the New Testament accounts of the resurrection we find that the evangelists themselves declare that Jesus' body *did not* remain in the tomb but was raised to glory. We cannot prove, however, that the Christian understanding of Jesus' resurrection corresponded to what really happened. This is a question that only faith can answer.

When we compare this text to Luke 24:1–11, we note that it seems to correct the Lukan version about the disciples' reaction to the report of the empty tomb. In John we find that Peter and the beloved disciple hasten to confirm the testimony. Although they do not see Jesus, they are convinced. Note how John in a subtle fashion refers to the primary experience by Peter of the resurrection. The beloved disciple, who actually is the first to arrive at the tomb, becomes *the* representative of all believers. Although Peter is the first to see, the beloved disciple is the first to *see and believe!*

Compare this seeing and believing with Jesus' reply to Thomas in v. 29: "Blessed are those who have not seen and yet believe." But the disciples did not yet know the scriptures that Jesus must rise from the dead. The resurrection was willed by God, and the scripture is a guide to God's plan. Note that v. 10 tells us nothing of the attitude of Peter or the beloved disciple and serves to get the disciples off the scene and prepare the way for Mary Magdalene.

The focus of the narrative shifts back to Mary in v. 11, who is now standing at the tomb and sees two angels. (Note that vs. 2–10 almost seem to be an interruption to the story of Mary.) Mark and Matthew indicate that there was only one angel. The angels sit where Jesus' body had lain, one at the head and one at the foot. Mary wept because she thought someone had stolen Jesus' body. She observed the two angels, but they do not inspire in Mary the fear, amazement, and prostration which the Synoptic accounts tell of the women at the tomb.

Jesus appears to Mary, but she cannot grasp him, for the vision, though real, is not yet the fully revealed truth of the resurrection. But she goes to report to the disciples, "I have seen the Lord." Jesus says here, literally, "Stop touching me." Jesus is asking her not to cling to him. When Mary sees Jesus she thinks he has returned, as he had promised, and that he will stay with her and the other disciples and resume their former relationships. She tries to hold on to her source of joy. But she mistakes an appearance of the risen Jesus for his permanent residence with his disciples which will come only with the gift of the Spirit. And the Spirit can come only *after* he has ascended to God. Mary is commanded to go and prepare the disciples for that coming of Jesus when the Spirit will be given.

A basic element in the New Testament understanding of resurrection is that the risen Jesus is *not* restored to the normal life he had before his death. Rather, he now possesses eternal life and is in God's presence. Many of the New Testament references acknowledge the identity of the resurrection and the ascension, since from the moment that God raises Jesus up he is in heaven or with God. His appearances are made from heaven. The word "ascension" is used to describe exaltation and glorification by using spatial language.

Recommended work: Compare this narrative of the resurrection with those of the Synoptics and note similarities and differences. Read the commentary by Raymond Brown on the meaning of the arrangement of the grave clothes (*The Gospel According to John I–XII,* pp. 986–987). Do a word study of resurrection, ascension, and exaltation.

The sermon might follow the narrative of the text, with Mary coming to the tomb early while it was still dark to express her devotion to her buried Lord and ending with her witness to the disciples, "I have seen the Lord." The sermon should have as its goal to move the hearers from disbelief to belief in the risen and living Christ. It should deal with the leap of faith which is required and with the empty tomb, the grave clothes, witness of the disciples, and scripture. The sermon might tell of contemporary persons whose lives have been transformed by the power of the risen, living Christ.

Mark 16:1–8 (E) and alternate for (C)

The Sabbath had ended at sundown on Saturday. The women came to the tomb to complete the rites of burial. There are differences regarding the stone that sealed the tomb. Mark refers to it as a round stone, disk-shaped, which would be rolled edgeways in a gutter close to the opening of the tomb. But Matthew describes it as a large stone which an angel rolled back and sat upon. There were a variety of types of tomb arrangements, but the one described here seems to have been a main chamber with niches around the sides to receive bodies. The young man's clothing of a white robe indicates that he is a heavenly messenger. Our modern minds must adjust to the thought form of the ancient world in which the early church believed in the objective reality of angels, just as it believed in the reality of demons. Mark here describes the annunciation of the resurrection of Jesus to the women by the angel's message (v. 6). The angel uses human speech, and his words reflect the vocabulary of Mark and correspond to the usage of Paul and the early church.

The angel directs them to go tell Jesus' disciples that he is going before them to Galilee and there they will see him, as he promised. According to Mark, Galilee had for Jesus and his earliest followers a special status as the supreme holy place, while Jerusalem was the source of opposition and unbelief. Therefore the disciples expected the return of Jesus to take place in Galilee. There they expected to behold him in all the splendor of his returned appearance.

Many scholars think v. 8 ended Mark's Gospel and the remaining verses were added later by an editor. The reference to the disciples being afraid seems to mean overwhelming awe which is the pervasive consequence of amazement (v. 5) and of their trembling and astonishment. This fear resulted in their flight and silence (v. 8).

Recommended work: Compare this account with the other resurrection narratives. Read the accounts of Jesus' appearances in Galilee.

The sermon might follow the movement of the text from amazement to fear and trembling as a result of the news of Jesus' resurrection. The goal of the sermon should be to bear witness to the risen Christ so that hearers may come to a personal faith in the living Christ and follow him.

Isaiah 25:6–9 (C)

Acts 10:34–43 or Isaiah 25:6–9 (E)

Since the Isaiah passage is an alternate for (E), we will deal only with the Isaiah reading here.

Our pericope follows a psalm of thanksgiving in vs. 1–5. Many scholars think our reading ends at 10a rather than with v. 9. The theme of vs. 6–8 is the feast for the nations, followed by Israel's song of thanksgiving in vs. 9–10a. The same author who wrote 24:21–23 seems to be responsible for this description of salvation. The nations are drawn into salvation. This is a passage dealing with End time events. It begins with a reference to "this mountain," meaning Zion. The nations of the world will be welcomed to Zion. There the Lord will make a feast, which was a part of the messianic expectation. The very best food is set before the nations, including fat delicacies flavored with the marrow, old wine fermented well and still on its lees, though strained before being poured. Reflect on how this table fellowship brings the nations into fellowship with God.

In the Hebrew Scriptures the image of the pilgrimage of the nations to Zion has the same position as the idea of mission in the New Testament. The New Testament records the sending out of messengers to tell the good news of the concealed revelation of God in the crucified and risen Christ. In both the Hebrew Scriptures and Judaism the idea of the salvation of the nations is a marginal one. But both the Hebrew Scriptures and the New

Testament look forward to the acceptance of all nations into fellowship with God. Otherwise the honor of God would not be maintained. Nor could peace among the conflicting nations be conceived of otherwise.

For the nations, this will bring an end to their suffering and mourning. They mourn the dead who have fallen in the great battles of history. God will take away the veil of covering with which they have covered their faces as mourners.

The image of death being swallowed up is drawn from Canaanite mythology. God will destroy death and take away the cares of all who gather in Jerusalem. God will bring in an era of peace. Until this future time of peace arrives, however, Israel lives as the people of the God who created heaven and earth and guides stars and the destinies of the nations, but lives also as nation among nations, often as an outcast nation subject to the Gentiles. The prophet announces hope based on God's spoken message.

Then in vs. 9–10a there is a song of thanksgiving. Its main theme is that the hope that the prophet has put in God has not been disappointed. The clear intention of this song is to counter any doubts aroused by the contrast between the present situation of Israel and the extraordinary changes anticipated. On that future day the people of Jerusalem and Jews from the whole world will gather to Zion for the enthronement of their God. They will cry out again and again that their God in whom they had hoped is now in their midst. Therefore they call on each other to rejoice because God's hand now rests on Zion, taking possession of it and guiding and guarding it.

Recommended work: Read chapter 25 in its entirety and background material on this era of Israel's history in a Bible dictionary.

The sermon might deal with the image of all the nations gathering to Zion where God will give a great feast and end sorrow and suffering. It might show how Jesus inaugurated this new age which is yet to be consummated in the future at the End time. The sermon might deal with Israel's hope for salvation which we see fulfilled in Jesus Christ. When he returns in power and glory we can say, "We have waited for him; let us be glad and rejoice in his salvation" (v. 9). Meanwhile we live "between the times" of Christ's coming and his coming again.

1 Corinthians 15:1–11 (C)

Our pericope is a restatement of Paul's gospel against the background of the reports that some Corinthians were denying the resurrection. The death, burial, and resurrection of Jesus are fundamental doctrines of the tradition which Paul preached in the churches he founded and are foundation stones of the Christian faith. Paul says that Christ died for our sins according to the scriptures, referring to Isaiah 53 and the Suffering Servant of the Lord. As for the resurrection, the apostles cited passages such as Psalm 16:8–11. Paul may also have thought of Jonah 2 and Hosea 6:2.

Then in vs. 5–11 Paul appeals to those who were witnesses to the risen Christ, such as Cephas (Peter), the Twelve, five hundred, James, and the apostles. Then he appeared to me, says Paul, as to one "untimely born." Notice that Paul omits the appearances to the women who were first at the tomb and mentions only those whom Jewish law would accept as responsible witnesses, which excluded women. Note that Peter and the Twelve rank first as the most responsible witnesses. There is some question about the reference to the apostles, some scholars saying it means the Twelve and others saying it includes a larger distinct group of authorized witnesses to the resurrection.

The literal meaning of the Greek for "one untimely born" is "an aborted fetus." When applied to an adult, the phrase means an object of disgust and horror. The phrase might be translated "as to one hurried into the world before his time." It may be that Paul took this phrase from the lips of his adversaries and that it suggests an unformed, undeveloped, repulsive, and possibly lifeless fetus, and might refer to Paul's supposed deficiencies as a Christian and apostle, and also might refer to his physical appearance.

Paul gives all the credit of his life and ministry to God, saying that it is by the grace of God that he is what he is. He says he worked harder than any of the others, but again it was the grace of God with him which enabled him to so work.

Recommended work: Reflect on Hebrew Scripture references to Jesus' death, burial, and resurrection.

The sermon should bring to bear the witnesses not only of those whom Paul mentions but also of the women mentioned in the Gospels who witnessed the resurrection, especially Mary Magdalene, who was first to bear witness. The sermon should deal with the evidence of scripture and the witness of the Spirit of the living Christ in our lives which affirms that the resurrection is true as it seeks to lead hearers to faith in the living Christ.

1 Corinthians 15:19–28 (L)

Our pericope is part of the larger section of vs. 12–34, which set forth the significance of the resurrection. Paul argues that if Christ has not risen, then the apostolic preaching is a waste of time and all Christian faith is fruitless.

The meaning of v. 19 is somewhat difficult to discover. It is difficult both to translate and to interpret, and several alternatives have been proposed. Perhaps the best choice is to take it just as Paul writes, meaning that if Christ was not raised, then Christians would be without any prospect that Christ's life would be manifested in them. They would be seeking only a figment of their imagination and in fact embracing death.

The "but" of v. 20 is a hinge on which the thought turns. What goes before reminds readers of what life without Christ would be. Now Paul declares that Christ has indeed been raised from the dead. There is no Christian affirmation without this basic declaration of the resurrection of Christ.

Paul uses two images from the Hebrew Scriptures in elaborating on the consequences of Christ's resurrection: (1) The resurrection can be pictured as the firstfruits, like the first sheaf of the harvest brought to the temple on the first day following the Passover celebration. The one sheaf symbolized the whole harvest which was given by God and now consecrated to God. Christ's resurrection symbolizes the resurrection of all who belong to him. (2) The motif of Adam as a "type" of Christ is mentioned next. Those who are in Christ will share his victory over death, even as those who are only in Adam are destined to die as a consequence of sin.

Note that vs. 24–28 have been called a "little apocalypse" and should be read alongside 1 Thessalonians 5:1–11, since both stress the already fulfilled aspects of God's purpose in Christ as well as those yet to be fulfilled. We should not separate this passage from others that emphasize the same idea. Consider how Paul assumes that his world lies under the dominion of angelic or demonic rulers, probably as a result of Adam's sin or of humanity's sin. But Christ's rule will defeat these powers which are already doomed. He will vanquish death, personified by Satan.

Then in v. 27 Paul uses the language of Psalm 8:6 to set forth the thought of the final subordination of all things to God. Paul does not qualify the divinity of Christ. It seems that Paul's thought here is that Christ as the representative of redeemed humanity is the Son of man who acknowledges the sole sovereignty of God. It was the denial of this supremacy of God the Creator which constituted Adam's fall into sin.

Recommended work: Read the entire chapter and reflect on how our pericope carries forth Paul's argument for the resurrection and its significance.

The sermon might follow the moves and images of the text, leading from rejecting the denial of the resurrection to the affirmation of the coming End time when God may be everything to everyone.

Colossians 3:1–4 (RC)

Colossians 3:1–4 or Acts 10:34–43 (E)

Our pericope is part of the section of Colossians 3:1–17, which deals with the true Christian life. Note the strong contrast between the things that are above and the things that are on earth. We should understand this contrast in view of the descriptions that have gone before of material religious practices (2:20f.), which stand in opposition to Christ's victorious presence where Christ is seated at the right hand of God.

Then in v. 4 Paul makes a definite reference to the future resurrection, although all along he has stressed the present resurrection with Christ. (In connection with this verse, see John 14:6; 1 John 2:28; 3:2.)

Recommended work: Read chapters 2 and 3, noting the contrasts between life lived as if one belonged only to this world and life lived in Christ.

The sermon should follow the contrasts of the text between the things that are above with Christ and the things on earth, pointing to the return of Christ when all believers will appear with him in glory.

Theological Reflection

As we might expect, the theme of the texts on this Easter Day is the defeat of death by Christ's resurrection. The Isaiah 25 text points forward to the time when God will swallow up death forever and God comes to save God's people.

Children's Message

You might tell the John 20 account of Mary coming to the tomb as she might have told it to her grandchildren, sharing the astonishment and joy that she felt.

Hymns for Easter Day:

Jesus Christ Is Risen Today; "Christ the Lord Is Risen Today"; The Day of Resurrection!

Easter 2

Psalm 133 (C)
Psalm 148 (L)
Psalm 118:2–4, 13–15, 22–24 (RC)
Psalm 111 or 118:19–24 (E)

Acts 4:32–35 (C)
Acts 3:13–15, 17–26 (L)
Acts 3:12a, 13–15, 17–26 or
Isaiah 26:2–9, 19 (E)

1 John 1:1–2:2 (C)
1 John 5:1–6 (L) (RC)
1 John 5:1–6 or Acts 3:12a,
13–15, 17–26 (E)

John 20:19–31

Meditation on the Texts

Gracious God, we thank you for the gift of Jesus Christ who died on the cross and was raised for our salvation. May we not be faithless but believing. Although we have not seen the risen Christ as Thomas and the disciples did, we thank you for the gift of faith by the power of the Spirit. God of our fathers and mothers, who glorified your servant Jesus, we repent of our sin and turn once again to you. We pray that we may be of one heart and soul with other Christians, sharing our material goods as any have need, so that there will not be a needy person among us. We know that you are light and in you there is no darkness at all. We know that if we walk in the light, as he is in the light, we have fellowship with one another and the blood of Jesus your Son cleanses us from all sin. We know that if we sin, we have an advocate with you, Jesus Christ the righteous, who is the expiation for our sins and those of the whole world. By this we know that we love your children when we love you and obey your commandments, O God. We rejoice that the victory which overcomes the world is our faith, a gift from you by which you give your grace. Amen.

Commentary on the Texts

John 20:19–31

Our pericope spans three sections: vs. 19–23, which tell of an appearance of the risen Christ to the disciples; vs. 24–29, an account of another appearance to the disciples, with Thomas present; and vs. 30–31, the conclusion to the Gospel, and the meaning of these signs. (Chapter 21 is an appendix or epilogue.)

Notice that v. 19 begins "On the evening of that day," meaning Easter Day. John's attention is still fixed on Easter. We find in 1 Corinthians 15:5 a reference to the appearance to the disciples.

We cannot tell whether John means that only ten disciples (the Twelve minus Judas and Thomas) were present or additional disciples were there also. This episode and the one that follows make up the conclusion to the history of the exaltation of Christ. Note the contrast of this conclusion with what goes immediately before it.

It seems the disciples met behind locked doors on that Easter evening out of fear of what the Jews might do to them now that Passover was almost over. They were probably discussing the events of the day as reported by Peter and Mary Magdalene. Jesus came into the midst of this fearful little group without doors being opened or even a knock being heard. His entry was abnormal and miraculous.

Jesus greeted them with the conventional Jewish greeting of "Peace to you." The "peace greeting" came to be part of Christian social life as well as a permanent part of

Christian worship. Immediately after giving the peace greeting, Jesus showed the disciples his hands with wound prints and his side with the spear wound visible. Thus his identity was established and the result was joy in the disciples' hearts when they saw the Lord. Jesus again spoke to them and then gave them a commission: "As the Father has sent me, even so I send you" (v. 21). The disciples' mission in the world was to be Jesus', and Jesus' mission was to be theirs.

Jesus then breathed on the disciples and said to them, "Receive the Holy Spirit." In contrast to the morning of that day when Jesus had not yet gone to the Father (v. 17), he has now received the glory which was his with God from the foundation of the world. Therefore Jesus can now give the Holy Spirit, and does. We cannot harmonize this account with Luke's in the Book of Acts of the day of Pentecost. John and Luke each set the giving of the Spirit in a certain historical scheme based on the sources each was using. Here John is saying that the Holy Spirit speaks to human beings in their totality about God, but only in terms of the life, work, death, resurrection, and return to the Father of Jesus who was the Son. What Jesus says on that Easter evening presupposes that he has returned to the Father to share his glory, according to John. For John, the resurrection, ascension, and coming of the Spirit all take place on the same first Easter Day. Remember that the authors of the Gospels are concerned primarily with historical mysteries and only secondarily with chronologies and statistical circumstances.

Jesus does more than announce that the Spirit is given. He actually *gives* the Spirit as he breathes on the disciples, even as God breathed upon the first human. Thus the new creation has begun.

For a detailed discussion of the meaning of v. 23, see commentary on John by John Marsh (*Saint John,* Westminster Pelican Commentaries [Philadelphia: Westminster Press, 1978]). The thrust of the verse is that the gift of the Holy Spirit, which is Jesus' life, is the sole means by which the disciples can declare the forgiveness of sins. The church embodies Christ's mission of forgiveness but only as Christ's life is breathed into the church.

Thomas was not with the disciples on that first Easter evening, but when he heard that the Lord had appeared to them he refused to believe until he saw the physical evidence on the Lord's body. Thomas stands for all those who doubt; hence the nickname "doubting Thomas." But when the living Christ appeared eight days later in the house, he said to the disciples, "Peace be with you," and turning to Thomas, invited him to touch and see the wounds of his crucifixion, urging him to be not faithless but believing. Note how the resurrection narrative builds up to a dramatic climax: the evidence of the empty tomb, a vision of what it symbolizes, and the vision which becomes concrete in the experience and acceptance of grace, and empowerment for mission. Then there is incorporation through faith in Christ's glorification through suffering. And finally the response of faith: "My Lord and my God!"

We are not told whether or not Thomas actually touched Jesus, and the point is immaterial. Note that it is the doubter, Thomas, who makes the most complete affirmation of Christ's nature to be found in the Gospel. Jesus gives a beatitude, describing those blessed who have believed without seeing. The only motive for faith is the Word itself, the gospel, which is the power of God. Miracles, touching, historical evidence, and other things can only assist the seeker of faith. But the preaching of the gospel and the grace of God at work by the Spirit brings the gift of faith.

John concludes his Gospel on this note of belief and sets forth the evidence of the gospel and its signs as a witness to lead to faith in Jesus as the Christ (Messiah), the Son of God, which leads to faith. Life in his name is life in the person of Jesus. It is to share in his life and so become identified with him that his eternal life becomes the reality of the believer's life.

Recommended work: Compare this account of the gift of the Spirit with that in Acts. Do a word study of signs, peace, forgiveness, and Holy Spirit.

The sermon might develop moves from the skepticism of Thomas, who represents the modern doubter with a scientific mind-set, to the empowering of the church by the gift of the Spirit and giving of mission, to the affirmation of faith by Thomas. The thrust of the sermon should be to lead hearers to make a confession of "My Lord (ruler) and my God" although they have not seen the evidence or touched the risen Christ.

Acts 4:32–35 (C)

Our pericope begins a section that continues through 5:11 dealing with the sharing of goods. One of the distinctive marks of the early Christian community was that it took care of the needy, as indicated in Romans 12:8. But only in Jerusalem do we find this kind of communal living which was similar to that of the Essenes, and it was practiced only for a limited time.

Our text is the second major summary of the church's life, which parallels that in 2:42–47. Luke says that the company of those who believed were united in one heart and soul, indicating the inner unity of the believers (see Deut. 6:5).

We must realize that this sharing of possessions was voluntary and not required. Also, there is no indication that this was the beginning of a new economic order. The laying of money at the apostles' feet reflects an ancient custom in the transfer of possessions or of religious dedication of an offering to the gods.

There are two distinct ideas in this passage: (1) Things were possessed in common in the Jerusalem church and (2) there were individual possessors who sold what was theirs for distribution to the needy. Note that the first idea reflects the Greek ideals of community life at that time. In v. 32 we have the same interpretation of Christian fellowship in terms of a community of goods as is indicated in 2:44. We may view Luke's "communistic ideal" as a characteristic of the ideal first church, rather than a continuing norm for Christian communities. This ideal may have been influenced by actual contemporary ventures in Jerusalem and/or by Greek speculation.

While Karl Marx claimed that most human attitudes and actions can be traced to economic sources, Luke, though not a Marxist, was a realist. He described a community in which people did not give top priority to possessions. It reflects Jesus' teaching that "where your treasure is, there will your heart be also" (Matt. 6:21). The temptation to make money our god is one of the chief temptations of our "bottom line" mentality. The early church made putting love into action, not money itself, the bottom line.

Recommended Work: Compare this section with 2:44f. and scan the rest of Acts for ways by which the church expressed its unity of soul and heart.

The sermon might deal with the power of the resurrection to transform our attitudes toward both money and people, putting people and their needs above greed. This text might be applied to the church as it ministers to street people and the homeless today. One church converted a classroom for housing transients for two nights and others in need of temporary shelter. Other churches are pooling their resources for a more intentional sharing of their goods with the needy, motivated by Christian love.

Acts 3:13–15, 17–26 (L)

Acts 3:12a, 13–15, 17–26 or Isaiah 26:2–9, 19 (E)

We will deal with vs. 12a–15 and vs. 17–26. This is part of Peter's second sermon, in which he gives a fuller account of the Christian message. It was delivered in a portico of the temple.

The kerygma begins with v. 13, and Luke shows the continuity of the church with Israel by using hallowed titles of God. The Greek word translated "servant" can be translated "child," but in the Greek version of Isaiah 52:13 this same word is used for the Suffering Servant of the Lord. Jesus is interpreted as fulfilling the ideal of the Servant of Isaiah 53. Now the Servant has been glorified and is called the Righteous One. He is contrasted with Barabbas the murderer, while Jesus was the "Author of life." Jesus' own resurrection points forward to the resurrection of all the faithful. The apostles are witnesses to the death and resurrection of Jesus.

Next, Peter applies his message to the present situation of his hearers. He says the crucifixion was committed in ignorance, a common theme of Luke's. But it was in accord with the plan of God. Another of Luke's themes is that Jesus should suffer, reflecting Isaiah 53.

The sermon is a call for repentance and conversion, although baptism is not mentioned.

The "times of refreshing" refers to the blessings of the End time which will come with the return of Christ. Note that vs. 22–23 are a composite quote based on Deuteronomy 18:15, 19 and Leviticus 23:29. This uniting of biblical material may reveal that what we have here is an early collection of Hebrew Scripture texts used by early Christian preachers.

Samuel was the anointer of David, the type of the messianic king. The covenant with Abraham refers to Genesis 22:18, suggesting that the blessing to all the families of the earth is granted through Jesus. Note that the idea of the Servant's being sent first to Israel is typical of Luke.

Recommended work: Compare this sermon with Peter's sermon in 2:14f. and other sermons in Acts.

The sermon might take v. 19 as its thrust, calling for hearers to repent and turn again to God, that God may blot out their sins and send times of refreshment.

1 John 1:1–2:2 (C)

Our pericope consists of 1:1–4, which is the introduction; 1:5–10, which deals with the right attitude toward sin; and 2:1–2, which is part of the section of 2:1–6, which deals with obedience. Compare 1:1–2 with Genesis 1:1 and John 1:1, all referring to the beginning. The "we" here is the apostolic group.

The phrase "word of life" refers to Christ. The mentioning of the evidence of the senses is an attempt to refute the gnostic heresy that Christ only seemed to be in human flesh but was "spiritual."

The purpose of the writing of the epistle (1:3–4) is the attainment of fellowship or oneness with Christ and Christian joy.

Then in 1:5–2:29 the author deals with the meaning of what is implied in fellowship with God, dealing with walking in the light.

Notice the contrast of light and darkness. Christ is the light, the revelation of God. Light is truth, darkness is error, referring primarily to the moral realm of human conduct. No one whose life is not compatible with God's can really be in divine fellowship. Fellowship with God demands fellowship with one's fellow human beings as its condition and sign.

The union we have with God is the result of the redemptive work of Jesus Christ (v. 7).

The theme of 1:8–2:2 is that of avoiding sin. While in principle the Christian should be and remain entirely free of sin, in fact the possibility of sin is always present and cannot be ignored. A fundamental difference between the teaching of the apostles and that of the Gnostics had to do with the nature of evil. Gnostics claimed that evil was only ignorance or misfortune for which one is not responsible. Christ came into the world to bring knowledge (*gnōsis* in Greek) of the truth. Thus one only needs illumination, not forgiveness, according to Gnostics. This notion is still prevalent in our scientific age with its emphasis on knowledge and self-knowledge as the key to the good life.

But Christ the righteous is the expiation for our sins and the sins of the whole world.

Recommended work: Do a word study of expiation, fellowship, and sin.

The sermon might contrast the gnostic view of salvation (which is still with us) with the New Testament teaching of salvation by the expiation of sin by Christ's death. The sermon might deal with the reality of sin in our lives which cannot be denied and the good news of Jesus as our advocate with God. Christ's blood, not the knowledge he brought, cleanses us from all sin.

1 John 5:1–6 (L) (RC)

1 John 5:1–6 or Acts 3:12a, 13–15, 17–26 (E)

Our pericope is part of the section of vs. 1–12 dealing with victorious faith which issues in eternal life. It relates faith to love. In the foregoing passage, the author shows what he means by the love that is rooted in faith, and now he goes on to expand on the nature of this faith that gives meaning to love. Earlier in 4:20 the author says that the proof of the love of God consists in the love of one's brothers and sisters, and now in vs. 1–2 he asserts that the love of God consists in obedience to God's commandments as a sign of this love for others. The love of God and neighbor cannot be separated.

The love that makes us children of God cannot exist apart from genuine Christian faith. The author refers to the "children of God" (v. 2) in order to stress that this love is a dimension of the love of God. The person who loves the parent or begetter also loves the child.

Now the sign of this love is obedience to God's commandments (vs. 3–4). Because the Christian is born of God, he or she possesses all the power needed to overcome all the hostile forces that would prevent obedience to God's commands. Faith in Christ gives the victory and is the source of the Christian's power (v. 4).

Then in vs. 5–6 the significance of this true faith is clarified even further by another formula of Christology. In v. 5 the great principle of faith in Jesus as the Son of God overcoming the world is set forth in the form of a question. Compare the mentioning of "believes" in v. 5 with "our faith" in v. 4, and 4:15 and 5:1.

Jesus came by water and blood (v. 6). He was not only a Spirit-filled revealer but also a redeemer who through his death made eternal life possible for human beings. The water stands for Christ's endowment with the Spirit at his baptism and the gift of the Spirit to the church (John 3:5). The blood stands for Christ's entrance into his supreme power and glory and for the benefits of his death which are now available for the church through the Lord's Supper. The Docetists and others denied the death on the cross or its significance. The author is careful to stress that Christ came by and with the blood (see John 19:34–35). Note that v. 7 should be included with our pericope, since it stresses that the Spirit's witness is to the water and the blood and is the truth.

Recommended work: Read the whole section of vs. 1–12 and compare with what has gone before in the letter. Do a word study of water, blood, faith, and love.

The sermon might deal with the relationship between love for God and love for neighbors in response to God's love which gives us the victory. This victory is given to those who believe that Jesus is the Son of God who came by water and blood, the Spirit, and death on the cross. Salvation is not a matter of ideas about God but of trust in God's saving acts in Jesus in history. The sermon might be titled "Victorious Faith."

Theological Reflection

In this Eastertide we will naturally expect to find in our passages an emphasis on the resurrection and its effect. The Acts 4 passage indicates that the one heart and soul and sharing of possessions was the result of the great power that came upon the disciples as they testified to the resurrection of the Lord, and great grace was upon them. In the Acts 3 text Peter proclaims the gospel of Jesus' death and resurrection and calls the people to repent and turn again to God, that their sins may be forgiven. The John 20:19–31 passage tells of Jesus' appearance to the disciples on the first Easter evening and the gift of the Holy Spirit to them, their commission to go into the world, and their charge as the church to forgive or not forgive sins. It tells of Jesus' appearance to Thomas and the disciples eight days later and his affirmation of faith in the risen Lord who is God. Both passages from 1 John deal with the implications of the risen Christ for Christian living, including forgiveness of sins and victory over the world.

Children's Message

The discussion with the children might be about Thomas who doubted and represents many people who want to touch, feel, taste, or use other senses only to be sure of something. Thomas doubted that Jesus had risen from the dead until Jesus came and stood with the disciples and invited Thomas to touch his hands and side where he was wounded on the cross. Thomas may or may not have touched Jesus, but suddenly he came to believe in the risen Jesus, exclaiming, "My Lord and my God!" This is the goal for each of us to believe in Jesus with all our heart and to follow him. The whole letter of John is written to lead us to this kind of faith so that we may have life in Jesus' name, life now with God and life beyond the grave.

Hymns for Easter 2

Thine Is the Glory; Strong Son of God, Immortal Love; Hark! the Glad Sound, the Savior Comes.

Easter 3

Psalm 4 (C)
Psalm 139:1–11 (L)
Psalm 4:2, 4, 7–9 (RC)
Psalm 98 or 98:1–5 (E)

Acts 3:12–19 (C)
Acts 4:8–12 (L)
Acts 3:13–15, 17–19 (RC)
Acts 4:5–12 or Micah 4:1–5 (E)

1 John 3:1–7 (C)
1 John 1:1–2:2 (L) (E)
1 John 2:1–5 (RC)

Luke 24:35–48 (C)
Luke 24:36–49 (L)
Luke 24:36b–48 (E)

Meditation on the Texts

We thank you, O God, for the revelation of yourself in Jesus Christ who died for our sins and was raised for our salvation. Thank you for calling us to preach repentance and forgiveness of sins in Christ's name to all nations. But without the promised Holy Spirit we are powerless to fulfill our commission. Strengthen us by your Spirit to be witnesses to the saving events of Jesus' life and passion. We repent of our sins, turning again to you, that our sins may be blotted out and that times of refreshing may come from the presence of you, O Lord. As we reflect on your love for us which enables us to be called children of God we praise and adore you. We rejoice in the assurance that when Christ appears we shall be like him. We know that we may be sure that we know Christ if we keep his commandments. Whoever keeps his word, in that person, truly, love for you, our God, is perfected. Amen.

Commentary on the Texts

Luke 24:35–48 (C)

Luke 24:36–49 (L)

Luke 24:36b–48 (E)

The reading of vs. 35–49 includes all of the above pericopes and spans three sections: v. 35 is the ending of the road to Emmaus appearance, vs. 36–43 tell of Jesus appearing to the disciples in Jerusalem, and vs. 44–49 contain Jesus' final commission. Note that vs. 36–53 are a literary unit, since they recount one appearance of the risen Christ. The real recognition of Christ does not come until v. 52, where, after being instructed by Christ from scripture, they finally worship him. We should note the parallelism between this section and that of the Emmaus road incident. In comparing the two, we find in each an appearance of Christ which is not comprehended, an instruction based on scripture which then leads to a revelation, a meal (taken by Jesus alone in vs. 42–43), and finally his departure (not by vanishing but by ascension in the case of the disciples). In our pericope Christ gives a commission to the disciples, an element not found in the Emmaus incident.

This is the third appearance of the risen Christ in Luke's resurrection accounts and it takes place in Jerusalem on the same evening as the discovery of the empty tomb, just after the two disciples return from Emmaus with their report of meeting the risen Christ. In our pericope Christ appears to the house church of his followers. They are bewildered, astonished, and unbelieving at this point. Note carefully how much this episode resembles that of John 20:19-29. Both accounts agree that Jesus appeared in bodily form which was not subject to ordinary, physical restrictions. Yet, both emphasize the solidly corporeal nature of Christ's resurrection body.

Our pericope lacks the dramatic suspense of the Emmaus story primarily because Luke has embellished aspects of it. Note especially the three forms that Luke's embellishment have taken: (1) the multiple description of the reaction of the disciples when confronted by the risen Christ (they are terrified, startled, full of doubt, incredulous, overjoyed yet wondering); (2) an apologetic theme, as Christ invites them to touch him, look at his hands and feet, his flesh and bones, and asks for something to eat and proceeds to eat it in their presence; and (3) the instruction of the disciples through an explanation of scripture.

The Greeks of that time tended to think of reality in terms of abstractions and universal truths, while the Jews were always particular and concrete in regard to reality. This concreteness finds expression in materialistic imagery such as in our pericope. For a Jew, a disembodied spirit could only seem to be a ghost, not a living being. The authorities of that time would certainly attempt to explain away the claims of the disciples that they had seen the risen Christ by arguing that they had only seen a ghost. Thus, Luke has an apologetic motive in this story. Near the end of the first century a heresy called Docetism (from the Greek word for "seem") grew up which denied the reality of Christ's human life, claiming rather that the divine Christ descended upon the human Jesus at his baptism and then withdrew again *before* his crucifixion. We find in the Epistles and Gospel of John references to this heresy as they attempted to refute it, and it is likely that for this reason Luke also wanted to indicate the identity of the risen Christ with the flesh and blood Jesus.

Luke thus develops in his own form a tradition of early Christianity, and it is just another way in which he builds up the assurance for the reader Theophilus. Luke is far more realistic than John, both of whom were coping with the same problem of the identity and physical reality of the risen Christ who appeared to the disciples. John does it by introducing the story of Thomas, who is not mentioned in this Lukan account. The Thomas story is an afterthought, it seems.

Since one rule of interpreting scripture is to relate it to what other scripture teaches, we must balance this view of the resurrection body with that of Paul in his letter to the Corinthians in which he says that the physical body which is sown is perishable but the body which is raised is a spiritual body (1 Cor. 15:1ff.). Luke emphasizes the identity of the risen Christ with the crucified Jesus, as Jesus showed the disciples the nail prints and ate before them. Paul makes it clear that the resurrected body is a transformed body. Christ is the man of heaven, the firstfruits of the dead.

The risen Christ claims a basis in scripture for the preaching in his name of repentance for the forgiveness of sins to all the nations and the rising of Messiah on the third day. But as Joseph Fitzmyer points out, "It is impossible to find any of these elements precisely in the OT, either that the Messiah shall suffer, or that he is to rise, or that it will happen on the third day. This is Lukan use of the OT in the service of his christology" (Joseph A. Fitzmyer, *The Gospel According to Luke,* Anchor Bible [Garden City, N.Y.: Doubleday & Co., 1985], p. 1581).

The disciples are commissioned to undertake the missionary work of the church, with a stress on their task to witness, and to stay in the city until the gift of the power from on high, the Holy Spirit, is received. In the Greek the word for "power" is put emphatically at the end of the sentence. Power in Jesus' ministry is mentioned in 4:14; 5:17; and 9:1. For the Hebrew Scripture background, see Isaiah 32:15 and Wisdom 9:17. Jerusalem had been the goal of Jesus' missionary wanderings and now it is cited as the focal point, thus shifting from being the goal to being the starting point from which the gospel will spread to the end of the earth.

Recommended work: Reflect on this resurrection appearance and that of the other Gospels, and compare it with Paul's description of the resurrection body. Reflect on v. 41, in which Luke says the disciples were still disbelieving from joy and wonder, in which Luke makes joy the excuse for the disciples' disbelief and compare with v. 11 and with 22:45, where the disciples' sleep is explained as a result of grief.

The sermon might begin with v. 35, which ends the Emmaus appearance story and begins the Easter evening appearance in Jerusalem, indicating that Jesus appeared to the disciples in the ordinary events of daily life such as the breaking of bread. Then the sermon might follow the moves of the passage, leading up to the commissioning to preach in Jesus' name to all the nations after receiving power. The church today is sent to preach the gospel after being equipped with the Holy Spirit, proclaiming repentance and the forgiveness of sins.

Acts 3:12–19 (C)

Acts 3:13–15, 17–19 (RC)

See Easter 2, (E) and (L).

Acts 4:8–12 (L)

Acts 4:5–12 or Micah 4:1–5 (E)

Our pericope is part of the larger section of vs. 1–31, an account of the arrest and release of Peter and John, the first of many occasions on which the apostles courageously defended their faith before the authorities. In v. 5 it seems the ''rulers'' were priests, who with the elders and the scribes composed the Sanhedrin, or council. The high priest was head of the council. It was made up of seventy priests, scribes, and elders. Annas was high priest in A.D. 6–14 and Caiaphas was his son-in-law. So Caiaphas, not Annas, was the official high priest at that time. Neither Alexander nor John is mentioned elsewhere. One text reads Jonathan instead of John and this would refer to the son of Annas.

The court sat in a semicircle, with the disciples of the learned men in the front three rows. The disciples Peter and John are set in the midst of them, with the lame man as the chief witness. This was a preliminary inquiry and there was no charge. The Sanhedrin was the supreme religious and civil tribunal. A deputation of the Sanhedrin had earlier inquired of Jesus by what authority he had cleansed the temple (Luke 20:1, 2).

Remember that Peter had earlier denied Jesus three times, intimidated by a lowly slave maiden, but now, empowered by the Holy Spirit, he courageously faced the Sanhedrin itself and speaks. He witnesses to the death and resurrection of Jesus, hence the special relevance of this text for Eastertide. While the crucifixion is the act of human beings, the resurrection is God's action, for God raised Christ from the dead (v. 10). Peter described Jesus as the stone that was rejected by the builders, a reference to Psalm 118:22. It could be either the capstone on the top of the building or the cornerstone in the foundation. The latter seems the case. It is this solid foundation which makes possible the superstructure of life. Thus God's power extends far beyond healing a lame man to the giving of salvation to the whole world. There is no other means of salvation, declares Peter. In this cornerstone, Jesus, is true safety to be found. Note the variety of terms used in this passage showing its completeness, such as to make strong in 3:16 and to give healing, cure, and so forth, in 4:9, 10, 14, 22.

In an age of pluralism and relative values the exclusive claim of the scriptures and the Christian faith may seem arrogant. But to those who have come to know Christ and have experienced forgiveness and healing they know that the claim is true that only in Christ is there salvation.

Recommended work: Compare Peter's actions here with those when he denied Jesus at his trial and note the difference the Spirit makes. Compare Peter's boldness to that of martyrs for the faith through the ages.

The sermon should set the scene in the minds of the hearers, then proceed to show that the cross and resurrection are at the heart of the gospel and there is no salvation outside of Christ's name (nature). Only in Christ do we have forgiveness and reconciliation to God and to one another. The sermon might be called ''Christ—The Head of the Corner,'' showing how faith in Christ's resurrection is the foundation of the Christian religion.

1 John 3:1–7 (C)

This is part of the section of vs. 1–10, which deals with filial relation expressed in correct conduct. It is part of the larger section of 2:28–3:12, in which children of God are contrasted with children of the devil. The separation of the two is a sign of the last hour, and the difference will be especially clear at the time of Christ's second coming. At that time the righteous will be revealed like him as pure, loving, and obedient in keeping God's commandments. This is the Christian's confidence and hope. The foundation of this is in vs. 1–2, in which the author says that it is God's love in making us God's children which produces a resemblance to God now and in the age to come. This resembles John 1:12: "But to all who received him, who believed in his name, he gave power to become children of God."

Reflect on the bold metaphors that the Gospel of John uses of begetting and birth to describe Jesus' intimate relation with God and the believer's relation with the Father and the Son as found in John 1:12–13, 18, and 3:3–16. Remember that these metaphors were used extensively by the Gnostics and for this reason New Testament authors use similar language to refute them. Gnosticism taught that the "seeds" of the divine being were scattered among human beings throughout the world and Christ came to collect and return them to God through revealing secret knowledge. They divorced a person's moral condition and behavior from this predestined return of the "seed" to its divine source. The hope we have of complete moral likeness to Christ is what motivates purity (v. 3).

The epistle writer takes pains to point out that "no one who abides in him sins" (v. 6). The reason? God's nature (literally, seed) abides in the person (v. 9). The author does not mean that the person born of God is sinless (1:10) but rather that such a person is moving in the right direction of doing what is right and loving the neighbor (vs. 7, 10). Note that love is the true test of whether a person is born of God or not. Sin is not a matter of nature but rather of what one does, of conduct. Sins refer to habitual and constant acts.

Recommended work: Compare this passage with those in John's Gospel which deal with the same theme of being born of God. Do a word study of gnosticism, sin, righteous, and pure.

The sermon might deal with the contemporary "gnosticism" which says science and technology can save us and the various new age and similar religions in contrast to the Christian teaching that love and doing right are the test of whether or not one is right with God. It should hold up the hope of being like Christ at the End time, which motivates us to purity of life. The sermon should link faith and moral conduct.

1 John 1:1–2:2 (L) (E)

1 John 2:1–5 (RC)

Since 1 John 1:1–2:2 was dealt with last week, we will briefly comment on 2:3–5 only. The thrust of these verses is that obedience to God's commandments tests whether or not we know God and also measures the perfection or completeness of our love for God. It stresses the need for congruence between word and deed, between saying and doing. The person who keeps God's word is one in whom the love for God is perfected or brought to completeness. This is the supreme proof that we are in God. The fundamental difference between the teaching of the Gnostics and the apostles was focused on the nature of evil. The Gnostics held that evil was just error or ignorance. It was a misfortune for which no one could be held accountable. They claimed that Christ came into the world to bring knowledge (*gnōsis*) of the truth; thus all one needed was illumination, not forgiveness. We can see a parallel with this in the modern trust in science and technology to save humanity.

But the New Testament sees the root of evil in sin, which is a deliberate rebellion against God. God sent Jesus into the world to be the expiation of our sins and those of the whole world. We must abide in and walk in God's way in order to perfect or complete our love and fellowship with God.

Recommended work: Combine this commentary with that of 1 John 2:1–2 from last week, looking for progression of thought.

The sermon might focus on the acid test of the Christian faith: obedience to the word of God, resulting in a walk of life like that of Christ.

Theological Reflection

During this Eastertide the theme of resurrection and its implications for Christian living permeate the readings. Luke gives an account of Jesus' appearance to the disciples on Easter evening and his commissioning them to preach to all nations. The reading from Acts 3 deals with Jesus' death and resurrection and a call to repentance. The Acts 4 passage tells of Peter and John's boldness, empowered by the living Christ, before the Sanhedrin. And the 1 John readings deal with the risen Christ who is coming again and our living as children of God.

Children's Message

The talk with the children might be about the miracle of Jesus' resurrection. A little girl asked at the coffin of her great-grandmother why "Granny" couldn't come back to life. The Christian hope is that she can in the age to come when we are raised with Christ to a new life. Jesus was crucified, but God raised him from the dead and he appeared to the disciples. He is coming again at the End of this age, when we will become like him.

Hymns for Easter 3

The Strife Is O'er, the Battle Done; Hail, Thou Once Despised Jesus; Jesus Christ Is Risen Today.

Psalm 23 (C)
Psalm 23 or 100 (E)
Psalm 118:1, 8–9, 21–23, 26, 29 (RC)

Acts 4:8–12 (C)
Acts 4:23–33 (L)
Acts 4:(23–31) 32–37 or Ezekiel 34:1–10 (E)

1 John 3:18–24 (C)
1 John 3:1–2 (L) (RC)
1 John 3:1–8 or
Acts 4:(23–31) 32–37 (E)

John 10:11–18 (C)
John 10:11–16 (E)

Meditation on the Texts

Gracious God, we thank you for Jesus, the noble and model shepherd who came that we might have life and have it abundantly. We thank you that he laid down his life for us, his sheep, and that he is a faithful shepherd who does not flee when the wolf comes. We know him and he knows us, even as you know him and he knows you, O God. We who are from the "other sheep," the Gentiles, rejoice in hearing his voice and in being included in the one flock led by the Good Shepherd. We thank you that Jesus laid down his life voluntarily and took it up again, empowered by you. May we always love in deed and truth, not in word or speech only. You are greater than our hearts and know everything. We know that you abide in us by the Spirit which you have given. May we be filled with the Holy Spirit so that we may speak your word with boldness. May we so be united in one heart and soul by your Spirit that we will share our worldly goods and there may be no needy person among us. We thank you for the examples of Barnabas who sold a field and gave the money to the apostles for the caring of the poor. Amen.

Commentary on the Texts

John 10:11–18 (C)

John 10:11–16 (E)

Our pericope is part of an entire chapter that focuses on Jesus as the shepherd who gave his life. The preacher is urged to read the whole chapter and Ezekiel 34 before studying the pericope itself. Jesus fulfills the promise in the Hebrew Scriptures that God will come to shepherd God's people, as indicated in Isaiah 40:11; Jeremiah 23:1–6; and Ezekiel 34, especially v. 11.

Jesus calls himself the good shepherd. The Greek word used in v. 11 means beautiful in the sense of an ideal or model of perfection. Recall that it was used in 2:10 of choice wine. Noble or model shepherd is a more precise translation than is good shepherd. David was called the handsome shepherd in a literal translation of 1 Samuel 16:12.

John uses the phrase "lays down his life" in contrast to "give one's life" as Mark has Jesus say. To lay down one's life may reflect the rabbinic term "to hand over one's life" and is rare in secular Greek. The shepherd of that time frequently risked his life to save the sheep (see 1 Sam. 17:34f.; Isa. 31:4).

The image of Jesus as the Good Shepherd is a familiar one from pictures and stained-glass windows, and it is perhaps the most loved image of Jesus. Originally it meant far more than what a shepherd with a sheep in his arms can convey. In our modern society we have lost the connection between the shepherd and the office of ruler, an image that Ezekiel used forcefully. The simple figure of a shepherd with a sheep does not confront the viewer with the profound life-and-death issues resulting in Jesus' sacrificial death which John gives us in this figure. Read carefully vs. 10–15 to discover the profound and ultimate issues that the figure of the good shepherd is meant to convey to us.

The real issue between the true and the false shepherd is that of life and death. The false shepherd is a thief or a hireling. The false shepherd (ruler) usurps the place that is reserved for God alone and does this by stealing the kingdom. This shepherd's work leads to death. By contrast, the true shepherd Jesus comes to govern the people in the right way. He brings them into proper submission to God, thus ensuring that they not only will have life but will have abundant life, life fuller than they can find under any other rule.

But Jesus' rule alone does not convey the abundant life. It is given only as Jesus the noble shepherd lays down his life for the sheep. Notice that it is not a matter of Jesus being the ruler of the people who only happens to lay down his life for his sheep. Rather, as the true ruler of God's people he lays down his life. His sacrifice is part of his office, and part of his reign consists in giving himself for those he governs. In surrounding pagan religions there were new year rituals in which the dying and the rising of the king were celebrated. But in Israel we find the final fulfillment of the human idea of a king who dies for the life of his people. Recall the Servant of Second Isaiah who gives his life as a ransom for many. Note that Israel's ruler or shepherd is yet the servant of all and as servant he suffers to liberate his people and give his life for the sins of many (see Isaiah 53).

Examine the contrast between the good and the bad shepherd as they relate to the sheep. The good shepherd knows and loves the sheep as his own, while the bad shepherd works only for wages and cares nothing for the sheep. When real danger, such as the wolf, comes, the bad shepherd flees and leaves the sheep to be attacked and killed. Notice especially the mutual love of the good shepherd and the sheep. The good shepherd not only knows and loves the sheep but they know and love him, in a mutual relationship like that of God the Father and Jesus the Son. Thus when dangers come, the good shepherd is ready and willing to give his life for the safety of his flock. Here is the supreme fulfillment of authority and rule by the shepherd: the one who rules is the one who sacrifices his life.

The flock of Jesus consists not just of those who are called out of the flock of Israel but also the sheep not of that flock, namely, Gentiles, whom Christ must bring and make into one flock. In v. 16 there is an alliteration in the Greek that is best translated as "There shall be one sheep-herd, one shepherd." The text supposes that there will be one single church made up of both Jews and Gentiles led and ruled by one Good Shepherd.

Verses 14–15 repeat the parallel between the relationship of Jesus and his disciples and that of Jesus and God. Both of these relationships are characterized by mutual knowledge, love, and life-giving care. This is the quality of loving care which unites the sheep in the one flock.

We should not assume that God began to love the Son only when the Son had offered himself upon the cross, as v. 17 might seem to say. Rather, the point John is making is that God's eternal love for the Son rests upon the Son's eternal sharing of God's love for human beings. This love is expressed in the incarnation, and as the incarnate Son, Jesus offers himself on the cross.

Jesus then says that the power to lay down life and to take it again is a charge received from God. But this does not make the laying down of his life any easier or less filled with terror for him. God loves Jesus the Son because he will obediently lay down his life, which is the only way his life may be eventually retained. He must, paradoxically, lay down his crown in order to secure it! And this laying down must take place while Jesus is still in the flesh. The New Testament, we should recall, does not think of the resurrection as a circumstance that follows Jesus' death but of the *essential completion* of the death of Jesus. For John, the passion, death, resurrection, and ascension compose *one* indissoluble saving action of return to God. In order for Jesus to give life through the gift of the Spirit, Jesus must rise again. Thus resurrection is the very purpose of his death. As Jesus says in John 12:24, a grain of wheat must die if it is to spring up again and bear fruit.

In vs. 17–18 Jesus is said to be the one who takes up his life again. The usual New Testament affirmation is that God *raised him,* not that Jesus rose from the dead on his own power. But, and this is the key, in John's thought the Father and the Son possess the same power. Therefore it matters little whether or not the resurrection is attributed to the action of the Father or of the Son. Later trinitarian theology built on this profound theological insight. Reflect on the fact that v. 18 describes Jesus' death and resurrection as commanded by God. This is the ultimate proof that when Jesus lays down his life in order to take it up again, his motive is not a self-seeking one, since it is God who willed that the death of Jesus should lead to resurrection and return to the Father.

Recommended work: Compare our pericope with the whole chapter's thrust. Read an article in a Bible dictionary on sheep and shepherd. Reflect on how our pericope expresses the saving action of Jesus in his suffering, death, and resurrection. Be especially aware of the ruling function of the shepherd as well as the caring function.

The sermon might follow the images and moves in the text itself. A brief description of the interaction of a good shepherd and flock might set the stage, since many people in urban settings are unfamiliar with the nature of sheep. The thrust of the sermon should be on Jesus' giving up his life for the sheep and being raised from the dead that we might have life and have it abundantly. The sermon should invite hearers to hear Jesus' invitation to know, love, and follow him.

Acts 4:8–12 (C)

See Easter 3, (L).

Acts 4:23–33 (L)

Acts 4:(23–31) 32–37 or Ezekiel 34:1–10 (E)

We will deal with 4:23–37, which includes both of the major readings of (L) and (E). The Ezekiel reading for (E) is especially fitting as background for our reading from John today but will not be dealt with here, since it is an alternative. Our reading spans two sections: 4:1–31, which deals with the arrest and release of Peter and John, and 4:32–5:11, which describes the sharing of goods in the early church.

In vs. 23–31 we have the prayer of the apostles which preserve early liturgical traditions. The prayer's conclusion in vs. 29–30 reveals that it grew out of the events being described and therefore is not a formula prayer from an earlier time. It may be that Luke composed this prayer to fit the situation, influenced by Hezekiah's prayer in Isaiah 37:16–20 and by Psalm 2:1 which was used of Jesus' passion. Peter and John, after their release, return to their friends, perhaps just to the apostles, or it may have included the 120 (1:15). We don't know where they met, but when the group heard the report of the Sanhedrin's warning, they lifted their voices in praise and petition to God. The prayer resembles Semitic poetry as do the poems of Luke's birth narrative. The prayer begins with ''Sovereign Lord,'' which translates a Greek term from which our word ''despot'' is taken. The term emphasizes the mighty power of God.

Quoting Psalm 2:1–2, the prayer finds the fulfillment of this in the life of Jesus. Note that the reference to Jesus combines two ideas about Christ, namely, that he is the servant described by Second Isaiah and that he is the anointed Messiah. For Luke, these two ideas are united, since he pictures Jesus as the Messiah whose mission demands his humble acceptance of the servant's role.

The giving of the Spirit (v. 31) resembles the Pentecost story of wind and fire in that the ground shook. These external events symbolize the great power released as the disciples are filled with the Holy Spirit. Note the notion that the Spirit comes only sporadically, as in v. 8. Here the disciples do not speak in tongues, but the Spirit enables them to speak the word of God with boldness. They proclaim the good news of God's actions in Jesus Christ.

We dealt with vs. 32–35 in (C) for Easter 2. The example of Barnabas selling a field and giving the money to the apostles is cited in vs. 36–37. His real name is Joseph. Scholars are not sure about the origin of his surname in Aramaic. It could mean son of Nebo, son of a prophet, or son of encouragement. Since the poverty of the Jerusalem church in its early days was well known, the act of Joseph/Barnabas would make a lasting impression on the tradition.

Recommended work: Compare the giving of the Spirit (v. 31) with other accounts of the giving of the Spirit such as on Pentecost and on Easter evening. Compare the account of vs. 32–35 with similar accounts, such as 2:43ff.

The sermon might move from the release of Peter and John and their prayer to the gift of the Spirit (v. 31), to the sharing of material goods and the specific example of Barnabas. It should motivate hearers so to pray that they too may be empowered by the Spirit to speak God's word with boldness and to share material possessions with those in need. The resurrection of Jesus was the core of their message, and great grace was upon them all. The Christian faith has been called the most materialistic of all religions and this pericope bears this out. God's grace moves people to share their material goods with those in need, an urgent message for our age when a few have so much and so many have so little of this world's goods.

1 John 3:18–24 (C)

1 John 3:1–2 (L) (RC)

1 John 3:1–8 or Acts 4:(23–31) 32–37 (E)

Since 1 John 3:1–7 was dealt with in the (C) reading last Sunday, it will not be repeated here. For 1 John 3:8, see John 8:44; Acts 13:10; and Hebrews 2:14 for similar ideas. The point of v. 8 is that sinfulness is the work of the devil, whose works Christ came into the world to destroy and did destroy. The reference to the devil being a sinner from the beginning must refer to salvation history beginning with the Fall in Genesis 3.

The 1 John 3:18–24 passage beings with a call to put faith into action. "Word" refers to intention without deed. "Speech" means hypocrisy, not truth. Compare with James 1:22. The Christian's assurance is set forth in vs. 19–24. The word "this" in v. 19 refers to the love mentioned in v. 18.

The word "truth" in v. 19 is equivalent to "of God" (see 1 John 3:10). The thrust of v. 20 is that God who knows everything judges human beings by the abiding relation of love to others rather than by our moods. "Heart" in this context is equivalent to our word "conscience." When our hearts do condemn us, we can take confidence from our consciousness of being of the truth. God who knows all things is plentiful in mercy and forgives those who are truly God's.

If we are not conscious of having sinned (vs. 21–22), so much the more will we be confident of God's favor. As Christians suffered persecution in the early centuries, their only assurance was that they were following Christ's example and the confidence of a good conscience before God (see 1 Peter 2:21–25).

The commandments are summed up in faith and love (vs. 23–24), which will be the theme of the final part of this letter. The name meant the nature or character of the person, in this case, Jesus Christ. Obedience to God's commandments guarantees continued communion with God (see 2:17). And a further guarantee of God's presence is the possession of the Holy Spirit which is explicitly mentioned here for the first time.

Recommended work: Compare the theme of belief in the name of Jesus and love with John 6:28–29; 13:34; and Acts 16:31, as belief and love are basic ingredients of obedience.

The sermon might follow the moves of the text, climaxing in v. 24 with the assurance of the Spirit that we abide in God.

Theological Reflection

During Eastertide we find the resurrection theme especially prominent in the texts. The John 10 passage tells of the shepherd who gives his life for the sheep and takes it up again, a charge Jesus has from God. The Acts 4:23–37 passage relates the power of the Spirit of the living Christ in the disciples, making them bold to speak God's word and to share their goods. The Spirit gives us confidence that God abides in us.

Children's Message

The talk with the children might be about Jesus, the good shepherd and a model for all shepherds who love his sheep enough to die for them. You might contrast the good shepherd with the bad shepherd who flees from the wolf. Psalm 23 might be read or recited together.

Hymns for Easter 4

The King of Love My Shepherd Is; Take Thou Our Minds, Dear Lord; Christ Is Made the Sure Foundation.

Easter 5

Psalm 22:25–31 (C)
Psalm 22:24–30 (L)
Psalm 22:26–28, 30–32 (RC)
Psalm 66:1–11 or 66:1–8 (E)

Acts 8:26–40 (C)
Acts 9:26–31 (RC)
Acts 8:26–40 or Deuteronomy 4:32–40 (E)

1 John 4:7–12 (C)
1 John 3:18–24 (L) (RC)
1 John 3:(14–17) 18–24 or
Acts 8:26–40 (E)

John 15:1–8 (C)
John 14:15–21 (E)

Meditation on the Texts

O God our help in ages past, and our hope for the ages yet to come, we thank you for Jesus Christ the true vine. May we always abide in him and so be nourished in order to bear much fruit. We confess that apart from him we can do nothing. May we so bear much fruit that you, O God, may be glorified. Even as Christ is the vine and we are the branches, we pray that we may so abide in him and his words in us that whatever we ask it shall be done for us. Grant to us wisdom and skill in interpreting the scriptures for those like the Ethiopian who are seeking to know the good news of Jesus. May we, like Paul, declare how we have seen the Lord who spoke to us and then preach boldly in the name of Jesus. We pray for the church, that it may have peace and be built up. May the church walk in the fear of you and the comfort of the Holy Spirit and be multiplied. Enable us to love one another even as you, O God, have loved us. We know that if we love one another, you, O God, abide in us and your love is completed in us. Amen.

Commentary on the Texts

John 15:1–8 (C)

Our pericope is from the first of three sections of a chapter that describes the pattern of the Christian believer's life. Our reading is part of vs. 1–11, which focus on the believer's relation to Christ, one of abiding in him, as branches are connected to a vine. Jesus is the true Israel. He fulfills the calling which the old Israel had failed. The church is the New Israel. It is to bear fruit which springs from actual incorporation with Jesus through prayer and loving obedience, which results in joy. This fruit which the church is to bear is described by Paul as "love, joy, peace, patience, kindness, goodness, faithfulness, gentleness, self-control" (Gal. 5:22, 23). The second section of the chapter, vs. 12–17, deals with the relationship of believers to each other, one of love; the third section, vs. 18–27, focuses on the believer's relationship to the world, which means separation from the world and bearing witness to Christ in the power of the Holy Spirit to the world. Thus, in order to understand our pericope we should reflect on it in its wider context, not of a "Jesus holding my hand in the garden alone" religion, but a robust, vital relationship with the living Christ which nourishes believers to love one another and to bear witness to Christ in an alien world.

If we read only vs. 1–8, we may get a false romantic posture of the church toward our cultural context. But by reading the whole chapter, we must face up to the abrasion that is inherent in biblical faith as noted in vs. 18–27. The Christian faith involves risks, persecution, and the hatred of the world which is over against Christ and his church. We should be aggressive in setting forth the biblical position of both the church and the believer in the world rather than giving a false romantic view which the lectionary readings in isolation from their context may give.

171

Jesus says, "I am the true vine" (v. 1). (For a detailed explanation of the "I am" passages of John, see Raymond E. Brown, *The Gospel According to John I–XII*, pp. 534f.) In John's Gospel, Jesus speaks of himself in seven instances in an "I am" figurative way: "I am the bread of life . . . the light of the world . . . the (sheep) gate . . . the model shepherd . . . the resurrection and the life . . . the way, the truth, and the life . . . the (real) vine." Recall that there are "I am" statements in Revelation as well as in John. John draws on symbolism from the Hebrew Scriptures that describe the relations of God to Israel, while in Revelation the words are taken directly from passages in the Hebrew Scriptures.

Note that there is nothing futuristic about this description of the branches and the vine, in contrast to many other passages of the Last Discourse which picture union with Jesus as belonging to the future. In our pericope the disciples are *already* in union with Jesus and the stress is on *remaining* in that union. Jesus does not hint of his departure, nor are there themes characteristic of the Last Supper. Some scholars think the description of the vine and branches in vs. 1–6 was originally in another context, perhaps spoken on the road between Bethany and Jerusalem in conjunction with the cursing of the fig tree where Jesus points to the notion of none bearing fruit (Matt. 21:19).

In the Hebrew Scriptures the imagery of the vine was associated not only with the community of Israel but also with the image of the individual. Thus John's transferral of a collective image (Israel) to a person is anticipated in Ezekiel's vine symbolism. Note that in the Hebrew Scriptures the symbolism sometimes shifts back and forth between Israel as a vine to that of vineyard, and there is other symbolism of Israel as a plant or tree. Therefore Jesus' use of the vine or plant as a symbol for a divine/human relationship would not be strange. The radical idea is that Jesus himself is the *true vine* which replaces old Israel. Jesus mentions God, his Father, to justify his claim.

The true vine, the church, would and must bear fruit, meaning evangelize. The relationship of vine and branch conveys to the disciples the nature of their profoundly intimate relationship with Jesus Christ. We might liken it to the relationship between a hand and an arm in our urban, technological society divorced from agricultural images. The hand must be joined to the arm and nourished by a blood flow in order to do its work. But the church's growth is not a simple plant that is allowed to grow untended. There must be dressing and pruning of the vine, meaning that the members of the church will always live under Christ's judgment. And the test of fruitfulness, the carrying out of the church's mission, must be faced. If the disciples live in intimate relationship with Christ and his words (v. 7), words that speak of his death, departure and return, his humiliation and glorification, and the disciples *abide* in Christ, then they may ask anything they will and it will be done for them. The key to this is abiding in Christ. To abide in Christ is to be controlled by Christ, to obey him, and this results in asking only those things in accordance with his will. It means to believe that Jesus' suffering and death and resurrection are an essential part of his ultimate triumph over the world. For the church to bear fruit means more than evangelistic success in the numbers game. It means to be with the Lord in word and deed, in action and suffering and in joy, and in defeat and victory. Only this manner of bearing fruit glorifies God. To remain in Christ is the only way to attain heavenly joy, and that belongs to the life of the Father and Son. The disciples are to spend themselves so that others may share this life. This is the whole purpose of Jesus speaking to the disciples in the way he has done.

Jesus' Father is the vinedresser who cares for both the vine (Jesus) and the branches (his disciples). In this metaphor Jesus states the intimate relationship between Christ and his disciples. Note that it is not possible to depict as forcefully the intimacy between Father and Son as that between them and the disciples.

The branch that bears no fruit may, at first glance, seem to be the Jews, but in view of the words "of mine" it refers to the apostate Christians. There are two actions in pruning: he takes away . . . he prunes.

Jesus says the disciples are already made clean by the word he has spoken to them, and the cleansing here seems to point to the cleansing that Jesus gave them when he washed their feet at the Last Supper. Word and deed go together, and the act of washing alone is inoperative. The final unity of word and deed is in the crucifixion and resurrection of the Lord. The proclamation of this saving action manifests God's gift of salvation.

In v. 4 a better translation would be "Abide in me even as I abide in you," which has a thrust of seeking unceasing loyalty from the disciple. The disciple who ceases to abide in Christ is like the branch that no longer is attached to the vinestock. Such a branch is no longer alive; it is just a piece of wood to be cast on the fire. There does not seem to be an implication of eternal fires of judgment in this v. 6, however. A person is able to bear fruit and to prove to be a disciple only as that person remains in Christ.

Recommended work: Read an article on vine and vineyard in a Bible dictionary. Reflect on other symbols of abiding and unity, such as that of a hand attached to the arm.

The sermon should develop the image of the vine and branches as a symbol of the vital relationship of the believer and Christ. The sermon might develop moves that deal with the pruning of the branches that do not bear fruit and the fruit borne by branches dwelling in the vine, Jesus. The climax might be that it is in bearing much fruit that persons prove to be Jesus' disciples.

John 14:15–21 (E)

Our reading is part of a chapter that focuses on the believers' relation to the glorified Christ. In vs. 12–17 Jesus says that greater works will be done by the believers through prayer, obedience, and the Holy Spirit or Counselor. They will be able to do these greater works of a more exalted kind because redemption has been achieved in Jesus' death and resurrection. The Counselor is mentioned in v. 16, which translates a Greek word translated "advocate" in 1 John 2:1. Then in vs. 18–20 Jesus says that the Spirit imparts Christ's life and unites believers to God (see Acts 2:33: "Being therefore exalted at the right hand of God, and having received from the Father the promise of the Holy Spirit, he has poured out this which you see and hear"). Then in vs. 21–24 Jesus stresses that fellowship with the risen Christ is dependent on love which is expressed in obedience.

Note that "If you love me" (v. 15) is the condition that underlies the development of the whole discourse to the end of v. 24. That which binds the disciple to the Lord is not an act of intellectual assent, not secret knowledge as the Gnostics taught, but rather the bond of love. Love for Christ means seeking the glory of God and means accepting the duties of the work of the Son, namely, obedience to the instructions of the Lord.

The person so bound to Christ is promised the Counselor whom Christ will request from God. As long as Jesus has been with them he has been the disciples' counselor. But now he is going away. Therefore they need another Counselor of comparable stature. Jesus prays to God for the Counselor who is even the Spirit of truth who will remain with the disciples forever. Thus Jesus' departure by death, resurrection, and exaltation will not leave them unsupported and unguided. This Spirit of truth will guide them and set them off from the world. Even as the world cannot see Jesus for the Son of God he is, so the world cannot discern the Spirit either. The world cannot either see the Spirit or know him. But the disciples will know the Spirit, for he will be dwelling in them.

The disciples need not fear being left desolate like orphans, for the Lord will come to them (v. 19). Soon Jesus will be put to death and thus pass out of human sight. But the disciples will know that he is in the Father and they are in him and he in them as they enter a new life based on new conditions. "In that day," says Jesus, using a term that was almost a technical one in Jewish thought employed to refer to the last days when God would bring all God's purposes to pass. But John's interpretation of Jesus' message here does not intend to refer to the End of time as usually understood. Rather, this is a subtle reference to Christ's resurrection and his coming to dwell with the disciples in the church, as well as to Christ's return at the End of the age. According to Jesus' thinking, history does not finally lose its meaning when the End, which lies beyond history, comes.

Rather, history here and now becomes possessed of ultimate significance only because the End time fulfillments are to be found within history. What Jesus says in vs. 1–3 is not just a promise of coming at the last day to gather his disciples to an eternal home rather than a historical one. Rather, his departure and return would be fulfilled in the one act that would combine both crucifixion and glorification, defeat and victory. The permanent dwellings are to be found in the time of the disciples' earthly pilgrimage and are to endure beyond the bounds of physical death. Jesus is the place where we meet God, and to be in Christ now is to be in him forever.

Jesus says he will love the disciple who keeps his commandments and will manifest himself to him. The word "manifest" is significant and is peculiar to this chapter of John. It is used of Hebrew Scriptures' theophanies, or revelations of God. What John wants us to understand here is that the theophany of the Hebrew Scriptures is fulfilled in the very different manifestation of God in the coming and return of Jesus the Son. The person who has Jesus' commandments is the one who has really come to understand them.

Recommended work: Do a word study of Spirit (Counselor), truth, theophany, and love.

The sermon might focus on loving Christ and what this means for believers now and in the age to come. Love is the key word in this passage and so is the work of the Spirit of truth. The sermon might deal with ways we express our love for Christ by keeping his commandments in our daily living, and with the Spirit who guides and strengthens us to do this.

Acts 8:26–40 (C)

Acts 8:26–40 or Deuteronomy 4:32–40 (E)

The events of this story take place on a road that runs south from Jerusalem to Gaza. Gaza is located southwest of Jerusalem on the route to Egypt and was a very old Philistine city. A revelation through an angel is a favorite theme of Luke's. Note that the angel in v. 26 performs the same function as the Spirit in v. 29. The Ethiopian eunuch was a Nubian from an area south of Egypt. Luke pictures him not as a Gentile but as a proselyte who had been to Jerusalem to worship and is reading one of the prophets. He need not be thought of as a castrated male who was excluded from the temple but rather as an important man, a foreigner, though possibly a Jew. He was a powerful person as the queen's minister. But he lacks the power to understand the word of God. However, he is willing to be instructed by Philip regarding the good news of Jesus (v. 35). Candace was the title of the queen, not her name.

In the ancient world, reading was done aloud. When a copy of an ancient manuscript was read, the words needed to be spelled out and this was more easily done reading aloud. It takes a good deal of sophistication to read silently, although with modern print this is done more easily. The Ethiopian was reading the great prophecy of the Servant of the Lord from Isaiah 53:7b–8a. This is one of the first plain uses of this passage in referring to Jesus. The term "servant" is not applied to Jesus here, nor is there reference to Jesus as servant bearing our sins. Luke, rather, is stressing his belief that the Hebrew Scriptures had been fulfilled in the suffering and resurrection of Jesus.

The lamb which is dumb refers to Jesus who was silent at his trial. The prediction that Jesus' life as servant would be taken up from the earth was fulfilled in his resurrection and ascension and exaltation.

Philip preached the good news to the Ethiopian, which may have included a demand to repent and be baptized (2:38). Some manuscripts add a call to confession and the eunuch's response, which is a footnote in the RSV. The purpose of this is to moderate the abruptness in which baptism is administered without instruction or evidence of faith.

Following the baptism, the Spirit sends Philip on his mission of preaching the gospel to all the towns until he came to Caesarea. The eunuch went on his way rejoicing, the usual response to conversion and forgiveness of sins. Eusebius, a church father, says that the Ethiopian returned home and became an evangelist. The record of his conversion moves Luke nearer to the evangelization of the Gentiles, a subject dear to Luke. Ethiopians were regarded by the Greeks as living on the edge of the world, and a Roman expedition went there in A.D. 61–63 to explore the Nile. The point that Luke is making here is that very soon after the risen Lord's commission to the disciples, their witness had reached the end of the earth!

Philip seems to have settled down in Caesarea, and he appears next in the narrative twenty years later (21:8). He, by then, had become a family man with four daughters, each a prophetess, who carried on their father's work of evangelizing.

Recommended work: Locate the action and movement of Philip and the eunuch in a Bible atlas and read the Isaiah passage and commentaries on it.

The sermon might follow the movements in the text from Philip encountering the Ethiopian, responding to his request for guidance in understanding the scriptures, and bringing him to faith in Jesus, which resulted in the conversion and baptism of the eunuch. The thrust of the sermon should be to move the hearers so to understand the scripture that they too may come to faith or deeper faith in Jesus and so go on their way rejoicing and, as tradition at least tells us, evangelizing others!

Acts 9:26–31 (RC)

This is an account of Paul's first visit to Jerusalem, although in Galatians 1:15–20 Paul implies that his first visit was three years *after* his conversion. We shouldn't be surprised that Paul had difficulty joining the disciples in Jerusalem, since he had persecuted the church. Note the dramatic way Barnabas mediates for him. It seems that Luke is anxious to present Paul as filling the role of Stephen, another one who disputed against the Hellenists. Luke describes Paul's dispute with the Hellenists. The response was swift and violent: they sought to kill Paul. (Preachers today get angry letters and responses but few threats on their lives.) In the eyes of the Hellenists, Paul was a traitor to their cause of persecuting the Christians.

Paul was saved by his friends who put him on a ship to Tarsus, Paul's home city and a leading center of culture.

The result of this persecution against Paul was that the church had peace, was built up, and was multiplied. The church through the ages has survived and often flourished under persecution but languished in times of affluence.

Recommended work: Read Paul's account of his visit to Jerusalem and his activities recorded in Galatians. Compare Paul to Stephen in their dispute with the Hellenists and the outcome for each.

The sermon might follow the moves of the text, giving some background of Paul and his persecution of Christians in Jerusalem. The sermon might encourage hearers to witness boldly to their faith in spite of difficulties and should remind them that the church survives better under persecution than affluence.

1 John 4:7–12 (C)

1 John 3:18–24 (L) (RC)

1 John 3:(14–17) 18–24 or Acts 8:26–40 (E)

Since 1 John 3:18–24 was dealt with in the (C) reading last week it will not be repeated here.

The 1 John 4:7–12 passage is part of the section of vs. 7–21, which deals with the blessedness of love. Note that vs. 1–6 dealt with the first rule of the double commandment in 3:23, namely, that we should believe in the name of God's Son Jesus Christ. Now in vs. 7–12 the second part of the great commandment is discussed, "that we should love one another, just as he has commanded us." Here the motive for mutual love is the knowledge of God and the sharing of God's life which such knowledge makes possible. Our love is not the condition of our fellowship with God. Rather, it is the sign of it. God's love is revealed in God's sending the Son into the world as the expiation or atonement for our sins.

Recommended work: Do a word study of love, perfected, and expiation.

The sermon might focus on the invitation the author gives to "love one another" which is grounded in the fact that love is of God. The sermon might use images of God's love for us in our personal experiences in family, community, and church, and ways we can love one another in daily living. By our loving one another, God abides in us and God's love is completed in us. God's love for us is prior to our love for God and others and is basic and should be emphasized.

Theological Reflection

Again there is a focus on the work of the risen and living Christ in these passages. The John 15 passage deals with the necessity of abiding in Christ in order to bear much fruit and prove to be his disciples, a relationship whose bond is love. In the John 14 passage Jesus assures the disciples of his continuing love and presence with them by the power of the Counselor after he has departed by death, resurrection, and ascension. Luke in the Acts 8 passage relates the evangelizing work of Philip in leading the Ethiopian to faith in the living Christ by the work of the Spirit, which involved his being baptized and going on his way rejoicing. The 1 John 4 passage focuses on love, God's love for us which is the basis and motive for our love for God and others. This love of God was made manifest in God's Son who is the expiation for our sins by his death and resurrection.

Children's Message

The talk with the children might be about Philip telling the Ethiopian the meaning of the Isaiah passage describing the Servant of the Lord. The Ethiopian was a high official with great power, but he lacked the power to understand the meaning of the scripture. Philip explained it, and the man came to faith in Christ, was baptized, and went on his way home to Ethiopia rejoicing. Legend has it that he evangelized what was thought of then as the edge of the world. We can help others understand the message of God's love for them and so find joy.

Hymns for Easter 5

In Heavenly Love Abiding; Thine Is the Glory; Blessed Jesus, We Are Here.

Easter 6

Psalm 98 (C)
Psalm 98:1–4 (RC)
Psalm 33 or 33:1–8, 18–22 (E)

Acts 10:44–48 (C)
Acts 11:19–30 (L)
Acts 10:25–26, 34–35, 44–48 (RC)
Acts 11:19–30 or Isaiah 45:11–13, 18–19 (E)

1 John 5:1–6 (C)
1 John 4:1–11 (L)
1 John 4:7–10 (RC)
1 John 4:7–21 or
Acts 11:19–30 (E)

John 15:9–17

Meditation on the Texts

We pray, O gracious and loving God, that we may keep Christ's commandments and so abide in his love, even as he has kept your commandments and abides in your love. We thank you that Christ has loved us even as you have loved him. As we remember Jesus' love which went even to laying down his life for us on the cross, we thank you for this supreme love. We know that Christ has chosen us and appointed us to go and bear fruit and wills that our fruit should abide. By the power of the Spirit enable us to obey Christ's command to love one another. And may we know Christ's joy in our lives in all its fullness. When we recall the persecution of Stephen and the early Christians we thank you for being with those who were scattered and enabling them to preach the Lord Jesus. We rejoice that a great number believed and turned to Christ as their Lord. Thank you for the work of Barnabas and Saul in preaching, teaching, and building up the church especially in Antioch. May we emulate the early Christians who determined, everyone according to her or his ability, to send relief to those in need. Help us to test the spirits to see whether they are from you, O God. We thank you for the assurance that every spirit which confesses that Jesus Christ has come in the flesh is of you, O God, and that we have overcome the spirits which oppose God. And by this we know that we abide in Christ and he in us because he has given us of his own Spirit. We love, because you, O God, first loved us. May we continually express our love for you in love for our neighbors whom we have seen. Amen.

Commentary on the Texts

John 15:9–17

Our pericope continues the theme from last week on the pattern of the believer's life. The thrust of our reading is the relation of believers to one another, which is one of love, a quality of love determined by Jesus' death. Jesus commands the disciples to love one another. If they obey, then fellowship with Jesus (vs. 14, 15) and fruit bearing and prayer (v. 16) will result from such obedience to love. The shapers of the lectionary have omitted vs. 18–25 (vs. 26–27 are used for the Day of Pentecost, Year B) which express the abrasive side of the Christian life: opposition from the world and persecution like that which Jesus endured. By omitting this and similar passages the shapers of the lectionary have created a romantic posture of the church toward the culture. This omitted material would be of special encouragement and comfort to Christians suffering persecution today. The preacher may want to draw from vs. 18–25 or even include them in the reading in order to give a more balanced interpretation of Jesus' message.

Verses 9–17 are really an interpretation of the idea of bearing fruit set forth in v. 8.

However, this connection may not have been original. Note that although the imagery of the vine and branches occurs again only in v. 16, the whole message of vs. 9–17 is very much related to that image. The theme of love is developed more strongly in vs. 9–17 than anywhere else in John. It is closely related to the motifs found in 1 John (compare with our readings for today and recent Sundays). Remember that in 6:57 we hear that life is passed from the Father to the Son in order that the Son might communicate life to others. Now in v. 9 it is *love* that is passed on from Father to Son and then from Son to disciples. This is entirely fitting, since Jesus is speaking in the hour when he showed his love for his own to the very end. See how the words "love" and "life" are somewhat used interchangeably.

We should be conscious of the fact that by love John does not mean something primarily emotional. Rather, love is not only ethical but comes close to being metaphysical. The love commanded here is not a matter of unity of will resulting from an affective relationship. Rather, it is a *unity of being* resulting from a divine quality. Love, for John, is related to being or remaining in Jesus.

The last part of v. 9, "abide in my love," puts a demand on the disciples to respond to Jesus' love in a similar fashion to v. 4 which demands abiding in Jesus' love in response to his cleansing. Note that the theme of love which is introduced in v. 9 is further developed in v. 10 which associates love and commandments. Love and obedience are mutually dependent, since love arises out of obedience and obedience out of love. Thus love, for John, is not mystical, as the Gnostics taught when using the image of the vine, but is mutually related to love.

The refrain "These things I have spoken to you" (v. 11) marks the transition from vs. 7–10 to vs. 12–17. While the theme of joy is mentioned in passing here, it will be further developed as the central focus of 16:20–24. See how joy is said to flow from both obedience and love as Jesus' own joy springs from his union with God. That union is expressed in both love and obedience. "My joy" is like "my peace," and both are gifts of salvation. Note here and elsewhere how often in John joy is linked with the saving work of Jesus. The risen Christ will fill the disciples with joy as he greets them with "Peace" in 20:19–21.

The verb tense in v. 12, a present subjunctive, indicates that the love the disciples are to have for one another is to be continuous and lifelong. Jesus commands love to be "as I have loved you." The aorist tense in Greek used in v. 13 indicates completed action and points to the supreme act of Jesus' love.

Notice that Jesus says "This is my commandment," not "commandments." All that follows from this can be summed up in the one implication, namely, that Christians *owe love to one another.* They are bound together as a body of disciples in order that their mission to the world might be more effective. This is not to narrow love from a universalism into a Christian churchly parochialism.

There is no greater love than that of one person laying down his or her life for another. The Carnegie Hero Fund Commission makes annual awards to individuals who have either risked their lives or given their lives to rescue one or more persons from drowning or other death-dealing circumstance. The preacher would do well to consult newspapers in a public library for records of this award over recent years.

Jesus' death is held up as a model of the intensity of the love the disciples are to have for one another. It should be pointed out that vs. 12–13 have become one of the great justifications for Christian martyrs.

Verse 14 indicates that the love of which v. 13 speaks is to be constitutive of those whom Jesus loves. Note that John's statement that Christian love is to be of the kind that Jesus expressed in laying down his life for his friends is the equivalent to the Synoptic demand that the disciples should take up their cross and follow Jesus (Mark 8:34–35 and parallels). If the disciples can understand this, then they will have crossed over the great divide that marks off the life of the New Israel from that of the old and that of the world. To understand what was involved in Jesus' death is to enter into a new set of relationships going beyond that of Lord and servant/slave to that of friend and friend. The symbol of foot washing had emphasized this (13:14). However, this did not prevent Jesus from acting in the very reverse of the master/slave relationship in washing their feet. In doing this, Jesus transformed the relationship and exposed it for what it really was all along.

It has been entirely on Jesus' initiative that all of the disciples have been called into the intimacy and strength of the community of faith (v. 16). The purpose behind this calling was that the disciples might go and bear fruit and their fruit should abide. Here Jesus speaks to all Christians who are of the elect or chosen of God (Rom. 8:33; Col. 3:12; 1 Peter 2:4). The Twelve are models for all Christians in both having been chosen and in being sent to bring the word to others.

The Twelve are being given a mission that all Christians must fulfill, which includes bearing fruit and remaining in Christ. Note that the "This I command you" of v. 17 is a variant of "This is my commandment" in v. 12 and is used in place of the refrain "I have said this to you." The latter is used by John to close several of the divisions of this Last Discourse. Consider how appropriate the "Love one another" command at the end of this passage is as it concludes a section so concerned with love. Note the striking contrast of this love with the world's hate in the section that follows, which is omitted by the lectionary. The contrast of hate of the world sets off the quality of Christian love and reveals the abrasive aspect inherent in the biblical faith. To love is to be set apart from the world as a follower of the King of love still living in a world of hate.

Recommended work: Do a word study of love, abide, servants, and friends. Contrast this passage with the one that follows in 15:18–16:4a.

The sermon might develop images and follow the moves in the passage but also contrast the love that Christians are commanded to have for one another with the hatred the world will have for them. The sermon might draw from contemporary instances of individuals who have lain down their lives for friends and then point to Jesus who gave his life for us. The preacher may want to point out that since love is commanded, it is not something the Christian can boast of or claim to originate. Rather, we are to love as Christ has loved us in his death and resurrection and then to bear fruit for Christ. We are so to abide in Christ that whatever we ask in his name (nature) he may give it.

Acts 10:44–48 (C)

Acts 10:25–26, 34–35, 44–48 (RC)

Since vs. 25–26 introduce the sections of vs. 34–35 and vs. 44–48, we will not comment on them. Acts 10:34–43 was dealt with in the Easter (E) reading. In the vs. 44–48 passage we have an account of the gift of the Spirit which is the result of Peter's speech after the conversion of Cornelius. Notice that 11:15 says the gift came at the very beginning of Peter's sermon, but in Luke's account the sermon had been completed. The gift of the Spirit *before* baptism is unique. The speaking in tongues was the proof that the Holy Spirit fell before baptism (v. 46). This was an external display of the Spirit's presence.

The Jewish Christians with Peter are amazed that God's gift is conveyed to Gentiles. Now the experience of Cornelius and his household is generalized.

Once the believers have received the Spirit, baptism cannot be withheld from them (v. 47). The rite is understood, as in the experience of Jesus (Luke 3:21–22), to involve both water and Spirit. Peter commands the believers to be baptized, acting as the apostolic supervisor, but does not perform the rite himself. Baptism is in "the name of Jesus Christ" rather than the trinitarian formula.

Notice that the descent of the Spirit on these Gentiles is outwardly manifested much as it was on the day of Pentecost when the original disciples received the Spirit. The Gentiles were considered "lesser breeds without the Law" and yet they too received the Spirit. The gift of the Spirit was not regarded as a substitute for baptism in water. Rather, baptism in water was the fitting response to the act of God in giving the Spirit. No one seems to have suggested that Cornelius be circumcised, which served as an appropriate precedent when this issue was raised at the Jerusalem council (Acts 15:5–11).

Recommended work: Compare this gift of the Spirit with that at Pentecost and on Easter evening and other occasions.

The sermon might focus on the spread of the gospel and the gift of the Spirit to the Gentiles, a breakthrough for the Christian faith as it moves out of Judaism into the Gentile world. The power of the Spirit to transform lives today should be the thrust of the sermon. It should seek to lead hearers to faith in Christ and the empowering of the Spirit and baptism.

Acts 11:19–30 (L)

Acts 11:19–30 or Isaiah 45:11–13, 18–19 (E)

This is the account of the mission to the Greeks in Antioch. The immediate events leading to this mission were Stephen's death and the ensuing persecution. Antioch was located on the Orontes River in Syria. The modern city is Antakya, located eighteen miles upstream. Antioch was founded in 300 B.C. and quickly became a city of great importance. At the time of Luke's account it was the third largest city in the Greco-Roman world, after Rome and Alexandria. It was a great commercial center as well as a political capital. It was located between the urbanized Mediterranean world and the eastern desert and because of this was more cosmopolitan than most Hellenistic cities. It was here at Antioch that Christianity first displayed its cosmopolitan character. The congregation included both Jewish and Gentile Christians. The evangelization of the Gentiles is described in v. 20. In Luke's thinking, the spread of the Christian faith is a slow process, moving out like ripples from the center at Jerusalem. Now it reaches this great center of Greek culture that has a population of some 800,000 noted for its blatant paganism.

The content of the message of the men of Cyprus and Cyrene was "the Lord Jesus." The Greek may mean they were preaching Jesus as the Lord, the lord of their lives in contrast to the lords of the Hellenistic cults. Notice that the term "Lord" is used three times in the passage.

The expression "The hand of the Lord was with them" (v. 21) is a typical one from the Hebrew Scriptures which recognized divine assistance and support.

Barnabas is sent from Jerusalem to supervise the Antioch church where he plays a role similar to that of Peter and John in Samaria. We get the impression that Saul (Paul) has dropped out of the picture for Luke, but actually he has been busy in Syria, Cilicia, and maybe even farther west on a mission similar to that at Antioch.

The disciples were first called Christians there, which has led to much debate by scholars over the meaning of the word. The ending "ian" suggests that the bearers of the name are followers of Christ. We cannot tell whether the name was one the Christians devised or whether it was given them by outsiders as a nickname.

An even greater problem is that of the sending of relief to Jerusalem by the hand of Barnabas and Saul. Famine did occur in various parts of the Roman Empire during the reign of Claudius (A.D. 41–54), but it is not likely that it occurred all over the world, since it would have affected Antioch as well. Note that the passage introduces two classes of church officials: prophets and the elders. Prophets were charismatic leaders who though associated with Jerusalem and Antioch were not restricted to a local church. The elders seem to have been local officials, and we find their background in Judaism (4:5, 8). They may have been appointed by the apostles.

It is significant that it was at Antioch, where believers were first called Christians, that an offering was given for famine relief in Jerusalem. Every one of the disciples gave according to his or her ability. It seems they allocated a fixed sum out of their income or property as a contribution to this fund and Saul and Barnabas were delegated to take it to the mother church in Jerusalem.

Recommended work: Reflect on the effects of persecution and martyrdom in the early church and compare the effects of it with affluent, comfortable American society on the spread of the gospel.

The sermon might follow the action in the passage leading up to the giving of the offering for famine relief in Jerusalem, thus expressing in a material way the spiritual commitment of the believers to love God and neighbor. The sermon might connect genuine Christianity with the act of giving to others in need, contrasted with self-centered religion concerned only for the wants and whims of a local congregation.

1 John 5:1–6 (C)

1 John 4:1–11 (L)

1 John 4:7–10 (RC)

1 John 4:7–21 or Acts 11:19–30 (E)

We dealt with 1 John 5:1–6 in Easter 2, (L) and (RC). We dealt with 1 John 4:7–12 in Easter 5, (C). Here we will comment on 4:1–6 and 13–21 only. The first passage, 4:1–6, focuses on the issue of discernment of truth and error. The second section, 4:13–21, is part of a section that deals with the blessedness of love in vs. 7–21. It presupposes the affirmation in v. 8 that "God is love."

Notice in 4:1–2 the contrast between spirits and powers claimed by false prophets and the Holy Spirit. This is a polemical passage in which the group attacked, along with its heretical doctrine, is probably not much different from that described in 2:18–27. It may be that the Ebionite denial of Jesus' Messiahship is the only heresy intended here, but it is likely that the docetic/gnostic issues are involved also. The source of this error is spirits, and their spokespersons are false prophets. The test of a Christian confession is: Jesus Christ has come in the flesh (v. 2).

In vs. 4–6 the victory of the children of God is set forth. There are two kinds of humans: those who are of God and those of the world. Whoever knows God listens to us, says the author.

Our passage of vs. 13–21 consists of two sections. The message of vs. 13–18 is that the Holy Spirit testifies that Jesus, the Son of God, has revealed his Father as love and when this love is matured in us then fear of judgment is eliminated. Verses 19–21 declare that love originates in God and failure to love is visible evidence of a break with the unseen God and a violation of God's commandment to love the brother and sister.

The author of this epistle here establishes the certainty of our abiding in God by bringing together various earlier considerations and combining them with the present treatment of the theme of love in greater depth. Notice that vs. 13–18 have connections both backward and forward.

The words "by this" in v. 13 look forward, since not only does our mutual love prove that God abides in us but the personal experience of God's own Spirit is concrete proof of this. Compare this verse with 3:24 and with Paul's statement in Romans 8:15–16, both of which affirm that the Spirit is the evidence that God abides in us and we in God.

Then we have another proof that God abides in us and we in God: the true confession that we make. "Whoever confesses that Jesus is the Son of God, God abides in him, and he in God" (v. 15). God's own Spirit enables us to testify that the Father has sent the Son. Reflect on the phrase "We have seen and testify" (v. 14) which expresses the common witness of the church and not that of a special group of eyewitnesses (compare with 1:1–5).

Recommended work: Read all of chapter 4. Reflect on the contrast between false spirits and the Holy Spirit and the ways of knowing that we abide in God.

The sermon on vs. 1–6 might focus on the affirmation that Christians are of God and therefore have overcome the false spirits. It might develop the contrast between false spirits today, new age religion, various isms, and of course the ever-present nationalism and greed for money and power which are false spirits.

The sermon on vs. 13–21 might center on the affirmation that "we love, because he first loved us" (v. 19). Our love for God and others is a response to God's prior love in Christ. The sermon might point especially to the critical relationship between love for God and love for neighbor (vs. 20–21).

Theological Reflection

The theme of love is prominent in the readings for today. The John 15 passage has the major thrust of Jesus' commandment to love one another. The Acts 10 passage deals primarily with the giving of the Spirit to the Gentiles, their believing and being baptized. The Acts 11 passage deals with the spread of the gospel to the Greeks and the relief offering to Jerusalem, an expression of love. Love is prominent in the passages of 1 John.

Children's Message

The talk with the children might be about the fact that followers of Jesus were first called Christians at Antioch, perhaps as a nickname, meaning belonging to Christ. Point out that Christians there sent an offering to poor Christians at Jerusalem suffering from a famine, thus expressing the love that followers of Christ have for one another.

Hymns for Easter 6

In Christ There Is No East or West; Love Divine, All Loves Excelling; We Are One in the Spirit.

Easter 7

Psalm 1 (C)
Psalm 47 (L)
Psalm 103:1–2, 11–12, 19–20 (RC)
Psalm 68:1–20 or Psalm 47 (E)

Acts 1:15–17, 21–26 (C)
Acts 1:15–26 (L)
Acts 1:15–17, 20–26 (RC)
Acts 1:15–26 or Exodus 28:1–4, 9–10, 29–30 (E)

1 John 5:9–13 (C)
1 John 5:9–15 or
Acts 1:15–26 (E)
1 John 4:13–21 (L)
1 John 4:11–16 (RC)

John 17:11b–19 (C)
John 17:11–19 (RC)

Meditation on the Texts

We thank you, gracious God, for Jesus' prayer that we might be one with all Christians even as you and he are one. We pray that the joy of the living Christ may be fulfilled in us. We recognize that the hatred of the world toward us is due to our not being of this world but belonging to Christ. Keep us from the evil one, O God. Consecrate us in your truth, we pray. We rejoice that we have the Son and therefore have life. We confess our faith in the name of the Son of God and are assured that we have eternal life. When we pray, we ask that we may always pray according to your will, for we know that if we ask anything according to your will you hear us. As we remember the first disciples who sought out godly leaders to lead the church, we pray that in our own time we may follow your guidance in securing leaders for your church. Amen.

Commentary on the Texts

John 17:11b–19 (C)

John 17:11–19 (RC)

Our pericope is part of Jesus' high-priestly prayer contained in chapter 17. The whole prayer falls into three parts: (1) Jesus' prayer for himself, vs. 1–5; (2) Jesus' prayer for his disciples, vs. 6–19 (of which our reading is a part); and (3) Jesus' prayer for the church universal, vs. 20–26. In contrast to the few brief prayers of Jesus in the Synoptic Gospels, here is an extended prayer offered by Jesus. Earlier, in 11:41–42 and 12:27, we have two brief "cries" of Jesus offered in times of great tension which resemble the prayers of the Synoptics. Jesus' prayer here is more serene and meditative and gathers up the themes of the discourses that have gone before. The thrust of the prayer is Jesus' consecration of himself as the mediator of salvation. In the prayer we have both the final resolution of Jesus' obedience to the death which will be his glorification, and an intercession for the fruits of his work after his ascension.

Jesus prays for the disciples who will be left in the world after his ascension (vs. 11). He prays that they may all be one, even as he and God, the Father, are one (v. 11b), that they may have joy (v. 13), that they may be victorious over the evil one (v. 15), and that they may fulfill their mission of representing the Christ to the whole world (vs. 18–19).

This prayer must be the prayer of *all who follow Jesus.* Some scholars see in it an exposition of the Lord's Prayer of the Synoptic Gospels. Notice that in both prayers there is a strange lack of reference to the Spirit.

Our pericope begins with Jesus saying that he is no longer in the world. He can say this because the cross is so imminent that he speaks of it as if it were already past. Jesus can pray that he is no longer in the world and then in v. 13 pray that he is coming to the Father. In other places in the discourse Jesus is said to be going to the Father, but here he speaks directly to God and so "coming" is more fitting. He prays "Holy Father," which could be translated "O Father most holy." Recall that God is called the "Holy One" of Israel in the Hebrew Scriptures and is addressed as holy in Jewish prayers.

Jesus prays that God will keep the disciples safe, meaning keep them safe from the contamination of the world. They are to be both marked with and protected by the divine name which had been given to Jesus.

The original idea in holiness is separateness, being set apart, and distance. The attribute of holy is especially fitting when used here of the One whom Jesus calls Father who is to "keep" those who are separated from the world, who are isolated in the world, as his own. Thus the "Holy Father" will keep his own "holy" in the midst of the world. He prays that God will give the disciples a protection he can no longer give. Notice the play on words in the line "None of them is lost (perished) but the son of perdition": perish and perdition. "Son of perdition" refers to Judas and is a Hebraism meaning "one closely identified with perdition."

(Note the reference to replacing Judas in our Acts 1 pericope for today.) In the New Testament, perdition often means damnation. Thus the reference here to Judas refers to him as one who belongs to the realm of damnation and is destined to final destruction. In the Gospels, Judas is seen as the tool of Satan, and we are told that Satan entered Judas' heart, prompting him to go out to betray Jesus. In some passages Judas is described as a devil (6:70). "That the scripture might be fulfilled" reflects what seems to have been an attempt by the early Christians to find passages in the Hebrew Scriptures to explain Judas' betrayal.

The reference to "these things" (v. 13) seems to refer to the early part of the prayer rather than to the whole last discourse of Jesus. Jesus speaks these things so that the disciples "may have my joy fulfilled in themselves," another instance in this discourse in which full joy is mentioned (see 15:11 and 16:24). In the writings of the rabbis full joy was a concept of the End time.

Jesus says he has given the disciples the Father's "word." Some scholars think the use of "word" in the singular refers to the divine message as a whole, in contrast to the plural which almost always means precepts. But both the plural and the singular of "word" appear in 14:24 without an apparent distinction of meaning. "Word," "words," and "commandments" are sometimes used interchangeably.

Jesus affirms that the disciples are "not of the world, even as I am not of the world" (v. 14). In John's thought, Christians are begotten from God and are chosen out of the world. They are citizens of another kingdom; therefore Satan has no more hold on them than he does on Christ their master. Jesus prays that God will sanctify them in the truth, praying that the disciples may be exempted from Satan's authority. Note that sanctify or consecrate (v. 17) corresponds to holy (see Heb. 9:13). Here Jesus is praying that God will make the disciples God's own separate possession, set apart and cut off from the world and its power. God will do this by the power of truth, which recalls the words of v. 3, referring to "the only true God." Therefore God's word as spoken by Jesus and revealed in the Word (Logos) is also reality. Recall that truth has power to act, to set free. Here truth is both the agency of the consecration and the realm into which the disciples are consecrated. Now the purpose of this consecration is to prepare the disciples to carry on Christ's work, just as Christ has himself first been consecrated to fulfill God's mission (10:36).

Then the prayer continues as Jesus prays saying that even as God has sent him into the world, so he has sent the disciples into the world (v. 18). The consecration in truth is not just a purification from sin but is a consecration to a mission. They are consecrated because they are being sent into the world. The church is the body of Christ and replaces Christ after he is gone and manifests him as still present. The final verse of our pericope again stresses this ultimate connection between the consecration to service of Christ and of his disciples. Jesus here consecrates himself, another example of the same power possessed by God and by Jesus. He prays they may be consecrated in truth. Truth is used here without the article, and the meaning here is not that much different from that with the article in v. 17. However, here truth is more the realm of the disciples' consecration than the agency of that consecration. Thus Jesus consecrates himself and is therefore the agent in consecrating the disciples. By consecrating himself in death to God, Christ achieves in reality for his disciples that consecration for holy service which the old rite merely symbolized (see Heb. 10:10). Note the similarity of John's thought here to that of Hebrews. Compare this passage with 13:14 in which the disciples' obligation to serve under the constraint of the master's example is emphasized in a similar way.

Recommended work: Compare the ideas and images in our pericope with those in Hebrews which describe Jesus as the high priest who makes intercession for his disciples. Do a word study of holy, consecrate, truth, and world.

The sermon might follow the movements of the passage as Jesus prays for the disciples (for us today) that they may be one and then prays that they may be kept from the evil one (compare to "deliver us from the evil one" of the Lord's Prayer), and consecrates the disciples for mission to the world. The sermon might deal with the abrasive aspect of the gospel, expressed in Jesus' words that the world has hated the disciples because they are not of the world, even as he is not of this world. The thrust of the sermon should be on the church's mission to the world, sanctified and empowered by the living Christ.

Acts 1:15–17, 21–26 (C)

Acts 1:15–26 (L)

Acts 1:15–17, 20–26 (RC)

Acts 1:15–26 or Exodus 28:1–4, 9–10, 29–30 (E)

We will deal with Acts 1:15–26, which includes all of the primary readings above. The theme of the reading is the restoration of the Twelve, following the earlier defection of Judas. The Eleven remained together, but the action in this passage is the restoring of the sacred number of Twelve, corresponding to the twelve tribes of Israel, anticipating the coming of the new age.

The witnesses of the ascension return to Jerusalem and enter the upper room. The list of the Eleven in v. 13 is identical to that of Luke 6:14–16 except for order. They prayed that Jesus' promise would be fulfilled and are joined by the women and family of Jesus in their prayer. This is the background for our pericope. Peter makes a speech to about 120 brethren in this period between the ascension and Pentecost. Luke inserts information about the death of Judas (see the John 17 reading for today).

The number of 120 may be the result of the notion of the rabbis that leaders of a community should compose a tenth of the total. Thus 10 times 12 equals 120. Also 120 Jewish males were the number required to form a synagogue with its own council. So now the disciples have enough people to form a legitimate community. Thus from Luke's point of view all is done in faithfulness to Judaism. Peter's speech is one that is designed for Luke's readers, as are all those in Acts. We do not have a tape-recorded account of Peter's speech. Rather than asking whether Peter really gave this speech, we should ask what Luke is trying to say to his readers in a period much later than that of Peter and how this contributes to the plot or movement of the story of Acts.

The information about Judas here is not consistent with that of Matthew 27:3–10. Early tradition had a number of stories about Judas' fate.

Peter says that Judas' place among the Twelve had to be filled, since scripture required it (v. 20). The first quotation is from Psalm 69:25, which speaks of the desolation of the habitation of the wicked, used here regarding the desolation of the field or farm that Judas purchased, thus implying his death. The second quotation is from Psalm 109:8 and it was used to insist that the vacant office of Judas be filled.

Therefore two candidates are put forward who meet the requirements of being eyewitnesses who had been with Jesus from the baptism of John until the day Jesus was taken up into heaven. This would include the resurrection. The apostles' primary task was to become witnesses to the resurrection. Note Luke's concern for a firsthand witness. This is his way of guaranteeing the authenticity of the account he puts in Peter's speech. This election of Matthias lets Luke define who an apostle is (vs. 21–22), and note that Paul would not share these qualifications.

The selection is made by casting lots. This was done by writing the names of the candidates on stones, putting them in a container, and shaking it until one fell out. The person whose name was on it was thought to be selected by God. Matthias is chosen, but we do not hear of him again in the story. This method is not used again in the early church.

Note the irony of Peter's speech in telling of Judas' betrayal when he himself denied and cursed his Lord. Here at the beginning the church encountered failure and deceit.

Recommended work: Compare Peter's speech with other speeches in Acts, noting differences and similarities.

The sermon might deal with the issue of church leadership, the failure of humans to be faithful, and the church's coping with this by facing up to the failure and selecting another who is qualified. The qualifications of an apostle should be pointed out and compared with qualifications today of a personal faith in the risen Christ and obedient discipleship in one's daily life.

1 John 5:9–13 (C)

1 John 5:9–15 or Acts 1:15–26 (E)

1 John 4:13–21 (L)

1 John 4:11–16 (RC)

Since the 1 John 4:13–21 and 11–16 passages were dealt with in the (E) reading for Easter 6, they will not be discussed here.

The 1 John 5:9–15 reading spans two sections: vs. 1–12, which deal with victorious faith which issues in eternal life, and vs. 13–21, which form the conclusion of the epistle.

The reference to the testimony of men (v. 9) is to the testimony to Christ given by the Baptist in John 5:32–36. But the author declares that the testimony of God is greater, because a father can speak with more authority about his son than can anyone else. Note that v. 9b and its connection are not very clear. But the emphasis is on the objective and varied and continuous testimony of the Father to the Son which begins with his mighty works and other signs he performed (John 5:36).

In addition to these outward testimonies, there is an inward one: within the one who puts his or her faith not in doctrine but in a person, the Son of God (v. 10). In v. 10b we have the converse of this: the one who does not believe God or trust God's word, who had thus made up his mind that God is a liar.

In vs. 11–12 the benefits and the content of the testimony of the inner kind are defined in terms of eternal life, a favorite concept of the author which dominates the epistle. The tense of "gave" (v. 11) indicates that the author has Christ's historic life in mind. Reassurance is found in the evidence that we abide in God: our own love, our true confession, and the activity of the Spirit within us.

Note that v. 13 is a more emphatic statement of v. 12 and is the real conclusion of the epistle. Compare it to John 20:31 which is the real conclusion of the Gospel. But here v. 13 is transitional to what follows: sure knowledge. The Christian life is a joyful confidence and unrestrained speaking, either in witness, approach to God, or as stressed here in the judgment and in bringing requests to God. Note especially the conditions set here for God's answer to prayer.

Recommended work: Compare v. 13 with John 17:3; 20:31; and compare v. 14 with Matthew 7:7.

The sermon might focus on prayer and what praying according to God's will means, showing how prayer is our final confidence of victory over evil.

Theological Reflection

We continue the Eastertide emphasis on the living Christ with the prayer of Jesus in John 17 for the disciples who will be left in the world after his ascension, that they may be united with God and with one another. The Acts reading points to the church's filling Judas' place in order to carry forth the mission of the risen Christ. And the 1 John 5 passage focuses on victorious faith and prayer, both following Christ's victorious resurrection.

Children's Message

The talk with the children might be about prayer, pointing to Jesus' need to pray not only for himself and his work but for us his disciples. Prayer might be described as both listening to and talking with God. Jesus prays that we may be kept from temptation to think and do bad things. God hears our prayers as they are in accord with his will. A brief prayer might conclude the talk, giving thanks for each child and her or his family.

Hymns for Easter 7

Jesus Shall Reign Where'er the Sun; God of the Prophets!; Christ Is the World's True Light.

Psalm 104:24–34 (C)
Psalm 104:25–34 (L)
Psalm 104:1, 24, 29–31, 34 (RC)
Psalm 104:25–37 or 25–32;
or 33:12–15, 18–22 (E)

Ezekiel 37:1–14 (C)
Acts 2:1–11 (RC)
Acts 2:1–11 or Isaiah 44:1–8 (E)

Acts 2:1-21 (C)
1 Corinthians 12:3–7, 12–13 (RC)
1 Corinthians 12:4–13 or Acts 2:1–11 (E)

John 15:26–27; 16:4b–15 (C)
John 7:37–39a (L)
John 20:19–23 (RC)
John 20:19–23 or John 14:8–17 (E)

Meditation on the Texts

Gracious God, we thank you for the gift of the Counselor promised by Jesus who bears witness to Jesus. We thank you for the Spirit who guides us into all truth and declares the things that are to come. He has taken what is Jesus' and declared it to us, and for this we are grateful. We thank you that you have put your Spirit within us and given us life. Ezekiel saw the vision of the valley of dry bones which were given flesh and breath and made to stand on their feet. We know that you are God, for you have raised us from our graves of bondage to sin and given us life and freedom. As we recall the day of Pentecost, when the disciples were all together in one place and your Holy Spirit came upon them, we celebrate the empowering of the disciples for mission. May your Spirit fall anew upon us, that we may go forth to bear bold witness to your saving acts in Christ Jesus our Lord. We thank you for the gifts of the Spirit and remember that all gifts are inspired by the one and same Spirit. We who are baptized into Christ are members of his body and are therefore one and we drink of one Spirit. We thirst for the living water and therefore come to Christ to drink and be filled with the Spirit. Amen.

Commentary on the Texts

John 15:26–27; 16:4b–15 (C)

Our pericope spans two sections: chapter 15 deals with the pattern of the Christian believer's life, and chapter 16 focuses on the Christian's relation to the world.

We must read 15:26–27 against the background of the preceding verses in which Jesus charges that the world's hatred means it is guilty of sin (another example of the abrasive character of biblical faith). Now the theme of the Counselor is introduced to prepare the way for the description of the Paraclete (Counselor) in 16:8–11. There the Paraclete establishes the guilt and sin of the world. The world will persecute the disciples because they belong to Jesus, and so the Counselor is sent in Jesus' name to counter this. The Paraclete represents Jesus' presence among human beings, and so in hating the disciples who are the dwelling place of the Counselor the world is striking out at Jesus' continued presence. The Counselor/Spirit is invisible to the world. Therefore the only way his witness can be heard is through the *witness of the disciples*.

The disciples are the unique witnesses of Jesus because they have been with him. They must bring his word into the world (see 14:26; 16:13–14). This also agrees with the other references in John to the witness of the disciples in the postresurrection period. Since Jesus is the supreme revelation of God to human beings, there can be no witness to the world except the witness that Jesus bore. The witness by the Counselor through the disciples only interprets that.

Thus the disciples, by living the life that Christ has made possible, by being the church which is the continuation of Christ in this world, are the continuing witness to his work. This is at the same time the witness of the Spirit because it is the Spirit who is sent by the Son from the Father who will be the heart of the church. The reference to the disciples' being with Jesus from the beginning could, when considered from John's viewpoint, refer to Christians who have been faithful to Jesus since their conversion.

Then in 16:1 Jesus gives his own prophecy of the future in order to bolster his disciples' faith. By thus being forewarned they should be better prepared for what will be the church's future. Jesus foretells that the disciples will experience what the blind man experienced (9:22, 34) who was excommunicated from the synagogue. By the time this Gospel was written the separation of synagogue and church was complete. Jesus says that everyone who kills them will think they are doing a service to God. The persecution of the church by both Jew and Gentile will be religiously motivated, although misguided. Paul before his conversion is a prime example of this. A commentary on Numbers 25:13 says that anyone who sheds the blood of the godless is like one who offers a sacrifice. We must remember, however, that similar statements can be found in Christian sources. To the shame of the church, it must be admitted that Christians have fulfilled Jesus' prophecy of good men doing evil deeds. But such evil cannot be justified by a right understanding of God's nature.

The hour (16:4) probably means the hour of the persecutors. Jesus reminds the disciples to remember these things he has told them.

Recommended work: Read other passages that describe the role of the Counselor/Paraclete and compare them with this passage. Do a word study of Holy Spirit/Counselor.

The sermon might focus on the Counselor/Spirit of truth and his work in witnessing to Jesus. The Spirit is given to enable the disciples then and now to persevere in their faith in spite of persecution by the world. The sermon might be applied to people undergoing trials because of their Christian commitment.

John 20:19–23 (RC)

John 20:19–23 or John 14:8–17 (E)

See Easter 2, (C).

John 7:37–39a (L)

Our pericope is part of a chapter whose theme is Jesus, the water of life. The setting is the Feast of Tabernacles (or Booths) which commemorated the wilderness wanderings and began on the fifteenth of the seventh month (our September–October). For seven days of the feast, water was carried in a golden pitcher from the Pool of Siloam to the temple to remind the worshipers of the water from the rock in the desert (Num. 20:2–13). It also served as a symbol of hope for the coming deliverance by Messiah: "With joy you will draw water from the wells of salvation" (Isa. 12:3). See how dramatically Jesus proclaims that he is the source of living water, symbolizing the Spirit: "If any one thirst, let him come to me and drink" (v. 37). Thus Jesus is the true water of life. The prophet foretold "For I will pour water on the thirsty land, and streams on the dry ground; I will pour my Spirit upon your descendants, and my blessing on your offspring" (Isa. 44:3; also see Isa. 55:1). Those who believe in Christ become channels of living water (life) to others through Christ's Spirit given at Pentecost. The Spirit could be given in its fullness only *after* Jesus was glorified (crucified, risen, ascended). The Spirit is a mark of the messianic age (Joel 2:28–29; Acts 2:14–21 [part of our scripture for today]).

Recommended work: Reflect on the references to water and Spirit in the Hebrew Scriptures mentioned above. Do a word study of water and Spirit.

The sermon might develop the images of water and Spirit as they relate to life given by God through faith in Jesus Christ. There is a twofold movement in the text: all who thirst are invited to come to Jesus and drink, and then those who believe in Jesus become channels of life to others. The preacher might mention examples of persons who are channels of life, such as parents, teachers, friends, missionaries, health care professionals, or ministers.

This vision takes place in Babylon when Ezekiel is led out by the spirit into a plain on which may have remained bones of those who had fallen in an earlier battle. There he has a mystical experience which symbolizes his mission to the exiles in Babylon, namely, that through prophesying they will receive a *new spirit* which will enable them to rise from their lost hope and in turn to lead a new life back in the land of Israel. The bones are the exiles who have lost all hope of resuscitating the kingdom of Israel. They have no more hope of restoring Israel than of putting flesh on these dry bones and calling it life. The Hebrew word *ruah* means "spirit, breath, or wind," which enables the prophet to engage in a constant wordplay here. (Pronounce the word *ruah* while holding your hand near your mouth and you will feel the breath which the word symbolizes.) The four winds (v. 9) may refer to God's omnipresence.

In v. 10 we have a very imaginative and unusual scene, yet this vision has no direct connection with the Christian doctrine of resurrection. There is no reference here to the resurrection of individuals, although this concept is not far removed from it. In v. 11 the explanation of the dry bones is given, namely, that they are the whole house of Israel whose hope is lost.

The discouragement of the people is to be countered by the powerful word of God who alone knows that they can live (v. 3). In this vision we find a very effective symbol of the way in which every despairing refusal by persons to live may be overcome by the consoling forces of God's promise.

Then in v. 12 the metaphor shifts from bones to graves. The revival of the nations now resembles a corpse made to rise out of its grave. The land of exile is seen as a grave, where death dwells. In Ezekiel's vision the action of God in bringing out the people from exile (exodus) in Babylon, the great graveyard of nations, is directly related to the return of the home country of Israel which is the land of life. The opening of the grave (vs. 13–14) is the breaking through of the prison door of Babylon and bringing forth those who were in the grave. See how the rest of the words of the lamentation in v. 11 are contradicted, since according to this promise hope *must live* once again and death set free its captives. This act leads to a fresh knowledge of God's nature and to inward fellowship with God. This is repeated in vs. 13–14.

This vision and prophecy of Ezekiel gives the exiles much more than words of comfort. He points not to what they can do for themselves in exile but to the superhuman and miraculous power of God who is calling the lost to new fellowship. The exiles were desperate. But God comes in all God's mysterious power and makes a breakthrough beyond the forces of death.

Ezekiel emphasizes individual responsibility as a key to life with God whose ways are fair (18:25ff.), and this provides a motive. The Lord can act and should act.

Recommended work: Reflect on how this vision of hopelessness may represent the feeling of hearers caught in a deteriorating marriage, in drug or alcohol addiction, in a mental depression, or in another seemingly hopeless situation.

The sermon should develop the images of dry bones, the giving of breath and flesh to the bones, and the new life and freedom which Ezekiel's vision gives for living today. We live by images, and the sermon should enable hearers to see new possibilities with God they never had alone. The Christian message of new life by Christ's Spirit should be included in the sermon, which ties in with the Pentecost theme for today.

Acts 2:1–11 (RC)

Acts 2:1–11 or Isaiah 44:1–8 (E)

Acts 2:1–21 (C)

This is the description of the well-known Pentecost event in vs. 1–13, plus part of the Pentecost discourse which includes vs. 14–40 (the first of the so-called missionary discourses). The preacher may want to preach from this text on the Day of Pentecost or will certainly want to refer to this event if another text is chosen.

According to Jewish tradition, the law was given on this day which came seven weeks after Passover. The chapter begins "When the day of Pentecost had come" or "When the day was fulfilled" as it might be translated. This introduction raises a red flag that we have reached an important date in Luke's history of the Christian church. Recall that the same formula was used to announce the birth of Mary's child in Luke 2:6 and was used for the inauguration of the exodus/journey of Jesus in Luke 9:51. This phrase is thus a guidepost for the beginning of a major stage in Luke's sacred history. In our pericope it signals the new era of the church which the giving of the Spirit inaugurates.

Although Pentecost is often referred to as the "birthday of the church," it would be more accurate to refer to Easter as the birthday even of Pentecost, since Pentecost must be read within the context of Luke 24 which tells how the risen Christ was made known to the disciples at Emmaus in the breaking of the bread, how he opened their minds to understand the scriptures, and commanded them to stay in the city (Jerusalem) until they were clothed with power from on high. Luke separated the resurrection, ascension, and Pentecost on purpose. But the three are inseparably related, since at Pentecost the power of God which was made manifest at the resurrection and ascension of Christ is bestowed upon God's people. In earlier years the church, as it observed the liturgical year, linked these three events more closely. In more recent years the liturgical reforms have sought to place the liturgy for Pentecost within the context of the fifty-day celebration of Easter.

The day of Pentecost was named such because it came on the fiftieth day after the presenting of the first sheaf to be reaped of the barley harvest which put it on the fiftieth day from the first Sunday after Passover. (The word "pentecost" comes from the Greek word for "fiftieth.") It was known as the "feast of weeks" or "the day of the firstfruits." However, later it was observed as the anniversary of the giving of the law on Sinai, a date that can be arrived at from Exodus 19:1. The disciples were in the house that may have included the upper room of 1:13, but we cannot be sure.

The disciples were all together in one place when suddenly the room was filled with what seemed like a great gale of wind from heaven. We have no way of knowing whether it was heard only by the disciples or was audible to others. The wind symbolized the Spirit of God. Recall from the Ezekiel passage for today that when God commanded Ezekiel to prophesy to the wind and called it to blow on the dead bones in the valley the wind was the very breath of God which filled them with new life (Ezek. 37:9–14). Recall also the words of Jesus to Nicodemus in John 3:8. Could it also be the same wind that on the first morning of creation swept across the dark waters (Genesis 1)?

In addition to the wind which was heard, there were tongues as of fire which rested on each disciple (v. 3). Recall that John the Baptist had foretold that Christ would baptize with the Holy Spirit and with fire (Luke 3:16). Also, God's presence had been symbolized by the burning bush which appeared to Moses (Ex. 3:2–5). The spiritual meaning of this has been expressed by Charles Wesley in his hymn "O Thou Who Camest from Above." The preacher may want to use all or part of the hymn in the sermon and/or use it in congregational worship. We cannot tell how far the "tongues as of fire" was meant to symbolize the other tongues in which the disciples later spoke.

We are left with a mystery about the sensible phenomena, but the inward experience of the disciples was plain: they were filled with the Holy Spirit and began to speak in other tongues. The spiritual baptism which John the Baptist had foretold was now an accomplished fact. The disciples would be filled with the Spirit on later occasions (4:8, 31). But this experience of the baptism in the Spirit was an event that took place once for all. In the Hebrew Scriptures, when people were possessed by the Spirit of God they prophesied (Num. 11:26). At Pentecost the filling with the Spirit resulted in prophetic speech of a peculiar kind: utterance in "other tongues." While the other tongues in Corinthians was an incoherent form of speech (1 Cor. 14:1–33), here Luke seems to think of the gift of foreign languages as though the story of the tower of Babel had been reversed, as some scholars think. Others doubt this is what Luke had in mind. One thing is clear, that the first gift of the Spirit is the gift of speech in different languages enabling the disciples to proclaim the gospel.

Then the scene shifts from inside the upper room to outside on the street, where the gospel was drawing a crowd. There "Jews, devout men from every nation under heaven"

(v. 5), were being confronted by the church for the first time and the result was that they were bewildered (v. 6). It appears that the tongues were various languages of the nations since the foreigners heard in their own native language. The gift of the Spirit replaces the parousia in Christian consciousness as the Spirit inaugurates the era of church and mission, the new age of salvation history.

The ecstatic speech made the onlookers think the disciples were drunk with new wine. This prompts Peter to explain in a sermon what had happened (vs. 14–36). He says it was only the third hour, 9:00 A.M., thus too early to be drunk! Then he quotes from the prophet Joel, who foretold the gift of the Spirit upon all flesh as a mark of the messianic age (Joel 2:28–32). The Spirit is given to "all flesh," not just to chosen individuals as in the past. It seems Acts assumes that all Christians receive the Spirit.

Recommended work: Compare the gift of the Spirit at Pentecost with other accounts of the Spirit coming upon the disciples. Compare the tongues here with those Paul writes about in 1 Corinthians.

The sermon might follow the movements of the text from the disciples gathered in one place awaiting the power that Jesus promised, to the sound of the wind and tongues as of fire, the filling with the Spirit and speaking in other tongues, to the response of the onlookers and Peter's explanation. The goal of the sermon should be to enable hearers to receive a greater measure of the Spirit to empower them for mission.

1 Corinthians 12:3–7, 12–13 (RC)

1 Corinthians 12:4–13 or Acts 2:1–11 (E)

Our pericope spans two sections: vs. 1–12 deal with spiritual gifts and vs. 12–31 focus on the church as the body of Christ and its members. Paul makes the point that ecstasy is not enough to prove that one is moved by the Holy Spirit as he refers to the highly emotional orgiastic practices in some pagan cults (v. 2). Then in vs. 4–11 he points out that the real test is whether or not the gift of the Spirit comes from the one God and contributes to the common good (v. 7). Note the hint of the Trinity here: Spirit, Lord, God in vs. 4–5 (which might be referred to next Sunday, Trinity Sunday).

Paul emphasizes the variety of God's gifts to the church, their single source although there are wide differences, and their common purpose which is the good of the entire community rather than that of isolated individuals.

Paul gives special place to wisdom and knowledge as gifts of the Spirit, since these gifts were conspicuously absent from the Corinthian church in spite of their claims otherwise. Faith here means the intensity of faith which some manifest in the church, for example, in healing miracles and other mighty works. In vs. 10–11 Paul ends the list of the gifts of the Spirit with those most highly prized by his readers. He insists that God provides the church with people who can distinguish between spirits and with others to interpret them. He points to the complementary relationship of the whole membership of the church.

Then in vs. 12–14 Paul describes the church as the body of Christ which has many members, yet is one body formed of all who were baptized with one Spirit and made to drink of one Spirit. There are parallels to Paul's figure of the body in other ancient writings, but Paul makes a special Christian application of the figure here.

Recommended work: Do a word study of Spirit, body, knowledge, and wisdom.

The sermon might focus on the unity of the church in the one body of Christ composed of members with a great variety of gifts which are to be used for the common good.

Theological Reflection

On Pentecost we should expect the texts to spotlight the gift of God's Spirit and the Spirit's work. This is the case of all the texts, and the preacher would do well to reflect on their common theme and how their messages relate to one another.

Children's Message

The preacher may want to talk about the church as Christ's body which is one although composed of many members with a great variety of gifts. You might mention gifts that are used in worship and the church program and other gifts that children have which can be used for the common good.

Hymns for the Day of Pentecost

Come, Holy Ghost, Our Souls Inspire; Holy Spirit, Truth Divine; O Thou Who Camest from Above.

The Sundays After Pentecost

Color: Green. But other colors or combination of colors may be used, such as red, purple, and white. Red, symbolizing the fire of the Holy Spirit, might be used for evangelistic services. White is used on Trinity Sunday and Christ the King Sunday, the first and last Sundays of this season.

This part of the nonfestival half of the Christian year has been called a variety of names: Season After Pentecost, Kingdomtide, Ordinary Time, and others. (The other nonfestival portion of the Christian year comes between Epiphany and Lent.) Each Sunday stands on its own, and you have some freedom in selecting the passages on which to base your sermon. One suggestion is to follow a nine-year cycle, preaching on the Gospel one cycle, on the Epistles another, and on the Old Testament lesson the third cycle.

Or you may choose from among the three readings in selecting the text for the sermon, using the Gospel one Sunday, the Epistle another, or the Old Testament lesson. Another choice is to follow a semicontinuous reading, using either Old Testament, Epistle, or Gospel readings for the sermon for a period of time. By following one reading from a narrative of the Bible, such as the life of David, the congregation may build interest in a kind of miniseries of sermons on a person or theme of the Bible. Another choice is to depart from the lectionary (after preaching through years A, B, and C) during some or all of ordinary time in order to address specific issues or books of the Bible that are omitted from the readings of the Common Lectionary. For example, you might preach a series on one or more of the minor prophets, or on the Book of Esther (not included in the lectionary), or on the psalms. Or the series might be on the basics of the Christian faith, dealing with topics such as the Lord's Prayer, the Apostles' Creed, the Sermon on the Mount, or the Ten Commandments. A series might deal with some current social issues. You may want to use subjects requested by the congregation, such as death, why the innocent suffer, or life after death.

The lectionary readings are determined by the days within which a Sunday falls on the calendar. For instance, the readings for a particular Sunday will be designated for the Sunday between two dates (e.g., "August 14–20") regardless of the date of Pentecost.

Because this half of the church year is less structured, congregations may be creative in celebrating each Sunday. Point out that the color green symbolizes life and growth in nature and thus can symbolize the growth of Christians and congregations.

There are possibilities for preaching "occasional sermons" which respond to particular civic occasions or to the congregation's life, such as a church anniversary, July 4, Labor Day, or Thanksgiving. When this is done, an appropriate scripture reading is selected and substituted for the Gospel, Epistle, or Old Testament reading from the lectionary that Sunday. When Communion is celebrated, you may want to select an appropriate passage of scripture if those of the lectionary are not fitting.

By way of overview, it should be pointed out that the Christian year is *not* a sequential following of the life of Jesus from cradle to grave and beyond. Rather, the pattern of the Christian year is *a theological ordering of the church's commemoration of God's saving action.* The reforms that have occurred in recent years since Vatican II have been directed to returning the Roman Catholic Church to earlier practices rather than introducing innovations. Thus, what may seem new is usually the restoration of an ancient practice of the Christian church that had been dropped during the centuries.

Trinity Sunday

Psalm 29 (C)
Psalm 149 (L)
Psalm 33:4–6, 9, 18–20, 22 (RC)
Psalm 93 or Canticle 2 or 13 (E)

Isaiah 6:1–8 (C)
Deuteronomy 6:4–9 (L)
Deuteronomy 4:32–34, 39–40 (RC)
Exodus 3:1–6 (E)

Romans 8:12–17 (C)
Romans 8:14–17 (L) (RC)

John 3:1–17 (C)
John 3:1–16 (E)
Matthew 28:16–20 (RC)

Meditation on the Texts

Grant us a new vision of your glorious presence in our midst, O God, and open our ears to hear your question, "Whom shall I send, and who will go for us?" May we answer with Isaiah, "Here am I! Send me." We pray that we may love you with all our heart, soul, and might and that we may teach these words diligently to our children. No other God has spoken out of the midst of the fire to the people and they still lived. We thank you for your mighty acts of deliverance in history. We have been led by your Spirit to put to death the deeds of the body and are led by your Spirit. By the Spirit bearing witness with our spirit we are children of yours, and heirs of yours and fellow heirs with Christ provided we suffer with him that we may also be glorified with him. We stand on holy ground in your presence, O God, and we confess that in Jesus Christ we have seen you in the Word made flesh. We pray that we may be bold in proclaiming the good news that you loved the world so much that you gave your only Son that whoever believes in him should not perish but have eternal life. For we know that Jesus came into the world, not to condemn it, but that the world might be saved through him. May we do what is true and thus come to the light, that it may be clearly seen that our deeds have been wrought in you, our God. Amen.

Commentary on the Texts

John 3:1–17 (C)

John 3:1–16 (E)

Our pericope is part of the section of vs. 1–21 in which Jesus deals with official Judaism. The Pharisees were the most devout of all Jews. Also, as a "ruler of the Jews," Nicodemus was a member of the Sanhedrin, the official Jewish court composed of seventy priests, scribes, and elders presided over by the high priest.

This discourse with Nicodemus is the first oral exposition in John of the revelation brought by Jesus. In concise form it gives the principal themes of this revelation. Nicodemus is mentioned only in John (7:50 and 19:39) and he represents a group among Jewish leaders who but hesitantly come to believe in Jesus. He is not just symbolic. His name was not unusual among Jews even though it was a Greek name. It seems John uses Nicodemus to illustrate a partial faith in Jesus based on signs. John has prepared the way for this in 2:23–25. This illustration follows in a logical fashion the example of a firmer faith revealed in the disciples at Cana and the complete absence of faith of the Jews at the temple. (John is less interested in a perfect chronological sequence than to develop a logical sequence to fit his purpose.) See how Nicodemus' approach to Jesus, though well intentioned, is theologically lacking. In the ancient period of the church, Nicodemus' visit was looked on as part of the Pharisees' attempt to trap Jesus.

John has placed this discourse in his Gospel in a skillful way. He has written of the incarnation of the Word, John the Baptist has borne witness to him as the Lamb of God, and Jesus has begun to gather disciples based on their recognizing him as Messiah. The first miracle of changing water into wine symbolizes the transcendence of all Jewish religion in the self-offering of the Lamb of God. Jesus cleanses the temple to demonstrate that the whole sacrificial system of Judaism will be replaced by Jesus as the one true sacrifice in his death and resurrection. Many believed in Jesus because of the signs he did. Now John puts the story of Nicodemus at this point, for he is exactly the sort of Jew who is ready to believe in Jesus but is incapable as a Jew of full commitment to Jesus as Messiah and Son of God. The sermon on this text might be "So Near and Yet So Far from Salvation."

John recalls the detail that Nicodemus came by night because of its symbolic meaning, namely, that darkness and night point to the realm of evil, untruth, and ignorance (9:4; 11:10). Remember that Judas went from the light of the upper room into the darkness to betray Jesus, in contrast to Nicodemus, who comes out of the darkness into the light (vs. 19, 20). His coming at night may be due either to his fear of fellow Jews or to the fact that it was the custom of rabbis to stay up at night to study the law. Nicodemus is a genuine seeker of the truth who is hampered only by the religious climate he is in.

Nicodemus opens the conversation and calls Jesus "rabbi." Nicodemus confesses his belief that Jesus is a teacher who has come from God. Here is a man who has all the insight but also all the limitations that the Hebrew Scriptures have when isolated from the New Testament. Jesus tells him that "unless one is born anew, he cannot see the kingdom of God" (v. 3). The kingdom is entered, not by moral achievement, but by a transformation brought about by God. To "see" is not used primarily in its literal sense here, seeing what there is to be seen, but its real thrust is *to experience.* The meaning is to experience by possession or, better, by *being possessed.* This involves much more than insights from the Hebrew Scriptures. Jesus compares this radical newness of the Christian experience to that of being born anew. Note that the adverb "anew" is deliberately ambiguous, and the direction the conversation takes from here on depends upon this ambiguity (a typical Johannine method). "Anew" can mean either "from the beginning, completely" or in a physical sense "from above," meaning from heaven. The direction of the dialogue derives from Nicodemus taking "anew" to mean a second time, while Jesus means "from above," referring to birth by the Spirit. So the Christian's second birth is a birth by God's Spirit. Even as one can become an adult only by first being a child, so a person can become a citizen of heaven only by being a child again, being born again.

Nicodemus might have raised the more logical question with Jesus of whether salvation is possible through keeping the law, since the rabbis taught that when all Israel kept the law perfectly, then the kingdom of God would come. But Jesus moves the conversation immediately to another level, saying that salvation in the kingdom requires a new birth, a birth not merely in a baptism of water as called for by John the Baptist but through the working of the Spirit.

A birth "from above" is possible only through faith in the Son of man and Son of God, namely, Jesus. Then Jesus proceeds to illustrate this teaching by using a sign from Moses the lawgiver. When the Israelites sinned in the wilderness through unbelief they were afflicted with serpents. Many of the Israelites died. But Moses interceded with God and God gave them a sign—the standard of the bronze serpent. Whoever looked on it would live (Num. 21:4–9). Now John uses this symbol both to refer to Moses raising up the serpent and passively to refer to Jesus who was raised up on the cross. John makes the term include Jesus' exaltation and glory as well. Luke in Acts 2:33 and 5:31 used it this way. Thus passion and action are spoken of by the same words. "Lifted up" means both defeat and victory, suffering and glory. The cross is a cursed thing, like the serpent itself. But whoever believes in the Son of man "lifted up" will have eternal life.

See how the discourse with Nicodemus becomes a pointer to the final sign of Jesus' death and resurrection. It also recounts the broad themes of the Gospel prologue: light and life have come into the world through God's only Son, and those who receive him and believe in his name are reborn by God. Thus the distinction between those who believe and those who do not is proof of the arrival of the final judgment. God does not make the judgment. But God ratifies the judgment that persons make for themselves for or against Jesus.

In v. 16 the word "loved" is in the aorist tense, which implies a supreme act of love. Compare this to 1 John 4:9, where love expresses itself in action. Then, so much "that he gave," which is the result of God's love, is in the indicative, the only instance in John. Its use in classical Greek stresses the reality of the result: that God *actually* gave the only Son.

The word "gave" refers not only to the incarnation but also to the crucifixion when God gave Jesus up to death. The background of this seems to be the Suffering Servant of Isaiah 53:12, which in the Greek translation says the Servant was given up for their sins.

For John, Jesus is sent to the world in contrast to the Synoptics, where Jesus is sent to Israel. "The world" has an intentionally ambiguous use here, indicating that God has a universal love for all God's creation, but the ability properly to reciprocate that love is the gift of God to human beings. God's purpose is to save the world, not to condemn it.

Recommended work: Do a word study of born anew, Spirit, eternal life, and world. Read the account of Moses lifting up the serpent in the wilderness and its effect on the people.

The sermon might follow the conversation of Nicodemus and Jesus with its ambiguities and clarifications. The thrust of the sermon should be to lead hearers to believe in God's only Son and thus have eternal life. The image of the lifting up of the serpent and its saving power and Jesus' being lifted up both on the cross and in his exaltation and glory should be described. (The preacher might lift up a cross to dramatize this.) This is an opportunity to make the gospel simple and plain so that everyone can understand and accept it as the preacher proclaims what Martin Luther called "the gospel in miniature."

Matthew 28:16–20 (RC)

This reading, like some others today, takes up the theme of the Godhead: three persons in one God, a topic we would expect on Trinity Sunday. The command of Jesus to baptize "in the name of the Father and of the Son and of the Holy Spirit" is the only explicit command of Jesus to baptize. Recall that the first disciples baptized "in the name of Jesus Christ," not in the threefold name (see Acts 2:38). The doctrine of the Trinity is implied rather than explicit in scripture. It was hammered out in debates and councils of the church through the ages. Although there is a mystery about God that humans can never penetrate, we cannot keep silent but must speak of the God who has spoken to us in Jesus Christ by the Holy Spirit.

Verse 19 is one of the few instances in the New Testament where the names of the three persons of the Trinity are explicitly mentioned. Many scholars question whether or not the trinitarian formula found here was original at this point in Matthew's Gospel. However, trinitarian formulae of a liturgical nature are found in Paul's writings and were used in the early church by the end of the first century in a setting much like that in which Matthew's Gospel was written. This verse probably comes from the life and work of the church some fifty years *after* Jesus' death, or about A.D. 83. Evidence for this is the fact that if Jesus had given this command at the end of his earthly ministry "to make disciples of all nations," then the opposition in Paul's time to the admission of the Gentiles would be unexplainable.

Here in this verse Matthew gathers up the loose ends of the Gospel and points ahead to the life and work of the church. The disciples are told to teach what Jesus had commanded them. In this pericope Matthew sets forth the main themes of his interest more fully than anywhere else in the Gospel. Jesus has complete authority in heaven and on earth. Jesus sends forth the disciples to (1) make disciples, calling those who will follow Jesus and be the bearers of his word and authority, (2) baptize the new disciples in the trinitarian name, and (3) teach those who follow to obey Jesus' commandments in all their fullness.

Recommended work: Reflect on the themes of the pericope and the major themes of

Matthew. Read in a Bible wordbook or dictionary articles on Godhead and Trinity. See **197**
Donald M. Baillie, *God Was in Christ* (London: Faber & Faber, 1956, pp. 133–134) for help
in developing the sermon.

The sermon might seek to explain how the church came to develop the doctrine of the
Trinity, showing, as Baillie does, how the church accepted the God of the Hebrew Scriptures who they believed was revealed in Jesus of Nazareth who came back to them in the
power of the Spirit after his death, resurrection, and ascension. The sermon should challenge hearers to go forth into the world on the mission that Jesus gave the first disciples.

Isaiah 6:1–8 (C)

Some scholars think this describes Isaiah's call to be a prophet, but it is possible that
some of his other prophecies should be dated before it. The significant thrust of this
passage is the strength of Isaiah's sense of being commissioned by God. God lays a
message on him which is not congenial to him. Notice that this is not a casual encounter
with God. Nor is there a voluntary response to a divine call. God's hand rests heavily on
Isaiah, and as he finds himself in God's presence he cannot resist accepting what is laid
on him.

This is one of the best-known passages of prophetic literature, and in it we have the
most vivid and detailed account given in the Bible of the making of a prophet. The
autobiographical narrative which begins here continues in 8:1–8. Isaiah 8:11–18 indicates
that Isaiah has, for the time being, suspended his pronouncement of oracles.

King Uzziah died in 740 or 739 B.C. Isaiah sees the Lord in the temple of Jerusalem,
perhaps at some great annual feast. He has a vision of the heavenly court in the earthly
temple which was the chosen place of the divine dwelling. The heavenly and the earthly
dwelling were intimately bound up together, and there Isaiah becomes aware of the
holiness of God. The seraphim are members of the heavenly court who acclaim the
holiness of God, one of the characteristics of Isaiah's image of God. They praise God and
carry out divine commands. They may have been thought, like the cherubim, to have
been animal/human creatures, and both are subordinate to God.

God's presence is expressed in an earthquake which shakes the temple (see Amos 1:1
and Zech. 14:5 for mention of a large quake). Smaller tremors were not uncommon. The
effect on Isaiah of finding himself in God's presence was that he was shattered. He
becomes conscious both of his condition and that of his people—an uncleanness which
cannot stand in the face of God's holiness. It includes but cannot be equated with
sinfulness. The ancients believed that to see God was to die unless God protected the
person. God mediates cleansing, and Isaiah hears the heavenly deliberations which indicate the reason for the vision. Now that Isaiah is cleansed by God, he can speak for God
(v. 7). He hears the heavenly deliberations which ask for a messenger and he volunteers
(v. 8). He is given a commission to proclaim disaster, but it will fall on deaf ears. We are
not given the details of the message, but it must have been a grim one to evoke from
Isaiah the cry, "How long, O Lord?" (v. 11).

Recommended work: Read chapter 13 in entirety. Compare this vision and call to that
of other prophets and to that of Jesus at his baptism.

The sermon might follow the movements of the passage itself: vision of God, vision of
self and community and their sin, assurance of pardon, vision of service, and obedience
to God's call.

Deuteronomy 6:4–9 (L)

See Pentecost 24, (C) (RC).

Deuteronomy 4:32–34, 39–40 (RC)

Here is a description of God's unique revelation. The question in v. 32 refers to the
mercy and faithfulness of God described in v. 31. Our pericope is part of the conclusion to
the first address of Moses. Moses reminds the people of God's unique actions and

revelation in history. No other god has ever saved a people or revealed the divine being or given such a law as God has done with and for Israel is the implied answer to Moses' question. God has acted in this tremendous historical display in order to form a disciplined people who would obey God. Since God has acted to form a people, Israel has every reason to keep God's commandments. "There is no other besides him" (v. 35) is the major thrust of the passage.

Notice that the passage closes with the conventional promise of the author of Deuteronomy of long life in the land (v. 40). But the real thrust of this unit is the calling to memory of God's presence and power, with which Israel is joined in awesome intimacy. God's election of Israel was based on God's love, and Israel's obedience should, therefore, be motivated by a love that responds to God's love.

Recommended work: Review vs. 1–40 and reflect on God's saving actions with Israel through the years. Reflect on how Israel's God was unique among the gods then and now.

The sermon might develop the tension in the passage between the uniqueness of Israel's God and other gods, specifically God's saving actions in history, which call for obedience from God's people today as in the period of the author. The promise is long life in the land. The sermon should include the Christian message of eternal life as the reward for obedience to the God revealed in Christ, the unique God among all gods.

Exodus 3:1–6 (E)

This is the account of the theophany of the bush in which Moses is on the sacred mountain, evidently Sinai but called Horeb here. The angel is the messenger of God who manifests God's presence, a characteristic of this strand of material in which the personal presence of God is usually visualized in some way. Here the angel of the Lord expresses a vital sense of personal confrontation and the urgency of God's call.

The root Hebrew word for "bush" (literally, thornbush) comes from the same root as "Sinai." The burning of the bush may have been due to a natural phenomenon. In popular religion, fire was a sign of God's presence (the fire by night that led the Israelites). The holiness of the place is indicated by the command to Moses to take off his shoes, a practice observed by Muslims on entering a mosque today.

Recommended work: Compare this theophany with others in the Hebrew Scriptures, such as Isaiah's vision in today's reading, and with God's revelation in Jesus Christ in the New Testament.

The sermon might begin with a description of our secular age which no longer is aware of the holy in the midst of the ordinary of life. The preacher might read and draw on books by Frederick Buechner which deal with recognizing the holy in daily living. Moses was open to God's presence, responded by taking off his shoes, and hid his face out of fear. But we have beheld God in Jesus Christ and are called, not to hide in fear, but to go forth in faithful obedience.

Romans 8:12–17 (C)

Romans 8:14–17 (L) (RC)

The thrust of this passage is the Spirit and sonship. Paul says that the Spirit does not make slaves of us but sons (and daughters). The word *abba* in Aramaic means "Father" and is the word that Jesus used in his own prayers and it passed into the worship of the early church.

The function of the Spirit is to give a new relationship with God, a high level of privilege. Some Greeks called it "deification." Paul rejects that term. But he does affirm that the Spirit enables Christians to become sons (and daughters) of God.

The Spirit prompts our prayers (v. 16) which is proof of our being children of God. While God is the creator of all humans, all humans are not God's children until they are led or moved by the Spirit into an experience of faith. We are adopted, referring to a common practice among the Romans when there was no heir for a person's property.

The Spirit's function is to witness. The Spirit creates a consciousness of the new and special relationship to God. The adopted persons become fellow heirs with Christ who might be called a natural son of God. This is provided we suffer with Christ in order that we may also be glorified with Christ. Suffering is not an option for a Christian which may be rejected. We are not told the suffering to expect, but it may well include experiencing malice and misfortune as Christ suffered, in addition to suffering as a result of our sin.

Recommended work: Do a word study of Spirit, adoption, and witness.

The sermon on Trinity Sunday from this text will find the references to Father (Creator), Spirit, and Christ pointing to the three persons of the Godhead. The sermon might deal with the actions of these three as they related to human salvation.

Theological Reflection

Look for references to the three persons of the Godhead in the texts for today, either implied or explicit, or for accounts of God's revelation to humans.

Children's Message

The talk might be about John 3:16 and the good news of eternal life through faith in Christ.

Hymns for Trinity Sunday

Come, Thou Almighty King; Holy, Holy, Holy!; O Worship the King.

Pentecost 2

Ordinary Time 9

Proper 4

Psalm 20 (C)
Psalm 81:1–10 (L)
Psalm 81:3–8, 10–11 (RC)
Psalm 81 or 81:1–10 (E)

1 Samuel 16:1–13 (C)
Deuteronomy 5:12–15 (L) (RC)
Deuteronomy 5:6–21 (E)

2 Corinthians 4:5–12 (C)
2 Corinthians 4:6–11 (RC)

Mark 2:23–3:6 (C)
Mark 2:23–28 (L) (E)

Meditation on the Texts

Creator God, we thank you that the Sabbath was made for us and not we for the Sabbath. May we always strive to do good on the Sabbath, to save life, and to worship and honor you our God. Forgive us for legalism which puts laws and things above persons and their needs. We confess that we have too often ignored the sanctity of the Sabbath which you have given as a day set apart for remembering that we are made for communion with you and not for work or pleasure. Enable us to find more constructive ways to enjoy you on the Sabbath as we anticipate the coming eternal "Sabbath" rest with you in heaven. Holy God, may we always strive to preach not ourselves but Jesus Christ as Lord, with ourselves as servants of your people. We thank you for the transcendent power which belongs to you and enables us to face trials and persecutions so that the life of Jesus may be manifested in our bodies. You have anointed servants like David in the past to lead your people. May your Spirit come mightily upon us to empower us for ministry. We thank you for your covenant with us and for the commandments to guide us in covenant living with you and others. Amen.

Commentary on the Texts

Mark 2:23–3:6 (C)

Mark 2:23–28 (L) (E)

Our pericopes are part of the larger portion of the text of 2:1–3:6. It shows the growing opposition to Jesus which leads to the Pharisees' plot in 3:6. The thrust of 2:23–3:6 is Jesus and Sabbath laws. The question about the Sabbath is dealt with in 2:23–28. The second part, 3:1–6, is a miracle story that presents a problem and evidence of a cure, but controversy is at the center of the story. Note that in 2:24 the Pharisees attack Jesus by attacking his disciples. They accuse the disciples of doing what is not lawful on the Sabbath, namely, plucking grain.

For Mark, the argument of the Pharisees with Jesus about the Sabbath played a critical role in Jesus' ministry and was one of the things that led to his death. And Sabbath observance was still a very important issue at the time Mark was writing as the Christians were separating from the synagogue. But in our time the pendulum has swung so far to the other extreme that very few Christians attempt to keep the Sabbath holy, set apart for God. As we delve into the text, let us continually ask what is God's word for our congregation in a secular society.

The setting of the first part of our pericope is a grainfield. It could be wheat, oats, or some other cereal. The time is the Sabbath, which is the key issue of the debate that follows. Now a Jew was allowed to pluck grain that did not belong to him so long as only the hands were used. The disciples rubbed the heads of grain in their hands, according to Luke's version of the incident. This meant they were doing something unlawful, threshing grain (see Deut. 5:12–15 of our lectionary for today).

A Mishnaic tractate interpreting Exodus 34:21 made reaping and threshing among the classes of work forbidden on the Sabbath. However, even the Hebrew Scriptures made exceptions to its own regulations (see Lev. 24:8). Note that although only the disciples break the law, the Pharisees ask Jesus their accusatory question (v. 24). They hold him responsible for his disciples' actions, and Jesus does not object to this. Jesus answers the Pharisees' charge in a typical way among rabbis, asking a counterquestion and making an appeal to 1 Samuel 21:2–6.

King David was held to be the very model of piety, but even he, when hungry and in hardship, had frequently transgressed the law for both himself and his followers. David thus demonstrated that the law, in exceptional cases, could be regarded as subordinate to human needs. The law was for the good of human beings, so if the good of a human was furthered by violating the law, then a lower law was broken for the sake of a higher one, namely, the necessity of human bodily needs in the case of both David and Jesus' disciples.

We see that Jesus' reply to the Pharisees' charge of breaking the Sabbath consists of three sayings: (1) the incident recorded in 1 Samuel 21:1–6 in which human need takes precedence over the law, (2) the principle that "the sabbath was made for man, not man for the sabbath" (2:27), and (3) the claim that the Son of man is lord even of the Sabbath. The latter affirms the authority of Jesus, the Son of man, to reinterpret the Sabbath law. It also claims that the Sabbath remains God's day and the proper use of it is determined by the Son of man. The Son of man as a human knows human needs best. But as a divine being he has the authority to say how the Lord's day should be used. (Note that while Mark refers to "Abiathar," both Matthew and Luke omit his name. But Abiathar was not the high priest associated with David. There seems to be some confusion between Abimelech and his son Abiathar in the Hebrew Scriptures.)

The second incident involves the healing on the Sabbath of a man who had a withered hand. It is a miracle story that includes a controversy which takes center stage. Note that Jesus speaks directly to the man (3:3, 5b), giving him an authoritative word. Consider the unusual response of the onlookers whose hardness of heart grieved Jesus. Note that Jesus' opponents do not speak in this scene, but they watch him closely in order to accuse him. Jesus boldly confronts their repressed hostility, telling the healed man to come to him and then to stretch out his hand. Jesus confronts the congregation and the Pharisees with the intention of the Sabbath and what constitutes Sabbath observance.

Note the conspiracy between the religious leaders and the political leaders that results as they plot to kill Jesus (3:6). This forms the climax and conclusion of this section of 2:1–3:6 and points forward to the passion narrative which is the climax of the entire Gospel. See how in this healing miracle the Sabbath, which was created by God to enhance life, becomes the occasion for plotting the death of Jesus who is lord of the Sabbath!

Recommended work: Do a word study of Sabbath. Read a commentary on Deuteronomy 5:12–15. Reflect on how secular society has ignored or misunderstood the meaning and purpose of the Sabbath. Recall strict Sabbath keeping in periods of church history such as the Puritan days in this country.

The sermon might focus on the purpose of the Sabbath as a day of rest and how this might be reclaimed for Christians in contemporary secular society. The sermon might show how legalism can distort its meaning. But so too can it be distorted by our ignoring or disobeying the commandment to observe the Sabbath as a day of worship, rest, and service to others. The sermon should take into account both the necessity for some people to work on the Sabbath and our responsibility not to demand more people to work than necessary. The sermon on this commandment may be one of the most difficult ones to preach among all the commandments.

1 Samuel 16:1–13 (C)

Our pericope is a sequel to chapter 15 and tells of the anointing of David. It may be a counterpart to the anointing of Saul. Olive oil was used in anointing kings. Although priests and prophets were sometimes anointed, this ceremony was more relevant for kings. A king was sometimes called "the Lord's anointed" or "the anointed one." This title was also applied to the ideal future king in the term "Messiah" (*Christos* in Greek, hence Christ). So in the anointing of David we have a foreshadowing of the anointing of the ideal future king, the Messiah, which Christians see fulfilled in Jesus of Nazareth. Note that the description of the anointing "in the midst of his brothers" (v. 13) does not seem consistent with the action described in 17:28. Ancient writings, like some modern writings, are not always consistent (see *The New Yorker* magazine's section "Our Forgetful Authors").

Note the suspense with which the story is told out of fear of Saul (vs. 2–3). Also note the local color reflected in vs. 4–5, telling of the meeting with the elders.

One of the main points the story makes is that the choice of David, the youngest son who was out keeping the sheep and was an unlikely candidate for kingship, underlines the freedom of God's election. In comparing this anointing with that of Saul earlier, we note that both involve a secret anointing which is commanded by God. Both are young men, who until the time of their anointing were known only as sons of their father.

As in the case of Saul, the action of anointing David, like that of many of the judges, includes the spirit of the Lord coming upon him then and for the future. This action points to the anointing of Jesus, the king of the final age, who at his baptism is filled with the Spirit of God (Mark 1:10 and parallels). Now Samuel can leave Bethlehem, since his mission is accomplished. But left unanswered are questions of the completion of the sacrifice, the feeling of the brothers, elders, father, and David himself. Such are considered nonessential by the author.

Because the narrative is not concerned with such details, the main thrust of the story becomes even clearer. David is the long-foreseen, preelected, and thoughtfully anointed one. From now on David is known as the man with whom the Lord is: "and the LORD is with him" (v. 18). The anointing of David is the theological foundation for the rise of David and his whole future life.

Recommended work: Compare David's anointing with that of Saul and of judges. Do a word study of anoint and of King David.

The sermon might relate David's anointing by God's Spirit, symbolized by the anointing with oil to that of Jesus' anointing by the Spirit at baptism and with the believer's anointing by the Spirit at his or her baptism. We are elected by God, unlikely though we may be, for a particular mission of obedient service in the world. As God called David and used him in spite of his sin with Bathsheba and other sins, so God can use us as we repent and turn to God, following God's guidance by the Spirit.

Deuteronomy 5:12–15 (L) (RC)

Deuteronomy 5:6–21 (E)

Since Deuteronomy 5:6–21 is an account of the Decalogue that differs only slightly from that in Exodus 20:2–17, a text commented on for Lent 3 in the (C) reading, it will not be repeated here.

2 Corinthians 4:5–12 (C)

2 Corinthians 4:6–11 (RC)

Our reading is part of a chapter whose theme is the ministry of the apostle Paul. In vs. 1–6 Paul deals with his faithfulness to the gospel, and in vs. 7–15 he deals with life through death. Our reading spans part of both sections.

Paul seeks to refute the accusation that his preaching had been too much concerned with himself (vs. 5–6). The church at Corinth had forced him to talk about himself, so it is easy to see how some people could draw this conclusion. Recall that Paul had advised his converts to imitate him (1 Cor. 4:16; 11:1). When persons preach the gospel, then or now, they cannot completely dissociate themselves from the gospel they preach. Their words and actions either further or hinder the message they proclaim. We recognize that the gospel is not an abstract truth, like a mathematical formula, but is a way of life to be lived. The one proclaiming the message is involved in the message, which means there will be times when the Christian will get in the way of the message. Although the truth of the gospel does *not* depend upon the purity of the lives of those who proclaim it, the immediate appeal will depend upon the purity of the proclaimer.

Paul rejects the accusations against him and affirms the essence of the gospel, namely, Jesus Christ as Lord, which appears to be the earliest creed of the church. Only Christ is Lord of Paul's life. It would be logical for Paul to say that he is therefore Christ's slave. Instead, he moves directly to say he is the servant of the Corinthians for Christ's sake. While it may be easy for us to say, "I am Christ's slave," few want to be the slave of another person. Americans especially feel they are as good as the next person. But the Christian community is not one in which each person asserts his or her rights and argues for being as good as the next person. Rather, one of the radical aspects of the Christian community is that it functions only when each believer behaves as a slave to all the others (see Mark 10:42–44). If the Corinthians could understand the meaning of this slavery of Paul's, then their accusations against him would be seen for what they really are and would disappear.

Paul affirms the light that comes from God through Christ (v. 6). See how Paul piles up words in v. 6. They pour out like a flood because he is overwhelmed with the greatness of God in Christ. Paul focuses on light and seeing, a good response to accusations of underhandedness and veiling. Recall that Paul saw a blinding light on the road to Damascus and was converted by this symbol of the glory of Christ streaming into his heart. The gospel is light and brings light and knowledge to all who open up to it. The light is the glory with which Christ and God shine. The brightness of God is seen in the face of Christ who is the likeness of God. And the glory of God which we see in the exalted Christ cannot be separated from the glory revealed in the cross.

Paul completes the section of vs. 1–6 on a high note. Now he begins in v. 7 by declaring that he has this treasure in earthen vessels. To all appearances, Paul's life was no more than an earthenware vessel—a clay pot, as it were. However, precious things were often kept in such. What does Paul mean by the treasure in his own earthen pot? It is not an immortal soul or divine spark, for this was a Greek, not a Hebrew, philosophical concept. We find the answer in the preceding paragraph. This treasure is a combination of Paul's ministry, the light that shone in his heart when he became a Christian and the knowledge of the glory of God in the face of Christ, all closely related in Paul's life beginning with his Damascus road experience.

The success of Paul's ministry and the vital nature of his Christian existence come not from his own ability and dedication but from the transcendent power of God. Note the four vivid contrasts in vs. 8–9. We cannot tell what Paul had in mind here, but he may be referring to trials listed in 11:23–28. Here he does not seem to be thinking primarily of physical suffering but rather of mental anguish over those he loved who got into trouble. Paul relates himself to the death of Jesus (v. 10).

While Paul does not deliberately seek suffering, it comes to him as he lives as a Christian and it results in the life of Jesus being seen in him (v. 11). Paul preaches Christ crucified. One of the main ways in which Paul does so is by showing Christ's life in his life. Both the death of Jesus and his life are visible at the same time in the life (read body) of Paul. We might expect Paul to say next, "So you should also be finding the same in yourselves." Instead, he introduces a surprising contrast: death at work in Paul, and life in the Corinthians. Paul's dying is not for himself but for others. In our dying with Christ, Christ's risen life shows itself in us and the result is that that same life appears in those with whom our lives are involved, or at least in some of those lives. This is a mutual process in which each Christian should be bringing help to others and receiving help from them.

Recommended work: Read and reflect on the entire chapter. Do a word study of light, glory, and life.

The sermon might follow the movement of the text itself, climaxing in v. 12, where Paul says that life is at work "in you." The sermon might deal with some of the ways in which Christians today are afflicted and with how they are sustained by God's power working in them.

Theological Reflection

The Mark and Deuteronomy readings deal with the Sabbath and what it means to keep it holy. The 1 Samuel reading deals with David's anointing. Paul discusses and defends his ministry in the 2 Corinthians passage.

Children's Message

The story of David being anointed might be told, or it might be dramatized after it is rehearsed with the children.

Hymns for Pentecost 2

This Is the Day the Lord Hath Made; The First Day of the Week; O Day of Rest and Gladness.

Ordinary Time 10

Proper 5

Psalm 57 (C)	**2 Corinthians 4:13–5:1 (C)**
Psalm 61:1–5, 8 (L)	**2 Corinthians 4:13–18 (L) (E)**
Psalm 130 (RC) (E)	
	Mark 3:20–35
1 Samuel 16:14–23 (C)	
Genesis 3:9–15 (L) (RC)	
Genesis 3:(1–7) 8–21 (E)	

Meditation on the Texts

We thank you, O God, for the gift of music which can refresh our spirits and bring joy and peace. We remember David's gift of playing the lyre which brought Saul relief from suffering from mental illness. The mystery of evil continues to haunt us as it continues to distort lives and relationships. In our anxiety due to sin we have attempted to hide from you, our God. Forgive us when we have confused the Holy Spirit and the evil spirit of Satan. May we always seek to do your will and thus be true members of your family, O God. We rejoice in your raising Jesus from the dead and the assurance that you will also raise us from the dead. We thank you for your grace which extends to more and more people and so increases thanksgiving. May we never lose heart although our outer nature is wasting away. We know that our inner nature is being renewed every day by your Spirit. We suffer afflictions now, but these prepare us for an eternal weight of glory beyond all comparison. We look, not to the things that are seen, but to the things that are unseen and are eternal. Amen.

Commentary on the Texts

Mark 3:20–35

Our pericope tells of an incident in Jesus' Galilean ministry, the description of which extends from Mark 1:14 to 8:26. In 3:13–19a, the section that precedes our pericope, the Twelve are chosen. Now Jesus deals with questions about his power in vs. 20–30 (some commentators include 19b also) and the question of who are his mother, brothers, and sisters (vs. 31–35). One uniting theme of our pericope is that of Jesus' real family, since vs. 20–30 deal with accusations against Jesus of using Satan's power to cast out demons, implying that demons are part of Jesus' life.

Notice that in Mark, Jesus makes few explicit claims for himself, rather, he submits to the judgment of the crowds, the disciples and religious leaders, and his own family. And he is thus submitted to the reader's judgment also. Consider the evidence that Mark's Jesus presents: deeds and words of power and authority. But he presents these in an attitude of lowliness and waiting. He allows others the possibility of misunderstanding him. Note the two erroneous judgments about Jesus that our text presents (vs. 21 and 22) and then the true one to which it points. In the last verse Jesus expresses his inherent authority as he makes a promise that shifts the question from *who Jesus is* to the equally important question of *who we may become.*

Some translations include "Then he went home" of v. 19b as a part of v. 20. That gives us the setting, which remains the same to 4:1. It is a house, perhaps that of Simon and Andrew in Capernaum.

Mark tells us that the "crowd came together again," which indicates that the ordinary unprejudiced common people flocked to Jesus, perhaps recognizing his goodness and godlike character. They are contrasted with Jesus' own family and the religious leaders, the very ones we would expect to flock to Jesus but who did not. They even attributed his actions to evil sources. His family thought he was "beside himself," which is another expression for mental derangement (v. 21), and went out to seize him. The scribes from Jerusalem said he was possessed by Satan and that he used Satanic power to do his supernatural works. It was just such attitudes that brought Jesus to the cross. Mark analyzes these attitudes and shows that they are due to sin of the most serious kind. Notice also the contrast of Jesus' family with "whoever does the will of God" of v. 35. The scribes have an attitude which is the *sin which never has forgiveness* (v. 29). There is no forgiveness, because they have rejected the very source of forgiveness, namely, the Holy Spirit. In Mark's Gospel this theme of the rejection of Jesus the Son of God who came to his own, both family and nation, but is rejected is played out. Mark shows how this attitude of rejection of Jesus not only was groundless but was positively sinful. Up until this point we have no motive suggested for such sin. And it remained a mystery for the early church. In the next chapter Mark deals with how those who made the charges that Jesus was possessed by an evil power could make them. Sometimes it is suggested in the Gospel that the ones making these charges were under the influence of Satan or were blinded by God. In v. 23 Jesus calls the people who are accusing him and speaks to them in parables, preparing for the parables in chapter 4. Mark's theory is that the result, if not the purpose itself, of the indirect way of teaching by parables by Jesus was to make it possible for those who heard both to misunderstand and to reject what Jesus taught. In these brief parables of our pericope we have a clue to the fact that Jesus' parables were not usually concerned with timeless truths, "earthly stories with heavenly meanings," as they have been called. Rather, Jesus' parables are concerned with the End time battle on behalf of the kingdom.

The two parables of vs. 24–26 and v. 27 may have originally been independent of each other. Both indicate that Jesus' activity in healing and working miracles was so remarkable that some supernatural power had to be involved. But the crucial question is, Whose power? God's or Satan's? Jesus argues that he could not be under the influence of Satan, since his activities are exactly opposite those of Satan, who brings madness and broken- ness, disease and falsehood. Jesus argues that if he was indeed under the influence of Satan, this would mean that Satan was working *against* Satan. There would be a civil war within the forces of evil itself. But this would mean the destruction of Satan's realm by his own divisions. But Satan is not such a fool. So Jesus refutes the charges that his activities are inspired by Satan.

Jesus' second parable (v. 27) is based on a proverbial saying that one cannot rob a strong man without first overpowering him and tying him up. Although the ruler of demons is strong, Jesus is clearly robbing him as Jesus' exorcisms and healings reveal, for they demonstrate that Jesus releases those who have been slaves of Satan. "The strong one" has a long history, as indicated in other scripture passages, such as Isaiah 49:25. The stronger one in the parable is the Messiah who is armed with God's own power. Mark interprets the various activities of Jesus as so many episodes in the working of the Spirit of God in the encounter of Jesus with the hostile powers.

Verses 28–30 are a pronouncement by Jesus and should be read in the light of the teaching of the rabbis who often said certain sins were so heinous that those who commit them have no part in the age to come. Mark is saying here that no matter how heinous various sins might be, from a Christian standpoint the one absolutely heinous sin is blasphemy against the Holy Spirit. Note that v. 30 makes clear what Mark understood by such blasphemy, namely, saying that Jesus, God's Son, is possessed by an unclean (evil) spirit. It is calling good evil, and evil good. Those who rejected Jesus cut themselves off from the possibility of salvation, for they attributed his work to Satan and rejected the Holy Spirit who makes forgiveness possible.

The story of Jesus' family in v. 21 and vs. 31–35 reveals that they were far from recognizing that his ministry was the work of God, the acid test of being within the family (kingdom) of God. To fail to recognize this is to put oneself *outside* the fellowship of the church in which salvation is realized. According to Jesus, natural relationships of kinship are of no worth in securing a place in God's family. Even his mother and brothers and sisters must enter through doing God's will, not by claiming kinship! God's reign and family was, for Jesus, not an abstract concept or theological proposition but a personal fellowship made up of men and women who obey the will of God. Note that the focal point of the passage shifts from Jesus to the crowd and thus to the reader. Jesus addresses the reader in saying "Whoever does the will of God is my brother, and sister, and mother." This was difficult for both Jews and Jewish Christians to comprehend. But it was the basis for the church's mission to the Gentiles, and it is the invitation and promise of the church today. The person who both hears and does the word of God may become a true member of God's family and thereby a relative of Jesus!

Recommended work: Do a word study of demons, Beelzebul, unforgivable sin, and Holy Spirit. Reflect on this passage in the light of Jesus' continued battle with his critics and the demons which bound and destroyed persons.

The sermon might contrast the attitude of the unforgivable sin, rejection of the Holy Spirit, with doing the will of God. One leads to eternal destruction, the other to eternal life in the family of God. One involves calling good evil, the other demands daily obedience to the will of God which brings true kinship with Jesus in the family of God. Thus the sermon might be one of contrasting these two, using illustrations from contemporary life.

1 Samuel 16:14–23 (C)

This is an account of David's winning a position at Saul's court and marks the beginning of the story of Saul's mental illness which the ancients attributed to an evil spirit. (Compare with the Mark reading for today in which the scribes attribute an evil spirit to Jesus; also see Luke 11:24–26, which deals with unclean spirits.) Note especially the good relations between Saul and David, as described in vs. 21–22.

In the Bible the stories of the men and women of God are told usually as a history of the Spirit of God at work in and through them. This is true of Saul, whose career brought to an end the period of the Judges. Recall that when he was anointed king, the Spirit of God was with him. Only when he is rejected does the Spirit depart from him. Although he continues as king, he is without the divine legitimation. Saul not only is no longer ruled by the Spirit of God, but an evil spirit continually tormented him. While it was not permanent, it continually came into him. Mental illness in the ancient world was attributed to an evil spirit. Notice especially in v. 16 that the evil spirit is said to come from the Lord, a surprising statement. But, for the Hebrew, all things, in the end, are caused by the one God. Where else could such a spirit come from? Remember that Satan is spoken of only three times in the Hebrew Scriptures; one of them is in Job 1 in which the accuser is subordinate to the Lord. So it is with the evil spirit. Note also that Saul's illness, while in all likelihood a form of mental illness, is described theologically rather than in terms of psychology or psychopathology.

Saul was held in high esteem at his court, as evidenced by the concern of his servants who hit upon the remedy of music to relieve his suffering from the evil spirit. They suggested a man skillful in playing the lyre, which is not a harp but a smaller instrument.

Then one of the attendants recalls meeting David, a son of Jesse, who was skillful in playing, a man of valor, a man of war, prudent in speech and a man of good presence. In addition, "the Lord is with him," he said. Thus David is attractive both in character and appearance. Saul was constantly looking out for good soldiers: "When Saul saw any strong man, or any valiant man, he attached him to himself" (14:52b).

Saul has a very favorable picture of David and immediately sends messengers to have David brought to the court. His kingdom extends beyond his own tribe at least to Judah, where David lives. There is no hint that Saul knows that David was anointed earlier (v. 13). And it does not seem that either Jesse or David fears that Saul's request is in any way connected with the anointing. Jesse sends presents to Saul as an act of homage to the king, not because of anxiety.

So David comes to the court, and in keeping with his character described earlier, he quickly wins the heart of Saul and later the hearts of Saul's son and daughter. David enters the king's service in a military capacity, but his main task is to use his skill in music

(v. 23) to help Saul when Saul is possessed by the evil spirit. Thus the goal of Saul's servants is achieved.

But this episode has far greater meaning. In a real sense it continues the anointing of David and shows how Saul, who is rejected but is still the bearer of the office of king, takes the newly chosen one into his court. Neither David nor Saul is aware of David's election by God. But this move of David to Saul's court is one of the first steps toward the throne which will be David's, according to the will of God.

Recommended work: Read a sketch of the lives of David and Saul in a Bible dictionary. Reflect on the mystery involved in the bringing of David, who will supplant Saul as king, to Saul's court. Do a study of God's providence.

The sermon might deal with the mystery of God's working in our lives, as illustrated by Saul's calling David to his court to enter his military service and play the lyre to relieve his suffering. The sermon might explore the providence of God as it relates to the lives of the hearers. Many people are struggling to make sense of their lives which so often are skewed.

Genesis 3:9–15 (L) (RC)

Genesis 3:(1–7) 8–21 (E)

Since the 3:8–19 passage is dealt with in Pentecost 21, (C), it will not be repeated here. The preacher may consult a commentary for vs. 20–21, which tell of Adam naming Eve and the Lord making garments of skins for Adam and Eve.

2 Corinthians 4:13–5:1 (C)

2 Corinthians 4:13–18 (L) (E)

Note that chapter 4 describes Paul's ministry as an apostle and 5:1–10 continues his reflection on his sufferings and constant peril.

Paul begins our pericope by quoting Psalm 116:10 to confirm that it is faith which sustains his preaching. This is a reference to the courage and faithfulness of the psalmist in the midst of troubles. Paul has faith in a coming salvation which is shared with the Corinthian readers as members of the body of Christ. Consider that Paul does *not* think of his own salvation apart from that of his converts. Nor can he think of the benefit of his suffering and consolation apart from them (1:6–7).

Although the outer nature is wasting away, the inner nature is being renewed every day, says Paul. Neither Paul nor the Corinthians lose heart, since Paul considers all his sufferings as a "slight momentary affliction" which is preparing him for an eternal weight of glory.

Then in 5:1 Paul uses an image of this life as a tent and compares it with the life to come which is described as a heavenly and eternal house not made with hands. He may be drawing on the words of Jesus in Mark 14:58. The tent life of the Israelites was commemorated in the annual Feast of Tabernacles. So Paul contrasts the Christian's present existence with the future mode of being prepared by God as he speaks of death and resurrection. This building is the "spiritual body" referred to in 1 Corinthians 15:44–50.

Recommended work: Compare this passage with all of chapter 14 and Mark 14:58. Review Paul's sufferings described in 2 Corinthians 11:23f.

The sermon might contrast this earthly life which Paul describes as temporary like a tent and involving affliction with the life to come described as a building from God, a house not made with hands and eternal. The thrust of the sermon might be courage for living in the here and now in the light of God's promises for the future. This is not escapism but realism from a Christian's perspective of the End time which shapes our present life.

Theological Reflection

Both the 1 Samuel and Mark readings deal with evil spirits. Also the Genesis 3 passage deals with the sin of Adam and Eve in disobeying God. Paul in the 2 Corinthians passage contrasts the present life with his momentary afflictions with the eternal life yet to come which he compares to a building from God, eternal in the heavens. Mark describes the questions about Jesus' power and his defense that he is not possessed by Beelzebul, for his works are destroying the works of evil. Jesus declares that doing the will of God is the way to entering God's family and true kinship with him.

Children's Message

The story of David being invited to Saul's court to play the lyre to calm King Saul's suffering might be told. The role of music in our lives to bring joy, hope, and peace might be emphasized. The church musician might help with this story.

Hymns for Pentecost 3

O Happy Band of Pilgrims; Jesus, Lead the Way; How Sweet the Name of Jesus Sounds.

Pentecost 4

Ordinary Time 11

Proper 6

Psalm 46 (C)
Psalm 92:1–5 (6–10), 11–14 (L)
Psalm 92:2–3, 13–16 (RC)
Psalm 92 or 92:1–4, 11–14 (E)

2 Samuel 1:1, 17–27 (C)
Ezekiel 17:22–24 (L) (RC)
Ezekiel 31:1–6, 10–14 (E)

2 Corinthians 5:6–10, 14–17 (C)
2 Corinthians 5:1–10 (L) (E)
2 Corinthians 5:6–10 (RC)

Mark 4:26–34

Meditation on the Texts

We thank you, O God, for giving your people images of hope, like the noble cedar on the lofty mountain. You make the dry tree flourish. You bring down the mighty nations, like Egypt of old, which was proud but has been cast out. As we reflect on the love of David for Saul his enemy and for Jonathan we are given a hint of your love which surpasses all human love, even love for our enemies. We are always of good courage because we know that if the earthly tent we live in is destroyed, we have a building from God, a house not made with hands which is eternal. In our present life we sigh with anxiety. We know that while we are at home in the body we are away from the Lord and we walk by faith, not by sight. We would rather be away from the body and at home with the Lord. We must all appear before the judgment seat of Christ where we will all receive good or evil according to what we have done in the body. As we reflect on your kingdom on earth we face a mystery. We know that its growth is beyond our understanding or control. Yet we can at times recognize its progress and take part in it. Though the kingdom begins in a small way, like a tiny mustard seed, yet it grows to greatness. May we hear your word in the parables of scripture and obey you. Amen.

Commentary on the Texts

Mark 4:26–34

Our pericope spans three sections: vs. 26–29, the parable of the seed; vs. 30–32, the parable of the mustard seed; and vs. 33–34, the conclusion of the preaching in parables division. Note that a section of miracles begins with 4:35 and continues through 5:43. The preacher is urged to read all of chapter 4 and especially reflect on vs. 10–12, which give the purpose of parables.

The parable of the seed resembles the parable of the sower (vs. 1–9) in that both are essentially stories pointing up the contrast between the inactivity of the farmer *after* sowing and the harvest, which symbolizes the fulfillment of the kingdom of God. The parable assures us that the kingdom will come because it has already broken into this world in the ministry of Jesus. It cannot but produce a harvest, just as seed grows of its own accord. The central thrust of this parable is found in v. 29, which says that when the grain is ripe the farmer "at once . . . puts in the sickle, because the harvest has come." The prophet Joel compares the great wickedness of the Gentiles to a harvest that is ripe and to vats that overflow (Joel 3:13). Consider how the details of the growth of the seed (v. 28) seem to be essential to the parable.

In this parable the stress is on the *inactivity* of the farmer after the sowing. Remember that the modern scientific idea of a "law of nature" that works itself out because of a programmed inner pattern but apart from God was foreign to the thought of Jesus. The Greek words emphasize that the farmer's life follows his usual round of activities after sowing. The Greek word for "scatter" is in the aorist, indicating completed action, while "sleep" and "rise" are in the present, stressing the *unbroken* and undisturbed way in which the activities and sleep and rising go on after the sowing is completed.

There have been a number of different interpretations of this parable. They include taking it as an allegory, or focusing on the seed, or the period of growth, or the harvest, or the contrast between sowing and harvest. I take the thrust to be on the contrast between sowing and harvest as the most likely meaning, since in v. 29 the hint of the Joel passage suggests that the harvest is the aspect that is significant for interpreting the parable. It also hints at other images of harvest in the Hebrew Scriptures. So it is a parable of contrast pointing up that even as seedtime is followed by harvest, so the present kingdom of God, hidden and ambiguous as it may be, will nevertheless be fulfilled in a glorious "harvest." Recall that harvest in scripture is used as a symbol for the end of the world, especially in regard to its judgment aspect. However, judgment does not seem to have been a key concept in the original form of this parable.

Mark uses the parable here as an answer to discouragement. The disciples need not be overly anxious about the kingdom, since the seed was being sown and it is God who produces the harvest and the kingdom's fulfillment, in spite of the hindrances and few results now. The disciples probably applied this parable to their own evangelistic work. God's kingdom does not come abruptly but grows from hidden beginnings. This parable may have been used to explain why Jesus did not attempt to use force to establish the kingdom, since this would have meant harvesting the grain prematurely.

Next is the parable of the mustard seed (vs. 30–32). Although the parable says that the mustard seed is the smallest of all seeds, which was proverbial at that time, it is not the smallest. Jesus uses the mustard seed to contrast its insignificant beginnings with the surprisingly large size of its mature bush, ranging from six to eight feet in height. There in its branches birds of the air could light. Note our Ezekiel 17:22–24 passage for today of the cedar tree. Mark interprets these words about the birds in the branches to imply that the preaching of the gospel would bring all nations within the realm of the kingdom. The thrust of the parable is to prevent us from judging the significance of the results of our work for the kingdom by the size of its beginnings. Mark seems to apply this both to Jesus' ministry and to the evangelistic work of the early church. In reading the beginnings of the modern missionary movement with William Carey in India, we can see how this parable is accurate, since from that small beginning the gospel was preached to the whole modern world.

The oriental mind would not have been concerned with the process by which the seed becomes the full-grown plant. It would, rather, focus on the *contrast* between the small beginning and the large ending, two greatly different situations. However, the notion of the growth of the seed does play a part in interpreting the parable. There is an organic continuity between the beginning of the kingdom laid in Jesus' ministry and the future kingdom which would include Gentiles as well as Israel.

Then the conclusion comes in vs. 33–34. A number of commentators find some inconsistency between these verses and think that v. 33 indicates the original purpose of the use of parables, while in v. 34 we have Mark's own understanding of parables as stories designed to veil the truth from outsiders. Jesus spoke the word to the people as they were able to understand it. This indicates that they could understand parables to some extent. But v. 34 seems to say that the parables were unintelligible unless "solved" like a puzzle and that only the disciples could solve them.

Note that earlier, in vs. 13–20, Jesus explained everything to them, thus showing the allegorical meaning of the parables. But Mark says in this conclusion that only the disciples received a solution to the parables and in this gained a clue to the secret of God's kingdom. This is true of the whole of Jesus' teaching as well as of the parables. When Jesus explained the parables, this was just one moment in the process by which Jesus gave the disciples clues to the kingdom.

Recommended work: Do a word study of parable in a Bible dictionary. Compare these parables with those of the Ezekiel passages for today.

212

The sermon might focus on the two parables and the clues they give to our understanding of the kingdom and the encouragement they give for our work of the church today. Discouragement is, perhaps, the devil's greatest instrument in defeating the work of Christians. Yet Jesus promises in these parables that the growth of God's kingdom is beyond our understanding or control. And from very small beginnings great things can happen!

2 Samuel 1:1, 17–27 (C)

In v. 1 we have the setting for the dirge that David gives over Saul and Jonathan in vs. 17–27. Chapter 1 takes up where 1 Samuel 30 leaves off. Note that chapter 1 contains a different version of Saul's death than the one given in 1 Samuel 31. The latter is more likely the accurate story.

From the 1 Samuel pericope last week we know that David played the lyre, and tradition connects him with the composing of various psalms. Although the text we have apparently has been altered in transmission over the years, the basic thrust of the dirge remains. Here is great lyric poetry, although there is no specific religious reference. But even so, this almost perfect poem which appears at the beginning of the history of Israel reveals the importance that poetry played in Israel's life even from this early period.

We don't know what the "Book of Jashar" was, but it probably was a collection of poems (see Josh. 10:13). It may also be translated "Book of the Upright."

This dirge, or lament for the dead, is not written in the verse form of this type of literature. The real feeling of this lament is found not in the beautiful artistic form in which it is written but in the genuine expression of mourning, especially felt where Jonathan is mentioned.

The repetition of the phrase "How are the mighty fallen!" (v. 19) in the refrain in v. 27 is characteristic of a lament. The young men of Israel have fallen in war. The image of the sword that devours (v. 22) was common in Hebrew Scripture. Note that the bow was Jonathan's weapon, while the spear was Saul's.

There is a special poignancy in the lament over Jonathan, David's dear friend. David praises both Saul and Jonathan for their bravery and courage and idealizes their united spirit in life and in death (v. 23).

There is an appeal to the women of Israel in v. 24 which reminds us of the fact that Saul gave them spoil after victories in war. Saul fought all of his life. This reference to the women reminds them of their debt to Saul over the years.

Compare v. 25 to vs. 19 and 27 which share a common theme of the mighty who have fallen.

Confirmation of David's feelings about Jonathan is found in 1 Samuel 19–20. The Hebrew word for "wonderful" here means "be wonderful" and particularly "beautiful" here.

Recommended work: Scan the life of David, Jonathan, and Saul in a Bible dictionary. Do a word study of the lament poetry.

The sermon should give an overview of the lives of Saul, David, and Jonathan as background for understanding this lament. The sermon might reflect on the mysterious way in which David comes to the throne through the death of both Saul and Jonathan, which began a new day in the history of the people of God.

Ezekiel 17:22–24 (L) (RC)

Our pericope is part of a chapter that contains two distinct divisions dealing with the allegory of the cedar and the eagle. Events of contemporary history are given in vs. 1–21, while vs. 22–24 point to a messianic restoration. Many commentators view this last section as a later addition because of the promise of restoration. However, it fits so well with the first section in both style and context that it forms a unit with it. It is written not from the viewpoint of captivity but from that of the long-range fulfillment of God's saving activity and resembles 2 Samuel 7:13.

The whole chapter is in the form of a fable in which eagles plant a vine, then God plants a cedar. The story's meaning is found in vs. 11–21.

We may view vs. 22–24 as a supplemental allegory. The sprig from the lofty top of the cedar refers to a descendant of Jehoiachin who will be planted on the lofty mountain, namely, Jerusalem. There it will grow into "a noble cedar; and under it will dwell all kinds of beasts" (v. 23). As a result, all the trees of the field (read nations) will know that Israel's God is the Lord of the nations. This section may have pointed to Zerubbabel the grandson of Jehoichin who, some hoped, would restore David's monarchy.

Recommended work: Read the entire chapter and locate this within the history of Israel.

The sermon might focus on Israel's messianic hope as pictured in the cedar on the mountain Jerusalem and then show how this hope was fulfilled in Jesus Christ, the long-awaited Messiah. It might mention the rule of David whose beginning is found in our 2 Samuel 1 text.

Ezekiel 31:1–6, 10–14 (E)

Another allegory of the cedar, which should be compared to that of chapter 17 (above), is based on an ancient myth from Babylon. The date is June 21, 587 B.C., and the message is that Egypt's fall, like that of Tyre's, is due to its pride and unreliability. Pharaoh is pictured as a towering tree, a cedar in Lebanon. See how scorn is heaped on the pro-Egyptian propaganda through this image of a tree that is full of great pride, which spells its doom. Although the tree is taller than others in the garden, it is cut down (v. 12). Some scholars think that the allegory here has been influenced by Babylonian myths, but its origin was in a fable, not a myth. Note that vs. 10–14 are essential for understanding vs. 1–6, for they continue the symbolism and contain the message.

Recommended work: Locate this allegory in the history of Israel and Egypt and world events of that time. Reflect on how this message may relate to our nation and other nations today.

The sermon might focus on the theme that pride goes before a fall, since pride is basically rebellion against God who is Lord of the nations. The sermon might be a call to repentance as a nation and a turning to God in humble obedience expressed in care for the poor, weak, and oppressed of the world rather than trust in military might.

2 Corinthians 5:6–10, 14–17 (C)

2 Corinthians 5:1–10 (L) (E)

2 Corinthians 5:6–10 (RC)

We dealt with 2 Corinthians 5:1 in the (C) reading last week. Paul continues the theme from chapter 4 of his sufferings and continuing peril. Here he draws on the images of life as a tent and as a building from God to discuss death and resurrection.

Paul writes in vs. 1–5 about longing for the inheritance, meaning the resurrection of the spiritual body described first as a heavenly house and then as a heavenly garment. Then in vs. 6–10 he describes the coming judgment. Paul hopes that Christ will come and that he will be given his new body before having to put off the old one so he will not be naked (v. 3). Paul believes that the End will come soon and he hopes to experience his heavenly dwelling before experiencing death. He does not speculate about an intermediate state between death and the general resurrection at the End.

While Christians are never completely away from the Lord absolutely, nevertheless while they are in the body in this life they are to some degree separated from the Lord (vs. 6–8). Paul can persist in good courage because he knows he is supported by the Spirit. He longs for the consummation of Christ's kingdom and for his own death. But this is not escapism, because he seeks to please Christ here and now while waiting to be at home with the Lord.

The last judgment is an essential element in Paul's expectation, and it is not a threat but an encouragement (v. 10). All are accountable to God, and while salvation is by grace in Christ, the works one has done will be submitted to Christ's judgment.

Recommended work: Compare this passage with 1 Corinthians 15 and Romans 8. Do a word study of heaven, resurrection, and last judgment.

The sermon might follow the moves of the passage, with the climax being pleasing the Lord now and being at home with him after death. The message should help hearers sort through the Christian understanding of the life to come.

Theological Reflection

The 2 Samuel passage is a lament of David for Saul and Jonathan. Both Ezekiel passages deal with images of the cedar as they apply to Israel and Egypt respectively. Mark recounts two of Jesus' parables of the kingdom using seed and its maturity as images. Paul expresses his faith in the life to come after death in the 2 Corinthians pericope.

Children's Message

The talk with children might use a mustard seed and a grain of wheat. Tell the two parables and explain that Jesus is teaching that the growth of God's rule in our hearts and in the world is beyond our understanding or control, just as we cannot understand or control the growth of the seed. The tiny mustard seed becomes a large plant. In Palestine it could be eight to ten feet tall and birds could light in it. From small beginnings God can bring about a great ending, as love is multiplied and God's rule increases.

Hymns for Pentecost 4

How Firm a Foundation; Love Divine, All Loves Excelling; Come, You Thankful People, Come.

Ordinary Time 12
Proper 7

Psalm 48 (C)
Psalm 107:1–3, 23–32 (L)
Psalm 107:23–26, 28–31 (RC)
Psalm 107:1–32 or 107:1–3, 23–32 (E)

2 Samuel 5:1–12 (C)
Job 38:1–11 (L)
Job 38:1, 8–11 (RC)
Job 38:1–11, 16–18 (E)

2 Corinthians 5:18–6:2 (C)
2 Corinthians 5:14–21 (L) (E)
2 Corinthians 5:14–17 (RC)

Mark 4:35–41 (C)
Mark 4:35–41; (5:1–20) (E)

Meditation on the Texts

Lord Christ, who stilled the storm on the sea, thus revealing your power over nature, still, we pray, the storm within our hearts and in our world. We have been tossed about on the waves of life and at times we have felt we were sinking. May we hear and trust your words, "Peace! Be still!" O God, we thank you for David the shepherd king whose kingdom you established over Israel. We reflect on his life and rule as it foreshadows the rule of Christ as messianic king. As we recall Job, may we learn from his experience with you that you are the creator and ruler of all and you have set boundaries for the sea. With Paul we are convinced that One has died for all, that those who live might live no longer for themselves but for Christ who for their sake died and was raised. May the love of Christ always constrain us in our ministry. Enable us to be faithful ambassadors of yours. Strengthen us for our ministry of reconciliation. We rejoice in knowing that if anyone is in Christ, that person is a new creation. May we always remember that now is the acceptable time, the day of salvation. Amen.

Commentary on the Texts

Mark 4:35–41 (C)

Mark 4:35–41; (5:1–20) (E)

In this account of Jesus stilling the wind and the sea we see that Jesus' authority extends to the world of natural forces. This miracle follows the four parables in 4:1–34. Some commentators think the stilling of the storm was based on a personal recollection of Peter. If it is, it has been reworked to an extent that it is almost impossible to discover the basic original account apart from its creedal interpretation in the church. The basic account is found in vs. 37, 38a, 39, and 41a. It was an early confession of the church of Jesus' power as a miracle-worker. This basic account was expanded by adding vs. 35–36, 38b, 40, and 41b. The mention of the boat in the story is a hint of the church, since the church was often symbolized by a boat, like the ark, in which we are saved.

Note especially the stress on the storm and the need for faith. Together these make this episode a lesson in discipleship under stress. The use of the present tense in v. 41b points to the fact that Jesus' power still operates in the church.

The miracle must be read against the background of ideas and stories from the Hebrew Scriptures. One myth of the ancient world, shared at one point by the Jews, said that the original act of creation consisted of God engaging in a desperate but final battle with the forces of chaos and evil symbolized by the waters of the sea. The implications of this contest are that the ability to control the sea and to still storms was seen as a characteristic of divine power. The image of a storm was used as a metaphor for evil forces active in the world, especially persecuting the righteous, a condition only God's power could overcome, and the confidence of a religious person was pictured in terms of faith that even in a terrible storm God would save him or her (note Ps. 107:23–32; 65:5; and Isa. 43:2).

In addition to this, the Hebrew Scriptures say that the ability to sleep peacefully is a sign of perfect trust in God's providential care (Prov. 3:23, 24; Job 11:18–19). There were times of personal or national distress when it seemed as though God had forgotten the people and no longer watched over them. In such periods God was said to be "asleep" and they did not hesitate to call on him to wake up and help them (Ps. 44:23–24; 35:23; Isa. 51:9a). We can more easily understand this miracle story if we keep this background in mind.

Sudden and violent storms on the Sea of Galilee were common then and still are today as winds sweep down from the mountains into the valley. Jesus was asleep in the boat because he had perfect faith in the divine power to keep him safe. But the disciples revealed that they were of little faith on that occasion, as on other occasions. The storm threatened to sink the boat and they were terrified. When they saw Jesus sleeping, they thought he was indifferent toward their danger and woke him with a rebuke (v. 38). When awake, Jesus performed a miracle of stilling the waves with a command "Peace!" and rebuke "Be still!" This caused the disciples to be filled with a different kind of fear and awe. Now they realized they were in the presence of One who had divine power and could command even wind and sea (v. 41).

The question of the disciples, "Who then is this, that even wind and sea obey him?" (v. 41) would have found a ready answer among the early Christian congregations. Early Christians would see in this miracle story evidence that Jesus was God's agent of the End time, if not actually God. Jesus had power to protect and save the church as he had the disciples in the boat. Although Jesus may have seemed indifferent, as God seemed indifferent at times, to the suffering of God's righteous servants, the truth is that God in Christ does hear and answer prayer for deliverance from danger. Christ would not be indifferent to their prayers, even if their faith was imperfect. Christ could and would deal with the forces oppressing the early Christians then and in all ages, for he was armed with God's own power.

Jesus slept on the high deck at the stern with his head on the leather seat used by the rower or helmsman, apart from the splashing waves. The word translated "Be still" literally means "Be muzzled" and is the same word used at 1:25 in speaking to the unclean spirit. It may have been commonly used by wonder-workers to bind hostile powers, in which case the storm would be seen as the work of demonic powers. Jesus' silencing them was another battle in his struggle against God's enemies.

Faith, in Mark's Gospel, means recognizing that Jesus is Christ and Son of God but also, as here, it means primarily the trust which the disciples lacked when they feared for their lives and cried out for help. A better translation of v. 40 would be "Are you still without faith?" (Today's English Version). Jesus addresses both the storm outside and the storms within the reader when he says, "Peace! Be still!" He asks us today why we are afraid and asks us to trust the God we see in him.

Recommended work: Compare this text with the Job reading for today regarding the whirlwind. Do a word study of faith, peace, and miracles.

In shaping the sermon, the preacher may want to follow the moves of the text itself, building to the climax of asking who is Jesus who is able to control wind and sea and showing that he is also victor over sin and death by his cross and resurrection. The sermon might deal with the contrast between our little faith in the storms of life and God's power to save and deliver us. Almost every person encounters a storm of accumulated disasters and disappointments in a brief time which threatens to sink one's "ship."

2 Samuel 5:1–12 (C)

This is the account of David becoming king of all Israel and Judah, a story that continues through v. 16, telling of how he captures Jerusalem and makes it his capital. While this passage is not entirely clear, it is of very great importance, since in it the promise to David is fulfilled: he becomes king of all the people and his capital is Jerusalem, a kind of neutral place between Israel and Judah. What follows later is only confirmation, assurance, and consequence of this action of becoming king.

We find in vs. 1–12 two very significant actions: David is made king and he takes the city of Jerusalem for his capital. Earlier, in 2:4, David had been anointed king of Judah and now he is anointed by the elders of Israel. Understand, however, that this did not mean the coalescing of the two kingdoms. They remained distinct states. But David ruled over these two kingdoms by the strength of his personality. Later the two drew apart.

David is the only logical choice for king of the two states, since he is connected with Saul's family by blood. He has already led the troops and in effect has exercised the role of king, and God has promised to make him king. The active and responsible men of the tribes take what seems like a preliminary action, and then in v. 3 we learn of the action of the elders, a higher and official body. David concludes a covenant with them, indicating that he takes pledges of their loyalty. This is an act of homage in which they recognize David as king. They anointed David as the sanctuary at Hebron. By this act David becomes king in the full sense. Note that this brings about not a united state but a personal union involving Israel and Judah.

David made a wise choice in picking Jerusalem for his capital since it stood at the border of Judah and Israel and was outside the influence of any tribe and was not previously occupied by Israelites. Because of its location, neither Judah nor Israel could feel that it was at a disadvantage. This reveals the political shrewdness of David. He is named shepherd of Israel and prince over Israel. The shepherd figure was frequently used of Israel's king. The reference to the blind and the lame is obscure. It may mean that the city could be defended by anyone, even the blind and the lame. Some commentators think the water shaft was the way in which Joab entered the city, but this is seriously questioned. The city of David is Zion, the city he captured from the Jebusites. The Millo refers to a rampart or earthwork, very likely to the north of the city.

Hiram and the Phoenicians supplied personnel and materials to build David a palace. David thus draws foreign attention to himself and finds respect and recognition. Notice that David exalted his kingdom for the sake of his people Israel. His power and status continue to grow, "for the LORD, the God of hosts, was with him" (v. 10).

Recommended work: Compare David's anointing with that of Saul. Do a word study of anoint, shepherd, and life of David.

In developing the sermon, the preacher may follow the moves of the text leading up to the statement that David exalted his kingdom for the sake of his people, as a godly ruler should do. The sermon might indicate David's political strategy in choosing Jerusalem for his capital, the city held sacred by Jews, Christians, and Moslems. The preacher will want to point to Jesus who fulfilled the ideal messianic king role and who rules not by military might as David did but by sacrificial love.

Job 38:1–11 (L)

Job 38:1, 8–11 (RC)

Job 38:1–11, 16–18 (E)

While many commentators once thought that chapters 38:1–42:6 were editorial additions, more recent scholarship has discovered their linguistic and literary relationship to the main body of the poem of Job. The first discourse is in 38:1–40:2, which contains our pericope. The whirlwind was a frequent setting for a divine appearance (Ps. 18:7–15; 50:3; Ezek. 1:4). Recall that throughout the book, Job has asked why misfortune has come his way as a human being. God now offers him the right to challenge the divine rule (vs. 2–3). Note that we have the key section of the whole book in 38:1–42:6.

In this key section God does not make a single statement, other than in mere description; rather, God poses a series of unanswerable questions to Job. A critic like Job should know what he is talking about and a person who would correct God must have divine knowledge. God pretends that Job has such divine knowledge and proceeds to cross-examine Job on the divine activity of the universe: "Where were you when I laid the foundation of the earth?" (v. 4). But if Job cannot give even the simplest answer, then how can he and God debate more weighty matters? So the argument goes. How can God explain the greater mystery of God's providence and treatment of God's own people? In all of nature there are marvels and mystery. Although through the wonders of science we know far more than Job did about nature, we nevertheless are baffled by the inner secrets of nature. (I heard two scientists at Rice University some years ago discuss the mystery of why water *expands* when it freezes to form ice and thus floats to the top instead of sinking, in contrast to most materials that shrink as they get colder.)

Two things emerge from this debate: one is the loving concern of God for the many creatures, particularly those independent and far removed from humans, and the second is the infinite variety and richness of creation, even of things that seem to humans monstrous and strange. But each has a place in God's wise ordering of creation and God takes pleasure in them. The analogy is true also of the moral order, where God's ways are not those of humans.

God asks Job if he knows the history of creation, how it all started? God asks, "Who is this . . . ?" referring to Job. Is he another god, a rival? To this point, all that Job has done is to darken counsel, meaning the sum total of God's plans and works. Job has brought this on in 13:22.

Job obviously was not present at creation when earth, sea, and light were made. The earth is described as a building planned by an architect (vs. 4ff.). Then the sea is pictured as a baby which needed God's tender care (vs. 8ff.).

Then in vs. 16–18 Job is asked whether he knows his way around the cosmos. God knows the abyss leading to the underworld, where darkness is kept and light is kept (vs. 17, 19).

Notice that God does not pass judgment on Job as either innocent or guilty. God does not prescribe any medicine of salvation or immortality for him; rather, God simply overwhelms Job with God's infinite power. The various riddles of creation are put to Job, forcing Job to contemplate the marvels of all creation.

Recommended work: Do an overview of the Book of Job in a Bible dictionary and reflect on the major themes of Job. Compare them to questions people ask today about why bad things happen to good people, and so forth.

The sermon might explore the questions God puts to Job out of the whirlwind regarding the mysteries of creation and the mystery of God's providence. The sermon might pose the questions of the hearer regarding God's moral order and deal with them in the light of both Job and the cross and resurrection.

2 Corinthians 5:18–6:2 (C)

2 Corinthians 5:14–21 (L) (E)

2 Corinthians 5:14–17 (RC)

We will deal with 5:14–6:2, which is inclusive of the above three pericopes. Our passage is part of the larger section of 5:11–6:13 in which Paul gives a further defense of his ministry. Paul begins in 5:14 by saying that the love of Christ, meaning Christ's love for us, controls us. This is the real controlling factor in Paul's life. Those who are loved by Christ will in turn love both those who love them and others. But too often love is thought of as powerless. The cross is seen to betray weakness. But in Paul's view love has a power all its own, not a power measured in terms of human strength or force. The love of Christ is revealed in his death for all.

What Paul means by "therefore all have died" is not obvious. Interpreters are clearly divided on the meaning, and the context does not give a clear meaning. Paul is not giving a doctrine of the atonement here; rather, he is insisting that the consequence of Christ's death and resurrection is that Christians no longer live for themselves but for Christ. They have died to self.

Once Paul thought of Christ as just another man put to death on the shameful cross.
But now he has a personal knowledge of him as the risen Lord who is head of a new creation into which believers are incorporated (5:16–17). Now Paul can no longer judge anyone from a human point of view, "according to the flesh" literally. Since becoming a Christian, Paul is convinced that God's new creation has begun.

In Romans 8:1–8 Paul affirms that those who are in Christ Jesus no longer live according to the flesh but according to the Spirit. Christ's death calls forth a deep and abiding response on our part. We can make such a response because Christ not only died but was raised for our salvation. As we live by the life of Christ, his love controls us.

We have in 5:16–21 one of Paul's greatest passages in which he traces out the nature of his ministry. This follows Paul's stating what Christ means to him in vs. 11–15. This passage of vs. 16–21 is packed full of basic theology.

It deals with the new life in Christ, God's working of reconciling the world to himself in Christ, the atonement, the role of ambassadors for Christ, and Christ's role in taking our sin upon himself so that we might become the righteousness of God. (See Ernest Best, *1 Peter,* New Century Bible Commentary [Grand Rapids: Wm. B. Eerdmans Publishing Co., 1971], for a detailed discussion of reconciliation, ministry of reconciliation, ambassador, etc.)

Paul says he is Christ's ambassador. An ambassador is one who has full power to speak for the government he or she represents and can commit it to a plan to act. With being ambassadors goes a serious responsibility to live a new life worthy of Christ.

Paul applies the term "reconciliation" not to the reconciliation of separated peoples but to their reconciliation with God. All true peacemaking, in Paul's view, involves peace with God. But when this is found, then it should be expressed in making peace with one another. Peace with God and peace with our neighbors go together (Matt. 5:23–24).

Then in 6:1–2 Paul exercises the ministry of reconciliation of 5:18 as he appeals to the Corinthians. This continues Paul's defense of his ministry. The "day" Paul writes about is today, a day that will continue until Christ returns. Often these verses are applied to unbelievers to urge them to repent and believe, meaning now is the time for "them" to repent. But Paul here is writing to *believers!* Salvation, according to Paul, is not a once for all instantaneous event but is a continuing process. One is not to accept the grace of God in vain but to live by grace each day.

Recommended work: Do a word study of reconciliation, ambassador, and righteousness of God.

The preacher may want to focus on the task of ministry, both ordained and lay, drawing on what Paul has to say about his own ministry. The controlling love of Christ guides the ministry of reconciliation as ministers are ambassadors for Christ. The urgent appeal in 6:1–2 gives greater impetus to the message. Christians are not to accept the grace of God in vain but should live now and every day as new persons in Christ.

Theological Reflection

The 2 Samuel passage is an account of the anointing of David as king of Israel and Judah and his taking the city of Jerusalem to be his capital. God promised him kingship and David acts to make this a reality. In the Job passage God questions Job about the mysteries of creation and the moral order, implying that many aspects of life are beyond human understanding. In the 2 Corinthians passage Paul makes a further defense of his ministry, pointing to basic aspects of ministry such as the controlling love of Christ, the new life in Christ, God's work of reconciliation and calling humans to declare this message, and his work as an ambassador for Christ. Mark gives an account of Jesus' stilling the storm, revealing his power over wind and sea and by implication his power to still the storms within human hearts as well as the storms at sea.

Children's Message

The story might be about Jesus' sleeping in the boat during a storm that terrified the disciples and how Jesus calmed the wind and the sea. The power of Jesus over nature and over the storms in our lives should be described. When we feel angry, frustrated, and all out of sorts, if we turn to Jesus and ask him to calm us, he will.

Hymns for Pentecost 5

Jesus, Savior, Pilot Me; The King of Glory Standeth; Give to the Winds Your Fears.

Ordinary Time 13
Proper 8

Psalm 24 (C)	**2 Corinthians 8:7–15 (C)**
Psalm 30 (L)	**2 Corinthians 8:1–9, 13–14 (L)**
Psalm 30:2, 4–6, 11–13 (RC)	**2 Corinthians 8:7, 9, 13–15 (RC)**
Psalm 112 (E)	**2 Corinthians 8:1–9, 13–15 (E)**
2 Samuel 6:1–15 (C)	**Mark 5:21–43 (C)**
Lamentations 3:22–33 (L)	**Mark 5:21–24a, 35–43 (L)**
Wisdom 1:13–15; 2:23–24 (RC)	**Mark 5:22–24, 35b–43 (E)**
Deuteronomy 15:7–11 (E)	

Meditation on the Texts

We praise you, O God, who have created us in your image and given us life. We thank you for Christ the divine physician who healed the woman with a flow of blood and who raised Jairus' daughter from the dead. Grant us the faith to be healed and to be raised from the dead in the resurrection. We recall that David the king danced before you with all his might. May we so rejoice in serving you that we may dance our way through life, praising and giving thanks for our days for your gift of salvation in Christ. For with the writer of Lamentations we know that your steadfast love never ceases and your mercies never come to an end. Great is your faithfulness. Though we suffer grief, you will not cast us off forever but will have compassion. We know you do not delight in the death of the living, for your righteousness is immortal. May we have a special concern for the poor and give to them freely. May we always open wide our hands to our neighbors, to the needy and the poor. For we have known your grace in Christ Jesus who though he was rich became poor so that by his poverty we might become rich. May we know the grace of giving to those who have less than we have. Toward this end, we dedicate ourselves anew to you, our God. Amen.

Commentary on the Texts

Mark 5:21–43 (C)

Mark 5:21–24a, 35–43 (L)

Mark 5:22–24, 35b–43 (E)

In the longer passage of vs. 21–43, which forms a unit, we have the account of Jesus' raising Jairus' daughter and his healing of the woman with a hemorrhage. The longer reading is recommended, since cutting out the miracle of healing the woman destroys the unity of the action in which Jesus is called to heal a girl at the point of death, takes time out to heal a woman with a flow of blood, and then arrives *after* the girl has died but raises her from the dead. In this passage we have an example of Mark's technique of insertion which he is fond of. It serves the purpose of raising the suspense level and intensifying the severity of the problem from serious illness to death. The healing of the woman serves the purpose also of elaborating on the meaning of faith, the kind of faith needed in the story of Jairus. Notice how each story, set over against each other, sheds light on the other! And we see how Jesus interrupts the journey to heal the daughter of a synagogue leader in order to heal a ritually unclean woman. The significance of raising the daughter is in-

222

creased by the fact that she dies while Jesus is speaking with the woman, thus making it necessary for the girl to be raised from the dead. (Here is another example of the way in which some shapers of the lectionary have done damage to a unit of scripture by cutting out essential verses.)

Each of the two stories has the structure of a typical miracle story, but each is broken in an important way. The raising of Jairus' daughter differs from the usual miracle story in two ways: first, the description of the seriousness of the problem is greatly expanded as Jesus confronts death itself. Next, Jesus commands the people to give the girl something to eat. This differs from the usual miracle story but may be included as evidence that she was really restored to life, since ghosts do not eat. More likely it suggests that Jesus was dealing with the twelve-year-old girl, not as a case, but as a little girl for whom the warm and human Jesus greatly cared.

In the story of the healing of the woman, the healing is complete by v. 29. She was past all human help. But she touched Jesus' garment and her flow of blood is stopped, evidence that the cure has taken place. This is only half the story, however. Up to this point it reads like an account of superstition or magic, since the woman was healed by personal contact with Jesus or faith in him, just by touching an object, Jesus' garment. But Mark does not leave the story there. Jesus wants personal contact with her, so he stops his journey to look around and see who has touched his clothing. The woman shows courage by staying, although she has been ostracized as unclean. She comes with fear and trembling, and Jesus speaks a saving word to her which includes not only health but "shalom," peace. The most important part of this healing miracle is found in the uncharacteristic expansion of vs. 30–34.

Examining more closely the raising of Jairus' daughter, we note that Jairus was one of the rulers of the synagogue, a title used of the supervisor of worship and more generally of the prominent members of the synagogue. He came trusting that Jesus could lay hands on her and make her well and live (v. 23). The Greek words used here could mean "be saved and gain eternal life." This is significant in relationship to vs. 41–42, where the Greek words for "arise" and "got up" are the usual Greek words for "resurrection."

Note in v. 26 the put-down of physicians, a common theme in popular stories of the ancient world.

There seems to be a deliberate ambiguity in v. 27 regarding "the reports about Jesus." The Greek literally means "the things concerning Jesus," which could include the religious truth about Jesus and his ministry.

The reference to power going forth from Jesus should not be thought of as something impersonal and physical, such as an electric current which goes automatically, independent of Jesus' control. Jesus perceived that "power had gone forth from him." The power is the personal power of the personal God. Although it does not seem that Jesus had made a decision here regarding the power, God does, for God controls this power. The cure does not happen automatically but by God's own personal and free decision.

While earlier commentators thought that Jesus knew who touched him (v. 30), and that he asked just to make the woman confess her faith, it seems more likely that Jesus did *not* know. Rather, he sought information, not to make the miracle stand out, but because he wanted to draw the woman's imperfect faith away from his clothes to himself. She was seeking a cure apart from a personal relationship with Jesus. But Jesus sensed the difference of the healing touch from an ordinary touch.

Mark does not say why the woman was afraid, but it was probably because of her fear when she realized that a miracle had been performed on her. Jesus told the woman that her faith had made her well. So she hears Jesus ratify with his words what she had already learned from experience. And he told her to go in peace.

Then in v. 35 comes the tragic news that Jairus' daughter is dead. This raises the question of Jairus' faith in Jesus' healing power and his power to raise the dead. The messengers reveal their lack of faith also.

But Jesus "tuned out" what they said and told Jairus, "Do not fear, only believe" (v. 36).

Faith was the necessary prerequisite for a miracle and was an essential demand of Jesus' preaching. The present imperative is used in the Greek here to denote continued action of believing. So Jesus commands not just a single act of faith but a continuing steady attitude of faith. The father has already shown his faith in the act of coming to Jesus, and now he must go on believing. But before Jesus' resurrection, faith could not have meant an act of belief in Christ as a divine person. Rather, during his ministry faith meant a receptivity to God's healing word proclaimed by Jesus plus a confident self-abandonment to God, since God's saving power was being exercised in and through Jesus.

Jesus tells the weeping parents and others that the little girl is not dead but sleeping. Some commentators have thought this meant that the family had prematurely concluded that the girl was dead. Mark and his contemporaries saw this incident as a raising from the dead and interpreted it as such. Jesus pays no attention to the great weeping but concentrates on giving a lesson in word and deed on the true meaning of death. We cannot tell whether Jesus meant by reference to her sleeping that we should take this literally or take it theologically, meaning that her death was only a sleep. For Mark, Jesus' miracles symbolize the passage from death, meaning bondage to sin and Satan, to new life. But the people laughed at Jesus (see Acts 17:32).

The verb in Greek for "got up" (v. 42) is used of Christ's resurrection. The amazement of the crowd is unusually strong. Jesus charges the people not to tell anyone about the miracle, a command that is odd, since it is impossible to fulfill. Many commentators think this is an instance where Mark has artificially inserted his theory of the messianic secret. Or Mark may have thought this sight which was too sacred for all to see ought not to be lightly described to the general public.

Recommended work: Compare this resurrection with that of the raising of Lazarus and others in the Bible and with Jesus' resurrection. Compare this passage with parallels in Matthew 9:18–26 and Luke 8:40–56.

The sermon might follow the moves in the text, with the building of suspense when the woman with a flow of blood stops Jesus on his way to heal the girl who was sick and then the news that the girl is dead and the suspense over whether Jesus can restore her to life. The preacher should deal with the raising of the girl in the light of Jesus' resurrection and relate it to our own death. The sermon might point out the way Jesus dealt with interruptions (which we preachers are always complaining about!). The sermon might deal with the relationship of faith, healing, salvation, and life.

2 Samuel 6:1–15 (C)

This is the account of the bringing of the Ark to Jerusalem, which David wished to do in order to add to the prestige of Jerusalem. The presence of the Ark containing the Ten Commandments given to Moses would make Jerusalem a religious as well as a political and military center. The Ark was the sacred object of the northern tribes, and when it arrived in Jerusalem it became the symbol of the national God. The transfer of the Ark was one of David's most important deeds (see 1 Sam. 7:1 for a previous account of the Ark).

It seems Uzzah paid with his life for presuming to touch the Ark, although he apparently was trying to steady the cart when the oxen stumbled. Remember that, for the Hebrew, God was the direct cause of everything that happens. Only after the house of Obed-edom is blessed by the presence of the Ark does David venture to move it to Jerusalem. We can't be sure whether David was angry or afraid (vs. 8–9), but he probably was afraid.

David offered sacrifice after the first six paces (but not each six paces). This was permissible, and only later was this function restricted to priests. David and others engaged in religious dancing, a practice used in worship in African churches and other churches where "interpretive dance" is done. Dance was used from earliest times to express religious faith and enthusiasm, as David does here. The word for "dancing" here is connected with the word for "circle" and refers to a rotating movement. In vs. 16 and 21 words are used that indicate quick hopping and springing.

Recommended work: Read the earlier account of the Ark and its symbolism for the people. Do a word study of dance in the Bible.

The sermon might follow the text as it builds to the climax as David dances before the Lord with all his might as the Ark is brought to Jerusalem. The sermon might deal with the religious significance of things and places and our response in word and action. The church processional today is a carryover from the religious dance of worship, and in black churches often there is a kind of dancing in processing down the aisle.

Lamentations 3:22–33 (L)

Our reading spans two sections: vs. 1–24 deal with the basis of hope and vs. 25–39 with the lesson to be learned. In chapter 2 the question of who can comfort Jerusalem in its unprecedented disaster is asked, and now in vs. 1–24 the answer is given. The whole of chapter 3 consists of an acrostic in three parts, with three verses to each letter of the Hebrew alphabet.

The basis of certainty that God will hear and rescue Jerusalem is God's steadfast love. The basic meaning of the Hebrew has to do with committed, loving loyalty to a covenant obligation. The word is used in the plural here. It points to specific events and actions of God and is parallel to faithfulness (vs. 22–24). Note the concrete thinking expressed here.

The poet knows that God's wrath is not God's final act but must be seen within the greater and final context of God's steadfast love. The poet is confident that God's eternal covenant with Israel applies to him personally as an individual (v. 24). When a lament was spoken in the sanctuary during a time of deep distress it was answered after a period of vigil by an oracle pronouncing salvation (v. 26).

Then in vs. 25 and 26 we have a transition to the next section of the poem. To seek God originally meant to go to the sanctuary. "Wait," as used in worship, may have referred to a vigil before an oracle of salvation. But the sanctuary is gone. Note that v. 27 is a typical wisdom maxim which may mean that the author is primarily concerned with the younger generation which is Israel's future.

The poet declares that the first move toward salvation lies in accepting the situation for what it is (v. 28). There is reticent realism in v. 29b.

When one accepts judgment one can come to know the basically good purpose of God which undergirds judgment (vs. 31–33). God's steadfast love is always the same and is the source of what to humans, in our sin, seems like wrath. But when one accepts and repents (vs. 28–30), God's steadfast love is the basis of hope.

Recommended work: Read chapters 2 and 3. Compare with Psalm 56 and the story of Job.

The sermon might deal with the mystery of God's wrath and steadfast love as they are experienced by sinful human beings. It might deal with Job as an example. The sermon may help hearers repent and submit to God and thus to acknowledge God's righteousness and mercy in the trials of their daily living.

Wisdom 1:13–15; 2:23–24 (RC)

In 1:12–15 the author states that God has made humans for immortality, and 2:21–24 refutes the false reasoning of the preceding verses which arises from wickedness and the failure to know God. Note that 1:13–15 insists that God is not the author of death. Rather, God's creation and all that conforms to God's will is made for life and immortality. The author says that righteous living leads to immortality.

The misguided folk of 2:6–20 who advocate an unrestrained pagan kind of hedonism have failed to recognize that in a future life righteousness will be rewarded. Notice the argument in 2:23 which says that since humans were made in God's image (Gen. 1:26, 27), they are therefore by nature immortal. Death is the work of the devil. In 2:24 we find that the devil is for the first time in the history of Jewish thought identified with the serpent of Eden (Gen. 3:4, 19).

Recommended work: Reflect on this passage in the light of the cross and the resurrection and the New Testament view of death and human life.

The sermon might deal with the misguided folk of our society, like those of the author's described in vs. 6–20, in the light of the teaching of scripture about death and immortality.

The sermon should draw on the Genesis passages relating to the creation of humans and the origin of evil death.

Deuteronomy 15:7–11 (E)

This is part of a section that deals with the conduct of a holy people in chapters 14–15. The sabbatical release is treated in 15:1–18. This seems to be addressed especially to the landed classes, who were conservative by nature and were probably instigators of the Josian reform. Note the humanitarianism of this passage which is so relevant for today, both in the United States and in third world countries.

Note that vs. 7–11 are in the form of casuistic law and are more exhortations than laws in the strict sense. Every seventh, or sabbatical, year there was to be a cancellation of all debts owed by fellow Israelites. This covered loans outstanding at the close of the year. The whole principal of the loan ceased to be owed, not just the year's payment on the principal. (See Ex. 23:10–11 and Lev. 25:1–7.) The cancellation of debts is only on the fiftieth, or jubilee, year according to Leviticus 25:8–55.

The author tells the reader to ignore the year of release, thus making the loan a gift. But we do not know how generally this law was practiced, if at all.

Recommended work: Read the whole chapter and compare with other passages that deal with the jubilee. Do a word study of poor, needy, and oppressed. Reflect on the John 12:8 saying of Jesus and Deut. 15:11.

The sermon might deal with poverty locally and around the world and efforts to relieve it. Draw on the 2 Corinthians 8 passage in which Paul urges giving to the needy so there may be equality. This passage cuts across the grain of our "get yours" capitalist economic order and calls for a radical reexamination of God's ownership and our stewardship of possessions.

2 Corinthians 8:7–15 (C)

2 Corinthians 8:1–9, 13–14 (L)

2 Corinthians 8:7, 9, 13–15 (RC)

2 Corinthians 8:1–9, 13–15 (E)

We will deal briefly with vs. 1–15, which include all of the above readings. The pericope spans two sections: vs. 1–5 focus on the example of the Macedonians in giving to the poor in Jerusalem, and vs. 6–15 deal with motives for completing the collection that the Corinthians had begun earlier. The central thrust of the whole passage is: give generously, as the Macedonians give. While some Corinthians may have prided themselves on their riches, Paul points to the extreme poverty of the Macedonians but God's grace nevertheless overflowed in a wealth of liberality. The grace of God is responsible for the Macedonians' self-dedication and joy in giving, and Paul holds them up as an example.

Paul is a master psychologist and praises the Corinthians for excelling in so many ways and then calls them to excel in the gracious work of giving to the poor in Jerusalem. They were Gentiles being asked to give to Jewish Christians. The ultimate motive for giving is Christ's own self-giving, who came down from heaven, becoming poor for our sakes so that by his poverty we might become rich.

The poverty of Christ is not his earthly life but refers to the voluntary giving up of heavenly riches by the preexistent Christ (Phil. 2:6–11). God's love in action in Christ is the supreme motive for sacrificial giving by Christians. The proof of genuine love lies in the Christian's readiness to give, not in the amount, according to Paul. The key is the intention to offer the gift without reservations. Paul refers to the experience of Israel with the manna in the wilderness in which there was equality, an ideal for Christians to strive toward in all ages.

Recommended work: Compare this passage with the Deuteronomy reading on aiding the poor and Jesus' teaching about the poor in Mark 14:7, where Jesus says you can do good to the poor "whenever you will." Study the commentary by Ernest Best (*1 Peter,* New Century Bible Commentary [Grand Rapids: Wm. B. Eerdmans Publishing Co., 1971]) on this passage.

The sermon might follow the moves of the passage, dealing with the example of the generosity of the poor Macedonians, the example of Christ, and the grace of God in Christ, the ultimate motive for generosity. This could be an "out of season" stewardship sermon on the Christian's standard of giving: Christ's love.

Theological Reflection

The Deuteronomy and 2 Corinthians 8 passages share a common theme of concern for the poor from a theological perspective. Mark tells of two miracles of Jesus dealing with faith, salvation, healing, and life. The 2 Samuel, Lamentations, and Wisdom passages have differing themes which we have earlier cited.

Children's Message

The story might be told of Jesus being called to heal the twelve-year-old girl, only to find her dead when he arrived. Jesus called her forth from the dead, and he gives us life now and after we die. For he has overcome death by his resurrection.

Hymns for Pentecost 6

Lord of the Dance; Lift Up Your Heads, O Mighty Gates; We Thank You, Lord, for Strength of Arm.

Ordinary Time 14
Proper 9

Psalm 89:20–37 (C)   **2 Corinthians 12:1–10 (C)**
Psalm 143:1–2, 5–8 (L)   **2 Corinthians 12:7–10 (L) (RC)**
Psalm 123 (RC) (E)   **2 Corinthians 12:2–10 (E)**

2 Samuel 7:1–17 (C)   **Mark 6:1–6**
Ezekiel 2:1–5 (L)
Ezekiel 2:2–5 (RC)
Ezekiel 2:1–7 (E)

Meditation on the Texts

We thank you for your assurance, O God, that your grace is sufficient for us. Your power is made perfect in weakness, and when we are weak, then we are strong by your power. For the sake of Christ, enable us to be content with weaknesses, insults, hardships, persecutions, and calamities. We thank you for the special moments when we have felt your presence in a way we cannot describe to others. Forgive us for our unbelief when we, like Jesus' family and neighbors, have become so familiar with holy things and persons that we have been skeptical. Teach us true faith. Teach us humility. Teach us to trust. Help us to be aware of your Spirit sending us to speak your word to a people who have rebelled against God, to the secular mind which rejects the holy. May we be faithful in speaking your message whether the audience hears or refuses to hear your message. We recall your servant King David who sought to build a house for you, but you built a "house," a dynasty, for him. We thank you for your kingdom, to which David's kingdom points, for your kingdom is forever. Amen.

Commentary on the Texts

Mark 6:1–6

This passage is an account of Jesus' rejection at home. Although there were some apparent exceptions, Jesus usually required faith on the part of those who sought healing for themselves or others. The incident is the conclusion of the section of Mark running from 3:7–6:6 whose theme is Jesus and his own. This section forms a transition from Jesus' ministry among the crowds in 1:14–3:6 to his ministry among his close disciples found in 6:7–8:33.

The Greek word translated "own country" can also mean homeland. Here it refers to Nazareth, but it also hints at the final rejection of Jesus by his people. For Mark, this rejection of Jesus had profound significance. The early church was puzzled by the refusal of Jesus' own people to believe the gospel, in contrast to the Gentiles, who were accepting it in increasing great numbers. The problem also involved the credibility of the claim that Jesus was the long-expected Messiah when his own people, the Jews, flatly rejected this claim and refused to believe the gospel. The church responded by following the hint found in Isaiah 8:14–15 which refers to one who would become a stone of offense and a rock of stumbling, causing many to stumble and fall and be broken. This involved the mysterious providence of God by which the Messiah would be for the Jews a stumbling block and snare which would throw them off the right track into error and sin (see Romans 9–11). Following Jesus' crucifixion, the thing that offended the Jews most was the accursed manner of his death (1 Cor. 1:23). All of Mark's Gospel is concerned with the offense of Jesus for the Jews and showing that they had no basis for this except in their blindness and sin. People put blasphemous interpretations on Jesus' activities (see 3:21–22). In our pericope we find that as Jesus' ministry in Galilee draws to a close his own neighbors of Nazareth are forced to make a decision about his claims. They also take offense at him (v. 3), using the same root word as used for "stumbling" in Romans 9:33; 1 Peter 2:8; and 1 Corinthians 1:23.

The people of Nazareth halfway believe and marvel but do not fully believe. This partial belief makes them even more irritated and incredulous. They knew that Jesus' teaching was wise, but he was just an ordinary person whom they knew well, and they knew his family. They do not want to believe. (A minister friend went back to become pastor of his home church after finishing seminary and confided to a friend later that as he looked out on the congregation the first Sunday he realized he had made a mistake going home!) Not only was Jesus rejected as a prophet but overfamiliarity with him also hindered his healing. (See parallels to the prophet saying in Matt. 13:57; Luke 4:24; and an indirect one in John 4:44. Only Mark includes a reference to Jesus' own kin and his own house.) Mark thereby emphasizes the scandal of Jesus' rejection by his own kinfolk, an echo of 3:21, 31–35.

The New Testament record is that Jesus again and again was rejected by his own people. The human reaction to rejection is anger, outrage, self-pity, and hurt. John 1:11 says that Jesus "came to his own home, and his own people received him not." The theme of rejection dominates our pericope, and the dominant emotion on the part of both Jesus and his townsfolk is astonishment (vs. 2, 6).

See how the context and form of this account bring out the true character of the rejection. Jesus has earlier done mighty works and has revealed great wisdom in his preaching, and they cannot but admire him (v. 2). They ask the right questions about the meaning and origin of Jesus' power and wisdom (v. 2). But note the abrupt change between vs. 2 and 3 as the questions do not receive their real answer and the wonder does not translate into genuine faith. The Nazareth neighbors remind themselves that Jesus had been a tradesman of their town, and his family and origin were well known to them. The Greek word here translated "carpenter" means a worker in stone, wood, or metal. The church fathers were divided on the exact trade. It may be that Jesus was the village builder and thus would have done a certain amount of carpentry in building. This is the only place where Jesus' occupation is mentioned. Matthew records that Jesus' father was the carpenter, and Luke leaves out this detail completely. Justin in the second century wrote that Jesus had made wooden plows and yokes.

It is rather strange that Jesus' mother is named but not his father. This leads us to assume that his father had been dead for some time. The brothers of Jesus are mentioned also in 3:31; Acts 1:14; and elsewhere. Roman Catholic commentators say that "the exact relation of these four to Jesus is not known (cousins? half brothers?), but the doctrine of perpetual virginity of Mary is the basis for stating that they are not sons of Joseph and Mary and not the real brothers of Jesus" (*The Jerome Biblical Commentary,* vol. 2, p. 796, sec. 167). A Protestant scholar comments that the mentioning of Jesus' brothers here and elsewhere "demonstrates that the New Testament knows nothing of the perpetual virginity of Mary" (Eduard Schweizer, *The Good News According to Mark,* p. 124).

The Greek word translated "took offense" is the basis for our word "scandal" and in 4:17 is translated "they fall away." At the time Mark used the word, it had developed a technical meaning to describe the effect of Christ's death on Israel. The Greek literally means something that trips a person up or snares a person or animal into a trap. By Mark's time the word was applied to people who, when confronted by Christ, found an excuse for not believing in and following Jesus.

There are parallels to v. 4 in Greek authors. This saying from Jesus must have given courage to early Christian missionaries as they were confronted by consistent Jewish denial of Jesus' claims to be the Messiah. Although it is strange and terrible that people should reject Jesus as God's final agent of salvation, this action is only an extreme example of what has happened again and again in human experience. It is possible that Mark added "and among his own kin, and in his own house" in order to make the saying fit the context here more exactly.

Jesus could not do a mighty work or miracle among his hometown folk because of their unbelief. A genuine miracle always established fellowship between God and human beings in that it seeks faith, stirs up questions, and gives answers. In addition, Jesus did not work miracles unless the miracle would lead to such dialogue. The mention of their unbelief underlines the fact that the pivotal point is the question of faith.

Recommended work: Do a word study of faith, miracle, and scandal in a Bible dictionary.

The sermon might deal with the dangers of overfamiliarity with the sacred which can lead to unbelief. The sermon might caution against taking holy things too casually and rejecting the sacred when we find it in the commonplace. Faith should be the focus of the sermon. Faith is the key to fellowship with God through Christ.

2 Samuel 7:1–17 (C)

Our pericope is part of the section, chapter 7, that deals with David's desire to build a temple, a "house" for God, but God wills to establish for David an everlasting dynasty, a "house" that shall be established forever. The key to understanding this pericope lies in the play on the various meanings of the word translated "house." Note that in vs. 1–2 it means a place, in vs. 5, 6, 7, 13 it means a temple, in vs. 11, 16, 19, 25–27, 29 it refers to a dynasty, and finally in v. 18 it means family status. Reviewing the history of David's dynasty, we find that it was not everlasting as promised but fell in 587 (586) B.C., most likely before the author of 2 Samuel wrote this. We can account for the dialogue here by taking it as a "dream" of a literal restoration of the kingdom of David which at the same time anticipated the kingdom of God, which, of course, is the only kingdom that lasts forever.

Our pericope is part of a later theological commentary that was put into an early historical account in an effort to explain why David was not chosen by God to build the temple in spite of his great power and fame and dedication to God. Our reading seems to have been based somewhat on Psalm 89 (see also Ps. 132:11–12). Verses 4–17 are usually referred to by commentators as the prophecy of Nathan, while vs. 18–29 are called the prayer of David. The author ignores the temple at Shiloh (v. 6).

This passage is very significant, since it is the basis of royal messianism in the Hebrew Scriptures. Note carefully how Nathan reverses his initial message to David that he should go and build a house for God (to house the Ark symbolizing God's presence) (v. 3). In a dream that same night Nathan receives a word from the Lord that instead of David building a house for the Lord, the Lord will build a house, meaning a dynasty, for David. Note in vs. 5–7 that an indifferent or even hostile attitude toward the temple is expressed, with a preference indicated for the tent to house the Ark, as used in the desert. Verse 13, which does reveal a favorable attitude toward the temple, may be, in fact, a later addition to the account. The builder in v. 13 is Solomon, David's son.

Note that the promise to David is a personal one. His house, or dynasty, is to be an everlasting one and Israel will enjoy peace and security. God assures David of God's favor to his dynasty which shall be established forever (vs. 14–16).

Recommended work: Review the lives of David and Solomon. Do a word study of Ark and temple, using a Bible dictionary.

The sermon should contrast the temporal nature of David's dynasty with the everlasting kingdom of God. This promise to David was the beginning of the royal messianism which found its fulfillment in Jesus the true king whose kingdom is established forever. The sermon might deal with the temptation to deify nation or state over against the kingdom of God which is the only everlasting kingdom.

Ezekiel 2:1–5 (L)

Ezekiel 2:2–5 (RC)

Ezekiel 2:1–7 (E)

Our pericope should begin with 1:28b and continue through 2:8a, which is the first of five commissions given to Ezekiel in 1:28b–3:27. We note immediately the use of "son of man,'' which here is a nonmessianic term. It is found ninety-three times in Ezekiel alone and stresses the finite dependence and insignificance of humans before God's infinite power and glory (compare with Ps. 8:4). The author contrasts God who is unchangeable with humans who are transitory. And there is a contrast between God's might and human weakness.

The word ''spirit'' here means the Spirit of the Lord. The spirit enters Ezekiel to bridge the gap between God and humans and the spirit gives strength to Ezekiel to listen to the word from God, to ''stand up.'' Here and elsewhere Ezekiel is conscious of being moved by the spirit of God. The role of the spirit before the exile was to fill the heroes and prophets with a physical power beyond their normal powers so that their physical actions seemed ecstatic and out of control (Judg. 6:34; 11:29).

In the case of Ezekiel the spirit is usually exercised on his psychic powers and often just in the sense of making him more attentive to God's presence and the meaning of God's message to him.

Although the people may ignore Ezekiel's words (v. 5), although they come from God, nevertheless the prophet's presence speaks of bold realities which cannot be ignored (v. 7).

Recommended work: Do a study of the life of Ezekiel. Do a word study of spirit in the Hebrew Scriptures and of prophet. Scan the other four commissions given to Ezekiel.

The sermon might deal with the role of the preacher today to proclaim God's message even when it is unpopular and is rejected by a rebellious people. The secular culture of America is rebellious against God, as revealed in movies, drama, novels, and media reporting. The secular mind has invaded the church, and members are often more oriented to the secular world than to the biblical worldview. With Ezekiel, clergy and laity alike need to listen to God speaking to us and then boldly proclaim that message to a rebellious world.

2 Corinthians 12:1–10 (C)

2 Corinthians 12:7–10 (L) (RC)

2 Corinthians 12:2–10 (E)

Our pericopes are part of the section of vs. 1–13 whose theme is strength in weakness. The shapers of the lectionary have cut off the section at v. 10 without losing any essential meaning of the passage. The theme of this pericope is found in 11:30, where Paul says: ''If I must boast, I will boast of the things that show my weakness.'' Although Paul feels there is nothing to be gained by boasting, he thinks he is compelled by his accusers to tell of his experiences of ecstasy which were given him, especially his vision of the third or highest heaven. He remembers the exact time—fourteen years ago—which indicates how sharply this experience was etched in his consciousness.

Paul expresses a touch of humor when he says he must boast but ''there is nothing to be gained by it'' (v. 1). The boasting here is a continuation of his boasting which began in 11:16, an action the Corinthians have forced on him. There is some uncertainty about the Greek text of v. 1, but the main thrust of Paul's argument is clear. This is an unusual aspect of Paul's life to discuss, his visions and revelations, and it may be that the Corinthians had introduced the topic. They may have expected qualified leaders to have had such visions and revelations (in this context we may equate the two). Or it may be that Paul's rivals claimed to have had such, thus forcing Paul to defend the authentic nature of his ministry by sharing his own visions and revelations. In the ancient world, and among some religious sects today, such revelations are regarded as a special sign of God's favor. (Among the Old Regular Baptists of eastern Kentucky where I worked one summer, a requirement for church membership was a dramatic vision or dream. When one man shared his dream before the congregation, he was asked how often he had such dreams and he replied, ''Whenever I eat boiled cabbage for supper!'')

Paul says that at least once, some fourteen years earlier, he had such a revelation from God. Reading between the lines, we see that Paul did not have such experiences on a regular basis. The one he shares here was a very personal one which he had kept private until now. Paul's rule of thumb was that unless sharing such an experience was helpful in building up the church, then there was no point in talking about it. This section of Corinthians was written about A.D. 56–58 it seems, thus dating his revelation about A.D. 42–45. But we don't know anything about Paul's life at that period and therefore cannot relate this revelation to any other event of that time.

In other places Paul tells us about some other spiritual experiences, the best known being his conversion on the road to Damascus (Gal. 1:11–16; 1 Cor. 9:1; 15:8). Also there was the revelation that led Paul to go to Jerusalem to advocate the admission of Gentiles into the church (Gal. 2:2). Acts also records experiences in 16:9; 18:9; 22:17–21; and 27:23. Because these spiritual experiences had a direct bearing on the advance of the gospel, Paul found it imperative to tell their basic message.

We cannot equate this vision with Paul's conversion on the road to Damascus which had occurred some twenty years or more earlier. This present revelation seems to have been one that was beyond words, of things that cannot be told (v. 4). Paul was not allowed to pass on what he had heard or seen, but commentators have speculated on it through the ages. The terms Paul uses indicate that it was more an aural than a visual experience. He refers to himself in an oblique way: "I know a man in Christ" (v. 2), but it is obvious that Paul is referring to himself. At Paul's conversion Christ came down to him. But here Paul is taken up, raptured, into Christ. He says the man was "caught up into Paradise," indicating that he thought of himself as being passive during the experience. God caught him up. Paul was given his vision and revelation in the "third heaven," or Paradise. The Jews believed in many "heavens," usually seven in number, but sometimes only three, as indicated here. The third was the highest, reached by passing through the other two, and can equally be described as Paradise, as the RSV translates it. Paradise for the Jews often meant the place of the righteous who had died. It may be that Paul saw and was told about the place of the afterlife rather than being given a preview of future events and the parousia when Christ returns. (One is moved to speculate about the relationship of Paul's experience to contemporary "out of body" experiences and the experiences of near-death in which people have felt they have died and passed on to the next life but then are brought back to this life.)

To keep Paul from being too elated by this revelation God gave him a thorn in the flesh, a messenger of Satan to harass him. God did not take away this thorn but allowed Paul to see its real purpose, which was to keep his rapture in true perspective. Paul could not boast about the spiritual experience that had been given him, just as he could not boast about the thorn that had been given him also.

The nature of his thorn in the flesh is not known but has been much debated. Some scholars have proposed that "thorns" meant malaria, or an eye disease, or stammering, or epilepsy, or a spiritual affliction that kept him from feeling secure from Satan's wiles. It was possibly some physical malady that was chronic and painful.

The grace of God was sufficient for Paul in his weakness. Paul could do nothing about his thorn in the flesh, but this experience led him to let God bring strength for his life. He knows both the heights of spiritual revelation and the depths of Satan's messenger and lives between the two by the grace of God. Even greater than the vision of Paradise is the assurance in the here and now that God's grace is sufficient for him in all circumstances.

Recommended work: Review the life of Paul in a Bible dictionary. Reflect on Paul's whole life and how God's grace sustained him.

The sermon might focus on the assurance that God's grace is sufficient for us, as it was for Paul. The preacher might outline the life of Paul showing how God worked in Paul's weakness to make him strong. The grace of God for our difficult times should be emphasized.

Theological Reflection

The readings from Mark and Ezekiel deal with rejection of God's agents. The 2 Samuel reading tells of God's promise of an everlasting dynasty for David which we see fulfilled in Christ and his kingdom. The 2 Corinthians reading stresses God's grace which is sufficient for all circumstances.

Children's Message

The talk with the children might be about the life of the apostle Paul who was afflicted (handicapped) with an unknown illness but found God's love to be sufficient for his every need. You might mention some handicaps that people today endure in a similar way.

Hymns for Pentecost 7

God Moves in a Mysterious Way; Make Me a Captive, Lord; Jesus Shall Reign Where'er the Sun.

Ordinary Time 15
Proper 10

Psalm 132:11–18 (C)	**Ephesians 1:1–10 (C)**
Psalm 85:8–13 (L)	**Ephesians 1:3–14 (L) (RC)**
Psalm 85:9–14 (RC)	**Ephesians 1:1–14 (E)**
Psalm 85 or 85:7–13 (E)	
	Mark 6:7–13
2 Samuel 7:18–29 (C)	
Amos 7:10–15 (L)	
Amos 7:12–15 (RC)	
Amos 7:7–15 (E)	

Meditation on the Texts

We bless you, O God and Father of our Lord Jesus Christ, who have blessed us in Christ with every spiritual blessing in the heavenly places and destined us in love to be your children through Jesus Christ. We rejoice that in Christ we have redemption through his blood, the forgiveness of our trespasses. You have made known to us in all wisdom and insight the mystery of your will. We have been sealed with the promised Holy Spirit which is the guarantee of our inheritance. As we remember David's prayer and your promise to build a dynasty for him, we rejoice that in Christ you have established an everlasting kingdom. May we always seek to speak your message, especially when it is an unpopular one with the power figures. We have heard your call to preach the gospel and to minister in Christ's name. May we be faithful to our mission. Amen.

Commentary on the Texts

Mark 6:7–13

This is the account of the commissioning and instruction of the Twelve (see Matt. 10:1–14; Luke 9:1–6). Earlier, in 3:13–19, Jesus chooses the Twelve and invites them to live intimately with him, following his way of life and declaring his message. Here Jesus gives the disciples authority with him over evil destructive forces. Like him, the disciples are not to be self-seeking or engage in violence. They were to proclaim Jesus' message of repentance (see v. 12 and 1:14–15). Jesus' sympathy for human suffering is revealed in v. 13, where Jesus commissions the Twelve to cast out demons and to anoint the sick with oil and to heal them.

When compared with Matthew's account, this passage seems to share with it a common tradition which included as a unit three actions: (1) the institution of the Twelve, (2) the sending out of the disciples, and (3) a discourse of Jesus to the disciples as they depart. Notice that Mark has separated action 1 from action 2 and has greatly shortened action 3. The result is that Mark's account is not so much an account of the disciples' preaching as it is a preparation for Jesus' revealing himself to them as the Messiah.

Reflect on how Mark composed 6:7, 12–13 as a parallel to the earlier 3:13–19, and similar to 1:17–20. Comparing Mark and Matthew, we note that Mark, for literary reasons, places the mission charge *after* Jesus had begun to preach in parables, while Matthew places it *before* that point in Jesus' ministry. It seems that Jesus did not begin to use parables until *after* he had experienced a certain disappointment with the crowds that followed him. Jesus' use of parables reveals a kind of withdrawal from the crowds, noted in fact in v. 7.

The disciples have spent some time of preparation with Jesus, hearing his words (4:1–34) and witnessing his miraculous works (4:35–6:6). Now the time is right for them to become active in Jesus' ministry in both word and works. Note that the conditions that the instructions presuppose are those found in Palestine, while by the time and place of Mark's writing the instructions have lost much of their relevance and practical application. How could Paul have carried out his tremendous missionary enterprise if he had obeyed these commandments of Jesus to the letter? For Mark's church, the instructions had only limited practical application for missionaries of that time. But it was different in the churches of Palestine where conditions for missionary work had not changed much. There Jesus' instructions continued to be practicable. Matthew and Luke were able to describe them more fully than Mark. From the accounts of Matthew and Luke we learn that the message the disciples were commanded to proclaim was the coming of the kingdom, a kingdom that was expected to break into history at just any moment. For this reason they had an urgent need to spread the news as quickly as possible and therefore needed to travel light and not be detained by audiences who rejected their message.

Jesus both authorized the disciples and gave them power. Their mission was communal, and they go out two by two. There is no one charismatic person. Their going two by two both validates their witness and is an example of their participation in a community of faith. While they incarnate the community, they are also agents of Jesus who sends them. Just as Jesus came out to announce the gospel of God (1:14–15), so now he sends them to preach repentance and to heal. Traveling light was also a sign that they relied on God alone to accomplish their mission.

When the disciples arrive in a village they are to accept the first hospitality offered rather than shopping around for the best room and board! The discipline expressed in such practical matters helps them keep their focus on their task.

The disciples' act of shaking the dust off their feet was a warning to the people who rejected them. It was used by pious Jews when returning to Israel from a Gentile land to symbolize separation from any ritual defilement that might cling to them. For the disciples the act was a formal disavowal of fellowship. And as Jesus suffered rejection by his own people (6:6), so his disciples are urged not to waste time trying to convince those who refuse their message. Rather, they are to move on. To reject the disciples, however, was a serious matter.

The pericope closes with an account of the fulfilling of Jesus' instructions (vs. 12–13). They went out and preached repentance, cast out many demons, and anointed with oil many who were sick and healed them. So their work included preaching, exorcising demons, and healing. Their message resembles John the Baptist's in that it was a call to repent.

The promise of Jesus to the disciples was fulfilled as the power of God became evident in their preaching and ministry, in spite of their weaknesses. The essential thing was the power that God conferred on them, as it remains the essential element for preachers today.

Some scholars think that the disciples' preaching was limited to a mission of repentance in the light of the coming passion of Christ. After Jesus' death and resurrection they could fully understand the good news and could preach a message of salvation. The fuller message of the imminence of God's kingdom is reserved to Jesus, while the disciples, like John the Baptist, preach repentance.

Recommended work: Read and reflect on parallels to this commissioning in the Gospels. Compare and contrast them, and compare with the commissioning of Amos in our reading for today.

The sermon may follow the moves of the text and apply the thrust of Jesus' commissioning to disciples today. The message may point out our need to "travel light" and live simply as Christians, witnessing in word and deed to the good news of Jesus Christ. It is a communal task, not a solo mission, and we are strengthened and encouraged as we work with others in bearing the good news.

2 Samuel 7:18–29 (C)

Our pericope is a continuation of the passage from last week dealing with David's wish to build a temple and God's plan to establish through David an everlasting dynasty (chapter 7). Notice that "house" is the key word in the passage and is used in a variety of meanings. In v. 18 it means family status, and in other parts of our passage it means dynasty. In the first part of the chapter it also had the meaning of palace and of temple.

God has assured David of divine favor in vs. 1–17. Now David, in reply, offers this touching prayer of praise and thanksgiving before the Ark. Compare the message of v. 23 with Deuteronomy 4:7, 34; Psalm 44:2–3; and Psalm 89.

This prayer, apparently made in the tent of the Ark, is certainly royal and worthy of David. David sits or lies on the ground to offer the prayer. The thrust of the prayer is a thankful acceptance of God's promise. See how it begins with a recalling of the guidance that David has already received from God. Then David says that God has spoken of David's house "for a great while to come" and has shown him "future generations" (v. 19). This act of grace on God's part is a sign of God's feelings toward David.

Personal prayers were often enlarged to take in the people and the community in some of the psalms, such as Psalms 22 and 130. The people were also mentioned in Nathan's prophecy.

Notice the parallel between the promise that the house of David will be forever and that the election of Israel to be the people of God will be forever. Both will magnify God's holy name forever. By the promise of Nathan, the house of David and the people of God are bound together eternally (vs. 13–16). While there are aspects that apply to the history of the time, the promise also points far beyond Israel's own history to the kingdom that Christ proclaimed and inaugurated. Note that David closes his prayer with the petition that God will fulfill what is promised "for ever" (v. 29).

In this passage we see a contrast between David and Saul. Saul's "house" ended in disgrace. While David's historical dynasty fell in 587 (586) B.C., his "house" anticipated the kingdom of God which is the only eternal kingdom. This passage points up the central significance of the time and person of David. The spotlight falls on the fact that God is with David, and David is king only by the grace of God.

Recommended work: Read and reflect on chapter 7. Scan the life of David in a Bible dictionary.

The sermon will need to include the events in vs. 1–17 in order to give the background for David's prayer in vs. 18–29. The sermon might deal with the grace of God by which David the shepherd boy became king and received God's promise of an everlasting dynasty. The sermon could help hearers reflect on the grace of God working in their lives as they respond in obedience and gratitude in prayer.

Amos 7:10–15 (L)

Amos 7:12–15 (RC)

Amos 7:7–15 (E)

Amos was a native of a small Judean village of Tekoa who was both a shepherd and a dresser of sycamore trees. He came on the scene about 760–750 B.C. Jeroboam II was king in Israel, and many thought that his peaceful reign was a sign of God's special favor which they deserved because of their generous support of the official shrines. Amaziah was the official priest of the royal sanctuary at Bethel in Israel. Our pericope of vs. 10–15 is an account of the encounter between Amos of Judea and Amaziah and is the only prophetic biography account in the book. It may be divided into three sections: (1) the priest's report to Jeroboam the king (vs. 10–11), (2) the priest's command to Amos (vs. 12–13), and (3) Amos' answer to the priest (vs. 14–17, including two verses beyond our pericope).

In vs. 7–9 Amos recounts a vision of a plumb line which he sees as a symbol of Israel's being warped beyond correction. The plumb line was a cord with a weight on the end used by builders to make certain that walls were vertical. Israel had been built correctly but was now out of line with God. God will judge Israel by letting Israel be devastated by the sword. Amos does not name a historical protagonist. God will be the executioner of judgment, for the covenant has been broken by Israel and God will no longer pass over Israel's sins.

Then in vs. 10–15 Amaziah reports to King Jeroboam that Amos has conspired against him in prophesying that Jeroboam shall die by the sword and Israel must go into exile away from his land (v. 11). The shrine at Bethel was the sanctuary of the king and the temple of the kingdom. Amos' message is seen as the first step in a strategy to overthrow the king. In past crises the predictions of prophets had been followed by internal revolts. Amaziah refers to all of Amos' speeches as his "words."

Amaziah tells Amos to leave the land. He had authority over the cult at Bethel and command over the cult priests who functioned there. He didn't want trouble out of Amos, so he gives him a way out: prophesy no more and flee to his homeland of Judah. Amaziah has no concern for the truth of what Amos was preaching but was focused only on the decency and order of the cult at Bethel. "Eat bread" could mean earn his living by practicing prophecy, thus implying that Amos should earn his bread by prophesying in his own land of Judea. He may have received gifts and fees from individuals and royal courts. The stress is on "there," pointing Amos to go back home and prophesy there but not at Bethel.

The issues of interpreting v. 14 are beyond the scope of this commentary. For details, the preacher is referred to the Old Testament Library volume by James L. Mays, *Amos, A Commentary* (1969). I take the conversation between Amos and Amaziah to be in the past tense. The stress of Amos' answer falls on the command of God to prophesy, which Amos uses to counter Amaziah's command to leave the country.

Amos had once been a shepherd, but now he is a prophet. He had also been a dresser of sycamore trees, which probably involved puncturing the forming fruit so that it would grow large enough to be edible and would be sweet. The fruit was smaller than the fig and was food eaten by the poor. It was seasonal work. (This suggests that Amos was a kind of migrant worker before becoming a prophet!) Amos rejects the idea that he is a member of the prophetic guilds which seem to have capitulated to the pagan practices of local places of worship. The chief interest of these professional prophets was their fees. Amos has no interest in being a prophet for fees. He speaks God's word of warning and judgment, which puts him at risk. But so have true prophets in all ages!

Amos stands in the tradition of prophets such as Elijah whose exclusive task is to declare what God reveals to them. Such a commission does not have geographical boundaries, as Amaziah suggests it should. God had commissioned Amos from Judea to prophesy to God's people Israel. Amos rejects any authority other than God, including the advice and command of the king's official priest, Amaziah. Amos even puts him under God's jurisdiction.

Recommended work: Read all five visions of God's judgment in chapters 7–9. Compare Amos with Jeremiah and with Jesus, Peter and Paul, and others who spoke God's message to hostile audiences.

The sermon might focus on the contrast between true and false prophets in our time, compared with Amos and Amaziah. Amos was a "layman" who responded to God's call to prophesy in Israel. The sermon should encourage Christians to speak and act for justice when it is the unpopular thing to do and when job and security are at risk.

Ephesians 1:1–10 (C)

Ephesians 1:3–14 (L) (RC)

Ephesians 1:1–14 (E)

The longer reading spans the salutation (vs. 1–2) and a liturgical preface (vs. 3–23) which includes our pericope with its hymn in vs. 3–14. It is part of the thanksgiving section of chapters 1–3. The preacher is referred to the commentary by J. L. Houlden, *Paul's Letters from Prison,* Westminster Pelican Commentaries (Philadelphia: Westminster Press, 1978), for a discussion of the setting, audience, time, place, and author of Ephesians. Most contemporary scholars do not think that Paul wrote this letter but that the author was a typical religious man of his time, probably a Jew in upbringing who was familiar with the Hebrew Scriptures and with current religious philosophy. He was a Christian who had found in Christ and the fellowship of his church the fulfillment of his dreams. The author was a Paulinst, not only sharing Paul's doctrine but also aware of inheriting Paul's authority and the need to exercise it. Note that he wrote in the name of Paul alone without mentioning any associates. Paul usually mentioned the persons who were with him. This calls attention to the authority the writer claims for himself.

While vs. 1–2 may look like a typical Pauline opening, a closer examination reveals some differences. The RSV puts the phrase "who are at Ephesus and faithful" in the margin, since it was not part of the original text, thus pointing up the uniqueness of this letter. All other letters attributed to Paul are addressed to specific congregations, not to a general Christian audience. The Greek is somewhat strange, although the RSV smoothes this out. The Greek word for "saints" is an adjective used as a noun and is parallel in meaning to "faithful." We would expect these two words in our text to be joined by "and." But they are not. A phrase "who are" translates a participle between them. Saints are people called of God and set aside for God's service. Saints are also faithful believers in Christ Jesus. One of the author's concerns in the whole letter is to define what true belief in Christ who is the head of the church really requires. Saints may have three possible definitions, however: (1) Christians in general, the usual meaning in the New Testament, (2) Jewish Christians, or (3) the angels. But usually the term refers to God's people, consecrated to God's service.

All of the Pauline greetings are adaptations of current formulae found in Greek and Jewish letters.

Then in vs. 3–14 we have a hymn in praise of God for God's great acts in Christ. The theme of vs. 3–8 is God's purpose to bless. "Blessed be the God . . . " is the commonest expression of Jewish piety expressed in the berakah, or blessing. Note that it is not a blessing from God to humans but an act of praise expressed by humans before God for some action on God's part in the past (such as creation or redemption) or for some desired action in the present such as the provision of food or the expected kingdom. This type of prayer was used by Jews on all kinds of occasions, such as over bread at a meal, or when there was some special good fortune, or in Solomon's prayer at the inauguration of the temple. Prayers from the synagogues of the New Testament time reveal examples that begin "Blessed art thou, O Lord our God."

This is the only letter in which the phrase "in the heavenly places" occurs in the New Testament (v. 3). It is used five times in this letter to describe the cosmic sphere where Christ rules and the place to which Christians have been raised to new life in Christ. But it is also a place where the powers of evil and darkness are yet active.

The meaning of spiritual blessing in v. 3 becomes clear in vs. 4–6. It refers to God's eternal purpose by which God has willed that all humans should be holy and blameless and should grow to their full stature as children of God. Here holiness and blamelessness refer primarily to the believer's election to sonship (v. 5), not just to moral purity.

In all of this hymn there is an emphasis on the sovereign freedom of God and on Christ's role as the one who reveals and mediates God's grace. It is in Christ that God's purposes have been set forth and realized. Notice how the phrases of this section are crowded onto each other in an effort to express the overflowing blessing of God.

Then in vs. 7–8 we have a further description of the blessing and Christ's function as its agent. Note the reference to redemption through his blood, referring to Christ's death on the cross which effects the forgiveness of our trespasses.

That all things are united in Christ is the theme of vs. 9–10, and that all things are created for God's purpose is the theme of vs. 11–14. God wills that humans live for the praise of God's glory. This is another fixed liturgical and doctrinal expression common to this opening section.

Note the important place the Holy Spirit has in the doctrine of Ephesians. "Sealed" probably points to Christian baptism when a Christian is inwardly consecrated to the service of God and incorporated into the church. Inheritance refers to all the future blessings to which a Christian may look forward.

Recommended work: Scan the whole Letter to the Ephesians and read an introduction to it in a commentary or Bible dictionary.

The sermon might follow the movement of the passage with its emphasis on the blessing that God has given us in Christ. The sermon should help hearers understand that salvation is God's purpose and is made possible through the death of Christ. The "over and above" of God's gracious salvation should be stressed.

Theological Reflection

The 2 Samuel passage is David's grateful prayer to God for God's promises. The readings from both Amos and Mark are concerned with speaking a message from God in the face of opposition. The Ephesians reading deals with God's graciousness in establishing the church of Jesus Christ and salvation given in it by God's eternal plan.

Children's Message

The talk might be about prayer and might refer to King David's prayer of thankfulness. It might deal with prayer as conversation with God, not just asking God for something.

The talk might conclude with a prayer that includes things and persons for which the children are thankful and petitions they wish to offer.

Hymns for Pentecost 8

Glorious Things of You Are Spoken; O Master, Let Me Walk with Thee; Praise, My Soul, the King of Heaven.

Ordinary Time 16
Proper 11

Psalm 53 (C)	**Ephesians 2:11–22 (C)**
Psalm 23 (L) (RC)	**Ephesians 2:13–22 (L)**
Psalm 22:22–30 (E)	**Ephesians 2:13–18 (RC)**

2 Samuel 11:1–15 (C)	**Mark 6:30–34 (C)**
Jeremiah 23:1–6 (L) (RC)	**Mark 6:30–44 (E)**
Isaiah 57:14b–21 (E)	

Meditation on the Texts

We thank you, O God, for Christ the Good Shepherd who cares for the sheep and nourishes us with the Bread of Life. We thank you for his care when we have wandered like sheep without a shepherd. Forgive us when we have not trusted your providential care of our lives. We remember the gracious abundance of the miracle of the feeding of the five thousand and give thanks for your abundant grace which more than meets our needs. We confess our sins of using others. We recall how David used Bathsheba and Uriah and sinned greatly. We ask forgiveness for our treating people as means to our selfish ends rather than as persons made in your image. May we never be found false shepherds who scatter the sheep. We rejoice that we who were alienated from the commonwealth of Israel and strangers to your promise, without hope, have been brought near in the blood of Christ. We affirm that Christ is the cornerstone of the holy temple in whom we also are built for a dwelling place of yours in the Spirit. We are grateful that you dwell both in the high and holy place and with the person of a contrite and humble spirit. We rest in the assurance that you will not contend forever, nor always be angry. For from you proceeds the Spirit, and you have made the breath of life and in Christ have healed us. Amen.

Commentary on the Texts

Mark 6:30–34 (C)

Mark 6:30–44 (E)

The theme of vs. 30–44, the longer reading, is the feeding of the five thousand (see Matt. 14:13–21; Luke 9:10–17; and John 6:1–13). This miracle of the feeding of the five thousand is the only miracle given in all four Gospels, although there are two doublets of feeding of four thousand in two Gospels. It appears that this story of Jesus' feeding of the multitude was a favorite of the early church and was told in a number of different contexts. The literary structure reveals that this pericope and that of 8:1–10 of the feeding of the four thousand frame the third division of Jesus' Galilean ministry. It is introduced by the sending of the Twelve. Reflect on the two feeding miracles which are interpreted by the discussion about bread found in 8:14–21.

The disciples gave a report of their missionary work, telling Jesus "all that they had done and taught" (v. 30). We are not told anything about the content of their report. Nor are we told the location of the place to which Jesus took the disciples, since such matters do not interest Mark. The Greek word translated here as "lonely" also means "desert." It is the Greek translation of the word used in Hebrew Scriptures for the wilderness. For Mark, the fact that the miracle took place in the desert is of the essence of the miracle.

Scholars have wondered whether or not the people on foot could have reached the place where Jesus and the disciples landed before they did. But the boat may not have gone to the eastern shore of the sea of Galilee as some think. It may have headed a few miles north or south, which would mean that the crowd could keep the boat in view and even be waiting on the shore when it arrived.

Jesus went ashore and saw a great throng. He had compassion on them because they were "like sheep without a shepherd," and he began to teach them. Earlier, in v. 31, Jesus gave the disciples "rest" as a shepherd provides rest for sheep after a journey to new pasture. Thus we see the figure of the End time shepherd introduced here in the person of Jesus. Relate this image to the Jeremiah reading for today about the bad shepherds and the good shepherds of God's flock, Israel. Rest is also an image of the Hebrew Scriptures to describe the entrance of Israel into the promised land after forty years in the desert. Also recall the shepherd motif in Psalm 23. Jesus is moved with compassion to give the people food for their spiritual hunger by teaching them "many things." In the teaching Jesus brings God's revelation to the people.

The disciples asked Jesus to send the people away to buy themselves something to eat. But Jesus tells them to give them something to eat themselves. While the Israelites were in the wilderness, they saw many proofs of God's power and should have trusted God to provide food (Ps. 78:8–20). The disciples had seen many signs of God's power working through Jesus and should have trusted that power and known that it would furnish them power to give to the people there in the desert. Their reply recalls a similar one by Moses in Numbers 11:13, 21–22.

We cannot completely understand the meaning of the symbol of the fish in the story, but we know that the fish was a "sign" found in the early church. Many of the Christians were fishermen, and fish with bread would have been a common meal. Bread and fish appear together in art in the catacombs as a symbol of the Eucharist. The Greek word for "fish" made an acrostic for affirming faith in Jesus as Son of God and so was used as a secret code word. The fish was a Christian symbol of great importance.

The mention of green grass may be just an allusion to Psalm 23, or it could indicate an eyewitness account which would date the event in the early spring about the time of Passover. The people were seated by hundreds and by fifties, which may point to Moses' dividing the Israelites into groups of 1,000, 100, 50, and 10. According to some scholars, the same divisions are to be made at the messianic banquet to come.

The original gestures of Jesus appear to have been expanded by further details taken from the Eucharist (v. 41). Looking up was the usual Jewish posture for prayer. He blessed God, broke the loaves and gave them to the people, and divided the two fish among them all. The report that they all ate and were satisfied recalls the provision of manna in the desert which was sufficient. The leftovers are a sign of God's super-abundant gifts (see Ex. 16:19–24). The twelve baskets left over are enough to feed the twelve tribes of the new Israel. Since there is not the usual expression of wonder associated with other miracles, this may indicate that Mark tells this story not so much as a miracle story but more as a messianic sign whose purpose is further to reveal to the Twelve who Jesus really is.

Recommended work: Read and compare parallel feeding miracles in this and other Gospels. Read an account of the gift of manna in the desert and compare it with this feeding.

The sermon might follow the moves of the text and apply the message to life today as we trust in God to provide abundantly for both spiritual and material needs. Miracles by their nature cannot be explained but only accepted in faith. This text would be especially fitting for a worship service celebrating the Lord's Supper. Jesus showed compassion by teaching "many things" and by giving spiritual and physical nourishment at the feeding.

2 Samuel 11:1–15 (C)

This account of David and Bathsheba paints the portrait of David "warts and all." It is revealing of the nature of biblical narrative that even heroes and godly persons like David are shown as sinners saved by grace and not as superhuman creatures. We are dismayed by this story in that David with his apparent piety could yield to such gross sins of adultery and what amounts to premeditated murder. The account astonishes us with its openness about David who is the type of the Messiah. In 2 Chronicles 20 we find that this incident is omitted! But the fact that it is included here indicates that the ancient writer saw God's plan advanced, not by sinless persons, but by God working through people like David despite their sinfulness.

In vs. 2–3 the story begins in an exciting fashion and is joined into the account of the Ammonite war (see 2 Chronicles 20:1). As the action begins, David has left the siege of the capital to Joab and remains in Jerusalem. The time is summer, and David has an upper room where he can enjoy the cool afternoon breeze. In the late afternoon he comes out on the flat roof of the palace and sees Bathsheba bathing outdoors. Some blame her for bathing in a place where she could be seen and think she may have done this deliberately to attract the king's attention. Even if she had, this would not excuse David's conduct.

He asked who she was and was told her father's and husband's names. Uriah was one of his very prominent officers. The speed of the action now picks up. She is called to David's quarters, and the liaison goes as planned. The author here places responsibility on David for the act, and David also later acknowledges it. Purification was required after the monthly menstrual period. The ancients thought this was an especially likely time for conception.

David finds himself in a predicament when he learns the consequences of his adultery. It has danger even for him as king, since the king in Israel, unlike pagan kings, does *not* stand above the law. He has Uriah summoned, tries to get him to go to his house and have intercourse with Bathsheba so that the child that is born later will appear to be Uriah's. The term "wash his feet" may mean just make himself comfortable. There is an allusion in the Hebrew word for "feet" to the male genitals. David makes a present of food to put Uriah in a good frame of mind. Now it is very possible that Uriah had learned of the adultery, perhaps from the messenger who went to and fro, and it may have become gossip in the court. But Uriah is loyal to his fellow soldiers and is true to the religious obligations that the holy war lays on him not to have sex with his wife during the war (see 1 Sam. 21:4). This refusal to give in to the king's wishes is Uriah's weapon and revenge. However, this will also trigger his death.

As the plot thickens, we see that for David there is only one way to solve the problem: eliminate Uriah. Note the different stages of David's sin, which are told only as bare facts devoid of feelings (vs. 14–15). David writes the "Uriah letter" and sends it by Uriah to Joab, thereby adding further insult to the injury. Some commentators think David wrote only the first part up to the phrase about hardest fighting (v. 15) and left it to Joab to read his fuller meaning into it. But the order is not executed in the way suggested by the letter as we now have it.

Recommended work: Reflect on the way in which one sin by David leads to another. Note how David is held responsible for his actions in the account.

The sermon could seek to show how the grace of God is even greater than our more grievous sins. David is not cast off by God but is later confronted by God's prophet Nathan: "You are the man" (2 Sam. 12:7). David confessed his sin against God, and Nathan assures him he shall not die. Thus the sermon should tell more of the story than just our pericope and should deal with sin in the light of Christ's death and resurrection to free us from bondage to sin. The excuse of the comedian "The devil made me do it" does not hold up in God's moral order. Each person is responsible before God for sinful acts.

Jeremiah 23:1–6 (L) (RC)

See Christ the King (Proper 29).

Isaiah 57:14b–21 (E)

This is one of the postexilic poems. The theme here is comfort for the afflicted. A mysterious voice fills the air around the prophet and the beginning lines appear to quote Isaiah 40:3–4. Notice the rich theology in v. 15 dealing with the nature of God and combining the idea of an exalted eternal holy God with God's imminence with those who are crushed and dejected. The word in Hebrew for "dwell" (v. 15) is drawn from the desert days when Moses and Israel lived in rough tent dwellings. The point is that God lived with God's people during that time and shared their hardships. The same word later came to be used only of God's dwelling with the people in the temple. It always alludes to the desert days when Israel lived in tents and God was there with God's people.

In v. 17 we are told that God says, "I hid my face and was angry." Nothing is nearer to eternal damnation than the terrible silence of God which leaves the satisfied person centered and satisfied on self. Then in v. 18 God assures the sinner that God will heal him and lead him and requite him with comfort. This promise is fulfilled in the next verse. The literal meaning of "requite him with comfort" is "give him peace" (see Eph. 2:17 in our pericope for today).

Then in vs. 20–21 we have lines that are anticlimactic after the preceding promise and may have been added by leading wise men of postexilic Israel.

Recommended work: Compare with Isaiah 40:1–4. Reflect on how God in the trinitarian doctrine is both high and exalted but also nearer than hands or feet by the Spirit.

The sermon might deal with the theme of consolation, showing how in Christ God's justifiable wrath is not unending. The sermon should speak to contemporary needs for assurance of God's healing as an act of grace in which in spite of our sins we are restored to wholeness with God.

Ephesians 2:11–22 (C)

Ephesians 2:13–22 (L)

Ephesians 2:13–18 (RC)

The above readings are parts of a chapter whose theme is Christ's benefits for both Gentiles and Jews. The distinction between Jew and Gentile has been removed in Christ (v. 11; see Col. 3:11). The reader is urged to keep in mind the sudden change that God's power has made in Gentiles who were once estranged from God. Now the terms "circumcised" and "uncircumcised" are obsolete. Circumcision was the eternal sign of the covenant, and "uncircumcised" came to refer to those who did not belong to God's people. This sign was external only and did not necessarily indicate an inner attitude or a genuine distinction from Gentiles. The word for "Gentiles" means the nations, that is, all the non-Jewish people of the world who were without hope without Christ. They did not have the Jewish Messianic hope.

But now the reconciling work of Christ has worked to bring those who were alienated from God's people, Israel, into relationship with Christ Jesus in the blood of Christ. This points to the power of Christ's death to reconcile all peoples to God in the new covenant.

Christ has not only broken down the hostility between Jew and Gentile and made them one but has also reconciled both groups to God in one body, namely, the church (vs. 14–16). This unity in one body is based on the participation of Jews and Gentiles in one Spirit. Those who were once strangers (vs. 12 and 19) are now fellow citizens with the saints (those set apart for God) and members of the household of God.

The foundation (v. 20) was laid by the apostles and Christian prophets, and the whole structure depends upon Christ as the cornerstone. "Cornerstone" was a term used to refer to Messiah (see Isa. 28:16). Paul may have been thinking of the universal church and looking back to its beginnings. We are not told the exact placing of this cornerstone in the building, but it has a cohesive and unifying position as well as function.

Ephesians sees this as a growing building (v. 21). The members who make up this building are living stones, according to 1 Peter 2:5. Then the emphasis in v. 22 is on the role of the members who as living parts contribute to their mutual growth and that of the whole church.

Recommended work: Read and reflect on the whole chapter.
The preacher may want to follow the action in the passage and develop the images the

author uses in applying the text to the hearers. Unity in Christ of all peoples should be the thrust of the sermon.

Theological Reflection

David alienated himself from God by his sin, but later he confesses and his sin is forgiven. This is a theme in Isaiah and Ephesians which deals with God's mercy in healing and uniting those who were alienated. Mark tells of Jesus' compassion for those who were alienated, like sheep without a shepherd, and how Jesus met their spiritual and material needs.

Children's Message

The talk might be about Jesus' feeding of the five thousand in which there was so much food that twelve baskets were left over. God's superabundance in providing for our needs may be stressed.

Hymns for Pentecost 9

Christ Is Made the Sure Foundation; Savior, like a Shepherd Lead Us; We Are One in the Spirit.

Pentecost 10

Ordinary Time 17

Proper 12

Psalm 32 (C)
Psalm 145 (L)
Psalm 145:10–11, 15–18 (RC)
Psalm 114 (E)

2 Samuel 12:1–14 (C)
Exodus 24:3–11 (L)
2 Kings 4:42–44 (RC)
2 Kings 2:1–15 (E)

Ephesians 3:14–21 (C)
Ephesians 4:1–7, 11–16 (L) (E)
Ephesians 4:1–6 (RC)

John 6:1–15 (C)
Mark 6:45–52 (E)

Meditation on the Texts

Gracious God, who forgives the repentant sinner, may we, like David, confess "I have sinned against the LORD" and look to you for pardon. May we have the courage of Nathan in preaching to declare "You are the man/woman" in confronting sin. As we recall the ministries of Elijah and Elisha we join with Elisha in praying for a double share of the spirit that filled Elijah. We pray that we may be strengthened with might through your Spirit in the inner person, that Christ may dwell in our hearts through faith and that we may know the love of Christ which surpasses knowledge and be filled with all the fullness of your being, O God. May we each use the grace given to us for the building up of the body of Christ until we all attain to the unity of the faith and the knowledge of Christ your Son, to the measure of the stature of the fullness of Christ. As Christ fed the five thousand by the Sea of Galilee, so may we be fed on the living Bread, even Christ himself. In recalling the terror of the disciples when they saw Jesus walking on the sea, may we hear his words in our times of terror, "Take heart, it is I; have no fear." Amen.

Commentary on the Texts

John 6:1–15 (C)

Since this is a parallel record to the feeding of the five thousand dealt with in Mark 6:30–44 last week, the preacher is referred to the commentary there. John uses the material in a different way from Mark, however. One of John's goals is to exploit the symbolic potential of the feeding miracle, bringing out explicitly what is already implicit in the Synoptic account. In the Synoptics the feeding miracle is already a symbol of the Eucharist and contains liturgical and sacramental allusions that bear this out.

Notice that vs. 14–15 are not in the Synoptic tradition but contain important historical information given only by John. The people recognize in the miracle that Jesus is the prophet like Moses who has come to form the New Israel. But they do not have a depth of perception about this. The result is that the people want to take Jesus up and make him an earthly king, their Jewish Messiah. But Jesus rejects such efforts. Jesus fled back to the mountain alone. It is not probable that the disciples shared the messianic enthusiasm of the crowd.

With these differences in the feeding miracle as John describes it, the preacher might follow the action in the text, with an emphasis on the gracious superabundance which Christ supplied the people (v. 13). The sermon might deal with the false and true nature of Jesus' Messiahship. The thrust of the sermon might be to lead hearers to confess faith in Christ as the true king whose kingdom is from heaven and who is ruling by his Spirit in the world today.

This is the miracle of Jesus walking on the water, with parallels in Matthew 14:22–33 and John 6:16–21. All three accounts place this miracle *after* the bread miracle when Jesus' popularity in Galilee is at its peak.

The messianic expectation, mentioned by John 6:15 but only hinted at by Mark, is essential to this event. Mark says that Jesus made his disciples get into the boat and go before him. The continuing contrast between Jesus and the Twelve is indicated here by their reluctance to leave. There is some question about the command to go to the other side, Bethsaida, since it was at the northeast end of the lake rather than opposite them. They may have set out to go the short distance to Bethsaida but were driven by the wind on a southwest course to Gennesaret.

Jesus withdraws from the Twelve to pray. This hints that messianic fervor stirred up by his last miracle may have confronted him with a temptation to depart from his true messianic role. Mark tells us that the boat was in the middle of the sea. He uses a word that in the Greek translation of the Hebrew Scriptures is used in connection with the passage through the Reed Sea. While none of the accounts mention a storm, we are told that the wind was against them. The fourth watch was between 3 A.M. and 6 A.M. Mark says Jesus "meant to pass by them," which suggests the way in which Jesus appeared to his disciples. Compare this with Job 9:11, where God is said to pass by (make himself known). Thus Jesus' action is a divine revelation. But the disciples thought Jesus was a ghost, a reaction similar to that to the risen Christ.

The disciples were terrified. The word for "terror" indicates fear in the face of an extraordinary vision or message. But Jesus spoke to them. What he said emphasizes the character of this miracle as one of revealing God in Christ to the people. Jesus tells them, "Take heart, it is I; have no fear." Take heart means to take courage, be bold. The phrase "It is I" is an answer to the disciples' question in 4:41 of who Jesus is. His answer is reminiscent of God's self-revelation in Exodus 3:14; Isaiah 41:4; and 43:11. In the Second Isaiah passages the phrase stresses God's transcendence and faithfulness to the promises of salvation. In using the phrase "It is I," Jesus is designating himself as the divine agent of God's salvation.

Jesus tells them not to be afraid. This is another phrase found in accounts of God's revelation to humans (Gen. 15:1; Dan. 10:12, 19).

The disciples were utterly astounded and did not understand about the loaves, says Mark. The disciples miss the real meaning of Jesus' acts because of their lack of faith. If the disciples had understood the mystery of the miracle of the feeding of the five thousand, they would have known who it was who came walking on the sea. Mark says their hearts were hardened, which is usually said of the Jews, but here Mark applies it to the disciples. They were not able to perceive the deeper meaning of Jesus' revelation of himself in both signs and parables.

Recommended work: Read the parallels to this miracle in Matthew 14:22–33 and John 6:16–21 and compare them. Read an article on miracles in a Bible dictionary.

The preacher may want to consider several approaches to developing a sermon from this passage. One would be to deal with fear and Jesus' assurance that because he is present we need not fear. Another is to deal with faith versus the hardness of hearts of the disciples. Or the sermon might follow the moves of the text and show how this miracle story seeks to reveal Jesus as divine with power over nature itself.

2 Samuel 12:1–14 (C)

This is the account of Nathan's confronting David with his sins of adultery and murder and David's repentance. Nathan tells the now well known parable of the pet ewe lamb. Nathan shows great courage in confronting David with his sin, which was condemned even by standards of that day. Israel's king was responsible to God for his actions. Notice that in telling the parable Nathan draws David into an untenable position (vs. 5–6). When David has taken the bait Nathan declares, "You are the man." ("Thou art the man" in the KJV is even more dramatic.) It appears that David has taken over Saul's harem, a common practice in that time. Now he has taken the wife of one of his leading soldiers, Uriah.

The prediction of evil (v. 11) could well have been added by an editor, according to a number of commentators. The neighbor who is referred to is probably Absalom (see 16:21–22). According to the law of exact retaliation, an eye for an eye and a tooth for a tooth, David should have died for the arranged murder of Uriah. But instead, God's judgment falls upon the child, as a kind of "favor" to David, as understood by the mind of that day. But note that the sin is against the Lord. The child will die because David has utterly scorned the Lord. God sets the moral standards. Nathan's word of judgment from God is tempered with the promise of forgiveness. God does not desire the death of the sinner, as Ezekiel 18:23 and 32 indicate. Rather, God seeks that humans turn from their wickedness and live.

David's sin not only is against God but has effects on the world around him. The death of the child shows how God feels about the plain transgression of the commandments, and its purpose is to prevent those who think that God is unjust from saying so. The judgment on the child may seem unjust to us today, but it was not in the thinking of David's time.

Recommended work: Reflect on the whole account of David and Bathsheba from last Sunday and today.

The sermon may begin with the setting of the parable of the ewe, with David having just murdered Uriah and taken Bathsheba for a wife, and then build to Nathan's confrontation with David and God's assurance of pardon for his sin. The death of the child in David's place may be difficult for contemporary Christians to accept and may need to be given special attention in the sermon. The forgiveness we have in Christ for the most heinous sins should be stressed, for this passage may open the way for hearers to confess their sins and receive God's pardon.

Exodus 24:3–11 (L)

These verses are part of the ceremony of ratifying the covenant found in chapter 24. In the whole account there are two sections: vs. 1–2, which continue in vs. 9–11 and point to Moses' special role as covenant mediator. But in vs. 3–4 we have the first version of the covenant ratifying rite which emphasizes the people's participation. In the first the action takes place on the mountain after Moses ascends to the top, leaving his comrades below. In the second, the action takes places at the foot of the mountain. The covenant is ratified by a sacrificial meal in the first section and by sprinkling with blood in the second. Both agree on the special covenant given Israel and its solemn acceptance by the people. The seventy elders represent the people. Although the passage says "they saw the God of Israel" (v. 10), we are at once told of what was "under his feet." The traditional belief was that if a person saw God directly, the person would die. So it seems we have an exception to this belief here, since God "did not lay his hand on the chief men of the people."

The ritual serves to unite the two parties to the covenant: the Lord, whose presence is symbolized by the altar, and the people. According to the thinking of the ancients, blood was effective in bringing about community between God and humans. Moses splashes half of the blood against the altar and the other half on the people. After Moses had written down all the words of the Lord, he took the book containing them and read it to the people and they responded with a solemn vow to do the words and be obedient to God. Now the covenant between God and the people is a reality. Even so, the new covenant of the New Testament was ratified in blood, namely, that of Jesus on the cross (Matt. 26:28).

Recommended work: Read articles on blood, sacrificial meal, and covenant in a Bible dictionary.

The sermon might deal with the text in the light of the new covenant in Jesus Christ which this action foreshadows. The preacher may want to develop the images of the passage and the moves. The hearers should be led to join with the people in vowing to be obedient to God. The Lord's Supper is foreshadowed by the sacrificial meal in which God is present with God's people to renew the covenant.

This account of the multiplication of the loaves is a most striking parallel to the miracles of feeding in the New Testament. The firstfruits were the loaves made of grain milled from the recent harvest. The phrase in v. 43, "Thus says the LORD," is followed in v. 44 by the common formula for the fulfillment of such a promise.

Not only were the hundred men filled with bread but they had some left, just as food was left over in Jesus' feeding miracles. This superabundance points to the graciousness of God, who supplies our needs over and above what we require! Thus there is no need to be anxious or greedy or despairing, for God cares for us.

Recommended work: Read the feeding miracles of Jesus.

The sermon might draw on both this text and that of John 6:1–15 and show how this account foreshadows the miracles in John. The message should stress God's gracious providence which cares for us "over and above" our actual needs.

2 Kings 2:1–15 (E)

Our passage is part of a chapter that deals with the taking up of Elijah into heaven and being succeeded by Elisha. The Elisha cycle, as it is called, extends from 2:1–8:15, although some would extend it even to 13:21. The thrust of the author here is to establish the authority of the prophets and to show the fulfillment of their prophecies. To do this he selects material from his sources, without much concern for chronology or the probability of the stories.

The power and the greatness of Elijah are expressed by the ancient writer in terms of legend and miracle. According to scripture, only Enoch and Elijah were counted worthy to be taken up by God without seeing death. "Sons of the prophets" refers to members of a prophetic order, not to actual sons.

Elijah took his mantle, rolled it up, and struck the water and the water parted (v. 8) and so reproduces the miracle that Moses performed at the Red Sea and Joshua at the Jordan. The double share (v. 9) refers to the rule by which the eldest son in a family received a double share of his father's inheritance. Elisha asks that he be recognized as the principal spiritual heir of Elijah.

In v. 12 Elisha is saying that Elijah was more important and more powerful than chariots and horsemen. Notice also that the teacher and student relationship is represented in terms of father and son. The title "father" was given to a man of religion from ancient times. The prophet's spiritual strength is of greater value in defending Israel than are Israel's chariots.

Although it is not said explicitly, it is implied that Elijah did not die (v. 12). Elijah was expected to return before the End time when Messiah came.

Elisha parted the waters and is acknowledged as the leader by the sons of the prophets.

Recommended work: Scan articles on Elijah and Elisha in a Bible dictionary and compare their lives.

The sermon might deal with passing on the prophetic tradition and would be very appropriate for an installation or ordination service for clergy. The preacher might tell the story and show how Elisha demonstrated by miracles that he was in the tradition of Elijah. The sermon could deal with the responsibility of Christians to take up where others before them have left off in serving God as teachers, preachers, lay leaders in the church, and leaders in the community.

Ephesians 3:14–21 (C)

Our pericope contains a prayer for wisdom in vs. 14–19 and a doxology in vs. 20–21. "For this reason" (v. 14) recalls the argument beginning with v. 1. The usual position for prayer was standing, as scripture indicates; thus, kneeling would be a more solemn and intense attitude for prayer. There is a play on words in the Greek words for "father" and "family" (vs. 14–15): *patēr*=father; *patria*=family. God is the origin of all fatherhood. The author prays for the inner person, praying that the reader may be strengthened with might through his Spirit in the inner man (v. 16). The inner man means the same and translates the same words as "inmost self" does in Romans 7:22. Both refer to the essential person-hood. When this is yielded to the powerful working of God's Spirit it can become completely new.

The innermost self is made new by the Spirit of Christ as he dwells within and as the life, opened to Christ's presence, is rooted and grounded in love. In the Pauline tradition, Spirit and the risen Christ were interchangeable terms. The risen Christ *is* the source of the Spirit.

The reference to breadth, length, height, and depth (v. 18) is from Stoic philosophy and referred to the totality of the universe. While knowledge was highly prized by the Greeks, the author says the experience of the love of God revealed in Christ surpasses all such human knowledge.

Then the closing doxology (vs. 20–21) places the church and Christ Jesus side by side. It celebrates God's infinite generosity and God's glory both in the church and in Jesus Christ. The author is saying the same thing in saying "in the church" or "in Christ Jesus," since they necessarily complement each other.

Recommended work: Watch for gnostic terms which the author twists and to which he gives a new Christian understanding, such as "knowledge" or "family in heaven."

The sermon may be structured as a prayer for the contemporary hearers, that God would bless and strengthen them. It might be titled "The Love of Christ Which Surpasses Knowledge." And the sermon might end with the doxology in the text.

Ephesians 4:1–7, 11–16 (L) (E)

Ephesians 4:1–6 (RC)

The theme of vs. 1–16 is the unity and growth of the body of Christ. We will deal with vs. 1–7 and 11–16. Note that the doxology in 3:20–21 marks the end of a section. Now chapters 4–6 take up the practical applications of the earlier material for the Christian life. We have here the ethical implications of chapters 1–3. The reference to "prisoner for the Lord" in v. 1 invokes again the authority of Paul. The writer appeals to the true basis for Christian ethics, namely, God's call to Christian unity, peace, and love, and the gift of the spiritual gifts for use in the common interest.

Christians have been called to their new life in Christ. They have a vocation to be Christian. Those called are to live a life worthy of their calling. They are to live it in all humility. For pagan Greeks, humility was not a virtue but was a vice, mean-spiritedness. But Christ raised humility in service to others to a dignity by his own example of life and acts. Unity is the distinguishing mark of the church and of all creation. The Spirit is the inner source of Christian life and is continually moving all members of the church toward that which promotes peace and harmony. Remember that the central thrust of Ephesians is *Christian unity*.

Then in vs. 4–7 there is a wonderful sevenfold formula of unity. Jewish emphasis on the one God influenced the early church greatly as the people remembered God, who dwelt within their faith community. The slogans found in these verses recapitulate arguments found in chapters 1–3, suggesting that the unity of the Spirit is a gift which is a gift of God and is already present in the church. Faith here points to the totality of Christian doctrines and practices. Christians are bonded together in one God and Father (v. 6).

The author explains in vs. 7–16 that within this basic unity there are diverse gifts from the risen Christ. These enable each member to contribute in a unique way to the growth and progress of the church. (Rom. 12:3–8 and 1 Cor. 12:1–13 give similar lists of gifts.) But in Ephesians the gifts are in the universal church, not just in local communities of faith. The gifts are concentrated in specific offices within the church, and no mention is made of individual charismatic gifts of tongues, healing, and so forth. For Ephesians, the risen Christ is the source and distributor of the gifts in contrast to other passages where it is the Spirit or simply God. And in Ephesians there is a vertical picture of the body of Christ:

Christ is the head who gives life and unity to the members joined to his body. In 1 Corinthians there is a horizontal picture, with head, hands, feet, and so forth, all pointing to Christians having gifts because of the working of the one Spirit in all.

In v. 11 specific gifts are listed. Apostles and prophets are mentioned first. Ephesians saw these as a select group on which the church was founded, who guaranteed the revelation. This group is now closed, according to Ephesians. Then in vs. 12–16 we have the collective goal of the church's various ministries. They are related to the life of the Christian community, not just to the faith of individual Christians.

The body of Christ is built up as its members attain to unity in Christ which is founded on a common faith in Christ (vs. 12–13). In contrast to the rampant individualism in contemporary American religion, Ephesians saw the church as a whole which attains mature manhood, the measure of the stature of the fullness of Christ.

The role of apostles, prophets, evangelists, pastors, and teachers is "to equip the saints for the work of ministry, for building up the body of Christ." This is a splendid description of the function of church leaders and professionals. They are to equip the saints (all Christians) for the work of ministry.

The goal is stated in a negative fashion in v. 14. They are to prevent the disintegration of the church which takes place when members go after false doctrine in a childish way and have no steadying anchor (an image of a boat tossed about on the waves by the wind).

In contrast to this kind of shifting mind the Christians are to speak the truth in love. As earlier, in 2:21–22, the author indicates that there is no life without growth, at least by implication. He affirms once again that all growth comes from Christ, who is the "head, into Christ." Love is used in a dynamic sense by the author, referring to the activating directive force behind the gifts. It moves Christians to exercise their gifts in view of building up others in the community rather than using gifts for private edification. "In love" here means the same as "in Christ." Reflect on the fact that Christ did not seek to please himself but put his own interests aside in order that all of his life might be directed toward the goal of building up a community, the church.

Recommended work: Read chapters 1–3 to reflect on how 4:1–6:20 reflects the ethical implications of the chapters.

The sermon might follow the prayer of the text and be addressed to the hearers as it asks them to maintain the unity of the Spirit in the bond of peace. Or the sermon might deal with the dynamic, growth aspect of Christian living or with the gifts of Christ and how they are to be used.

Theological Reflection

The 2 Kings 4 text links up with the John 6 feeding miracle. David in the 2 Samuel text is an example of a sinner who, when confronted by sin, confesses to God, repents, and is forgiven. The Exodus passage tells of the ratification of the covenant by blood and a sacrificial meal. The 2 Kings 2 passage relates Elijah passing on his prophetic role to Elisha.

The Ephesians 4 reading is a prayer for Christian living in its dynamic, growing aspect. The Ephesians 3 pericope is a prayer for wisdom summed up in knowing the love of Christ and being filled with the fullness of God. Mark recounts the miracle of walking on water and the failure of the disciples to understand Jesus' acts because of lack of faith.

Children's Message

The story with the children might be about Jesus appearing to the disciples walking on water, their fear, and his assurance "Take heart, it is I; have no fear." You might ask the children about their fears and offer the assurance that Jesus is with us at all times to give us courage to overcome our fears.

Hymns for Pentecost 10

Guide Me, O Thou Great Jehovah; O Sing a Song of Bethlehem; O Christ, Our Savior, Who Must Reign.

Pentecost 11

Ordinary Time 18

Proper 13

Psalm 34:11–22 (C)
Psalm 78:23–29 (L)
Psalm 78:3–4, 23–25, 54 (RC)
Psalm 78:1–25 or 78:14–20, 23–25 (E)

Ephesians 4:1–6 (C)
Ephesians 4:17–24 (L)
Ephesians 4:17, 20–24 (RC)
Ephesians 4:17–25 (E)

2 Samuel 12:15b–24 (C)
Exodus 16:2–15 (L)
Exodus 16:2–4, 12–15 (RC)
Exodus 16:2–4, 9–15 (E)

John 6:24–35

Meditation on the Texts

O God, feed us on the true bread from heaven, even Jesus Christ who is the bread of life. We recall how you fed your people in the wilderness with manna. Help us not to murmur against you or fail to trust you to provide for our daily bread. May we not be content to labor for the food which perishes but rather seek the food which endures to eternal life. May we feast on the teachings of Jesus as we are nourished by living in daily communion with the living Christ. By your Spirit enable us to put off the old nature which belongs to our former manner of life and is corrupt and renew us in the spirit of our minds. Grant us courage to put on the new nature created after your likeness, O God, in true righteousness and holiness. And so may we, like David, repent of our sins and turn from them with hatred and turn to you in trust and obedience. Amen.

Commentary on the Texts

John 6:24–35

Our pericope is part of the larger section of vs. 22–71 whose theme is Jesus, the bread of life. Notice that the people seek after Jesus to get more bread (vs. 22–25). Earlier, in v. 15, we saw that the people tried to proclaim Jesus as the Jewish messiah but this was aborted. The more persistent people continued to look for Jesus, for they knew he had not gone with his disciples but they could not find him on the other side of the lake. Their reasoning led them to proceed to Capernaum, where Jesus and his disciples made their headquarters.

The crowd was curious about Jesus coming to Capernaum (v. 25). Jesus confronts them with the fact that they sought him, not because they saw signs, but because they filled up on the loaves. The signs pointed to Jesus as food for the soul. But they had failed to perceive the true meaning of the signs. Recall the woman who was confused about the water Jesus promised (see 4:15).

Jesus begins a discourse in v. 27 in which he sets forth the theme using the metaphor of bread to speak of doctrine, even as bread symbolized the Torah in Jewish thought. Jesus tries to raise their consciousness from being concerned about material bread to seeking the bread that leads to eternal life (v. 27).

Jesus says they should always be working for this bread just as they work for earthly bread. Jesus refers to himself as the Son of man who will give the bread of life. "Son of man" is Jesus' favorite term for himself in John and in the Synoptics. He apparently drew it from Daniel 7:13–14. There the one like a son of man represents the people Israel, but a glorified Israel, namely, the kingdom of God. So in using this term to refer to himself, Jesus designates that he himself is the very embodiment of salvation. The title implies that Jesus is a man who lives with the glory of God and is a mediator in whose being heaven and earth meet.

God has set his seal on the Son of man. The Son is in the world to do the work of God alone and to give humans the life which is God's gift through the Son. Here life is symbolized by bread.

Then in v. 28 we see that the people have misunderstood the nature of the miraculous food and think it involves performing a work of God. Jesus seeks to clarify this by pointing out that they cannot really *do* God's work, but their only task is to accept in faith Jesus who is sent by God.

The people again misunderstand and think they are being asked to put faith in Jesus in order to credit something he is about to say (v. 30). The people demand a sign, and from v. 31 it seems the sign they want is a supply of bread. The crowd introduces the theme of manna as a pattern for the sign. So the people challenge Jesus to produce manna or its equivalent as a sign.

This is very understandable if they thought of Jesus as the prophet like Moses. There was a popular expectation that in the final days God would again provide manna. This was connected with the hopes of a second exodus. The expectation also developed that the messiah would come on Passover and that manna would begin to fall again on Passover.

The people fail to realize that Jesus has identified this bread from heaven with himself. They ask for a continued supply of the heavenly bread, which makes relevant Jesus' response. Jesus declares, "I am the bread of life" (v. 35). He goes beyond the background of the Hebrew Scriptures in speaking of himself as the bread from heaven. He points to himself as incarnate revelation. Because the people have misunderstood and think he is speaking only of material bread, Jesus begins the great Bread of Life Discourse which follows.

When Jesus says, "I am the bread of life" he promises that this bread, like the water of life (4:10), will satisfy hunger and thirst forever. This is the first "I am" formula with a predicate, which is so characteristic of John's Gospel.

Recommended work: Compare the question-and-answer format of our passage with that of John 4:9–26. Reflect on other "I am" passages in John and see how they relate to eternal life.

In preaching on this passage, the minister may want to follow the images and moves within it, dealing with the questions and answers of the people and Jesus. The sermon will climax in Jesus' affirmation that he is the bread of life with an invitation to hearers to feed on this bread which endures to eternal life and is given by Jesus. The sermon might contrast material bread and the eternal bread that Jesus offers.

2 Samuel 12:15b–24 (C)

This continues the story of God's punishment of David for his sin with Bathsheba. Instead of requiring the life of David, God diverts the death penalty to the child. God's judgment, falling on the child, was, in the thinking of that age, a special favor to David. Note that the description of David's penitence is in keeping with his simplicity found in 6:21–22 and his idea of realism found in vs. 20–23. David seeks to ward off the death of the child through acts of special prayers, a special fast which seems to last during all of the child's illness, and he puts on sackcloth and lies on the ground. He also does not wash or anoint himself. All of this points up David's complete self-abasement. His trusted officials try to tear him away from his acts by which he seeks to move the Lord to "repent." But he failed completely.

The child dies, but no one dares tell David. It seems the court may have tried to keep the news from him because they feared he might take some drastic action. The text implies that they fear David might commit suicide (v. 18). But David finds out and when his servants confirm the news he gives up the attitude of a mourner and again goes to the sanctuary dressed in his usual clothes and calls for food. It seems he has anticipated mourning for the child during his time of penitence when he sought to change

God's plan for the child. Those around David could hardly understand it. It seemed shocking.

David declares that he cannot bring the child back but must finally go to him. This does not express hope in a future life but simply his belief in the immutability of death. David expects to go to the land of Sheol, the land of no return, not heaven as we understand it. Sheol was the cavity under the earth where all the dead go. Notice that the child was accepted, as it were, as a sacrifice and a confirmation that nothing more would happen to David himself.

David and Bathsheba then had another child, a son they named Solomon. And the Lord loved him. The grace of God shines over this child and over David too. Solomon is given a second name, Jedidiah, meaning "beloved of the Lord."

Recommended work: Scan the whole story of David and Bathsheba up to this point. Look up "repentance" or "penance" in a Bible dictionary.

The sermon may well follow the story itself, showing how the mind-set of that day felt that sin had to be punished and in this case the child suffered the penalty due David. (Some regard Psalm 51 as an expression of David's experience.) The sermon should reflect the Christian understanding of repentance and pardon made possible through Jesus' death and resurrection.

Exodus 16:2–15 (L)

Exodus 16:2–4, 12–15 (RC)

Exodus 16:2–4, 9–15 (E)

We will deal with vs. 2–15, which are part of the section of 15:22–16:36 whose theme is crises in the wilderness. (Note that the account of manna is referred to in the reading from John for today.) Chapter 16 tells of the provision of food by God in the wilderness. The setting is probably the Sinai Peninsula. The account may be seen as a paradigm of human ingratitude and longing for "the good old days" in preference to living in precarious freedom with all its risks. It is an example of nostalgia for a life that has been idealized but never existed. The Israelites murmured against God as they remembered the seasoned food of the fleshpots of Egypt. Notice that the people's murmuring is a constant motif. In response to it, God promises prompt relief.

Manna and quail are provided to nourish them. We can find both phenomena in the peninsula today. Manna is a honeydew excretion given off by two species of scale insect that infest the tamarisk thickets. The substance drops to the ground and becomes firm in the cool of the night but has a low melting point of 70 degrees. Thus it must be gathered before the sun makes it melt. Bedouins of the area consider it a delicacy because of its sweet taste. Quail fly each year from their home in northern Europe to winter in Africa, passing through in September and October going south and returning north in May and June. Because of their long flights over water, they are forced to land, exhausted, on the peninsula, where they can easily be captured.

Since the Israelites do not know what to make of the manna, they ask "What is it?" Some scholars think the derivation of the name manna comes from the word for "what," which may have come from the Canaanite dialects. So the divine gift came to be known simply as "what." Moses told them it was the bread that the Lord had given them to eat. The thrust of the section is that God always gives what is needed for the nourishment of the people at the moment, the daily bread (see Lord's Prayer), no more and no less. In the famous John 6:31–59 section on the bread of life, John notes that the desert manna was a type of the Eucharist itself. Both are gifts from a gracious God to nourish and sustain his people.

Recommended work: Read articles on manna and quail and wilderness wandering in a Bible dictionary. Compare this account with our passage from John for today.

Ephesians 4:17–24 (L)

Ephesians 4:17, 20–24 (RC)

Ephesians 4:17–25 (E)

We will deal with vs. 17–25 only, since vs. 1–6 were dealt with last week in the (RC) (L) and (E) readings. In the whole section of 4:17–5:20, the author makes an appeal to hearers to renounce pagan ways.

We should read in conjunction with vs. 17–19 Paul's message in Romans 1:21–25. The author speaks of putting off the old life and putting on the new in terms of casting off old, filthy clothes and putting on new clothes. He tells the people no longer to live as the Gentiles do in the futility of their minds, darkened in their understanding and alienated from the life of God by the ignorance that is in them because of their hardness of heart. This harsh condemnation of the moral life of pagans may have been drawn from ordinary Jewish criticism of pagans.

The old nature they are to put off is life that was led with human resources only. Today we might call it "the secular life." Many human weaknesses caused permanent spiritual death, as Romans 8:13 notes. It seems that the terms "put off," "renew," and "put on" are drawn from a baptismal liturgy. In the baptismal ceremony the candidate removed his or her old clothes, was plunged into water, and then was brought up and given new white clothing, symbolizing the new, purified life in Christ. Thus the outward signs signified the inner change that took place by the power of the Spirit. The baptized person had put aside the old life and now put on the new life in Christ.

The "new" human being of v. 24 points to the incorporation into Christ of the person as a part of the new humanity, renewed by the Spirit. The person is incorporated into Christ himself as the new Adam. This new humanity connotes the attainment of all that humans were intended to be when God first made humans in God's own image (see Gen. 1:27). Recall that Adam means "man."

Then in vs. 25–32 the author outlines the new motivation for a good moral life that belongs to all who share Christ's renewed humanity. No longer is it just a matter of right and wrong but of a consciousness of how our actions can affect our brothers and sisters in Christ. We are to speak the truth with our neighbor, since we are members one of another. The neighbor here is almost certainly the fellow Christian. In Jewish tradition the command to love the neighbor as oneself (Lev. 19:18) was applied only to relations with other Jews. But Jesus' teaching in Luke 10:25–37 and other Gospels breaks down the barrier and applies it to all people.

Recommended work: Read the whole section of 4:17–5:20 and reflect on the very down-to-earth practical issues the author is taking up here. Reflect on how this is a message for a congregation today.

In planning the sermon, the preacher may want to focus on the contrast between the old life which is to be put off and the new life, renewed by the Spirit of God, which is to be put on. The sermon might raise the consciousness of hearers to realize that we are living in a basically pagan culture whose morals and values often run counter to those of the Christian faith. The preacher might even dramatize the sermon by wearing an old, wornout jacket or other piece of clothing while talking about the old nature, then putting it off and putting on a new piece of clothing to illustrate the new. The sermon should point up the critical need to speak the truth to one another, which is one of the foundation stones of community life.

Theological Reflection

There is a tie between the passages from Exodus and John, since both refer to manna from heaven. John records Jesus' saying that he is the bread of life, the one who nourishes believers, even as manna was material nourishment for the Israelites. The 2 Samuel passage describes the repentant David seeking to change God's judgment on the child born to David and Bathsheba. When the child dies, David no longer grieves. Another child, Solomon, is born to Bathsheba and David. And God loved Solomon. The Ephesians passage contrasts the old life alienated from God with the new nature created in the likeness of God in true righteousness and holiness.

Children's Message

The talk with the children might use the Exodus passage and tell how God supplied food to the Israelites in the wilderness. You might describe the manna, called "what" in Hebrew, which is still collected, and the quail which migrate from northern Europe to Africa each winter and can easily be caught when resting after a long flight. God is faithful to provide our daily bread. We pray in the Lord's Prayer for our "daily bread," meaning food enough for the next day.

Hymns for Pentecost 11

Break Thou the Bread of Life; The Church's One Foundation; Deck Thyself, My Soul, with Gladness.

Ordinary Time 19
Proper 14

Psalm 143:1–8 (C)
Psalm 34:1–8 (L)
Psalm 34:2–9 (RC)
Psalm 34 or 34:1–8 (E)

Ephesians 4:25–5:2 (C)
Ephesians 4:30–5:12 (L) (RC)
Ephesians 4:(25–29) 30–5:2 (E)

2 Samuel 18:1, 5, 9–15 (C)
1 Kings 19:4–8 (L) (RC)
Deuteronomy 8:1–10 (E)

John 6:35, 41–51 (C)
John 6:41–51 (L) (RC)
John 6:37–51 (E)

Meditation on the Texts

Gracious God, you have forgiven us through Christ's death and resurrection. Help us not to grieve the Holy Spirit in whom we were sealed for the day of redemption. Let us put away all bitterness, wrath, anger, clamor, and slander. We pray that we may be kind to one another, tenderhearted, forgiving one another as you have forgiven us. May we give no opportunity for the devil. We thank you for Jesus, who is the living bread come down from heaven. May we feed upon him by faith and so be nourished for eternal life. We rest in the assurance that those who are drawn by you to Jesus will be raised up at the last day. Forgive us when we have despaired of life as Elijah did in the wilderness. May we trust your providential care of our lives as you provided for Elijah a cake and water in the wilderness. Amen.

Commentary on the Texts

John 6:35, 41–51 (C)

John 6:41–51 (L) (RC)

John 6:37–51 (E)

Recall that v. 35 was part of last week's reading from John. The thrust of the verse is that Jesus is God's gift of sustenance for now and for eternity. Jesus said earlier (3:13) that the Son of man was the only person who has come down from the Father. Although the reader may understand this to mean that Jesus is the bread of life come down from heaven (6:33), the crowd does not understand. So Jesus must say directly, "I am the bread of life." This means that Jesus is the revealer of the truth, the divine teacher who has come down from God to nourish humans. Thus Jesus claims to personify divine revelation. In saying that those who believe in him shall never be hungry or thirsty, Jesus is setting forth the same thought that he will give in 11:25–27 where Jesus says, "I am the . . . life." The symbols of bread, water, and life, when possessed by faith, enable a person to see natural hunger, thirst, and death as insignificant. Notice that the basic reaction to Jesus' calling himself the bread in vs. 35–50 is that of belief (vs. 35, 36, 40, 47) or is one of coming to Jesus, which is synonymous with belief. Only in v. 50 does Jesus say that anyone must eat the bread of life. But eating does appear again and again in vs. 51–58. Note also that there is a parallel for the bread of life in the symbol of living water in chapter 4. Water is also a symbol for revelation.

The Jews murmured or grumbled at Jesus, as their ancestors had done after God gave them manna in the wilderness. The crowd adopts a hostile attitude toward Jesus, and so

John refers to them as "the Jews." John uses this term for the representatives of Judaism, especially its leadership in Jerusalem, which proved to be hostile to Jesus and his teaching.

Compare the reaction to Jesus in v. 42 to that of Mark 6:2–3. The people reject Jesus' claims to have come down from heaven, because they know Jesus' parents. Christian readers of John will recall that Christ was conceived of a virgin and is divine. Rather than dealing with the protests, which are side issues, Jesus insists on what he said earlier in vs. 37–40. If the people would only respond to God's grace, they would believe rather than wasting time and effort in pointless protests. Note that in v. 37 there is a note of election by God in that all who are given by the Father to Jesus will come to him. In order to come to Christ, one must be brought by the grace of God. And those who accept this grace will not be cast out of God's kingdom (v. 37). The will of God is that those who believe will be safe in the kingdom of God and shall share in the resurrection at the End. While John stresses eternal life as a present reality, he never surrenders the idea of a final End time expressed in Jesus' words (vs. 44, 54).

The reference in v. 45 to those "taught by God" is to Isaiah 54:13, words that will be fulfilled in believers who hear God and learn. Notice how election and free will are expressed here: the believer must answer God's grace with a willing spirit.

Only Jesus has seen God (v. 46). Jesus is the only mediator, and only in him does one see God (see 14:9). And so the believer comes to have eternal life (vs. 47–50). Jesus again repeats that he is the bread which came down from heaven who gives eternal life in a way the manna in the wilderness could not give. The people then ate and died. But one who eats the living bread "will live for ever," says Jesus. The bread that Jesus gives for the life of the world is his flesh. Jesus uses the term "flesh" where Paul uses "body." There is a eucharistic theme in v. 51, the reference to eating the bread which is his flesh. Jesus the One who became flesh, assuming our complete human nature, offered himself to God in death. In doing so, he released his life for the life of the world. Jesus speaks of the bread which he shall give for the life of the world, referring to his voluntary death (see 1 Cor. 13:3). There is a suggestion here of a connection between the Eucharist and the death of Jesus.

Recommended work: Read the whole of 6:22–71 in which Jesus is portrayed as the bread of life and see how our pericope fits into the entire section.

The sermon might follow the moves and images of the text as Jesus calls himself the bread of life and the living bread come down from heaven. The sermon should seek to lead hearers to believe in Jesus and thus have eternal life. Jesus' death on the cross, "the bread which I shall give for the life of the world," makes salvation possible. In the Eucharist we receive Christ anew by faith as we eat and drink of the bread and the cup, symbols of his life poured out in his death.

2 Samuel 18:1, 5, 9–15 (C)

The theme of this pericope is the death of Absalom, David's son. Absalom had raised military forces against his father's standing army. In vs. 1–8 we learn of the battle in the forest of Ephraim. David's army leaders are all experienced and loyal. We learn that Absalom is somehow caught in a tree. The popular notion was that he was caught by his hair, based on 14:26 which tells of his long hair. But our text indicates that his whole head was caught, perhaps in the fork of a tree limb. Joab, the commander of David's army, was told by "a certain man" of Absalom's plight. Joab asked the man why he did not strike Absalom to the ground. But the man refused to strike the king's son, since David had asked protection for the young man Absalom. But Joab never failed to deal a fatal blow when he thought it would be to either his or David's advantage to do so. The soldier's reasoning seems quite valid. He understands the consequences that killing the prince would have on himself, since he would be left alone by Joab in the decisive hearing before King David. And he confirms the widespread notion that nothing could remain hidden from the king.

But Joab breaks off the conversation, takes up three darts, and thrusts them into the heart of Absalom while he is still alive in the oak. His act seems to be only a symbolic action which then leaves open the way for the killing of the king's son by ten young armor-bearers. The three darts may point to the complete and definitive character of the act of Joab, but the final death-dealing blows are given by a group of warriors. Thus the execution is performed by the troops as a whole and would not be blamed on one person alone (see Josh. 7:25). Some scholars think that v. 15 is unnecessary and may have been added later, since the blows of the armor-bearers seem unnecessary.

Recommended work: Read the whole account of David and Absalom's conflict. The rebellion of Absalom against his father for selfish power is the opposite of Jesus' submission to his Father in selfless obedience.

The sermon might contrast the relationship of the young man Absalom in his rebellion with that of Jesus and his submission. The sermon should picture the terrible dilemma that David faced with his rebellious son, whose life he wanted spared but whom his trusted army leaders saw must be executed. This death was in vain. But Jesus' submission to death was for our salvation.

1 Kings 19:4–8 (L) (RC)

This is the account of Elijah on Mt. Horeb after his victory over Jezebel and the prophets of Baal. By a miracle Elijah arrives at Horeb, where the Lord revealed the law to Moses. The traditional site of Mt. Horeb, which probably is not intended here, was some two hundred miles to the south. The names of Horeb and Sinai were used for the same mountain by different traditions. Jezebel had almost overnight turned Elijah's triumph to ashes and wiped out his long campaign to turn Israel back to God. So Elijah is in despair and asks God to take his life (v. 4). God, however, not only will comfort but will strengthen Elijah. He receives rations from an angel who touched him and told him to arise and eat (see 17:6). Since the distance to Horeb was some three hundred miles, Elijah could have traveled it in less than the forty days mentioned here.

Recommended work: Reflect on the whole life of Elijah by scanning it in a Bible dictionary.

The sermon might focus on human despair in the face of apparent defeat and God's rescue in a miraculous way of his prophet. It might help people who face despair because of a seemingly impossible situation, loss of job, divorce, loss of health, and so forth, to take hope in God who provides the courage to endure and be renewed.

Deuteronomy 8:1–10 (E)

Our reading is part of chapter 8 which deals with the temptation to pride and self-sufficiency. Moses warns the Israelites that success in the promised land of Canaan will tempt them to forget their complete dependence upon God's mercies during the wilderness wandering. This remembrance marks the end of the stage of Israel's history that began with the covenant at Horeb and marks the beginning of a second stage which begins with the covenant in Moab. The call to remember the desert experience of forty years is a theme of the prophets (Amos 5:25; Hos. 2:14–15). The wilderness experience was one of trial and influenced Matthew's story of Jesus' temptation in the wilderness.

God fed the people with manna. Jesus, in Matthew 4:4, points out that humans live authentically only when sustained by God's word and law. This theme is already implied here in strong theological terms: "Man does not live by bread alone, but . . . lives by everything that proceeds out of the mouth of the LORD" (v. 3). Moses reminds the people that even as a father disciplines a son, so the Lord disciplines his people, and then Moses calls the people to keep the commandments of the Lord by walking in his ways and fearing God.

Then in v. 7 the theme of the fertile land is repeated, the fulfillment of God's promises to their ancestors. But there is a warning in v. 11: "Take heed lest you forget the LORD your God."

Recommended work: Reflect on the comparison between Israel coming into the promised land and the early settlers of America arriving here in what was called "the New World," which they expected to be like a promised land.

The sermon might follow the moves of the passage from wilderness to fertile promised land to the danger of forgetting God. The prophetic message for our American culture is to beware that we not forget God but keep God's commandments by walking in God's ways and by fearing God.

Ephesians 4:25–5:2 (C)

Ephesians 4:30–5:2 (L) (RC)

Ephesians 4:(25–29) 30–5:2 (E)

Our pericope is a portion of the larger section of 4:17–5:20 which is the author's appeal to the Ephesians to renounce pagan ways. In 4:25–32 we have an outline for the new motivation for a good moral life. This new life belongs to all who share in Christ's renewed humanity. As background for 4:25, see Zechariah 8:16 and Romans 12:5. No longer is it a simple matter of right and wrong but rather one of respect for our neighbors in Christ and realizing how our actions impact them. Lying means lack of trust to members of the same body, and to give up stealing should be the occasion for beginning honest work.

There is a reminder in 4:28 of the constant emphasis Paul places on sharing material goods with the poor. In 4:29 the motivation for avoiding foul language is the idea that good speech can impart grace to others. The author connects injury to one's neighbor with a lack of respect and reverence for the Spirit who dwells in people of faith (4:30). The reference to being sealed in the Holy Spirit points to the use of a seal as a common sign of ownership. Followers of pagan gods often branded themselves with the name of the deity to whom they belonged, much as today one might be tattooed with "Mother" or the name of one's wife or girlfriend. Baptism is the visible sign of incorporation into Christ by the power of the Spirit.

This new life is one motivated by love. We find reaffirmed in 4:32–5:2 the reality of God's love given in Christ. Christians are to forgive one another as an expression to others of the same forgiving grace that Christ has shown us.

"Be imitators of God," the author exhorts readers (5:1). Note that 5:1–2 is included in what went before, namely, forgiving one another, and so readers are to imitate God's way of forgiving. "Children" does not refer to youngsters but connotes the imitation of qualities, as in the Sermon on the Mount. Jesus exhorts his listeners to be children of their Father in heaven by showing forth God's universal love for all people. Christ is the perfect model of a child of God.

Christ loved and gave himself up for us. The supreme moment of Christ's life was his giving up his life on the cross. Since he laid down his life for us, so we ought to lay down our lives for our neighbors (see 1 John 3:16).

The mention of fragrant offering and sacrifice points to the sacrificial system of the Hebrew Scriptures. An individual needed a priest as a go-between who would make an offering to enable the worshiper to find access to God. Now Christ is that mediator. The offering is the gift of himself for human beings. Christians are to walk in love even as Christ loved us.

Recommended work: Read the whole section of 4:17–5:20 and reflect on the concrete aspects of living that are considered and compare them to similar aspects of living today.

The sermon might focus on the theme of walking in love as Christ loved us, putting away destructive thoughts and actions and becoming imitators of God. The sermon might deal with the various pagan ways mentioned here and how they have parallels in contemporary life. But the major stress should be on the positive aspects of forgiving one another, loving, speaking the truth, and so forth.

Theological Reflection

The theme of bread or manna occurs in the John reading, 1 Kings, and Deuteronomy. The preacher who chooses the Gospel for the sermon may want to relate the 1 Kings and

Deuteronomy texts to it as they reveal how God provided nourishment for the people. The
2 Samuel text deals with the rebellion of Absalom against David his father and the killing of
Absalom by Joab and soldiers. The reading from Ephesians deals with renouncing pagan
ways and living a life motivated by love, imitating God.

Children's Message

The talk with the children might be about anger, an emotion we all feel but may not
know how to deal with constructively. The Ephesians text tells us to be angry, to own our
anger, but not to sin by nursing it. Rather, we should not let the sun go down on our
anger. You might tell a story about a boy or a girl who became angry and dealt with anger
in a positive way.

Hymns for Pentecost 12

Break Thou the Bread of Life; Jesus, Thou Joy of Loving Hearts; Bread of the World.

Pentecost 13

Ordinary Time 20

Proper 15

Psalm 102:1–12 (C)
Psalm 34:9–14 (L)
Psalm 34:2–3, 10–15 (RC)
Psalm 147 or 34:9–14 (E)

Ephesians 5:15–20

John 6:51–58 (C)
John 6:53–59 (E)

2 Samuel 18:24–33 (C)
Proverbs 9:1–6 (L) (RC) (E)

Meditation on the Texts

O God, help us to look carefully how we walk, not as unwise but as wise persons making the most of the time. By your Spirit enable us to understand what your will is for us. And may we be filled with the Spirit, rejoicing with one another in the harmony of song and praise and always and for everything giving thanks to you in the name of our Lord Jesus Christ. We thank you for Jesus Christ the living bread who came down from heaven and gave his flesh for the world on the cross. May we be nourished for everlasting life on this living bread. As we eat and drink of the flesh and blood of Christ may we so believe and be assimilated into him and abide in him forever. As we recall the tragic death of David's son Absalom and David's grief, we are reminded of Jesus who willingly gave his life for us in obedience to you his Father. May we ever eat of the bread and drink of the wine of wisdom and leave simpleness to walk in the way of insight. Amen.

Commentary on the Texts

John 6:51–58 (C)

John 6:53–59 (E)

Our pericope continues the theme of last week, Jesus the bread of life, and (C) overlaps by including v. 51 again. Jesus declares that he is the living bread from heaven. He says that the bread which he shall give is his flesh. This is a way of saying that he is the One who became flesh and in doing so assumed our complete human nature. Jesus offered himself to God in death as the bread "which I shall give for the life of the world," and in doing so released his life for the world. (For further comment, see last Sunday's material on John.)

Notice that in v. 52 some of the Jews take Jesus' words about eating his flesh literally. Recall a similar response to the idea of rebirth in the conversation with Nicodemus, and the idea of living water when Jesus talked with the woman at the well. There was a Jewish saying of "eat someone's flesh," which meant to slander the person (Ps. 27:2). This did not help them understand Jesus' meaning here. The question of the Jews "How can this man give us his flesh to eat?" has been debated by theologians at various times in the church and is still a cause of division among Christians. We must understand the symbolic meaning of these words of Jesus.

John Marsh defines the meaning of Jesus' statement thus:

So in speaking of eating his flesh and drinking his blood Jesus is saying that unless men come to live by his death, and find their own real life in accepting the destiny that his own life has marked out as characteristic for the disciples, they cannot find the way to the life he has come to bestow. Entry upon "life" in this world, and an inheritance of *life* in the world to come are both bound up with man's relationship to the self-offering of Jesus in his sacrifice. (John Marsh, *Saint John,* Westminster Pelican Commentaries [Philadelphia: Westminster Press, 1978], p. 306)

Consider that the true food is Christ's flesh and the true drink is his blood. These alone satisfy human hunger for spiritual nourishment. Without these the human person dies spiritually, although the person may continue to live in the flesh. But with them the person lives the authentic life here and now and also in that life which lies beyond history in the world to come. The notion of eating a person's flesh would be abhorrent to a Jewish audience, and the suggestion of drinking blood would be even more so since blood as food was forbidden under the law. Flesh and blood were the common Hebrew Scriptures expression for human life. These two elements are partaken in the Eucharist, stressing the idea that the whole living Christ is received.

Jesus says that the person who eats and drinks as indicated abides in Christ and Christ in that person. To have Christ dwell in one is not to have one's personality divided but instead to find true integration of personality for the first time. Christ dwelling within a person enables the person to share in the divine unity. God, who is the source of life, has sent Jesus to the world with his mission.

Then Jesus says, "He who eats me will live because of me" (v. 57). This opens up the mystery of the Eucharist for the Christian who knows that Christ comes to him or her by faith "in the breaking of the bread." The possession of Christ is the earnest of eternal life in the resurrection, and this means that the Eucharist is an End time sacrament. Receiving the flesh and blood in the Eucharist means that the believer receives the shared life of God by faith.

Verse 58 sums up the preceding argument. Jesus began to speak of bread in v. 33, pointing to the true bread of God which manna only hinted at. The metaphor of eating in the passage has gradually been brought to a point where it can be transcended: eating manna, bread, flesh, blood, and "me." These direct our thoughts to the reality which is to have unity in communion with God through the Son. Eternal life is gained in so feeding upon Christ. Jesus taught this in the synagogue in Capernaum.

Recommended work: Reflect on the eating theme of the whole passage and its meaning for receiving Christ into one's life. Read articles on the Eucharist and on the breaking of bread. The Eucharist was early called "the breaking of the bread," from actually breaking up a loaf in the celebration of the sacrament. Compare with the Synoptic accounts of Jesus' breaking the loaf at the Last Supper and in the feeding miracles. Contrast Jesus as the bread which gives life with the manna which came down but left those who ate it to die eventually.

The sermon might follow the metaphor of eating through the passage as Jesus refers to himself as the living bread from heaven which, when eaten, gives everlasting life. Contrast this bread with the manna which the Israelites ate and later died. The preacher will want to relate this passage to the Eucharist. In the Eucharist the flesh and the blood of Jesus are eaten and Christ comes and abides in the believer. Flesh and blood serve to make real the presence of Christ to the believer.

2 Samuel 18:24–33 (C)

Our pericope is part of the section of vs. 19–33, dealing with the grief of David after Absalom's death. David was sitting between the two gates of the city, not sitting in the gatehouse itself but in a space between the outer and the inner gate. From that vantage point he could keep in touch with the watchman who was stationed where the gate was joined to the battlements. We can almost feel the tension and sense the anxiety between David and the watchman.

The watchman reported the running of a solitary man, which implied good news, since many soldiers running would have indicated a rout of fugitives. But soon a second man appears. The first man is soon recognized as Ahimaaz. He is the first to bring the news of the victory. David replies with an inquiry about Absalom. But Ahimaaz lacked the courage to tell the king of his son's death, as Joab had foreseen. So it is left to the Cushite, an Ethiopian slave, to break the sad news. He has less presence of mind. He was familiar with the language at court. He gives an answer to David's renewed questioning, and from this somewhat elliptical answer suddenly the truth bursts upon David (v. 33). David cries out that he would rather have died in his place. There may be seen a foreshadowing of Jesus who died for others, obedient to his Father, rather than dying in vain rebellion against his father as Absalom did. Then David was deeply moved with grief over Absalom his son whom he had never been able to understand during his life. In his deep distress David momentarily forgot his military victory and public responsibilities.

Recommended work: Reflect on the whole David and Absalom story. Compare and contrast their relationship with God the Father and Son.

The sermon might follow the action of the text, leading up to the tragic news of Absalom's death and David's deep distress. David's cry that he would rather have died in Absalom's place adds to the tragic nature of the events. The preacher may want to compare and contrast Absalom's rebellion and death with that of Jesus who died for us and said that there is no greater love than that of laying down one's life for a friend.

Proverbs 9:1–6 (L) (RC) (E)

We have what may be called a poetic allegory in which wisdom is personified as a gracious hostess. Our reading is from Proverbs 9, which deals with the banquets of Wisdom and Folly. Here Dame Wisdom invites the unwise to her feast.

The seven pillars were like those supporting the roof of a huge banqueting hall. Recall that seven was symbolic of perfection. Wisdom's house is the world, and the pillars mentioned here are the pillars of heaven.

Wisdom mixed spices with her wine, which was done to increase the flavor. Recall that meat and wine were festive foods which contrast sharply with the bread and water of Folly's table (v. 17). Wisdom invites the simple, the very ones for whom Proverbs was written. (Proverbs seems to have been a kind of training manual for young sons of aristocrats.) Notice that Folly addresses the simple in the same words (v. 16).

Wisdom invites the simple to leave simpleness and live and walk in the way of insight. The banquet that Wisdom gives would remind the Israelite of the End time banquet promised by God (Isa. 25:6; 55:1–5). For Christians, the banquet points to the wedding feast of Matthew 22:1–14 and of the messianic banquet when Christ returns at the End of the age. The eucharistic banquet is an anticipation of the heavenly banquet. This text ties in with the John 6 text (and John 2). Christ gives the wine of wisdom and the bread of teaching. Christ also gives his sacrificial flesh and blood for nourishment for everlasting life to all who believe. This is the true wisdom, to know Christ and abide in him forever.

Recommended work: Reflect on Wisdom and contrast with Folly in this chapter.

The preacher may want to relate the feast that Wisdom offers to the simple to the bread and wine which Christ offers to the believer. To "eat and drink" at Wisdom's feast is to live and walk in the way of insight. To eat and drink of Jesus' flesh and blood is to abide in him and gain everlasting life.

Ephesians 5:15–20

Our pericope is the final part of the section that runs from 4:17 to 5:20 which is an appeal to the reader to renounce pagan ways. Our passage develops the theme of the wisdom of God which Christians should manifest through wise actions, alertness to God's inspiration, and an eagerness to follow God's designs. Some scholars think that v. 15 reflects a practice within the Christian community of rebuking one another as a form of discipline within the church. If this is the case, then the thrust of this verse would be to be thoughtful about how one behaves in order to avoid being rebuked.

The author urges the reader to walk "not as unwise men but as wise" (v. 15), pointing to wisdom as understanding what the will of the Lord is (v. 17). Recall the personification of wisdom in the Proverbs reading for today where wisdom invites the simple person to walk in the way of insight. And Proverbs 9:10 points out that "the fear of the LORD is the beginning of wisdom, and the knowledge of the Holy One is insight." There is a strong Jewish tradition which defines the beginning of wisdom as "the fear of the LORD" (Ps. 111:10).

Notice that the text says "the will of the Lord," while in other Pauline literature "God's will" is indicated. It may be that "Lord" and "God" have been so closely connected in the author's mind that he used "the will of the Lord" in this instance.

Note that the way to discover the will of the Lord is to "be filled with the Spirit" (v. 18). This is not a private matter but takes place in the Christian fellowship, as the context suggests. Paul, writing to the Corinthians, goes into some detail to explain the link between Christian wisdom and the Spirit and discusses how the Spirit enables the Christian to comprehend "the thoughts of God" and so know the will of God (see 1 Cor. 2:6–16). Seeking the will of God is one of the most basic actions of Christians, and it is only by relying on the Spirit from God that we can discover God's will. We find God's will through the Spirit speaking through scripture, through prayer, and in the fellowship of Christians.

The author warns against being drunk with wine, apparently a reference to some religious sects that used alcohol in order to bring about an ecstatic state in which people thought God was speaking to and through them. The author may have had Proverbs 23:30 in mind: "Those who tarry long over wine, those who go to try mixed wine." The pagan practice of getting drunk on wine may have slipped into the Christian congregations, which Paul warned against in writing to the Corinthians: "For in eating, each one goes ahead with his own meal, and one is hungry and another is drunk. . . . Shall I commend you in this? No, I will not" (1 Cor. 11:21–22).

It seems that the religious ecstasy produced by the Spirit was sometimes confused with drunkenness, as on the day of Pentecost (Acts 2:13). It was probably a favorite criticism that pagans made of Christians. And there may have been some instances that justified the criticism.

The joyful fellowship of Christians should be the result, not of being drunk on wine, but of being filled with the Spirit which moves Christians to encourage one another and praise God with music. They are to sing hymns to the exalted Christ. Recall that at about midnight in prison Paul and Silas were praying and singing hymns to God (Acts 16:25). Paul urges the Colossians to praise similarly through singing psalms, hymns, and spiritual songs with thankfulness in their hearts to God (Col. 3:16). It may be that the reference to "giving thanks" (v. 20) refers to the Eucharist, which was so called for the thanksgiving at the heart of the rite. But we cannot be sure that this is the meaning here.

Recommended work: Reflect on the Christian life described as a "walk," and recall that the early Christian movement was called "the way."

The sermon might contrast the life of the unwise with that of the wise. The unwise live in present evil days, are foolish, and get drunk with wine. But the wise look carefully how they walk, understand the will of the Lord, and are filled with the Spirit, addressing one another in hymns and making melody to the Lord. The wise persons always and for everything give thanks in the name of the Lord Jesus Christ to God the Father. This contrast could be fleshed out with illustrations from contemporary life. The urgency of "making the most of the time" should be stressed.

Theological Reflection

The Proverbs and Ephesians readings link up the wisdom theme. The 2 Samuel reading focuses on the death of Absalom and its effect on David his father. In the John passage Jesus continues the theme from last week of declaring that he is the bread come down from heaven who gives life forever. To eat and drink of Christ is to assimilate him into our lives and abide in him.

Children's Message

The Ephesians passage might be the focus of the talk with the children, with its caution to look carefully how one walks, to be wise, not foolish, and to strive to understand God's will for us. The urging to sing and praise God with all your heart might lead to the children joining in the singing of a familiar song or hymn.

Hymns for Pentecost 13

Lord, Enthroned in Heavenly Splendor; O Holy City, Seen of John; 0 Lord, Who Hast This Table Spread.

Ordinary Time 21

Proper 16

Psalm 67
Psalm 34:15–22 (L)
Psalm 34:2–3, 16–23 (RC)
Psalm 16 or 34:15–22 (E)

2 Samuel 23:1–7 (C)
Joshua 24:1–2a, 14–18 (L)
Joshua 24:1–2, 15–18 (RC)
Joshua 24:1–2a, 14–25 (E)

Ephesians 5:21–33 (C)
Ephesians 5:21–31 (L)
Ephesians 5:21–32 (RC)

John 6:55–69 (C)
John 6:60–69 (L) (RC) (E)

Meditation on the Texts

We thank you, O God, for the words of Jesus which are spirit and life. With Peter and the disciples we affirm our faith in Jesus who has the words of life and we have come to know that he is the Holy One of you, O God. We pray that we may live in mutual subjection to one another, loving one another as Christ loved the church and gave himself up for the church. We thank you that you have created us male and female and gave human beings the institution of marriage in which a man and a woman become one flesh. May we always fear you and serve you in sincerity and faithfulness. We thank you for the covenant you have made with us in Jesus Christ. May we with Joshua of old affirm, "As for me and my house, we will serve the LORD." We remember your servant David, your anointed who was the sweet psalmist of Israel. We thank you for the everlasting covenant made with him and fulfilled in Jesus Christ. Amen.

Commentary on the Texts

John 6:55–69 (C)

John 6:60–69 (L) (RC) (E)

Our pericope continues the theme of Jesus as the bread of life which runs from 6:22–71. Since 6:55–59 was dealt with last week, we will comment on vs. 60–69 here.

The "this" of v. 60 probably refers to the whole preceding discourse in which Jesus speaks of himself as the bread of life, meaning the source of life. However, we should note that the mention of flesh in v. 63 does not concern the eucharistic flesh of vs. 51–58. Some commentators think v. 60 followed immediately after v. 50 at one time. In v. 50 Jesus claimed that he was the bread of life which had come down from heaven, and then in v. 60 we learn that the disciples are indignant about this and murmur, just as the crowd had murmured earlier in v. 41 about the same claim. Many scholars think that vs. 60–71 refer not to vs. 51–58 but to vs. 35–50.

Note that all the references in vs. 60–71 concern hearing or believing in Jesus' teaching. The disciples cannot bear to listen to Jesus' claim to have come down from heaven. In v. 60 the same Greek verb for "hearing" is involved twice. In the first part of the verse it has the meaning of "hear without acceptance" ("they heard") in contrast to the end of the verse, where it means "to hear with acceptance" ("listen"). This latter has the flavor of hear and obey.

The disciples found Jesus' words to be a hard saying, just as they did not understand his words and actions at the Last Supper until *after* his resurrection when he revealed himself in the breaking of the bread (John 21:1–14). The Greek word for "hard" has a double meaning of fantastic and offensive. In v. 60 the phrase "can listen to it" could also be translated "can listen to him," with "him" referring to Jesus.

Jesus knew in himself that his disciples murmured at his saying about being the bread of life come down from heaven. The Greek literally means "knew in himself," and it implies supernatural knowledge.

In vs. 61–62 we find that the disciples reveal their lack of the faith needed by those who are to follow after Jesus (v. 64). They cannot believe that Jesus could really be the bread (source of life) come down from heaven. If they cannot believe this, then what will they make of the even greater mysteries connected with Jesus' return to God? These mysteries will be the focus of the second half of the Fourth Gospel. The consequences of these mysteries are spelled out for the true disciples of the Lord. But for those who refuse to believe, the seeing of these mysteries can only mean a repetition of seeing without understanding (see v. 36).

Notice in v. 62 that Jesus says, "If you were to see," implying that the disciples might not see his ascension. The ascension refers to going to the Father (17:5). Jesus' ascension is through crucifixion and resurrection.

Jesus declares that it is the spirit that gives life, in contrast to the flesh which is of no avail. The necessity of grace is emphasized here. Only the Spirit can give life and can give an understanding of this life. The verb for "gives life" was used in John 5:21, and it is found some seven times in Pauline books. Both 2 Corinthians 3:6 and 1 Corinthians 15:45 point to the Spirit giving life.

The term "flesh" in this verse (v. 63) does not mean "my flesh" of v. 55 but has the meaning of flesh as found in 1:14 and 3:6, where it refers to human nature. The contrast is between the flesh which is subject to death and the words of Jesus which give life through the power of the Spirit. Recall the contrast in Isaiah 40:6–8 of the flesh which is grass versus the word of our God which will stand forever. This Isaiah passage was used in the early church.

Note that the "I" of "I have spoken" (v. 63) is emphatic. Deuteronomy 8:3 relates the words of God to manna: "Fed you with manna; . . . that he might make you know that man does not live by bread alone, but . . . by everything that proceeds out of the mouth of the LORD."

Jesus knew of the unbelief that was before him, even among the Twelve, and so he emphasizes that faith is impossible without God's motivation (vs. 64–65). Jesus knew what was in the hearts of human beings from the beginning of the ministry. And he knew who would betray him, that is, who would hand him over.

From that time many of the disciples no longer followed Jesus. This rejection anticipates the general rejection and the judgment that is passed on it, as noted in John 12:37 and 47–48. (Compare with Matt. 11:20–24.)

Jesus pointedly asks the Twelve whether they also wish to go away, extending the challenge of faith to them. He recognized that there was one among them who would betray him. This is the first time the Twelve, as such, are mentioned in John. The phrasing of Jesus' question implies a negative answer.

Peter speaks for the Twelve and asks, "Lord, to whom shall we go?" Then he declares that Jesus has the words of eternal life and that they have believed and come to know that he is the "Holy One of God." (Compare this with Mark 8:27–30 and Matt. 14:33.) The disciples walk by faith, which means a daily renewal of loyalty and belief. It is sustained by a daily renewal of the Spirit's gifts. Note the relationship of belief to knowledge which is a matter of continuing interest. John sees knowledge as the relationship of conscious communion which follows belief. To believe may mean the act of first putting one's trust in a person or a statement. In this case, belief is a single historical act. But belief can also mean a settled disposition of the whole person's life as it is centered and given to a person or a cause. Peter uses the word "believe" in the first sense. He uses the word "know" for what happens to the consciousness of relationship that develops as the believer follows Jesus Christ. The person comes to know something about Jesus, namely, that he is the Holy One of God. Although the disciples had not yet come to know Christ in all his fullness, they are moving toward this knowledge because they not only have seen Jesus but have believed in him.

Recommended work: Compare this confession with those in Mark and Matthew. Reflect on the negative as well as the positive responses to Jesus as some drew back and no longer followed, while others confessed their faith.

The sermon may follow the action in the text as it deals with the hard saying of Jesus as the bread come down from heaven and moves to his affirmation that his words are spirit and life. Jesus and his words call for a decision for or against him. The sermon should lead hearers to affirm with Peter and the disciples that Jesus has the words of eternal life and that he is the Holy One of God.

2 Samuel 23:1–7 (C)

This is a hymn of praise which is presented here as the last words of David. It is in the style of Jacob (Gen. 48:21–49:2) and Moses (Deut. 33:1). Although it claims to be an oracle spoken by the spirit, it deals with a common theme of wisdom literature, namely, that the wicked perish while the just prosper. This psalm is in the style of Psalm 1 and Proverbs 4:10–19.

We have already noted the theme of the perpetuity of the dynasty of David (v. 5) which is promised in chapter 7. However, the dynasty of David was not everlasting but fell in 587 (586) B.C. But the author may have been anticipating the kingdom of God, which is the only eternal kingdom.

David is called the sweet psalmist of Israel. David is both the anointed and a man with a gift for writing poetry. Thus he is qualified to bear the divine spirit and to mediate the divine word. As a sacral figure, the king can be said to be filled with God's word.

God's gracious gifts to a just ruler are climaxed with the everlasting covenant. The results of God's dealings with David are life-giving, producing blessings as does the beginning of the rains. Recall that in 2 Samuel it is often emphasized that the Lord is with David. This is the key to understanding the guidance of David's life.

In vs. 3b–4 the poem uses two similes, that of the rising sun and that of the effect of rain. They should not be forced together. The first simile deals with the saying of God proper and what is said of a righteous ruler. Notice the comparison with the rays of the rising sun. Malachi 4:2 speaks of the "sun of righteousness," drawing on images from pagan religions of the East, where the sun was associated with righteousness.

The second simile is still used in the East. Following a long summer's dry period, the rain makes the young grass sparkle. This points to God's dealings with a ruler. The results of God's covenant with the house of David are life-giving.

But standing in sharp contrast to those who receive God's blessings are the godless, who are like thorns which are thrown away and burned. The children of the devil are compared with thorns which can only be managed with an iron spear (v. 7). At the end of David's life all the "thorns" of opposition that had goaded him had been withered and burned.

In this brief poem we are shown the essential elements of David's character and life, pointing to God who is with David and his house. (Note 2 Samuel 22.)

Recommended work: Reflect on the whole life of David and the importance of God's abiding presence with him.

The sermon might focus on the secret to David's life which was God's presence with him. God made with him an everlasting covenant, which points to the fulfillment in the kingdom of God. The sermon might stress that the only life or house that is secure is that which is grounded in God's abiding presence. In Christ we have the assurance that he is with us always to the close of the age (Matt. 28:20).

Joshua 24:1–2a, 14–18 (L)

Joshua 24:1–2, 15–18 (RC)

Joshua 24:1–2a, 14–25 (E)

Our pericope is part of vs. 1–28 which describe the covenant at Shechem. The generation of Israelites that had conquered the promised land now enter into a covenant with the Lord which resembles that which their ancestors entered at Sinai (Ex. 24:7–18; 34:27–28). Shechem was named for its location between the two "shoulders" of Mt. Ebal and Mt. Gerizim. The shrine there may have contained the Ark of the Covenant, but there is no certain evidence for this. Joshua gathered all the tribes of Israel there and they presented themselves before God. Joshua reminded them of God's call to Abraham and other ancestors and God's guidance through the generations of Israel.

Then in v. 14 Joshua calls the people to fear the Lord and serve the Lord in sincerity and faithfulness, putting away all the gods of their past. It is evident from v. 15 that non-Israelites are being brought into the faith of Israel's God. This freedom of choice for conquered peoples is not found in treaties of kings of that time outside the Bible.

Then in vs. 16–18 we find material in the language of the covenant renewal in the Book of Deuteronomy. It appears from v. 16 that the people are already Israelites, in contrast to v. 15.

The people recalled God's gracious act of delivering them from bondage in Egypt and preserving them through the wilderness and bringing them into the promised land. They declare, "Therefore we also will serve the LORD, for he is our God" (v. 18).

Notice how strange vs. 19–24 seem after Joshua's exhortation found in v. 14. Some scholars think this section was composed by someone who had already witnessed the exile, which would account for the emphasis on failure to keep the covenant. Therefore the people are called as witnesses (v. 22), which is contrary to the ancient practice that a witness *not* be one of the contracting parties. It may be that vs. 19–24 are a later rhetorical expansion, but the dating of the origin lies in doubt.

So Joshua made (literally, cut) a covenant with the people that day (v. 25). Covenants were cut, referring to the slaughter of animals as part of the covenant ritual (see Ex. 24:3–8), and the parties of the covenant passed between the divided parts of the animal. Since the Canaanite god Baal was worshiped at Shechem, the city had covenant associations for Canaanites as well as for Israelites.

Recommended work: Read an article on covenant in a Bible dictionary. Reflect on this decision to unite in serving and obeying God and the actual religious practice of Israel over the centuries of breaking covenant and disobeying God. But God was faithful to the covenant and gracious to forgive when Israel repented, which can be a parallel for reflecting on God's dealing with us today.

The sermon might focus on the challenge that Joshua gives the people and the affirmation that "as for me and my house, we will serve the LORD." The preacher may want to point out the false gods which attract us today and the importance of making a conscious decision to choose and obey God. The note of judgment on those who persist in turning from God to serve other gods should be stressed (v. 20). This is part of the abrasiveness of the biblical message which too often is overlooked.

Ephesians 5:21–33 (C)

Ephesians 5:21–31 (L)

Ephesians 5:21–32 (RC)

We will deal with the longest passage, vs. 21–33. It is part of the section of Ephesians that extends from 5:21 to 6:9 dealing with the Christian household. The relationships of husband and wife are dealt with in our pericope, followed by children and parents in 6:1–4 and masters and slaves in 6:5–9. The general principle set forth here in all these relationships is that of mutual subjection (see Phil. 2:3: "Do nothing from selfishness or conceit, but in humility count others better than yourselves"). The applications that follow in this section are based on this principle.

In the light of the modern feminist movement and the changing structure of marriage and family life, the text should be interpreted with special care. We should avoid drawing conclusions for marriage today from what were cultural values of the past. Instead, we may focus on theological and biblical principles which may be applied to married life today.

The mutual subjection is based on reverence for Christ: "Be subject to one another out of reverence for Christ" (v. 21). This is the guiding principle of the "table of household duties" which follows. This table is modeled on similar instructions found in Paul's letter to the Colossians (3:18–4:1). But there is a different focus here, namely, the duties of wives and husbands are seen as a reflection and symbol of the mutual relations of Christ and his church. This gives the author a means for expounding on this new aspect of his doctrine of the church. It is interesting to note that the author here is following a formula found in Hellenistic philosophical literature which often concluded the discussion of a doctrine with a social code dealing with one's duties to the gods, country, and its rulers, and duties to one's own household.

As we reflect on this passage, we should keep in mind that the author's main concern is to define the nature of the church as he finds a parallel to Christ and the church in the institution of marriage. There are two basic convictions about marriage here: (1) According to Genesis 2:24 husband and wife become one flesh in marriage (5:31) and (2) the husband is regarded as head of this body. Paul writes that "the head of every man is Christ, the head of a woman is her husband, and the head of Christ is God" (1 Cor. 11:3). The author exhorts each marriage partner in the light of the above convictions. The wife is urged to be obedient and respectful of her husband, while the husband is to love, nourish, and cherish his wife. The husband's own life is completely identified with his wife's (v. 28), and for this reason the husband should love his wife as he loves his own body.

Christ, who is both head and savior of the church, loves the church with a self-sacrificing and sanctifying love. What is stressed is the church's duty to give unconditional obedience to Christ. The author identifies the authority of Christ with that of God. Note that Christ's Lordship over the church is very closely related to Christ's love for it expressed and given in his death on the cross. The church is considered the bride of Christ and is presented to him washed and dressed for marriage (vs. 26–27). Notice how easily the idea of the church as the body of Christ merges into the idea of the church as Christ's bride, particularly in the light of the Jewish understanding that marriage creates a complete union between husband and wife.

The "washing of water with the word" (v. 26) points to baptism as a sacramental act. The word probably refers to the baptismal formula. Baptism with water and word is the entrance into the church fellowship, and by it Christians are called to service of God.

The meaning of v. 32a is best conveyed by "this mystery is great," meaning of great significance. Note the different way in which mystery is used here in contrast to other places in the letter. Here it refers to the figure of the church as Christ's bride, which the author finds in Genesis 2:24. Elsewhere it refers specifically to the unity of Jews and Gentiles within the church. The author emphasizes "I am saying . . . ," which shows he is offering his interpretation of the passage from the Hebrew Scriptures in contrast to the interpretation of others. The author sees that the Genesis passage has now received its true meaning as it points to the union of Christ with the church.

The author does not suggest servile capitulation of the wife to her husband; rather, reciprocal responsibility is to be the controlling principle in marriage and other household relationships. The witness of equality in Christian marriage and family life has been one of the most effective means of evangelism in pagan cultures, since it stands in sharp contrast to nonbiblical marriage practices.

Recommended work: Do a word study of marriage in a Bible dictionary.

The sermon might develop the image of the love of Christ for his church as the guiding principle for husbands and wives in the marriage relationship. The preacher will need to interpret the text in the light of the culture in which it was written, a male-dominated one. Or the sermon might focus on the doctrine of the church found here.

Theological Reflection

The 2 Samuel passage is a hymn of praise about the perpetuity of the dynasty of David, contrasting the just person with the godless. The Joshua pericope is a call for decision to fear and serve God. The John reading deals with the decision to reject or follow Christ and

Peter's confession. The Ephesians passage has the themes of Christ and his church and the mutual relationship of husband and wife in Christian marriage.

Children's Message

The talk with the children might be developed from the Joshua passage and the many decisions about loyalties we make. The talk might point out that the decision to love and serve God is the most important one anyone can make.

Hymns for Pentecost 14

Love Divine, All Loves Excelling; God of Our Fathers, Whose Almighty Hand; God of Our Life.

Ordinary Time 22

Proper 17

Psalm 121
Psalm 15 (L) (E)
Psalm 15:2–5 (RC)

1 Kings 2:1–4, 10–12 (C)
Deuteronomy 4:1–2, 6–8 (L) (RC)
Deuteronomy 4:1–9 (E)

Ephesians 6:10–20 (C)
James 1:17–18, 21–22, 27 (RC)

Mark 7:1–8, 14–15, 21–23

Meditation on the Texts

We thank you, gracious and forgiving God, for cleansing our hearts by the power of the Holy Spirit. We know that nothing outside going into our lives can defile us, but the things that come out of us are what defile. We pray that we may be strong in you, O Lord, and in the strength of your might. Enable us to put on your whole armor and so be able to stand against the wiles of the devil. As preachers, may we take the helmet of salvation and the sword of the Spirit which is your word. We seek to pray at all times in the Spirit with all prayer and supplication. Help us to put away all wickedness and to receive with meekness the implanted word which is able to save our souls. May we practice religion that is pure and undefiled, religion that is more than devotional exercises. We pray that we may obey your statutes and ordinances and teach our children the saving acts you have done for us. And when our end comes, may we, like David, encourage those who follow us to keep the charge you have given and walk in your ways. Amen.

Commentary on the Texts

Mark 7:1–8, 14–15, 21–23

This selection of readings is from a passage that deals with the tradition of the elders and makes up a second collection of the teaching of Jesus. It reveals Jesus' controversy with the Pharisees. In this reading we see that the religious leaders were mainly concerned with the details of ritual, in contrast to Jesus who had compassion on human suffering. Note that vs. 1–8 deal with the problem of unwashed hands and vs. 14–15 and 21–23 deal with the issue of kosher food. The Corban vow is the subject of vs. 9–13, which are not part of our pericope.

Mark does not attempt to locate this section in specific time or place and it is a composite piece with no simple obvious theme. Much of it deals with the issues of defilement, either real or imagined. The whole section reveals Jesus' reaction to Judaism of that time.

The passage begins with a question that the Pharisees put to Jesus. Since they had come from Jerusalem, they had some kind of official status. This indicates how serious the outcome of the debate might be. Notice how specifically the question is put: Why do some of the disciples eat without ritually washing their hands? Handwashing was but one aspect of the wider demands of the Pharisees' code. For Christians of Mark's day, it seems to have been a pressing issue. The Jews believed, of course, that the written law contained in the first five books of the Hebrew Scriptures was absolutely binding. Through the years an oral code developed whose purpose was to ensure the complete observance of the written law. Learned scholars, rabbis, or scribes had developed this oral code. In Jesus' day this had become a large collection of probable or undisputed law which was oral, not written. This is the tradition of the elders cited in v. 5. The Sadducees rejected this oral code, while the Pharisees put it in equal place with the written law. So the question was put to Christianity of how it would deal with the oral code.

The fact that Mark explains Jewish customs indicates that he was writing for Gentile readers. Mark himself may have been outside the group that had personal knowledge of these customs, since some aspects of his explanation are not accurate. For example, he says that all Jews practiced a custom that only strict Pharisees observed (v. 3).

The conflict with the authorities is increasing in this second official investigation of Jesus (see 3:22 for the first). The violence of the reply (vs. 6–7) expresses the hostility between the church and the synagogue of Mark's time. So we may view this whole section of vs. 1–23 in the larger arena of the early church's struggle with Jewish law.

Jesus quotes Isaiah 29:13. The Moffatt translation brings out the meaning more clearly than does the RSV: "Yes, it was about you hypocrites indeed that Isaiah prophesied." Jesus accuses the Pharisees of leaving the commandment of God and holding fast to the human rules.

Then in vs. 14–15 Jesus points out that the things that go into a person do not defile the person; rather, the things that come out are what defile.

And the thought is continued in vs. 21–23, where Jesus stresses that it is what comes out of a person which defiles the person, things like evil thoughts, fornication, theft, and murder. A better translation than "evil thoughts" would be evil devisings which produce degraded acts and vices. The items in the list of evil in v. 21 down to "wickedness" are all in the plural, indicating acts of fornication, acts of theft, and so forth. The word "envy" literally means "the evil eye" and may have a reference to the evil glance which casts a spell.

Notice the importance that Jesus places on life-style in this passage. Jesus puts no importance on the ritual washing of hands and such matters but goes to the heart of the matter with his stress on one's way of living.

Recommended work: Compare our passage with Matthew 15:1–20. Also read Matthew 23:25.

The preacher may want to contrast the two life-styles presented in the text, one of human origin and the other from God. The sermon might deal with outer appearances and inner integrity. The text speaks a very straightforward word to contemporary culture which has rejected God's commandments. In applying the text to life, the preacher will want to point to the cross and resurrection as the source of power for overcoming the wickedness within the human heart.

1 Kings 2:1–4, 10–12 (C)

Our reading is from the early part of 1 Kings 2 which tells of the death of David and the destroying of persons who threatened the reign of Solomon. In vs. 1–4 Solomon is warned by David that he must follow the law of Moses, namely, the Deuteronomic law. However, the author does not doubt that the dynasty promised by God will endure regardless. But history reveals that the rulers after Solomon were not always faithful and as a result they were punished by the division of the kingdom and by the destruction of Israel. Finally the judgment of God was expressed in the destruction of the temple and the captivity of the Davidic king and the people of his kingdom.

It seems that vs. 10–11 are based on 2 Samuel 5:4–5. We are told that both David and Solomon (1 Kings 11:42) reigned forty years, which was a round number, and here it indicates a full career. Note that Jerusalem is now called the city of David.

Recommended work: Review the life of David in a Bible dictionary.

The preacher may want to focus on David's admonition to his son Solomon to be strong and show himself a man and walk in God's ways. In his dying counsel David reminded Solomon of God's promise to establish his word and to continue David's throne. But human sin brought about the downfall of kings, the temple, and Israel. But God did not forsake Israel. God has redeemed the people by the death and resurrection of Jesus

Christ, establishing a kingdom forever, in contrast to David's dynasty which fell. God is faithful even when we are unfaithful.

Deuteronomy 4:1-2, 6-8 (L) (RC)

Deuteronomy 4:1-9 (E)

Our reading is part of the conclusion to the first address by Moses in vs. 1–40. In the chapters that precede this, Moses reminded the people of what the Lord had done for them, and then in this chapter he appeals to them for faithful obedience. The thrust of these verses is that obedience to God's law is the one condition for life in Canaan and testifies to the gift of wisdom that God has bestowed on his people.

Notice the caution not to add or take from the instructions (v. 2). This points to a strictness not found in Israel before and may reflect the new emphasis during the exile on the written tradition for the Israelites in exile. The main thrust is not so much a literal inspiration as it is an emphasis on obedience to God's laws which too often had been ignored.

The warning against disobedience in v. 3 is emphasized by citing the story of the Israelites who were destroyed by plague when they followed the pagan god Baal of Peor. Numbers 25:1–9 tells how they joined in licentious rites with the Midianite women.

Then the passage builds to a climax in vs. 7–8 with its rhetorical questions about Israel's God being unique among all the gods. These questions set the stage for the remainder of the speech.

It seems that v. 9 is connected with vs. 10–24, but the lectionary has joined it with vs. 1–8. It repeats the warning to the people to take heed and keep their soul diligently and not to forget what they have seen God do in history and to teach these things to their children. Note the role of memory and tradition with reference to the exodus and Horeb (Sinai) event.

Recommended work: Scan the preceding chapters and the remainder of this chapter. Reflect on the uniqueness of Israel's God in relationship to other gods.

The sermon might focus on the uniqueness of Israel's God as a God who has acted to redeem the people and given them laws to follow. The uniqueness of God revealed in Jesus Christ crucified and raised should be included. The sermon might stress the necessity of teaching to our children what God has done.

Ephesians 6:10-20 (C)

The thrust of this passage is Christian warfare against evil, both satanic powers and hostile heavenly powers. Note how the Christian is equipped with God's armor for the battle. The main message of the whole letter is the triumphant Lordship of Christ, and in this passage we see how it relates to the Christian in the world. Notice the style here of inspired exhortation which resembles liturgy or oratory more than an epistle. The assumption behind the whole passage is Christ's victory over the evil powers of the cosmos. This victory at present is mainly a heavenly victory which is not yet fully realized in earthly matters. However, those who belong to Christ are assured of the final victory over evil. During the present time, however, they must continue the struggle against evil until victory is complete. While they have the task within the church of growing into Christlikeness, their warfare is a work that faces outward to the world. It is warfare! This battle against evil is also evangelism and persuasion. But the primary thrust is warfare against the cosmic powers, not specifically against human beings. However, those who are enslaved by these cosmic evil forces needed to be liberated. Christians have a message of salvation to proclaim to others (v. 17). And at the heart of the message is Christ's ultimate victory over the cosmic forces of evil. The Christian is equipped with God's gift of righteousness (v. 14). In Ephesians we have both doctrine and its moral application. We find this particularly in the present passage as the message of peace and salvation (vs. 15, 17) and its application in the spiritual warfare are described.

The exhortation ''Be strong in the Lord'' reveals that the Christian's power depends upon God's infinite power. God gives the Christian the armor for the spiritual battle (v. 11). The image of the whole armor of God is based on the armor of a fully armed Roman soldier of that time. This image also reflects the descriptions of God arming himself as a warrior to defend his people in the Hebrew Scriptures (see Isa. 59:17 and Wisd. 5:17–20). The basic equipment of the Christian is the truth of his or her faith and the word of God (vs. 16, 17). God's armor which is handed over to the Christian includes the breastplate of righteousness (v. 14) and the helmet of salvation (v. 17).

The battle is not against flesh and blood, meaning human beings or human nature, but against principalities and powers, rulers of this present darkness and the spiritual powers of the heavenly places. Here in Ephesians these powers are hostile to human beings, while in Colossians they do not necessarily seem to be hostile. The world of darkness may be another group of hostile spirits. Spirits were thought to have control over human events, an attitude that produced a fatalism among pagans. They felt a kind of futility in trying to overcome evil forces and destructive events. The good news that the Christian faith brings is that Christ has won the victory over all the powers of evil by his death and resurrection. Thus Christians have a new freedom from such evil forces.

The devil is the chief of the evil powers (v. 11). While devil is mentioned here and in 4:27, the term is not found in the unquestioned writings of Paul. (Such stylistic differences point to a Pauline follower as the author rather than to Paul.) The evil day was the future day when Christians expected the struggle of God with the devil to reach its final battle and the victory would be God's.

Salvation is the Christian's helmet, and the Spirit which dwells within is the Christian's sword for the battle. That the Spirit gives the Christian the message to speak is instructive for the preacher today.

The Christian is urged to pray at all times in the Spirit and to keep alert with perseverance (v. 18). Christians are to pray for one another. In an interview, Bishop Desmond Tutu in South Africa told me of a woman who was continuously praying for him and that this gave him courage. Christians are to be alert in praying for their comrades in this spiritual battle. We are members of an army, not Lone Rangers fighting alone with the bad guy in the town, as in westerns. Therefore we must express our concern for all who are fighting in the Lord's army to help support them. Such persevering prayer is a valuable asset in standing firm.

The author mentions the mystery of the gospel (v. 19) which is the doctrine set forth at the beginning of Ephesians. The mystery refers to God's purpose which has been to this point concealed but is now openly declared in Christ. References to mystery are found in both Jewish apocalyptic writing and in the Qumran literature as well as in the Greek mystery cults and gnostic sects.

The author says he is an ambassador in chains for the gospel (see 2 Cor. 5:20 and Acts 28:20). In Philemon (v. 9), Paul says he is an ambassador and now a prisoner also for Christ Jesus. The word for "chains" here refers to the leg iron that bound the prisoner to the soldier. Note the visual image of an ambassador who wears leg irons as he pleads his Lord's cause as an ambassador. While an ambassador was inviolable in the law of all nations, here is an ambassador who is in bonds. (Since the author seems to be a Pauline writer rather than Paul himself, he nevertheless draws on Paul's experience in prison, perhaps as an attempt to make the letter seem to be from Paul's own hand.)

Recommended work: Compare this passage with 1 Corinthians 16:13 and 2 Timothy 2:1–3 and reflect on the images used there and in this passage.

The sermon may be an exciting action sermon in which the images of armor and the battle with cosmic evil are described, with the Christian having the assurance of ultimate victory through Christ. The preacher might come from behind the pulpit to point to the various pieces of armor and how they function in this spiritual battle. The exhortation to pray for one another and to keep alert might be a final word. Christians live as resident aliens in a culture more and more controlled by the forces of evil. The battle lines are more clearly drawn than ever before between the Christian faith and the demonic forces which tear down human lives and community. The sermon should be as concrete and specific as possible.

The theme of vs. 17–18 is that all good gifts come from God, while the theme of vs. 19–27, which contain the remainder of our pericope, is the way to pure religion. God gives only good and perfect gifts, says James. For God is the Father of lights who not only is light but creates light and the heavenly bodies that give light (see Gen. 1:3 and Ps. 136:7–9). We cannot be certain of the meaning of "with whom there is no variation or shadow due to change," but it may serve to contrast the light of God which does not change with that of heavenly bodies which are subject to change.

In v. 18 "the word of truth" refers to God's creative power. It is by this power that we were made the firstfruits of all God's creatures. Or this may mean that God's creative power continues to give us new life by the power of the gospel so that we might be the firstfruits of the promised new age in Christ (see Rom. 8:19–23).

Then in vs. 21–22 James points out that the way to true religion is not clear but is obstructed by filthiness and wickedness. In order to receive with meekness the implanted word, the Christian must put aside such evil. The implanted word is able to save one's soul, and this inner core of true religion is the source of piety and godly action. This implanted word consists of Christian teaching, along with the law of liberty (v. 25) and the royal law (2:8).

Christians are to be doers of the word and not hearers only (v. 22). This is a key idea of the whole passage, since it points to true religion as involving action, not just thought. The verses that follow provide illustrations and practical examples of doing the word.

The pious Jews and Pharisees of that time insisted on ritual purity and spotlessness (see our Markan pericope). In fact, this was required in all ancient religions. A characteristic of such true religion is works of justice and charity, such as visiting widows and orphans (v. 27). Implied is that the visit is to aid them with both justice and material goods. In addition, pure religion means avoiding involvement in the wickedness of society. Christians are aliens in a culture that is over against the Christian faith. This is becoming more and more evident in American culture as the mass media, in movies, television programs, novels, magazines, and newspapers, impact our lives with filthiness and wickedness. Here is a clear call to live a life that is pure and undefiled and that consists of more than devotional exercises.

Recommended work: Compare Jesus' teachings in the Sermon on the Mount (Matthew 5) with those of our pericope. Note the contrast between the life as firstfruits of God's creatures and the life lived in wickedness and filthiness.

The sermon might hold up the contrast between the Christian life brought forth by the word of truth and endowed with good gifts from God and the life lived according to the world's filthiness and wickedness. The preacher will want to stress being doers of the word of God and not just hearers and might draw on vs. 23–26 and other passages of James to illustrate this teaching. The sermon should point to justice and charity as marks of true religion and might use Matthew 25:31–45 to illustrate this.

Theological Reflection

The readings from Mark and James deal with defilement and with true religion. Jesus stresses following the commandment of God rather than the tradition of human beings. The 1 Kings passage tells of the death of David and his charge to Solomon his son to be strong and keep the charge of God and obey God's laws. The Deuteronomy passage calls the people to keep the commandments of God in the light of God's saving acts on their behalf. They are to teach them to their children and grandchildren. The uniqueness of Israel's God is emphasized. The theme of the Ephesians passage is Christian warfare against evil forces in which the Christian is urged to be fully equipped with God's armor. James stresses being doers of the word and not hearers only and describes the nature of true religion as that of justice, charity, and keeping oneself unstained by the world.

Children's Message

The talk with the children might be from the Ephesians pericope and the armor that the Christian wears in the battle with evil forces. The *Star Wars* movies captured the imagination of many, and here is a description of the cosmic battle between God's people and the principalities and powers and rulers of this present darkness. The preacher should assure the children that God has already determined the outcome of the battle with evil in Christ's death and resurrection and that the outcome is victory.

Hymns for Pentecost 15

Give Me, O Christ, the Strength That Is in Thee; A Mighty Fortress Is Our God; Soldiers of Christ, Arise.

Ordinary Time 23

Proper 18

Psalm 119:129–136 (C)   **James 1:17–27 (C) (E)**
Psalm 146 (L)   **James 1:17–22, 26–27 (L)**
Psalm 146:7–10 (RC)   **James 2:1–5 (RC)**
Psalm 146 or 146:4–9 (E)

     Mark 7:31-37

Proverbs 2:1–8 (C)
Isaiah 35:4–7a (E) (L) (RC)

Meditation on the Texts

We long for greater understanding of your law, O God. From you alone come our help and our redemption. You give us wisdom and understanding. Open our eyes and unstop our ears, that we may be able to take in the wonder of your creation. We give thanks to you for Jesus who did all things well, even making the deaf to hear and the mute to speak. We pray for the grace to speak in love and to be slow in anger. Strengthen us to be doers of the word, visiting the lonely and the afflicted, even as you have come to us in Jesus Christ. Amen.

Commentary on the Texts

Mark 7:31–37

Jesus had gone northward from Tyre to Sidon and now he turns southeastward past Caesarea Philippi and through Philip's territory to reach a place on the eastern shore of the Sea of Galilee in the territory of the Decapolis. Some scholars think Jesus took such a circuitous route in order to avoid entering the territory of Antipas at this time.

This miracle is described only by Mark. Matthew may have known of it but omitted it, some think, because it seemed magical. There are parallels to the miracle of healing the deaf-mute man in Jewish and pagan sources.

The man who was brought to Jesus was deaf and had an impediment in his speech. The Greek word used to describe him means "blunt" or "dull" and thus can mean both deaf and dumb, and it can also be used with regard to sight or intelligence. Here it means deaf. Those who brought him asked Jesus to lay his hands on him, a common way of healing. Jesus took the man aside from the multitude to deal with him in private. Jesus put his fingers into the man's ears. He spat and touched the man's tongue. In the ancient world, saliva was believed to have curative powers. Then Jesus looked up to heaven, sighed, and spoke to the man. Looking to heaven and sighing were, like the laying on of hands and using saliva, common gestures used in healing. Even so, Jesus' sighs indicate the strong emotion he felt as he waged war against the power of Satan which caused the impairments. He seeks divine aid in urgent prayer. Jesus then said to the man "Ephphatha," meaning "Be opened." This word could also mean "Be released" as well as "Be opened." At once the man's ears were opened and his tongue was released, so that he could hear and speak clearly. Jesus' command to the man shatters the fetters by which he had been bound by Satan. The man who had been shut up by deafness and impairment of speech is now being released by the power of God working through Jesus. Verse 35 implies that the man had an impairment of speech, perhaps stuttering, rather than being unable to speak at all.

Jesus charged the people to tell no one of the miracle, but the more he bid them to be silent, the more they told of what they had seen! Jesus was up against a kind of "Murphy's Law" in which the more he tried to prevent the messianic secret from being told, the more those around him told it!

The popular reaction to this miracle was very great. The people exclaimed, "He has done all things well; he even makes the deaf hear and the dumb speak" (v. 37). Some may have seen it as the fulfillment of Isaiah 35:5–6. Others may have thought of it as a new creation (Gen. 1:31).

This healing can be coupled with that described in Mark 8:22–26. Just as 7:31–37 concludes the series of events including the feeding of the five thousand, so 8:22–26 ends the series containing the feeding of the four thousand. One thing that both miracles have in common is that the cure was accomplished with difficulty and not instantaneously. Both concern miracles that figure in Isaiah 35:5–6, which is in the Old Testament reading today for (E), (L), and (RC). Mark seems to have regarded these miracles as a pair.

Mark seems to imply more than just the healing of the man who was deaf and dumb by this miracle. Mark is saying that true faith and all true confession of Christ is a miracle. Note that the ears were healed first, and then the tongue, which is a reminder that it is only as the church *hears* the word of God that it has a message to speak! The miracle has eschatological significance. It leads up to the christological confession of Peter in 8:29 and the subsequent teaching about it (8:31–33).

We are not told whether or not the man who was healed followed Jesus. But Jesus met the man's needs and in doing so revealed his own glory.

Recommended work: Look up other instances of healing in the Gospels and consult Bible dictionaries to learn more about what may have been involved in the methods used by Jesus.

The sermon can point out that when the deaf man with the speech impediment was brought to Jesus, Jesus took him apart from the crowd for the healing. Jesus was concerned for the man, not for the impact any healing might make upon the crowd. Jesus felt deeply about the man, as expressed by his sigh. Then the man found wholeness of body and spirit because of his faith in Jesus.

Proverbs 2:1–8 (C)

The entire second chapter of Proverbs deals with the fruits of the search for wisdom. Understanding and morality are both results of this search. The introduction (vs. 1–4) presents the condition—if you seek wisdom. The rest of the chapter describes the consequences: you will find wisdom (vs. 5–8); you will understand righteousness (vs. 9–11); you will be guarded against bad companions (vs. 12–15) and against immorality (vs. 16–19); and you will dwell with the upright (vs. 20–22).

The introduction points out that the search for wisdom demands a receptive and expectant attitude. One must be attentive with senses (ear) and reason (heart) and must be actively searching for wisdom. The search for wisdom demands total commitment which sacrifices everything else. Only those who are pure in heart can find wisdom. In v. 1 the "commandments" are a synonym for wisdom and the means for achieving it. But the reference here is not to the body of laws contained in Israel's covenant.

The greatest gift of all is "the knowledge of God" (v. 5). The Lord is the source of wisdom and gives knowledge and understanding. In this text it is impossible to determine whether God is synonymous with wisdom in its fullest sense. The metaphors used in this passage show the influence of the rest of the Old Testament. God is affirmed as the giver of wisdom, the protector of those who walk in integrity, the one who preserves the way of the saints (vs. 7–8).

Recommended work: Look up wisdom in a Bible dictionary.

The sermon might begin with what it means to understand the fear of the Lord. Then it might move to the affirmation that God gives wisdom and upholds those who walk in the paths of justice. If you seek wisdom from God, God will give you wisdom and guard your ways.

This pericope is best understood in the context of the verses that precede and follow it. This passage along with the preceding chapter describes the restoration of Zion after the exile. Therefore these two chapters probably originally belonged with chapters 40–66. The transformation of nature is a prominent feature, as is the highway along which God leads the people home to Zion. Just as God's judgment has burned and ruined (ch. 34), so now God's redemption makes the desert bloom (35:1–2). God's people see the glory of God.

The despondent (vs. 3–4) should take heart, for God is coming to rescue them. Those who have been blind will see, the deaf will hear, the lame will be healed, and the dumb will sing for joy. God's broken people will be whole again. This picture of the coming new age came to be associated with the work of the expected Messiah. The reading from Mark 7:31–37 for today tells of Jesus healing a man who was deaf and had an impediment in his speech, which was a sign that Messiah had arrived in Jesus Christ.

Deutero-Isaiah has more than one prophecy of joy and of the transformation of the desert into a forest. This image recalled the first exodus and journey through the desert from Egypt to Canaan. But that exodus would be surpassed by the victorious journey from Babylon to Jerusalem. The desert will now be covered with trees and flowers (vs. 1–2).

The Jews who had doubted God's power and who were fainthearted will see what is promised to all peoples (Isa. 40:5), the revelation of "our God." The exclamation "Behold, your God . . . " is a quotation from 40:9. The phrase "vengeance comes" brings to mind Isaiah 34:8a. In this way the prophecy against Edom is linked with the prophecy of salvation.

Beginning with v. 5 the instruction to the messengers and the promise of salvation is concluded, and now the author is once again speaking to the reader. In v. 6 there is something new and original. We cannot be sure how the author intended vs. 5 and 6 to be interpreted. Was he thinking only of bodily healing or also of liberation from prison? Could it be prison of spiritual blindness? There is rejoicing at both the beginning and the ending of this first train of thought (vs. 1–6). It can be assumed that it is joy in God, although this is not explicit.

In vs. 6b–10 our attention is turned again to the desert with the assurance that it will no longer hold the terrors for travelers it held in the past and that water will be plentiful. The author assures the people that there will not be any lions or jackals or other dangerous beasts along the highway to Zion. The redeemed will travel along this highway (v. 8) which God has prepared. They have been set free by God's coming and God's act of revenge upon the nations. Instead of fear and weakness, there will now be joy and gladness. For sorrow and sighing shall flee away (v. 10).

Recommended work: Compare this passage with Isaiah 40 and with the accounts of the first exodus through the wilderness, described in the book of Exodus.

This passage proclaims that God will come to bring salvation to the people. In the sermon, comparison might be made with this promise and the miracle of Jesus described in the reading from Mark for the day. Thus the prophecy has found fulfillment.

James 1:17–27 (C) (E)

James 1:17–22, 26–27 (L)

See Pentecost 15.

James 2:1–5 (RC)

The thrust of this passage is that Christians must not show partiality but treat all persons equally, just as God has treated all without partiality. In v. 2 the word translated "assembly" means literally "synagogue," which was where the early church had its roots. For parallel passages dealing with God's special concern for the poor in this world, see Psalm 35:10; Luke 6:30; and 1 Corinthians 1:26–29. The 1 Corinthians passage says:

> For consider your call, brethren; not many of you were wise according to worldly standards, not many were powerful, not many were of noble birth; but God chose

what is foolish in the world to shame the wise, God chose what is weak in the world to shame the strong, God chose what is low and despised in the world, even things that are not, to bring to nothing things that are, so that no human being might boast in the presence of God.

There is no place for class distinctions in the church, since Christ himself humbled himself and took the form of a servant (Phil. 2:5–7). To show partiality is to reveal that a person is divided in mind, like the judges who give unjust and corrupt decisions. God has chosen the rich in faith, not the rich in material goods, to be the heirs of the kingdom. The rich, on the other hand, were often the oppressors of the poor who dragged their debtors into court (v. 6). By filing lawsuits, they blasphemed the "name" of Christian (v. 7). It would seem that the readers of this letter were among the poor in that they are addressed directly in vs. 6 and 7.

This passage is particularly relevant in our global village in which the gap between the haves and have-nots is growing at an increasing pace. In contrast to the situation in the church addressed by James, through the ages the church has often been captive of the rich and powerful and taken the side of the haves against the have-nots. Special seats for the landowners were provided in the balcony of Scottish churches, while the common folk sat down below. In America in the days of slavery, blacks had to sit in the slave gallery in the balcony. When churches were supported by pew rents, the rich obviously were able to rent the better seats and leave for the poor the less desirable seating or only standing room. The church often sides with the rich owners against the poor workers, and management against labor. The church today must examine itself to discern where it is continuing to discriminate against the poor and show partiality toward the rich.

Recommended work: Look up the words "rich" and "poor" in a concordance and compare what the Bible has to say about each.

The sermon might raise the question of whether our churches today show partiality between rich and poor. What might be done to put into practice the teaching of James?

Theological Reflection

The reading from Proverbs tells us that the search for wisdom brings us both understanding and morality, and the greatest gift of all, the knowledge of God. The Isaiah passage describes the restoration of Zion. The healings mentioned there foreshadow the healing by Jesus described in Mark of the man who was deaf and dumb. Mark's miracle story has overtones beyond the healing of the one man, in that it points to the church's need to hear God's word and then speak that message to the world. It has an eschatological thrust as it points to the coming age when Satan will be defeated. The passage from James 2:1–5 reminds us that just as God does not show partiality toward people, neither should we favor the rich or put down the poor. Rather, God has chosen the poor in the world to be rich in faith and heirs of the kingdom.

Children's Message

The children probably have seen homeless people in the streets, or at least have seen some pictures of them. Ask how they think such a person would be welcomed in the sanctuary of the church on Sunday morning. How do they think Jesus would respond to such a person? If their home were destroyed and their clothes lost, how would they like to be treated? Jesus said the foxes have their holes and the birds have their nests, but he had no place to lay his head.

Hymns for Pentecost 16

O for a Thousand Tongues to Sing; Great Is Thy Faithfulness; Strong Son of God; Immortal Love.

Ordinary Time 24

Proper 19

Psalm 125 (C)   **James 2:1–5, 8–10, 14–17 (C) (E) (L)**
Psalm 116:1–6, 8–9 (RC)   **James 2:14–18 (RC)**
Psalm 116:1–8 (L)
Psalm 116 or 116:1–8 (E)   **Mark 8:27–38 (C) (E)**
                                 Mark 8:27–35 (L) (RC)

Proverbs 22:1–2, 8–9 (C)
Isaiah 50:4–9 (E)
Isaiah 50:4–10 (L)
Isaiah 50:5–9a (RC)

Meditation on the Texts

We turn to you, O God, because you have surrounded us with your love as the mountains are around Jerusalem. In you alone do we find our strength and true wealth. When we become discouraged because of the triumphs of the wicked, help us to remember that they will reap the consequences of their deceits. Enable us to be your faithful servants, sustaining the weak and enduring suffering for your sake. May we have the faith to put our trust in you and in Jesus who is the Christ, your chosen one. Give us the courage and the trust to take up our cross to follow him. Help us to express our faith in doing works of love for others, loving our neighbors as ourselves, in the name of Jesus who became poor for our sake. Amen.

Commentary on the Texts

Mark 8:27–38 (C) (E)

Mark 8:27–35 (L) (RC)

This passage opens the second major section of Mark. The series of deeds and incidents in the life of Jesus that were related in the first part of the Gospel raised the question, "Who then is this, that even wind and sea obey him?" (4:41). What Jesus had done in his ministry was so amazing that even ordinary people who were not disciples were prompted to ask, "Who is this who does such amazing things?" At the very least, they answered it by saying that he must be some very great figure. But when Jesus put the question directly to the disciples, Peter answered for them all: "You are the Christ [Messiah]." These words sum up the Christian understanding of Jesus.

In Matthew's account of this event, Jesus enthusiastically responded to Peter's affirmation (Matt. 16:17). But this is not the case here. According to Mark, Jesus' reaction to the confession is guarded. He charges them to tell no one about him. The word for "charged" (v. 30) has in Greek the normal meaning of "rebuke" which suggests that there is a hint of censure in Jesus' reply to Peter, and perhaps even displeasure at this open confession of faith.

This report of Jesus' request for silence is another evidence of the messianic secret of Mark's theology. But even such a response is a tacit acceptance of their description of who he is. But Jesus carefully avoids identifying himself as Messiah. Jesus rejected the title of Messiah because the general assumptions at that time about Messiah were that he would accomplish his work by the exercise of brute force in one form or another. This concept of Messiah held that he would achieve his victory by overpowering his opposition, not submitting to it and experiencing suffering and defeat.

To counter this conception, Jesus outlines the kind of Messiah he has come to earth to be, referring to himself by the usual term "Son of man." The Son of man must (1) suffer many things, (2) be rejected by the elders and the chief priests and the scribes, (3) be killed, and (4) after three days rise again (v. 31).

This strategy for the completion of the Messiah's mission on earth was shocking to Peter and the disciples. Peter took Jesus aside to rebuke him. But Jesus turned to Peter and the rest of the disciples, in effect speaking to them all, and replied, "Get behind me, Satan! For you are not on the side of God, but of men" (v. 33).

Peter's confession of faith and the subsequent interchange about the role of the Messiah lead up to the radical teaching about discipleship to the multitude as well as to the disciples (8:34–9:1). Jesus says that anyone who would come after him must deny himself and take up the cross and follow him. The Romans forced a condemned criminal to carry a part of the cross to the place of execution, hence the metaphor. The present form of the saying may reflect the work of the early church as it looked back on Jesus' crucifixion. Jesus then offers a paradox: whoever would save his life will lose it; and whoever loses his life for my sake and the gospel's will save it (v. 35). Then Jesus asks what gain is it to have the whole world, only to lose one's own soul. And he warns that whoever is ashamed of him and his words in this adulterous (perhaps a metaphor for idolatrous) generation, of him will the Son of man be ashamed when the Son of man returns in glory at the End of the age.

Recommended work: Look up the term "Messiah" in Bible dictionaries and trace its development through the Old and New Testaments.

The sermon might begin with consideration of the confession of Peter that Jesus was the one expected by the people, the Messiah. Then the difference between their expectations and Jesus' warning of suffering and death might be explored. What does it mean for the disciples, and all those who would follow Jesus, to deny themselves and take up the cross? What is the meaning of the promise that Jesus offers to those who will follow?

Proverbs 22:1–2, 8–9 (C)

The Book of Proverbs came into its present form about 350 B.C. It is classified as wisdom literature because it deals in practical matters of living. The sayings were transmitted from parent to child, scholar to scholar, friend to friend, and, over the years, were gradually refined and sharpened and compiled into the present collection. The section of Proverbs from 10:1 to 22:16 is the core of the book and often attributed to Solomon. Any proverb written by Solomon would have to have been composed by 931 B.C., when he died.

In today's reading, Solomon stresses the great value of a good name, established through ethical behavior, over against riches. And he says the favor or goodwill is better than silver or gold. In the market economy of capitalist America, with its emphasis on the "bottom line" rather than moral decision and ethical behavior, these words of Solomon are particularly relevant. Youth must be trained in value judgments and taught that ethical behavior is far more valuable than dollars, in spite of the message of the mass media to the contrary.

Solomon warns that the person who sows injustice will reap calamity. We are seeing this on an international scale, as the injustices against third world nations result in tragedy not only for them but for the world village. The world economy links the peoples and nations of the world together like mountain climbers tied together on the same rope. If one falls, all will be pulled down.

But the person who is generous toward the poor and who is bountiful will be blessed. The God of the Bible takes up the cause of the poor over against the rich who oppress them. This verse reminds us of the Beatitudes of Jesus in which he describes what the blessed life of the kingdom is like.

Verse 1 is not a polemic against wealth but rather seeks to assert a hierarchy of values within which material wealth can make its contribution to a full life. Otherwise wealth may be a snare and a delusion. According to this scale, reputation is to be preferred over great wealth, and engaging personal qualities are to be valued more highly than silver or gold.

In v. 8 we have a typical expression of the doctrine of divine retribution—the person who sows iniquity will reap evil.

A sensitivity to the poor is commended in v. 9. This concern will be expressed in practical ways, like sharing one's food. The paradox in this verse is the fact that, because the benevolent person does not live to himself or herself and is not a prisoner of selfish desires and ambitions, that person achieves the highest degree of self-fulfillment. True blessedness is not to be found in going all out for self, with no concern for neighbor and the neighbor's well-being. The blessed person is the one who sees the brother or sister as one for whom he or she is responsible and who does acts of mercy for them. Such a person sees the world as a global village and shares bread with the person in need.

Recommended work: Consult a commentary on Proverbs to find out how this collection was developed and used by the Jewish faith and then in the Christian church.

The proverbs, as part of the wisdom literature, are part of the body of generally accepted axioms by which people live. The truth of them has been established by experience. They point to what is most valuable in life—not wealth but a good reputation. Such a reputation is gained by sharing with others, not attempting to bolster one's own security by defensive living. The sermon might pick up the suggested theme that sharing is done not only person to person but among peoples and nations.

Isaiah 50:4–10 (L)

Isaiah 50:5–9a (RC)

Isaiah 50:4–9 (E)

This selection is part of the third Servant song found in vs. 4–11. It is a song of faith sung by those who have learned from the prophets the meaning of Israel's tragic history. It reflects the experience of the Israelites in exile who have learned from their suffering, who submit with understanding to the humiliation of the exile and wait expectantly for God's coming act of redemption, which they are confident is near at hand. This song seems to have been composed by an Israelite to be sung by faithful exiles as an act of trust and belief. Notice that it is intensely individual in character. Its use in worship would probably aid the individual exile in identifying with the experience of Israel. But by singing the song in the assembly, the Israelite also found meaning in being one with the "servant." Hebrew thought moved easily from the individual to the group, even as Americans refer to Uncle Sam as an individual representing the people of the whole nation.

This Servant song is probably the easiest of all of those in Deutero-Isaiah to understand. It has been generally accepted as an individual lament in form. But since vs. 4–5a are not part of a lament, it can more accurately be called an individual psalm of confidence. The thrust of vs. 7–9 is a broad development of the main two motifs of the psalm: (1) the confession of confidence in God and (2) the certainty of being answered. Notice that the one who confesses unshakable confidence in God in vs. 5b–9 is the same one who is commissioned with an office of the word. So the whole passage, vs. 4–9, is the confession of confidence spoken by one who is mediator of the word.

Verse 4 and the first clause of v. 5 are the expression of one who has been called to hear and then to speak. This person is like a disciple, in that in both hearing and speaking he or she is obedient to God. God opens the disciple's ears to hear. God tells the disciple what to speak. The Servant has been awakened and aroused in order to hear God's word. The word is addressed to those who are prostrate, to Israel who is not in a position to hear the word. Thus the people Israel, like the Servant, must be aroused before they can hear the word that applies to their case.

In vs. 4–5a we have the call of the one who in vs. 5b–9 attests his faith in the office committed to him. Notice that the Servant who is entirely unable to exercise any control over the reception and transmission of this word is not supported by any establishment or institution. This utter dependence upon the word is the chief characteristic of the prophetic office here. A second distinctive feature of the prophetic office is that God's Servant is here described as one who is taught, a "disciple." The identification of God's Servant as God's disciple is the most important feature in the picture of the Servant here.

The Servant who is attacked and defamed because of his task develops in this song for the first time a new approach: he *assents to* and *accepts* this suffering. The Servant believes God wills his suffering and its acceptance. Note the glaring contrast between v. 6 and v. 7—I will not hide from shame, but I shall not be put to shame ("be ashamed" in KJV). God makes the Servant's face like a flint. He is enabled to resist the blows and the shameful treatment that he meets. This complete acceptance and it alone enables him to make his face hard as a flint rock.

We find expressed in vs. 8–9 in a very forceful way the certainty that the Servant feels that God is on his side. The terms—vindicate, contend, adversary, guilty—reflect the setting of a trial. From the opponent's point of view, the contest is already decided and the Servant's case is lost, since he has admitted defeat by accepting the blows and acts of shame. However, the Servant summons those who oppose him. These are the people who smite him and shame him and spit upon him. He calls them into God's law court, for he is convinced that God justifies him and that no one can condemn him.

In v. 9 the Servant declares and asks, "Behold, the Lord GOD helps me; who will declare me guilty?" He believes that those who mock and smite him will perish. But the question of whether there is the slightest possibility of any justification or rehabilitation for the Servant according to vs. 4–9 is left open. The question points forward to the final Servant song.

Recommended work: Review in a commentary all four of the Servant Songs—42:1–4; 49:1–6; 50:4–11; and 52:13–53:12—to find out how they describe the idealized Servant of God.

The sermon might open with the question of how a person is enabled to withstand opposition and even persecution for the sake of obedience to God. It is God who upholds the servant and enables him or her to accept the suffering. There might be a comparison with the reading in Mark calling the disciples to deny themselves and accept suffering in obedience to the call of Jesus to follow him.

James 2:1–5, 8–10, 14–18 (C) (E) (L)

James 2:14–18 (RC)

These verses will be considered together, with the exception of vs. 1–5 which were discussed in the previous Sunday's reading for (RC).

These passages deal with living the Christian faith in practical matters of giving respect to the poor and doing deeds of mercy to those in need. If God shows no partiality, neither should the disciple. Running through vs. 1–13 is the theme of the sin of deference toward the rich. Instead of a sustained argument, the section consists of a rather loosely connected group of reproaches, which were apparently written down as they came to the mind of the author. All of them find root in faith in the Lord Jesus Christ who ascended to heaven and reigns in heavenly glory.

After a digression in vs. 5–7 about God's choice of the poor, the author returns in vs. 8–9 to the theme of vs. 2–4. Verse 8 seems to respond to an objector who argues that the neighbor whom one is to love might actually be rich. But the answer given to this excuse is that such behavior would be praiseworthy if it were true, but the same attention that they show to the rich is rarely shown to the poor. By favoring the rich, they are not loving the poor neighbor as themselves, and thus are breaking the commandment. By failing at this point, they are transgressors of the law and rebellious against God.

The theme of faith versus works is taken up in vs. 14–18 but related to the previous discussion through the concrete example of doing works of mercy to those in need. If James is arguing against Paul, he seems to have misunderstood Paul's argument for faith over against works. For Paul, faith was not mere intellectual acceptance of monotheism which even demons could share with believers (2:19). Rather, for Paul, faith was self-surrender of the whole person to God, a surrender that cannot be "dead" or without moral actions in daily living. The polemic here is not against genuine Pauline theology but rather against a distortion of what Paul taught. Even Paul rejected such a distortion.

We find in vs. 14–17 a little parable that has its application in v. 17: "So faith by itself, if it has no works, is dead." "Be warmed" (v. 16) is to have warm clothing. The arguments in vs. 18–19 disregard vs. 15–17 altogether. The opening word of v. 18, "But," looks back to v. 14 and is a contrast to the "faith, not works" false doctrine the author is refuting. Verse 18 must be taken as a unit. Works can be shown and they will reveal the true faith which underlies them. The author assumes that both he and his readers are Christians. Thus he does not deal with the issue of the possible value of good works performed by unbelievers.

Recommended work: Consult a commentary to study the teaching of Paul about faith and works in Romans 3 and 4. Compare and contrast this with what James says.

The sermon can explore the differences between works and faith as presented in the reading. The question of how giving to the poor is an act of faith might be considered. How are works an expression of faith?

Theological Reflection

The various lessons contrast the way of the world with the godly life pictured in the Bible. In Proverbs, Solomon seeks to develop a framework of values in which material wealth can make its contribution to a full life. He stresses the importance of a good reputation and gaining personal qualities over against wealth. James stresses the need to treat all people the same, showing no partiality toward the rich. James argues that good works reveal true faith which motivates them. Isaiah presents a third Servant song in which the servant accepts suffering as part of his role in hearing and speaking God's message to weary Israel. He expresses confidence in God who vindicates him before his enemies. Such confidence is reflected in Peter's confession that Jesus is the Christ. Jesus corrects the misunderstanding of the disciples about what the Messiah must undergo in fulfilling his mission. Then he spells out the radical demands of Christian discipleship which call for denying self, taking up one's cross, and following Jesus. The paradox of finding one's life by losing it is described. And Jesus warns that those who are ashamed of him now he will be ashamed of when he returns in his glory.

Children's Message

Point out that some common names speak of character traits, for example, Peter means a rock or Dorothy a gift of God. Refer to the reading from Proverbs about the value of a good name. Help the children understand how one can gain a good name, a good reputation, by sharing with those who have less and being friendly to those who have no friends.

Hymns for Pentecost 17

In the Cross of Christ I Glory; O Love That Wilt Not Let Me Go; Glorious Things of You Are Spoken.

Pentecost 18

Ordinary Time 25

Proper 20

Psalm 27:1–6 (C)
Psalm 54:1–4, 6 (RC)
Psalm 54:1–4, 6–7a (L)
Psalm 54 (E)
Job 28:20–28 (C)

Wisdom 1:16–2:1, 12–22 (E)
Wisdom 2:12, 17–20 (RC)
Jeremiah 11:18–20 (L)

James 3:13–18 (C)
James 3:16–4:6 (E) (L)
James 3:16–4:3 (RC)

Mark 9:30–37

Meditation on the Texts

We give thanks to you, O God, because of the greatness of your care for us. You are our light and our salvation. In trust, we have committed our cause to you. We continually seek to know your holy purpose, that we may be sustained in the midst of our lives. We confess our inability to find true wisdom apart from you. Help us to know the wisdom that comes down from above so that we may live in peace. May we thus be enabled to follow you, and your Son, Jesus Christ, in humility and trust as little children. Amen.

Commentary on the Texts

Mark 9:30–37

We have here two closely related teachings, although they come out of different settings. In vs. 30–32, Jesus again speaks about his forthcoming passion; and in vs. 33–37, he responds to his disciples' discussion of true greatness.

Verses 30–32. In keeping with the general thrust of this second major section of Mark, we find Jesus seeking privacy with the disciples in order to give them further insights about what was to happen. This second prediction of Jesus' passion is shorter than that in 8:31–33 and makes no explicit reference to suffering or rejection. Although the briefest reference to the passion, it may be the oldest (see also Mark 10:33–34). In today's reading, Mark quotes Jesus: "The Son of man will be delivered into the hands of men, and they will kill him" (v. 31). This is a more all-inclusive statement than the other two predictions that Jesus made regarding his suffering in that here he says he will suffer at the hands of representatives of the whole human race! All are implicated in the death of the One who died for all. Thus, to the question of the spiritual, "Were you there when they crucified my Lord?" we must all answer, "Yes, I was there. My sins helped nail him to the cross."

Here Jesus refers to being "delivered into" for the first time. Some commentators see this as a reference to the treachery of Judas. But more likely it refers to the "delivering up" of Jesus according to the counsel of God (Acts 2:23; see also Rom. 8:32). The disciples fail to understand what Jesus is saying, because they are still thinking in terms of the conventional Messiah who will take over by force to bring in the rule of God. In Luke's account of this incident, the disciples are excused for misunderstanding, because the meaning of Jesus' death was still hidden from them (Luke 9:45). Matthew 17:23 omits any mention of the misunderstanding. Here Mark indicates that they were afraid to ask any more about it. Perhaps they remembered all too clearly the sharp rebuke given to Peter when he voiced his misunderstanding.

Verses 33–37. True greatness is the thrust of this passage. The house in Capernaum may have been Peter's house. In this intimate setting, we should be alert to special instructions Jesus will give to the disciples. When he asks what they had been discussing on the way, the disciples are too embarrassed to answer. They had not intended him to hear, and his question reminds them of his teaching about denial of self (8:31–34) which was in sharp contrast with their speculation about who will be the greatest. It would seem that the disciples have more than a mere intellectual misunderstanding about life in the kingdom of God. They have been following Jesus, but they have missed the essence of his message. So Jesus tries in a new way to illustrate the real meaning of true greatness.

His deliberate intent is indicated by his approach: (1) "he sat down," which indicates formal teaching; (2) "and called the twelve," which focuses the teaching on the disciples; and (3) "he said to them," which introduces the climactic saying: "If any one would be first, he must be last of all and servant of all" (v. 35). This saying about the first and the last is a reversal of the world's values and carries further the instruction given in the first passion prediction of 8:34–9:1. The measure of greatness by lowly service is a characteristic of Jesus who said that he came "not to be served but to serve, and to give his life as a ransom for many" (Matt. 20:28). Even as service was characteristic of Jesus, so it runs counter to the world and its values.

To reinforce his teaching on true greatness, Jesus took a child in his arms (the Greek leaves uncertain the age and sex of the child). Jesus' gesture with the child is striking, because children were held in low esteem in the Greco-Roman world. The word used here for "child" in the Greek is the same used of the Suffering Servant in the Greek version of Isaiah 53:2, "We heralded him as a child." Those who read this story as it circulated in the early church would see Jesus identifying himself as the lowliest, the least, and the servant of all as he embraced the child.

While we might expect Jesus to exhort the Twelve to be like children, which is what Matthew 18:3 records, Mark shifts the argument from being lowly like a child to urging the Twelve to receive a child in the name of Jesus. In v. 37, "in my name" means "because of who I am by my very nature." This passage gives a blessing to all who work with and care for children. However, "child" can also refer to anyone who has need of help, however insignificant, perhaps even others who would follow Jesus, as the verses that follow make clear. Thus, this incident forms a transition from the prediction of Jesus' passion to the series of loosely connected sayings that conclude chapter 9.

Recommended work: Compare this passage with Matthew 18:1–6 and Luke 9:46–48 to study further Jesus' teaching in regard to children.

The sermon might begin with the misunderstanding of the disciples about Jesus' prediction of his passion, then move to the teaching about true greatness. What does it mean to receive a child in the name of Jesus? What are the characteristics of a person who so receives a child? What does this teaching mean today in regard to the care of children in our society?

Job 28:20-28 (C)

This passage is one of the most impressive in all of the Old Testament. This poem about where wisdom may be found challenges our pride in reason and the scientific method. Wisdom is hidden from those who seek her in the physical world (v. 21) and even from the deities of the underworld (v. 22). If science and technology cannot provide answers to the search for wisdom, neither can religious techniques.

Because Job 28 is not written in the style of Job, nor immediately connected with its context, many scholars feel that it does not properly belong to the discourses of Job. Verses 1–13 develop the theme that people cannot find wisdom, wherever they look. Further, the deep and the sea do not know wisdom (vs. 14–22). The chapter concludes with the assertion that only God understands the way to wisdom (vs. 23–28).

Although God alone knows the way to wisdom, says the poet, he does not say that God created wisdom. Rather, he insists that God at the moment of creative activity took note of wisdom (vs. 25–28). Some feel that the hymn originally ended at v. 27. Up to this point, the kind of wisdom dealt with is a metaphysical type that is forever beyond human beings. But v. 28 speaks of practical wisdom as a way of life fully accessible to humans, which is summed up in (1) knowing the fear of the Lord and (2) departing from evil.

The question of the whole Book of Job, How can a person truly fear God the creator and truly depart from evil? remains unanswered. Human beings are unable to discover wisdom precisely because its price—the perfect fulfillment of the law—is beyond the reach of human beings.

Recommended work: Look up wisdom literature in a Bible or in an introduction to the Old Testament to see how this passage relates to that kind of literature.

The sermon can uphold the greatness of wisdom that is beyond human understanding; it comes only from God. How then can one find this wisdom? It is by fearing God, giving top priority to God.

Wisdom 2:12, 17–20 (RC)

The language of these verses suggested to the early church the circumstances of Jesus' crucifixion: "Let us lie in wait for the virtuous man"; "If the virtuous man is God's son, God will take his part"; "Let us test him with cruelty and torture"; "Let us condemn him to a shameful death." Therefore this passage can be used in conjunction with the story of Jesus' trial and crucifixion. But this text, like all texts about events before the cross, must be interpreted in the light of God's mighty acts of salvation in Jesus Christ. Along with the crucifixion, the good news of the resurrection of Jesus on the third day must be proclaimed to expound the meaning of both crucifixion and resurrection for Christian living today.

Jeremiah 11:18–20 (L)

The larger section of 11:18–12:6 of which this passage is a part is the first of six personal laments of Jeremiah. Here he complains of an assassination plot against him. He has learned that he is the unwitting object (gentle lamb) of the plot and so prays to God who knows all to protect him (v. 20). This lament wrestles with the problems of theodicy, how to reconcile the justice of God with the evil known in human experience. Jeremiah affirms the existence of God's justice (12:1) but then asks why the wicked who plot against his life seem to prosper. The overall thrust here is Jeremiah's impression that evil thrives on earth precisely because God is negligent or capricious. This reading might be used to counter the false piety that refuses to voice agonizing doubts.

James 3:13–18 (C)

James 3:16–4:6 (E) (L)

James 3:16–4:3 (RC)

Since the readings for (E), (L), and (RC) overlap that for (C), they will be discussed here in two sections—3:13–18 and 4:1–6.

True wisdom which comes from God and reveals itself in a good life is the focus of 3:13–18. In contrast to the earlier part of this chapter which speaks about the dangers of boasting, this section calls for a good life which demonstrates true wisdom. Where there is bitterness and rivalry, the boastful pretense to wisdom is a sham. Such wisdom, says James, is not from God in heaven above but is earthly, unspiritual, devilish (3:15). True wisdom is revealed in works, in daily actions, not in philosophical speculation. The word "meekness" here conveys a misleading sense in modern English, but in the Elizabethan English on which this version is based, "meek" and "gentle" were used as synonyms.

In sharp contrast to the disorder produced by false, human wisdom is the divine wisdom from above. The author describes this true wisdom with eight terms. Such a listing of items was a common procedure among Hellenistic teachers of rhetoric and ethics who made their pupils memorize lists of virtues or vices to be used in moral instruction. Such instruction had as its goal good conduct and the avoidance of evil. Such lists are not found in the Old Testament but were adapted for Jewish use in Hellenistic Judaism. This is not intended to be an inclusive list of moral virtues but is a list of terms relevant to the theme of wisdom. True wisdom is:

Pure. It is unmixed with evil. This is the basic quality underlying the items that follow.

Peaceable. It doesn't cause disorder, in contrast to false wisdom which does (3:16).

Gentle. It respects the feelings of others (see 3:13).

Open to reason. It is not locked into a position as is the person who says, "I know what I believe. Don't confuse me with the facts!"

Full of mercy. It shows mercy toward those who are in the wrong, seeking to win them back to the truth.

Producing good fruits. It produces good fruits in daily living.

Without uncertainty. It is single-minded, aiming for the truth as its goal.

Without insincerity or hypocrisy. It is honest in method, not trying to appear what it is not.

Verse 18 is the climax to this passage: the purpose of life, true righteousness, is found through seeking to live peacefully with others. Those who make peace will sow in peace and reap the harvest of righteousness.

In James 4:1–6 are listed wrongful desires, in contrast to the previously mentioned virtues of true wisdom. While the previous section pointed out the harm done by false wisdom, here James points out the far greater harm done by wrongful desires.

Although the wars and fightings of 4:1–2b are set in direct contrast to the peace of 3:18, the reference does not seem appropriate for Christian readers. The wars and fighting here do not seem to be just quarrels and disputes within the community of faith; rather, they seem to be literal wars which result in killings. The author sees the passions of desire, a cardinal vice among Stoics, as the underlying cause of wars, fighting, and killings. Verse 4 can be understood in the context of the prophetic understanding of the covenant as a marriage between God and Israel. This verse condemns the unfaithful as covenant breakers who have made friends with the world and are thus at enmity with God.

The origin of the quotation in 4:5 is not clear. There is no such text in the Old Testament or in other Jewish writing that has survived. In 4:6 the main thought seems to be that God, who yearns for the best for every person, gives more grace or special help to those fitted to receive it by their humility (see 1 Peter 5:5; also Ps. 138:6). The main thrust of 4:5 and 6 is to point out the deadly evil of unlawful pleasures and desire and to help the reader to overcome them.

Recommended work: Use a concordance and a Bible dictionary to do a word study of wisdom and desire.

Draw out the contrast that James makes between the results of earthly wisdom and those of true wisdom from God. The eight characteristics of true wisdom might become the backbone of the sermon, with illustrations given for each. Compare the wisdom described by James with the wisdom featured in the Old Testament readings.

Theological Reflection

The readings all deal with the nature of true wisdom. Wisdom is praised in Job as a virtue that only God can give, for only God knows where it can be found—in the fear of God and departing from evil. James contrasts earthly wisdom with heavenly wisdom and shows that God's gift of wisdom leads to a life of righteousness and peace. The second section of the James reading draws the contrast between true wisdom and the passions and desire which are the underlying cause of wars and killing. There is a kind of wisdom in the saying that God opposes the proud but gives grace to the humble (4:6). Jeremiah, in the face of the plot against his life, prays to God for protection and commits his cause to God. Mark tells how the disciples misunderstand what Jesus is saying about his death because their concept of Messiah is radically different from his and does not include suffering, death, and resurrection. Jesus then imparts wisdom to them as he describes true greatness in terms of being the servant of all. He acts out a parable with a child and blesses all who work with and care for "children," not only children who are young in age but anyone who has need of help and especially new disciples who are "children in the faith." To receive others in this way is to live by divine wisdom in the kingdom.

Children's Message

Television dramas often make heroes of persons who achieve their desires by violence. Call attention to the endless cycle of fighting in which such a person is trapped and point out the more excellent way of peace, reasonableness, and mercy in achieving good for all. Use people and events to illustrate the point.

Hymns for Pentecost 18

I Love Thy Kingdom, Lord; Be Still, My Soul; Jesus, Friend, So Kind and Gentle.

Ordinary Time 26
Proper 21

Psalm 27:7–14 (C)
Psalm 19:7, 9, 11–13 (RC)
Psalm 135:1–7, 13–14 (L)
Psalm 19 or 19:7–14 (E)

Job 42:1–6 (C)
Numbers 11:4–6, 10–16, 24–29 (E) (L)
Numbers 11:25–29 (RC)

James 4:13–17; 5:7–11 (C)
James 4:7–12 (E) (L)
James 5:1–6 (RC)

Mark 9:38–50

Meditation on the Texts

We seek your face, O God, because you have promised never to forsake us. Your ways are beyond our understanding. We confess our pride in thinking we can search out your secrets. Only in your presence, in direct encounter, do we find meaning for our lives. When we find the tasks you have given us to be too great for us to bear, may we, like Moses, find strength from you. Give to us a portion of your spirit. Give to us patience and wisdom to recognize that all who work in your name are our colleagues. Free us from pride and self-importance so that we may be able to give the cup of cold water and to be steadfast in love, as Jesus is compassionate and merciful. Amen.

Commentary on the Texts

Mark 9:38–50

This last portion of chapter 9 shows evidence of a complex redaction history. As we have it now, the text consists of two clusters of sayings, plus a concluding trio. An outline goes like this: (1) the unauthorized exorcist, vs. 38–41; (2) warnings against causes of sin, vs. 42–48; and (3) the conclusion, vs. 49–50. The passage is made up of originally independent sayings now linked together by catch words such as "in my name," "for," and "little ones." They are also linked in a general way by the subject matter.

A summary of this section is as follows: The disciples are to be characterized by (1) lowly service, (2) openness to Christians different from them, (3) care of those who are "little ones" or young in the faith, and (4) rigorous self-discipline. They are urged to be salty in the sense in which Jesus was salty (vs. 1, 35–37) in that he suffered and died in obedience to God. If they follow such a path, they will be at peace with one another (v. 50c).

The story in vs. 38–40 is linked to the previous section and to v. 41 by use of the phrase "in my name." This is the only place in Mark where John is mentioned alone. Some scholars have questioned the historicity of this story, since exorcisms were unlikely in the lifetime of Jesus. The point at issue in the story is whether or not to welcome a man who cast out demons in the name of Jesus but who does not belong to the apostolic group. He was not a part of the Twelve, the established leadership of the church. Jesus states categorically, "Do not forbid him." (This account might be contrasted with that in Acts 19:13–20.)

Then follow two "for" sayings ("for no one who does a mighty work" and "for he that is not against us") which urge the disciples to be gracious and generous in dealing with others who call on Jesus' name. In v. 41 a third "for" saying begins with a solemn "truly" and gives a promise of reward for anyone who does even a simple act such as giving a drink of water in the name of Christ. There were traveling missionaries and needy persons to whom the disciples had opportunity to show kindness in Christ's name. This giving and receiving of hospitality was to be given to all who follow Jesus and not to just an in-group.

Next are the warnings against causing one of "these little ones" to sin. The little ones may be children (v. 37) but also, or even primarily, new believers in Jesus. They might also be those who were acting in the name of Jesus, though not part of the inner group of disciples, or those offering seemingly insignificant services like giving cold water to the thirsty.

The three parallel sayings about hand, foot, and eye expand the teaching of v. 42. Anything that causes sin is to be put aside. In Jewish thought, there was the notion that an individual part might commit a sin. Some clever persons might even try to excuse themselves by pointing to their eye, foot, or hand as the responsible party to relieve themselves of punishment for sin. The harshness of these statements undergirds the importance of obedience (Matt. 5:27–30). Rather than following them literally, we are to be wholly committed to God. There is no merit in cutting off a hand, plucking out an eye, or cutting off a foot, although some persons have done this in an effort to rid themselves of sin and guilt. The thrust of this section is to free oneself from what might hinder fellowship with God.

The term for the "hell" mentioned here is Gehenna in Greek and refers to the valley south of Jerusalem where in the past offerings had been presented to idols. Since the prophets threatened the area with the judgment of God, it came to be associated with the place where the damned would be punished. We should not read into "hell" here later ideas of eternal punishment, nor should the sternness of Jesus' sayings be taken lightly.

In modern versions vs. 44 and 46 are rightly omitted, since they are textual variants not found in the early manuscripts. "Where their worm does not die, and the fire is not quenched" is from Isaiah 66:24. This vivid description of punishment held a fascination for ancient copyists who repeated it for the sake of emphasis.

The three sayings on salt are grouped together editorially to form the conclusion, but they are unrelated to each other in meaning. "For every one will be salted with fire" (v. 49) is not found in any other Gospel. It seems to teach the acceptance of suffering as a normal experience. The identification of salt with fire in v. 49 links vs. 43–48, and "salt" to the two sayings in v. 50. A textual variant is "and every sacrifice will be salted with salt." Evidently some early copyist noted the command in Leviticus 2:13, "With all your offerings you shall offer salt," and so inserted it here. Salt was used in ritual sacrifices and would be known to Mark's readers. Salt and fire both suggest purification.

The hardships that disciples undergo, perhaps persecution in Rome, are compared to the fire of a sacrificial offering which purifies or to salt which stings and smarts but has a preserving effect. On his way to Jerusalem, Jesus is the supreme example of the sacrificial offering that has been "salted with fire." Jesus sets the example for every disciple in that by his death he shows the costly obedience of discipleship.

The section concludes with an exhortation to "be at peace with one another." Compare this with the disciples' discussion with one another about who is greatest (9:33–34). If one fulfills the exhortations of the preceding verses, then one can live at peace with others.

Recommended work: Look up in a concordance the various texts in which salt is mentioned to see how the image is used in the Bible.

For the sake of unity, the sermon may need to focus on only part of the passage. For example, the main thrust of the sermon might be on the showing of hospitality and grace toward those who differ. This spirit reflects the spirit of Jesus and can indeed lead to peace with each other. Or the sermon might concentrate on the need for the disciple to accept the role of suffering, as one follows the example of Jesus.

Job 42:1–6 (C)

This passage gives us Job's confession to God. In it Job responds to God's second speech (40:6–41:34) and concedes his awareness of the purposefulness of God (v. 2). However, on the whole his replies seem anticlimactic. A reading of the Book of Job reveals Job's longing throughout the dialogue to confront God. Now when the opportunity comes, he can only utter a few unimportant platitudes. Note his complete surrender and humiliation. While courage and fortitude are virtues of the highest kind, the submissive Job does not display them here. Rather, he has a craven attitude, demonstrated by the replies he makes to God. Some scholars think that the replies of Job are not by the author of the dialogue.

A brief outline of the passage is: (1) beginning of Job's confessional response (v. 2), (2) God's first address quoted and Job's response to it (v. 3), (3) God's second address quoted (v. 4), and (4) Job's concluding words (vs. 5 and 6).

In v. 3a we find a quotation from 38:2. Job recognizes his finitude. There is an echo of the divine questioning in 40:7 in v. 4 which prepares for the confession that follows. Job is ready to denounce the pride with which he had challenged God.

Verse 5, "I had heard of thee by the hearing of the ear, but now my eye sees thee," is one of the best-known verses of Job and of scripture. In it we find the contrast between belief through tradition (hearing of the ear) and a living faith experienced through prophetic vision and confrontation with God (my eye sees thee). Although God has not justified what has happened to Job, God has come to him in person as a God who cares for a lonely man. Although Job is not vindicated, he has gained far more than the recognition of his innocence. Job has been accepted by the creator God who is ever-present. This encounter face-to-face with God makes vindication superfluous.

Most commentators see in v. 5 the supreme teaching of the entire book. All through the book Job has expressed almost as pedantic an academic knowledge of God as that of his so-called friends. His knowledge of a personal God had been challenged by the unjust suffering and disasters that befell him. He desperately searched for a formula that at the same time would preserve the justice of God and defend his own righteousness. His knowledge, from the hearing of the ear, led him down blind hallways to blank walls. While such traditional theology might satisfy a person's needs when health and affluence are the order of the day, it could not sustain a person struck by destitution, pain, rejection, and isolation from God.

In a sense, third world Christians are the Jobs of the world today. We might also include Christians who suffer for their faith in totalitarian countries. We Christians in the Western world have much to learn from our Christian brothers and sisters who go on believing in the face of political and economic oppression and personal suffering because of lack of medical care, food, housing and other basics of life. They are the Jobs who see God face-to-face and who, in this personal relationship, are sustained in spite of their destitution and hardships.

In v. 6 the word translated "despised" is a difficult Hebrew word which is intransitive and has the thrust of "to flow" or "to melt." The meaning here is "I flow into nothingness" or "I sink into the abyss of nothingness."

Job repents in dust and ashes. He is no longer egocentric. His desire at this point is no longer for righteousness—this is annihilated. Therefore he is truly able to repent. He repents, not from moral guilt, but from a reckless display of distrust of God. Job now trusts God and says in effect, "Thy will be done." This trust is a result of his personal communion with God and is the motivation for his repentance. Job's repentance means total dedication.

Recommended work: Review the development of the dialogue between Job and his would-be comforters and finally with God.

Job, like many people in history, had searched for an answer to the question raised by suffering that he honestly believed was undeserved. His prior knowledge of God had not been able to provide the answer, but now in a firsthand encounter Job's priorities are changed. No longer is understanding the issue. Now he opens himself in trust to God and knows in his heart the answer to life's questions.

Numbers 11:4–6, 10–16, 24–29 (E) (L)

Numbers 11:25–29 (RC)

In this pericope we have two stories: the full story of the complaints against manna which begins with v. 4 and continues to the end of the chapter, and the inserted story of the seventy elders (vs. 11–12, 14–17, 24b–30). The story of the manna has marks of being a composite. For example, note the differences between the threat in v. 20 and the actual punishment in v. 33.

The difficulty began with the rabble among the Israelites who had a strong craving for the rich foods they had enjoyed in Egypt in contrast to the manna they now subsist on in the wilderness. This rabble is mentioned in Exodus 12:38: "A mixed multitude also went up with them, and very many cattle, both flocks and herds." There were rootless people who had joined with Israel who did not share in the traditions of the patriarchs. This "rougher" element led the others in complaining against Moses and God: "O that we had meat to eat! We remember the fish we ate in Egypt for nothing, the cucumbers, the melons, the leeks, the onions, and the garlic; but now our strength ["throat" is better] is dried up, and there is nothing at all but this manna to look at" (vs. 4–6; see Ex. 16:3). They craved the variety of the seasoned dishes of Egypt.

The story in vs. 4–34 seeks to explain the place-name at the end: "Therefore the name of that place was called Kibroth-hatta-avah, because there they buried the people who had the craving" (v. 34). Nothing is known of the place now. The original meaning of the name could have been "the graves at the boundary." But for the writer who recorded this tradition, the meaning is "the graves of desire or craving." It appears to have been a place of a divine judgment (graves) inflicted on Israel for its sinful craving. This happened after the exodus and during the period of wandering. Although God provided manna for the people in the wilderness, and guided them, they craved something more and tastier. So they murmured.

The manna they ate was a resinous gum from the manna-tamarisk plant of the Sinai Peninsula. Eating it left the throat dry, a better translation of v. 6 than "now our strength is dried up."

Moses is enraged by the people's desire for more and better food but turns his anger, not toward the people as might be expected, but to God.

Then in vs. 12–13 we have one of the rare occurrences in which the connection between Israel and God is expressed by the idea of motherhood. This indirectly attributes the concept of femininity to God (see Isa. 49:15; 66:13). In v. 12b the image shifts slightly when Moses complains that he is supposed to be the nurse charged by the mother with the care of the child.

In vs. 14–17 we have a new section with a new thought, namely, that Moses alone cannot bear the burden of leading the people. He says to God he would rather be killed than live in such wretchedness. God responds by telling Moses to appoint seventy elders to assist him. The story presupposes the tradition about the tent of meeting. Moses is regarded as a charismatic leader who has the divine spirit, which is then shared with the seventy. The number seventy should be taken simply as a large number.

In vs. 18–24a the basic narrative is resumed about food. Almost in sarcasm, Moses asks where food enough can be found for this large company. God tells Moses that he will see whether or not God can fulfill the promise for him (v. 23). The story emphasizes the miraculous power of God to support a large population in the wilderness and is picked up in v. 31.

The narrative then returns to the appointment of the seventy. Moses gathered them round about the tent of meeting and God came down and spoke to Moses and conveyed some of the spirit of Moses to the seventy elders. When they received the spirit, they prophesied. While the KJV reads, "They prophesied and did not cease," the RSV is a correct translation of the Hebrew which means "They did so no more." The reference is probably to a prophetic frenzy which was at times a common characteristic of Semitic religions. Great importance was attached to it. That the spirit is not confined to certain officers or people is seen in the story of Eldad and Medad who did not go outside the camp to the tent but stayed in the camp and prophesied there.

Joshua asked Moses to forbid Eldad and Medad from being a part of the seventy, but Moses asked him if he was jealous for his sake. But Moses wished that all God's people were prophets and that God would put God's spirit upon them. Here we have an early conviction of the Old Testament that the Spirit "bloweth where it listeth."

Recommended work: Consult a commentary or an Old Testament history to learn more about how Moses led and organized the people during the wilderness experience.

This passage charts the course of the process of organizing to meet a need, then the defensiveness of the organization once it is formed. The administration of the whole company was too great a burden for Moses himself to bear. He appointed elders to help him—the institution was formed. Point out that God endorsed the new structure by endowing it with the divine spirit. But then those who were gifted by God assumed their gifts to be rights and protested when others outside their circle also displayed evidence of God's spirit.

James 4:13-17; 5:7-11 (C)

James 4:7-12 (E) (L)

This section exhorts readers to resist wrong desires and to submit to God, since God is stronger than the devil. The Testaments of the Twelve Patriarchs contain sayings similar to that in v. 7. They indicate that, if a person turns to God, then Satan or evil will flee away.

The promise of v. 8, "Draw near to God and he will draw near to you," is well known and is borne out in Christian experience. People draw near to God by repenting of sin, by rejecting the evil desires and pleasures in which they have indulged, and by rejecting the double mind which tries to serve both God and the world at the same time (1:8).

Cleansing the hands originally referred to ceremonial purity, but here it is used symbolically of not doing evil. Purifying the heart suggests the proper inward attitude toward God, a pure heart which enables one to see God. The text calls the sinner to put aside laughter and joy for the sake of mourning and sorrow for sins. Sin is not to be treated flippantly. The way to a proper relationship with God is through *humbling oneself* before God. Then God will exalt the person who does so.

Speak no evil is the thrust of vs. 11-12. This section is complete in and of itself, although it deals with evil speaking which is a result of evil desires and pride. When a person slanders another, that person, in effect, denounces the law which forbids such, as well as speaking evil against the neighbor (Lev. 19:16-18). In doing so, the person sets himself or herself up as a judge in place of God.

In vs. 13-17 the author rebukes those who plan their future with complacency, forgetting that God is the author and giver of life and that they live at God's mercy. Human life is as evanescent as mist, vapor, or smoke. The Lord refers to God, not Christ, in this section.

The author says that to know what is right but not to do it is sin (v. 17). This verse does not relate directly to what went before or what follows. The author must have thought it a saying worth repeating and so inserted it here. But there is a danger that we infer from the verse that sin consists in not knowing what is right. The connection between sin and ignorance is a Greek concept, not a Jewish or a Christian one.

James 5:1-6 (RC)

This passage lays a very sharp criticism on the rich. The last days (v. 3) have already begun, and in the light of the End time all earthly values lose their meaning. In vs. 2-3 the verbs are in the perfect, indicating that judgment has already taken place on riches. The gold has tarnished and the luxurious garments are moth-eaten.

If the rich have cheated their workers, they can expect no mercy. To defraud workers of their pay was a grave crime in Judaism (Lev. 19:13). The cries of those who are unjustly treated are heard by the Lord of hosts, or the Almighty (Judge).

We find in vs. 5-6 that the idea of the rich preparing their doom by their own acts is continued. They have fattened their hearts, as cattle are fattened before the slaughter. The selfishness of the rich has resulted in murder (v. 6). The term "righteous man" used here does not refer to a particular individual but is a generic term. It means any righteous person who has suffered.

The application of this passage to society today is obvious. Western countries are rich at the expense of the poor in the third world countries. The latter, working at minimum, subsistence wages, provide much of the labor to make the things enjoyed by the rich. Management and labor relations, the oppression of women in the work force who are paid much less than men for the same work, the suffering of children of single parents who go to bed hungry every night and lack medical care, and other aspects of contemporary life are addressed by this passage of James.

The final clause, "he does not resist you," points up the utter helplessness of the poor and thus heightens the guilt of the oppressors.

The sermon might point out the relationship between humbling one's self and drawing near to God and keeping wealth in proper perspective. Ultimately, we trust in God, not in what we can do for ourselves.

Theological Reflection

Job finds the answer to unjust suffering in a face-to-face encounter with God. He moves from an academic knowledge of God to an existential knowledge which satisfies his search for self-justification. The reading for (C) from James includes a reference to the steadfastness of Job. Numbers gives an account of the murmuring of the Israelites in the wilderness and God's miraculous power to support them. The selection of seventy elders to assist Moses reveals a theology of administration in which authority and power are delegated and shared with others. James is concerned with wrong desires and how to overcome them by drawing near to God. There is also a sharp criticism of the rich who oppress the poor and cause their death. The passage points up the folly of accumulating riches. The Markan passage contains a collection of proverbs that deal with discipleship. Jesus urges generosity and graciousness, self-discipline, and acceptance of hardship and sacrifice as disciples. Jesus exhorts the disciples to be at peace with one another.

Children's Message

The children may sometimes think they cannot do very much for Jesus and the kingdom. Remind them of what Jesus said about the value of giving even a cup of cold water in his name. Suggest various everyday acts of kindness they can do in the name of Jesus.

Hymns for Pentecost 19

Where Cross the Crowded Ways of Life; Just as I Am, Without One Plea; All My Hope on God Is Founded.

Ordinary Time 27

Proper 22

Psalm 128 (C) (RC) (L)   **Hebrews 1:1–4; 2:9–11 (C)**
Psalm 8 or 128 (E)   **Hebrews 2:9–11 (L) (RC)**
                              Hebrews 2:9–18 (E)
Genesis 2:18–24
                              Mark 10:2–16 (C) (L)
                              Mark 10:2–9 (E)
                              Mark 10:2–12 (RC)

Meditation on the Texts

We give thanks to you, O God, because you make secure and blessed the lives of those who walk in your ways. You have given us the joy of family life, calling us to live with spouses who become bone of our bones and flesh of our flesh. As Jesus took the children to himself, so you have enabled us to see the fulfillment of life in our children. You have reached out to us in many ways through the prophets and most fully in the life of your Son, even Jesus Christ. We take confidence because we have seen Jesus enter into our experience, even suffering and death, and know that you have made him the pioneer and perfecter of our faith. In his name we pray. Amen.

Commentary on the Texts

Mark 10:2–16 (C) (L)

Mark 10:2–9 (E)

Mark 10:2–12 (RC)

The setting for Jesus' teaching is given in v. 1, which is not included in the reading. Jesus and his disciples are leaving Galilee and moving into Judea toward Jerusalem. His teaching still attracts the crowds and those who seek to discredit him. In vs. 2–12 Mark records the test the Pharisees put to Jesus when they asked him if it was lawful for a man to divorce his wife. The question about divorce may have implications beyond Jesus' treatment of the law of Moses. Since they were in the area across the Jordan River, they were in the territory ruled by Herod Antipas. Antipas had ordered the execution of John the Baptist because John had criticized him for marrying his brother's wife. Verses 13–16 deal with the blessing of children and the rebuke of the disciples to the parents which made Jesus indignant.

The section on marriage and divorce (vs. 2–12) is a Gentile-Christian adaptation of Jesus' original teaching, reflecting the setting of the Markan community. The evidence for this is in vs. 11–12. In the Jewish community adultery was not a crime against the wife but against the other woman's husband. In Matthew 19:9 we find what is likely a more accurate statement of Jesus' teaching omitting the phrase "against her." He says, "And I say to you: whoever divorces his wife, except for unchastity, and marries another, commits adultery." While the wife did not have the right to divorce her husband in Jesus' environment, she did according to the customs of Roman society. Notice that Matthew omits any reference to the wife divorcing the husband, and Luke does not include any of this teaching.

The central issue of the text is the ideal of marriage set forth by Jesus. He cites Genesis

1:27 and 2:24 as revealing the real purpose of God regarding marriage from the time of creation. In the ancient world the sexual act, not love or the marriage ritual, was the thing that united a man and a woman in marriage. But the sex act alone is not enough to explain how two people can become one flesh (personality) in a marriage in which they become true companions. Jesus saw the uniting of a man and a woman as an act of God, an act so mysterious that one cannot explain it in human terms: "What God has joined together, let no person put asunder." However, to treat his teaching legalistically would be inconsistent with Jesus' own attitude toward the law.

The issue of marriage and divorce in Jesus' day, as in ours, was not a mere academic question discussed by the rabbis but was very much an existential issue. There were two positions on divorce in Jesus' time: (1) Rabbi Hillel and his followers practiced a very lenient interpretation of Deuteronomy 24:1 and permitted a man to divorce his wife for minor matters, such as burning his dinner or if he found someone he liked better; (2) Rabbi Shammai and his school of thought allowed divorce only on the grounds of adultery. Matthew 19:9 adapts Jesus' statement to the view of the stricter school of thought. The view of divorce that Mark gives, without any exception for adultery, is similar to that found in 1 Corinthians 7:10–11: "To the married I give charge, not I but the Lord, that the wife should not separate from her husband (but if she does, let her remain single or else be reconciled to her husband)—and that the husband should not divorce his wife."

The provision of Deuteronomy was one of mercy and justice, since it helped women by requiring divorce rather than mere abandonment. Deuteronomy 24:1–4 was a concession to the hardness of the hearts of people. It is likely that Jesus saw it as an excuse for irresponsible conduct and so adopted a stricter view of divorce. Jesus puts both sexes on the same level, in contrast to the Jewish law which allowed divorce only by men.

In vs. 10–12 we see again a characteristic of Mark's Gospel—the disciples need Jesus to give them a private explanation. Matthew does not mention any private teaching.

Jesus and the children who are brought to him are the topic of vs. 13–16. There is a poignant beauty about this passage, since Jesus was on his way to the cross and he knew it, yet he found time for children!

The children are brought to Jesus so that he might touch them and give them his blessing. It was customary to bring children to a great person, such as Jesus, on the child's birthday. But the disciples rebuked them (the parents). Apart from the Gospels, there is no expression of sympathy toward children in other Christian literature or in secular literature of that period.

The disciples fail to understand the relation of children to the kingdom and apparently want to save Jesus from embarrassing attentions. But Jesus rebukes the disciples. Perhaps they remembered his rebuke of Peter earlier when Peter sought to protect him from suffering. The disciples still have difficulty understanding what Jesus is doing. In this setting, Jesus expresses one of the best-known sayings of the Bible: "Let the children come to me, do not hinder them; for to such belongs the kingdom of God. Truly, I say to you, whoever does not receive the kingdom of God like a child shall not enter it" (vs. 14–15).

Jesus treasured certain qualities about a child: humility, obedience, trust, and an incapacity to bear grudges. To receive the kingdom of God as a child is to depend in trustful simplicity on the grace that God offers.

Recommended work: Look up marriage and divorce in a Bible dictionary to get a fuller picture of the biblical teaching on this important subject.

The sermon may begin with the ideal of marriage, as Jesus recalls the Genesis account. Then the provision of divorce for "hardness of heart" may be put into this context. The relationship of grace and forgiveness to the sin that leads to divorce might well be explored. The attitude of Jesus toward the children offers another insight into family life.

Genesis 2:18–24

In the first account of creation (Gen. 1:1–2:4a) the Priestly writer presents male and female as created together in one act. But the Yahwist in the second account (2:4b–25), of which this reading is a part, pictures the man as created first alone and put in the Garden of Eden to till it. But God recognized that it was not good for the man to be alone.

Man is social by nature, created in the image of God (1:26), who by nature is social, one God in three persons.

God creates the animals but none is suitable for the man as a helper. Nor does God intend to be man's "helper." None of the creatures is suitable, so there must be a new creature. This calls for a fresh creative act of God, which brings forth one of the profoundest images of the entire Old Testament. God makes woman out of man's essential stuff. Someone has commented that woman was made, not from man's head to be over him, or from man's foot to be under him, but from his rib to be equal and a companion to him. The deeper relationship between man and woman is pictured by the creating of woman from the man's rib.

The creation of woman is stunning and unpredicted. The two creatures of surprise, the man and the woman, now belong together. They are one in covenant in one flesh. The garden exists as the context for the human community in which the man and the woman are the first members.

God takes the role of "father of the bride" and leads the woman to present her to the man (v. 22). The man has an "Aha" experience. He instantly recognizes that the new creature, the woman, is one belonging completely to him (and by implication, he to her) and he gives her the name Woman. The naming here, as with the other creatures earlier, expresses a previous inward interpretive insight. From man, *ish,* is made woman, *ishshah.*

The narrator of the tale provides a short conclusion, or epilogue, in vs. 24–25. It explains the extremely powerful attraction of the male and the female being for each other. This strong attraction does not come to rest until the two again become one flesh in the child created by their union. The man and the woman were originally one flesh and thus by destiny belong together.

The statement about the man forsaking father and mother and cleaving to his wife does not fully reflect the patriarchal family customs of Israel, since in that setting the woman breaks from her family more than does the man. However, the passage could preserve something from an earlier matriarchal culture. Still, the point of the passage is not legal custom but natural drives.

Verse 25 serves a coupling function by pointing both backward and forward. The man and the woman were naked but not ashamed. Shame is the correlative of sin and guilt (3:7). They had not yet sinned and thus had no reason to fear that the body would show sin in them.

The Hebrew words for "one flesh" imply one personality. This is the ideal of companionship marriage in which two persons unite in love and form a third personality, their marriage. So the mathematics of marriage is both $1+1=1$ (the two become one flesh) and $1+1=3$ (the man and the woman retain their identities while still forming a third, their marriage).

One way of interpreting vs. 24–25 is as follows:

1. A man leaves his father and mother—severance.
2. He cleaves to his wife—permanence.
3. They become one flesh—union in companionship marriage.
4. They were both naked and were not ashamed—intimacy.

Recommended work: In a commentary, study carefully the comparison and the contrast of the two stories of the creation of humankind to appreciate more fully the nuances of the biblical understanding of humanity and sexuality.

The four points listed above could be used as an outline of the moves of the sermon. One might go on to relate this passage to Ephesians 5 in which the marriage partners are enjoined to be subject to one another in love.

Hebrews 1:1–4; 2:9–11 (C)

Hebrews 2:9–11 (L) (RC)

Hebrews 2:9–18 (E)

Hebrews 1:1–4 forms the prologue to the Letter to the Hebrews which declares the author's theme, the superiority of Christianity to Judaism. Note the sharp contrast between "of old" and "in these last days he has spoken to us by a Son." Yet the God who has spoken now is the same God who spoke in the old days. The Son in whom God now speaks is the exact counterpart of God (v. 3). The Son not only had part in creation (John 1:1–3) but continues to sustain the universe (1:3). After completing his priestly work of purification for sins, the Son was enthroned in royal splendor. Christ is a prophet in that God spoke forth in him, and Christ is also priest, the mediator, and king, the ruler.

These verses describe the progressive character of biblical revelation. God spoke to earlier generations by the prophets, but that communication was piecemeal and partial. Now God has spoken in full through the Son. "In these last days" (1:2) is an Old Testament phrase indicating the time of fulfillment.

"He sat down at the right hand of the Majesty on high" stresses the finality of the work of the Son. The right hand was the place of honor. The statement that Christ is enthroned at God's right hand echoes the words spoken to the Davidic king (Ps. 110:1). Here the enthronement is seen as evidence of the perfect and unrepeatable nature of Christ's sacrifice on behalf of the people. It is evidence of the finality of Christianity. Sitting in the presence of God was a royal prerogative of Davidic kings.

The Son is as much superior to angels as is his name, Son, more excellent than theirs (1:4–5). He is superior to the angels both by the title "Son" and by his exaltation to the throne of God. "Superior" is used thirteen times in Hebrews of Christ and his new order in contrast to what went before.

In 2:9–11 we find that the exaltation of Jesus is the consequence of his humiliation as described in 12:2, "looking to Jesus the pioneer and perfecter of our faith, who for the joy that was set before him endured the cross, despising the shame, and is seated at the right hand of the throne of God."

There are two difficulties in 2:9. First, the phrase "crowned with glory and honor" seems to interrupt the flow of the sentence. Unless the text has been disturbed, and it does not appear to be from manuscript evidence, then it is best to take these words as a parenthesis reminding the reader that the humiliation had a glorious outcome. The second problem is that the phrase "by the grace of God" appears as "apart from God" in some manuscripts. In Greek the words for "grace" (*charis*) and "apart" (*chōris*) are similar in spelling. The original meaning might be that Jesus tasted death for everyone except God. Or it may have referred to Jesus' sense of abandonment on the cross. But the wording "by the grace of God" fits well with the opening words of 2:10 and probably is the original. Note that "to taste death" does not mean to sample death lightly, as we might taste a gourmet dish, but rather to *experience* death (see Mark 9:1).

"But we see Jesus" is a great turning point for our approach to all of the experiences of life. Jesus is the answer God gives to our every human failure and is our hope when we despair. The pessimist reads the headlines of the daily paper or watches the evening television news and sees what happens as if there were a period, ending the story. But the Christian puts a comma there, for "we see Jesus" who is the Lord of the nations, the Prince of peace, the Hope of God to human beings.

In 2:10, "it was fitting" means that what happens was in accord with God's nature. The high destiny of human beings which is described in Psalm 8 is to be gained through the work of Christ. The idea of "to make perfect" is characteristic of Hebrews and means to make complete or bring to maturity. There is no reference here to a process leading to moral perfection but rather to Jesus' completely adequate qualification for leading people to full and complete salvation. It was fitting that God should achieve the goal of salvation for all human beings by the means of Christ's incarnation.

The word translated "pioneer" in Greek can also mean author and leader. Jesus is the pioneer, not in the sense of the lone hero breaking the trail to salvation but rather as the victorious leader of salvation.

Recommended work: Consult a commentary or an introduction to the Letter to the Hebrews to get a broad perspective on the way in which this book compares the life and work of Christ to the Old Testament.

Compare the way in which God had spoken through the prophets and the way in which God now speaks through Jesus, the Son of God who reflects the very glory of God. This same Son of God has entered into our human experience, even suffering death. But in his resurrection, we too share in the hope of salvation and life in the presence of God.

Theological Reflection

The Genesis account of the creation of man and woman provides the background for the Markan passage dealing with the ideal of marriage in which man and woman become one flesh. The theological thrust here is one of permanency, fidelity, and intimacy in marriage. Jesus blesses the children brought to him as a sign of his love for children. In doing so, Jesus expresses his love for a group ordinarily not held in high regard in society and thus expresses his unique kind of love. The Hebrews passage introduces the book with its theme of the superiority of Christianity to Judaism. The revelation of God in Jesus Christ who is the exact counterpart of God is an expression of the incarnation.

Children's Message

One artist has shown Jesus surrounded by children of many different races and nations. The preacher may want to use the picture, or some other illustration of children of various races, as a focus for the children's attention. If Jesus invites us all, large and small, black, white, red, and yellow, to share his love, then we also are called to share that love with all others.

Hymns for Pentecost 20

For the Beauty of the Earth; Thou Didst Leave Thy Throne; Look, Ye Saints, the Sight Is Glorious.

Pentecost 21

Ordinary Time 28

Proper 23

Psalm 90:1–12 (C)	Hebrews 4:1–3, 9–13 (C)
Psalm 90:12–17 (L) (RC)	Hebrews 3:1–6 (L) (E)
Psalm 90 or 90:1–8, 12 (E)	Hebrews 4:12–13 (RC)

Genesis 3:8–19 (C)	Mark 10:17–30 (C)
Amos 5:6–7, 10–15 (L) (E)	Mark 10:17–27 (28–30) (L)
Wisdom 7:7–11 (RC)	Mark 10:17–27 (28–31) (E)

Meditation on the Texts

O Lord, we thank you for the gift of eternal life through faith in Jesus Christ. We know that with human effort alone salvation is impossible but that all things are possible with you, our God. May we not be like the rich man who ran to Jesus asking what he had to do to inherit eternal life but went away sorrowful, for he loved possessions more than God. May we always consider Jesus, the apostle and high priest of our confession who was faithful over your house as a son. We pray that we may always strive to enter into your rest which you have promised. As preachers of the word we thank you for your living word which is active and sharper than any two-edged sword, piercing to the division of soul and spirit and discerning the thoughts and intentions of the heart. May we always seek you, the Lord, and live confident that you will be with us. We commit ourselves to seek good and not evil and to seek to establish justice for all people. As we pray, we ask for wisdom and understanding that we may serve you well in our time. We thank you for Christ who saves us from our disobedience. Amen.

Commentary on the Texts

Mark 10:17–30 (C)

Mark 10:17–27 (28–30) (L)

Mark 10:17–27 (28–31) (E)

This is the account of the rich man who came to Jesus and Jesus' teaching to the disciples on riches and the kingdom. The story of the rich man in vs. 17–22 is a unit. Note that vs. 28–30 seem to have been added as a result of the experiences of the church, perhaps its persecutions. Also note that vs. 23–27 may have developed slowly over a period of time and include one of Mark's favorite expressions in v. 23. This makes a transition from an individual case to a universal teaching. It seems that vs. 23b, 25, and 27 are traditional sayings of Jesus dealing with the dangers of riches. They seem to have been added, since vs. 17–22 deal with discipleship, not riches. If added, this was probably done before Mark was composed.

The man is sometimes called "the rich young ruler," since Matthew says he was a young man and Luke says he was a ruler and all three indicate he was rich. Mark calls him simply "a man." Every reader can identify with him, since Mark does not specify who he was. We might call him "everyperson."

It was common for students to ask rabbis about how to share in life and similar questions. This man wants to accomplish more than what an ordinary person does. It was common at that time to speak of inheriting (meaning receiving) what God had promised.

Israel, when true to its faith, recognized that the future inheritance depended upon God's gracious promise and that alone. Eternal life means the final existence in the presence of God beyond the grave. It is a radically new quality of life.

He called Jesus "Good Teacher," but Jesus rejects this title and says no one is good but God alone. The church did not regard Jesus' sinlessness as an unchanging attribute but as something that was manifested through Jesus' temptations. The church in this text seems to set forth the mystery it encounters in Jesus and says that Jesus does not call attention to himself but points to God who is greater.

Jesus reminds him of the commandments, pointing to those dealing with relationships to other people, and the man says he has observed them from his youth. Jesus did not take this as pride but loved him as he looked on him and then commanded him to "Go . . . sell . . . give . . . follow me." Jesus calls him to discipleship as the way to enter the kingdom and receive eternal life. Discipleship is a matter of total commitment. The man was unwilling to sell and give and follow, and the dismay on his face revealed his rejection of Jesus' call.

Then in v. 23 Mark stresses that what follows applies to every disciple and wants the reader to hear Jesus' call to respond in discipleship. In v. 24 we see how amazed the disciples were over Jesus' comment on the difficulty those who have riches will have in entering the kingdom.

It was thought at that time that wealth made possible the performance of religious duties such as the giving of alms and therefore the disciples are shocked to hear Jesus say that riches make it hard to enter the kingdom. The thrust of Jesus' teaching is that human beings by nature do not submit to God's rule. Submission to God is essential for salvation.

In v. 25 there is a proverb describing entrance into the kingdom by a rich man as being as impossible as a camel going through the eye of a needle. We must not try to explain this metaphor in an effort to remove its difficult teaching. We must see it as grotesque and thus even more impressive. The disciples are exceedingly astonished and ask who can be saved, meaning enter the kingdom. Jesus' teaching is relevant not only in the case of the rich man but to everyone. No one can enter the kingdom on her or his merits. Discipleship is a gift of grace which one can only receive obediently.

Peter told Jesus that the disciples had left everything to follow Jesus (but Peter took his wife on his missionary travels). Jesus' promise in v. 30 is remarkable, since it includes every aspect of human life. Jesus' demand to "leave all" for the kingdom is actually an invitation to find the gift of eternal life in the giving of oneself. Thus, following Jesus does not lead to poverty or an ascetic life but to the experience of real life, the life of wholeness. But such a life calls for a radical decision to trust in God and not riches or anything else. The reference to persecutions indicates that this happens to disciples here and now, along with fullness of life, but in the age to come life will be free of temptations and persecutions.

Recommended work: Do a word study of riches, astonished, and eternal life.

The sermon might deal only with the rich man and the temptation to let riches prevent our following Jesus and receiving eternal life. Or it might be developed using images and movements from the whole passage, with the climax coming in v. 30 with the promise of eternal life in the age to come. The sermon should draw each hearer in as "everyperson" who is confronted by Jesus to go, sell, give, and follow him.

Genesis 3:8–19 (C)

Our pericope is part of a chapter whose theme is the Fall. The whole chapter should be read in preparing to study our pericope. This story is a myth in that it conveys religious truth through metaphors and symbols. God is described in human terms as "walking in the garden" as an oriental ruler might do. The man and the woman hid from God among the trees. Anxiety moved them to hide. God asks, "Where are you?" which may be interpreted not only in terms of location in the garden but in terms of relationship to God. The man admits he was afraid because he was naked and so hid himself. When God asks if he has eaten of the forbidden tree, Adam accuses God by saying that the woman God gave him gave him the fruit and he ate.

In vs. 14–19 the story seeks to explain a number of things: why the serpent crawls rather than walks and why humans are hostile toward it, why women have pain in childbirth, woman's sexual desire for her husband (and her motherly impulse), and woman's subordinate position to man in the society of ancient Israel when this story developed.

Notice that work is not evil in itself but was affected by the human beings' broken relationship with God. Work became toil, and the ground was cursed. Humans are to toil all their days until they die and return to the dust from which they come. The relationship between the power of evil and human beings is one of enmity, as the story tells us, and this will continue throughout all generations. But in this continuing struggle, humans will gain the clearer victory (v. 15). There is a sense of optimism in this tradition which affirms that God's saving acts will prevail. This is the first vague message of victory, a victory Christians see revealed in Christ.

Recommended work: Read this passage in several translations and note their differences. Ask what "worldview" the story reveals regarding woman's relationship to man and sin and how this must be interpreted in the light of the whole of scripture and church teachings.

The sermon might show the results of human disobedience to God as related in this story and in society today: domestic strife, wars, famine, unemployment, and so forth. It should lead to an affirmation of God's victory over the power of evil through Jesus' death and resurrection. The sermon should stress how this victory over evil is manifested in the Christian's daily living.

Amos 5:6–7, 10–15 (L) (E)

Our pericope is part of the third of God's testimonies against Israel in vs. 1–17. Note that v. 6 is a call to seek the Lord and live lest God's judgment break out like a fire against the people. The northern kingdom is called the house of Joseph. The unjust judges turn justice into wormwood and destroy righteousness (v. 7).

The foundation of this righteousness and call for justice in the law court is the covenant relationship between God and Israel, although Amos does not use the word "covenant." Amos does not define righteousness, since it was so well known and stood at the core of Israel's life. Wormwood was a very bitter tasting plant. So Amos warns those who turn justice into wormwood that they are in danger of God who will break out like fire to judge.

Amos denounces judges who abuse civil justice and make the court process into injustice for the poor and oppressed. The gate was the public square just inside the city gate where both public meetings and courts of law were held. Verse 10 continues the denunciation of v. 7. The exploiters despise those who protest against their injustice (v. 10). They also abhor these protestors who speak the truth. Then in v. 11 there is a shift to the second person, which may indicate that a second oracle begins here.

In vs. 10–13 Amos focuses on the exploitation of the poor. Amos has pronounced judgment on those who exploit the poor (vs. 6–7), but now he adds "exactions" and "bribes" to his list of wicked acts against the poor. The exactions were extortions in the grain market, and the bribe (v. 12) perverted justice in the law court. In v. 11 Amos warns the profiteers that they will never enjoy the luxury of their "houses of hewn stone" and "pleasant vineyards."

In the coming evil time of God's judgment those who have tried to manipulate God and have done injustice will find that they have not been successful. Consider that "successful" is a preferred translation to "prudent." Those who have been "successful" will be shocked into stunned silence.

Amos issues a third call to seek and live (vs. 14–15). This is the prophet's final plea for right seeking. In v. 6 it was "Seek the LORD," and now Amos says, "Seek good, and not evil." Life is the reward for those who seek the Lord and seek good. The meaning of seeking good is to respond to God in obedience so that the Lord will be with you. The primary goal of God's people must be to seek good rather than evil, says Amos. Good includes a whole range of moral and spiritual possibilities, but in this instance it points to justice in the law court. Seeking good must become the inner motivation of life. It is not enough to avoid doing evil and simply do good. Israel must hate evil and love good!

Those who seek God and seek goodwill and are transformed in their inner character will form a remnant in the coming judgment. This expresses the hope that there will be some survivors in the coming judgment described in v. 3, where only a tenth will be spared. The remnant of Joseph here refers to all Israel which is seen as rather small (7:2). Amos' message goes directly counter to the claims of those who argue that Israel's present prosperity is evidence of God's presence in their midst. Rather, he calls the people to turn from injustice and to seek God and good.

Recommended work: Do a word study of righteousness, justice, good, and remnant. Do background reading of life in Israel at the time of Amos' prophetic ministry.

The sermon might deal with the images and moves of the passage, pointing out the injustices of our judicial system today and the ways in which bribes, extortion, and trampling on the poor take place. The message of Amos is especially relevant for American society in which the rich are getting richer and the poor and middle class are getting poorer. The hope of a remnant of the faithful points to the grace of God. The sermon should include a call to repentance and assurance of God's gracious mercy to those who turn from evil and return to God in obedience.

Wisdom 7:7–11 (RC)

Our pericope is a section of vs. 1–22a which describe how Solomon received wisdom from God. The preacher is urged to read 1 Kings 3:5–15 in conjunction with our pericope, since it tells of Solomon's dream and his request for understanding from God.

Solomon recognized his need for wisdom, prayed for and received it, and then valued it above all other gifts. Then, in v. 11, we learn that with this gift of wisdom Solomon received "all good things," including friendship with God (v. 14) and unerring knowledge of all that exists (v. 17).

In the first six verses of the chapter, Solomon recounts his birth and points out that his wisdom was not due to any inherited understanding. "For no king has had a different beginning of existence" (v. 5). This sets the stage for Solomon's declaration in v. 7, "Therefore I prayed, and understanding was given me." He prayed for wisdom because he recognized how important it was to obtain and possess it. He loved wisdom, portrayed as a woman, more than health and beauty. The source of Solomon's wisdom was God's wisdom. Solomon's wisdom is remembered best for his decision in the dispute between two women over a baby (1 Kings 3:16–28). Solomon displayed his wisdom best in such decisions rather than in the larger and more difficult matters of statecraft.

God answered the prayer for wisdom and with it came also all good things and uncounted wealth. Solomon rejoiced in them because wisdom leads them and is their mother (v. 12).

Recommended work: Do a word study of wisdom and prayer, and do a biographical study of Solomon.

The sermon might be directed especially to young people as they seek to set goals in life. The sermon might deal with examples of the foolishness of making money, pleasure, power, and fame one's god. God's wisdom might be described in a brief story and then commended as the greatest goal of all, for it includes friendship with God and all other things.

Hebrews 3:1–6 (L)(E)

In this passage Christ is portrayed as superior to Moses who also had been appointed by God and was faithful in God's house. The author stresses the transcendence of Jesus in comparison to Moses. While Moses was faithful in all God's house, Jesus as the Son of God received from God a higher standard and authority. While Moses represents the religion of the law and God's revelation through it, Jesus is the final revealer of God. Jesus' personal relation to God as "Son" (v. 6) confers on him an authority far greater than all other claims. We can read between the lines here the ongoing conflict between the Jewish community and the Christian community as Hebrews was being written.

Notice that the author calls the audience "holy brethren, who share in a heavenly call" (v. 1). This is another of the author's favorite terms, like "drawing near to God" and "running the race set before us." The "heavenly call" points to the End time aspects of the Christian faith. It reveals the inevitable tension at the heart of the Christian life between living here and now and our life with God yet to come at the End. We are drawn by Jesus into a pathway that leads to God, for Jesus is the apostle (one sent) and high priest of our confession.

The author of Hebrews sees his readers in a crisis situation much like that of Israel in the wilderness. The Christian life is a new exodus, and Jesus, not Moses, is the one who leads the way to a heavenly place of rest, God's eternal kingdom. But everything in this journey depends upon holding fast our confidence and pride in our hope (v. 6). Christians live in the last "Now" of time, since Jesus has announced the eternal order.

Recommended work: Do a comparison of the life of Moses and the life of Jesus, using a Bible dictionary. Do a word study of heaven, faithful, confidence, and hope.

The sermon might move in setting up a comparison between Jesus and Moses, showing how Jesus is counted as worthy of more glory than Moses, for he was faithful over God's house as a son. The sermon should show the tension between living as Christians here and now and our hope for eternal rest in the heavenly home. The key is holding fast our confidence and pride in our hope.

Hebrews 4:1–3, 9–13 (C)

Hebrews 4:12–13 (RC)

We will deal with vs. 1–3 and 9–13 which include both of the above selections. The thrust of vs. 1–12 is the rest which God has promised. Christianity is a life in which we, at every moment, are exposed to the cutting edge, the drastic operation of God's word (vs. 11–12). This is a living word and is active, meaning that it gets things done. The Word lays open our lives to God's judgment at every moment, so that we live a life that already has the nature of eternity in it.

The rest that God has promised will be given, but it remains for Christians to appropriate it (vs. 1 and 6).

The Sabbath rest, of vs. 9–10, points to God's rest after the work of creating all things (Gen. 2:2). But it also points forward to the eternal rest that God gives after the toils of this life are ended. This rest is for the people of God. It is not a temporary rest but God's own final and perfect rest, as v. 10 states.

Notice the contrast between the promise of Sabbath rest for the people of God, followed immediately by warning against the ever-present danger of disobedience (v. 11). The author personifies the word of God, saying that it is active and living. But the author does not even hint at a comparison of the word with Jesus Christ. Nor does it mean the Hebrew Scriptures.

There are many parallels to the word of God as a sword, found in Ephesians 6:17 and elsewhere. The Word here refers to God speaking.

Recommended work: Do a word study of word of God and of rest. The preacher may want to read an introduction to the Letter to the Hebrews to become familiar with the thought forms and images that the author uses.

The sermon may develop the tension between the promise of entering God's rest and the fear of failing to reach it through disobedience. Entering this rest depends upon faith. God's word sees into the hearts of all, for it is living and active. The good news of assurance of salvation attested by the Holy Spirit in our hearts should be declared.

Theological Reflection

The passage from Mark sets forth the demands of discipleship, especially in contrast to love of possessions. It points up that salvation is a miraculous gift from God, whether for a poor person or a rich man. The Genesis passage describes some of the results of Adam and Eve's disobedience, including pain in childbearing, the cursing of the ground, and toil in earning one's bread. Because of their disobedience, God makes death an inevitable fate that haunts humans throughout their lives. In the Amos passage the prophet calls the people to seek the Lord and to seek good and thereby live. He warns those who do injustice and oppress the poor that God's fire may break out against them and devour them. He promises that if they seek justice in the gate (courts), it may be that God will be gracious to the remnant. In the reading from Wisdom, the prayer of Solomon for wisdom is described. It is compared to other things he might have prayed for, but wisdom is superior to all. God granted him wisdom, and along with it God gave him friendship, and unerring knowledge of what exists, and all good things. The Hebrews 3:1–6 passage contrasts Jesus and Moses and urges readers to hold fast their confidence and hope. The Hebrews 4:1–3, 9–13 passage sets forth the rest that God has promised and the warning not to drift into disobedience of God. God's word is a living and active force and discerns the thoughts and intentions of all.

Children's Message

The Mark passage might be used, with the story of the rich, young ruler who came asking what he had to do to inherit eternal life. Jesus' story of how impossible it is for a camel to go through the eye of a needle may be told. The emphasis should be on God's gift of love and salvation which no one, rich or poor, can earn or deserve.

Hymns for Pentecost 21

Jesus, I My Cross Have Taken; God's Word Is like a Flaming Sword; Our God, Our Help in Ages Past.

Pentecost 22

Ordinary Time 29

Proper 24

Psalm 35:17–28 (C)
Psalm 91:9–16 (L)
Psalm 33:4–5, 18–20, 22 (RC)
Psalm 91 or 91:9–16 (E)

Hebrews 4:14–16 (C)
Hebrews 4:9–16 (L)
Hebrews 4:12–16 (E)

Mark 10:35–45

Isaiah 53:7–12 (C)
Isaiah 53:10–12 (L)
Isaiah 53:10–11 (RC)
Isaiah 53:4–12 (E)

Meditation on the Texts

Merciful God, we thank you for your Son who came not to be served but to serve and to give his life as a ransom for many. Forgive us when we have sought the places of honor here and now and in the kingdom. May we never forget that whoever would be great must be a servant and whoever would be first must be slave of all. We remember your Servant described by Isaiah who has borne our griefs and carried our sorrows. We see in Christ's life the fulfillment of the Servant's mission who bore the sin of many and made intercession for the transgressors. We thank you for Jesus who is a great high priest who has passed through the heavens, who is able to sympathize with our weaknesses. For he was tempted as we are, yet without sin. Let us draw near to your throne of grace with confidence so that we may receive mercy and find grace to help in time of need. Amen.

Commentary on the Texts

Mark 10:35–45

In this passage we find the ignorance of the disciples contrasted with true discipleship. James and John seek honor in the coming kingdom. But Jesus tells them they do not know what they are asking and then tells all the disciples that whoever would be great among them must be their servant. The passage concludes with Jesus' message that the Son of man came to serve and give his life as ransom for many.

In the immediately preceding passage Jesus gave his third teaching concerning the suffering of the Son of man who would rise after three days. Our pericope is given "on the road" as Jesus and the disciples go to Jerusalem where the passion will take place. The context of this passage reveals its importance in preparing the disciples for what will soon take place.

The ambition of James and John is revealed in our passage. Mark pictures them as selfishly seeking the chief seats in heaven, on Jesus' right hand and on his left. Jesus takes this occasion to teach all the disciples humility, and in doing so he puts the disciples, especially James and John, in a poor light. Luke omits the James/John part entirely, and Matthew alters the story to shift the stigma to the mother of James and John. But in doing so, Matthew does not make the story consistent (Matt. 20:20–28).

It seems that v. 45 is an explanation of what has been said earlier and was added by the church. Although we cannot identify any specific allusions to Isaiah 53 in the wording of this passage, it probably is based on the church's understanding of Isaiah 53.

The question of James and John about places of honor in the kingdom and Jesus' reply in vs. 38ff. show the amazing fashion in which God's way runs directly counter to all human thinking. Jesus asks the brothers if they are able to drink the cup that he drinks or to be baptized with the baptism with which he is baptized (v. 38).

The cup of suffering is an Old Testament metaphor. Often it is used to symbolize the pleasant or bitter experiences of life. The psalmist speaks of his cup overflowing with God's goodness (Ps. 23:5), and God's wrath must be drunk by Israel (Isa. 51:17). Here Mark indicates that James and John were willing to drink from Christ's cup of suffering, meaning their moral participation in his passion. In the *Martyrdom of Isaiah,* a second-century A.D. Jewish writing, the cup refers to martyrdom: "For me only God hath mingled the cup [of martyrdom]."

Baptism in v. 38 has been the subject of much debate among church scholars through the ages. The Greek word for "baptize" used here means "to drown." In its passive form it means "to go under." Here baptism is symbolic of death, as it is in other passages, such as Luke 12:50 and Romans 6:3–4.

In this context drinking the cup and undergoing the baptism of Jesus refer to the martyrdom of Jesus and the two disciples. But in other contexts their symbolic character would allow them to be interpreted as referring to any suffering for the faith, as in Psalm 75:8f.; Isaiah 51:17; and elsewhere.

The goal of the journey to Jerusalem is thus passion, not pilgrimage. Jesus will be hailed "King of the Jews," but his coronation will mean his death and his throne will be a cross. Mark does not say explicitly that Jesus knew all that was going to happen in Jerusalem ahead of time. Mark's text stresses Jesus' limitations rather than his divine power. When James and John ask Jesus to grant them to sit on his right side and on his left side in glory, he replies that this is not for him to grant. Not only the allotting of places of honor but also the date of his own return in glory are not within the power or knowledge of Mark's Jesus. The picture of Jesus that Mark paints for us does not elicit marvel from us over Jesus' foreknowledge; rather, it moves us to reflect on his sense of the purpose of his life and death. This purpose comes into sharp focus in v. 45: "For the Son of man also came not to be served but to serve, and to give his life as a ransom for many." This verse is the climax and conclusion of the discipleship section of 8:22–10:52. In these words of v. 45 Jesus interprets his ministry, indicating the meaning of his life and death. Some scholars question whether it is a genuine saying of Jesus or a statement from the early church. The real question is whether or not they are true. Scripture, especially Isaiah 53 as it describes the Servant of the Lord, describes Jesus in terms of his service and death for others. The greatest service of Jesus for humankind was his giving of his life as a ransom for many.

"Many" in Greek usage meant a large number but not all. In this verse it has a Jewish meaning indicating the multitude as over against the individual. Thus "many" does not mean that some might *not* be included, although this is a real possibility.

The word "ransom" in Greek was used to describe buying the freedom of prisoners of war, slaves, or condemned criminals. The sum paid was a "ransom." (Reflect on ransoms paid for kidnapped persons or hijacked planes today.) The process of setting the person ransomed free was called redemption. And the person who did the liberating was called the redeemer. Recall that Moses alone is called redeemer (deliverer) in the New Testament (Acts 7:35).

It may be helpful at this point to examine the structure of this passage which is parallel to other passion prediction units. It may be divided into setting (v. 32), prediction (vs. 33–34), misunderstanding (vs. 35–40), and instruction in discipleship (vs. 41–45). Our pericope is the third in a series of three passion units. The first is 8:27–9:1 set in Caesarea Philippi. The second, 9:30–50, is set in Capernaum. The third one, 10:32–45, has the fullest and most explicit setting and prediction of any of the three.

As you read the pericope, be conscious of how the text invites readers to identify with the Twelve as the stumbling and shaky servants of Jesus. Every reader of Mark can identify with some party involved in the death of Jesus. Each person who answers yes to the question posed by the spiritual "Were you there when they crucified my Lord?" can also be assured that he or she is one of the many for whom Christ gave his life as a ransom. So the text draws us readers into the action to hear both judgment for our role as sinners in the death of Jesus and also the good news that Jesus died for us while we were yet sinners.

The reference to redemption is found only here in the New Testament, in Mark's record of Jesus' ministry. The link between service and vicarious suffering would be a natural one for Jesus to make, influenced as he apparently was by the concept of the Servant in Second Isaiah 53:11–12 especially (part of our pericope for today). Compare the reference to "many" in this Isaiah passage and to the "many" of v. 45. In preparing a sermon on this passage, the preacher will find a study of Isaiah 53:4–12 relevant. Jesus' service was expressed in his atoning death for all people.

We should note in passing that there is considerable scholarly debate over whether or not v. 45 is original. The reader is referred to D. E. Nineham, *Saint Mark,* pp. 280–281, for a synopsis of this issue.

Jesus makes it clear in this pericope that true discipleship is marked by humble service and a pouring out of one's life for another. Jesus reverses the world's values and power structure to show that in the kingdom the one who would be great must be the servant and the one who would be first must be slave of all. This new norm of conduct calling for becoming the servant of all is made possible only by Jesus' own mission of service. The title "Son of man" (v. 45) shows Jesus' authority and reinforces the paradox of his voluntary lowliness.

Recommended work: Do a word study of servant and slave, ransom, cup, and baptize. The preacher may want to review Jesus' action in washing the disciples' feet at the Last Supper as well as his death on the cross as he demonstrated the meaning of lowly service.

The sermon may develop the moves found in the passage, proceeding from the request of James and John for seats of honor to Jesus' saying about the Son of man giving his life as a ransom for many, pointing out that the places on Jesus' right hand and left hand on the cross were occupied by robbers. The images of serving tables and washing feet may be used to illustrate Jesus' teaching. The sermon may move from acts of service to Jesus' supreme service in dying for many on the cross to the resurrection which means victory over sin and death and a new life for all who believe.

Isaiah 53:7–12 (C)

Isaiah 53:10–12 (L)

Isaiah 53:10–11 (RC)

Isaiah 53:4–12 (E)

Our pericope contains part of the fourth Servant song found in 52:13–53:12. In 53:1–3 we have a lament telling how the Servant's background and appearance were undistinguished and revealing that the Servant was rejected by people. Then in vs. 4–6 we are told that the Servant's vicarious suffering is the means of restoring all people to God. The word "whole" in v. 5 means general well-being and is based on the same root as "peace" in 48:18.

Then in vs. 7–9 we are told that the Servant suffers silently, in contrast to sufferers like Jeremiah and Job.

The reference in v. 6 to the people of God being like straying sheep is picked up in v. 7 with the lamb (literally, "sheep") led to the slaughter and the sheep ("ewe") being sheared. These metaphors of people being sheep remind us of Jeremiah 11:19. Such phrases are common in psalms and laments.

The Servant is unjustly condemned, executed, and is buried with the wicked, although he had done no violence. The reference to "rich man" is strange and the Hebrew word may be better translated "rabble" or "evildoers," as some scholars put it.

Notice how rapidly the images follow one another: trial, sentence, death, and burial. There is a problem with the text in v. 8d, and a better translation than the RSV might be, "With transgressors he [the Servant] was stricken to death." When this pericope has been misunderstood, the problem has usually been a result of failing to recognize that metaphors are used. If we take all of these phrases literally, the result is absurd. The metaphors change rapidly, which is characteristic of Hebrew poetry, and they change without being explained. Therefore we should read this passage for the impression it gives rather than seeking an exact description.

There is much that is obscure in vs. 10–12, but one thing is clear: the climax of the death and burial of the Servant in vs. 8–9 is found in renewed life: "He shall see his offspring, he shall prolong his days; . . . he shall see the fruit of the travail of his soul and be satisfied" (vs. 10–11). The Greek translation of v. 11a found in the Septuagint reads "after his travail he shall see light." Although victory was never enjoyed during the Servant's lifetime, it is proclaimed again (see 52:13–15 for the first time). In v. 11 God is the speaker announcing resurrection to the nation.

This Servant song ends as it glorifies the Servant for identifying so closely with his sorrowful fellow Israelites. Although he is sinless and this separates him from other human beings, he identifies with them. The Servant's divine gifts become the means of their salvation.

Recommended work: Do a word study of Servant of the Lord and a comparison of this Servant song with the others. Compare this passage with the Hebrews pericope for today.

The sermon not only should deal with the Servant as described by Second Isaiah in this passage who represents the people of God and their purpose but should proclaim Jesus Christ as the fulfillment of this role of the innocent one who suffers and dies for the guilty. The sermon should stress the metaphors of the passage and show that we are the sheep who have gone astray for whom the Servant died, bearing the sin of many. The resurrection and renewal of life by the Spirit might be the climax of the sermon.

Hebrews 4:14–16 (C)

Hebrews 4:9–16 (L)

Hebrews 4:12–16 (E)

We will deal only with 4:14–16, since the other verses were commented on in the previous Sunday's materials. The author calls Jesus "a great high priest," which is the only time this title is given him. He is called high priest or priest elsewhere. The main thrust of Hebrews is that of Jesus as the perfect high priest whose task it is to bring the voice of God to humans and to bring humans into God's presence. In order to do this, the high priest must know perfectly both humans and God. That is what Hebrews claims Jesus does. (Compare this passage with the Isa. 53:4–12 reading for today.)

Note that v. 14 begins by stressing the greatness and absolute divinity of Jesus, the Son of God. He is great in his essential being. The meaning of "who has passed through the heavens" may mean the heaven of the sky or the heaven of God's presence. Jesus passed through every heaven that exists and is in the presence of God. And Jesus is so great that heaven cannot hold him.

Since we have such a great high priest we are to hold fast our confession of faith in him. Jesus fulfills the two requirements for a priest: he is appointed by God, and he has the ability to sympathize with humans in their weakness.

At God's throne of grace humans receive mercy for past sins and find grace for their present and future needs (v. 16). Grace is the main characteristic of the rule of Christ. Christ rules through grace, unmerited love, not by armies or might. God's strength is expressed in Christ through grace.

Recommended work: Do a word study of priest and high priest, grace and mercy.

The sermon may develop the images of Jesus our great high priest who has identified with sinners yet remaining sinless, of Christ who was tempted as we are and who gave his life as a ransom for many. The message should be one of encouragement, offering the invitation to all to come near to God's throne of grace and receive mercy and grace for every need.

Theological Reflection

The graciousness of God is a theme common to our readings for today. God reveals divine grace to human beings through the Son of man who came to serve and give his life as a ransom for many, as Mark writes. Hebrews invites hearers to come near the throne of grace and receive mercy mediated through Jesus, the Son of God, our great high priest. The Second Isaiah reading describes the Servant of the Lord who bore the sin of many, making himself an offering for sin. This Servant's suffering manifests God's judgment on sin and mercy upon sinful humans.

Children's Message

One approach would be to talk about how we all want to sit in the front seat of the car next to Mom or Dad who is driving. James and John wanted the seats of honor in Jesus' kingdom. But Jesus told them that the greatest person must serve others. He washed the disciples' feet at the Last Supper and served others all his life. Jesus wants us to follow his example of loving service to others.

Hymns for Pentecost 22

Lord, Who Shall Sit Beside Thee?; "Seek Ye First the Kingdom"; You Servants of God, Your Master Proclaim.

Ordinary Time 30

Proper 25

Psalm 126 (C)	**Hebrews 5:1–6 (C)**
Psalm 13 (E)	**Hebrews 5:1–10 (L)**
	Hebrews 5:12–6:1, 9–12 (E)
Jeremiah 31:7–9 (C)	
Isaiah 59:(1–4) 9–19 (E)	**Mark 10:46–52**

Meditation on the Texts

Like blind Bartimaeus who was physically blind, we have too often been spiritually blind to our sin and your grace, O God. Forgive us, as we cry with the blind man, "Son of David, have mercy on me!" May we hear Christ say, "Go your way; your faith has made you well." And may we not only receive new spiritual sight but follow Christ on the way of life. By your Spirit enable us to go on to maturity in the Christian faith. May we be earnest in realizing the full assurance of hope until the end, being imitators of those who through faith and patience inherit the promises. May we no longer grope for the wall like the blind, like those who have no eyes, for Christ has come to open our eyes and set us on the path of eternal life. We come home to you, O God, like Israel returned, praising you and rejoicing. Amen.

Commentary on the Texts

Mark 10:46–52

The restoring of sight to Bartimaeus ("son of Timaeus" in Aramaic) is placed in a strategic spot in Jesus' journey to Jerusalem. It comes just before the Last Week, beginning with the account of Palm Sunday in 11:1 when Jesus enters Jerusalem. Mark wants his hearers to join the blind man in crying out to Jesus, "Son of David, have mercy on me!" and to hear Jesus' reply, "Go your way; your faith has made you well" and then follow Jesus on the way. Parallels are found in Matthew 20:29–34 and Luke 18:35–43, but they do not call the man by name. Matthew tells the story as the healing of two blind men rather than one. One unique thing in this healing story is the introduction of the title "Son of David" for Jesus.

This healing story is particularly significant for those who sit outside the church. Bartimaeus was an outsider. The story may help those who are lost in the crowd but are ready for a vital relationship with Jesus Christ. Some rebuked the blind man's cries, but Jesus, who is on his way to Jerusalem, takes time to call to him and heal him. The healing of Bartimaeus points to the power of Jesus to heal, make well, and restore those who know they are blind. Notice the eager persistence of Bartimaeus in calling out to Jesus and his springing up to come to Jesus. He models active faith. The story is a witness to Jesus Christ and a call to come, follow him. (Compare this text with that of Isaiah 59:9–19 for today describing Israel as being like those who are blind and have no eyes.)

Bartimaeus takes the initiative in crying out and chooses to make Jesus' way his own way. The story models the faith process: the call is mutual in that Bartimaeus cries out to Jesus and Jesus calls Bartimaeus. The outcome is critical and is the example that Mark wants the reader to follow, namely, to follow Jesus on the way.

This healing miracle forms the transition between chapters 8–10 dealing with discipleship and Jesus' encounter with the religious authorities in Jerusalem described in chapters 11–13. "On the way" is an appropriate conclusion to Jesus' teaching on discipleship to the Twelve. It also describes the act of discipleship, of being on the way through life with Jesus. The early church was referred to as "the Way": "So that if he [Paul] found any belonging to the Way, . . . he might bring them bound to Jerusalem" (Acts 9:2).

Notice Jesus' question, "What do you want me to do for you?" (v. 51) which links this passage with the preceding one when James and John ask Jesus to do whatever they ask (v. 35) and Jesus replies, "What do you want me to do for you?" (v. 36). While James and John make a misguided request, Bartimaeus corrects their ignorant question of Jesus by asking, "Master, let me receive my sight."

The restoring of sight and seeing function on two levels, the physical and the spiritual. Bartimaeus, an outsider, is given sight, while the disciples, who are insiders, are blind to the things of Jesus' passion and of the kingdom which are about to unfold.

The blind man's healing points ahead to 11:9 in that among those who followed and cried out "Hosanna!" is the healed beggar who followed Jesus on the way. He repeats twice his cry to the Son of David for help (vs. 47, 48), which is echoed by the cries of the crowd in 11:10, "Blessed is the kingdom of our father David that is coming! Hosanna in the highest!"

Note also that the blind man focused on the one thing he wanted more than anything else: sight. He anticipated that Jesus could and would heal him. Both his attitude and his actions are called "faith" by Jesus (v. 52). His faith is proved by his actions, which satisfies the test of the Letter of James: "So faith by itself, if it has no works, is dead" (James 2:17).

Mark knows that all disciples share the blindness of the disciples except when Jesus opens their eyes to understand. A person seeking spiritual sight must become aware of his or her blindness and must cry out with Christians of all generations, "Lord, have mercy," a cry known as the Kyrie Eleison. When such a person hears Jesus' call, then that person must take heart and rise, believe, hope, and pray. Then when Jesus heals the person's life, the person will follow Jesus on the way. Contrast the self-centered question of James and John with the humble but persistent cry for mercy of the blind beggar.

Recommended work: Compare this healing miracle with other healings of the blind and their responses. Scan previous and following chapters of Mark to understand the purpose of placing this healing story here.

The sermon might contrast the question of James and John with that of Bartimaeus and Jesus. The disciples misunderstand Jesus' teaching about his passion and resurrection, but Bartimaeus asks for sight, which, Mark implied, includes spiritual vision. The result is that the blind man sees and follows Jesus. The sermon should attempt to elicit the same response from the hearers: to ask Jesus for mercy and then to follow him in discipleship. The moves of the passage may guide the moves of the sermon, leading to discipleship on the way of life.

Jeremiah 31:7–9 (C)

This oracle describes the return of the exiles who have been scattered but now come home amid the joy of Isaiah. The oracles include vs. 7–14 of which our pericope is just a part.

Ephraim (v. 9) represented Israel's apostasy (Ps. 78:9–10; Hos. 4:17). Isaiah is aware of God's compassion for sinful Ephraim (Isa. 11:13). Jeremiah predicts that Ephraim will once again worship in Jerusalem (Jer. 31:6) instead of committing idolatry at Bethel. Recall that Ephraim was the second son of Joseph and Asenath and supposedly the ancestor of a tribe by that name. He and his brother Manasseh were adopted by their grandfather Jacob after he arrived in Egypt (Gen. 48:5). The tribe of Ephraim was situated somewhat west of the Jordan and south of Manasseh. It was located in a fertile and well-irrigated part of Canaan.

The hymn opens with a solemn call to joy, for God has bestowed salvation on the people. These people are the remnant (v. 7), meaning the small number who have escaped the calamity of captivity and who have been purified through the experience of the exile. They now constitute the New Israel which is faith to her God.

The "farthest parts of the earth" is synonymous with the north country, meaning Assyria where the exiles have been kept captive. Compare this with Isaiah 43:5–6. In this caravan are weak people, the blind, the lame, the woman with child and the one who is in travail. These weak people are a sign of the miraculous nature of the homecoming event.

The people come with weeping. Note the contrast between sorrow and joy here (vs. 7–8), which is also the central theme of Psalm 126, another hymn on the return from exile. In the reference to brooks of water (v. 9) we have an allusion to the rock incidents of the first exodus, noted in Exodus 17:1–7. This is not an occasional spring but a continuously flowing stream. The straight (or level) path is a symbol for Jeremiah of the facility of this march, in contrast to that of the first exodus. God speaks of being "a father to Israel," a symbol of God's favors for Israel during the period of the exodus (Hos. 11:1–4). Ephraim is God's firstborn, not because Ephraim is superior to Judah but only because God will renew this same fatherly love for Ephraim. A father's love for a child is a frequent image for God's loving care for God's people. In Isaiah 66:13 we find the image of a mother's comforting love for her child, a similar powerful and moving image of God's love.

Recommended work: Read about the exile in Assyria in a Bible dictionary. Compare this return home to the exodus by briefly scanning each and comparing and contrasting them.

The sermon might be on the theme of homecoming. The joy of homecoming which God makes possible is the thrust of the passage. Homecoming to one's home after going away to college, into military service, or living abroad might be an image to develop. Or homecoming to one's church or college for a special celebration might be described with the joys that accompany it. God's love, as a father for a child, is another image to draw on. The sermon might also point forward to the End time homecoming in heaven when we will return to God, outside of whom our souls can find no rest or peace.

Isaiah 59:(1–4) 9–19 (E)

Our pericope is part of an entire chapter which is a penitential liturgy and is one of the most obscure passages of Third Isaiah. Some scholars reject large sections of the chapter and others split it into independent sections. We affirm the unity of the chapter as we deal with it, however.

In vs. 9–15b we have a community confession of guilt in which the community admits that sin has put God's right and justice far from the people. They looked for light but found only darkness. This look for a sudden light insulted God. God would trust the people with external wonders only when they were prepared within to receive these gifts, gifts as a father might give a child. The people growl like hunted bears, refusing to give up, and they moan like helpless doves (v. 11). In v. 12 we see that sorrow always teaches the sinfulness of human misdemeanor. Israel's God is the Lord of joy.

In v. 13 note that the prophet condemns a practical abandonment and denial of God expressed by the violation of charity, justice, and honesty in human relationships.

Then in vs. 15c–20, which form another section, we learn that once humans recognize the full extent of their destitution they are ready to accept the full power of God's arm of redemption. Compare this to Isaiah 24–27. There is no human helper available to help Israel; therefore God intervened with every means at God's command. In vs. 18–20 we see that God brings judgment upon all God's enemies with irresistible fury and might to redeem repentant Zion.

The symbolic use of armor has greatly influenced later scriptural writing. Recall Ephesians 6:14–16 and other passages.

The general thrust of vs. 16–17 is that with no human aid to help in solving the problem of human sin, God intervened with every means at God's command, indicated by the breastplate of righteousness, the helmet of salvation. Note that this corresponds to the words of the lament in 63:5a: "I looked, but there was no one to help." God brings judgment on all God's enemies with might and fury that are irresistible in order to redeem repentant Zion (Jerusalem). The people are described by the name of the mountain on which Jerusalem is built. The description of the warrior and his battle equipment verges on the allegorical and anticipates the battle's outcome of victory. There will be salvation for the devout (v. 17a) but retribution upon the transgressors (v. 17b).

In v. 18 the two aspects of the arming described in v. 17 are further developed. God carries out retribution on God's foes.

In v. 19a we find words shaped into a pattern like those which usually form part of the description of an epiphany, a revelation of God. God's coming to punish foes takes place before the eyes of the entire world and terrifies them.

God will come like a rushing stream driven by the wind of the Lord (v. 19b). God's coming to judge shakes the cosmos.

Recommended work: Using a concordance, compare the description of armor in v. 17 with other descriptions in the scriptures. Do a word study of justice, righteousness, transgressions, and salvation.

The sermon might develop the images of human transgressions and injustice in society now, showing that evil in Isaiah's time is basically similar to evil in our time. Both result from turning away from following God. Only God can save and does act to come to judge God's foes. The sermon should include God's act in Christ's death to judge and break the power of evil and to offer the gift of a new life through faith in the risen Christ.

Hebrews 5:1–6 (C)

Hebrews 5:1–10 (L)

Our pericope continues the theme of Jesus as our high priest which was dealt with in the previous Sunday's passage also. It is part of 4:14–5:14, which focuses on this theme. In 5:1–10 we are told that Jesus is a priest by predestination and incarnate qualification. Jesus is contrasted with the priests and high priests of Jewish religion.

Note in v. 1 the reference to gifts and sacrifices, which are cereal and animal sacrifices. The ordinances for the high priest were intended to point to the higher ministry by which the true access to God could at last be realized. From this side of the cross we see that this was indeed realized in Jesus' death and resurrection by which he was both priest and victim, making perfect sacrifice for the sins of the world.

The Old Testament did not provide an atoning sacrifice for deliberate or defiant sins (note this in Num. 15:30 and Deut. 17:12 especially). Only unwitting offenses committed by the ignorant and the wayward could be atoned for. The sin with a high hand was the deliberate sin, and the one who sinned this way was to be cut off from among his people because the person had despised the word of the Lord and broken God's commandment. In priestly legislation, there was no provision for atonement of such deliberate and defiant sin.

The high priest had to offer sacrifice for his own sin as well as for those of the people, since he too is beset with weakness. A priest does not take the role upon himself but is called by God as Aaron was called. Even so, Christ did not exalt himself but was appointed by God as a high priest after the order of Melchizedek, the mysterious priest of the Old Testament (Ps. 110:4). We gather from Genesis 14:17–20 that this mysterious priest/king was greater than either Abraham or his descendant Levi (from whose tribe the priests were drawn). We know little about Melchizedek, since his ancestors, birth, and death are not recorded in scripture.

The author reminds us of Jesus' agonizing prayer in Gethsemane (vs. 7–8), a prayer that was heard in the sense that Jesus learned obedience to God by submitting to God's will, which involved Jesus' death and resurrection. The purpose of this section of vs. 7–10 is to show how intensely Jesus entered into our human condition. The author shows us what it was for Jesus to be a son and to be a priest, and to be both of these together. The author describes a *real incarnation,* and the passion of Jesus is understood in the deeply emotional character of Jesus' human experience and in the exquisite feeling presented to evoke feeling on our part.

Jesus was made perfect (v. 9), meaning that he completely fulfilled his divinely appointed training for priesthood. Recall that the idea of "to make perfect" is characteristic of this letter to the Hebrews and means to make complete or bring to maturity.

This perfect high priest, Jesus, became the source of eternal salvation in contrast to the temporary deliverance provided by Levitical law and priests.

Recommended work: Do a word study of perfect, sacrifice, priest, and eternal salvation.

The sermon might compare and contrast Jesus as the perfect high priest with the priests after the order of Aaron. The focus of the sermon might be on Jesus as the source of eternal salvation to all who obey him. The sermon might point to Jesus who learned obedience through what he suffered, revealing his humanity as well as his divinity.

Hebrews 5:12–6:1, 9–12 (E)

In 5:12–6:1 the author calls the readers to move from immaturity to maturity in the Christian faith. He deplores the spiritual immaturity of the readers and uses the image of "milk" to stand for rudimentary teachings. Solid food represents more advanced doctrinal teaching. The author has some misgivings about the capacity of his readers, as indicated in 5:11–14, and he takes the basic doctrines of Christian knowledge for granted, 6:1–3. Now he is resolved to move on to more advanced subjects. Notice in 6:4–6 that he says it would be useless to try to restore those who have left the faith and become apostate and are like worthless land. But he is confident that this is not the condition of his readers (vs. 9–12). Notice that only here does he call his readers "beloved."

The Christian community's work and love which are shown for God's sake is a continued service to the church as a whole. It is a sign they have not dropped out of the purpose of God. The author wishes to see in all the community a greater zeal of forward-looking and expectant faith. He wants them to realize the full assurance of hope until the end. He wants them to be not listless and uncertain but rather imitators of those who through both faith and patience inherit the promises.

Recommended work: Do a word study of mature, hope, and salvation. Reflect on persons in scripture or other literature who were so immature they needed milk and those who were mature and could take solid food as mature people.

The sermon might have as its goal motivating hearers to move forward in their Christian growth, moving from milk to solid food, able to distinguish between good and evil. It might hold out hope for realizing the full assurance of Christian hope until the End, when Christ returns.

Theological Reflection

The Jeremiah passage describes a homecoming of the exiles when God will assemble the dispersed to their homeland. They will praise God for deliverance, and the weak will return by straight paths by brooks of water. Isaiah describes Israel's transgressions and injustice and God's action to judge Israel's offenses. God intervenes with every means at God's command. The first Hebrews passage contrasts the high priests of the Levitical order with Jesus, the perfect high priest, who became the source of salvation. The second Hebrews passage seeks to motivate hearers to move from immaturity to maturity in the Christian faith. Mark relates the healing of blind Bartimaeus, a beggar of Jericho, who models response to Jesus. He cries to Jesus for mercy, springs up and comes to Jesus, and asks for his sight. Jesus healed him and sent him on his way well. Bartimaeus responded by following Jesus on the way.

Children's Message

The talk might be about the blind beggar Bartimaeus ("son of Timaeus"). He heard about Jesus and believed Jesus could help him. So when Jesus came by he cried out for mercy. Jesus had mercy, healed him, and then Bartimaeus followed Jesus. Jesus loved people, especially sick and handicapped people like Bartimaeus. He offered them a new life and called them to follow him. Jesus offers us mercy and calls us to follow him.

Hymns for Pentecost 23

If You Will Only Let God Guide You; God Is Love: Let Heaven Adore Him; Father, We Greet You.

Pentecost 24

Ordinary Time 31

Proper 26

Psalm 119:33–48 (C)
Psalm 119:1–16 (L)
Psalm 119:1–16 or 119:1–8 (E)
Psalm 18:2–4, 47, 51 (RC)

Deuteronomy 6:1–9 (C)
Deuteronomy 6:2–6 (RC)

Hebrews 7:23–28

Mark 12:28b–34 (C)
Mark 12:28–34 (35–37) (L)
Mark 12:28–34 (RC) (E)

Meditation on the Texts

We have heard your call to us, O God, to be your people and to love you with all our heart, soul, and might. We pray that this command may always be upon our heart and that we may teach it to our children diligently. We thank you for Jesus Christ the permanent priest who is able for all time to save those who draw near to you through him. We remember that he is a high priest who is holy, blameless, unstained, separated from sinners and exalted above the heavens. We thank you that he offered himself once for all for our sins. We recall that Jesus said that the first commandment of all is, "Love the Lord your God with all your heart, and with all your soul, and with all your mind, and with all your strength." And the second is, "You shall love your neighbor as yourself." Help us by the power of your Spirit, O God, to obey these commandments and so live in community with you and our fellow human beings. Amen.

Commentary on the Texts

Mark 12:28b–34 (C)

Mark 12:28–34 (35–37) (L)

Mark 12:28–34 (RC) (E)

Our pericope is the Great Commandment, and it appears in each year of the lectionary. This indicates its centrality to the Christian faith but also poses a challenge to the preacher to deal with it in a fresh, creative fashion in preaching. (For similar passages, see Matthew 22:34–40 and Luke 10:25–28; also note Deuteronomy 6:4–5, which forms a preface to and is part of the first commandment.) The second part of the first commandment is from Leviticus 19:18. The whole of Leviticus 19 gives concrete examples of how one is to love one's neighbor.

In previous arguments Jesus triumphantly answered a priest, a Pharisee, and a Saddu- cee. Now in this fourth pronouncement story Jesus is questioned by a scribe and answers him in such a way that "after that no one dared to ask him any question." The scribe does not appear hostile, and the question he asked was a popular one to ask rabbis at that time. The purpose of the question was to sum up in as short a form as possible the fundamental principle or principles of the law. For example, the famous rabbi Hillel, when asked a similar question, replied, "What you yourself hate (to be done to you), do not do to your fellow; this is the whole law; the rest is commentary, go and learn it." This was spoken about 25 B.C. The goal of all such attempts was to formulate the basic principle of the Jewish religion from which all other parts of the law could be deduced. In Matthew

22:40 Jesus says of these two commandments: "On these two commandments depend all the law and the prophets."

The answer Jesus gave to the scribe was satisfactory to him. We probably should not imply that Jesus meant any more by formulating this first commandment than other contemporary rabbis meant by such a formulation. But for Mark the importance of this commandment seems to be that the Christian church inferred from it implications that Judaism refused to draw, namely, that if the spirit of the law summed up in love for God and neighbor were kept, then all else might be ignored. We cannot determine whether such an attitude went back to Jesus or not. A complete discussion of the implications of this commandment go far beyond the limits of this or any other commentary. The preacher is challenged each year in dealing with this commandment to explore further implications for the congregation.

Although love for God seems to be a simple and basic teaching of the scriptures, it is found only in Luke 11:42 and parallels to our pericope and is seldom referred to in other parts of the New Testament. The New Testament places an emphasis on the *prior* love of God for humans from which human love for God is derived and takes its character (Rom. 5:8; 1 John 3:16; 4:9–11). God's self-giving love (*agapē* in Greek), revealed in Christ's death on the cross, is the quality of love that we are commanded to show God and other human beings.

The two commandments are interrelated at their core. True love for neighbor arises from our love of God, and, on the other hand, there can be no genuine love for God which does not express itself in love for neighbor. Both love for God and love for neighbor are grounded in monotheism, the worship of one God. This is the motive for morality.

In examining the text, we should regard the first half of v. 28 as a Markan composition. When Mark received the original story it probably began, "And one came and asked him. . . ." In asking "Which commandment?" the scribe was putting a question to Jesus that was debated a great deal among the scribes. Such a question may well have been asked Jesus without any attempt to trap him, which was the usual purpose of such questions from his opponents.

Remember that Jesus' work as a teacher plays a prominent role in Mark's Gospel. Jesus' answer to the scribe about the first commandment includes two significant areas of meaning. First, Mark's account of the Great Commandment is the only one that contains the opening words of the Shema (so named from its first word in Hebrew, meaning "hear"). Pious Jews repeated this confession of faith from Deuteronomy 6:4 (see our pericope for today) morning and evening from the second century B.C. on. In stating this commandment as the great one, Jesus affirms the oneness of God, following his Jewish heritage. In doing this, Jesus affirms monotheism, and the early church would be able to point to this when accused of polytheism by the synagogue. Opponents claimed that Christians worshiped three gods—Father, Son, and Holy Spirit. There have been times when emphasis has been put on Jesus only or the Spirit, and Jesus' words here call the church to remember the radical monotheism that Jesus affirmed.

Jesus' reply to the scribe sets forth *love* as the basis of Christian love and living. Consider that when Jesus is asked to name the *first* of all the commandments, he answers with not one but two commandments. But love is the operative verb in both. And love is stated in the imperative.

Jesus says you shall love the Lord your God with your mind, which was not included in the Old Testament text from Deuteronomy, although "mind" is often used in the Greek translation as an alternative for the Hebrew word for "heart." The addition of mind to the other aspects of loving God stresses the all-embracing character of the love commanded.

It may be that the two Old Testament passages that form Jesus' reply were thought of as constituting a single supreme command. Another explanation is that v. 28 is secondary and does not perfectly introduce the passage that follows.

The word "neighbor" (v. 31) is a key word. In the time of Leviticus it appears to refer only to another Israelite, but by the time of Jesus it was taken to include the resident aliens in Israel also. There is disagreement over whether it was interpreted more widely or not. Recalling Luke 10:29–37, the parable of the Good Samaritan, we may assume, as most commentators do, that Jesus understood "neighbor" in a completely unrestricted sense.

The command to love neighbor as one's self raises the question of whether or not

Jesus is assuming self-love here and making it the standard by which one is to love neighbor. Another interpretation is that self refers not to the individual as such but to one's clan. Thus one is commanded to love those *outside* one's immediate family group with the same love one has for those within! This is quite suggestive for preaching in an age that is so caught up with self-love and the provincial attitude that prevails in sophisticated metropolitan society as well as in remote villages.

Verses 32f. are found *only* in Mark. Their presence here means that the decisive saying of Jesus does not form the conclusion of the pericope. It may be that Mark retained these verses as driving home the complete identity of view between orthodox Judaism and Jesus' teaching.

The scribe sums up morality in terms of love for God and love for neighbor which he says is much more than all whole burnt offerings and sacrifices. Such service motivated by love involves other persons and is of more value than sacred actions which are specially rendered to God. This idea is found also in Hosea 6:6; 1 Samuel 15:22; and elsewhere.

Jesus tells the scribe he is not far from the kingdom of God. Although put in a negative way, Jesus' comment emphasizes the scribe's *nearness* to the kingdom. What was still lacking for him to be in the kingdom was an acknowledgment of Jesus, following of Jesus, and admission to the fellowship of the disciples.

It seems that v. 34b should be ascribed to Mark on linguistic grounds, since its purpose is to round off the series of pronouncement stories and to mark a pause in the activity before the final incident in this section.

Recommended work: Do a word study of love in a Bible dictionary. Make a study of commentary on the Deuteronomy and Leviticus passages on which Jesus' reply is based. Also do a word study of heart, soul, mind, and strength, and of neighbor.

The sermon might be titled "The Cruciform Shape of the Christian Faith: Love for God and Neighbor." The sermon might be introduced by the minister going to the center of the chancel and silently drawing, with arm and index finger outstretched, a cross, even rising on tiptoe to reach the top of the imagined cross. Then the sermon might begin by pointing out that love for God and love for neighbor are bound up together in the Christian faith according to Jesus' teaching here and elsewhere. Love for God might be illustrated by the story of the widow who gave two mites, the smallest coins of all, which was her whole living (12:41–44). She might have kept one for herself and given one, but her devotion and her trusting faith were expressed in giving all she had, little though it was. Love for neighbor is described by Jesus in the parable of the Good Samaritan and the parable of the sheep and the goats. Love is something you *do,* not simply something you feel, although the emotions are a very real part of love, as Jesus' reply indicates. The sermon should deal in images, perhaps drawing from true stories of self-sacrifice from the annual Carnegie Hero Awards to people who risked or gave their lives for others. Jesus' love for us in giving his life on the cross is the supreme expression of love for God and neighbor. Jesus loved God to the point of obeying God even to dying for the sins of the world.

Deuteronomy 6:1–9 (C)

Deuteronomy 6:2–6 (RC)

This pericope includes the verses on which Jesus' reply to the scribe is based in our reading from Mark. In preaching this text, one should connect it with the Markan text for today.

In chapter 6, Moses deals with the first of the Ten Commandments. Note that Moses is not just a legislator but is also a teacher and an expositor of God's will. In chapters 12–26 the statutes and ordinances are expressed in a sermonic appeal to do the will of God in various concrete situations.

Note in v. 3 that a characteristic theme of the author of Deuteronomy appears, namely, that reverent obedience will result in divine blessings of long life, welfare, and fruitfulness. God promised to Abraham and those after him a land flowing with milk and honey and other blessings. Canaan was called a land of milk and honey, foods that in the eyes of seminomads made it seem like a paradise. The phrase "a land flowing with milk and honey" is of Canaanite origin.

In the Jewish tradition, vs. 6–9 were known as the Shema, so named from its first word in Hebrew, which means "hear." In vs. 4–5 we have the Great Commandment, as Jesus called it in our Markan text. It is basically a restatement of the first of the Ten Commandments in a positive form. In contrast to pagan belief, Israel has only one God who is sovereign and unique. Therefore Israel is to have but one loyalty. Recall that heart for the Hebrew meant mind or will as we know them. The soul was the vital being or self (not the spirit in contrast to the body, as contemporary thinking sometimes defines it). Here "might" expresses the idea of loving God with all one's devotion.

The command to put this command on one's hand, forehead, and doorpost means that it is to be constantly thought about. It is to be the guiding principle for all living.

Recommended work: Do a word study of the Hebrew understanding of heart, soul, and might, and love. Compare this command with Exodus 13:9 and the Markan passage for today.

The sermon might focus on the Great Commandment as expressed here and in Mark, with implications for living as love for God and love for neighbor are linked together by Jesus.

Hebrews 7:23–28

The focus of chapter 7 is on the priesthood of Melchizedek in comparison with that of the Levitical priesthood. The preacher should read the whole chapter before concentrating on our pericope. The author says that the Levitical priesthood is inadequate because it is provisional and temporary, but a priesthood like that of Melchizedek is eternal and the office is not inherited or transmitted. Jesus stands in contrast to the Levitical priests because he is appointed with a divine oath and is immortal. Thus he holds his priesthood permanently. The author of Hebrews stresses that the supreme characteristic of Christ's office as a priest is that he is a priest not by the law of a physical commandment but because of his divine life. Here the author is appealing to Jesus' resurrection. Jesus is the priest of the resurrection who inaugurates a better hope by which we draw near to God. Notice in v. 25 the moving touch where the author says Jesus' indissoluble life is given in intercession for those who draw near to God.

The entire Letter to the Hebrews is dominated by one major Old Testament passage: Psalm 110. This psalm should be studied as background for this and other Hebrews pericopes. Psalm 110 exercised a great influence on early Christian thinking.

In vs. 26–28 we have a summary of the merits of Jesus our high priest who is Son of God. He is separated from sinners and exalted above the heavens. He is unlike other priests who offer sacrifices for their own sins as well as those of the people. Rather, Jesus our high priest is both priest and sacrifice who offered himself up for us all. He has been appointed priest by the word of the oath and made perfect.

Recommended work: Do a word study of priest, high priest, sacrifice, and perfect in a Bible dictionary.

The sermon might contrast Jesus our high priest who is both priest and perfect sacrifice with other priests of old who were limited by death and offered sacrifices for their own sins as well as those of the people. It might focus on Jesus' death on the cross once for all when he offered up himself. Jesus is the priest of the resurrection who always lives to make intercession for us. The sermon might call hearers to trust this high priest who always lives to make intercession for them.

Theological Reflection

Both the Deuteronomy and Markan passages focus on the command to love God with all one's being, and in Mark, Jesus adds a second command: to love one's neighbor as oneself. Jesus sees love for God and love for neighbor as interlocking and says there is no other commandment greater than these. The thrust of the Hebrews reading is on the contrast between human high priests and Jesus the perfect high priest who offered up himself and made a sacrifice of himself once for all. Jesus is able to save those who draw near to God through Jesus, again a focus on God's love for us. There is implied the thought that if God so loved us we ought to love God and one another in response.

Children's Message

The conversation with the children might be about why we love God: because God first loved us in Christ. Therefore we are commanded to love God and our neighbor. You might point to a cross in the chancel or carry a small cross to show the children how the vertical arm points upward to remind us of God who first loved us and whom we are to love. The horizontal arms point to other people around the world to remind us to love our neighbor as ourself. You might mention one or two concrete ways by which the children can express their love for God and neighbor in your church and its worship and work.

Hymns for Pentecost 24

Spirit of God, Descend Upon My Heart; My Faith Looks Up to Thee; Lord, as I Wake I Turn to You.

Ordinary Time 32
Proper 27

Psalm 146 (C)   Hebrews 9:24–28
Psalm 107:1–3, 33–43 (L)
Psalm 146:7–10 (RC)   Mark 12:38–44 (C)
Psalm 146 or 146:4–9 (E)   Mark 12:41–44 (RC)

1 Kings 17:8–16 (C)
1 Kings 17:10–16 (RC)

Meditation on the Texts

We praise you, O God, for your majesty, power, love, and justice revealed in Jesus Christ. We thank you that he appeared once for all to put away sin by the sacrifice of himself. We look forward with eager expectation to his coming again to save those who are eagerly waiting for him. May we have faith, as did the widow of Zarephath who obeyed Elijah's instructions and used her last "handful of meal" and "a little oil" to make small cakes for him, and for herself and her son, risking her last food supply. We remember the widow in the temple who gave her whole living, two copper coins, in trusting faith that you, her God, would provide. We pray that we may have such faith that we risk our very lives for your sake. Forgive us for our lack of faith. Forgive us when we have used religion, like the scribes of Jesus' day, for selfish and prideful purposes. We repent and turn to you, O God, for pardon through Christ our Savior. Amen.

Commentary on the Texts

Mark 12:38–44 (C)

Mark 12:41–44 (RC)

Our longer pericope consists of two parts that contrast human pride with humble trust: vs. 38–40 deal with the scribes and human pride and include Jesus' warning not to be like them; vs. 41–44 are the account of the widow's offering of two mites, her whole living, which she gave to the temple treasury.

I suggest that the preacher include the longer pericope in both the study and the sermon, since the warning against the scribes acts as a foil against which the account of the poor widow's offering and humble trust stand in sharp contrast. The warning against the scribes and their pride strikes against clergy pride and privilege today as well as that of lay members. The warning is linked to what went before by the reference to "scribes" (v. 35), but it also links with 9:42f. which refers to those who cause a "little one," a disciple, to sin. Jesus attacked the teaching of the scribes in vs. 35–37, and now he directs his judgment against their actions. The impact of both sections is to reinforce the teaching of vs. 1–12 that the leaders and teachers of Israel have been unfaithful husbandmen. Thus, they deserve the condemnation in store for them.

Jesus was teaching "a great throng" (v. 37b), which may indicate the mass of the people. The charge against the scribes is, first, that they like to go about in long robes. This outer garment was worn by ordinary people, but the scribes wore a distinctively large version! The proper time to wear them was at prayer and during the performance of certain scribal duties. In this passage Jesus indicates that the scribes liked to parade their piety by wearing them continually.

A second charge is that the scribes like salutations at feasts indicating that they expected to be honored because of their religious superiority. There was a rule that a man should "salaam," offer peace to his superior in knowledge of the law. A third charge is that the scribes wanted the best seats in the synagogues. At that time it was becoming customary for the elders to sit *facing* the congregation. And the fourth charge about seats at feasts is dealt with by Jesus in Luke 14:7–11. Seating was according to learning, although later it was made according to age.

Jesus says that they also devour widows' houses and for a pretense make long prayers. It appears this means that the scribes took large sums of money from credulous old women as a reward for the prolonged prayer which they professed to make on their behalf. From a study of history we may gather that religious leaders in every age (not just present television evangelists) have been known to make undue use of their influence over wealthy women in the cause of religious projects (see Josephus and others). Some scholars disagree with this meaning, however. To balance this judgment, it must be said that there were many very good scribes. These sayings reveal a hostile attitude toward Judaism and rabbis. Compare this with Jesus' parable in Luke 18:10–14, which pictures a Pharisee of the time. Jesus seems to be describing the scribes as examples of holding human religious achievements in high esteem.

The poor widow who gave her all, which was two copper coins, stands in contrast to the scribes who pride themselves on their religiosity and draw attention to their piety. Some scholars, including Nineham, explain this story of the widow in the temple as being originally a Jewish parable which Jesus took over in his teaching. Later it was shaped and made an incident in his life. There are a number of close parallels in Jewish and pagan sources of a poor woman offering a handful of flour or some other thing and being praised for her gift which was all she had. I accept it as an authentic event in Jesus' life. If it isn't, it certainly expresses Jesus' point of view toward the poor who trust God completely.

Compare the scribes who devour widows' houses with the good widow here who gives her whole living. The story points out that the true gift is to give everything we have. See how this story sums up what has gone before in Mark's Gospel and is a bridge to the story of the passion in which Jesus gave everything for human beings.

The details of the story are not as precise as usual in such accounts. We cannot be certain about what is meant by "the treasury." It is generally thought to be a kind of trumpet-shaped receptacle for offerings. One document says there were thirteen such "treasuries" placed around the wall of the court of the women. There is a mystery about how Jesus knew what the widow gave and that it was her whole living. If the story Jesus told was based on a Jewish parable in current use, then it may be that Mark had no precise notion of what "treasury" was intended.

The two copper coins she put in were leptons. The Greek word *leptos* literally means "a tiny thing." The coin was often referred to as "the widow's mite," since mite indicates a very small thing. The value can be estimated from the fact that 128 leptons made a denarius, a laborer's daily wage.

The fact that she gave *both* coins is very significant. She might have kept one and given one, which would show a human prudence in looking out for herself. But she gave both coins, her whole living. And in doing so, she gave "more" in sacrifice than did all those who contributed out of their abundance. The wealthy who gave to the treasury were probably guided by the law of the tithe and the tradition of how it was figured. But she was not. She gave her whole living.

That this teaching is directed to the church we can gather by the fact that Jesus called the disciples to him (v. 43) to teach from her example. The widow's gift foreshadows Jesus' gift of "his whole living" which he is about to make on the cross, so she becomes a type of him who though rich became poor, so that by his poverty we might become rich.

The widow stands as a model for all disciples, while the scribes serve as a warning to the crowd in general. The teaching of the example of the widow gains more power through the way Jesus himself lived and died, and, by the power of the resurrection, now lives again in those who truly hear him.

Recommended work: Do a word study of scribes and widow. Compare the widow's gift with the giving of others in Jesus' ministry, such as Zacchaeus, the rich young ruler,

Mary Magdalene, and the gift of ointment (John 12:3). Compare with the widow in 1 Kings 17:8–16.

The sermon might contrast the false piety of the scribes who loved to display their religiosity with the humble piety of the poor widow who gave her whole living. The sermon should point to the trust in God and faith which cast her on God's mercy which her action reveals. The widow of 1 Kings 17:8–16 is another example of such trust in God.

1 Kings 17:8–16 (C)

1 Kings 17:10–16 (RC)

This story of the widow of Zarephath foreshadows the trusting action of the widow who gave her two coins to the temple treasury, as recounted in Mark's Gospel reading for today. In a sermon on either text, the preacher may want to point to the example from the other text.

Our pericope is part of a larger account of the affairs in the northern kingdom. It features both Elijah and Elisha and is found in 1 Kings 17–2 Kings 10. The source material was brought to Judah by refugees from Israel. Note especially the element of the miraculous in these stories such as the meal and oil that never ran out. Remember that the people of Elijah's day did not have our modern concept of the uniformity of nature. The miraculous in the story is a part of the author's method.

Many believed that the Canaanite god Baal controlled the rain, but Elijah sought to show that it was really Israel's God who controlled it (v. 1). Elijah told Ahab there would be neither dew nor rain for years except by his word as God's prophet. Thus, there was a drought in the land which caused the brooks to dry up and created greater poverty, as the widow reveals.

The village of Zarephath was on the Phoenician coast in territory beyond that controlled by Ahab. It is now called Ras Sarafand, located seven miles south of Sidon. The fact that Elijah goes there may indicate he has already clashed with Ahab, as 18:10f. suggests. The reference to Zarephath belonging to the Sidonians suggests a date *before* Assyria took Galilee from Israel in 734 B.C.

To understand the act of the widow in feeding Elijah we need to realize that the position of widows and orphans with a breadwinner or male protector was very precarious. The marriage of a widow by her late husband's brother was not designed to relieve the widow but rather to provide an heir to the name and property of the dead man. While a childless widow was the responsibility of the family, a widow-mother like this woman had no such provision. She depended on charity.

In this account Elijah's dependence of the widow-mother is indeed poignant. She was gathering sticks to build a little fire to cook her last piece of bread for her son and herself before they died of starvation. The word for "jar" here refers to a storage jar for meal of about one pint capacity. It would have a groove for a thong, and a pair of small handles.

The unfailing supply of meal and oil was a motif found in the ancient Near Eastern descriptions of kings, where the king was thought of as the dispenser of the water of life. This points to the saga character of the Elijah story. Some think the supply of oil and meal was replenished by the widow's better-off neighbors who were touched by her generosity.

This story is a typical prediction/fulfillment story. The prediction is in v. 14, and the fulfillment is in v. 16. See Luke 4:24, which alludes to this story.

Recommended work: Read an article on miracles in a Bible dictionary, and read about the life of Elijah.

The sermon might follow the moves of the story, stressing the prediction (v. 14) and the fulfillment (v. 16). The trust of the widow in God and God's prophet Elijah is the central thrust of this passage. Her trust was rewarded by God's provision for the needs of her and her son. The sermon might point to our need to rely more fully upon God in daily living and to trust God as we face the unknown future. Jesus' teaching in the Sermon on the Mount about not being anxious about food and clothing might be used in illustrating this kind of trust in God's providence.

Our pericope is part of a larger passage that deals with the characteristics of the sacrifice of Christ. It may seem surprising that the things in heaven need to be purified by the blood of Christ. They, like the things of Jewish worship under the old covenant such as the book, sanctuary, and ritual furnishings, all need to be purified by Christ's death. The author was writing to Jewish Christians who may have missed in the spiritual worship of the Christian faith the many holy things and actions of the Jewish religion. He says to them, in effect, that Christianity has its own sublime, though invisible, sanctions which are given by a greater sacrifice, Christ's death. The stamp of the cross is on the book of the new covenant, the heavenly Zion, and the New Israel, the church. The things in heaven represent realities that exist here and now for Christians through Christ.

The point that is being made here is that the sacramental element is found throughout Christianity even as it is in Judaism. But its sanctions in the blood of Christ are much greater, although they are not material.

Reflect on how the author contrasts the sacrifice of Jesus with the limited, local, impersonal, external, and forever repeated rites of the Jewish religion (vs. 24–25). Jesus' sacrifice was once for all in history.

The real thrust of the author's message is in v. 24, where he repeats what has already been proved, namely, that Christ has penetrated into the very presence of God on our behalf. Christ's service in the heavenly sanctuary is permanent.

In vs. 27–28 the author uses a human analogy again. It is appointed for all humans to die once, and after that comes the judgment, says the author. Even so, Christ having been offered once will appear a second time. Note especially that this is the *one* explicit use of the term "second coming" in the New Testament. In other places where the "parousia," meaning "presence," is mentioned, it is not called a second coming, although the idea may be contained in it.

The author has combined his dominant idea of Christ as the priest who introduces us to the heavenly sanctuary with the primitive End time events which move in terms of a time sequence. The author was a primitive Christian who wants to arouse his readers to a sense of urgency and crisis. The time is short. Christ will definitely return. Therefore be ready for him, "eagerly waiting for him." Christ will return to judge. For those who are ready, the judge will be their savior.

The phrase "appointed for men to die once, and after that comes judgment" (v. 27) suggests that for each individual, judgment follows death immediately. This is consistent with the author's thoughts elsewhere.

Recommended work: Do a word study of sacrifice, sanctuary, second coming, and judgment.

The sermon might deal with the once-for-all death of Christ for our sins in contrast to sacrifices before him which had to be repeated. The sermon might then point forward to Christ's coming again and our need to be eagerly waiting for him by prayer and obedience to his will. Christ will come to judge, but for believers he comes as savior!

Theological Reflection

The 1 Kings and Markan pericopes picture trust in God's providential care in terms of widows who act in faith, casting themselves on the mercy of God. The widow in the Markan passage is a Christ figure who gives her whole living, as Christ later would give his life for others. In Hebrews the author contrasts Christ who made a sacrifice once for all with previous sacrifices which had to be repeated. Christ put away sin by the sacrifice of himself, and he is coming again at the end of the age to judgment. But for those who early await him he comes as savior.

Children's Message

The talk might be about the widow who gave her last two coins to the temple treasury. You might have two shiny pennies to show the children, pointing out that the widow put in two copper coins that were almost worthless for buying anything. But she gave more than the rich who contributed out of their abundance, because her sacrifice was greater. She gave her whole living. She might have kept one and given the other. But she gave both, trusting in God to care for her. You might tell the children that the widow shows us that Jesus praises sacrificial giving, regardless of how small our gift might be.

Hymns for Pentecost 25

Now Thank We All Our God; Love Divine, All Loves Excelling; If Thou but Trust in God.

Pentecost 26

Ordinary Time 33

Proper 28

Psalm 145:8–13 (C)
Psalm 16 (L)
Psalm 16:5, 8–11 (RC)
Psalm 16 or 16:5–11 (E)

Daniel 7:9–14 (C)
Daniel 12:1–3 (L) (RC)
Daniel 12:1–4a (5–13) (E)

Hebrews 10:11–18 (C)
Hebrews 10:11–14, 18 (RC)
Hebrews 10:31–39 (E)

Mark 13:24–32 (C)
Mark 13:1–13 (L)
Mark 13:14–23 (E)

Meditation on the Texts

O God, we confess that we often become fearful because of the wars and rumors of wars, earthquakes, and famines. We wonder if world events are out of control and fate is our only god. But we take heart from the assurance of Jesus that the Son of man is coming again with great power and glory. We know that his words will not pass away. Although we do not know the time of his coming again, we pray that we may be faithful servants, eagerly expecting his return. We remember the vision of Daniel, who saw one that was ancient of days and who saw one coming like a son of man. We thank you for the assurance that your kingdom is an everlasting one that shall not be destroyed. May we be among those who are wise and shall shine like the brightness of the firmament. We thank you for Christ who offered himself for all time as a single sacrifice for sins and is seated at your right hand. May we always seek to live in covenant with you our God, and we pray that your laws may be on our hearts and minds. Amen.

Commentary on the Texts

Mark 13:24–32 (C)

Mark 13:1–13 (L)

Mark 13:14–23 (E)

These three pericopes cover vs. 1–32. Chapter 13 is sometimes called "the Little Apocalypse," but, as we will note later, this is not entirely correct for several reasons. Verses 1–2 foretell the destruction of Jerusalem, while vs. 3–37 deal with the End of the age.

The setting for this discourse, which is Jesus' longest "speech" in Mark, is found in vs. 1–4. The secrets to the End of the age are given only to the four senior disciples, according to Mark's account. For Mark, this teaching was not a part of Jesus' public teaching or his special instructions to the Twelve. Andrew is included in the inner group with Peter, James, and John. Remember how they followed Jesus from the time he called them (1:16–20) until now. He said "Follow" to them, and now he adds the command "Watch" (v. 37).

The disciples' question about the destruction of the temple is linked to the End of all things. Jesus' reply to their question makes a clear distinction between the two, however. The destruction of the temple is associated with the End of this era and the coming of God's kingdom. The temple was destroyed in A.D. 70 by the Romans, but the End of the age did not occur.

As you read this chapter in preparing to preach on a particular pericope from it, notice the characteristics of apocalyptic thought found in it: dualism of good and evil, God and evil; visions of cosmic upheaval; a deterministic and pessimistic view of history; the anticipation of the End of this world in a great and imminent crisis. Note especially the Old Testament passages quoted in the chapter, particularly from the Book of Daniel (see the pericope from Daniel for today). Daniel is quoted in vs. 14, 19, and 26. There seems to be a parallel to 2 Thessalonians 2 and some passages in Revelation. This chapter of Mark resembles in both form and context Daniel 7–12. As we analyze it, we see that it is a composite, containing some genuine sayings of Jesus that were expanded and adapted to current community needs in written form before the church put them into Mark's Gospel.

This chapter is Jesus' farewell discourse to his disciples. The central thrust of this final order that Jesus gives to the disciples is to watch for the coming of the Son of man. It presupposes that the church will be very aware of the absence of its Lord and at the same time will have an intense yearning for the renewal of his presence. Mark 13:30–31 meets this yearning with the certain hope founded on Jesus' promise. The chapter functions within the whole Gospel to give a sense of urgency to the church's mission and to give a future dimension to its loving fellowship.

This farewell discourse functions here as John 14–17 does in the Fourth Gospel, as the Great Commission in Matthew 28:16–20 does for Matthew's Gospel, and as Jesus' resurrection appearances both in Jerusalem and on the Mount of Olives do in Luke 24:36–49 and Acts 1:6–11.

In order to understand this chapter better we must put ourselves in the place of the original hearers of this Gospel in the last third of the first century. Many of the things mentioned in it were known to them from their own experience, such as those mentioned in vs. 6–8, 9–13, 14–20, and 21–22. It is almost certain that the destruction of the temple in A.D. 70 had already occurred. And Jerusalem very likely was also destroyed. The hearers of the Gospel were familiar with the kind of speech attributed to our Lord, a familiarity gained from the Hebrew Scriptures and later Jewish writings. The apocalypse was a literary form that was very popular and widely known at the time. In such a writing the author shared visions granted to him or her, visions in which readers could see contemporary events or events about to happen. The purpose of such visions was to give hearers courage that no matter how hopeless things might seem, God was nevertheless in control and would soon vindicate both God's own honor and God's servants in a dramatic fashion. Such apocalypses were almost always attributed to some great religious figure of a previous era.

A second kind of literary writing was that of the farewell discourse such as that made by Jacob, Moses, Samuel, David, and others who, knowing they were about to die, called family, friends, and, in some cases, subjects to hear what we could call their last will and testament. This farewell speech would include a summary of the past events and a survey of the things yet to come, including sufferings and dangers, along with an exhortation to continue faithful in the face of them. Farewell discourses and apocalypses were both believed to depend upon divine revelation, thus giving them authority for the period to which they spoke and for the future.

As we noted at the beginning, Mark 13 differes somewhat from the usual apocalypse, although commonly called "the Little Apocalypse." It does not correspond exactly to a farewell discourse either. Rather, it combines characteristics of both farewell discourses and apocalypses. It differs from the usual apocalypse in that it does *not* rest on any vision. There is little fantastic imagery. And the tone of warning that runs through it also sets it apart from the normal apocalypse which usually has a thrust of encouraging its readers and raising hopes. But Mark 13 is more concerned with *restraining* hopes, as noted in vs. 6f. Some scholars call this a warning speech in apocalyptic terms. Compare it with 2 Thessalonians 2 which was designed to hold back overeager expectations aroused by contemporary events. Mark has designed this speech to curb the fanatical apocalyptic feelings he expected as an immediate sequel to the disasters of A.D. 66–70. However, it must be said that it contains apocalyptic imagery and is concerned with the End of the world, which set it apart from most of the farewell discourses cited in the previous paragraph.

While vs. 5–37 appear to be a composite, we may accept it as giving us substantially our Lord's teaching. We may not have his exact words, for they may have been modified somewhat in the course of transmission. But they do give us a discourse that represents the mind of Jesus. (For further discussion of the authenticity of this chapter, see C. E. B. Cranfield, *The Gospel According to St. Mark,* and D. E. Nineham, *Saint Mark,* ch. 13.)

The first pericope (L) is vs. 1–13. As noted earlier, vs. 1–4 give the setting. In vs. 5–13 we have a warning of the miseries that will precede the last days. Note that vs. 5–6 parallel vs. 21–23 and may be two versions of a traditional warning. Compare to 1 John 2:18: "Children, it is the last hour; and as you have heard that antichrist is coming, so now many antichrists have come; therefore we know that it is the last hour." Then in vs. 7–8 there is an expectation of strife and natural disasters at the End, which is typical of apocalyptic thought. See how the theme is carried over in vs. 24–25. According to this point of view, salvation comes at the darkest moment—a kind of "The darkest hour is just before dawn" and "There is a silver lining behind every cloud" thinking. Revelation continues this kind of thinking in which things get progressively worse until, suddenly, they are all over. This is a mark of premillennialist thinking in modern times.

Then in vs. 9–13 we have more standard apocalyptic material which reflects the problems of persecution, probably Roman persecution of Christians. Apocalyptic literature is persecution literature which urges the faithful to continue to hold fast to their faith to the End.

Recommended work: Read critical commentaries on this chapter and section. Do a word study of apocalyptic writing and read farewell discourses of other biblical characters.

The sermon might focus on the thrust of the passage found in v. 13b: "But he who endures to the end will be saved." The sermon should deal with current expectations of the rapture or Second Coming, pointing out that only God knows the time when it will happen and that human speculation is futile. It should be an encouraging sermon, showing that God is in control of world history although chaos seems to prevail at times. It might be pointed out that such a passage has greater impact for persons undergoing persecution than for others.

The next pericope is *vs. 14–23* (E). In vs. 14–20 the desolating sacrilege (v. 14) is an apocalyptic code for something. That this has a hidden meaning is shown by the note "let the reader understand," placed in parenthesis in the RSV and quite out of place in a speech. It seems to refer to the same thing as Daniel 9:27 and 12:11, which is now thought to refer to an event of 167 B.C. Or it could refer to the desecration of the temple in the war of A.D. 66–70.

In v. 20 "the sake of the elect, whom he chose" is mentioned, which seems to be related to the chosen people concept. Although this may seem mysterious and unfair to our rational view of life, the doctrine of election is a necessary part of a theological system that understands God's salvation as a gift/act to rescue helpless humanity. Then in vs. 21–23, which parallel vs. 5–6, we have a traditional warning like that in 1 John 2:18.

Recommended work: Read critical commentaries on the passage. Do a word study of apocalyptic, election, and tribulation.

The sermon might compare the desolation at that time with that of today in various parts of the world. Our confidence in God's election and providential care should be a thrust of the sermon. Also, the sermon should warn against false prophets and point out that only God knows when the End will come.

The third pericope is *vs. 24–32* (C). The view of the universe expressed in vs. 24–25 is prescientific. These wonders of the sun and moon darkened, and so forth, are common themes found in apocalyptic writings.

In vs. 26–27 the picture of the Son of man coming in clouds with great power and glory was a popular early Christian expectation. Compare this with Acts 1:9–11 and 1 Thessalonians 4:17. The consummation of the End is described in language from Daniel 7:13, from one of the pericopes for today. We cannot be certain about what is meant by Son of man in Daniel, but here it refers to a superhuman person who is given divine authority and is filled with God's power and majesty. Clouds are associated with divine status. Recall that angels are messianic agents (v. 27). The gathering of the elect was a traditional idea; for Jews it referred to the gathering of Jews from the Dispersion to be united with the faithful remnant in Palestine.

Compare vs. 28–29 with 4:26–29 and James 5:7–8. It is a little parable which speaks for itself. Some scholars see that the explanation in v. 29 is secondary and think that the original reference of the parable was to the various actions of Jesus' ministry that pointed to the kingdom of God which was already manifesting itself.

In v. 30 "this generation" is to be taken literally. It may have originally referred to some specific event such as the destruction of Jerusalem. It seems to refer to the second coming of Christ here.

Many commentators think that the reference to Jesus' words not passing away in v. 31 was an early Christian claim on Jesus' behalf. It may have been an adaptation of his saying about the law found in Matthew 5:18 to his own teaching.

The point of v. 32 is that since no one except God knows the exact time of Christ's return and the End of the age, everyone should be ready at all times. This saying is important since it preserves an early tradition that even Jesus the Son did not have perfect knowledge of all things. But Mark is not trying to say that Jesus is inferior to God. He intends the opposite, since the Son is not classified among humans or angelic beings but is superior to both.

Recommended work: Study the meaning of apocalyptic literature in a Bible dictionary. Compare this section with vs. 1–23.

The preacher may want to follow the moves of the passage and use images from it. The idea of the elect should be dealt with and the stress on the eternal nature of Jesus' words and the uncertainty of the Second Coming. The sermon should conclude with the command of Jesus in v. 37 to "Watch" and should explain how Christians watch by avoiding the cares of this world and by seeking to be faithful disciples every moment, since Jesus' second coming may occur at any moment.

Daniel 7:9–14 (C)

The theme of this passage is the divine judgment. God is called the Ancient of Days and is pictured on his fiery throne surrounded by his court. As in an oriental court, the record books are examined and judgment is given. Scholars see a link in the Judge as "Ancient of Days" with other records from the past. Note in Daniel's vision that interest is focused first upon the Judge and the Judge is God, pointing to the author's monotheistic faith. The dress and the hair of the Judge are radiantly white.

The thrust of vs. 1–12 is that the Greek empire will be destroyed but the remnant of the other empires mentioned earlier will continue until absorbed into the final kingdom.

God will give the messianic king a universal and everlasting dominion (vs. 13–14). The meaning of this vision is that there will be a striking reversal of the fortunes of Israel and other nations by the power of God. In the image of the Son of man there may be a reference to the Messiah. The Son of man is a corporate figure here, and this image may merge with the thought of an individual Messiah. The Son of man image does not stress a human likeness but rather the representatives of the kingdom of God. This is a symbol of its divine character.

Recommended work: Do a word study of Son of man in a Bible dictionary, noting how Jesus used this name for himself and the meaning he gave it.

The sermon might focus on the Son of man and how this prophecy was fulfilled in Christ who reigned from a cross. His kingdom is an everlasting one that shall not be destroyed. The sermon should relate this to the Christians and world events that seem to reveal that evil is in control of history. The thrust of the sermon should be one of encouragement and confidence, since God has given the kingdom of Christ and it shall not be destroyed.

Daniel 12:1–3 (L) (RC)

Daniel 12:1–4a (5–13) (E)

Our pericope is part of the long section of 11:2b–12:4 in which the pages of the book of truth are turned for Daniel so that he may see what is to come. The section really begins with chapter 10. What is given is a selective account of recent history from the Persian period to a date in the latter part of the reign of Antiochus IV Epiphanes. This is the actual time in which the author was living, and the verses of our pericope give the prophet's forecast of what he believes is about to happen in the near future. The author pictures what the divinely appointed end will be like, namely, a climax in which Israel would be the center, indicated by the figure of Michael who was the patron angel of Israel. He is to play a decisive part on God's behalf.

The great tribulation will come to a head, but all those in Israel whose names are written in the book of life will escape. God knows God's own people! Then we have the prediction of a resurrection that has only one parallel in Hebrew scripture (Isa. 26:19). A key word here is "many," and how we interpret it reveals whether we are to think of a general or limited resurrection. The author is not concerned with the problem of life after death or the fate of the individual. Rather, he points to the kingdom of God. God will do justice to the martyrs for their faith but also to the apostates. We probably should not read into this a doctrine of heaven and hell. But the author has prepared the way for a doctrine of the final judgment and the irrevocable separation of the good and the evil.

Recommended work: Do a word study of Michael, book of life, and resurrection.

The sermon might deal with this vision of the End time events, and it should be balanced with other scriptural views of the End. The Christian belief in the resurrection and judgment should inform the sermon in addition to this vision of Daniel. A note of hope and assurance for all who have faith in Christ should pervade the sermon.

Hebrews 10:11–18 (C)

Hebrews 10:11–14, 18 (RC)

The longer pericope of vs. 11–18 concludes the formal argument that began with v. 1 and reiterates two points made earlier: (1) Christ's sacrifice was a single offering for all time which perfects for all time all who are sanctified (v. 14) and (2) it achieves the goal of the new covenant in the forgiveness of sins. Note that in vs. 12–13 the author uses quotations from his favorite Psalm 110. He bases his whole argument on scripture, and vs. 16–17 are a climax from his point of view.

Note that Christ sat down at the right hand of God (v. 12). A priest stands but a king sits, and Christ is both as indicated in 1:3. The author has set out to prove that Christ's death once and for all made a perfect sacrifice for sin. While priests stood to repeat their sacrifices, Christ sits in triumph awaiting the final defeat of his enemies.

The perfect referred to is not moral perfection as such but is the perfect sacrifice on Christ's part and the perfect assurance of forgiveness this made possible. Moral perfection is implied though.

The single offering perfecting both worship and the worshiper achieves the goal contemplated by the new covenant: the forgiveness of sins.

In vs. 16–17 the author quotes from Jeremiah 31:33–34 but with some slight changes. The Holy Spirit speaks for God: "I will remember their sins and their misdeeds no more."

Note the negative form of v. 18 which prepares for what will follow. The new covenant in Christ's death assures full and final remission of sins.

Recommended work: Do a word study of priest, sacrifice, new covenant, sanctified, and perfected.

The sermon might follow the moves of the passage with an emphasis on Jesus' once-for-all sacrifice on the cross to make forgiveness possible. The sermon might deal with the images of the covenant and new covenant in Christ's death for our sins. This makes further offering for sin unnecessary.

Hebrews 10:31–39 (E)

A warning is given in v. 31 followed by encouragement and assurance based on the past record of the audience to whom Hebrews is written. Notice that greater details are found here than elsewhere. The persecutions the readers endured cover a fairly wide range, but martyrdom is not on the list. The implication is that they are not now facing such persecutions, but their past record shows they were able to endure such trials. What they need in their present circumstances is a similar endurance (v. 36). They have but a short time to wait (v. 37). The author quotes from Habakkuk 2:3–4, a passage Paul used also. But the author uses the original meaning of faithfulness here rather than Paul's interpretation of faith righteousness over against works righteousness.

The author adds a final word of assurance in saying, "But we are not of those who shrink back and are destroyed" (v. 39). And then he introduces with his usual clever manner the theme of the next chapter: "those who have faith and keep their souls" (v. 39). What follows in chapter 11 is the well-known description of faith and how it was lived out in great leaders of old.

Recommended work: Do a word study of confidence, endurance, and will of God.

The sermon could well follow the images and the movement of the passage. It should put stress on continuing to be faithful in present trials as were the hearers in the past testing. Everyone needs words of encouragement to endure faithfully until Christ's return, and the sermon should give encouragement based on faith in Christ who has conquered sin and evil and been raised from the grave victorious.

Theological Reflection

The theme of the Markan passages is the End of the age and the urgency to live watchful lives until Christ returns. It is both a kind of apocalypse and a farewell speech designed to encourage the disciples. The Daniel 7 passage foretells the coming of "one like a son of man" to whom the Ancient of Days gives dominion and glory and kingdom, a figure that Christians see fulfilled in Christ. His kingdom shall not be destroyed. The Daniel 12 passage is a vision of Israel's triumph over its enemies, a time of trouble and a deliverance of Israel, at least those whose names are written in the "book." This is essentially a reassuring and hopeful vision, although Daniel's vision includes the book that is shut up until the end. In the Hebrews 10:11–18 passage Christ is portrayed as both priest and king. As priest Christ offered himself as the sacrifice for sins to perfect all those who are sanctified. It is a message of assurance of the new covenant made in Christ which makes forgiveness of sins possible once for all. The Hebrews 10:31–39 passage gives encouragement to the readers by reminding them of their past victories which should inspire present endurance. The author says they need to endure only a little while before Christ's return, in which interim they are to do the will of God and receive what is promised.

Children's Message

In the conversation with children you might draw on the Hebrews 10:11–18 passage and the covenant that God has made with us in Christ. You might describe priests of that time who offered up sacrifices of animals and fruit of the field in order to worship God. But Christ who was both priest and victim offered himself once for all to make forgiveness possible. He was crucified but God raised him from the grave, and he is alive and present with us by the power of the Holy Spirit. If we trust in Christ, God forgives our sins and makes us new.

Hymns for Pentecost 26

O Worship the King; Come, Thou Almighty King; Lo! He Comes with Clouds Descending.

Pentecost 27

(Lutheran only)

Psalm 111   Hebrews 13:20–21

Daniel 7:9–10   Mark 13:24–31

Meditation on the Texts

We look forward with eager expectation, O God, to the coming again of the Son of man when he comes with great power and glory. May we be among the elect who will be gathered from the ends of the earth to the ends of heaven. We rejoice in the assurance that although heaven and earth will pass away, Jesus' words will not pass away. We remember Daniel's vision of the Ancient of Days before whom thousands stood and the court sat in judgment. When the books of judgment are opened, we pray that our names will be found there. You, O God, are the God of peace who brought again from the dead our Lord Jesus, the great shepherd of the sheep by the blood of the eternal covenant. We pray that you may equip us with everything good, that we may do your will, as you work in us that which is pleasing in your sight, through Jesus Christ, to whom be glory forever and ever. Amen.

Commentary on the Texts

Mark 13:24–31

See Pentecost 26, (C).

Daniel 7:9–10

See Pentecost 26, (C).

Hebrews 13:20–21

This is one of the best-known passages of Hebrews. It is a beautiful benediction and doxology and includes one of the few references to the resurrection in the book. Note how it sums up ideas expressed more fully earlier: Christ's sacrifice, the establishment of a new covenant, the life of the Christian as a combination of both the work of God and the Christian's own work.

This stately prayer/doxology introduces not only the resurrection of Christ but also the figure of the shepherd. In the preceding chapters the author has not dealt with the resurrection, since it is the entrance of Christ into the true Holy of Holies which is so essential to his analogy. We may assume that the figure of the shepherd is from liturgical usage. Although we would expect the author to write something like ''our great high priest,'' he writes of the great shepherd instead. The shepherd figure is drawn from the Hebrew Scriptures from passages like Isaiah 40:11; Ezekiel 37:24; Zechariah 9:16; and Psalm 23. We may compare it to 1 Peter 5:4.

Note that the final clause ''by the blood of the eternal covenant'' shapes the thought in the familiar framework of what has been written earlier in Hebrews. Although there is a beauty about these verses, they are rather awkward as a conclusion to the book. Reflect on the doxology which refers to God who works in the believer that which is pleasing in his sight ''through Jesus Christ.'' Compare this to 1 Peter 4:11.

Recommended work: Do a word study of shepherd, covenant, and will of God. **335**

The sermon might be modeled on the scripture passage itself and thus be a prayer/sermon for the hearers that God might equip them with everything good so that they might do God's will. The thrust of the sermon might be on doing the will of God, equipped by God who works in and through persons through Jesus Christ. The death and the resurrection of Christ make possible this new life in covenant with God. Through faith in Christ we become sheep of the risen Christ who is the great shepherd. We are to follow wherever he leads us. The sermon might offer specific ways of following the great shepherd and of doing God's will in the here and now.

Theological Reflection

The Daniel passage pictures God as the Ancient of Days who judges. The Markan reading calls us to expectant waiting for Christ's return as the Son of man who comes in power and glory. His words, all the things he taught, will not pass away. In Hebrews 13 we have a prayer/doxology with the resurrection of Christ and Christ as the great shepherd introduced into the book for the first time. The thrust of the passage is that the hearer may be equipped by God to do God's will as God works in the person through Jesus Christ.

Children's Message

The talk with the children might be about Jesus as the great shepherd. You might remind them that Jesus said he was the good shepherd who cares for the sheep and does not run away from the attack of wolves. We are Jesus' sheep who are to follow him always. He loves us and laid down his life for us his sheep. God raised him from the dead, and he is present with us. God wants us to follow Jesus and to live by the law of love.

Hymns for Pentecost 27

Father of Peace and God of Love; Ah, Holy Jesus, How Hast Thou Offended?; The Lord's My Shepherd.

Christic the King

Ordinary Time 34
Proper 29

Psalm 93   **Revelation 1:4b–8 (C)**
Psalm 93:1–2, 5 (RC) **Revelation 1:5–8 (RC)**
         Revelation 1:1–8 (E)

Jeremiah 23:1–6 (C)
Daniel 7:13–14 (L) (RC) **John 18:33–37 (C)**
Daniel 7:9–14 (E)   **John 18:33–37 or Mark 11:1–11 (E)**

Meditation on the Texts

We hail Christ who was called "the King of the Jews" as our king also. He said he was born to be king and came into the world to bear witness to the truth. As we meditate on his life, death, and resurrection we pray that we may be of the truth and hear his voice. O God, we thank you for him who loves us and has freed us from our sins by his blood and made us a kingdom, priests to you our God to whom be glory forever and ever. May we be watchful always for his coming with the clouds. We acknowledge you Lord God as the Alpha and Omega, the one who is and who was and who is to come, the Almighty. We thank you for Christ the righteous Branch which you raised up for David, a king who deals wisely and executes justice and righteousness in the land. We thank you for his life and obedience, even to death on a cross, by which he reveals his kingship from the tree. For he rules by love and not by earthly power or might. Amen.

Commentary on the Texts

John 18:33–37 (C)

John 18:33–37 or Mark 11:1–11 (E)

Only the John passage will be dealt with, since the Mark 11 is an alternate for (E).

On this Christ the King Sunday all pericopes focus on the kingship of Jesus. The Jeremiah passage calls kings "shepherds," but the reference to the leaders of Israel is clear. The Daniel passage foretells the coming of the Son of man who will be given dominion over all forever, which we see fulfilled in the kingship of Christ. Revelation calls Jesus the "ruler of kings on earth" who is coming with the clouds at the End.

The religious leaders charged Jesus with political treason, saying he claimed to be King of the Jews. But Jesus is king of truth. His kingdom is not of this world but of God's. He is in the world but not of it.

Our pericope is part of John's passion narrative. The setting is the trial of Jesus before Pilate. The passage of vs. 33–37 begins with Pilate entering the praetorium again, calling Jesus to him and asking, "Are you the King of the Jews?" These are the first words of Pilate to Jesus in all of the Gospel accounts. Here "the Jews" refers to the Jewish nation and does not have the special meaning John usually gives it of the hostile Jewish authorities. Some think the title "King of the Jews" was first used by Hasmonean priest/kings who were the last really independent rulers of Judea before Rome conquered it. The Jewish historian Josephus applies the title to Herod the Great. It was probably kept alive during the Roman rule as a designation for the expected liberator of the Jews. The older title "the king of Israel" was also used of Jesus. It may be that in Pilate's question the "you" is emphatic, expressing Pilate's unbelief that one so humble and unassuming as Jesus could be accused of claiming such a title.

Nothing in the narrative that goes before this passage prepares us for Pilate's question. It seems John presupposes that Pilate had more definite information about Jesus than is indicated by v. 30 in which the religious leaders accuse Jesus of being "an evildoer." The only charge the Roman rulers would have taken seriously was the charge of being the leader of a nationalist movement. The events that John describes in 6:15 and 12:12f. may have been the basis for denouncing Jesus as such a leader. Note the political overtones in the account of Jesus' trial, beginning with 18:12 and continuing to 19:22. The overtones are both paradoxical and ironic. For example, the preliminary hearing before the high priest resembles an investigation rather than a trial, and no specific charge is formulated. The Jewish authorities simply hand Jesus over to Pilate, accusing him by implication of being "an evildoer." But as the trial by Pilate moves along, the issue becomes clear that Jesus' kingship challenges that of Caesar! But neither Pilate nor the Jews believe that Jesus is the King of the Jews, and, as our pericope indicates, Jesus certainly rejected any such claim to be a temporal ruler. Since the hypocrisy of the Jews is quite evident to Pilate, he mocks them when they object to that title, a title he ordered placed on the cross. It is also clear to Pilate that Jesus is innocent. Nevertheless he yields to the fear of his own political position when the Jews cried out, "If you release this man, you are not Caesar's friend" (19:12).

In vs. 34–35 Jesus asks Pilate, "Do you say this of your own accord, or did others say it to you about me?" Here is the accused putting Pilate on trial! Jesus offers Pilate the opportunity of speaking his own convictions rather than being the channel for the hatred the world has consistently shown Jesus and the light he brought into the world. Pilate takes a serene attitude toward Jewish matters, however (v. 35).

Then in v. 36 Jesus responds to Pilate, explaining that his kingship is not of this world but is a kingship nonetheless. Jesus has a kingship not of this world as 1:10 points to: "He was in the world, and the world was made through him, yet the world knew him not." John does not give much emphasis to the idea of Jesus as king, but it is a common theme from the Synoptic tradition and early Christian preaching, both of which reflect Jesus' own identification of himself as the One who fulfilled the Hebrew Scripture ideal of messianic king.

Jesus does not answer Pilate's question of "What have you done?" in v. 35 but rather answers the question, "Are you the King of the Jews?" asked in v. 33. And when he answers, it is not in terms of kingly title, but rather he speaks of his kingship or kingdom being not from the world. Jesus' kingdom, like his disciple, is not of this world, although it is in it. Remember that for John the ultimate goal of the disciples is to be withdrawn from this world, as indicated in 14:2-3: "In my Father's house are many rooms; if it were not so, would I have told you that I go to prepare a place for you? . . . I will come again and will take you to myself, that where I am you may be also."

Jesus says that *if* his kingship were of this world, then his subjects would fight so that he would not be handed over to the Jews. So we are not explicitly told that a kingdom which is not of this world actually has subjects. Jesus would not think of his followers as being subjects in the sense of being servants, as an earthly king has. Earlier, Jesus told the disciples, "No longer do I call you servants, for the servant does not know what his master is doing; but I have called you friends" (15:15).

Jesus does have subordinates (v. 36), and the Greek term is used of temple guards. But these subordinates do not fight as temporal guards do for their king. Recall that in Matthew 26:53 Jesus says he could call on angels to fight the world on its own terms but he chooses not to do so. In Luke 1:2 and in some other places the same Greek word is used to refer to the apostolic ministry.

Then in v. 37 Pilate again asks for a direct answer about his being a king, and Jesus replies, "You say that I am a king." Note that Jesus gives a qualified reply, as he also does in Mark 15:2. According to Pilate's understanding of a king, Jesus is not a king. So here is another instance of John's use of irony. But in another sense Jesus is a king, as he says in v. 36: "My kingship is not of this world." The essence of Jesus' kingship is to testify to the truth (v. 37). He says that he has been born and has come into the world to bear witness to the truth.

See how Jesus calls on Pilate to take a stand, implicitly, on the side of truth. To choose truth is to choose life, as Jesus says in 5:25: "Those who hear [the voice of the Son of God] will live."

To sum up, Jesus does not deny that he is a king, but this title is not one that he would spontaneously select to describe his role and mission in this world.

Recommended work: Do a word study of king, kingdom, and truth. Compare and contrast the images of king given in the pericopes for today.

The preacher might develop the sermon by following the dialogue between Pilate and Jesus, showing how their understanding of king differs radically. It might climax with a picture of Jesus reigning from the cross, as the king of love who was lifted up to draw all people to himself. Jesus commands the loyalty of his followers/friends by loving them and giving his life for them, not by using physical force. The sermon might deal with Jesus' kingship in the hearts of humans today by the power of the Holy Spirit who makes his love real in their hearts and thus draws forth their obedience.

Jeremiah 23:1–6 (C)

Daniel 7:13–14 (L) (RC)

Daniel 7:9–14 (E)

For the Daniel passages, see Pentecost 27.

The key to understanding this passage lies in the term "shepherds," which refers to kings and other leaders of the people. Earlier, in 22:22, the prophet says Israel's shepherds (leaders) shall be "shepherded" by the wind. Now the prophet pronounces a "woe" on the shepherds who destroy and scatter the sheep.

Our pericope is part of the messianic oracle of vs. 1–8. God reproaches Judah's leaders for scattering Judah but promises to establish a righteous branch of David's line to rule over a restored Israel. This coming king will be responsible to God and will not be a puppet king like Zedekiah. Notice how this messianic picture differs from the later militant nationalism described in 16:14–15.

This passage is one of several short pieces that comment on the problems of leadership in the community, calling them shepherds, and looking to the future new king on the throne of David. Note that in vs. 1–4 there are general criticisms of the leaders of Judah. God promises to gather a remnant of his flock out of all the countries and bring them back to their fold, where they will be fruitful and multiply. Not only are the kings condemned but also all the ruling elements of Judah are charged with destroying and scattering the flock. It is the leaders who are responsible for the deportation of the people. While no specific social evil is pointed out, a general description of social disruption is portrayed. The shepherds are blamed for the fate of the sheep, yet they are threatened with the same fate. Recall that the deportations exiled primarily the leaders of Judah. While the shepherds are blamed for scattering the flock in v. 2, God assumes responsibility for the scattering in v. 3. This is a theologizing of the exile which allows for the possibility of return. God who drove out may also later retrieve. In Ezekiel 34 we find the images and theology of this in a more developed form. If only the people's leaders were blamed, the people's fate would be permanent, for the leaders would be powerless to bring about their return from exile. But since it is Israel's God who is ultimately responsible for their scattering, this same God will gather together all the exiles and restore them to their own land, their "fold." God will make them prosperous. God will set responsible leaders over the community who will maintain the welfare and unity of the people and in this way proper leadership (shepherds) is restored to God's flock.

The second division of the pericope is vs. 5–6, which is a mixture of both prose and poetry. The future king of David's dynasty will rule justly and wisely. There is a wordplay here on the name of Zedekiah ("Yahweh is righteous"). The pronouncement of Jeremiah here legitimates Zedekiah and promises peace and security. This oracle might be taken as an inaugural celebration of Zedekiah's rightful claim to be king. But another approach sees a wordplay on the name Zedekiah and the righteous Branch. The oracle sets the celebration in the future and foretells the coming of one who will practice justice. This section reflects the period of salvation expected in the postexilic era and so can hardly refer to Zedekiah himself, according to this alternate view.

There is a contrast between the wise rule of the coming king with that of Zedekiah who is a puppet king of the Babylonians. His foolish behavior as the leader helped bring about the ruin of Jerusalem.

The new king's name will be "The Lord is our righteousness or vindication." There is an emphasis on the vindication of the nation as a whole. We see in this prophecy Jeremiah's image of messianism which at that time was a very simple and undeveloped notion. The king who is coming is called simply the Branch, as he often is called in the Hebrew Scriptures.

Recommended work: Do a word study of righteousness, Branch, remnant, shepherd, and Zedekiah.

The sermon might focus on this image of the coming righteous Branch of David who will execute justice and righteousness which was fulfilled in Jesus Christ. Christ is the messianic king who is the good shepherd in contrast to the unfaithful shepherds who scattered God's flock. God gathers the remnant and blesses them, caring for them and none will be missing. We see this being fulfilled in God's calling human beings by the Spirit to salvation in the church in which Christ is recognized as king and savior.

Revelation 1:4b–8 (C)

Revelation 1:5–8 (RC)

Revelation 1:1–8 (E)

The longer passage is composed of the prologue to the Revelation to John, vs. 1–3, and the introductory salutation, vs. 4–8. The authorship of Revelation is debated by scholars, but we will refer to the author as "John" for convenience' sake. The revelation came to John by an angel speaking for God through Jesus Christ. An alternative title to the book is "An apocalypse of John of the Divine Word." "Servants" (v. 1) may refer to the prophets.

We might translate "what must soon take place" (v. 1) as "the events that are destined to happen soon." Compare this to Daniel 2:28–29. Predestination is one feature of apocalyptic literature, which is also found in Luke's Gospel, and in both it points to divine destiny and decree. "Soon" is another mark of apocalyptic writing, since it is crisis literature and urgency is a characteristic of such writing. Compare with 2 Thessalonians 2:2f. and other passages and note that the crisis seems more urgent in Revelation than anywhere else in apocalyptic writings.

"Blessed . . ." is the first of seven blessings pronounced upon the hearers of this message. "The time is near" is a strong motive for obedience. John writes to the seven churches in Asia. Recall that the number seven designates completeness, perfection, and totality and was especially sacred in Judaism.

Jesus Christ is called the faithful witness, the firstborn of the dead, and the ruler of kings on earth. This affirmation of Jesus as ruler of kings makes him "king of kings." Thus this passage is particularly fitting for Christ the King Sunday.

God says, "I am the Alpha and the Omega . . . who is and who was and who is to come, the Almighty" (v. 8). God is the beginning and the end of all things.

Recommended work: Do a word study of apocalyptic, seven, blessed, and predestination.

The sermon might center on Jesus as the ruler of kings on earth and the Lord of history, and relate this to the other pericopes for today. It might deal with the mystery of God's working in history to bring about God's purpose in spite of human disobedience and evil forces.

Theological Reflection

The image of the king is clearly set forth in the readings for today and ties them together. Jeremiah speaks of the righteous Branch of the line of David who is to come, the messianic king, and Christians see this fulfilled in Christ. Jesus tells Pilate that his kingship is not of this world and he came into the world to bear witness to the truth.

Children's Message

The talk with the children might be about Jesus as a different kind of king from rulers of this world. He has no tanks, planes, guns, or bombs to enforce his rule. Rather, he rules our hearts by the power of love, and his kingdom is not from the world but from heaven.

Hymns for Christ the King

Ancient of Days; At the Name of Jesus; God, the Lord, a King Remaineth.

Notes

Notes

Notes

Notes

Notes

Notes

Notes

Notes

Notes

Notes

Notes

Notes